The Children of Ash and Elm

NEIL PRICE

The Children of Ash and Elm

A History of the Vikings

ALLEN LANE
an imprint of
PENGUIN BOOKS

ALLEN LANE

UK | USA | Canada | Ireland | Australia
India | New Zealand | South Africa

Allen Lane is part of the Penguin Random House group of companies
whose addresses can be found at global.penguinrandomhouse.com.

First published in the United States of America by Basic Books, an imprint of Perseus
Books, LLC, a subsidiary of Hachette Book Group, Inc. 2020
This edition first published by Allen Lane 2020

005

Print book interior design by Amnet Systems

Printed and bound in Great Britain by Clays Ltd, Elcograf S.p.A.

A CIP catalogue record for this book is available from the British Library

ISBN: 978–0–241–28398–1

www.greenpenguin.co.uk

For the *fylgjur*, all of them

CONTENTS

Contents

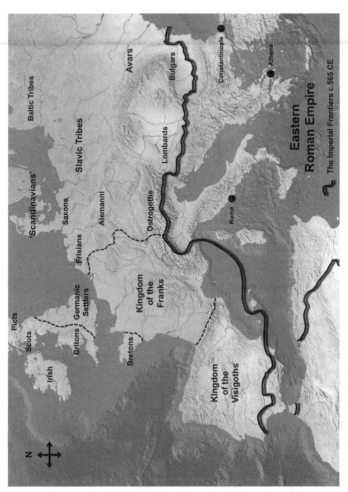

Map 1. Simplified political and ethnic geography of Europe c. 565 CE, showing the changes resulting from the preceding decades of crisis. The borders of the Eastern Roman Empire are depicted as they stood at the death of the Emperor Justinian. Map by Neil Price.

Groups mentioned in
Getica and Widsith

(Unnamed groups)

◯ Tribe, population density

N

Håløyger

Skridfinner

Vino-finner

(Helgeland)

(Namdalen)

Trøndere

(Jämtland)

(Medelpad)

Romser

Finner

(Hälsingland)

NORWAY

(Valdres)

Heder

SWEDEN

(Hardanger)

Hader

Raumer

Svear
(Fjärdrundeland)

Horder

(Närke)

Lid-
Vikinger

(Värmland)

(Södermanland)

Grener

Öst-götar

Ryger

Raner

Euner

Egder

Ö-gröter

Västgötar

Tjuster

Goter

(Tveta)

Fjärer

Haller

Finn-
veder

(Värend)

Eowum *(Øland?)*

DENMARK

Berger

Luguder

(Blekinge)

(Göninge)

0   200 km

Map 2. Scandinavian tribal groupings, legal districts, and kingdoms, from sources dating c. 500–1350 CE, including the *Getica* of Jordanes (c. 551) and the tenth-century English poem *Widsith*. Map by and © Ingvild T. Bøckman and Frode Iversen, Museum of Cultural History, University of Oslo, used by kind permission.

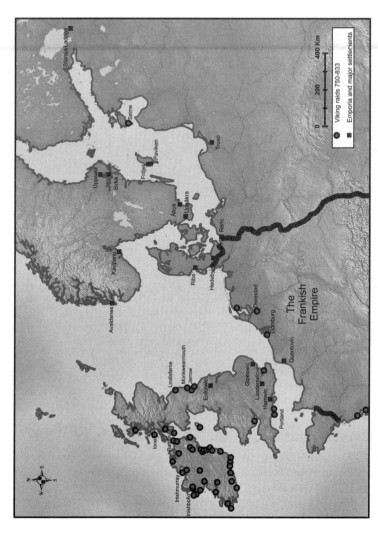

Map 3. Places assaulted in the first phase of Viking raiding, 793–833 CE, with the European coastal emporia and the major settlements of Scandinavia. Map by Ben Raffield and Daniel Löwenborg.

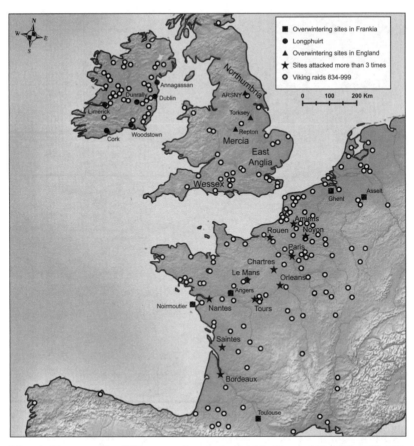

Map 4. The successive Viking assaults on the British isles and Frankia, 834–999, with the bases established in Ireland, in England, and on the Continent. Map by Ben Raffield and Daniel Löwenborg.

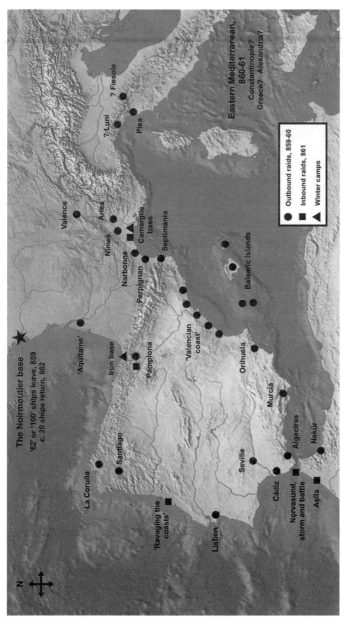

Map 5. The great Mediterranean raid of c. 859–862, allegedly commanded by Björn Ironside and Hástein. The path of the Viking fleet can be traced southward from its base at Noirmoutier in the Loire estuary, around the coasts of Frankia and Iberia, and into the Middle Sea itself; three years later, a third of the ships made it home, having spent time somewhere in the eastern Mediterranean and fought the passage of the Gibraltar Straits (Nörvasund). Map by Neil Price.

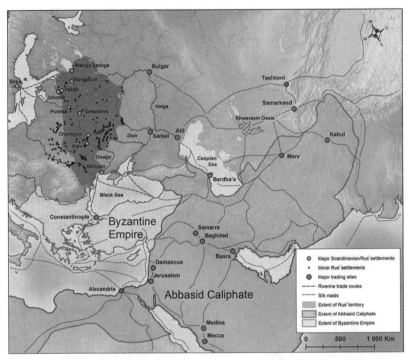

Map 6. The Viking diaspora in the East, to Byzantium, the Steppe, and beyond. The river routes from the Baltic to the Black Sea, dominated by the Rus', connected seamlessly with the caravans of the Abbasid Caliphate and the Silk Roads, extending far into Asia. Map by Ben Raffield, Daniel Löwenborg, and Neil Price.

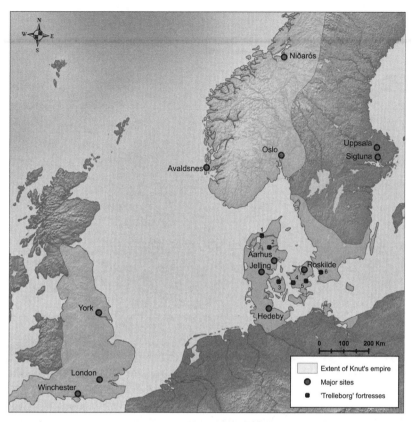

Map 7. The later Viking Age in Scandinavia and the North Sea, from the reign of Harald Bluetooth (c. 960–987) to the 'empire' of Knut the Great (c. 1016–1035). The six known 'Trelleborg'-type circular fortresses are shown: (1) Aggersborg, (2) Fyrkat, (3) Nonnebakken, (4) Trelleborg, (5) Borgring, (6) Borgeby. Map by Ben Raffield and Daniel Löwenborg.

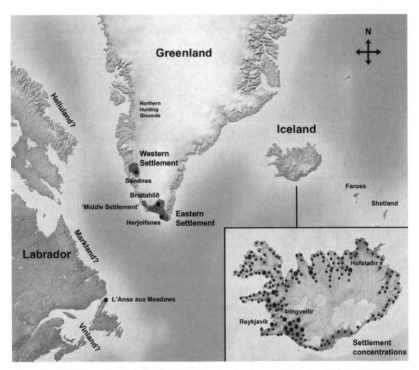

Map 8. The Norse in the North Atlantic. Iceland was settled c. 870 and quickly attracted a large population. Just over a century later, Icelanders founded the Eastern and Western Settlements in Greenland, and in turn sailed to what is now eastern Canada. The precise location of the regions they named Helluland, Markland, and Vinland can only be estimated, and L'Anse aux Meadows on Newfoundland remains the only confirmed Norse settlement in North America. Map by Neil Price.

A NOTE ON LANGUAGE

A GREAT DEAL OF THIS book concerns beings, places, and concepts whose names in use today ultimately derive either from the Old Norse language (actually a shorthand term for a complex array of dialects and linguistic branches from Iceland and Scandinavia, dating to the Middle Ages and earlier) or from the modern tongues of the Nordic countries. This can be a complex soundscape to navigate, and there is no simple way that it can be normalised in an English text while also doing justice to its original variety. I have opted for readability and convention over consistency, and the language has been simplified here in several ways.

Two Old Norse (and modern Icelandic) letters have been anglicised, except when quoting texts in the original and certain names: Þ/þ or thorn, as 'th' and pronounced as the first two letters of '<u>th</u>ought'; and Ð/ð or eth, spoken more softly as in 'brea<u>the</u>' but usually rendered as 'd'. In the same way, the Old Norse æ diphthong has been separated 'ae' and is pronounced approximately 'eye'.

Norse acute accents on the vowels have mostly been retained in names: long á is pronounced 'ow', and thus *há* (high) is spoken 'how'; é is 'ay', like the first letter in the alphabet; í is a long 'ee'; ó is a higher, more defined version of the regular sound, spoken like 'owe' and conveying emphasis; ú is long and deep, like the vowel in 's<u>ure</u>' said with a rolling Scots accent. In Old Norse, y is also a vowel, pronounced approximately like 'ew' as in the colloquial expression of disgust; the accented ý stretches it out.

In place-names and personal names, the modern Scandinavian letters å, ä/æ, and ö/ø have been used where appropriate, with the slight differences between Swedish and Danish/Norwegian. These are pronounced in English approximately as follows: å like 'oar'; ä/æ like 'air'; ö/ø like 'err'. The Swedish letter ö has been used for ǫ, the Old Norse o with ogonek.

Some academic works—including many of my own—use the Old Norse nominative for proper names, even when this is rendered grammatically problematic by the present-day English context. The most common example, also including some of the letters and accents mentioned above, is probably the name of the god Óðinn (pronounced '<u>Owe</u>-thinn'). With some exceptions, this and other similar cases (such as his son Þórr) are anglicised here, thus 'Odin' and 'Thor'.

Quotations from Old Norse texts are mostly rendered in English without the original, although occasionally I have retained the medieval words as well, especially in verse. When properly recited in appropriate surroundings, Viking-Age poetry can taste like cold iron on the tongue, its complex rhyme schemes building upon one another like layers of frost—treacherous but beautiful. We gain something old and true in this language, even if only understood in translation, and for that reason I have included a selection here.

PROLOGUE: DRIFTWOOD

The gods' footprints stretch out behind them in a meandering line, clear in the sands by the shore of the encircling ocean. Its waves crash and foam beside them, in their ears its roar. The beach is utterly unmarked by the passage of others because there are as yet no humans in this world.

It is three brothers we see walking: Odin—the most powerful and terrible of them all—and his siblings, Vili and Vé. They go by many names, which will become a common thing in their divine family of the Aesir.

Peaceful and still though it seems, everything around them has been built from blood, the earth and the heavens fashioned—literally— from the dismembered body of a murder victim. The universe as crime scene: it is an unsettling story, full of strangeness, violence, and contra-dictions, a tale whose truths must be felt rather than merely explained and understood. We shall explore it in time, but for now, in its after-math, all is quiet. They are curious, these gods, always restlessly inquir-ing into the nature of the things they find in their shiny new creation. What is that? And this? They are also lonely, in this place that as yet lacks spirit, sense, and colour.

But now the gods are on the strand, and they have seen something by the water's edge.

Two great stumps of driftwood have washed up with the tide, the beach otherwise empty under the immensity of the sky. Odin and his

1

brothers approach them, turning over the trunks in the sand with effort. And it is then that they understand what is inside, as a sculptor perceives the carving within the block of raw stone, waiting to be released. The three gods work their hands into the wood, moulding, planing, shaping it along the grain. A cloud of shavings and dust. They grin at each other, swept up by the joy of making. Slowly the things inside become visible, forming under the pressure of divine fingers. Here is an arm, and there a leg, and at last, the faces.

First, a man—the first man—and then a woman. The gods stare down at them. It is Odin who moves now, exhaling into their mouths, giving them life; they cough, start to breathe, still trapped inside the wood. It is Vé who opens their eyes and ears, sets their tongues in motion, smoothes their features; wild glances, a babble of noise. It is Vili who gifts them intelligence and movement; they shake themselves free of the stumps, flakes of bark falling.

Last of all, the gods give them names, their substance transformed into sound. The man is Askr, *the ash tree. The woman is* Embla, *the elm.*

The first people in the world look around them, astonished, listening to the silence and then filling it with speech, shouts, laughter. They point at the ocean, the sky, the forest, at more and more, naming them all, laughing again. They begin to run, away from the gods watching them, off along the sand, farther and farther into their new home until they are lost to sight. Perhaps they wave to Odin and the others, perhaps not, but they will see them again.

From this couple are descended all of humankind, down through the millennia to our own time.

The Vikings enjoy a popular recognition and interest shared by few other ancient cultures. More or less everyone has at least heard of them. Over just three centuries, from approximately 750 to 1050 CE, the peoples of Scandinavia transformed the northern world in ways that are still felt today. They changed the political and cultural map of Europe and shaped new configurations of trade, economy, settlement, and conflict that ultimately stretched from

1. The Vikings and the Victorians, incarnate. An extraordinary drawing from 1895 by Lorenz Frølich, of the gods' feast as related in the Old Norse poem Lokasenna, 'Loki's Quarrel'. The Aesir gods appear as a cross between barbarian banqueters in the Classical mould and rather prim contemporary diners, while Loki plays drunk uncle, all in a Rococo room under what seems to be a chandelier. Image: in the public domain.

the eastern American seaboard to the Asian steppe. The Vikings are known today for a stereotype of maritime aggression—those famous longships, the plunder and pillage, the fiery drama of a 'Viking funeral'. Beyond the clichés there is some truth in this, but the Scandinavians also exported new ideas, technologies, beliefs, and practices to the lands they discovered and the peoples they encountered. In the process they were themselves altered, developing new ways of life across a vast diaspora. The many small-scale kingdoms of their homelands would eventually become the nations of Norway, Sweden, and Denmark, which are still with us, while the traditional beliefs of the North were gradually subordinated by Christianity. That initially alien faith would fundamentally change their view of the world, and the Scandinavian future.

In a literal sense, the Vikings are of course people of the past, dead and gone—but at the same time they inhabit a curiously haptic kind of prehistory, one that appears to return whatever pressure is applied to it. Many have been tempted to put their fingers on the scales of hindsight and imagined that the impulse to do so came not from themselves but through the revelation of hidden truths buried by time. Medieval monks and scholars reinvented their pagan ancestors either as nobly misguided forebears or as agents of the devil. In the manuscript illuminations of Romance literature, with a kind of Orientalist prejudice, they became Saracens, enemies of Christ depicted with turbans and scimitars. In Shakespeare's England, the Vikings were taken up as violent catalysts in the early story of the kingdom's greatness. Rediscovered during the Enlightenment as a sort of 'noble savage', the figure of the Viking was enthusiastically adopted by the nationalist Romantics of the eighteenth and nineteenth centuries. Searching for their own emerging identities, Victorian imperialists scoured Scandinavian literature looking for suitably assertive northern role models, expressing the manifest destiny of the Anglo-Saxons through their Nordic cousins. The logical end of that trajectory came a century later, when the Nazis appropriated the Vikings in pursuit of their racist fictions, elevating them as a spurious Aryan archetype; their modern successors still plague us today. Elements of the broad Pagan community now seek a spiritual alternative that draws inspiration from Viking religion, with Tolkienesque flavourings added to a cloudier Old Norse brew. All these and many more, including today's academics and the audiences for historical drama, have taken the fragmentary material and textual remains of the Vikings and recast them in moulds of their choosing. At times it can seem that the actual people have almost disappeared under the

2. Where it all went wrong. A recruitment poster for the SS, advertising a rally in Nazi-occupied Norway in 1943. The political appropriation of the Vikings could not be more obvious. Image: in the public domain.

cumulative freight they have been made to bear. One recalls *Brideshead Revisited* and Anthony Blanche, "*Oh, la fatigue du Nord*".

What unites most of these perspectives is that they privilege the observer, looking in on the Vikings from the outside, and ignore how they themselves saw the world. This attitude has a long pedigree, and in fact dates back to the writings of the Vikings' victims, who can hardly be expected to be unbiased. Ironically, even the people with whom the Scandinavians came into contact (often at the point of a sword) were not always entirely sure whom they were really dealing with. To take a single example from the late ninth century, after a vicious war with an entire Viking army, King Alfred of Wessex in southern England could still entertain a non-combatant Norwegian merchant at his court, asking question after question: Where did they come from? What did they do? How did they live? The king was not alone in his uncertainty and curiosity.

Those same puzzles continued to be debated for the next thousand years, accelerating in the last two centuries or so with the growth of academic enquiry and scholarship. Here again, though, the focus has largely tended to be on what the Vikings did rather than on why they did it. There is a sense in which this viewpoint is looking through the wrong end of the historical telescope, defining (and often judging) a people solely by the consequences of their actions rather than the motivations behind them.

This book takes the opposite approach, working from the inside looking out. The emphasis here is very firmly on who the Vikings really were, what made them tick, how they thought and felt. Their dramatic expansion will not be ignored, of course, but its context, its origins, are at the core of what follows.

Where better to begin, then, than with the creation itself? The tale of the gods fashioning the first humans from stumps of wood, on the shores of the world ocean, has roots that extend very deeply into Norse mythology. For all the fearful confusion about their identity among those they encountered, in the Vikings' own minds there was never any doubt at all: they were the children of Ash, the children of Elm.

INTRODUCTION: ANCESTORS AND INHERITORS

WHAT DOES 'VIKING' ACTUALLY MEAN? Should it be used at all, and if so, how?

The Scandinavians of the eighth to eleventh centuries knew the word—*víkingr* in Old Norse when applied to a person—but they would not have recognised themselves or their times by that name. For them it would perhaps have meant something approximating to 'pirate', defining an occupation or an activity (and probably a relatively marginal one); it was certainly not an identity for an entire culture. Even then, the word was not necessarily negative or always associated with violence—these overtones would begin to accrete round it in the centuries after the Viking Age. Similarly, it did not refer exclusively to Scandinavians; it was also applied to Baltic raiders in general, and the word was even used in England. By the same token, the Vikings' targets were by no means only outside Scandinavia; maritime robbery with violence rarely respects such proprieties. Even as late as the eleventh century, a Swedish runestone could commemorate a man—one Assur, son of Jarl Hákan—"who kept the Viking watch", standing guard against incursions from the neighbours.

The exact derivation of the term is unknown, but the most widely accepted interpretation today builds on the Old Norse *vík*, a bay of the sea. Thus Vikings may originally have been 'bay-people', their ships waiting in concealment to strike at passing marine traffic. Another alternative links the term to the Víken region of south-western Norway, from which the earliest raiders were once believed to have come; this too may have some validity.

In the modern Nordic languages, *vikingar* or *vikinger* is still used only in the exact sense of seaborne raiders, while in English and other tongues it has come to serve for anyone who had, as one Cambridge scholar resignedly put it, "a nodding acquaintance with Scandinavia 'in those days'". There have been many attempts to get around the problem, with little success (such as the late historian who ranted for several pages about what he saw as his colleagues' terminological carelessness, only to content himself with 'Norsemen'—thereby excluding Swedes, Danes, and, indeed, women). Some scholars now use lowercase 'vikings' to mean the general populace, while reserving title case for their piratical acquaintances. In this book, big-V 'Vikings' is employed through-out but defined through context.

This is much more than semantic nitpicking. In speaking of a Viking Age at all, using a term that would have surprised the people supposedly labelled with it, there is a sense in which histori-ans have created an unhelpful abstraction. Of course, the past has always been divided into conveniently manageable chunks of time, but when scholars argue about when the Viking Age 'started', this is not the same as debating, say, the origins of the Roman Empire, which was very far from a retrospective concept.

It is good to bear in mind that no other contemporary peoples ranged over the then-known Eurasian and North Atlantic world to the same degree as the Scandinavians. They travelled through the territories of some forty-odd present-day countries, in docu-mented encounters with more than fifty cultures. Some scholars have tried to claim that in this the Vikings were in no way remark-able or significant in themselves, merely the regional manifestation of Continental mobility and general trends in the reorganisation of the post-Roman economy—essentially a kind of burgeoning early medieval European Union with some particularly aggressive negotiators in the north. It is true that raiding and maritime warfare undoubtedly existed around the Baltic and the North Sea for centuries (and probably millennia) before the time of the Vikings. However, there is no doubt that the flow, scale, and range of seaborne piracy gradually but dramatically increased from the 750s onwards, culminating in the full-blown military campaigns of the ninth and tenth centuries that would shatter the political structures of western Europe. At the same time, there were parallel and intertwined movements of colonialism, trade, and exploration, especially to the east. In short, the 'Viking Age', hindsight construct of researchers though it undoubtedly is, has genuine validity.

There have also been other attempts to write the Vikings out of history, ironically focussing on how they have been written into it. The idea is that this piece of the past was 'colonised' by the future and bent out of shape to suit its needs—essentially that the Vikings were creations of later peoples' imaginations. This makes little sense to me. Yes, nationalist Romanticism, Victorian imperialism, and their even darker European successors all certainly had an impact on how the Vikings were seen afterwards, but they actually say nothing at all about what really happened between the mid-eighth and eleventh centuries—only about how it was subsequently appropriated and sometimes weaponised (which, of course, should not be ignored).

With all this ambiguity and such a long background of sociopolitical abuse, it is therefore vital to be clear that the concept of the Viking Age has a testable, empirical reality that can be illuminated by close study. The three hundred years from about 750 CE onwards were above all else a period of social transformation so profound as to ultimately shape northern Europe for the next millennium—a process that in itself justifies the notion of a discrete Viking Age.

Synthesising all this is a daunting prospect. A narrative track, running chronologically, is necessary to understand the events of these three centuries in context, but there is no single strand to follow across the vast and varied arenas of the Viking diaspora. There have been longer books than this one written solely on Scandinavian interactions with what is now European Russia, to take just one example, and the same can be said of the rest of their world. Inevitably, something will be lost when using such a wide-angle lens. Readers seeking detailed discussion of Viking art, typologies of artefacts, ship-building methods, and much more have many well-illustrated, technical studies to choose from and can use the references at the back of this book as a point of entry. Similarly, if the Scandinavians encountered more than fifty cultures, even a thousand words on each would easily take half a book of dry description alone. While the bigger picture is always in the background as one walks with the Vikings, the most productive focus can be on simultaneities, on snapshots and brief visits in different times and places.

This approach opens up new possibilities but also acknowledges limits. In particular, the notion of Viking exceptionalism (which is not the same as difference) is problematic and, I believe, should be avoided where possible. To take an image that they would have liked, northern European folk tales often revolve around a search for someone's secret name (the fairy story of Rumpelstiltskin is an obvious example). The Vikings have left clues to theirs, the true self hidden beneath the surface. A strong sense of the numinous place courses through Norse poetry and even runic inscriptions, created by minds in tune with their environment. The same mind-set is visible in their material culture, in every available surface—including the human body—covered in interlaced designs, writhing patterns, animals, and other images that were imbued with meaning. Their world hummed with life, but its boundaries, both internal and external, were in many senses more permeable than ours, always and constantly connected by winding paths to the realms of the gods and other powers.

However, alongside the stories that unfold throughout this book, it is important not to lose sight of the absences, the things that are *not* known. Some of them are details; others are funda-mental. The resulting gaps can seem curiously random. It is possi-ble to fill these blank spaces but only through informed speculation (and history is nothing if not a suppositional discipline, sometimes akin to a sort of speculative fiction of the past).

Little is understood, for example, of how the Vikings measured time. Their music and songs are a mystery; here there is a poten-tial starting point in the few surviving instruments, with tonal qualities that can be reconstructed, but what the Vikings did with them is another matter entirely. It is unclear where women were believed to go when they died. Why was so much silver buried in the ground and never recovered? These and other questions go on and on, and have vexed scholars for centuries. Some questions are more tentative, and their answers may be unknowable. But they are still worth asking. If you truly believed—in fact, *knew*—that the man living up the valley could turn into a wolf under certain circumstances, what was it like to be his neighbour? What was it like to be married to him?

We will probably never speak the Vikings' secret name, but if we are open to their voices, to their concerns and ideas—in a word, to their minds—I believe it is possible not only to truly explore these ancient lives, but to write a new story of how we became who we are. This, then, is the Viking Age of the children of Ash and Elm: a set of vantage points from which to look out over people, place, and time, inevitably finite but also in constant motion. Of course, it is also in a sense *my* Viking Age, informed by more than thirty years of research but—as with the work of any professional student of the past—equally constrained by my own biases and preconceptions.

But how to get there? In practical terms, what sources of evi-dence can be used to get closer to the Vikings?

Like many fields of scholarship, Viking studies is occasionally convulsed by interdisciplinary squabbles, especially between those who work with texts and their archaeological colleagues who approach the past through things and places—an argument that never really settles, but just keeps rumbling along like the irregular tremors on a fault line. The production of text is, of course, also a deeply material act—the cutting of signs into stone or wood, or painting them with a quill onto vellum—a process that requires direction, effort, resources, preparation, all naturally with purpose and social context beyond simple communication. Some of the very rarest sources, such as the great epic poem *Beowulf*, for example, exist in only a single manuscript; they are, quite literally, artefacts.

Students of the Vikings tend to specialise in one particular bandwidth of signals from the late first millennium, but they need to be conversant with many more, often stretching far later in time: archaeology, saga scholarship, philology, runology, the history of religions—the list goes on, now with increasing contributions from the natural and environmental sciences, including genomics. A knowledge of the modern Scandinavian languages is essential, as is at least a working familiarity with Old Norse and Latin.

As an archaeologist myself, it is hardly surprising that much of this book is based on the results of excavations and fieldwork. Whether concerned with objects, buildings, burials, or samples for scientific analysis of varying kinds, all this essentially relates to *things*—or to use the academic term, 'material culture', which captures it quite well.

Some of these things, especially the contents of graves, have survived because the people of the time made deliberate arrangements for their disposal: put simply, they have been found because they were intentionally left where they were placed. In burials it is possible to directly encounter the Vikings themselves, in the form of their skeletal or cremated remains. However, for the most part, what archaeological studies uncover are fragments, broken and badly preserved, that have survived by chance through loss, abandonment, discard, or decay. These include the occupation layers of settlements with all the bits and pieces that found their way into the ground over the years that people lived there: smashed pottery, food waste, things that were dropped or else left behind when it was finally time to move on. Archaeologists also find traces of the buildings themselves, preserved as dark outlines in the soil where timbers have rotted away or as the holes that once held posts supporting roofs and walls. On rare occasions there are stones from foundation sills, or the trenches where they had lain before somebody took them away for recycling.

Archaeology is a highly interpretive undertaking, a constant balancing of probabilities and alternatives. One can speculate with varying degrees of confidence, but it is not always possible to be sure. An essential prerequisite for a good researcher is the willingness to be wrong, the invitation of constructive critique. Nevertheless, while conclusions must be framed carefully, it is pointless to caveat everything to oblivion, to believe that it is impossible to really know anything about the past. In this, archaeologists are aided by an impressive theoretical apparatus, one that is always evolving and contentious and quite often impenetrable from outside, but vital nonetheless. It can be positively astonishing, and uplifting, to compare our understanding of the Viking-Age (and global) past even fifty years ago with what we know now. The Vikings I studied in college in the 1980s were quite different from the people I teach undergraduates about today, and the same will certainly be true of their students in turn. This is how it should be.

There are other issues too. Common to most archaeological sites is the question of preservation, which largely depends on the local soil types and their relative acidity. Stone is the material most impervious to damage, although it may well have become chipped or eroded if exposed to the elements over a long period of time. Metal and ceramics are both quite likely to have survived (albeit corroded or otherwise degraded), while bone is only variably preserved. Rarest of all are the organics—things made of textile, leather, wood, and the like—which have almost always disappeared except when the soil is waterlogged or else in other ways excludes oxygen.

This all applies to things in the ground, but archaeologists also record the visible landscape—most obviously for the Viking Age in the form of earthworks, fortifications, or burial mounds but also including standing stone monuments, field boundaries in the form of ditches or drystone walls, and so on. The topography itself may have changed, as rivers have altered course, shorelines have risen or fallen, wetlands been reclaimed, and in rare cases where natural events such as volcanic eruptions have effected more drastic impacts—but the evidence is there. As landscapes can be 'read', so can what lies hidden beneath them, using non-destructive reconnaissance techniques such as georadar and a variety of electromagnetic methods that can penetrate the soil to reveal buried features, trenches, postholes, and hearths.

As we combine excavation, field survey, and geophysical prospection, the wider arena of Viking-Age settlements can be pieced together, down to the minutiae of people's lives. This can reveal how they lived, what they wore and ate; it can show the things they made and used. Archaeologists can reconstruct what their homes and farms were like, how people made a living and sustained themselves, and can gain an idea of their economies. One can also paint a sketchy picture of family structure and social hierarchies—an approximation of political systems and the way in which power may have been manifested. Archaeology can furthermore recover ritual activities, both for the living and the dead, that can open windows into the mind and the landscapes of religion. Not least, all this can also illustrate how these peoples of the Viking Age interacted with each other, both within the huge territory of what is now Scandinavia and also far beyond.

Over the past half-century, archaeological science has dramatically altered our understanding of the past, in the Viking Age no less than for other time periods. The analysis of strontium and oxygen isotopes in human teeth and bones can locate the places where people spent their formative years, tell us whether they moved around, and also reveal what they ate. Materials science can identify objects and substances so badly preserved that previously their nature could only be guessed at. Scientific analysis can trace the origin of the metals, clays, and minerals used in manufacturing; the species and habitats of the animals whose fur, bones, and ivory were employed as raw materials; and exact dates from the growth rings of trees, sometimes giving the year and even season of an event. Archaeologists can excavate a sunken ship in Denmark and determine that it was built in Ireland. Analysis of ancient DNA can make reliable sex determinations of the dead, tease out their family relationships, and even reveal the colour of their eyes and hair; it also makes possible the wider tracking of migrations and larger demographic change. Environmental studies can recreate the flora of settlements and landscapes, determine whether an area was cultivated or under forest and what crops were grown, and provide a scale for alterations in land use over time.

No single specialist can master all these fields, but the combined teamwork of archaeologists in the field, laboratory, and library now has greater potential for recovering the lives of past peoples than ever before.

But the evidence for the Viking Age relies on more than this material culture and the other natural and physical traces of the time, although the data is varied and always growing. What about written sources? The cultures of Scandinavia at this time were predominantly oral in that they did not make literary or documentary records—the Vikings never wrote their own histories. This is not the same as being illiterate; the use of runic script was widespread in the North from its beginnings in Roman times to a flowering of inscriptions in the Viking Age itself. Nonetheless, this material is limited. There are thousands of brief memorials and epitaphs carved in stone, sometimes with a few lines of poetry, and also rare examples of everyday notes and labels scratched into slivers of wood. But there are no lengthier texts from inside the Viking-Age societies of the North.

Instead, their culture is what is called protohistoric, in that its 'history' comes from what some of their foreign contemporaries wrote about them. This, however, presents problems that are in many ways at the core of all the modern stereotypes of the Vikings, for the obvious reason that most sources of this kind were authored by people on the sharp end of their aggression. The bulk of these records take the form of court annals, usually compiled in Latin, for the ruling dynasties of western Europe. A number of different texts, often named after the monasteries where they were produced or kept, cover the Frankish and Ottonian (German) Empires on the Continent, and variant Old English manuscripts of the so-called *Anglo-Saxon Chronicle* cover England. There are counterparts from the Arab world, especially the Caliphate of Córdoba in Andalucía, and from the Byzantine Empire that ruled from Constantinople, to name but a few.

To these can be added the drier legal documentation of land grants and charters, some of which preserve incidental information of the Vikings' activities, such as references to the sites of their former defensive works or camps. There is also the law itself—the early medieval regional legislation written down a century or more after the time of the Vikings but often encoding a variety of useful information that is clearly very old. The same cultural milieu also produced a smaller number of more personal texts written by monks and priests, travellers, diplomats and merchants, spies, poets, and others who encountered the Vikings at home or abroad.

All these kinds of documents will be taken up in the following chapters, but it is important to understand two of their qualities above all else. First, although they originate in contemporary and sometimes eyewitness accounts, in their present form they were almost all compiled, edited, or transcribed at a later date, and critical questions must be asked of that context. Second, while they often give the appearance of straightforward reportage, they are always written with a purpose—frequently outright propaganda, not only showing their authors in a favourable light that casts shade on the Vikings but also to the disadvantage of other neighbouring kingdoms or peoples. In short, they must be treated with care.

Besides the broadly contemporary written sources, there are perhaps the most famous tales of all: the extraordinary body of Icelandic texts that has given the North its own literary tradition. For many people, the Vikings are so synonymous with 'the sagas' that they are surprised to discover that, in fact, these vivid narratives date from centuries after the events they claim to describe. For anyone wanting to understand more about the Viking Age, coming to grips with these texts is a complex matter.

Saga simply means 'story', literally 'what is said', both in Old Norse and in the modern Scandinavian languages. As with any storytelling tradition, there are numerous narrative styles and genres, composed at different times and places and for a wide variety of purposes. The first Old Norse sagas were written down in Iceland during the late 1100s, more than a hundred years after the nominal end of the Viking Age. The tradition continued for centuries thereafter, although with a creative floruit in the 1200s, and new sagas were still being composed beyond the Reformation and into early modern times. The deceptively simple term thus embraces a range of texts from formal histories to bedtime stories for listeners around the hearth, with many stops along the way.

The two genres of saga-writing most often cited in connection with the Vikings are the sagas of Icelanders, also known as the family sagas, and the so-called *fornaldarsögur*—literally 'stories of ancient times' but more often referred to as the legendary sagas. Both genres are actively concerned with the Viking Age, but in different ways and with varying degrees of reliability, although the question of their 'accuracy' depends on one's approach to these medieval texts.

The sagas of Icelanders usually focus on individual families of settlers in that young North Atlantic country, and frequently on a smaller region such as a valley or district. The colonists' gene-alogical heritage is traced in detail, not only back to the settlement of Iceland but to their earlier ancestry in Scandinavia. The sagas vividly follow these people's lives and adventures, sometimes over decades, and in the process sketch a compellingly convincing picture of Iceland at the time: a unique political experiment, a republic of farmers in an age of kings. Feud and revenge are common themes, with neighbourly quarrels escalating to theft and murder, as competing lawsuits attempt to stem the tide of inter-generational violence that usually follows. These themes are interwoven with affairs of love and war, and the full range of human emotions in tightly wrapped rural communities with international contacts. Beneath the skin of most of the tales beats a steady pulse of magical contacts with the Other World, of sorcery and seers, of spirits and supernatural beings, although rarely the gods in any direct sense. From the tenth century onwards (according to the sagas' internal chronologies), such activities are increasingly contrasted, and sometimes conflicted, with the growing influence of the 'White Christ', their name for the figure of Jesus. All these events are often played out against uneasy tensions with the royal families of Norway, who were watching Iceland with territorial envy, and the ever-present backdrop of political events in a wider world.

As their name implies, the legendary sagas include elements common to tales of the fantastic—heroes battling monsters, the curses of evil witches, and so on—but often inserted into stories that nonetheless bear some connection to known history. In particular, the legendary sagas sometimes include narratives that ostensibly concern events long *before* the Viking Age, stretching back to the time of the great migrations when the post-Roman map of Europe was violently transformed. Figures such as the Hun warlord Attila appear (rather approvingly), along with fifth- and sixth-century kings and military leaders struggling for dominance. Unlike the family sagas, in these stories Iceland is not always the primary focus, and they span the European world with extensions far into the East.

There are other, more contemporary forms that deal with the time of the saga-writers themselves, including the *Sturlunga saga*, a collection relating the political fortunes of the eponymous family; the Bishops' sagas; several flavours of Christian morality tales; and more. Medieval Iceland was far from isolated, and there are also sagas that clearly bear influences of the European fashion for chivalric Romance, with stories of dashing knights rescuing princesses from dragons and the like. Even the popular epic of the Trojan War was recast in an Old Norse version, *Ektors saga*, which revealingly focusses on the doomed Homeric hero rather than on his assassin, Achilles—perhaps an insight into Scandinavian notions of martial honour.

There is also another important category of Old Norse text, namely poetry. This too comes in several different varieties, sometimes composed as free-standing verses but more often as commemorations of events or, most of all, as praise poems. Poetry was also used as a medium for the storage and communication of mythological lore and as a repository of heroic tales.

Unlike the prose texts of the medieval sagas, it is generally agreed that the Old Norse poetic corpus may be considerably older and could actually preserve the voices of the Viking Age. This is because of the extremely complex structure and rhyme schemes of Norse poetry, which mean that if the verses are to function at all they need to be remembered and repeated largely intact. Poetic ability was a very highly prized quality in the Viking Age, an admirable skill for a well-rounded person to master, and especially for anyone aspiring to leadership. This too has contributed to the poetry's survival. Individual memory—the legacy left by a good name after one's death—was crucial, and was deliberately fostered by the upper strata of society who either composed verses in their own honour or else acted as patrons to those who could do it for them. These professional poets were the famous skalds, and it must be said that they did their job: the subjects of their elegant, commissioned boasting are still being talked about a thousand years later.

There are three main sources of Old Norse poems, one of which is the saga corpus itself, which occasionally preserved them as the reported speech of the protagonists. Much of the rest has survived in two medieval Icelandic works known as *Eddas*. The word's derivation and meaning are uncertain—many explanations have been proposed—but either by definition or metaphorical allusion it seems to refer to the production of poetry.

One of them, known as the *Prose Edda*, is a discrete work by the scholar, historian, and politician Snorri Sturluson, written sometime around the second or third decade of the thirteenth century and preserved in several later manuscripts. Snorri's *Edda* is literally a handbook for poets, a manual of style divided into three sections with a prologue, the whole text covering genre and metre, with discourses on the subject matter appropriate to different occasions and purposes. Containing a huge wealth of information as prose asides, the key fact is that Snorri mainly makes his points through quoted example. The *Prose Edda* thus in a sense belies its name, in that its pages are filled with poems, cited whole or as fragments and often with the authors' names. Some of the material is known from other sources, but much of it comes only from Snorri. The text is especially rich in skaldic verse, allusions to mythology and the traditional religion, numerous fragments of tales, and lists of alternative poetic terms for a wide range of things, including supernatural entities (such as the many names of Odin, for example). Snorri's *Edda* is one of the most remarkable literary documents of the Middle Ages.

Alongside this handbook is another medieval work known as the *Poetic Edda*, although (as for Snorri's book) this is a modern title. Largely preserved in two manuscripts with variations between them, alongside later copies, this is a wide-ranging collection of anonymous verses with mythological and heroic themes. Little is known of how they came to be collated in this way, by whom, or why. It has even been speculated that the main manuscript (the so-called Codex Regius, kept in Reykjavík) was the work of a collector of curiosities, which might explain why it is a physically small, scrappy little book made of reused parchment—hardly the stuff of prestigious record. Who knows what made a thirteenth-century Icelandic Christian so carefully preserve the core tales of her or his pagan past, but it is fortunate that they did. The poems are ambiguous, elusive, and hard to interpret, and they speak obliquely of powerful sacred knowledge for the already initiated. They are also difficult to date, although the earliest are thought to have been composed towards the end of the Viking Age, building on more ancient models. For all its complexity and source-critical problems, the *Poetic Edda* is *the* primary foundation for what is known of Norse mythology, cosmology, the tales of the gods and goddesses, and the great heroic lays of the North. Fragments of 'Eddic' poems also appear in Snorri's writings and occasionally in sagas, making a corpus of some forty works altogether.

With the exception of runic inscriptions, all the surviving Old Norse texts date to the centuries *after* the time of the Vikings, and were written down by Christians. They are, therefore, separated from the pagan Viking Age they claim to describe by significant barriers of time, culture, and ideological perspective. Many of the sagas are also focussed on Iceland, either by narrative locale and/or production, thus introducing a geographical bias into what must originally have been a much wider, pan-Scandinavian world of stories. Furthermore, each text was unique and written for specific reasons, not all of them immediately obvious to a modern reader. Even to this, one must add the vagaries of preservation: texts have become corrupted through faulty copying over time (we almost never have the 'original' manuscripts); passages have been lost, edited and changed, or simply censored; and, of course, the matter of a work's survival at all is never assured. Sometimes the fragmentary nature of a text is obvious, as well as how and why. On occasion the names of sagas that have not survived are known, along with brief summaries of their contents. In many cases it is impossible to know what has been lost.

Before approaching the sagas, or indeed any other works of Old Norse prose and poetry, it is necessary to answer a deceptively simple question: what do you want to do with them? For many studying a saga text, whether from the perspective of literary or material research, there is often (as Tolkien put it with regard to *Beowulf*) "disappointment at the discovery that it was itself and not something that the scholar would have liked better". As the name implies, the sagas were stories first and foremost, meant to be told aloud, but for their intended hearers they also had a context. Viking lives were structured around relationships, not just within families but between them, and extending much further across society in webs of mutual dependence. The sagas anchored people in time and gave them a link to the past—to what Tolkien again called "that sense of perspective, of antiquity with a greater and yet darker antiquity behind".

This perception has not disappeared. Part of the family sagas' dislocating effect on a modern audience is the way they *feel* so real, as if they somehow let the reader experience what it meant to be alive in that alien world, in all its laconic drama and heightened sense of things. In Iceland, their homeland, the sagas are even now entirely living works, familiar to all. Everyone can (and should!) enjoy these tales as the true masterpieces of world literature they undoubtedly are—but it is when one wishes to go beyond that, to 'use' them in some way, that more fundamental issues arise. The most basic question of all is one of focus: are we interested in the actual, real, lived Viking Age that the sagas have as their theme, or do we want to know how this ancient experience was mediated and appropriated in the medieval environment of the sagas' composition and social context? These are utterly different questions.

A reasonable first step must be to ask whether it is even possible to perceive genuine Viking-Age lives under the medieval textual patina, or if they were present to begin with. It is worth considering what a fully negative answer would mean. Even the most sceptical of literary researchers, those who generally reject the Old Norse texts as viable sources (however remote) for the actual Viking Age, do not always go on to confront the question this viewpoint requires: why, in that case, would medieval Icelanders have created—over several centuries—the most remarkably detailed, comprehensive, and consistent corpus of historical fiction in the world? While some have argued for Christian allegories in the sagas—the Odinnic warrior-poet Egil Skalla-Grímsson as an avatar of St. Paul, for example—why the elaboration of such a device when the Norse were perfectly capable of assimilating the biblical stories directly? If the intention was retrospectively to link Christian virtues with ancestors who could still be admired because they could not have been expected to know better, how does this explain a genre of storytelling that at its moral core promotes a pagan view of life utterly at odds with the prevailing norms of medieval thought? Far beyond the hazy golden age of an *Iliad* or the commissioned foundation myths of an *Aeneid*, these are entire cycles of tales that deal in detail with the doomed nobility of people from whom the Church of the saga-writers' times would have recoiled.

This book rejects that viewpoint as far as the Old Norse texts are concerned, and attempts a clear-eyed but not uncritical journey along the other path—the one we hope will lead us to the world of the Vikings themselves; we will not linger very long in its later, medieval shadow. Nevertheless, the obstacles in reading the sources in this way are considerable. Broadly speaking, medieval writings of all kinds can almost *never* be read as straight-up, trustworthy, and reliable reportage of what they claim to describe. There is always an agenda of some description, although the degree to which this is true is individual to each text, and always debatable. The sagas and other textual products of the Old Norse mind are marvellous indeed but must be interpreted with an abundance of caution; we must always be aware of the gaps (sometimes more like chasms) in the knowledge they can impart.

The sources provide terms of reference, but before proceeding it is necessary to set down some terms and conditions—of social context, intellectual responsibility, and ethics. Just as anyone's experiences of living in the present are always subjective, the same is true for history and its study. The Vikings could easily serve as exhibit A.

Over the centuries, a great many people have eagerly pressed the Vikings into (im)moral service, and others continue to do so. However, this intensity of interest also reveals that their ancient lives still speak to us today. I strongly believe that any meaningful twenty-first-century engagement with the Vikings must acknowledge the often deeply problematic ways in which their memory is activated in the present. Viking scholars will recognise the feeling of yet another piece of fact-resistant nonsense surfacing in public or private discourse, and it is therefore important to be unequivocally clear here at the start.

The Viking world this book explores was a strongly multicultural and multi-ethnic place, with all this implies in terms of population movement, interaction (in every sense of the word, including the most intimate), and the relative tolerance required. This extended far back into Northern prehistory. There was never any such thing as a 'pure Nordic' bloodline, and the people of the time would probably have been baffled by the very notion. We use 'Vikings' as a consciously problematic label for the majority population of Scandinavia, but they also shared their immediate world with others—in particular, the semi-nomadic Sámi people. Their respective settlement histories stretch so deeply into the Stone Age past as to make any modern discussion of 'who came first' absurd. Scandinavia had also welcomed immigrants for millennia before the Viking Age, and there is no doubt that a stroll through the market centres and trading places of the time would have been a vibrantly cosmopolitan experience.

The Vikings cannot be reduced to a template, but if abstract concepts can describe their impact upon and interactions with the world around them, then one should look to curiosity, creativity, the complexity and sophistication of their mental landscapes, and, yes, their openness to new experiences and ideas. To seriously engage with the Vikings and their time is to embrace all these, and absolutely not to flatten them with stereotypes. They were as individually varied as *every* reader of this book. At the same time, no one should look away from what we would see as their less palatable sides, particularly the aggression that, in part, fuelled their movement into the wider world—beyond the clichés of 'Viking raiders', this aspect of the early medieval Scandinavian cultures was very real. They were warlike people in conflicted times, and their ideologies were also to a marked degree underpinned by the supernatural empowerment of violence. This could take extreme forms, manifested in such horrors as ritual rape, wholesale slaughter and enslavement, and human sacrifice. We should not read the Vikings backwards from our own time, but anyone who regards them in a 'heroic' light needs to think again.

At the core of any modern relationship with the Vikings must be a commitment to clarity. To observe that these Northern peoples really did bend the arc of history is neither to approve nor condemn, but simply to acknowledge an ancient reality with legacies still perceptible today.

Conventional studies of the Vikings tend to be organised regionally, preserving the artificial notions of 'western' and 'eastern' arenas of activity that are actually just scholarly legacies of the Cold War, with its more-or-less impermeable barrier stretching across Europe. Thus one is usually guided sequentially through the British Isles, the Continent, and the North Atlantic from the first raids to the Battle of Stamford Bridge in 1066, followed by a separate chronological tour of the East over the same period. Along the way in works of that kind, one may also find discrete themes neatly packaged (such as chapter 4, "Religion").

This book attempts something different, not only in terms of promoting the Vikings' worldview but also by emphasising that it was *the same people* traversing that great map of cultures and encounters—no Iron Curtain for them. In addition, their lives must be seen as a seamless whole, blending 'religion', politics, gender, subsistence, and all other aspects of existence into a general perception of reality itself—quite simply the way things seemed to them to be. What, for some, is 'background', building up to what the Vikings accomplished out in the world, is here the point itself.

The text is in three main sections, following an approximately chronological track but acknowledging contemporaneity as well as sequence.

The new home in which Ash and Elm awakened was called *Miðgarðr*, or Midgard, literally the 'Middle Place' (the inspiration, by the way, for Tolkien's Middle Earth). This, of course, is our world too, though the Vikings saw it rather differently. Its geographical limits do not seem to have been defined by any means other than experience and travel. The first part explores this realm through the Vikings' sense of self, and of their environment, and begins by delineating the contours of this landscape both on the ground and inside their heads. It explores their unique understandings of personhood, gender, and the place of the individual in the many dimensions of the cosmos. This also involves meeting the other beings with whom the Vikings shared these spaces.

The Scandinavian experience is traced from the wane of the Western Roman Empire and its interactions with the Germanic tribes beyond its borders, through the turbulent years of the fifth and sixth centuries to the new order that was built on the remains of the old. The social arena of the early North is described here: the material culture of everyday life, the settled landscape, and the overarching structures of politics, power, ritual, belief, law, and war. The borders between the living and the dead are explored, alongside the human relationships with the invisible population around them. The timeline here takes us up to the ninth century—roughly the middle of the Viking Age as conventionally reckoned.

The second part goes back to the early 700s, but follows a different path to seek the major sociopolitical developments and demographic factors that slowly combined to trigger the Viking phenomenon itself. This was the time of the raids and their gradual escalation from isolated attacks to invasions of conquest, in the ever-present context of expanding trade networks. The maritime culture of Scandinavia, the rise of the sea-kings, and the development of uniquely mobile pirate polities are the focus here. The beginnings of the diaspora can be traced in all directions: along the eastern rivers of silver to Byzantium and the Caliphate of the Arabs, creating a new identity in the warrior-traders known as the Rus'; west into the British Isles; south into the Continental empires and the Mediterranean; and through the opening up of the North Atlantic. This section follows these events to the start of the tenth century in a series of parallel, simultaneous narratives.

Part three moves the story to the mid-eleventh century, as the Viking phenomenon diversified across the northern world. Its consequences included an urban revolution in the Scandinavian economies and the reorganisation of the countryside, paralleled by the consolidation of royal power and the rising influence of a new faith. Abroad, competing Viking power bases and kingdoms were established in Frankia, England, Ireland, and the Scottish Isles. The flowering of the Icelandic republic led to westward voyages to Greenland, and the European landfall in North America. In the East, the Rus' state expanded ever further. By 1050 or so, the lines of modern Norway, Denmark, and eventually Sweden, too, were already clear, the Scandinavian peoples beginning to take their place on the stage of Christian Europe.

The Viking Age did not 'end' with particular events in specific times or places any more than it 'began' with them. Instead, it became something else with another shift in perspective, with new points of view as the Scandinavians moved into their many different futures. This book started with driftwood on a beach as the first human couple stepped onto the sand, the beginning of us all. At its close is the final battle and the end of the cosmos, the Nordic apocalypse—the Ragnarök. Wolves will swallow the sun and moon, the white-hot stars will sink into the sea and shroud the world in steam, the powers of the night will pour through a hole in the sky, and the gods will march to war for the last time.

But there is a long way to go before then, and the path takes many turns. It begins at the trunk of a tree.

THE MAKING
OF MIDGARD

1

THE HOME OF THEIR SHAPES

TAKEN AT FACE VALUE, THE world of the Vikings appeared much the same as that of everyone around them: individuals, looking roughly like you and me but in different clothes, going about their business and moving through landscapes and settlements that—albeit rustic-looking—would still be intelligible all these centuries later. But that is all it was, surface, a screen masking something very different, very old, and very odd.

Any attempt to understand the Vikings must first delve beneath that deceptive exterior to get inside their minds, even inside their bodies. What is found there, and its implications, provides the first key to truly seeing the world through their eyes.

The Vikings were not alone, but very much shared their world with a multitude of 'Others'—not just other humans, but other things altogether. The most obvious were the gods, and the plural form in itself set them apart from the monotheistic cultures of the great Continent to the south. They were also familiar with those divinities' servants (some of them utterly terrifying) and a whole host of other beings, spirits, and creatures that have survived under the comforting label of 'folklore' but at the time were very real.

This question of reality is important because the Vikings did not *believe* in these things any more than someone today 'believes in' the sea. Instead they *knew* about them: all this was as much a natural part of the world as trees and rocks. That these beings could not be seen need not have been significant.

This shadowy population beside whom the Vikings walked also spanned more worlds than one, and here is another difference: the Scandinavians were situated at the centre of many realms of existence—far beyond the familiar binaries of 'good' and 'bad' afterlives found in many religions. In the Viking mind, these worlds were all other places for other inhabitants, but ordered and connected in a manner that made them accessible if you knew the right paths to take.

At the most fundamental level of all, inside every Viking-Age person was not just some abstract 'soul' (if that is to your spiritual taste) but several separate and even independent beings. Each one was a component of the whole individual.

Taking the Vikings 'at face value', then, would have been a big mistake, though one made by many of their contemporaries. A few, especially Christians, seem to have realised exactly who and what the Vikings were, and usually recoiled from the knowledge. But there is no need to do so today. By looking at the Vikings with open eyes and open minds, it is possible to enter their world.

There is no fully comprehensible geography of the Norse cosmos, nothing that really makes coherent sense in the poems and stories. This may be a product of the tales' long and rough journey down to us over the centuries, but equally it may reflect a lack of clarity or even concern at the time. We should not read too much into this because, after all (taking just one religious example), how many of even the most devout Christian faithful today can sketch an accurate map of the afterlife? It is also important to understand that the Norse had never heard of 'the Norse myths'. The collections now conveniently packaged under that name in our bookshops are the syntheses of far later times, compiled after their fossilisation as text by people who were not entirely sympathetic to what they contained. These are very different from the lively, organic world of oral stories that changed in the telling and probably also varied considerably across the valleys, plains, mountains, and waterways of Scandinavia.

The names and natures of the worlds, and their beginnings, are described in a number of mythological texts collected in the *Poetic Edda*, as well as in longer narrative form by Snorri in his prose handbook. His information is particularly difficult to assess precisely because it *is* so detailed, so rich. Why should this canny Christian politician, acutely aware of his place in the world, take such pains to record the intricacies of a dead religion that was anathema to the Church whose interests he upheld? The answer perhaps lies in the fact that the spiritual themes in the skaldic poems he cites were almost all marshalled in a single cause: the praise of kings and the recording of their deeds. If those mythological allusions and metaphors were not actively maintained, there would be no possibility of properly understanding and perpetuating the heroic royal histories. This may be why Snorri wrote his *Edda*—to activate that resource in the service of memory harnessed for political ends. Fortunately for Viking scholars, Snorri's loyalty to the idea of Scandinavian monarchy gifted us a trove of knowledge of these other worlds. Always indirectly, in the course of questions and answers or as knowledge grudgingly imparted, a fragmentary picture emerges—but it is, barely, enough.

At the centre of it all was a tree, *the* Tree, that spanned all the worlds and joined them together. A great ash, its name was Yggdrasill, literally the 'Steed of the Terrible One'. The latter was one of the many names for Odin and a hint of the tree's wider properties, for it did not just connect the realms but also served as a road between the realms for those who knew how to ride it. That the first man was made of the same substance may not have been coincidence, implying some subtle quality of humanity that infused the universe.

In the beginning there had been nothing but the grassless void of Gin-nungagap, an emptiness that stretched forever. Though not quite empty, for deep within it lay a sleeping potential, a power and presence inside the absence, waiting to be awakened. To the north (directions are important here) was the icy space of Niflheim, the 'dark world'. To the south lay Muspellsheim, in flames. Rivers of poison, the Élivágar, flowed from a spring in Niflheim and froze in Ginnungagap. As the sparks from Muspell's fires met this ice, it began to melt and, in the process, change—the slowly falling droplets taking shape and form. The first being in all creation was made: the frost giant, Ymir. He was soon joined by something else, something very different, and her name was Authumbla—a great hornless cow that shambled about in the vacancy. Her milk kept the giant alive.

Just as with the first humans who would later emerge from the driftwood, the gods themselves had a similar beginning. As cattle do, Authumbla liked to lick the salty rime that formed on the blocks of ice dotting Ginnungagap, and it was under her tongue that the first of them woke to life. On the first day, his hair was revealed; on the second, his head was freed; on the third, he stepped out of the ice and into the cold. His name was Búri, the ancestor of the Aesir, the divine family. Soon more and more creatures appeared in this desolate place. Somehow more giants coalesced from the sweat beneath Ymir's arms. One of his legs mated with the other and produced a child. Among these progeny were Bölthorn and his daughter, Bestla, the ancestors of the giants.

It is hard to know how the people of the Viking Age perceived these stories, with their strangeness, contradictions, and apparent absurdities. Did they sagely nod their heads at the mysteries, at ancient wisdom imparted to the privileged? Did they laugh? Were these deep, legendary truths for the elders or yarns for the very young? The one certainty is that, in one form or another, the tales survived for centuries down to our own times: someone, in fact a great many people over the years, must have felt them to be very important indeed.

Búri, too, mysteriously had a son—Burr. From his union with the giantess Bestla came the first of the Aesir. Their sons were Odin and his two brothers, and it is they who began to shape the worlds. It was done through murder, carefully planned.

The three young gods lie in wait for Ymir. They ambush him, kill him, literally rip him apart. Ymir's blood rises and rises, drowning all the giants but two, Bergelmir and his wife, who float away on a raft. He and his kind, the frost giants, will make their own world; they will return, and they will remember what Odin and his brothers have done.

As the blood begins to recede, the gods drag Ymir's corpse into the centre of Ginnungagap. From the giant's torn flesh, they make the land. His hair becomes the trees, and the waters flow from his blood— all the rivers and lakes filling red. His bones are the rocks and mountains; his teeth, his molars, are the boulders and scree. Above it all is the dome of the sky made from the vault of Ymir's skull. To support its heavy weight, the gods set four dwarves at the corners of the earth: their names are Austri, Vestri, Nordri, and Sudri—the cardinal points. Then they throw clumps of the giant's brain into the heavens, forming the clouds.

Around it all the gods set a great fence made of Ymir's brows and eyelashes—a defensive boundary for the world, a mighty seawall against the encircling ocean of blood. They call this palisade Midgard, the name by which the whole earth will be known, the place of Ash and Elm.

This final component of Midgard, its boundary, is an example of a central concept in the Viking mind that is encountered throughout their view of the world. The suffix *-garðr* literally means an enclosed space, somewhere set about with a border. In the Scandi-navian languages even today the word *gård* simply means 'farm', and this is its basic sense—a settled place, a *bounded* place, even a whole world; in the same meaning of enclosure, it is the root of the modern English 'yard'. This idea of being inside the wall, as distinct from what is beyond and therefore outside one's control, is at the core of Viking-Age concepts of settlement and order. It is an insight into their way of thinking.

As yet, Midgard was dark, but the gods brought lights snatched from the molten embers of Muspellsheim and placed them around the firmament. At first the heavenly bodies were confused; in the words of the *Seeress's Prophecy*:

> Sól [the sun] did not know
> where she had her home.
> Máni [the moon] did not know
> what strength he had.
> The stars did not know
> where their places were.

Then the gods brought order to the sky. Ymir's skull began to glow as the chariot of Day rode across its vault, illuminated by the sun; her brother Máni followed the horses of Night to complete the cycle (just in passing, as another insight into the Norse mind-set, it is worth noting the unusual sex of the heavenly bodies, the sun female and the moon male). To set the pace of sun and moon, even now, they are both chased by wolves, a hunt that will never end until the Ragnarök, the final battle and the fall of all things.

It is then that Odin and his brothers go walking along the beach, where the driftwood is waiting. Where we are waiting.

As Midgard and its people took form (the time frame is as ambig-uous as ever), the other worlds around them were brought into being, the great ash in their midst. To some degree, there are at least relative locations. Up above was *Ásgarðr*, or Asgard—another bounded space—literally the 'Place of the Aesir', in other words, the home of the gods. This was a vast, rolling landscape of fields and forests, mountains and lakes, essentially a divine mirror of the human world below in which everything was appropriately scaled up in both size and grandeur, as befitting its residents.

A road, or rather a bridge, ran between the realm of the gods and the home of humans: the rainbow, arcing across the worlds. Its name was Bifröst, the 'shimmering path', and according to the poems it blazed with flame. Known too as the 'Aesir Bridge' and the 'Powers' Way', it was also a line of defence against the giants. Beneath it raged two mighty rivers, Körmt and Örmt, always in torrential flood.

Flowing water also divided Midgard from the realm of giants, Jötunheim (sometimes found in the plural, 'Giant-worlds'), that lay to the east. Somewhere on this boundary was also Járnviðr, 'Iron-Forest', where giant troll-women gave birth to the wolves that, at the end, will swallow the heavenly bodies.

Even farther east was *Útgarðr*, Utgard, 'the Place Outside', a wilderness literally beyond the worlds of humans, gods, and giants, as its name implies. There is little detail in the stories, but Utgard seems to have been a churning, dark, and formless space, the home of things that could not be relied upon—trolls, monsters, and evil powers. It was nowhere you'd want to go. In the texts, both the world of giants and the world beyond move steadily northwards as the medieval source material gets further away in time from the Viking Age, perhaps a reorientation that reflected one of the Christian locations of hell.

The Norse, too, had a special realm for the dead, although there is no contemporary suggestion that it was bad or a place of punishment. The name of this world was Hel, disconcertingly close to its negative Christian equivalent; the exact relationship between them, if any, is unknown, but Christian overtones can clearly be seen in the later sources. Some philologists have argued that in Old Norse the original name instead related to something underground—essentially a metaphor for the grave, which would make sense. According to Snorri, the path to Hel lay north and down. It was certainly a realm below, stretching nine leagues into the ground, through nine worlds of death, with Niflhel, 'Dark-Hel', at the bottom. It was bounded by a great fence, Nágrind, or 'Corpse-Gate', with a terrible hound at the door. To get there one had to cross a river churning with knives and swords, and clashing blocks of ice, over the golden-thatched Gjallabrú bridge, which was guarded by a giantess.

Connecting all these realms, again, was the great ash tree, Yggdrasill. There have been numerous attempts at visualising the spatial relationships of the Norse worlds, all of them speculative and some plunging into New Age fantasia with careless abandon. Were they formed as concentric discs, one inside the other, moving outwards in two dimensions like ripples from the thrown stone of the World Tree? Or were they a stack, a vertical tier of realms threaded on Yggdrasill's trunk like a spindle? Perhaps they perched on its individual branches. According to the *Grímnir's Sayings* poem, the tree had three roots that covered respectively the worlds of humans, giants, and the dead; Snorri has it slightly differently as they stretch over the gods, the giants, and Niflheim.

Yggdrasill was evergreen, unlike its earthly counterparts, and was nourished from three springs at its roots. Again, the sources differ, but it seems clear that at least two of them rose from wells. Beneath the root that led to the realm of the frost giants was the Well of Mímir, guarded by a being of the same name. Its waters contained all wisdom and could be drunk from the Gjallarhorn. The root of the gods rose into the sky (says Snorri, following the contradictory physics of the Norse cosmos), but under it was the Well of Urd, the 'spring of fate' that was also the location of the Aesir assembly. The third root went down into the dark world, feeding from the spring Hvergelmir, 'the bubbling cauldron', in which all the worlds' rivers had their source.

Clearly, some of the Norse cosmology was based in physical nature—after all, almost everyone has seen Bifröst, the rainbow bridge, at one time or another. Similarly, the volcanic landscapes of Iceland, where most of the sources were written down, are a natural backdrop to the volatile mix of fire and ice from which the worlds were formed. The Tree may also have a manifestation in everyday perception. Relatively little is known of how the Vikings understood the night sky, the stars, and the constellations; beyond a few ambiguous references in Snorri, which some dismiss while others take seriously, there is little to go on. However, one Icelandic scholar is convinced that Yggdrasill can be read as an interpretation of the Milky Way—surely a plausible idea, especially when one escapes the nocturnal light pollution of our cities and sees its majesty rearing overhead, impossibly vast, with its cloudy arms spanning the sky like branches.

The shape of the Norse worlds can be dimly perceived across centuries of distance, the great Tree connecting them through the void. But what of their inhabitants?

The extent to which the Vikings have suffered from stereotyping is more than matched by how their gods and other supernatural beings have been perceived. In the popular imagination, the divine world of Asgard holds a single hall: Valhalla (actually a Victorian misspelling of Valhöll), home of Odin and famous worldwide today as 'Viking heaven', the destination of the worthy dead and synonymous with the Norse afterlife itself. However, the myths are clear that Valhöll was only one of many such residences, as each of the major gods lived on their own estate. These would have been understood as a main hall and surrounding huts, barns, and stables for the household and the animals—god-sized reflections of the manors of the elites in Midgard. Asgard was very much a landscape, a world in its own right.

The literal origins of the oldest gods, emerging from the primal ice, by no means account for all the Norse divinities. They came from two families, the Aesir—of whom Odin is the head—and the Vanir, who in some strange way seem to be the older of the two, despite the fact that they do not appear in the basic creation myth. The Vanir were gods of the earth and its riches, representing the dependent relationship between humans and the land in an agricultural society. The Aesir were distinct, with a more patriarchal family structure and a greater propensity for violence (which is not to say the Vanir were entirely peaceable). The *Seeress's Prophecy* describes how the families at first clashed in a mighty war, with fighting that shook Asgard, resolved only after complex negotiations and the giving of hostages.

It is unclear what the two divine families really signify, or even whether that is a meaningful question. Are the Vanir the remnants of the supposed earth-based religions of the Bronze Age and the early Iron Age, many centuries back in the past? Is the war of the gods a magnified image of turbulence in the real human world and (in the artificial terms of historians) a metaphor for the fifth-century transition to the 'late Iron Age'? Some scholars certainly think so, but it is far from clear what the more distantly prehistoric Scandinavians really believed. Despite extraordinary archaeological evidence amassed over the past two centuries and analysed in depth, we cannot be sure. The sun and the cycle of the celestial bodies were important, as were liminal places such as bogs and wetlands, a suggestion of chthonic powers below. All this was referenced in material culture, depicted in art, and honoured through water offerings of gold, costly metals, food, animals—and sacrificed humans. There seems to have been a clear concern for propitiation, a sort of sacred insurance policy for agricultural prosperity, individual fertility, and probably success in war. The people of the Iron Age were hardly alone in such preoccupations, but it is not difficult to fit the Vanir into this picture.

In the tales, the Vanir joined the Aesir after a truce was declared in their war, and thereafter they appear together in Asgard—an image of a society remade? The particular qualities of the older gods then emerge as specific skills and attributes alongside those of their new cousins, rather than differences that fundamentally separated the families.

The head of the Vanir is Njörd, a fount of wisdom and provider of abundant crops, full catches of fish, and a fair wind in the sails. As patron of farmers and sailors, he would have made an appropriate high god back in the Bronze and early Iron Ages. His hall is Nóatún, the 'ship enclosure'. Right from the start, this founding figure embodies one of the main aspects of the Vanir as they appear in the sources—a disconcerting, and disapproving, taint of sexual deviance. His children are Freyja and Freyr, and their mother was Njörd's own sister. In turn, they, too, were rumoured to be lovers as well as twin siblings. While open carnality was certainly a Vanir trait, the notion that it was a negative one may well be a Christian intervention in the sources. Freyja, in particular, was exactly the sort of sexually independent woman that terrified the Church.

Freyr appears in the texts as a lord of rain and sun, the god in the corn, rider of a golden boar, and master of a special ship that could be folded into a pocket. For some reason he is often associated with giants and can be found both fighting and courting them. His attempt to seduce the giantess Gerd, conducted by proxy, is made with violent and abusive threats. Freyr is very much a sexual being, and an eleventh-century description of what seems to be his image in a temple describes him as endowed with a gigantic erection. His hall is at Álfheim, 'Elf-home'.

His sister, Freyja, is routinely imagined as a goddess of fertility, and sometimes even love, as if she were a sort of Viking Venus. Such clichés bear little resemblance to how she emerges in the tales. Freyja is primarily an embodiment of women and every aspect of their lives, agency, and potential, including childbirth. Above all, she is a being of power, one of the greatest of the deities. Always in control, she defies the attempts of gods, dwarves, giants, and others to objectify and coerce her. She drives a wagon pulled by cats. Freyja's sexuality is at the core of her being, for her enjoyment and use, sometimes with affectionate overtones but also as manipulation and a means of violence. Although married to Ód, her husband is virtually absent from the mythology, and Freyja instead takes many lovers (according to Loki, she has slept with every elf in Asgard, as well as all the Aesir). She bought the necklace of Brísingamen by bedding its four dwarf smiths in turn, and was much courted by giants. She seduced kings, coaxing them to a fatal mistake; she divided her affections between rivals, driving them to mutual destruction; she exploited the lust of others for her own material gain. Some of the other gods, especially Loki, attempt to slut-shame her with accusations of promiscuity; Freyja ignores them all. It is clear that her body and favours are hers alone to command (which is probably what annoyed the gods) and also that she has little regard for the opinions of others. She is also very much a deity of the battlefield and its aftermath. Contrary to the general assumption that the Viking warrior dead went to Odin in Valhöll/Valhalla, only half of them actually found a posthumous home there; the remainder travelled to Freyja in her great hall of Sessrúmnir, 'Seat-Room'.

Similar attitude problems (both ancient and modern) tend to afflict the other goddesses, to whom connotations of 'fruitfulness' and 'fecundity' have also become so regularly attached as to constitute a sort of reflexive trope. Thus Idun, the keeper of the golden apples that ensured the gods' eternal youth, is seen as a passive goddess of 'plenty' rather than as the one holding the very lives of the immortals in her power. She was not the only goddess with influence over destiny and fate. Frigg, whose husband was Odin, acted as a manager of Asgard and held sway over its disposition; others bowed to her authority, which was her own rather than an allowance bestowed by a male god. Yes, the goddesses were beautiful, just as stereotype would have it, but in a way that inspired terror as well as desire.

Among the Aesir, the leading figure is clearly Odin, although whether he really is the lord of all is often left ambiguous in

3. A Power on the throne? This tiny cast silver chair with occupant was found by metal detector in 2009 near the royal site of Lejre in Denmark. Dating to c. 900, its details of ravens, wolves, and the fact that the figure is one-eyed (confirmed by microscopic analysis) suggest that this may be Odin on his seat of power, Hlidskjálf. The fact that the figure is wearing what would conventionally be interpreted as women's clothing only deepens its interesting ambiguity. Photo: Ole Manning, © Roskilde Museum, used by kind permission.

the written sources. He has over two hundred names: he is Mask, he is Third, the Hawk, Victory-Tree, Ghost-Lord, Ripper, Battle-Screamer, and so many more. Odin is a war god and a killer, shaking his spear, Gungnir. He is the protector of kings and outcasts, but also a consummate liar. He may grant you the beautiful gifts of poetry, or trap you with betrayal. He will probably sleep with your wife or, just possibly, your husband—a being of contradictions and seduction, unwise to trust. But wisdom is his prize, his hunger (he gave his eye for it), and there are few things he will not do to really *know*. In particular, he speaks to the dead through spells and makes bodies on the gallows talk. Odin is skilled at teasing open the seams where the worlds join, just enough to slip through, riding his eight-legged stallion whose name, Sleipnir, means the 'sliding one', its teeth etched with runes. He is the supreme master of sorcery, sending out his mind and memory in the form of ravens to scour the worlds for news. Odin has several residences as befits a king: Valaskjálf, Gladsheimr, and, of course, Valhöll, the 'hall of the slain'.

The leaders of the Aesir were largely related, albeit through the most tangled of family trees. Thor was Odin's son by a giantess in one of many liaisons outside his marriage to Frigg. Thor was the strongest god, lord of wind and weather, caller of storms and thunder. A great belt doubled his already prodigious brawn, and his iron gloves gave him power, especially to wield his famous hammer, Mjölnir. Amulets in the shape of this weapon have been found throughout the Viking world, and he was clearly venerated by humans. Thor was the scourge of giants; one poem is simply a list of his many victims, and these encounters make up the bulk of the myths. His hall is Bilskírnir, which Snorri calls the largest building ever made, with 540 rooms. He shares it with his wife, Síf, whose blonde hair was the envy of all who saw it and used by poets as a metaphor for gold.

Baldr, the bright god, is the son of Odin and Frigg, with his hall at Breidablikk. Beloved by all things, he is thereby impervious to damage. Baldr's unexpected death, engineered by Loki at the hands of his unknowing, blind brother, Höd (another of Odin's sons), set in motion events that will in time lead to the end of the worlds. Höd will in turn be slain by Váli, yet another son of the war god by yet another goddess, Rindr—layers within layers of family killing.

Then there is Ull, the archer, tracker, hunter, skier, and son of Síf (although not, it seems, with Thor). Ull appears hardly anywhere in the myths and yet is found in sacral place-names across Scandinavia, especially in Sweden. His cult seems to have been widespread once. Snorri says, "He is good to pray to in single combat". Ull's hall was at Ýdalir, and he used a shield as a boat.

4. Hammer of the gods. Thor's sacred weapon, Mjölnir, seems to have been adopted as a symbol of his cult relatively late in the Viking Age, perhaps in reaction to the Christian use of the cross. Found as pendants and on amulet rings, these items are among the most common objects connected with the traditional religion. This example from Købelev, Lolland, Denmark, bears the helpful runic inscription "Hammer". Photo: John Lee, © National Museum of Denmark, used by kind permission.

Heimdall, the horn blower, has his residence at Himinbjörg. It lies by the end of Bifröst, guarding the rainbow bridge against the inevitable moment when the giants will finally come to war on Asgard. His stories are buried in obscurity, but he was evidently very old when the somewhat contradictory tales were finally written down. Heimdall is the son of nine mothers; he has golden teeth; he can see for a hundred miles; he can smell the grass growing. He will spend eternity as the watchman at the wall until the rooster Gullinkambi ('golden comb') crows that the Ragnarök has begun.

Týr, whom Snorri says was yet another son of Odin, but other sources have descending from giants, is one of the oldest gods, with roots going far back in Germanic prehistory. He was known for his courage and bravery, although with very little detail, and his cult was popular (to judge again from place-names). Like the other great gods, he has given us a day of the week. After Sunday and Mo(o)nday, Týr's Day comes before the day of his 'father' Odin (Woden's Day) and then the days of Thor and Freyr. The week ended with a day that in English is named after a Roman god, Saturnus, but in the Scandinavian languages is still *lördag*, derived from the Old Norse word for a hot thermal spring—in other words, bath night, a lovely insight into Viking habits of hygiene.

And finally, there is Loki, one of the most prominent beings in the mythological tales but also something of a mystery. Born of Laufey, one cannot even really say if he is a god at all. Some see him as a demi-god and trickster, a classic figure with parallels in many other cultures, but this kind of nomenclature may not help in understanding him from the perspective of the Vikings themselves. Loki changes form, appearing as a fish, a bird, or an insect as he chooses. With the giantess Angrboda, he fathered monsters, including the wolf, Fenrir; the Midgard Serpent; and Hel, who keeps the dead. In the shape of a mare, he gave birth to Sleipnir, Odin's horse (an act of truly troubling perversity in the Norse mind). In the many, many tales about him, he causes unending mischief for the gods and stirs up trouble with the giants, only to almost always solve the resulting mess himself. He is handsome and humorous, sly and malicious, all at once. It was Loki who cut off Síf's original hair, and then made a deal with the dwarves to make her new locks that shone like gold but grew from her head; he also had an affair with her, to Thor's fury. Having caused Baldr's murder, Loki will at last be bound in the entrails of his own son, poison dripping on his face forever, until the Ragnarök, when all chains are broken. At the end, he will steer the ship of the dead against the gods.

The lists of the Aesir are long. The goddess Sága in her hall at Sökkvabekk, 'Sunken Bank', where she drinks every day with Odin. Skadi, daughter of the giant Thjazi but also named as one of the goddesses, first married to Njörd and later the lover of both Odin and Loki—homesick in Njörd's hall by the sea, she eventually returns to her beloved mountains and her residence in Thrymheim. Forseti, Baldr's son, in his gold and silver hall at Glitnir.

Many of these gods had children, with giants or their spouses, and often in so many combinations that the family structure is truly complex. There are also many more deities mentioned only once or twice—a name and nothing else, occasionally a brief glimpse of what they must have been, but incomplete and difficult to see. Bearded Bragi, a god of poetry, married to Idun of the apples. Fulla, the goddess-handmaiden of Frigg, and keeper of her secrets. Vídar, son of Odin and the giantess Grithr, who will avenge his father's death at the Ragnarök. Eir, a goddess of healing. Gefjon, in some tales a goddess of virginity, in others a lover of one of Odin's sons. A poetic list of *ásynjur*, the goddesses, is the only source for some of them: Sjöfn, inciter of passion; Lofn, the comforter; Vár, goddess of the oath; Vör, an embodiment of awareness; Syn who guards the doors, whose name means 'refusal'; Snotra, the wise; Gná, the messenger, whose steed can cross the sea and sky.

Some of them were probably relics by the time of the Vikings, perhaps just names even then. They would have resonated, certainly, but as distant echoes of old beliefs from the ancestral memory-world that the Scandinavians always perceived behind them in deepening layers of lore and heritage. It should never be forgotten that the Vikings, too, had a past; they told its stories, and they were not averse to mystery themselves.

The sheer variety of the many tales raises an important issue. Beyond the gods' individual personalities and qualities, their adventures that make up many of the myths, is the more basic question of what they actually *do*. Outside the great monotheistic faiths, we have somehow become accustomed to divinities being gods *of* something, sole personifications of the weather, the harvest, the hunt, and the like. This is not true for the Aesir and Vanir, as many of them embodied several things at the same time, often overlapping with each other in their interests and activities (rather like us, in fact). There were certainly gods of war, for example, but each of them related to it in a manner that suited their personalities. In this context, Thor was brute force and the business of fighting; Odin was planning, command, luck, and frenzied aggression; Freyja was malice, the calculated viciousness necessary to prevail against odds; and there were others, too, more personal in their allegiances and favourites.

It is clear that the Norse gods were not necessarily particularly admirable by modern lights, and perhaps the Vikings felt the same way. While the Aesir and Vanir could lend their support to human schemes and individuals, this was mostly on a whim, almost for amusement. They could also be crude, stupid, appallingly prejudiced in our eyes, violent, and cruel—the gods as essentially a quarrelsome family, largely indifferent to humans other than as objects of temporary interest. There is a parallel to be found here between the residents of Asgard and the older pantheons of the classical Mediterranean cultures, the squabbling Greek deities of Mount Olympus and their Roman descendants, and this prompts a larger question that bears closer examination: can a genuine connection be traced between Viking beliefs and those of classical antiquity?

There are certainly many points of resemblance, not only in the divine families but also details of the mythology itself. In the Greek cosmogony, as related by Hesiod around 700 BCE, the worlds began in *chaos* (as a specific, original term) that had the sense of a yawning void—just like Ginnungagap. Even the continuation of the creation story is similar, at least in part, with gods spontaneously generated or birthed through improbable couplings, and a cosmos created from bloody murder and dismemberment. Other elements can be linked too, such as the great hound that guards the doors of Hel, matching Cerberus in the Greek underworld, and there are more to be found.

Some scholars do see the Norse gods as later shadows of antique precursors, something that has especially been argued for Odin. Others trace the lineage of Asgard back further still, and controversially, to the dimly perceptible religions of the Indo-Europeans, who are argued to have originated either on the Asian steppe or in Anatolia thousands of years before the time of the Vikings. There are reasonable comparisons that can be made, which also begin to bridge the immense spans of time involved. For instance, some rituals recorded for the Vedic period of Bronze Age India (c. 1500–500 BCE) are remarkably close to some Norse practices. Ultimately, however, the chronological and geographical gulf is vast, and the links are tentative at best.

At some level there is undoubtedly a web of cultural inheritance, by no means confined to religion, that links the prehistories of many Northern peoples, and this may well extend beyond Europe itself. However, when we look deeper at specific times and places, unique qualities emerge—and this is hardly surprising. Individual similarities notwithstanding, there are many more respects in which the spiritual world of Viking-Age Scandinavia differed markedly from what had gone before (even the classical parallels are but isolated cases). When reviewed together in all their marvellous complexity, the products of the Norse mind form a category all their own, and we should approach them that way.

To take just one example from the realm of the gods, it seems hardly appropriate to speak of a Norse 'pantheon' at all, at least in the classical sense of the term. With the exception of the poem *Loki's Quarrel* and a handful of other stories such as the death of Baldr and some elements of the *Seeress's Prophecy*, the Norse divinities rarely even seem to meet or interact with each other in the mythic tales. The world of Asgard seems to have been every bit as cosmopolitan as its human mirror below, its population building up over time with incomers from all over—a remarkably faithful reproduction of Midgard, in fact.

One other dimension of the gods' lives is intriguing. Strangely, Asgard also contained temples, cult buildings where *the gods themselves made offerings*—but to what or whom? The mythology of the Vikings is one of only a tiny handful in all world cultures in which the divinities also practised religion. It suggests something behind and beyond them, older and opaque, and not necessarily 'Indo-European' at all. There is no indication that the people of the Viking Age knew what it was any more than we do.

The idea of a related power to the gods also connects to their own Others, the giants. They are present in the cosmogony right from the beginning—in fact, from before the first god appears. They are primal beings and recur throughout the many stories of divine adventures as enemies of Asgard. In revenge for Ymir's death, the crime at the core of the Viking world, the giants' hatred of the Aesir will extend to the Ragnarök itself when their armies of frost and fire will invade the gods' home. There have been many attempts to understand what the giants 'mean'. Unlike the gods, they do not seem to have impinged on the human world of Midgard at all, but they are part of the deepest, oldest strata of tales. Are they spirits of the wilderness, the ultimate adversaries? Do they represent the Sámi, partnered with the Norse gods but distinctively different? Are the endless couplings of giants and Aesir somehow symbolic of royal ritual marriages, uniting the constituencies of a realm? We simply do not know, but the giants are indivisible from the wider arena of the great powers.

One concept above all was central to the gods' relationship with the human world and intersected with the lives of its other, supernatural inhabitants: the idea of fate. Governing beings of every kind—mortal and divine, living and dead—was the preordination of the future; it lay at the heart of the Norse mind-set. For the Viking-Age Scandinavians, fate did not represent the absence of choice but rather the manifestation of a pre-existing truth. Free will existed, but exercising it inevitably led to becoming the person you always, really, had been.

Fate was embodied in many forms, but none clearer than the Norns, female supernatural beings of immense power who were responsible for the unfolding of individual destiny. As ever, the sources are mixed and ambiguous, combining Eddic and skaldic verse with Snorri's prose. Most often mentioned are the three women—Urd, Verdandi, and Skuld—whose names arguably have connotations of the past, present, and future (or perhaps just different perspectives on *being*). 'Urd' at least has clear overtones of 'Fate', and the three Norns lived in a hall by the well of that name at the root of the World Tree that connected to Asgard. Every day they took moist clay from the water's edge, smearing it on the trunk and branches to keep Yggdrasill cool and healthy. In some poetic descriptions they are giantesses, in others young girls; their relative age is uncertain, but one should not trust too easily in the cliché of 'maiden, woman, crone' that often attaches to them. In the skaldic verse, the Norns appear as metaphors of judgement, lawyers of life bringing a kind of ultimate arbitration of fate.

The Norns worked their power in the shadows, invisible, although sometimes appearing in dreams. Their fingernails each bore a rune, the symbols of secrets. The Norns often are depicted weaving fate on a loom, another motif common to several mythological traditions. On an upright loom, the warp of a textile always has a pattern, inherent from the beginning and determined by the threading of the heddles. It is made by the decisions of the weaver, but cannot be fully perceived until the cloth nears its finished state. It is an elegant metaphor for the essential outline of a life, revealed through human experience, ending only when the last thread is cut.

Some Eddic poetry refers to many more Norns linked to types of beings besides humans—including elves, dwarves, and even gods. Occasionally there are references to 'good' and 'evil' Norns who are responsible for different twists of fate, although it is unclear if this should be taken literally. Snorri says that the Norns of the Aesir visit each human child at birth, shaping the course of its days to come. It may be that this multiplicity of Norns is the truer Norse picture and that the idea of a primary trinity is influenced by classical models, perhaps filtered through Christian writers.

Alongside the major celebrities of the Norse 'pantheon', the other supernatural beings best known today are the Valkyries. They, too, were agents of fate, but as their name—'choosers of the slain'—implies, their province was war. The Valkyries are exceptionally well attested in the written sources, both prose and verse, from the late ninth century into the 1300s and beyond. Images that arguably represent them are commonly found in the iconography of the Viking Age, and there is no doubt they were a genuine part of the belief system. Like the Vikings themselves, the Valkyries have also been obscured by centuries of appropriation and stereotype.

In the literature the Valkyries are servants of Odin and select the bravest warriors to die in battle. This might hardly seem positive but was, in fact, a compliment to those they chose because it meant they would join the war god in Valhöll. As the slain prepare for the Ragnarök, they are served mead by the Valkyries as hostesses of the hall, and perhaps offered more personal comfort. The Valkyries are described as armed with spear, sword, and shield, armoured in mail, and sometimes helmeted. They ride horses through the sky; when you see dew on the grass, it is sweat fallen from the flanks of the Valkyries' steeds. The battle-women occasionally don the skins and wings of swans, permitting them flight. In the Eddic poems, Valkyries at times adopt an individual human hero, protecting him in combat and often falling in love—but it is at this point (if not earlier) that they begin to merge with what would become their legend.

An internet image search reveals 'Valkyries' endlessly recycled today through the male gaze, usually depicted as voluptuous young women with big swords and minimal clothing. These dreary

5. A woman of war. This silver-gilt, tenth-century figurine from Hårby, Denmark, is the first three-dimensional image of an armed female known from the Viking world. The subject is unclear—whether a Valkyrie, a war-goddess, a human warrior woman, or some other martial being—but her sword and shield are unequivocal, with the characteristic knotted hairstyle that seems to have been the primary female marker in Viking art. Photo: John Lee, © National Museum of Denmark, used by kind permission.

tableaux bear little resemblance to the demons of carnage in Norse mythology, but they dimly echo what the medieval Christian mind seems to have found in the Valkyries. Clerical men, in particular, had fantasies of their own and created the image of them as love-lorn heroines. Recast as beautiful women, armed and armoured, they were an exciting subversion of both medieval realities and the chivalric ideal. In the Old Norse heroic poems, they overcome obstacles to rescue or at least mourn their human boyfriends, even embracing their revived corpses in the grave. The later frisson of

Gothic horror seems not far away, with appropriate appeal to the Victorians, and it is these Brünnhildes who enjoyed a long afterlife to populate Wagner's *Ring* and its analogues. However, this version of them has little place in the Viking-Age consciousness or that of earlier centuries, from which the Valkyries originally emerged.

These 'primal' Valkyries did not visit the battlefield, swooping gracefully down to bear away their chosen heroes; instead, they were unleashed upon it and personified its harsh realities. Indeed, they appear to have literally represented aspects of the fighting, as revealed by their names. We know of some fifty-two individual Valkyries, and there are many, many more anonymously subsumed in collectives. It is extraordinary, and telling, how many different terms for 'battle' and 'war' can be found in the Valkyrie names. Clearly, many of them embodied the condition of combat itself, often through the metaphor of a violent storm. The sense of swirling chaos is increased by the significant portion of the Valkyries whose names refer to noise, the overwhelming din and screaming confusion of a Viking-Age battlefield. Thus, we meet Göndul, the 'War-Fetter', who brought the freezing hesitation that could be fatal; perhaps the same is meant by Hlökk, the 'Chain', or Mist, the 'Cloud'. Around them move Hjalmthrimul, 'Helmet-Clatter'; Hjörthrimul, 'Sword-Noise'; and Hjlód, 'Howling'. There is Randgnithr, the 'Shield-Scraper', and behind her Skalmjöld, the 'Sword-Time'; Sváva, the 'Killer'; and Tanngnithr, 'Teeth-Grinder'. Other Valkyries' names focus on weapons in combination with different elements—Geirahöd, 'Spear-Battle'; Geirdríful, 'Spear-Flinger'; Geirskögul, 'Spear-Shaker'; and so on. Their many sisters' names include Battle-Weaver, Shaker, Disorder, Scent-of-Battle, Victory-Froth, Vibration, Unstable, Treader, Swan-White, Shield-Destroyer, Helper, Armour, Devastate, and Silence. The list goes on.

There is much to learn here concerning the realities of early medieval warfare, and also of the battle-spirits whom the Vikings believed governed its fortunes. The Valkyries were indeed handmaidens of Odin, but in the sense that befits the vicious servants of a god of war. There is only minimal evidence to suggest they were physically attractive, but plenty that implies they were terrifying. Perhaps echoing Odin's governance of the military mind, even the sight of Valkyries could be lethally mesmerising—as it says in the *Saga of the Völsungs*, referring to their role as shield-maidens, "looking at them was like gazing into flames".

As agents of fate, the Valkyries also have obvious links with the Norns, and Snorri even says that the "youngest" Norn, Skuld, rides with the Valkyries to choose the slain. In a strange battle poem called *The Web of Spears*, dating to either the tenth or eleventh centuries, a troupe of twelve horse-borne Valkyries are seen dismounting to enter a cottage. When the observer peeks inside, he sees them working an immense loom made of human body parts, weaving a cloth of entrails dyed with blood, using weapons for tools. The women sing verses that make it clear they are, in fact, weaving the outcome of a distant battle, the motions of their implements mimicking (and effecting) the dart and swoop of projectiles on the field. Here, the Valkyries and Norns are truly combined. When the cloth is finished, they tear it to shreds and ride off with the scraps.

The Valkyries were the essence of violence, unsettling and terrible.

Not all the shadowy, non-human denizens of the Norse world were as dangerous to know. Many were extensions of the natural beauty that surrounded the Scandinavians every day.

Beyond their vibrant cityscapes, to outside eyes the Nordic countries today are still a region of untrammelled peace, a vast canvas of forests, mountains, and waterways that is seemingly one of the last places in Europe to offer the true solitude of the wild. To a person in the Viking Age, such a view would be incomprehensible. Anyone moving through the landscapes of trees and rock, snow and ice, wind and water, would have understood themselves to be in the midst of teeming life—not just of animals and insects, but of something far more—that other population of beings with whom humans shared their world.

It is hard to find a collective noun for them, and even individual terms can be difficult in modern languages. One can speak of 'elves' and 'dwarves', for example, but it would be disingenuous to claim that such beings can ever be truly viewed now without thinking of their later incarnations in Tolkien and other fantasy media. At the same time, the characters of today's games and movies are very different from the *álfar* and *dvergar* that the Vikings knew. Creatures of this kind are important not just for their intrinsic interest, but because they played a far greater part in people's everyday lives than the higher powers of the gods and their servants. In modern Swedish they are called *väsen*, a general term that cannot readily be translated but encompasses the whole variety of 'supernatural beings', although here again there are problems in that their essence was *entirely* 'natural'; the Norse would not have made a distinction as we do in this regard.

My favoured term for them comes from modern Iceland (although with older precedents), where they are known as the *huldufólk*, the 'Hidden People', which is usefully vague but captures the correct distinction in that what divides them from us is mainly their discretion. In Iceland today, belief in the Hidden People just about survives (though to a much lesser degree than tourist brochures would have you think) as part of a deeper and more widespread respect for the spiritual currency of the past in relation to a landscape that is far from inert.

The *álfar*, or elves, were probably the most prevalent of the Norse nature-beings, and they were often in direct contact with humans. They could be influential in the prosperity of a farm, as they were able to harm livestock or crops if they chose, and keeping on their good side was highly advisable. The 'average' Viking-Age person probably rarely felt the presence of the gods, but putting butter out for the elves living in that rock behind your house was part of the farmyard routine. The *álfar* could heal the sick or make people ill.

They could bring luck or misfortune. Several sagas recount offering ceremonies for the elves—*álfablót* sacrifices held in halls at regular intervals—so they may have been part of the ritual calendar in a similar way as the holy days of today's world faiths.

Dwarves were distinct from the elves, though Snorri calls them *svartálfar*, or 'black elves', and seems to think they were related in some way. In the few secure images of them that exist, for example on carvings that depict familiar scenes from the legend of Sigurd, dwarves appear to look the same as humans. There is no sense that they were especially small, which was a medieval development. They lived mostly underground, and were very much creatures of stone. In the myths they emerge as skilled craftworkers, jewellers, and miners, masters of the mystical transformation of ore, minerals, and crystal into beautiful objects. There are no records of rituals held for them, and they seem to have been a broadly friendly presence in the human world. They kept to themselves.

Some otherworldly beings were more personal in their interactions with humans. The most important of them were the *dísir*, an ambiguous mixture of goddess and spirit who appear to have represented the ancestral heritage of families—perhaps the souls of its dead matriarchs. These supernatural women were often invisible, but they appeared in dreams and could also be perceived by those with the gift. They occasionally took on martial aspects, with shades of the Valkyries, or represented the prospect of victory as 'seen' before a fight. At other times they are guarantors of fertility, especially of the harvest. As tutelary spirits the *dísir* acted either singly or in groups, and sometimes appeared as cloaked riders. In dreams, the colour of their clothes, black or white, could portend good or evil. Such variants were known as *spádísir*, '*dísir* of prophecy'. There is a suggestion that these beings too had a special link to Odin. The word *dís* itself was a synonym for goddess and for women in general; it appears occasionally as part of female personal names, for example.

There were sacrifices held in their honour and even mentions of special buildings for that purpose—*dísasalir*, '*dísir*-halls'. In

Uppsala there was an annual market and *dísir*-assembly, the Disting, at which offerings were made "for peace and prosperity". Rather wonderfully, it has a continuous history and is still held today, each year in early February, but is incorporated into the Christian calendar at Candlemas.

Most of the invisible population are harder to categorise, and perhaps it is better not to try. The Norse called them *vaettir*, 'spirits', and the term seems to have meant as much or as little then as it does now. There were spirits of the land, the water, the sea, and the air. Those of the land were especially powerful, acting as guardians of place and perhaps also as stewards of its resources. One also reads of land-*dísir*, living in rocks. A law code recorded in the medieval Icelandic *Book of Settlements* notes how ships approaching shore must remove their figureheads so as not to frighten the spirits. Such legal strictures tend not to be frivolous, so this should be taken seriously.

Then there were the more dangerous beings of the wilderness, the trolls and *thurs*, a difficult word to translate but meaning something like 'ogre'. Much like the dwarves, they lived in stones and underground but in more remote places, and they were uniformly threatening. They are rarely closely described and more often seem to represent abstract hazards, an intimation of what could befall the unwary. By the Middle Ages, trolls had become nondescript monsters in stories to scare children at bedtime, but in the Viking Age, they were clearly 'real' enough. The sagas and poems use *troll*- as part of compounds that imply supernatural nastiness in general, sometimes with a suggestion of dark magic thrown in. Trolls were beings of Utgard, the realm beyond the borders. Almost uniquely among the invisible population, it is possible that an Iron Age depiction of trolls has survived on the Baltic island of Bornholm, in the form of grotesque little monsters made of stamped gold— lumpy creatures with faces in their chests, pointy ears, and oversized arms. Today they live on as tourist art and engaging silliness, symbols of the Nordic countries for external consumption, a long way from their origins as terrors of the wild.

As perceived and communicated today, the Viking Age is an intensely visual experience: the intricate interlace art, the sleek and predatory lines of the ships, the landscapes of burial and commemoration—and, of course, the people themselves as seen through several centuries of mediation in Romantic paintings, woodcuts, and reconstructions on the page and screen. Ultimately deriving from the accounts of the literate cultures whom the Scandinavians encountered on their raids and travels, especially the English, Franks, and Arabs, this is the 'othered' picture that has overwhelmingly formed the popular perception of the Vikings in our own times.

However, very different worlds were being built inside the Norse mind. Here is another distinction between appearance and reality, between the surface and what it conceals. From the problematic medieval written sources, and occasional mentions in Eddic and skaldic poetry, emerges one of the most remarkable aspects of the Vikings: the fourfold division of being and an extremely complex notion of what might loosely be called the soul.

If you met a Viking-Age Scandinavian in the street, you would have seen their *hamr*—her or his 'shell' or 'shape'—essentially what for us is the body. Conceived as a container for other aspects of the person, the *hamr* was the physical manifestation of what somebody was, but, crucially, *it could alter*. This is where the concept of shape-changing comes from, in the sense that the actual structures of the body were believed to flow and shift. But this was not true for everyone, only for the gifted (or, perhaps, the cursed). Most people stayed as they appeared, but some, in special circumstances—on certain nights, when stressed or frightened, in anger, or at times of extreme relaxation—could become something else.

For men with these abilities, the alternative form was most often a large predator, such as a bear or wolf (one of the most famous Vikings of all, the warrior-poet Egil Skalla-Grímsson, had a grandfather named Kveldulf, 'Evening-Wolf', with all this implied). Women seem to have borne a special affinity with water creatures, particularly seals, as we learn in tales of sea-wives and selkies that have parallels in many Northern cultures. Some women could change into birds. Whatever the form of these shifters, their eyes always stayed human.

Such individuals crossed the borders between people and animals. We do not know how they were really perceived by their contemporaries, but in our terms, they perhaps formed a very special kind of gender. Our own happily expanding spectrum includes many variations of the self, but they are all bounded by the human; the Vikings may have gone beyond even that, into what we now call posthumanism (but they got there first). However, it is possible, although strange to the modern mind, that such abilities were treated more as a sort of skill than anything else. Some people were good at carpentry, others had a fine singing voice, and your neighbour could become a bear when irritated.

Inside the 'shape' of a person was the second part of their being, the *hugr*, for which no modern translation really suffices. Combining elements of personality, temperament, character, and especially mind, the *hugr* was who someone really was, the absolute essence of *you*, free of all artifice or surface affect. It is the closest thing the Vikings had to the independent soul found in later world faiths, because it could leave the physical body behind. The afterlife beliefs of the Vikings, which they certainly had in elaborate variety, will be considered in due course, but it is less clear what part of a person 'moved on' after death. As far as one can tell, it was probably the *hugr*.

Crucially, some people with different, equally disquieting gifts could *see* these aspects of others. In the poetic fragment known as the *Ljóðatal*, the 'List of Spells', Odin boasts of his magical ability with a series of individual charms, and in one of them we see the true viciousness of his power:

I know a tenth [spell]:
if I see sorceresses
playing up in the air,
I can so contrive it
that they go astray
from the home of their shapes [*heimhama*]
from the home of their minds [*heimhuga*].

The spell is directed against the independent spirits of witches, sent out from their bodies on their mistresses' errands. Odin's charm is terrible in its severance of their very souls, cut away to dissipate forever.

In the Viking mind, somewhere inside each of us is also a *hamingja*, a remarkable being that is the personification of a person's luck. This was a very important attribute for the people of the North in the late Iron Age, as everyone's path in life was determined by fate but rode on a wave of luck. A woman or man who was lucky, and seen to be so by their contemporaries as a result of their success, was a fortunate—and respected—person indeed. It is no accident that Leif Eiríksson, allegedly the first European to land in North America, was also known as *hinn heppni*, 'the Lucky'. Interestingly, the *hamingjur* (in their plural form) could leave the body and walk about, mostly invisible except to those with the right kind of sight. There are saga accounts of men retreating from a coming battle because their opponents clearly had too many luck spirits with them, and nobody in their right mind would go against such odds. Curiously, a *hamingja* also had independent will and in extreme situations might even choose to leave its person. The English saying that someone's luck has 'run out' is actually using a Norse proverb—except that the Vikings meant it literally.

The last part of the fourfold soul was something else entirely: a separate being that somehow dwelled inside every human, inseparable from them but also distinct. The *fylgja* was a female spirit—*always* female, even for a man—and accompanied a person everywhere throughout life. How marvellous, and how utterly sub-versive of the male-focussed stereotype, that every single Viking man literally had a spirit-woman inside him.

The word *fylgja* means 'follower', although sometimes it is translated 'fetch' and equated with similar beings from neighbour-ing cultures. The *fylgja* was a guardian—a protector—but also the embodied link to one's ancestors (in some texts, they are strongly reminiscent of the *dísir*, and at times the two beings appear to be the same). She moved on at death, continuing down the family line (although exactly how is unknown—did the *fylgja* wait for the next to be born, or could a person inherit one long after birth?). In any event, everyone carried with them—through them—the spirit of their family, watching over them and guiding their steps. The *fylgjur* could not be seen other than in dreams, where they appeared with warnings and advice. Of all the Viking-Age spirit-beings, these have proved the most tenacious. Modern Icelanders roll their eyes at being asked by visitors, again, if they believe in elves—but question them about their *fylgjur* and you may be met with a level stare and perhaps a change of subject.

This sense of something utterly alien beneath the skin, occasionally manifesting itself in action or words, may have been one of the most significant differences between the Vikings and the people they encountered. Certainly for a European Christian, the composite soul with its shapes and shells would have been deeply unnerving. It may also have felt unnervingly familiar because pre-Christian Europe held many such beliefs, and they were deep-rooted enough to survive the coming of the new faith, buried in memory and folklore.

By now it should be apparent that the Vikings were decid-edly not the unsophisticated barbarians of stereotype. Equally, the mental (and, in their terms, the physical or natural) world they inhabited was not the same as that of the Franks, the Germans, or the English, to name but a few. When Continental Christians opened their doors in the morning, they did not see the work of elves, dwarves, and nature-spirits; their day was not ordained by the Norns; the dew on the grass was not sweat fallen from supernatural horses; a rainbow did not lead to Asgard and the sky-halls of the gods. Even battles, though bad enough, were not the playground of terrible war-women, screaming their rage and malice in the din. The Vikings, in short, were different.

2

AGE OF WINDS,
AGE OF WOLVES

THE VIKING AGE DID NOT begin with the famous raids on the
West, with longships beaching from rough seas to chase the
English and frighten the clergy. It did not even begin with Vikings,
a label that sometimes obscures more than it illuminates. The
world that Ash and Elm would populate took shape long before—
centuries further back in what archaeologists refer to as the Iron
Age. In order to understand the Vikings, it is first necessary to
uncover their own past.

The Scandinavians of the first millennium were living in the
shadow of their world's only superpower, the empire of Rome, in its
heyday and also through its long, slow decline. The imperial border
ran along the Rhine, cutting through the lands of the Germanic tribes
not far south of Denmark. Cross-frontier trade and exchange—of
ideas and attitudes as much as commodities—had been a staple of
Scandinavian life for hundreds of years, especially among the elites.

As the Western Empire started to fall apart into the fifth
century, this too affected the North. In Europe, Roman power

gradually dissipated and unravelled, taking new forms, breaking up old structures, and setting events in motion that convulsed the Continent. People were on the move: as militarised expeditions, as streams of refugees, in any way and for every reason that human beings leave their homes to seek new lives somewhere else. At the same time, Roman authority was partially absorbed, and enhanced, by its imperial twin to the east—what would later be termed the Byzantine Empire, with its capital at Constantinople (modern Istanbul). New politics, and new politicians, were on the rise and making their presence felt. These networks of influence and contact also reached Scandinavia, and the people of the North were always intimately connected with their surroundings.

The overall impact on the Scandinavians of these convulsive changes to the south was one of instability, of change, but also of opportunity—often for the few at the expense of the many. What archaeologists have long identified as the 'Migration Period', from the fifth to mid-sixth centuries, included protracted crises with far-reaching effects. Their impact was further accelerated by a terrifying climate disaster that no one could have foreseen, causing mass mortality in the North. The deeper origins of Viking-Age Scandinavia can be found in these social and political upheavals. The recovery from a half-century of trauma was the beginning of something different, a new order of warlords and their retinues, of petty kingdoms ruled from great halls— and the whole culture of mythologised, ritual power that supported them—that would ultimately set the stage for the Viking phenomenon.

Rome's slow fall created unpredictable consequences that, centuries later, led to the rise of the Vikings. In a very real sense, the 'new world' of Viking-Age Scandinavia began in a cold, unending winter beneath a darkened sun.

THE SCANDINAVIAN IRON AGE
CHRONOLOGY AND REGIONAL TERMINOLOGIES

Subdivisions	Dates	Norway	Sweden	Denmark
EARLY IRON AGE	500–0 BCE	Pre-Roman Iron Age		Celtic Iron Age
	0–400 CE	Roman Iron Age		
LATE IRON AGE	400–550 CE	Migration Period		Early Germanic Iron Age
	550–750 CE	Merovingian Period	Vendel Period	Late Germanic Iron Age
	750–1050 CE	Viking Age		

Rome was always a part of the 'long' Scandinavian Iron Age, as archaeologists term it. Even the current, conventional names for its chronological components are relative to the Empire, strangely beginning before its inception: the 'pre-Roman' period began around 500 BCE and extended to the fall of the Republic and the rise of the Caesars.

Like any imperial construct, at its apogee Roman power was a complex entity with regional administrations, a dispersed military, and an extended network economy. These elements operated with differing degrees of autonomy, and officials often pursued their own agendas alongside their formal duties. Riven by internal tensions and domestic conflict, the Empire also engaged in 'peace-keeping' missions within its borders and pacifying expeditions beyond its frontiers. All these things varied regionally and changed over time; the Empire was far from static. In the course of roughly two centuries—from the 370s to the 560s—this fluidity undermined the fabric of imperial power itself. The Western Empire began to fragment, at the same time as large numbers of frontier peoples, often characterised somewhat misleadingly as 'barbarian tribes', began to move.

The question of the failing Empire and this so-called Migration Period continues to vex historians and generate sometimes acrimonious debate, but a number of clear positions have nonetheless emerged. These essentially occupy points on a scale that at one extreme sees an imperial structure disintegrating under increasing external pressure from mobile raiders and militarised migrations, while the opposite perspective sees the gradual internal transformations of the Empire itself as stimulating the movements of border peoples. There is little doubt that it was a time of great change, from reversals of the strategic balance at critical points on the imperial frontiers, to new social structures emerging beyond the *Limes* (as those borders were called) in which the influence of Rome played a part. The Migration Period was no simple timeline of invasions and depredation, the classic European map misleadingly crisscrossed by arrows of different colours to mark the moving 'tribes'.

From the third century onwards, imperial cohesion was more or less constantly tested—from within as much as from without. Destabilising conflicts played out in Gaul, Spain, and North Africa throughout the early 400s, while Roman power steadily frayed under the onslaughts of Attila and his Huns. These actions, in turn, caused social displacement across the Empire while a succession of military usurpers attempted to seize the imperial throne. In reality, the 'fall' of Rome was no single process, and there are only isolated incidents that show a sharp decline at all (though some of them were dramatic, such as the sack of the 'Eternal City' itself by the Goths in 410). There were good years as well as bad, occasionally occurring at the same time in different parts of the Empire. For the citizens of the state and the people beyond its frontiers but still within its orbit, all this would have been felt in a myriad of ways, some sudden and others so slow acting as to be imperceptible as they unfolded.

Trade routes were realigned as certain goods ceased production or shifted markets, while others rose to fill the gap. There would have been shortages, certainly, things you could no longer find in the market, but also reorientations of commerce to meet changing demand or new economic realities. These processes were catalysts for more profound change, as settlement patterns and demographics shifted around them. In modern terms, one could think of successful roadside communities that see their prosperity erode as a new highway passes them by and the traffic leaves them behind.

People always move in troubled times, as insecurities seep into the fabric of daily life and both individuals and collectives face difficult choices. In part, the 'Migration Period' was just such a situation; people—in movements both large and small—took to the roads in search of positive change. Some were fleeing, and others were those they fled from. Most were looking for economic security, safety, and a quieter life, while a powerful minority were trying proactively to shape a world more to their liking. The whole was characterised by a loosening of (already decentralised) power and a constant process of local negotiation. Peoples and polities were working out ways to adapt and survive, forming new identities and ethnicities in the process.

In Scandinavia, human settlement had always been determined by the region's unique geography and topography: the mountainous fjords of Norway with their marginal agricultural fringes; the great forests, lakes, and fertile arable plains of Sweden; the low-lying landscape of Denmark, rich in farming potential and with total access to the sea. Once the viable agricultural land was settled and cleared for cultivation, the pattern of life stabilised into a landscape of scattered farms and small villages.

By the fifth century, life in Scandinavia centred on the longhouse, a staple feature of communities there for millennia prior to the time of the Vikings. Farms kept a range of domestic animals, including cattle, sheep, and goats, as well as horses and household creatures such as dogs. During the Migration Period, as earlier, humans and animals often shared the main dwelling, the livestock housed at one end of the structure in a byre divided into stalls along the sides with a central gutter down the middle. The warmth of the animals contributed to heating the building, a trade-off perhaps with the smells of manure and wet hides. Even now, many parts of rural Scandinavia are lined with low drystone walls that once divided the fields of the Iron Age, and marked out droveways where the livestock were taken to pasture each day. In the summer, animals ranged farther afield, up into the hills and mountains.

Barley and oats were the primary cereal crops, supplemented by small amounts of wheat. Other plants, such as flax, were also grown. It was a cyclical system, with hay from the fields feeding the animals, which in turn provided manure for the crops. In the course of the Iron Age, the simple technologies of these practices improved, leading to an expansion of the agricultural base of the region over the fourth and fifth centuries, and a steadily increasing population. The clearance of land for farming continued, with archaeological evidence attesting to the opening up of northern regions for agriculture. The most fertile soils, of course, supported the richest farms, and their products—especially a surplus that could be traded—became intimately linked to power and status.

In more marginal areas, marine resources and hunting made up a greater portion of the subsistence economy. Fish could be dried for the winter, and sea mammals such as seals, walrus, and whales were utilised in a variety of ways. The woodlands were populated by animals such as elk (the North American moose), bear, birds, and small game that augmented the hunters' diet and provided furs and skins.

Authorities more than capable of coordinated organisation had been in existence in the North since pre-Roman times. Social stratification had probably developed centuries earlier during the Bronze Age, due to the ability of certain groups to control the flow of imported raw materials used in the production of the metal. These levels of social complexity would continue to increase. It was also towards the end of the Roman Iron Age that burial customs began to change and cremation became the norm for disposing of the dead, a practice that was to remain throughout the pre-Christian period until the conversion process gained traction during the late Viking Age.

The Scandinavians' local and regional groupings (there is no adequate vocabulary—both 'tribes' and 'peoples' seem to fall short) had long interacted with the Empire, especially farther south. During the first centuries CE, at the height of Roman power, there is also good evidence for contacts between parts of Norway and the Gallic provinces, and a degree of trade is also detectible. Roman goods, such as glasses and high-end tableware, found their way into Scandinavia. It is clear that items of status were preferred as they conveyed a new social dignity on their owners by association with the distant imperial authority. Put simply, it was thought classier to drink wine than beer or mead.

Roman weapons have also been found, in quantity, as imports in what is now Denmark. It is a familiar strategy—in that the Empire sold armaments not to its immediate neighbours, but to those on *their* borders beyond, helping keep the frontier in check. That these societies were capable of relatively large-scale warfare is evident from the massive quantities of contemporary military equipment found in the bogs of southern Scandinavia. These deposits have been interpreted as offerings, presumably to supernatural powers, following the defeat of invading enemy forces. Several of these bog assemblages are composed of weapons and personal items of types characteristic of western and southern Norway, implying that this was where these particular attackers originated. It is hard to understand the exact nature of the communities that could mount such major maritime expeditions, or their exact reasons for doing so, but it seems plausible that a fairly extensive tribal or clan-based system must have developed by this time.

Some have argued that the military units that can be perceived in these deposits had been organised along Roman army lines. Danish bog finds dating from the late Roman Iron Age also indicate that groups from Sweden were conducting raids across the Danish islands and into the Jylland Peninsula (the largest part of modern Denmark, connecting with the Continent). Links with the Empire are also attested by high-status imported objects that would have functioned as visible markers of social elevation. Of particular note is the spectacular Roman cavalry mask from Hellvi, on the Baltic island of Gotland, that was probably made in the late second century but was found in a sixth-century context. How and when this helmet, which was originally intended for use in Roman cavalry displays and equestrian games, came to Gotland is a mystery, but the fact that this object was of great antiquity by the time it was deposited implies that it must have been an especially treasured or revered item that lent status and power to its owner.

In particular, many Scandinavians hired out as mercenary auxiliaries in the forces of the later Empire, organised along ethnic lines and thus forming units of warriors from the same point of origin. The constant movement of these potentially violent groups back and forth across the frontiers not only contributed to the importation of Roman influences in the North, but also created destabilising feedback within the Empire. Many of the 'migrations' ultimately had their origins in organised foreign militias and auxiliaries of this kind. A proportion of soldiers have always settled where they were demobbed (or had deserted), and the late Roman fallout was no exception.

The broader momentum of the Migration Period in Europe, and the demographic transformation in its wake, was considerable. But what did the fall of the Western Empire really mean for Scandinavia in the long term?

The overall picture through the Roman Iron Age and into the late 400s is one of growth in every area. It can be seen in the numbers and scale of farms and villages, in woodland clearance for cultivation, through trading connections, and in domestic economies. But this was to change. In seeking to trace the deeper origins of the social trajectories that would produce the cultures of the Viking Age, it is hard (and often unwise) to isolate individual events above processes. However, it has long been known that something unusually drastic happened to the north European world in the sixth century CE, signalled in the archaeology by a relatively sudden shift in the nature of the surviving record.

In the late 400s and the first half of the 500s, and especially towards the middle of the century, there is a remarkably steep decline in the number of settlements, graves, and, indeed, most other markers of human activity. In many regions of central and southern Sweden, for example, there was an almost total abandonment of settlement sites that had been occupied in some cases for millennia. Well over a thousand farms were deserted on each of the Baltic islands of Gotland and Öland alone. The same is true of cemeteries, which went out of use at the same time as the settlements they served. The rich burials and elaborate material culture of the preceding century or so also disappeared. There are corresponding discontinuities of production in ceramics and many other commodities. Most significantly of all, pollen analyses show that woodland grew back over what had once been cultivated fields. There is no doubt that these places were truly given up and left uninhabited.

Similar dislocations have been detected in the symbolic repertoire of Scandinavian art, in the rapid disappearance of styles and decorative schemes that had persisted for centuries. There is every reason to believe that much Iron Age 'art' was intensely laden with meaning, and thus that this was a shift in more than merely ornament and taste. Golden bracteate discs were buried in large quantities at this time, and other ritual practices sharply changed.

Taken together, these impacts represent a clear break with an earlier way of life, a fundamental difference not only in settlement patterns and economy but in beliefs—the structures of the mind. It is one thing to label this package of decline as the late Migration Period 'crisis'—but what actually happened, and what was the result? What could have caused such a deep-seated shift in the lives of the Scandinavians?

There is little evidence to suggest that expansion in the Migration Period went too far, as scholars once believed: it was not overexploitation of resources or unsustainable population levels. In fact, the farmers of the early Iron Age had a sophisticated understanding of their environment and its potential, as could be expected. Crops were rotated; a system of infield and outfield farming had been in place for centuries along with the use of natural fertilisers; and cereal production was mixed with animal husbandry on a large scale, adapted to the northern climate. There were regional variations in these patterns, of course, relating to the possibilities afforded by local weather and topography. What worked for people in the sunlit meadows of one valley might be inappropriate for their neighbours on the other side of the hills, more often in colder shadow. Clearly, the different regions of Scandinavia followed their own trajectories, influenced not only by environmental conditions and subsistence practices but also by the flavour of local politics.

Some scholars have suggested that progressive destabilisation was caused by warfare on the Continent, part of the factional fighting that erupted there as Roman authority declined. This pattern is familiar from more contemporary conflicts, as units long accustomed to lucrative employment and active combat find themselves adrift, sometimes turning against the same authorities who hired them, or returning home looking for trouble. Such situations risk creating a world of petty warlords and a kind of gangster culture— part bandits, part small but effective armies—undermining the work of social institutions and leaving chaos in the wake of their vicious civil engagements. In a culture that does not formally record its history, even the most profound trauma can disappear relatively quickly without leaving much material trace. However, such war bands *were* on the move in the North, and they must have been entering Scandinavia in some numbers. The recent discovery of a massacre site at the fortress of Sandby borg on the island of Öland is unique evidence of raiding that was probably much more commonplace. Whole systems of fortifications were constructed at this time along a maritime belt from Danish Bornholm to Gotland and also farther inland. These places were frequently attacked and burnt, and it is clear that a zone of conflict stretched from the Skagerrak to central Sweden.

Other researchers have suggested a major role for the Huns, who originated in the Caucasus. Their European invasions under Attila in the early fifth century brought not only violence but also influences of all kinds, including artistic ones, and new trains of thought. Their impact has been considered particularly important in the sphere of religion, with aspects of Norse belief paralleled in the steppe cultures. The zenith of Hunnic power was long over by the turbulent years of the sixth century, but it is significant that their memory remained vivid even long after the Viking Age itself. There must be a reason why the Horde features so prominently in the legendary sagas.

Another factor in the downturn is likely to have been disconnections in international trade and the mercantile economy, to which even robust systems are vulnerable if the external supply situation changes (especially if it does so relatively suddenly). Such disruptions occurred in the late fifth century and into the sixth.

For decades, scholars have tended towards extremes in their interpretations of what was happening in the 500s, whether to see these years as a crisis of near-catastrophic proportions or else to stress resilience and continuity. This not only oversimplifies the issue, but it also assumes that similar conditions prevailed everywhere and that the communities in different areas all reacted in the same way. This was far from the case. It is also important to emphasise that the 'sudden' decline visible in the archaeology is dependent on sometimes imprecise dating and chronologies, and that these processes nonetheless played out over decades at least, perhaps longer. The abandonment of cemeteries may have to do with behaviour rather than demographics, and these things can be hard to read. In both settlements and cemeteries alike, one must also consider the degree to which a 'decline' was in reality more of a reorganisation, but there is nevertheless no doubt that some kind of major social contraction was occurring. Clearly, the Migration Period 'crisis' must have had multiple causes that acted in combination, and it went on for a long time.

However, a growing body of collaborative work between natural scientists, historians, and archaeologists has revealed something else in the mix: a short sequence of events so enormous in scale and impact as to make them initially question if they could be real. It began with the environmental analysis of ice cores sampled from both Greenland and Antarctica, and the identification of significant layers of sulphate aerosols—the material that results from volcanic eruptions. At about the same time, refinements in tree-ring chronologies found that the dating of the aerosols corresponded to a short period of markedly reduced forest growth across large parts of the world. In turn, natural scientists noted that pollen data indicating woodland regression and the loss of cultivated land also matched this time period. More and more evidence accrued from multiple proxies clearly indicated either a single climate event, or perhaps several within a short number of years, that together took on major proportions.

Initially, the findings were dismissed by historians, one calling it "the latest Great Disaster theory". This swiftly changed. After years of patient work around the globe, volcanologists and climate modelers are now sure: in the years 536 and 539/540, there occurred at least two volcanic eruptions of almost unprecedented magnitude. The first of them may have been somewhere in the tropics, although the location has not yet been pinned down conclusively. The second was at Lake Ilopango in today's El Salvador, an explosion so vast that the entire volcano collapsed and left only the flooded caldera that can be seen today, large enough to contain the capital city.

It is estimated that Ilopango alone produced up to eighty-seven km^3 of ejecta, a figure big enough to induce double takes in even the most sceptical authorities (yes, *cubic kilometres*). The sulphate emissions may have measured up to two hundred megatonnes, significantly higher than those from Tambora (1815), which was the second-greatest eruption in history. The Ilopango eruption was among the ten largest on earth over the past seven thousand years, and remember, this was preceded by the 536 volcano, so far unlocated. New research also suggests these may have been followed by a *third* major eruption, in 547.

The effects were devastating, as the ejecta and sulphur dioxide aerosols reached the lower stratosphere and began to circle the globe. The sun's light was blocked in a hazy mist that allowed no heat to penetrate, while at night the heavens were filled with wavering curtains of fiery colour, like a sunset that went on for months (Edvard Munch's famous painting *The Scream* shows such skies, then a result of the Krakatau eruption).

Scientists refer to this phenomenon as the 'dust veil'.

The impact was not unlike that of a nuclear winter. Trees began to wither, their growth stunted, as seen in the dendrochronological record. Unseasonal cold gripped the northern hemisphere, with snow in the summer months visible in the Norwegian high-altitude data. The weakened sunlight most directly affected plant life of all kinds, including crops, quite literally taking out the food supply. Written sources from China and India describe harvest problems and disrupted weather patterns; the environmental evidence is consistent from North America to mainland Europe. In the Mediterranean world, writers among the Goths and other militarised imperial successors described the famine, riots, and slide into civil unrest that resulted from the failed harvests in the endless winter.

But in Scandinavia, the ecological consequences were far worse. There, the natural environmental conditions meant its people already subsisted at the limits of resilience; at the best of times, their agricultural production was acutely vulnerable to fluctuations in temperature and other climatic shifts. It seems clear that temperatures fell by at least two degrees, and possibly as many as three to four. Current (2019) estimates suggest a temporary temperature drop of perhaps three and a half degrees Celsius. In Norway, where only 3 percent of the land is suitable for farming in the first place, this would have been enough to render significant parts of the country uninhabitable through the collapse of viable cereal cultivation. The regression of woodland into what had once been food-producing fields shows that, in many places, agriculture itself had ceased. Acid rain caused by the eruptions may even have affected marine life, including fish catches, although to a lesser degree than the agricultural catastrophe.

The worst of these effects went on for three years. In 2016 a team of climate scientists suggested that the long-term, cumulative ecological impact of the dust veil persisted in varying degrees for up to *eighty years*.

We have seen the effects on settlement and farming patterns, the mass abandonment of dwelling sites and arable land, but what did this mean in plain terms? The farms were left vacant because the people were gone. The consequences of the dust veil quite literally killed them. Those who survived fought each other for what was left. To add to the region's misery, it is also possible that the Justinian plague pandemic that swept across Europe from 541 onwards also reached Scandinavia; it has so far been detected as far north as Germany.

Estimates of the population loss across Scandinavia rise as high as 50 percent—a number considered reasonable by both volcanologists and archaeologists—with tens of thousands starving to death as the major sources of food simply ceased to exist. For historical comparison, the bubonic plague (the 'Black Death') is thought to have ended the lives of 45–60 percent of Europeans in the mid-fourteenth century. In the Thirty Years' War of 1618–1648, perhaps a third of the Continent's people died. In the aftermath of both these events, it took well over a century for population levels to recover.

The situation in Scandinavia seems to have been so bad that it left a mark on religion itself, in what scholars call geomythology, whereby natural events and disasters are given meaning through their articulation in sacred tales. Geomythology is by its very nature an inexact concept: inherently unproveable, prone to confirmation bias, and hampered by a lack of precise dating in both textual and archaeological sources. However, there is a compelling case to be made for such a connection here, a paradox in which parts of the Viking Age may have originated, precisely, with the imagining of its end.

One of the more widely known narratives of the Norse myths concerns the fall of the worlds—the cataclysmic final battle at the Ragnarök in which gods and humans will perish forever. The prelude to the Viking apocalypse is actually quite specific in its details, as recorded in a variety of poems. Here is Snorri, from his *Edda*:

> First of all that a winter will come called Fimbulwinter.
> Then snow will drift from all directions.
> There will then be great frosts and keen winds.
> The sun will do no good.
> There will be three of these winters together
> and no summer between.

The description of this terrible distortion of the seasons, the Fimbulwinter, or 'Mighty Winter', is remarkably similar to the cycle scientists postulate for the immediate effects of the eruptions. In several of the Eddic poems, such as the *Seeress's Prophecy*, the same is found:

> Black become the sun's beams
> in the summers that follow,
> weathers all treacherous.

A few verses later one can read again that "the sun starts to blacken"; there are clear and surprisingly precise descriptions of a dimness in the heavens as a prelude to the Ragnarök. The "ruin of the moon" comes in the form of the wolf that has hounded it since the beginning. As the sun vanishes, the stars fall into the sea, where their heat raises a great steam that covers the sky.

There may be something similar in a neighbouring mythology, the *Kalevala* of the Finns, who have a legend of an ongoing darkening of the celestial bodies and the sky caused by the Mistress of the

Northern Land who captures the sun and moon. The descriptions are eerily alike:

> What wonder blocks out the moon
> what fog is in the sun's way
> that the moon gleams not at all
> and the sun shines not at all.
> [. . .]
> Still the sun is not shining
> nor the golden moon gleaming
> [. . .]
> The wealth [i.e., the crops] grows chilly,
> the herds get into a dreadful state
> strange to the birds of the air
> tiresome to mankind
> that the sun will never shine
> nor will the moon gleam.

Another version of the text, the so-called *Old Kalevala*, says that the sun was gone for years:

> Now the night was perpetual,
> long, dark as pitch, a deep place unreached by the sun.
> It was night for five years, no sun for six years,
> no moon for eight years.

It seems unlikely to be coincidental that at this time the image of the burning sun-wheel, which had been a central motif in Scandinavian sacral iconography for several thousand years, disappears. The sun had gone, and people turned to any alternative they could think of. The new offerings of gold bracteates (sun discs?) and other precious metals can be seen as crisis rituals, increasingly desperate attempts to invoke the aid of higher powers in averting the terrible

6. The setting of the sun. A so-called picture-stone memorial from the island of Gotland, dating to the fifth or sixth century and showing the characteristic burning disc thought to denote the sun, with the moon and stars. During the sixth-century climate crisis, such imagery disappeared as the sun lost its power, never to return in the Iron Age art of the North. This stone is from Sanda church and stands 3.5m high. Photo: Fredrik Sterner, Gotlands Museum, used by kind permission.

fracturing of society that was only gaining momentum. This too is visible in Old Norse poetry, not only with civil strife and fighting, but also in the destruction of the framework of custom and propriety. Again from the *Seeress's Prophecy*:

An axe age, a sword age
– shields are riven –
a wind age, a wolf age –
before the world goes headlong.

The poem specifies how brothers murder brothers, cousins "defile the bonds of kinship"—a reference to incest—and families are ruined. The crises of the mid-sixth century must have led in the North to a widespread sense of dissolution, as the social cement that bonded Scandinavian communities began to lose its effect. In many respects, the fabric of life evidently came apart.

An obvious argument against the dust veil as the model for the Fimbulwinter is that the Scandinavian world did not, in fact, end in the mid-sixth century. But this depends on perspective and hindsight—in a very real sense, one model of society really was destroyed in the upheavals of the time. It is clear that the volcanic winter was not the sole cause, perhaps not even the primary one. But it added fuel to an existing fire and certainly played a very significant role indeed. What emerged from the chaos *was* in a sense a new world, founded on quite different sociopolitical principles than the old. This renewal is also reproduced in the larger myth of the Ragnarök, of which the Fimbulwinter is the beginning—but that is to get ahead of ourselves.

Even veterans and civilian victims of modern wars would have difficulty contemplating the deaths of fully half the population, and the consequent collapse of social institutions. Today, even the worst disasters with the most appalling casualties nonetheless play out against a wider arena where these things are not happening. It is not hard to imagine how the Scandinavians of the sixth century felt that their whole world was falling into ruin, and slipping back into the primal emptiness from which it came. In a culture reliant on oral traditions for preserving and mediating history, it would not be surprising if, two hundred years later, the trauma was still clearly embedded in stories—a terrifying vision of endings and beginnings that were also part of a longer cycle. After all, the preordination of fate, the inevitability of the Ragnarök, and the gods' knowledge of their coming doom form *the* constant pulse of Norse mythology.

Not everywhere was equally affected, at both regional and local levels. In parts of eastern Norway, there are perceptible differences even from one district to the next, dependent on local topography, political structures, and the external factors of climate change. In the far north of Scandinavia, the picture is different again, perhaps due to the availability of marine resources that were less affected by the climatic events of the 530s and 540s. In some areas, there was no settlement abandonment at all, and few other signs of decline. Some areas suffered greatly, while others may actually have prospered at their expense—for example, there appears to have been a shift of power from western Norway to the eastern region around the Oslo fjord, today's Østfold and Vestfold with their sheltered access to the sea. Some even seem to have truly thrived, seeing an opportunity and adjusting a new reality to their own ends.

For the Scandinavians of the Migration Period, the 'Fimbulwinter' (in combination with other, slower-burning factors) was an ending—but also a beginning of something else, which is the key point. The new societies that built themselves up from the bleak landscape left behind by the years without summer did so on a new model, creating fundamentally different structures of power and community, and with them altered ways of life in which lay the seeds of the Viking future. Over time, then, archaeologists have come to see the transformations at the beginning of the late Iron Age not simply in terms of recovery, but more as deliberate choices, the adoption of new political strategies, and the emergence of new forms of power—specifically, the rise of militarised elites.

This new world was Midgard, the home of the people from whose collective consciousness it emerged: the Scandinavians. But what did it look like?

In the popular imagination, especially when contemplated from a distance, Scandinavia is still a place of ice and snow—the archetypal frozen North. The reality is very different, with variations in landform, climate, and seasonal conditions that are among the most extreme in the world. However, in one sense the stereotype holds true, in that it was the effects of the last Ice Age that created the landscape we still recognise today.

In all of Europe, Scandinavia was one of the areas where the glaciers lingered longest, burying the land under a mile thickness of ice even when much of the Continent was settled by mobile hunters, fishers, and gatherers. As the glaciers began their long melt around thirteen thousand years ago, when the North began to warm, it was their retreat that scoured out the fjords, rivers, and lakes that were to become so characteristic of the Vikings' homelands. This also set in motion another ongoing transformation that would continue for millennia, manifested in changes to the relative level of the sea. As the glaciers melted, they released water into the surrounding ocean at the same time as the relief from their immense weight caused the land itself to rebound and rise. The rate of change fluctuated and also differed by region, but the net result was a steady drop in relative sea level: since the time of the Vikings, parts of central Sweden have risen some five metres above the then waterline. This means that the people of the time experienced rivers that could take more boat traffic farther inland than these same waterways can today, deeper harbours offering better access to larger vessels, and lakes that have since become dry land. The process continues even now, as central Sweden rises at a rate of a few millimetres per year. In the Viking Age and the preceding centuries, the landscape was in places substantially different to its appearance today and had a great many more open bodies of water.

Of all the areas of Scandinavia, it is present-day Norway that most clearly bears the imprint of the ice. As the glaciers slowly moved westwards, they scored deep valleys into the bedrock, which then flooded and became the fjords that remain the defining feature of the Norwegian terrain. Over more than twenty thousand kilometres of indented shoreline, these products of the last glaciation have made Norway a supremely maritime environment, its population always largely dependent on the sea for their livelihood. Offshore, chains of small islands created sheltered passages that protected shipping from the worst of the ocean weather and turned the sea-lanes into a major transport route. The bulk of Norway's landmass is occupied by mountains that run in successive ranges to form a great north-south spine of high ground along the length of the Scandinavian Peninsula. The climate there has always been difficult and inhospitable, with lethally cold winters and deep snow cover that remains for many months of each year interspersed with cycles of frost and thaw. In the far north of the country is a tree-less zone of tundra, but farther south the fjords were bordered by woodland.

Sweden was naturally separated from Norway to the west by the mountain ranges. Spanning the Arctic Circle in the high latitudes, some 60 percent of the country is known today as Norrland (literally 'Northland') and lies within the taiga zone that ultimately stretches far to the east and on into the plains of Siberia. The landscape here is characterised by rolling hills covered with vast coniferous forests that made the region virtually impassable in the Viking Age. In northern Sweden, agrarian settlement was therefore largely restricted to the banks of the rivers that cut sweeping valleys eastwards to the sea—a pattern of subsistence broadly similar to that found along the Norwegian fjords.

In the central and southern regions of Sweden, the coniferous forests thinned out and merged with deciduous species, creating a more open woodland environment more akin to parts of the European Continent. Fertile clay flatlands overlying granite bedrock form the agricultural heart of the country, which is dotted with lakes that again resulted from the effects of glaciation. Gravel ridges left by the ice formed natural transport routes alongside networks of navigable waterways and rivers. The climate here was very strongly seasonal with a remarkable annual variation. In the late Viking Age, the time of the Medieval Warm Period, it would not have been unusual for a person living in central Sweden to experience a temperature range of fifty to sixty degrees Celsius in the course of a year, from snowy winter to blazing-hot summer.

The landscape of Denmark is markedly different from that of its northern cousins, consisting almost entirely of low-lying agricultural plains with light but rich soils, dotted with lakes, bogs, and marshes. In the Viking Age, much of the region's gently rolling terrain was covered with deciduous forest, but it was nonetheless a core producer within the Scandinavian agrarian economy. Although different in scale and topography, Denmark supported a maritime society just as extensive as Norway, and nowhere in the country is more than forty-five kilometres from the sea. Especially in the north, deep fjords penetrate the land, although they are bounded by gentle hills rather than mountains. Despite lacking the large game of its northern neighbours, Denmark combined the resources of the sea with the extensive cereal production made possible by the fertile soils of the plains.

During the Migration Period of the fifth and sixth centuries, it is estimated that some forty to fifty polities became established along the coastal regions and inland agricultural centres of Scandinavia. They can be traced in the archaeology, correlated (up to a point) with very dim reflections in later written sources, and linked to geographical areas largely defined by topography.

It is hard to know what to call them, these little centres of power. The first native ethnonym—a name for a people—that we have from Norway comes from the Viking Age itself and, in fact, from the first description of Scandinavia that has survived from one of its inhabitants. This is preserved in a remarkable English document that records the conversations between Alfred, the king of Wessex, and a visitor to his court in the 880s, as mentioned above in the prologue. Named there as 'Ohthere', he was almost certainly called Óttarr in his own language and seems to have come from the region around the Lofoten islands in Arctic Norway. According to the English scribe who recorded the encounter, Óttarr called his country Norðveg, which in Old Norse would have been approximately the same and retained the same meaning: 'the North Way'. This was quite literally the passage one followed to the north, clearly referring to a marine route along the coast of Norway. Those who lived there, Óttarr's own people, were the 'Northmen', and exactly the same sense is retained in the modern terms for 'Norway' and 'Norwegians'. In Óttarr's words, filtered through the Old English text:

> He said that the land of the Northmen was very long and very narrow. All that they can either graze or plough lies by the sea; and even that is very rocky in some places; to the east, and alongside the cultivated land, lie wild mountains.

It is hard to think of a more succinctly accurate description.

Unlike Norway, there is no known universal ethnonym used by the population living in what is now modern-day Sweden to describe their land, or themselves, during the first millennium CE. There is some evidence to suggest that both political and probably also ethnic identities were regionally oriented in the centuries immediately preceding the Viking Age. South-central Sweden, essentially the territories south of Norrland, was broadly divided between two folk groups, although it is difficult to accurately find a name that reflects the nature of their polities. Farthest south, spanning the great lake lands of Vänern and Vättern, and bordering on the forest barrier of Småland, were the Gautar or Götar (sometimes anglicised, problematically, as Goths). They occupied the region of Götaland, broadly reflected today in the eastern and western provinces of that name.

North of them, centred on the Mälar Valley and the extensive plains bordering it, were the Svíar, spelled today as Svear. There are many forms of the name, but one that has found common use is the Old West Norse *Svíþjóð*, the 'Svíar people', a term sometimes employed for their territory, Svealand. These are the people who came to give their name to the whole country (in modern Swedish, *Sverige* literally 'the kingdom of the Svear'). Despite nominal unification, Sweden would remain politically fragmented along these lines well into the Middle Ages, and the sociopolitical relations between Svealand and Götaland remains a divisive issue generating a degree of tension even today.

In all this, the political structures of the Viking Age in Sweden differ significantly from those of Norway, where the process of political unification began at a much earlier date, and even more so from those of Denmark, which seems to have achieved a degree of social and political cohesion long before its northern neighbours. The earliest record of the name Denamearc comes from the same English text mentioned above: the Norwegian Óttarr's description of his homelands and travels on the occasion of his meeting with King Alfred. The Latin term for its inhabitants, *Dani* ('Danes'), has longer antecedents, and it is clear from archaeological finds that a regional identity formed relatively early.

Part of the reason for this lies with geography, in the connection of the Jylland Peninsula with mainland Europe and the archipelago of more than four hundred islands that guards the entrance to the Baltic through the Skagerrak and Kattegat straits. This whole area developed very close social links at least half a millennium prior to the Viking Age, with a broadly coherent culture that extended from Jylland through the larger Danish islands of Sjælland and Fyn and onto the mainland of what is now southern Sweden. This latter region was separated from the central Swedish lake lands by a natural border of dense forest and hills, essentially today the province of Småland. The area to the south, consisting of Skåne and parts of Blekinge and Halland provinces, was considered to be culturally and politically part of Denmark until well after the Middle Ages and was not formally incorporated into the Swedish nation until the late 1600s.

Beyond the three main areas of Scandinavia and their coastal archipelagos, each of them divided into numerous small polities at the start of the Viking Age, there were also a number of major Baltic islands that supported their own distinctive cultures but were nonetheless part of the broader Nordic sphere. These include Bornholm, to the east of Danish Fyn; the islands of Öland and Gotland lying off the southern and central shores of Sweden; and the extended chain of the Åland islands between Sweden and what is now Finland. All enjoyed temperate climates suitable for agricultural settlement, and all were well-situated within maritime networks that extended across the Baltic and beyond.

This book is largely concerned with the majority population of what we now call Scandinavia. Problems of terminology and labelling aside, the Vikings were speakers of Indo-European languages, with ultimately north Continental origins, living in the territories of modern Norway, Sweden, and Denmark. But they were not alone there. Although they do not play a primary role here, the semi-nomadic Sámi people ranged widely as hunters, fishers, and gatherers and interacted extensively with their 'Germanic' neighbours.

The origins of the Sámi are unknown, although genetic and linguistic evidence suggests they migrated northwards from southern Europe into Scandinavia during the Stone Age. Much energy has been wasted on the acrimonious debate as to who 'arrived first' in the region and thus which of the Nordic or Sámi peoples may lay claim to being the indigenous population of Scandinavia. It is clear not least from language that the two groups had fundamentally different identities and cultures. In recent years, there have been suggestions that their ethnicity developed much later during the Iron Age, effectively as a division between a settled agrarian existence and a mobile hunting-based economy. However, although these different subsistence strategies certainly coexisted, there is no evidence that they were mutually exclusive and even less to suggest that they represent in themselves some kind of Sámi-Norse dichotomy.

By the Viking Age, it is entirely certain that the Norse and Sámi had both been established in Scandinavia for millennia. The

Sámi homeland today, known as Sápmi, ignores the geopolitical boundaries of the Nordic countries and stretches across the northern areas of Norway, Sweden, and Finland, with a small extension into Russia on the Kola Peninsula. In the Viking Age, however, the Sámi ranged much farther south. Burials conducted with what would elsewhere clearly be understood as Sámi rituals, the characteristic remains of circular tent encampments with central stone hearths, and isolated finds of objects decorated with art styles common among the Sámi have been found around Trøndelag county in the Norwegian central region and even just to the north of Oslo, and in central Sweden they were present in Uppsala. Identity is a more complex matter than patterns of ornament or the burial rites of the dead, but in combination the mass of data is compelling, especially contrasted with the surrounding settlements of equally typical 'Norse' type.

Some Sámi herded domesticated reindeer (the animal called caribou in North America) and used every part of the beast, including its milk for daily sustenance and ultimately its meat and the raw materials provided by its body. Others hunted and trapped for food and furs, or fished the rivers, lakes, and coasts. The Sámi were people of the mountains, as in their popular image today, but also of the waterways, the boreal taiga forests, and the tundra to the north.

Above all, the Sámi were people of the drum—the sacred instrument that was the primary tool of their *noaidi*, or what anthropologists would call a shaman. Their spiritual beliefs and practices were deeply connected to those of other circumpolar cultures, and differed markedly from those of the Scandinavians. In the early modern period when missionaries tried to convert the Sámi to Christianity, often by brutal force and the intentional destruction of their ancient spiritual values, a word was coined to represent the rapidly fading past of the old ways, encapsulating traditions that went back to the Viking Age and beyond: *goabdesájgge* (in the Lule Sámi language), the 'Drum Time'. Throughout the narratives of this book, it should always be kept in mind that the time of the Vikings was also the time of the drums.

Viking-Age Scandinavia thus supported two distinctive populations living in close proximity and in relative cooperation—occasionally in the same settlements or even households—but following their own ways of life and employing substantially different kinds of material culture. The Sámi seem to have taken little active role in the political consolidation of the North, although they were integrated in its economy. However, support from their communities in the forests and mountains may have been a critical factor in maintaining stability and a grip on power.

In Norway, the early polities centred on fjords, with a view towards control of the sea lanes, and on the small strips of farmland along the valleys. In Sweden, their areas were larger around the central and southern plains and lakes, but smaller and concentrated on the river mouths in the north, straddling the water routes down from the mountains. In Denmark—a region both spatially smaller and flatter, and also closer to the great power blocs of the Continent—the fledgling polities were larger still, following the shadowy push towards faster political cohesion that can be sensed there earlier in the Iron Age.

These realms in miniature seem to have been conceptualised as kingdoms, but very small ones to modern eyes. A key factor in the new structures of power was the right to own land, which in turn hinged on how that land was obtained. In the social order that rose after the 'Fimbulwinter', land tenure seems to have been newly concentrated into the hands of the few rather than the many and then parcelled out in a form of tenancy. Absentee landholding seems to have begun well before the dust veil in 536, but clearly accelerated afterwards. A transition of this kind may have occurred by force, or perhaps vacant farms—empty because their inhabitants were either dead or gone—were simply appropriated, another context in which the passage of arms may have provided its own legitimacy.

This de facto seizure of landed wealth was then enshrined in a complex layering of consolidation. It can be seen in the construction of great halls and 'royal' residences for the new 'monarchs'. It appears in the allocation of estates to trusted military retainers, whose loyal violence provided both the pathway to power and the ultimate guarantee of its retention. It can be perceived in the energetic support given to foreign and domestic exchange and markets, which provided luxuries needed to pay the retinues. It has left a trace in the creation of spurious ancestral traditions of rightful office—associated with the gods and mythical forebears, supported by religious rituals that honoured such divinities of war. And at its mortal conclusion, it was manifested in the building of burial mounds greater than any ever seen before, a permanent record of power unavoidably established in the landscape for all to witness. All this effort focussed on individuals, the self-appointed representatives of collectives that were in part their own creations, and as the first steps in the founding of family dynasties to carry them into the future.

The vacuum of Roman power that had once served as a political role model was consciously filled by these new elites, who even emulated the symbolic language of the former imperial authority— the divine lineages, portraiture, and a Scandinavian version of their grandiose monuments. This is not surprising because they or their immediate ancestors were well acquainted with the Empire and its visual world. They were never entirely cut off from what Rome became. Power in the North became synonymous with its display, in a visual language crude enough to make its meaning self-evident to anyone.

Given the ecological pressures of the sixth century and their aftermath, there is an entirely literal sense in which the new elites were products of their environment. More to the point, every self-styled Scandinavian 'king' thereafter made his environment an extension of himself, as he and his militias stamped their imprint on land and people alike. In the two hundred years immediately preceding the Viking Age, some version of this system was built up across the North and was augmented and consolidated by each successive ruler in every petty kingdom. This process also embraced all their war leaders, their men, and their families and tenants. Such rulers and peoples populate the poetry of the Viking Age, ancestral histories and tales that kept the past close. Although it is an Old English text, the epic of *Beowulf* tells an exclusively Scandinavian story of the Danes and Swedes and Geats, of their wars and rivalries, and of the honour-fixated culture that sustained them. Muddled echoes of the same shared memories, and sometimes the same individuals, appear in the Icelandic legendary sagas. In every case, the main protagonists are members of family dynasties: the Ynglingas, the Skjöldungas, the Völsungas, and others. They were the *nouveau riche* and self-made men of the late Iron Age, who had fought their way to power and made tiny worlds in their image. One historian has called such warlords "violent chancers", and he is right.

This way of life became encoded in monumental landscapes of mounds and great halls of which remnants can still be seen today at places such as Gamla (that is, 'Old') Uppsala in Swedish Uppland, Borre in Norwegian Vestfold, and Lejre near Roskilde in Denmark. They represent a confluence of factors familiar from more recent times, especially an emphasis on exclusivity and the importance of membership within a defined group. Their militaristic ethos thrived on notions of honourable companionship, bound through obligation and oaths of mutual support, and in a sense represented a refinement of identities that had been present in Scandinavia since at least the Bronze Age. Built around what one scholar has called "the warrior's beauty", it combined a violent aesthetic with sworn loyalty and a dazzling material culture of killing.

The royal mounds at Uppsala were all cremation burials, and thus the riches they once contained have been reduced to burnt fragments, but archaeologists can still reconstruct the golden collars, helmets, weapons mounted with garnets, and imported luxuries. From other sites, such as Högom in Norrland, it is possible to see the clothes they wore: whole suits of bright red cloth, with gold buttons, and gold and silver thread bordering the cuffs and hems. It would have caught the light as they moved; this was not clothing for the modest.

A few kilometres away from Uppsala is the grave-field of Valsgärde, the burial site of what appears to be an extended family group over the entire Iron Age. Some fifteen funerary boats have been found buried there, one per generation, with magnificent regalia: enormous shields, sometimes three to a grave, their boards covered with decorated mounts in the form of animals and interlace; heavy war spears; and gilded weapons decorated with the characteristic red-on-gold patterns of cloisonné garnets.

The ultimate symbol of the social code was the ring-sword, mentioned in the poetry and represented by many archaeological finds—a weapon with a literal gold ring locked into its hilt. This was the token of loyalty in battle, sworn and accepted, the mark of a war commander. In the great boat burials of the sixth and seventh centuries, most impressive of all are the helmets, each a war mask covering the face (and sometimes the entire head and neck in a curtain of mail). Their surfaces are composed of dozens of small plaques, each decorated in relief with scenes from Northern mythology. There are tiny fighting men on foot and horseback, monsters, winged creatures, shape-shifters, and what seem to be the war gods themselves. These men were a walking illustration of their ideology. The graves also contain the remains of fighting dogs, with spiked collars and chain leashes, as well as hunting birds trained to the wrist. The boats were surrounded by slaughtered animals, such as horses and cattle, which must have soaked the ground with their blood. Even the vessels themselves were decorated, the gunwales bristling with curving spirals of iron, perhaps leading forward as the mane of a figurehead dragon.

These were men whom nobody would fail to recognise, who stood out from the crowd wherever they went—a literal embodiment of hierarchy.

In Sweden, the first of these sites to be discovered—the boat burial field at Vendel, in Uppland—has given its name to a whole time period, c. 550–750, the two centuries that led into the Viking Age. Terminologies vary; in Norway the Vendel Period is known as the Merovingian, while in Denmark it is combined with the Migration Period as the Germanic Iron Age.

The new social order implicated everyone in the community, not just the predominantly male elites. At Valsgärde, the boat graves were interspersed with cremations and chamber burials, many of which contained women who were interred with high-status objects similar to those of the ship-lords. It is only modern prejudice that sees the 'spectacular' boat burials as being of greater importance than the others. Indeed, the poetry of these kingdoms explicitly celebrates the power of queens, the leading lights of the halls, bearing drinks in jewelled mead cups to the self-styled heroes.

The scale of these mortuary landscapes also needs to be appreciated. In the central Swedish provinces of Uppland, Södermanland, and Västmanland alone—the territories bordering Lake Mälaren and thus the gateway to the Baltic—there are nearly three hundred monumental burial mounds more than twenty metres in diameter. This is far larger than any conventional barrow, and these graves are the tombs of the new 'kings', their elite supporters, and the highest-ranking members of their retinues. The pattern is repeated in the west of Sweden, and on a much smaller scale in the north.

Mapping these burials allows us to estimate the size of the retinues that the warlords could command. Judging from the grave mounds, the Uppsala region could probably support forty to fifty leaders of the kind buried in the Valsgärde boats, backed up with a host of perhaps five to eight hundred warriors. If they wanted to take to the water, some fifty or so Valsgärde-type boats would be required to transport them. This was the 'army' that the Uppsala kings brought with them to war.

There are also aspects of the monumental burials that raise other questions, as some of the great boat burials contain Sámi tent covers made of birch bark with characteristic burnt decoration. These were used to swathe some of the funerary ships; from the Sámi perspective, this would turn the whole vessel into a burial wrapped according to their practice. It is hard to know what this means—perhaps a diplomatic gift, like a foreign dignitary laying a wreath at a modern politician's funeral, or something more interactive? A close relationship between the Scandinavians and the Sámi at the highest levels nonetheless seems established.

The social transformation of the North extended into the homes of the farmers, even the layout and design of the buildings changing to fit the new norms of domestic life. There was a shift from open-air communal feasting and the use of cooking pits to the interior culture of the hall, which was replicated on a smaller scale in the houses of the countryfolk and their families.

Built architecture was especially crucial to the new ideologies of the North, as these new dramas of power required expansive performative spaces to enact them. The rise of hall culture can be traced from this time. Essentially a development of the traditional Scandinavian longhouse, the living area was redefined as a communal space made for public display. Cooking areas were partitioned off at one end, out of sight, while the private quarters of the lord were at the other, also screened from the main hall itself. These structures had different entrances for guests of different rank, and sometimes reception areas or vestibules where armour and weapons could be removed before admittance.

Long fireplaces ran down the centre of the hall, with platforms on either side where guests would sit on benches. Later, after the fittings had been cleared, they would bed down to sleep there. Either at one end of the room, or at the middle of a long side, was the high seat of the hall's lord—the focal point. Guests were welcome; indeed, their presence was partly the point, bound up in the grim logic of obligatory and reciprocal hospitality that was part of the elite code. These were arenas for mutual recognition, for the telling of tales over feasts and drink (especially drink), for the giving and receiving of rings and other tokens of largesse with which the lord controlled his men, who in turn enforced his wishes among the people. Such buildings were also highly gendered places, replete with symbolism linked to the roles of men and women.

The hall had its own verbal currency, a special language of self-honour and commissioned public praise that best mediated the messages of power the building was designed to convey. The hall was the primary milieu of poetry and of its masters, the skalds. In a sophisticated oral society such as that of Vendel, and later Viking, Scandinavia, one of the poets' main tasks was to find memorable language in which to distill what was necessary to know, enabling people to retain what they needed of their collective past. This project grew with time, part of the self-perpetuating mechanisms that kept these societies in motion. Today we might ask what a poem 'means', but this would itself be meaningless for the work of the skalds. In sketching their complex word-pictures, they simply allowed the things they related to be more truly themselves.

There is a sense in which this story-world of the late Iron Age depended for its vitality on the stage set of the dwelling, the wavering circle of light around the hearth—whether in a farmer's longhouse or in the epic space of the hall. Indoors was the closeness of tellers and listeners, and outside, the dark. In the greatest early medieval poem of all, *Beowulf*, a famous building of this kind is almost a central character. Here, the hall is civilisation, light, fame, honour, memory, history, and joy—beyond its doors, and in the poem literally smashing through them, are the monsters of chaos and the night.

Many of the Old Norse poems set out detailed, complex narratives of kings' deeds and heroes' prowess, often contrasted with the less worthy acts of inferior men. They functioned through many elaborate metres and rhyme schemes, through imagery and wordplay. There is also the richly textured world of similes, or 'kennings', in which two or more nouns and descriptors are combined to evoke an object visually or metaphorically. Thus, the ocean was 'the whale road', a ship was a 'wave-horse', and a person's thoughts were 'waves on the shore of the mind-sea'. Trees were frequent metaphors for humans, almost certainly playing on Ash and Elm. In this poetic imagery, people were the 'trunks' that supported other things—thus men could be spoken of as 'trees of weapons', women as 'trees of jewels', and so on, while arms and wrists were 'branches' on which objects could alight like birds. When describing the play of light on weapons or armour, they saw it as being "like the sun on a field of broken ice". Again, anyone doubting the sophistication of the late Iron Age Scandinavian mind need only turn to its poetry, an inexhaustible fount of wonder. Such skills had a myth all their own.

At the end of the war of the divine families, the gods sealed the peace by spitting into a communal vessel, and from the saliva they made a man. His name was Kvasir; he knew the answer to every riddle and could untangle any puzzle of words. On his travels, Kvasir was waylaid and murdered by two dwarves, who mixed his blood with honey to make a mead that contained all the powers of poetry. After a series of evil deeds, the dwarves fell afoul of a giant and were forced to surrender the drink to escape with their lives. The fame of the mead spread, but it was guarded inside a mountain by the giant's daughter, Gunnlöd. Having tried to trick his way to a taste of the potion (a story that with characteristic brutality involves the murder of nine slaves), Odin eventually tunnelled inside the rock in the form of a snake, and seduced Gunnlöd. He stayed with her for three nights. She gave him three draughts of the mead, but he gulped it all down. Transformed into an eagle, Odin flew back to Asgard, evading the pursuing giants and vomiting the mead into containers the gods set out in readiness.

The tale has all the hallmarks of Odin: cunning, violence, sexual deception, theft, shape-changing, and victory. Ever after, the gift of poetry was in the god's power, and a true skald stood thus marked as a recipient of divine favour, appropriately established in the seat of a king.

The hall, and hall culture, was the machine at the heart of the new Scandinavian regimes. It is fascinating to look inside them.

Excavations at Gamla Uppsala over many years have revealed a sequence of extraordinary royal halls on raised terraces at the highest point of the site. Elevated over the surrounding plain, they would have been visible for kilometres, which is what 'Uppsala' means: the high halls. The main structure was fifty metres long and twelve metres wide, probably with two storeys—one of the greatest buildings of the North. The interior roof-supporting posts were whole trees, dug metres down into the underlying terrace. A wide processional ramp led up from the plain to its double doors, fully three metres across. At some point the structure had burnt, preserving many details intact, while fragments of its fittings had been carefully gathered up and buried as offerings of closure along the walls and postholes.

Providing the best picture yet of what such a building looked like, dozens of iron spirals were found along the wall lines and clustered around the doors—the smallest the length of a finger, the biggest as long as a forearm. The hall had been covered with curved iron spikes, jutting out from the timbers. They are identical to the ship-spirals in the nearby Valsgärde boat graves, suggesting this was something of an emblem for the people of the region. Even more exciting was the ironwork decoration on the doors: more spirals, flat against the wood, along with volutes and other patterns, the whole resembling medieval church doors (clearly, that tradition was much older than previously thought). And then there were the door hinges: actual spears, hammered into a curve round the door posts, laid so their blades would have rested flat on the door surfaces, the points towards the centre. The entry to the hall was thus through a portal of weapons, bringing to mind the description of Odin's own residence, Valhöll—another resonance for the Uppsala kings.

In Lejre, Denmark, the seat of the Skjöldunga kings of Sjælland (and possible location of the Heorot hall in *Beowulf*), rows of royal palace buildings have been excavated at the crest of the slope, towering over the plain as at Uppsala. Again, they are nearly fifty metres long, but here the complex is surrounded by the ancillary buildings, workshops, and cultic structures that archaeologists are only beginning to perceive at the Swedish sites. The dimensions of such halls varied with the climate. The biggest of all, at Borg in the Lofoten islands of Arctic Norway, is *eighty metres long*—the size of Trondheim's medieval cathedral, built centuries later. Few people today have ever seen timber construction on this scale, truly meriting the concept of epic space.

Such architecture was repeated across the North. Similar examples, if not quite so grand, occur at many sites. They are found at Borre and at Kaupang in Norway, where the place was known as Skiringssal, the 'Shining Hall'. Finds of lime kilns indicate that the halls at Tissø in Denmark had whitewashed walls, and something similar is described by the Roman historian Tacitus some seven hundred years earlier among the Continental Germanic tribes. These great buildings would have shone in the sun.

With the assistance of archaeology, some help from the written record, and a little imagination, one can picture the scene inside them. In particular, there are later descriptions such as a marvellous episode from the thirteenth-century *Saga of Egil Skalla-Grímsson*. Here, the famed warrior-poet and his men are being entertained at the hall of his mortal enemy, their hatred of each other churning beneath the iron-bound rules of hospitality. Fine food is served; the ale horn goes round and round in the dim, smoky light, where it's hard to make out exactly what is happening. The endless toasts; men passing out and throwing up, some making it to the doors, some not. Women warily watching, serving beer and food, trying to keep out of their way. Simmering tension one moment, drunken bonhomie the next; deadly violence always a possibility, spurred by a careless (or very deliberate) word.

Once again, we can turn to *Beowulf,* the entire epic poem a long-form encapsulation of this warrior ethos of the hall. Here is the young hero Wiglaf, son of Weohstan, defending his lord to the last and exhorting his companions to remember their oaths:

> I remember that time when mead was flowing,
> how we pledged loyalty to our lord in the hall,
> promised our ring-giver we would be worth our price,
> make good the gift of the war-gear,
> those swords and helmets, as and when
> his need required it. He picked us out
> from the army deliberately, honoured us and judged us
> fit for this action, made me these lavish gifts –
> and all because he considered us the best
> of his arms-bearing thanes.

This was the kind of verse declaimed around the hearth.

The firelight also had an unsettling effect that lent an otherworldly air to the lords of the hall. The poetry describes how they wore their helmets indoors, and the flickering orange flames of the hearth would have animated the covering of relief pictures on their tiny press-metal plaques. The warlords' faces were veiled with a mass of moving figures, dancing in the shadows. Again by firelight, some of the helmet images could also be seen to lack an eye, an effect achieved by selectively omitting the reflecting gold foil backing of the cloisonné garnets on their features—a one-eyed lord for the one-eyed god, Odin, the ultimate patron of the new royalty. This may even have been taken as a possession, almost a transformation.

The same effect was cultivated by visitors. In many of the halls, archaeologists have found tiny rectangular foils of pure gold, wafer thin and stamped with images. There are human figures, alone or in pairs, making formal gestures—pointing, an embrace, a kiss—or with their arms in such specific positions that they must mean something. The figures are usually in profile but occasionally are seen from the front. Their clothing and hairstyles are minutely depicted, an important source for our knowledge of fashion, gendered dress, and social signals. They carry staffs, weapons, horns, and cups. The figures stand within borders of beaded gold, or amidst interlace patterns. A few figures are not on foils at all, but are cut out freestyle like paper dolls in precious metal. Even fewer are very clearly not human, or divine, but something else entirely: strange, swollen shapes—monsters, perhaps, or beings of another world. The foils tend to cluster round postholes for the uprights that supported the roof, and would probably once have been fixed to the posts themselves with resin or some similar adhesive.

On the few occasions where the stamp matrixes used to mass-produce the foils have been found, it is evident there were particular motifs for individual hall complexes; in other words, a specific design denoted a single place or its people. Perhaps the foils were high-end business cards, or ambassadorial tokens, presented by visitors and then affixed in place in the host's hall. Multiple repeated foil images on the posts indicate return visits, and thereby a generous reception. The greater the variety of foils in one place, the more renowned the lord to have welcomed guests from far and wide. In the fire's glow, the foils, too, would have glittered, the towering roof posts appearing through the smoke as pillars of shining golden lights.

But in the end, how was all this paid for and maintained?

Long-distance trade was not new to Scandinavia. Bronze Age networks had once traversed Europe, and even after a contraction in the early Iron Age, the influence of the Roman Empire brought innovation and imports to the North. But those connections were also hit by the imperial decline—they were a real part of the Migration Period crisis and possibly even one of its causes. It has long been known that the pre-Viking warlords in some way managed to recharge, and even realign and extend, overseas connections, but recent studies have shown that these links stretched much farther than previously thought—beyond what not so long ago were imagined to be the borders of their world.

Excavations of Swedish jewellers' workshops have revealed caches of garnets, imported as raw material from India and Sri Lanka. Elephant ivory perhaps travelled along a similar path, either through the Persian Gulf and then overland on the caravan routes or via the Red Sea to the Mediterranean ports. Roman jewellery and glass, as well as Byzantine metalwork, came the same way. There are carnelian beads from Sindh, precious cowrie shells from Arabia, even lizard skins from Bengal. At the settlement site near the mound burials of Sutton Hoo in eastern England, the exact contemporary and equivalent to the Vendel grave-fields in Sweden, was a decorated bucket from Egypt. The list goes on, and archaeologists are only now starting to discover how these networks functioned and where they extended, by tracing the items that flowed through them. The latest suggestion, and a convincing one, is that in the sixth to eighth centuries the North actually formed the western terminus of the Silk Roads that ultimately stretched to Tang China, to Silla and the North-South States in Korea, and in the eighth century to Nara Japan.

The Scandinavian elites evolved careful strategies to access these commercial networks. To participate in such far-flung trade, they must have had a ready supply of goods that were in demand abroad. What were these things, and where did they come from? In the last decade of archaeological research, it has emerged that in addition to promoting prestige gift exchange and the use of foreign goods, the new rulers also set up mutually beneficial webs of long-distance trade *inside* Scandinavia—the resources of one petty kingdom usefully complementing the domestic wealth of another. In practice, even the products of remote areas of the North could be redirected to the rising kingdoms of the coasts, which could then funnel it into foreign commerce.

The discovery of this transactional economy means rethinking the structures of the farm itself, which governed how commodities were produced and moved—in particular, the traditional concept of the infield (the area immediately around the home farm where crops were sown) and the outlands. The latter have often been seen as pasture and grazing areas, usually in upland meadows, marginal environments nonetheless useful for animal husbandry that were utilised either at a distance from the farm or even seasonally in more inhospitable microclimates. It is now clear that the 'outlands' as a notional economic zone could in fact extend hundreds of kilometres from the points that they supplied, requiring a redefinition of what they were—and, most important, what they were for.

To take just a few examples, a tar-making industry grew up on a scale that steadily increased through the late Iron Age, with exports from the Swedish forests being moved out to the sea and serving a demand for the protection of timber and sails (a trade the Swedes would continue to operate far into the nineteenth century). Similarly, bear pelts turn up in southern Sweden from animals that had been hunted in the far northern forests, their skins taken along the coast from sites at the Norrland river estuaries. A parallel trade connected the trappers of Jämtland on the Norwegian border with consumers in the Swedish lowlands. All these areas were thus 'outlands' of farming communities on the other side of Scandinavia, just as much as the animal pastures a few hundred metres away from their infields.

The outlands even included the deep-sea fishing grounds of the Atlantic. Thus, a whale speared in the Arctic waters off Norwegian Lofoten could provide the bone for a gaming piece with which you could win at the popular board game of *hnefatafl* in Swedish Uppsala, or the plaque on which a Dane would smooth a linen shirt. The catalogue of such commodities is being extended all the time.

Not all of this is a product of the 'crisis' and its response. The hunting of elk and reindeer using pitfall traps, for example, clearly started accelerating in the 400s before the main settlement decline. The wholesale exploitation of the outlands that began to take off in the sixth century was thus in part an adaptation of trends that had already begun, although perhaps it was applied more readily in new contexts. It is clear that at least from the 500s (and perhaps much earlier), there were mercantile connections between the far north of Scandinavia and the south, between the east and west, and also into the European mainland. But the expanded domestic utilisation of the outlands (in this new definition of them) provided the trading goods to activate foreign exchange, especially in the form of skins and furs, and largely underpinned the expansion of the petty kingdoms.

The utilisation of the outlands from the sixth century onwards thus acted as a sort of experimental training ground for the larger mercantile expansion that would come to characterise the Viking Age. The difference is that in the pre-Viking period it seems the trade largely came *to* Scandinavia, perhaps through middle agents to a communal trading arena in the Baltic and along its shores. In the Viking Age, the Scandinavians themselves took the trade overseas and overland to its points of origin.

From the early 500s onwards, we can also detect a marked surge in iron production—used for weapons, armour, and the rivets that held ships together. Not only does this signal the same kind of new economic initiative that can be seen in other commodities, but the specific utilizations of iron are telling: Scandinavia was arming itself.

Throughout this period of profound changes, Scandinavia was far from isolated in Europe, and such developments were not confined to the North. There were active connections to what is now Poland, the German border region, northern Italy, Hungary, and beyond. Even if it is hard to be sure precisely what form these links took, there were mobile military forces constantly exploiting the profitable aftermath of imperial withdrawal. As the 'new North' began to take shape, the Merovingians were similarly fighting their way to carve out kingdoms in France with aspirations that extended into parts of southern Germany; the Lombards taking power across the Alps in Italy; the Saxons consolidating their grip along the Danish border region.

This same post-Roman period also saw the first settlements of north Germanic peoples in southern Britain, who over succeeding centuries would become the English and ultimately give rise to the nation that bears their name. Connections between the Norwegian and Swedish lowlands and eastern England were particularly close, and in some ways this link was never lost. The famous ship burial at Sutton Hoo, dated c. 625, contained a helmet, regalia, and weapon set that would not have been out of place in Sweden, and indeed seems at least in part to have been imported from Uppland. One of the picture plaques on the helmet was even pressed on a matrix made in the same workshop as one from a royal grave-mound at Uppsala, buried with rituals that indicate a shared set of values and political ideas. The thought-world of the pre-Viking period, whether scholars today call it the time of the Vendels or the Merovingians, extended seamlessly across the North Sea.

The point should not be overstated, but it is striking that the key tenets of the new societies that rose from the Migration Period crisis seem to have included a marked rise in militaristic ideology, infused with uncompromising codes of honour, oath-bound loyalty, and the obligations of violent redress. These values were expressed in the growth of an expansionist hall-based elite culture whose elevated view of itself was fuelled by a constant appetite for war. Underpinning it all was an ever-greater reliance on family and kin—a dependence on the ultimate redoubts of social cohesion and their unbreakable bonds. It is not hard to see all this as a bulwark against the distant memory of the sixth-century collapse.

These, then, were the building blocks of the Viking Age, set in place more than two hundred years earlier: the slow collapse of post-Roman power, its knock-on effects in terms of economic and military instability in the North, and the opportunistic gambits of those who tried to take advantage of them. An already unstable situation was tipped by the terrible thing that happened to the sky in the 530s—the dimming of the heavens that called into question the very foundations of the Northerners' beliefs in their gods. As the dust veil went on and on, "three of these winters together / and no summer between", and the crops died, the bonds of society itself began to slip. Then the starvation began, followed by the years of struggle for the scraps. Perhaps half of the entire Scandinavian population perished, the Ragnarök prefigured. Over the following decades and centuries, the North recovered but remade and reshaped itself into a different kind of world. The outline of almost everything to come can be traced back to this time: the social and political structures, the economies and connections to long-distance trade overseas, the rituals and frames of mind, and the propensity for violence.

3

THE SOCIAL NETWORK

EVERYONE IN VIKING-AGE SCANDINAVIA ULTIMATELY lived within the extended orbit of the farm and the family, and also within the social codes that bound them together. Most important of all were the bonds of kinship, whether by blood or acquired through institutions such as marriage. Men in particular were also connected by a special kind of formal friendship, and by political alliances embodied in personal ties. All these links were complex and far-reaching, but firm. Every aspect of life—from one's possible choice of partner to the ordering of the hearth and home, even what a person wore and ate—was dependent on the social network and someone's place within it. These structures, these relationships, and all the many, many objects in daily use lay at the absolute heart of the Vikings' social world—physically located around the farm and within the household. They must be explored together.

Some surprises quickly appear. Many Viking marriages were polygynous, for example—men were able to marry more than one woman, although women could each only take one husband. In addition, there was an institution of concubinage, which in the Viking Age was very far from the sexual subservience conjured by an Orientalist harem cliché; this, too, bound men and women to one another in complicated and varied ways.

Archaeology enables this social network to be reconstructed in detail, from the types of architecture to the food on the table, as well as the behaviour that went on there. It is perhaps here that the Vikings are revealed most clearly as the opposites of the 'hairy barbarian' cliché. In fact, Viking-Age men and women were well-groomed, even fastidious in their appearance—appropriately so because they lived in a thoroughly visual world. Their clothes, possessions, furniture, vehicles, and buildings were all decorated—as was their skin. The notion of 'art' does not do justice to this all-enveloping world of symbolism and display, and is just one more reason why the Vikings so often stood apart from their contemporaries.

The majority of the Viking-Age population encountered in the archaeology, and in the written sources, were 'free farmers', in the often-repeated trope. This is true, up to a point, but it is important not to mistake it for equality. The societies of the Viking Age were deeply stratified, with an individual's place in the stack largely dependent on the resources available to her or him—in the form of land, property and, not least, the support of other people. A landless person was only a half-step above the unfree and the utterly impoverished.

Kinship, family, was the glue that held the communities of the Iron Age together, which can be seen most sharply when it began to loosen, as in the crisis of the sixth century and its aftermath. Most people belonged to the rural middle class of *bœndr* (farmers), living within the protective environment of the *hjón*, the household. This was not always independent, but could encompass the concept of tenancy and an obligation to pay dues or tax of some kind to a lord. It also included the protective sphere of the family who sheltered under that cover.

This intimate bond between people was also extended to the land. Claims to ownership could be staked by the burial of personal possessions, which were sometimes broken to emphasise that the occupants were there to stay. It may be that deposits made within the property were for the ancestors, while those over the line were for other beings. In time, as such actions accumulated over the generations, together with burial mounds on the boundaries and stone memorials to mark out the borders, "the property owned the owners".

It is hard to know how many people lived in the 'average' Viking-Age household, but it was probably similar to the farmsteads of the preceding centuries. The usual guestimate for a smallholding is perhaps seven to ten individuals, comprising a nuclear family of parents and children, an elderly relative or two, and possibly two or three labourers. On the larger estates, the occupants might rise to thirty or forty, including extended family constellations together with retainers and a much greater number of enslaved people.

Family life was enshrined and perpetuated in the condition of marriage, but this concealed multiple layers of nuance. In the Viking Age, marriage was primarily a contract between families, rather than individuals. It represented a means by which kin structures, identities, and both social and political hierarchies were formed and adapted. The emphasis was on carefully planned relationships as much as on blood ties; indeed, the former may have carried more weight than the latter. A favourable marriage, for example, was not only essential to securing the social and political status of individuals and their relatives but also, in some cases, to ensuring survival during times of conflict. Men employed a variety of strategies to secure marriage partners that enabled them to dominate matters of family diplomacy. These in turn had implications for intra-household relationships, policy, and conflict.

Negotiations were complex manoeuvres, and girls could be betrothed early—as young as thirteen—although marriage was often delayed until the bride-to-be reached sixteen. In the *Saga of Gunnlaug Snake-Tongue*, one Jófríd is already a widow when she marries Thorsteinn at the age of eighteen. This was not unusual. Men were often much older when they married, which meant that, in time, many women became widows and remarried. Women retained their own property rights in marriage. Dowries were paid not by the bride's family, but by the groom's, as *mundr*, or bride price. In the *Saga of the Confederates*, a man laments that none of his daughters are yet married because no man is rich enough to afford them.

All these networks became more intricate, and loaded with potential consequence, the further one moved up the social scale. At these higher levels, marriages were first and foremost family alliances—leverage and collateral in power strategies designed to further the long-term interests of the elites. Actual marriage customs also seem to have varied in practice across the social strata, and what the nobility thought proper might have been very different to the way things were done 'in the country'. The *List of Ríg* Eddic poem describes an elaborate high-status wedding with fine linens and much ceremony. At the other extreme, an episode in the *Saga of Egil Skalla-Grímsson* relates how a farmer buys the daughter of another for an ounce of gold, for "a sort of marriage"; it is not hard to imagine the rest.

Divorce was not uncommon, and a wife could initiate proceedings as well as a husband. She could cite a variety of reasons, including simple dissatisfaction, all strongly in her favour. In the *Saga of Burnt Njál*, a woman leaves her husband due to his impotence, which was regarded as formal cause. In the *Saga of Gísli*, a woman threatens divorce when her husband objects to her adultery. Extreme poverty—the fault of the husband because he did not support his family—was also sufficient grounds. Violence within a marriage was a significant feature of divorce petitions, although the severity of the injuries cited in such cases is so great that it seems the threshold of tolerance for male aggression was high.

Of primary importance is the fact that Viking-Age marriages could be polygynous. The existence of this practice has proved controversial in academia, which is puzzling because the evidence is persistent; this perhaps points again to the resilience of stereotype, suggestive of the kind of Viking Age people are prepared (or not) to accept. There are references to men with multiple wives in the first-hand accounts of Arab travellers who encountered them in Russia in the tenth century. More than a hundred years later, around 1070, the German cleric Adam of Bremen wrote of the Swedes that "a man according to his means has two or three or more women at one time, rich men and princes an unlimited number". Earlier in the same work, he related the troubles of his friend, the king of Denmark, who had been censured for marrying his cousin, saying that soon after "he took to himself other wives and concubines, and again still others". This is first-hand information about a man Adam knew. It is significant that these sources seem to distinguish between wives and concubines.

Polygyny is also found in the Old Norse corpus to a limited extent. The Eddic *Poem on Helgi Hiovardsson* begins with a prologue describing the four wives of a king. In the *Saga of King Harald Finehair*, one reads that he "had many wives" in a passage that then goes on to name three of them. It is further specified that one of his marriages brought with it the stipulation "that he put away nine of his wives". A skaldic verse relates the various districts of Norway that these women came from, and earlier chapters make it clear that he had concubines in addition to his wives. In the *Saga of Harald Sigurdsson*, there is also a brief mention of the king taking a second wife.

Polygyny is really quite unambiguous in the Icelandic legal sources, continuing far into the Christian period (and it can hardly have been an innovation introduced by the Church). One lawspeaker was simultaneously married to a woman and her daughter. The pope was forced to write twice to the Icelandic clergy protesting against the practice (by the clergy, amongst others), and priests were buried with multiple wives and children as late as the 1400s, for example at Skríðuklaustur. The institution was euphemistically known as *bi-fruar*, translating approximately as 'side-wives'. Two Icelandic bishops were eventually canonised in part because they were the only clergymen to remain celibate in the entire country. Marriage was always subject to control as a primary tool of power, which is why polygyny lasted longer among the ruling class than the general populace.

The late Viking-Age corpus of runestone inscriptions from central Sweden includes many texts mentioning marital relationships, but almost none in which more than one wife is named. This is not as contradictory as it sounds. First, it is clear that polygynous marriages almost always have internal hierarchies of relative status between the wives, and it is by no means certain that anyone more than the 'first wife' would be named in inscriptions that often have to do with inheritance and land claims. Second and most important, the Swedish stones are almost all from the eleventh century at the end of the Viking Age, and they usually have a clear Christian context. Given the Church's outspoken and legally enshrined rejection of polygyny, it would be surprising if the stones *did* actually mention such relationships. There are two exceptions—from Uppinge in Södermanland and Bräcksta in Uppland—that both have inscriptions mentioning two wives of the same man. Numerous half-siblings are also mentioned on the central Swedish stones, presumably with mixed parentage, combined with the routine of several family sponsors for a single memorial. This contrasts with the inscriptions from the south of Sweden, which converted much earlier, and where only single sponsors are the norm.

Outside marriage and its prelude in betrothal, concubinage offered another kind of formalised relationship. The institution was important in the literal context of sexual politics, and embraced several categories of agreement by verbal contract, each with their own vocabulary. These included liaisons arranged for the purpose of connecting powerful families, strengthening political ties, or for fine-tuning the complex networks of mutual obligation that were central in Norse public life. Other types of these relationships were essentially confined to sexual companionship; a few involved bonds of genuine warmth from their inception (or grew to acquire them).

Viking-Age women did not formally initiate or drive these relationships, although it may be that, on occasion, they were a means by which emotional attachments could be shaped together with a degree of social sanction, outside what must sometimes have been loveless marriages. Nevertheless, in the legal codes it is clear that men (who made the laws) assigned themselves the dominant role in such arrangements. Furthermore, a woman who became a concubine thereby relinquished the right to obtain a bride price for her family, in that she was not getting married but was now 'spoken for'.

It is significant that a man could have more than one concubine, in addition to more than one wife, all at the same time. Each of the women involved, of every status, was bound to the one man alone. To the arguable extent that they can be trusted, the family sagas also include several of these relationships. In the *Saga of the People of Laxardal*, a married man purchases an enslaved woman to share his bed as a concubine. In the *Saga of the People of Vatnsdal*, another married man clearly has a formalised sexual relationship with a concubine, who later bears his child. In the *Saga of Burnt Njál*, the earlier extramarital affair of the titular character is openly acknowledged in front of his wife, again involving a child of that union.

Concubinage could be enforced against a woman's will, although this was technically illegal. There are instances where local rulers either kidnap the daughters of their tenants or otherwise leave them little choice but to hand the women over. They are usually held for a time and then released. There are suggestions that this is a power play—a form of protection racket—on the part of the elites, or even that the tenants are trying to curry favour (there are unequivocal cases where farmers offer their daughters to kings). Equally, there is poetic evidence that this practice might have to do with fertility rituals for which the lord was responsible as a divine proxy. The reality may well have been somewhere in between, or variable, but, in any case, without regard to female consent. The contemporary generalising word for concubine, *frilla*, continued into early modern times as a pejorative suggestive of casual sexual conquest, promiscuity, or even outright prostitution, all on terms defined by men.

The enslaved could also be concubines, elevated (though perhaps not much) above the sexual abuse that often accompanied their miserable station. The sagas mention a few who managed to use such relationships as a ladder to a better life, such as the Irish noblewoman Melkorka, who, in the *Saga of the People of Laxardal*, is seized on a raid and enslaved before eventually marrying in Iceland. In *Beowulf*, even the stately Danish queen Wealhtheow, mistress of Heorot hall, always bears with her a very different backstory as a war captive: her name has been suggested by some to mean 'foreign slave'.

Alongside marriage and concubinage, with their impact on kinship through connection, there was also another component of the social network in Viking-Age Scandinavia, which in the later written sources is termed *vinátta*. Literally meaning 'friendship', it had subtly different connotations to our modern concept. Norse *vinr*, 'friends' (the modern Scandinavian languages have *venner* and *vänner*), combined the closeness of 'brothers in arms' with the same kinds of complex ties as the social bonds of kinship. The mechanics and social impact of friendship, in this special sense, are clearest from the tenth century onwards, but its fundamental codes can also be perceived at the start of the Viking Age. While these were masculine networks, there was also a female equivalent; women, too, could draw on support systems among their 'friends'.

Viking friendship was yet another means of structuring mutual assistance, within communities that otherwise did not have fully reliable guarantees of security and support. The resulting overlap of social networks was the key to a (relatively) peaceful society. Friendship was cemented through gift-giving, as between lords and their retainers, with a legal obligation to reciprocate.

A key element of these relationships (for men) was an understanding of mutual protection—not just physically in battle but also in the sense of generally looking out for the interest of one's friends. This could include support in legal proceedings, but also fed into the complex dynamics of war. A man might be bound to a lord through vows of loyalty, the world of obligated violence that permeated hall culture. However, if a man's friend was seen to be present in an enemy host before battle was joined, there are references to truces being negotiated in order to avoid the delicate problem of forcing 'friends' to fight one another, and the consequent test of relative loyalties that would be to nobody's advantage. This in turn linked with systems of formalised friendship between chieftains and kings, and even with the gods.

Families—however composed—presuppose family life and the household that was its arena. The basic settlement unit in Viking-Age Scandinavia was the farm, the *garðr* or *gård*, the familiar concept that denoted an enclosed, inhabited place. It was here that (almost) everything happened in the cycle of rural life that was little different to that of later centuries. Some of the Eddic poetry even preserves a sort of homespun philosophy, a series of aphorisms about how to live on the land. From the *Sayings of the High One*:

> By the fire one should drink ale,
> on the ice one should skate;
> buy a lean mare
> and an unpolished blade –
> fatten the horse at home,
> but your dog at a neighbour's.

There would have been a central building, either a rectangular longhouse or a shorter structure, most likely built of timber. The roof was supported by upright posts forming three aisles inside, and the walls were made of wattle panels covered with clay daub.

Wood was not in short supply, and some wealthier people made their house walls of solid planks, either fitted horizontally between upright posts or resting upright on sill beams. If available, stone might be used as the foundation of a timber wall, keeping the wood from the damp of the ground. In areas of harsher climate, insulation was an issue, and the walls would be thicker, with stone cores and heavy coverings of stacked turf that might extend over the roof. Bark could also be used as a weather protection, even under roofs of thatch. For those truly with resources to spare, a great hall might be roofed with thousands of wooden shingles.

Most domestic activities took place in this communal space—eating, sleeping, and indoor craft work. The interior could be easily transformed, with bedding dragged out, blankets wrapped up, or things cleared quickly away. A few basic stools might have been available if an extra seat was needed. Possessions were stored in boxes and chests, securely locked (padlocks are a not uncommon find on excavations), or sacks. Meat and herbs were dried up in the roof, smoking over the fire. Things of all kind could be stored on platforms built into the rafters—not a formal second storey as such but a useful place to tuck loose items away. Foodstuffs were packed down, and often preserved, in barrels.

The central 'living room' of domestic buildings—whether the spacious chamber of a hall or the more cramped environs of a smaller hut or urban house—was poorly lit even in daytime. Illumination would come in via the door, in very rare cases through a small window covered in skin or shuttered, or as a shaft of light from a smoke hole. Oil lamps of clay, stone, or metal might be used, resting on a flat surface or pinned into the walls, their wicks giving a soft light. The main source of illumination, and heat, was the central hearth, banked up around stones and enclosed in a sturdy frame to prevent loose sparks straying—fire being a major hazard for all wooden buildings.

In the evenings, the fireplace was the community focus. This was the main cooking space where all meals were prepared, either in clay vessels laid directly in the embers, grilled and fried in iron pans, or suspended over the hearth in cauldrons on chains or tripods. Most of the pottery was very basic, but some used better-quality Slavic black wares. A wealthier home might have one or two ceramic vessels from the Continent, especially from Germany, that had come overland via the Danish border. These included glazed jugs, bowls, a kind of sieve, and even a type of Rhineland pottery decorated with silvery foil that would have glittered, especially when wet.

Meals were consumed around the comforting flames. When it comes to Viking food culture, somehow we still seem stuck with the tavern scenes of medieval movies, where everybody is roaring drunk or laughing heartily, tearing at hunks of meat with their teeth while a fight breaks out in the background. The reality was very different and included a varied and sophisticated cuisine.

Table manners were respected. Everybody in the Viking world carried a pocket knife—a small utilitarian item for everyday needs and especially for eating. Utterly ubiquitous, they are found in almost every burial, some richer examples embellished with decoration but all with the same practical purpose. As important as a knife was a hone to sharpen it on. These too have been recovered by the thousands, small rectangles of stone, often pierced with a loop for suspension. Many were merely practical, but others were made of banded, multicoloured slate chosen for its functional beauty. Regardless of appearance, whetstones remained an essential part of the everyday toolkit.

Large, pronged meat forks were used to serve from cauldrons and other big cooking vessels, but table forks for individuals were not known. Spoons and ladles were made of wood or horn, often decorated, and much of the food would be at least semi-liquid in the form of thick broths and stews, porridge, and gruel.

In simple households, food was served in wooden bowls or on platters. The better-quality tableware was turned on a lathe, resulting in a smooth surface with a pleasing grain; markets did a roaring trade in such products, which were produced by specialists with equipment to match. A more basic alternative was the hand-carved or hollowed-out wooden bowl, crude but effective, and perhaps with its own charm. Wooden plates and cutting surfaces would have been the norm even in higher-status households, although perhaps with carved decoration. A very few might have had metal dishes. For some meals, bread could be used effectively as a plate, soaking up the food placed on it before being eaten.

A whole doctoral thesis has been written just on Viking bread, and it is in the details of daily life like this that the vividness of their world really emerges. From graves and settlement contexts all over central Sweden, but especially from the Birka burials, at least nine distinctive types of bread are known. There were rectangular loaves baked in a form; round loaves threaded on a thin wire; oval buns; thin, soft, and foldable flatbreads made on a circular griddle pan—rather like a sort of Nordic tortilla to be stuffed with food; thin, circular wheels of dry, crisp flatbread with a central hole so they could be hung up for storage (you can still buy these all over Scandinavia today); at least two different kinds of biscuits; little balls of fried dough; and crunchy figure-of-eight-shaped snacks that resemble pretzels or, more particularly, the Swedish nibbles still called *kringlor*. They made their bread with hulled barley and oats, sometimes wheat for the thinner forms, and very occasionally rye.

The bread was made in familiar ways, all of which can be traced in the material culture of baking. The corn was ground into flour between rotary quern stones; dough was kneaded in wooden troughs, rolled and flattened, formed with the hands and in moulds. Some of it had pricked patterns on the surface (the iron dockers to make them have been found). Dough could be poached in boiling water, fried on long-handled griddle pans, or baked in clay ovens. One can even see how many times different loaves and cakes were turned, and whether they liked them with rounded sides, soft and chewy, or dry and crisp. At least some bread seems to have been flavoured with herbs, or with seeds sprinkled on top for decoration and flavour. But we do not yet know how typical this was: was Birka baking famed far and wide, could you get much the same anywhere, or did each region have its own traditions?

Meat was a popular part of the diet, judging from bone debris with characteristic butchery marks, found in middens and pits. Vikings ate mutton, goat, beef, and seem to have especially liked pork. Arab travellers in the East remarked how much the Scandinavians enjoyed this meat; not least, it was what was served to the dead heroes in Valhöll. Chickens were kept for both eggs and their flesh, while ducks, geese, and other waterfowl were hunted. Finds of narrow meat spits show that a kind of kebab was on offer at the supper table, and there were bigger versions resembling a sort of meat-spear for holding really large joints to roast over the fire. Elk and reindeer provided lots of tasty protein, and boar meat was prized. Sea mammals, including both seals and whales, could provide a nourishing supplement. Many kinds of freshwater fish were caught, and even deep-sea species were known. Herbs were grown in cottage gardens and used for flavouring food of all kinds. Bees were kept for honey. Milk products from cows, sheep, and goats included cheeses, whey, and soured dairy run-offs that could also be used as an alternative to salt for storing meat over the winter. They ate the delicious cultured dairy product called *skyr*, still popular in Iceland today as a sort of thick yogurt-like snack, sour but with a slight edge of sweetness (try it, if you can find some). Berries were widely available to pick in the woods (put them in your *skyr*!), along with mushrooms and tubers.

Unfortunately, only a little is known of what exactly the Vikings did with all this bounty. There are no runic recipes, but the sheer variety of food on offer suggests that the Scandinavians were no less creative in the kitchen than they were anywhere else. Given the influx of foreign traders and other influences from abroad, which intensified during the Viking Age, there is no reason to assume this did not include food customs. At least in the market centres, and maybe brought back to the countryside if people fancied a change, there were probably 'ethnic' dishes available. One also imagines that a foreign servant on the farm might make an innovative contribution around the cooking pit, perhaps longing for a taste of home.

All this was accompanied by ale, and mead made with honey. Both were drunk from horns, or tankards made of leather or wood. Custom sometimes dictated that these were emptied in one go, but there are also many textual references to a horn being passed around. Perhaps in irritated response to seeing the Christian blessing, in the late Viking Age there are descriptions of people making a hammer sign to Thor over their cup before drinking.

Milk was a weaker alternative, and perhaps stream water if available. On special occasions, *beor* may have been drunk, not really beer as the name implies, but apparently a kind of sweet concoction like a fruity wine, consumed from small cups. Some beverages were certainly very strong. Travellers from the Caliphate saw them drinking something that was rendered in Arabic as *nabīdh*, clearly alcoholic but of uncertain nature. People began to reel after a cup or two. At the funeral of a leader, which may have been an exceptional occasion in many ways, one such visitor saw people drinking solidly for ten days and noted that they sometimes *died* like this, with a beaker in their hands. He does not seem to have been exaggerating.

Wine was certainly known among the elites, as it had been from Roman times, although as an imported commodity it was both expensive and rare. In the richest graves there are delicate glasses brought in (or looted) from Frankia and elsewhere on the Continent. Sometimes they have been painstakingly repaired with metal clips, indicating how valued they were, not only in themselves but as status symbols for people who could afford to drink wine and acquire the paraphernalia that went with it. These vessels were often conical in shape and so could not be set down on a table. This has sometimes been taken to mean that even wine was drunk in one draught like ale, but more likely the glasses were either held constantly (and ostentatiously?) in the hand or else supported on some kind of wooden stand—another little window on etiquette. They held slightly less than a regular wine-glass today, in contrast to some bracing examples from the Migration Period that held more than half a modern bottle.

The Viking view of drinking reached its ultimate expression in the afterlife, as seen in the description of Valhöll, Odin's hall of immortal warriors. In the Eddic poem *Grímnir's Sayings*, the *einherjar*, as the dead men are called, are served ale from horns carried to them at the benches by the Valkyries. But the host himself, presiding over the nightly banquet of the slain, never even has to eat: "On wine alone does weapon-glorious Odin live". In the table manners of the ruler of the gods, we find the Vikings' ultimate fantasy of high-end luxury.

The consumption of food and drink was in due course followed by other needs (except perhaps in Valhöll). In the countryside, nature provided its own open-air lavatories, but on settlements, latrines were usually dug as deep pits in the vicinity of the dwelling structures. In urban settings, they were in the backyards. Often lined with wickerwork for stability, they sometimes had a stick or—the grand option—even a holed plank over the top to sit on. When almost full, the pits were simply filled in and sealed, and a new one was dug nearby. They are among the most unpleasant elements of early medieval life to excavate, especially if the ground is waterlogged, thus preserving everything inside the latrines in pristine condition, still moist and with its original bouquet; I once spent a nasty week trying to hold my breath while digging to the base of one in York. Inside are the clumps of moss used as toilet paper, the scraps of cloth that were the Viking equivalent of sanitary towels, and, occasionally, all manner of other objects that people had dropped while otherwise engaged but sensibly decided not to retrieve. Latrines are also an environmental archaeologist's dream: coprolites (preserved faeces) can be tested for intestinal parasites, reconstructing Viking-Age gut flora and health; remains of seeds, proteins, and other food detritus give clues to diet.

Around the meal, while some people discreetly went outside, others used the light of the hearth to carry on household tasks that did not require close vision, and, of course, they talked. There were also board games to play, such as *hnefatafl*, in which the aim was to take the king in strategic manoeuvres with pieces made of bone, antler, or glass. The hearth was also the arena of stories—in humble farmers' homes just as in the skaldic theatre of the halls. Musical instruments have been occasionally found, including the simplest wooden whistles and pan pipes, sometimes the bridge of a stringed lyre—these kinds of tones would have accompanied poetic recitals.

Children ran about and played, as they always have, and toys have been found on a number of sites: miniature wooden horses, one of them on wheels; wooden boats (several of these, so they must have been popular); balls made of rags; also some monster masks of cloth and leather, although they may have instead served some ritual purpose. There are even small swords and other weapons, made of wood and scaled down for tiny hands but following the same typologies of design as the contemporary adult versions; in other words, children wanted swords that looked like the ones that *faðir*—or, just possibly, *móðir*—had. From eleventh-century deposits in Lund, southern Sweden, archaeologists have even found fragments of a toddler-sized chair made of beech, with a wooden dowel that could be fixed in place across the front to prevent a little Viking from getting out. It is the earliest children's furniture to have survived in Europe.

These rooms were also very smoky. We know this not least from saga descriptions, which were probably based on medieval halls with essentially the same internal conditions. In the *Saga of Hrólf kraki*, for example, a woman has to leave the room urgently, and a friend excuses her behaviour by saying that she had become sickened by the smoke from the hearth; nobody is surprised to hear this. Clearly, fresh air was a necessity for everyone at some point in the evening.

When it was time for bed, the outer door was bolted or locked for security. In modest houses people just slept communally on the benches, or curled up by the hearth tucked in blankets. In the larger halls, privacy could be found behind interior screens, and there were even beds. These were quite short by modern standards, although Viking-Age people were of average stature in comparison with today's Europeans. Their beds were probably more to sit up in, bolstered by pillows and coverlets. In the sleeping alcoves of the later Icelandic longhouses, people clearly slept seated or on their sides with their legs drawn up. In the burials of the rich, we find cushions and duvets stuffed with down, providing luxurious winter warmth. In these contexts, feathers from chickens and crows have been found, and in the bedding of the highest elites, even from eagle-owls. In a high-status tenth-century grave from Mammen in Denmark, there was a special pillow that dipped in the centre but had extra stuffing either side; it could have been folded around the neck and shoulders for comfort.

In the morning, most people might wash quickly in one of the many bowls or basins that stood about, and comb their hair— hardly the stuff of unkempt Viking legend. Archaeology indicates a relatively high regard for personal hygiene. Combs, in particular, were a universal possession, made of bone or antler and kept in a special case to protect the finely cut teeth. They came in many shapes and sizes, often richly decorated, and their manufacture was a major industry that fed into long-distance trade in raw materials. One specialist in these objects goes so far as to place their design, crafting, and use at the centre of what he calls a "Viking way of life". Combs also attracted a rich symbolism, used to signify the individual and her or his presence. Finds of deliberately broken comb cases buried in the postholes of military buildings suggest an oath to remain in place: 'Here I stand'.

A much-quoted Oxfordshire chronicler, writing around 1220 but working from older sources, recorded that Viking men arriving in England combed their hair every day, washed once a week, regularly changed their clothes, and "drew attention to themselves by many such frivolous whims"—behaviour so astonishing that the English women preferred them to their husbands. Even the rare surviving three-dimensional images of Viking-Age men, such as a famous carved antler portrait from Sigtuna in Sweden, show carefully twirled moustaches and long hair neatly curled at the neck. Other depictions have men with straight-combed hair to their shoulders, and beards both tightly clipped and brushed to a goatee; one example shows dreadlocks and long beards. In the East, a Scandinavian commander in Byzantium was described as having a shaved head except for two long locks beside his ears, his ensemble topped off by a big red carnelian earring.

Women's hair is often depicted in a standard manner in the art: worn long and knotted behind in a loose ponytail. In some cases, the trailing hair reaches almost to the heels. Occasionally we have imagery that shows women from the front rather than in profile, and it seems the hair is then drawn to both sides in voluminous pigtails. There are other depictions of a centre parting and hair pulled back in a tight bun. What all these hairstyles have in common is that they are both careful and deliberate.

Personal grooming did not stop there. When an Arab soldier-diplomat called Aḥmad ibn Faḍlān encountered Vikings on the Volga in 922, he noted how "each man, from the tip of his toes to his neck, is covered in dark-green lines, pictures and such like". He must be writing of tattoos, apparently universal (*each* man) and full-body. This is in an eastern context, but the group had travelled there from Scandinavia.

Some men also filed their teeth. Research on Viking-Age cemeteries has turned up a remarkable discovery that a consistent 5–10 percent of the males, most of whom died under the age of forty, had dental modification. This took the form of V-profiled grooves

7. Dental modification. Horizontal grooves filed into the enamel of a Viking-Age man's front teeth; this example from Vannhög, Sweden. Photo by Staffan Hyll, courtesy of Caroline Ahlström Arcini.

cut into the enamel of the front teeth, making horizontal lines and occasionally chevrons. Some men had just one line, others several, sometimes on the same tooth. The grooves were probably coloured in with resin, visible as red lines across the teeth. A Viking grin would have been something to behold.

Dental modification seems to have been an exclusively male attribute and, furthermore, was confined to a specific constituency—those associated with ports of trade, stations on the travel networks of the Viking world, and the sea. In other words, the men who filed their teeth belonged to that portion of the Viking-Age community who lived on the move. The practice continued for at least two centuries; men could get their teeth filed in different patterns and on several successive occasions. It was a form of body art to which one added over time. What it *meant* is another matter about which we can only speculate, but it does seem likely that dental modification was in some way reflective of a particular lifestyle and, perhaps, of achievements within it. One thinks of traditional sailors' tattoos from more recent times, with variations for the seas a person had sailed, the styles and motifs relating to time spent in particular ports, and so on. Or did the filed grooves indicate something else—a mark of rank, of initiation or group affiliation, or even the number of enemies slain? It is hard to resist the notion that these markings in some way relate to a properly 'Viking' life in the exact sense of the term. There is little reason to suppose that tooth-filing always sent the same signals—there may have been many subtle variations of meaning that are opaque to us now, but were once easily intelligible to those in the know.

Lastly, we have a single reference to facial cosmetics in the writings of Ibrāhīm ibn Ya'qūb, a Jewish traveller from Spain who made a memorable trip through the market centre of Hedeby in Denmark. While there in the 960s, he observed, "There is also an artificial eye makeup. When one uses it, the beauty of both men and women is enhanced, and it never disappears". No more than this is known, whether it was a Danish fashion or more widespread, but my imagination is touched by an image so far from the Vikings I was once taught about.

Leaf through the pages of any well-illustrated book on the Vikings, or visit a market-festival with early medieval re-enactors, and it would be easy to think that the clothing and fashion of the period are well-known to us. This notion is thrown into sharp contrast by two discoveries made by metal detectorists in Denmark, as late as 2012 and 2014.

The first was uncovered in the late December frozen ground at Hårby, near Roskilde: a small figure in gilt silver, rendered in three dimensions (a rare thing in Viking art), in the form of a standing person armed with sword and shield. Details of the decoration suggest a date of about 800. The figure has the long, knotted ponytail conventionally taken as a feminine marker and has therefore almost universally been interpreted as a woman, but there are also gender ambiguities. The figure has not been given obvious breasts,

although we have so few three-dimensional human images that we
do not know whether this was artistic convention or even a Viking-
Age cultural preference for a flatter chest. Could this even be a
male-bodied individual with a transgressive haircut?

The clothing is also unusual and hard to gender. The Hårby
figure wears a pleated underskirt that seems to be ankle-length,
but the feet of the image are broken off so one cannot tell. Over
this is what appears to be a sort of singlet, with a deeply plunging V-shaped neckline and two thin shoulder straps that leave a
very wide-open area around the top of the arms. The undergar-
ment does not seem to extend above the waist, because the figure
is apparently bare-skinned under the 'vest'. Interestingly, the hem
of the singlet is not straight but instead cut at a slant down from
the figure's proper right to left. Apart from looking quite striking,
one effect is to leave less fabric at waist height by the right hand,
which holds the sword, while the wide arm-holes of the vest also
give good freedom of movement. As a sort of floor-length waistcoat
over the vest and skirt, the figure wears (perhaps) a straight-falling
cloak heavily ornamented in interlace designs, picked out in a kind
of black enamel called niello. The clothing of the Hårby figurine is
of a type never seen before.

The second object turned up in 2014 at Revninge in the east of
Denmark—a curious gilt-silver pendant just under five centimetres
long in the form of a human figure. The body is flat, in two dimensions, whereas the head swells into three-dimensional relief and is
pierced at the back with a hole for suspension. It too is a unique
object and, on the basis of the art-styles, can be dated to the beginning of the ninth century—the same date as the Hårby figure. The
Revninge piece is special for the extraordinarily detailed clothing
it wears (probably the most intricate example known), the surprises
thereby revealed, and the fact that like the Hårby figure, it gives
few clues as to the person's gender.

The figure wears an underskirt, over which is a belted long-
sleeved gown that comes down to the feet. The bodice is tight, and

8. The ambiguities of dress. The enigmatic figurine from Revninge, Denmark, with its elaborate clothing. Photo: John Lee, © National Museum of Denmark, used by kind permission.

there appears to be a shawl of some kind around the shoulders. Each item of clothing is rendered in a different style and decoration, which surely represents a variety of fabrics, patterns, and, perhaps, even colours. If one converts this image to reality, the effect must have been stunning. Over the shawl, the figure wears a multi-strand necklace. The hands are clasped just below the belt, either side of a 'buckle' that appears as a very large trefoil brooch. Such jewellery is normally thought to be worn higher up on the body, fastening a shawl, so its position here is unusual and unexpected.

There are excavated examples of Frankish trefoil sword fittings, almost as big as that of the Revninge figure, reused in Scandinavian contexts—perhaps this is one of those. Two lines, with roundels partway down, descend from the trefoil fastener, and it is not clear whether they are the long, pendant ends of the belt or the embroidered edgings of the gown. The figure's hair is worn drawn back in a bun, parted in the middle to leave the ears uncovered.

At first, the Revninge figure was almost universally described as female, and often as either a fertility goddess or a Valkyrie—the usual go-to clichés in the rush to label. But doubts soon crept in; in fact, there is little to indicate whether this individual is male, female, or beyond such binaries. In late Iron Age Scandinavian imagery, many ostensibly masculine figures are depicted with long jackets or kaftans, with a skirt-like lower section that flares out. They appear on the Vendel period helmet plaques, on several pendant figurines, and on the Gotland picture-stones, amongst numerous others.

Taking the two figurines together, Hårby and Revninge, one can look at the clothes, even reconstruct them to a degree, but in the end there is no way of knowing if these were even human fashions—and, if so, of what social status, although surely wealthy. If this was the clothing of a god(dess) or some other supernatural being, does the Hårby figure reveal a Valkyrie's face, perhaps for the first time? Is the Revninge image what a *fylgja* looked like, or a *dís*, those ancestral spirit-women of the North? These things would probably have been obvious to a Viking-Age person, but not to us. There is something to be learned from the fact that two finds of five-centimetre figurines have shifted, indeed undermined, scholars' presumed understanding of Viking-Age clothing. With this sounding of a note of caution, what is really known of dress at this time?

Most of what we have comes from imagery such as the huge number of human figures depicted on picture-stones (a kind of illustrated carving found only on the island of Gotland) and gold foils, and also from clothing fragments found in graves and preserved in the corrosion products of metal objects that once rested against the textiles. This information can be combined with jewellery and other dress accessories excavated from burials, with functions that can be guessed at from their positions on the body. This is a database that has been built up over more than a century of fieldwork and incorporates thousands of variant examples. The clothing itself has been reconstructed through the patient work of dedicated specialists, such as the staff of the Centre for Textile Research in Copenhagen and their colleagues at similar institutions.

Women of all social stations seem to have worn a basic, ankle-length shift of wool, or perhaps linen, although the latter would have required looking after. Such items were carefully smoothed on plaques of whalebone—often beautifully decorated with snarling animals—using oval 'slickstones' of hollow glass, green or blue, with a flat side to lay against the cloth. The shift had a vertical slit at the front neckline that was held together by a small brooch. These are found in every kind of metal, from lead to gold, depending on budget. For the poorest, this might have been the extent of their clothing.

Some women wore full-body over-dresses on top of the shift—a simple, practical outfit for everyday use. Those of higher status, however, seem to have preferred an apron-like garment that started at chest height and hung from the shoulders by thin straps that detached at the front. These were fastened above the breasts by two oval brooches, one on each side. The straps were gathered behind each brooch and fixed with a pin, although the join was concealed underneath the metal. As each brooch could be unfastened independently, enabling one side of the apron to be folded down while the undershirt was pushed aside, it is thought the design was an aid to breast-feeding. Inside the tortoiseshell shapes of the brooches, archaeologists sometimes find several layers of textile, as if a number of different items of clothing had been pinned under there simultaneously. Some women apparently wore additional panels of fabric suspended down their fronts—perhaps for display or as a pinafore to protect the rest of their clothes when undertaking tasks.

The oval brooch has become the single most common supposedly female marker in Viking-Age graves, where their presence is often used to determine sex if no human bone survives. They came in many different patterns and designs as well as materials—from bronze and copper alloy, with silver and gilt, all the way to actual gold. The art-styles used can be closely dated, which provides one of the prime chronologies for the period. Some of the brooches could be taken apart and had openwork upper surfaces, enabling cloth of a contrasting colour to be placed within, enhancing the effect. Many of the oval brooches were completely covered in decoration, twisting interlace, or mythical animals, sometimes in high relief.

Over the whole outfit, women might have worn a heavier gown that extended to the ground, with wide, deep sleeves. Some examples buttoned or otherwise fastened high at the neck, while others were cut away in front so the underlying dress, oval brooches, and beads would have been visible in the opening. Women wore a simple cap covering the hair and gathered under the chin, either of thin linen or, for the wealthy, made of imported silk from the Mediterranean, the Middle East, or even China. In some graves, we also find thin bands of silver worn around the forehead and temples either as a sort of tiara or, more likely, holding a headscarf in place.

Shoes and boots of leather have been found, some ankle-length and fastened with a simple toggled flap across the front. Others are laced around in a circle through multiple loops just below the top of the opening, not across the front like today's shoes. This was cheap, practical footwear, although some examples were decorated with coloured threads. High-end boots, by contrast, could be calf- or knee-length, made of heavy, tooled leather and decorated with interlace designs (one of my best excavation memories is of patiently revealing one in the thick, black mud of a waterlogged Viking town). Inside, knitted woollen socks, sometimes in the *nålebindning* technique, kept the feet warm and dry. Poorer people probably made do with grass and straw packed around their feet, ensuring both insulation and a snug fit.

A question seldom asked, and hard to answer, concerns how Viking-Age people *used* clothing; how did it make them feel—the combinations of fabrics, the sense of them on their skin, the circumstances in which they were worn? Just like us, the Vikings had fashion too, and dress was used to signal not only wealth and taste but also a great many other things, not the least of which was power (or the lack of it, in people who had less freedom to choose their own attire). Clothing conveyed achievement, but also aspiration. The international canvas of the Viking Age provided new sources of textiles and outfits with which to experiment, and new arenas to try them out. At least some of those who pursued a mobile life, with all its opportunities and risks, may have dressed as the kind of person they wished to be—and perhaps eventually became.

Necklaces of beads, sometimes in multiple strands, were hung between the oval brooches or sometimes just draped around the neck. Made of glass imported from the Mediterranean as raw materials and then reworked in the North, they were manufactured in a wide range of shapes and colours. By the middle of the Viking Age, finished beads of carnelian and other materials were entering Scandinavia from the Levant in large quantities. Ibn Faḍlān mentions how much the merchants he met prized such items, especially the dark green ones. Each of them had an actual coin value and thus acted as a walking statement of wealth. Archaeologists also find examples of amber and rock crystal beads.

A variety of ornamental brooches could be worn for display, much as today. There were zoomorphic ones, with animals and monsters, and others shaped like ships, horseback riders, and more. Pendants were worn in many designs—for example, formed as curling piles of so-called gripping beasts, rather strange creatures who seem to be smiling while strangling one another. There were also enigmatic figurines worn round the neck, little silver female figures holding horns (Valkyries, perhaps?), armed 'weapon dancers' (maybe Odin?), and many others, including a disturbing one from Sweden depicting a figure with a blank face and a single rectangular hole where its eyes should be.

After the beginning of the raids in the eighth century, foreign loot was sometimes repurposed as jewellery—book mounts from ecclesiastical volumes turned into brooches, English sword fittings similarly remade, coins pierced and hung on necklaces. In Norway there is an Irish or Scottish reliquary, almost certainly plundered from a monastery, that seems to have been used by a woman as a luxury box; it is inscribed in runes that read, "Ranveik owns this casket".

Female jewellery had many regional variations, preferred styles, and local fashions, but none more so than on the island of Gotland. Although the standard forms are found here, the majority of wealthier women replaced the oval brooches with animal-head fibulas, looking rather like bears or badgers, their long snouts resting on the shoulders. The shawl fastener was not a disc or trefoil brooch but a small round box, worn in the same way, that could be opened and used as a container. As with all the jewellery, these too came with varying degrees of elaboration and in a range of materials and finishes. The box brooches are particularly fascinating, as they may provide a clue as to the identity of the merchants ibn Faḍlān met on the Volga. Describing the women, he specifically says they wear a round thing like a box on their breast—were they Gotlanders? It would make sense given the geography of their travel route.

Both sexes wore finger rings, often chunky pieces with flat panels covered in ring-and-dot ornament. Arm rings were also worn, and were similarly patterned, as well as large chain-work collars of both gold and silver. These neck rings were heavy, dramatic, and very expensive. Ibn Faḍlān records such "bands of gold and silver" and that a man gave one to his wife for each ten thousand dirhams he possessed—an enormous sum.

In his meeting with Scandinavians out east, ibn Faḍlān describes the men thus: "I have never seen more perfect physiques than theirs—they are like palm trees, are fair and reddish, and do not wear the tunic or the kaftan. The man wears a cloak with which he covers one half of his body, leaving one of his arms uncovered". This accords well with the archaeological finds.

If they could afford it, men would have had an undertunic, probably of soft wool or more likely linen, a breathable fabric. Over this was worn a long-sleeved shirt with a high, wide neck opening, which would be pulled over the head. This overshirt was sometimes embroidered at the neckline and cuffs, and was slightly flared below the waist.

Trousers of the kind worn throughout the Iron Age were cut tight to the leg. To judge from grave finds, almost everyone wore a belt, probably a vital addition to a loose-cut waistline, and fragments of garments have been found with belt loops. Some of these surviving leggings have integral feet, like small children's pyjamas today, and this is also mentioned occasionally in sagas. Even when trousers were slightly fuller in cut, some men wore tightly wound bindings (essentially puttees) on the lower leg for insulation and ease of mobility. On picture-stones and in other imagery, as well as in written sources, we also find evidence for a distinctly eastern fashion in trousers that became popular in Scandinavia during the later Viking Age. These were made of extravagant amounts of cloth to produce a very wide, puffed appearance over the thighs and past the knee, with the fabric gathered in boots or with bindings to fit closely on the lower calf.

A special set of weaving techniques called *röggvar* attached extra pieces of fleece to the warp during manufacture, which were then teased out from the surface (rather like accidentally catching a thread from a wool sweater, though done deliberately) to make a tufted effect that was thought to resemble fur. There is some evidence that this could be used for producing a particularly exaggerated type of trousers, and it may be this that lies behind the nickname of the famous ninth-century Viking Ragnar lothbrók, his nickname meaning 'shaggy-breeches'. The effect would have been dramatic, and like some modern fashions its success must have depended on the charisma of the wearer to cross the line from ridicule to style.

Depending on the weather, an outdoor jacket of heavy wool, sometimes lined with fur, could be worn. Some of these were influenced by eastern fashion and more resembled kaftans, with the two sides overlapping in front and secured by a belt. The Scandinavians operating on the Russian rivers also went in for a kind of brocaded jacket, fixed with toggles or loops and with silverwork panels across the front.

Many of these fabrics could have been enlivened by embroidered patterns or other designs, probably of the sort familiar from the metalwork. Even buttons were decorated, with carvings on bone or cast ornament on precious metals. As well as other kinds of unisex jewellery, some men also wore necklaces, though these sometimes differed sharply from those worn by women. Pendants included carved bear's teeth, Thor's hammers, miniature weapons, and the like.

Interestingly, no Viking-Age clothing for either sex has ever been found with pockets, which has implications for the kinds of bags and other accessories necessary for carrying even small items.

Cloaks were pinned at the shoulder, either by a simple ringed pin (a uniquely Norse invention diagnostic of a Viking site) or a penannular brooch of varying elaboration. If a Viking-Age man wore headgear, he could choose from a simple woollen cap or, if he was feeling flush, a more elaborate conical cap made of silk and fur.

Children's clothing was essentially a miniature version of adult fashion, though tending more towards simple shifts and tunics for the very small. My favourite Viking-Age archaeological find from Iceland is a small pair of children's mittens in heavy wool, still attached to one another by a long string that would have run across the back and down inside the sleeves of a jacket. They would fit a two- or three-year-old, and one can picture some Viking-Age girl or boy playing in the cold and swinging their gloves around. At least they didn't lose them.

Everyday work took a variety of forms. Manual labour on the farm mostly involved sowing, manuring, and tending crops, to which can be added herding livestock and supervising their movements through the outfields.

Animals on the farm included cattle, pigs, sheep, goats, and sometimes chickens. Roosters play a clear part in Norse mythology, where their crowing heralds great events; on the farm they must have made a familiar start to the day. Horses were draught and riding animals but also expensive to keep. They were a prominent feature of many rituals, and consuming their flesh was regarded by Christians as such a peculiarly integral part of pagan practice that it was explicitly banned. In the Viking Age, horses were also trained to fight, and matches of two stallions kicking and biting each other (often to the death) are a popular sport in the sagas; there are even depictions of such violent contests on the Gotland picture-stones. Back on the farm, dogs were kept for both herding and hunting (and, in some cases, battle—as in the Valsgärde boat graves). Cats were bred both for companionship and also for their fur.

All this required tools, which were made of both wood and iron. Most farms would have had a basic smithy, staffed by two or three individuals: the firepit and the nozzles of bellows, the site of the anvil, and remains of waste products have all been found on many settlement excavations. In graves they find the rest: the tongs and hammers, clamps, wedges, and everything else sufficient for the production and repair of basic household ironwork, including sickles, blades of all kinds, household knives, horse gear, and other fittings. Some of the forge installations were mildly elaborated, with extras such as a unique bellows stone from Snaptun on the Norwegian border that was decorated with a carving depicting a male face with sewn lips, almost certainly the trickster god Loki—an appropriate choice for a fire shield. Most of the workshops, how-ever, were quite simple.

Excavations in the waterlogged environments of urban harbours—at places like Hedeby in Denmark and Birka in Sweden—have revealed the organic aspects of daily life that other-wise rarely survive, including wooden tools such as spades, mallets, and a curious kind of barrow that was not wheeled but carried by two people a little like a stretcher. There are lots of storage items, stout wooden chests, little boxes, and resin-sealed containers made of birch bark. And rope—so many kinds of rope. Objects seem to have been bundled together with twisted fibres, or carried about on harnesses for both humans and animals. Bulk goods were per-haps slung over a shoulder, or lashed onto carts. The sheer quantity of twined fixings, string, cables, and the like gives a vivid image of a practical society rushing about its daily business. Archaeolo-gists also find the wooden handles of cloth bags, similar to those used for craftwork and knitting today, alongside a range of leather satchels, shoulder straps, and knapsacks. Wood was used for pegs, toggles, and fasteners of all kinds.

All this activity churned up the ground, so regular pathways in the settlements were strewn with brushwood, planks over the worst parts, and—in some market emporia—even crushed stone. Everything was also covered in wood chips from all the timberwork. Once, in the Russian urban centre of Novgorod, where the water-logged soil preserves such things well, I breathed in the scent of fresh pine a thousand years old, the whole site just saturated in the fra-grance from all the woodworking waste lying where the Viking-Age carpenters had left it.

The domestic sphere of the dwelling and estate management was primarily under the control of women. The sourcing, prepa-ration, and serving of food took up an immense amount of time. Beyond this, however, one of the primary female activities was the manufacture and working of textiles, and their transformation into a range of products from clothing to sails.

Wool was cleaned, sorted, combed, and then spun using a spindle whorl and distaff until ready for the loom. In Viking-Age Scandinavia the upright, warp-weighted variety of loom was used, that stood slightly higher than an adult and usually was positioned near a doorway for maximum light. Many different kinds of textiles were produced; the most common was homespun *vaðmál*, which was also used as a standard medium of exchange. Several varieties of twill are found, as well as other patterns. There are also fragments of fabrics, usually cloaks, made in the *röggvar* techniques that created a 'fake fur' effect. Imported silk and brocade were used on luxury clothing for facings, decorated cuffs, and collars. Fur trim was used in the same way.

Most farms produced their own cloth and worked it up into the clothes required; there were bronze pins, bone needles, and scissors of all kinds. 'Shopping' in our sense would have been rare indeed, and expensive—possible only at a market or, perhaps, by purchasing from itinerant peddlers. Time-consuming but vital, textile production probably made up the greater part of women's daily activities.

Textile work at the higher end of the scale could also have other consequences, such as the role played by women as storytellers in their weaving and embroidery of pictorial wall-hangings. These visual narratives were stories just as much as the verbal tales, and thus repositories of social memory, politicised history, and religious lore. By controlling such media, women acquired yet another source of real power, potentially a subversive one. This was especially the case in the high-status hall environments in which such wall decorations were displayed.

And display was important. Just as every surface of the great halls of the post-Roman warlords (and their successors) was covered in decoration, so too in almost all aspects of Viking-Age material culture. Archaeologists have spent a lot of time studying 'art-styles', the changing trends in visual ornamentation that are used on metal, wood, bone, stone, leather, and textiles. A small library of books addresses this subject alone, charting the evolution of the Vikings' aesthetic expression from the eighth to the eleventh centuries. Six main stylistic groupings can be traced, partially overlapping in time and named after the sites where they were first identified.

They range from fine-line, slightly baroque carvings in the early Viking Age, to interlocking ring chains and gripping animals that over time develop into great striding beasts and dotted interlace. In the eleventh century, the interlace art, in particular, sprouted fleshy tendrils twined around elegant, stately creatures. Whole buildings could be covered in this carved, sinewy ornamentation. There are regional variations of these styles across Scandinavia and fusions with other cultural traditions (also with hybrid forms) out into the Viking diaspora—thus the so-called Anglo-Scandinavian styles of northern England, the Hiberno-Norse traditions of Ireland, and so on.

These art-historical schemes are useful and necessary, not least for the dating of objects and places in the absence of material for more accurate scientific analyses, but they should be studied in parallel with the human context in which they were employed. At only small risk of exaggeration, subject to constraints of time, tools, and budget, the people of the Viking Age decorated more or less everything possible. They wore clothes embroidered with ornament along with jewellery that was a mass of writhing creatures and patterns. All but the most basic wooden items were carved, sometimes elaborately. The same is true of metalwork of all kinds, with the most intricate decoration of all worked so fine that a loupe is necessary to even see it properly. The chairs they sat upon, the beds they slept in, the bowls they ate from, the wagons that carried them, the harness of their horses, the walls of their homes—images everywhere. Their armour and weapons, especially, were layered with visual symbols and pictorial codes.

All this had meaning. When one understands how to 'read' some of the interlace designs, untangling not only the different animals twisted together but also tentatively trying to match this with narratives from the mythologies and heroic tales, what emerges is a world of stories told in pictures. Some were intended for outward projection—for display and proclamation (of allegiances, opinions, or identities?)—while others were more private. There are even metalwork designs on brooches, for example, that only make sense when seen from the wearer's perspective, looking down at her or his own body. Like the illustrated ideologies on the Migration and Vendel Period helmets, this too is a message, a collective cultural statement of who the people of the North felt themselves to be. Seen from the outside, it helps explain why the Vikings were often perceived as being so different from those they encountered.

There were also differences within Viking-Age society. Outside their social networks, people of the time felt themselves to be surrounded by an invisible population of spirits and other beings, but there was also another, more tangible community of the marginalised and ignored, much closer to home. In a real sense, much of the 'Viking world' was built, underpinned, and maintained by the enslaved. For a millennium and more they have disappeared from the histories of the Viking Age, and it is time to restore them to their rightful place of prominence.

4

THE PURSUIT OF LIBERTY

ONE OF THE MOST ENDURING, and politicised, components of the Viking image is the notion of freedom—the adventure of a far horizon and all that went with it. But for many this was an unattainable hope. Any true reading of life in the Viking Age first has to come to terms with an aspect of everyday experience that probably represented the most elemental division in the societies of the time: the difference between those who were free and those who were not. Beneath the social network, any other distinction of status, class, opportunity, and wealth pales beside the most basic fact of liberty and the consequent potential for choice.

The institution of slavery had long antecedents in Scandinavia, probably going back thousands of years before the time of the Vikings. By the eighth century, there was already a considerable population of unfree people living in the North, their condition being largely a hereditary one built up over generations. In the Viking Age, this picture changed dramatically because for the first time Scandinavians began to make the active acquisition of human chattel a key part of their economy. This was one of the primary objectives of the Viking raids and military campaigns, and the result was a massive increase in the numbers of enslaved people in Scandinavia.

Let it therefore be clearly stated: the Vikings were not only slavers, but the kidnapping, sale, and forced exploitation of human beings was always a central pillar of their culture.

One reason why this reality has made so little public impact is that the conventional vocabularies of enslavement—as employed by academics and others working on, for example, the transatlantic trade of more recent centuries—have rarely been applied to the Viking Age. In particular, there is ambiguity in the terminology because in place of 'slave' a very different word has always been used: the Old Norse *þræll*—giving us the modern English 'thrall', which we now use as in being 'enthralled' by a person, a work of art, or an idea.

It is impossible to know how far back in Scandinavian pre-history the practice of slavery originated. Scholars have plausibly proposed that it was at least a Bronze Age institution, and perhaps was very old even then. There is no reason to believe there was any discontinuity in the use of unfree labour and involuntary servi-tude all through the Iron Age. For the Viking period, a judicious combination of archaeological and textual sources can produce a relatively comprehensive picture of slaveholding.

The term for enslavement was *ánauð*, meaning 'bondage' or 'compulsion'—the central sense is of people subjected by force and lacking free will. There is a basic Old Norse terminology of its degrees, preserved in the Norwegian *Gulathing* laws. An enslaved man was a *þræll*, a thrall. Within that category, there was a spe-cific term, *þjónn*, for a thrall who acted as a domestic servant. An enslaved woman was an *ambátt*. If she was primarily made to work with weaving, she was a *seta*; if her assigned tasks included baking, she was a *deigja*. There were also *fjósner*, 'stable-living thralls', a special category of enslaved people who not only looked after the animals but were also housed with them.

It is clear that a kind of intermediate state of servitude existed that was voluntary up to a point although entered into under considerable economic compulsion—for example, as a means of clearing debts. A person could also serve as a thrall for a fixed period, following a legal judgement against them for having committed a crime. The Norse system of thralldom was not always complete chattel slavery, but most of the enslaved had little agency. As two prominent Viking scholars observed fifty years ago, "the slave could own nothing, inherit nothing, leave nothing". They were not paid, of course, but in some circumstances they could be allowed to retain a small portion of the proceeds they obtained at market when selling goods for their owners. As a result, it was technically possible, though rare, for a thrall to purchase his or her freedom. They could also be manumitted at any time. Some scholars have argued from this that the number of actual enslaved people in Viking-Age society was relatively low. However, as more work has been done on the detailed European records of Viking slave-taking raids, the scale of the trade has been revised sharply upwards.

Some were born into slavery, if both of their parents were already enslaved, or if a freeborn man who impregnated their enslaved mother declined to acknowledge the child. Others were taken captive, either in raids often undertaken for that purpose or as prisoners of war. Although an enslaved individual might pass through many hands in a journey lasting months or years, it almost always began with violent kidnap. Behind every Viking raid, usually visualised today as an arrow or place-name on a map, was the appalling trauma visited upon all people at the moment of enslavement, the disbelieving experience of passing from person to property in seconds.

Not all enslaved people—indeed, perhaps only a small minority—were retained personally by their captors and put to work. The majority entered the wider network of trafficking and were transported to markets and points of sale in settlements across the Viking world and beyond. The enslaved were moved through the trading posts of Scandinavia as well as over longer distances to the emporia of western Europe. The practice was entirely legal in the Christian states. In time, slaving would also become argu-ably *the* main element of the trade that would develop during the Viking Age along the eastern rivers of European Russia and what is now Ukraine. There was no solid infrastructure of purpose-built slave markets, with auction blocks and the like. Instead, transac-tions are likely to have been small-scale but frequent, with one or two individuals being sold at a time in any circumstances that seemed viable.

The enslaved appear frequently in the sagas, where the men perform manual labour and carry out the everyday duties of the farm while women serve inside the house and take care of the ani-mals in the byre. The stories describe how enslaved women were sometimes exploited sexually by the men of the house, which could lead to tension with their wives. The numbers of thralls are hard to estimate, but two or three might be likely for an average-sized farm while large estates could house dozens.

One of the Eddic poems, the *List of Ríg*, is a curious work that purports to describe the divine origin of the social classes among humans. The gist of its plot is that the god Heimdall, using the name Ríg, visits three households in turn. One is humble and impoverished, the second is modest but well kept, while the third is wealthy and proud. Ríg spends three nights at each house, sleep-ing between the couples living there, and in due course a series of children are born—respectively the progenitors of the thralls, the farmers, and the elites. The poem includes a list of personal names appropriate to their station in life for each of the social classes. The 'first couple' of the slave class are called Thrall and Thír, the latter name meaning effectively 'thrall-woman'. Their sons' names trans-late as Noisy, Byreboy, Stout, Sticky, Bedmate, Badbreath, Stumpy, Fatty, Sluggish, Grizzled, Stooper, and Longlegs. The daughters are called Stumpina (a feminine form of the male equivalent, with the sense of a demeaning joke), Dumpy, Bulgingcalves, Bellowsnose, Shouty, Bondwoman, Greatgossip, Raggedyhips, and Crane-shanks. All clearly pejoratives, several of the names imply ill health and a lack of hygiene, and one clearly refers to sexual servitude. None of them acknowledge individual identity or personality.

The poem also gives the tasks of the enslaved: "they fixed fences, dunged fields, worked at the pigs, watched over the goats, dug the peat". The man Thrall also carries heavy bundles of kindling and plaits bast to make baskets. Their bodies are marked by manual labour, with wrinkled skin burnt dark by the sun, scabbed nails, gnarled knuckles, and dull eyes. Their bare feet are covered with soil.

Enslaved women were extremely vulnerable to sexual abuse at the hands of their owners, which they experienced as a constant hazard alongside the manual tasks of daily life. By definition, a slave-owner could not be charged with raping his own slave because, as property, she had no rights within his household, and her body was his to treat as he wished. There are saga references to visiting men being offered a slave-woman to 'borrow' for the night, and it seems that sexual hospitality was also part of the wider institution of generosity to guests. Rulers also actively rewarded their military followers with enslaved women, clearly stated to be destined for their beds. The skaldic praise poem *Hrafnsmál*, the 'Sayings of the Raven', in honour of Harald Finehair, notes how the king gives his men "gold from Hunland and slave-girls from the east lands".

Male slaves could also be exploited in this way. The thrall name translated above as Bedmate, Kefser (lit. 'servile sleeping-partner'), is masculine and listed among those for the male enslaved. The name Leggialdi, 'Longlegs', carries a sense of condescending approval—a sort of verbal wolf whistle—and is also masculine. Even the goddesses were known to sleep with male thralls, out of boredom, lust, or in one instance as a way of rebuking a husband.

At least part of the Viking slave trade explicitly depended on sex trafficking, especially in the East. Settlements were specifically targeted for the enslavement of women, while their menfolk were often killed on the spot. Young women were transported long distances to be sold as sex slaves and were routinely assaulted by their captors along the way. Aḥmad ibn Faḍlān, meeting Scandinavians on the Volga in 922, noted several instances of such abuse. His account is all the more brutal for being an eyewitness report. He makes it clear that the enslaved young women travelling with the merchants were chosen for their looks, with an eye for future sale as sexual servants. As part of the everyday routine, he describes the Vikings having sex with the women in groups—apparently while their wives look on, unconcerned. Even at the point of sale, a woman was sometimes raped one last time in the presence of her purchaser. Ibn Faḍlān's text should be compulsory reading for any-one tempted to glorify 'heroic' Viking warriors.

The Arab sources record that some of the Viking leaders in the East, as in the West, awarded female body-slaves to their men, in addition to other thralls for their domestic needs. Albeit cloaked in imagery of idle 'dalliance', the right to sexually exploit the unfree was seen as an obvious and unquestioned prerogative of wealth. For example, in the *First Lay of Helgi Hundingsbani*, an Eddic poem, someone insults a lord with the claim that all he's ever done is kiss slave-women at the grindstone. The same probably applied in the relationship between owners and owned on a small farm, simply at a reduced scale.

In the sagas, the status of the enslaved as property, rather than people, is ambivalent. In some instances, the narratives note per-sonal qualities in favourable terms—a thrall unusually skilled at a particular task, regarded as sensible and reliable, or especially good-looking. However, when the sagas' frequent motifs of neigh-bourly feuds begin to escalate beyond harsh words into violent action, this often takes the form of killing opponents' thralls, evidently seen as a peculiarly personal form of property damage. An alternative view of this grim value system comes again from Aḥmad ibn Faḍlān, who saw with his own eyes how thralls who had fallen sick while travelling were simply discarded as rubbish and left to die. If they wished, slave-owners could also kill their own thralls without penalty under the law. Elderly thralls too infirm to work, and unwanted children of the enslaved, may have been disposed of in this way.

The enslaved had very few legal rights, and in almost every case only appear in the law as property. Almost all compensation payments for injury or death were channelled to the owners, as the 'economic loss' was theirs. A couple of unusual exceptions stand out, both related to sexual offences against the wives of thralls. In the *Borgarthing* law of south Norway, a thrall who finds his wife in bed with another man is "to go to the brook and take a bucket-full of water and throw it over them and bid his marriage-kinsman sleep well". This pays lip service to the severity with which offences against the institution of marriage were treated in law for free people, but simultaneously manages to convey contempt by turning the enslaved's situation into a vicious joke. In Iceland, the situation was different; a cuckolded male thrall had the right to kill any man who had seduced his wife. What makes this especially unusual is that a slave-owner who regarded a female thrall as "his woman" (as the law states) could *not* kill any other man who slept with her, as their own relationship was unequal. Similarly, it was a shameful thing to die at the hands of a thrall.

A tiny handful of texts preserve the actual voices of the enslaved. One is an eleventh-century, highly decorated runestone from Hovgården, the royal estate on Adelsö island opposite Birka market town in Lake Mälaren, Sweden. The inscription honours the king's estate manager and is a rare example of people erecting a stone to themselves while alive:

> Read these runes! They were properly ordered cut by Tolir, the *bryti* in Roden, appointed by the king. Tolir and Gylla had them cut, husband and wife to their own memory [. . .] Hákon did the carving.

The key fact here is that a *bryti* was a special class of thrall, someone entrusted with much responsibility but unfree nonetheless. In other cultures there are many parallels of the enslaved rising to positions of sometimes considerable power, blurring the lines of what their status really meant. On Adelsö, Tolir had clearly been able to marry (although whether this had legal standing is another matter) and to afford a magnificent statement of his position as the royal servant.

Another stone of similar date from Hørning in Denmark tells a simpler tale, but perhaps more poignant:

> Tóki the blacksmith raised this stone to the memory of Thorgisl, son of Gudmund, who gave him gold and freed him.

A freed thrall occupied an ambiguous status that was not enslavement but not complete liberty either. All freed(wo)men were still obligated to their former owners and expected to support them, but were never regarded as fully the equal of freeborn folk. Former thralls also had lower rights to compensation in the law codes. The stone raised by Tóki indicates his profession—a handy, useful thing to be doing—but whether this was something new or a legacy of his former tasks as a thrall is unclear. In time, the children and grandchildren of freed thralls would gain the full rights of the freeborn.

The material reflections of slavery are meagre, but significant. At the most basic level, iron shackles have been found at the urban centres of Birka, Hedeby, and a handful of other sites connected with commerce. They are ambiguous items up to a point, in that some of them arguably could be used to restrain animals, but it is more likely they were designed to be placed around a human neck, wrist, or ankle. An Irish site has produced an extensive chain with collars. At Hedeby, the five collar finds have mostly come from the harbour area, suggesting either a loss directly off a ship's side, or perhaps that trading in the enslaved was taking place actually on the jetties.

9. A thrall's life. A Viking-Age slave-collar from the island town of Birka, in Lake Mälaren, Sweden. Photo: Christer Åhlin, Swedish History Museum, Creative Commons.

10. Realities of raiding. On this engraved stone found at the insular monastery of Inchmarnock in Scotland, what appear to be armoured Viking raiders are shown leading at least one bound captive to a waiting ship. Photo: Headland Archaeology Ltd, used by kind permission of Chris Lowe.

At least one image seems to depict the moment of enslavement. An engraved graffito on a slate from the insular monastic site of Inchmarnock in Scotland, provisionally dated to the eighth or ninth century, shows what looks to be the aftermath of a slaving raid. Three armed figures in chainmail, including one with a beard and an extravagant hairstyle, move around a waiting ship. The bearded figure is leading a captive, perhaps a male monk, whose hands are locked together, a leash of some kind around his neck.

A second such depiction is more formal in nature and comes from Weston in North Yorkshire. Found at the church there, this is a fragment of stone sculpture that once formed the upper arm of a freestanding cross. Originally of Anglian manufacture, it was recut in the ninth or tenth century in the Anglo-Scandinavian tradition. On one side, the cross arm is taken up by a frontal depiction of a helmeted male warrior with a battle axe in one hand and a sword in the other. On the opposite side, what looks to be the same figure still holds a sword, but his other hand is gripping a woman by the throat; her hands are together and may be bound. This is the only illustration of direct male violence against a woman anywhere in the Viking world—clearly, it was an unusual choice of motif and perhaps thought inappropriate. Other Northumbrian stone crosses in a similar tradition also depict armed warriors, and it has been suggested that they are either the patrons of the work or in some way reference militaristic scenes in the Bible.

Of the domestic lives of the enslaved, only a single archaeological discovery has so far been made in Scandinavia. It is not from the Viking Age but from the early first century CE, back in the Roman Iron Age; there is cultural continuity, however, and the find almost certainly preserves the remains of enslaved people in a household setting. At Nørre Tranders in Jylland, Denmark, archaeologists have found the burnt remains of a longhouse of the classic Iron Age type, of which only half—the byre section—survived. The building had been completely consumed by fire. Experimental archaeology has shown that within only three to four minutes of a blaze starting, the air inside such structures becomes lethally toxic due to the effects of smoke. If a fire began at night, while the occupants were asleep, they were unlikely to get out. Something like this seems to have happened at Tranders. The archaeologists uncovered the bodies of cattle and horses that had died in their stalls, and a flock of sheep and lambs bunched up by the north door, where they had apparently blocked the exit in their panic. The animals were not alone. The body of a man was found in the midst of the sheep; a second man and three children lay at the east gable after the line of animal stalls, perhaps where they died trying to break through the outer wall. Why would both adults and children be among the livestock like this? They appear to have been *fjósner*, 'stable-living thralls', that special category in the sources, enslaved people who lived with the animals they tended. Remarkably, the ruins of the longhouse had not been cleared away, but instead the entire structure—charred bodies and all—had been covered with a mound, effectively making a 'grave' of the whole building. It is notable, and perhaps eloquent, that evidently no distinction was made between humans and animals. The village continued in use, so for decades after the fire, its inhabitants had carried on their daily lives with a huge burial mound in the midst of their settlement, a tomb for the thralls. Whatever happened, the events of that night must have lived on in stories.

Most of the archaeological material is harder to read, in that it only indirectly reflects the presence of the enslaved. They would have needed housing and feeding, and their work must have been not only integrated into the economy but perhaps also a main driver of it. In the early Viking Age, for example, who serviced the rapid expansion of the labour-intensive tar production industry, along with the parallel rise in the exploitation of the outlands? Later in the Viking Age, there was further reorganisation of the economy in connection with an escalating need for sailcloth (and therefore wool, and so also sheep), with obvious implications for the consequent rapid rise in labour requirements. There were also developments in the built environments of the estates, with an increase in smaller structures (perhaps thralls' quarters?) in addition to the main halls and ancillary buildings. As raiding for slaves escalated, their work was needed to build, equip, and maintain the fleets used in such assaults, and so on in a self-reinforcing system.

A related question concerns the material culture *of* the enslaved, and whether there is anything in the archaeology of settlements that belonged to the thralls. This remains uncertain, but to judge from the finds made in contexts where it is known they worked—such as weaving huts and the like—it seems that there was no specific material marker of enslavement, but rather that the clothing and possessions of thralls reflected the lowest level of social status generally, and were perhaps indistinguishable from those of the poorest free people. It is also possible that what few items they 'owned' (because, in reality, they owned nothing at all) were cast-offs, unwanted by others but still an integral part of the general material repertoire of the time.

One of the earliest archaeological identifications of enslaved people was in the burial record, and the discovery of graves where the presumed primary occupant had been accompanied in death by one or more individuals who had evidently been killed during the funeral rites. This is far from common, but there are now dozens of examples across the Viking diaspora. Each burial is different, but as far as one can generalise, the graves contain a single person, usually male, interred according to the prevailing norms. The 'sacrifices' were then deposited either in the grave with the primary occupant—alongside or laid over the body—or at a higher level in the same burial mound. These individuals were often bound by the hands and/or feet and had been hanged, decapitated, or killed with severe blows to the head. One of the most graphic examples comes from Ballateare, on the Isle of Man, where a tenth-century Scandinavian high-status young man was interred in a coffin with a variety of weapons. His grave was covered by an elaborate burial

mound made of multiple layers of soil brought from different localities (his fields, perhaps?). When the mound was still unfinished,
the corpse of a woman aged twenty to thirty was laid on top; the
back of her skull had been removed with a single sharp force blow,
probably from a sword. Rigor mortis had set in by the time she was
brought to the mound, and she may have died up to seventy-two
hours earlier. Her body was then covered by the burnt ashes of a
horse, an ox, and a sheep before the mound was finally completed
and a post raised on top.

The suggestion that such unfortunate victims may be thralls,
and therefore essentially just more possessions of the dead, was
made early in the history of Viking archaeology. It has an obvious
logic but is hard to prove; some or all of them may instead have
been criminals, prisoners of war, or anyone else whose death was
deemed necessary by the community and appropriate to a public
ceremony. There is also no reason why the same explanation should
fit all the examples. In favour of the interpretation, however, are
the numerous, unequivocal descriptions of precisely this practice
in the Arab eyewitness accounts of Scandinavian funerals in the
East, where enslaved people of both sexes (but most often female
and young) are described as being murdered during burial rituals.
There are also Byzantine observations of identical practices, including the mass slaughter of war captives.

Recent work taking advantage of new scientific methods has
shown that there are, in fact, real differences between the 'primary'
burials and the executed individuals. An oxygen isotope study of
Norwegian Viking-Age burials of this type has found that the 'sacrificed' people had a markedly inferior diet to the other deceased,
presumably indicating a lower social status. A similar study of Swedish burials has found the same, with a much greater consumption
of freshwater fish among the victims. In addition, the study found
that several of these individuals had the familiar dental modifica-
tions of filed grooves. Was this actually a marker of enslavement,
akin to a brand on the flesh? Then again, many enslaved people

were once free; their condition could change, voluntarily or not. These sacrificed men may thus have been war captives, or the filing might mean something quite different in this context.

It seems reasonably secure that the people killed by the gravesides of others were of lower status, which strengthens the idea that at least some of them were thralls. Future work will no doubt illuminate this further, but it is clear that the miserable experiences of the enslaved extended, in some cases, even to the circumstances and manner of their deaths.

For the enslaved, the mid-eighth to mid-eleventh centuries CE were an utterly different experience from that of the free people around them. The Viking Age was very much a time of borders—between cultures and ways of life, between different views of reality, and between individuals, including at the level of liberty itself. It was also a period when those borders were transgressed, tested, and sometimes erased: this, too, is a fundamental part of what made these centuries so important.

The Vikings can be seen as if through a prism, each turn of the glass producing new people, new reflections. Everyone had their own identity—their self-image—and its outward projections; some of them were familiar to us, others frighteningly alien. Border crossing, in every possible sense of the word, was at the core of the Viking Age, and it is now time to move to the other side.

5

BORDER CROSSINGS

B EING HUMAN IN VIKING-AGE SCANDINAVIA was not a condition restricted to the externals of the body or the interior life of
the soul: there was also the individual nature of personhood itself.

Part of the Viking image today is a caricature of masculinity—
the long-haired warrior still incorporated into the logos or advertising for products appealing to a supposed ideal of manly behaviour.
This is matched in popular culture by an almost equally clichéd
image of the uniquely independent woman, activated either as an
allegedly 'Nordic' archetype or (more sympathetically) as a role
model for female self-confidence and emancipation. It is therefore
ironic that Viking-Age reality should embrace a true fluidity of
gender.

Patriarchy was a norm of Viking society, but one that was subverted at every turn, often in ways that—fascinatingly—were built
into its structures. The Vikings were also certainly familiar with
what would today be called queer identities. These extended across
a broad spectrum that went far beyond the conventional binaries of
biological sex, and even across the frontiers of what we would call
human. The boundaries were rigidly policed, at times with moral
overtones, and the social pressures laid upon men and women
were very real. At the same time, however, these borders were also

permeable with a degree of social sanction. There is a clear tension here, a contradiction that can be productive for anyone trying to understand the Viking mind.

Today we have developed a rich vocabulary of identity and preference, of sexual orientation and its infinite expressions, of our bodies and how we inhabit them, of our relationships with others, including our preferred forms of address—in essence, a terminology that at its best acknowledges and empowers who we each feel ourselves to be. We can also articulate what happens at the interfaces between these identities and society's reactions to them, for better or worse. In exploring the ancient equivalents of modern lives, it can be problematic to directly transfer today's perceptions onto the late Iron Age. Some scholars argue strongly that it is impossible to do so. The Old Norse languages did not contain words for many of the concepts we use; the people of the time may not have understood themselves in those terms or found such labels necessary; the social context was also different in some fundamental ways.

It is clear that Viking society quite emphatically set out expectations based on the normative concepts of male and female sex, expressed in standards of gendered behaviour for both women and men. Some of the sources (especially Snorri) convey information very much through a Christian, masculine filter, but there are less prejudiced texts.

There is a sense of an outdoor realm for men, while women's domain was inside the dwelling, but both these spheres were perceived as places of genuine power and authority. This distinction was not a literal one but instead referred to arenas of responsibility— thus 'the house', in practice, meant the management of the entire farm, both economically and socially. A wide range of indoor and domestic tasks were also the province of women, including kitchen and food-related activities of all kinds, textile work (a major endeavour, as we have seen), and the daily round of agricultural life. None of this was devalued through patronising notions of 'women's work'; by contrast, these were vital skills and activities in which ability carried respect. To take but one example, this can be seen clearly on a remarkable runic monument from about 1050, a stone from Fläckebo parish in Swedish Västmanland, set up in memory of a wealthy lady with the unique name Óðindísa ('Odin-woman', though using the spirit *dísir* as a metaphor): "There will come / to Hassmyra / no better housewife / who arranges the estate".

In addition, women had a primary role in the conduct of household and communal rituals—for example, by officiating at sacrifices to the elves and *dísir*. In a real sense, they also managed the spiritual economy of the people. This was another source of true social power, guarding the lines of communication between the community and the other worlds, channels that might need to be opened up at any time.

For men, the 'wider world' extended to the sea, hunting and fishing, metalworking and smithying, the public assemblies, commerce, law, and war. Above all, politics was the preserve of men. An influential study from the early 1990s argued that Viking society operated on a model that essentially divided the powerful from the disempowered, regardless of sex. Masculine roles were prioritised, but women could assume them if circumstances dictated (for example, in the case of widows with no adult men left in the family). Most scholars have moved away from the rigidity of this concept, emphasising instead women's relative independence and agency in their own right, but there is no doubt that at times they could take on male tasks and duties apparently without social prejudice. There are clear examples of women acting in the courts, owning and selling property, and conducting trade.

Some social arenas were strictly gendered, such as everything surrounding childbirth, in which there is no indication of male involvement at all. By contrast, women were most often exempt from direct reprisals in feud-based violence—although not, of course, from its consequences.

It is also just as productive and necessary to consider the traits that were shared *across* gender boundaries, in which identity was formed as much by social role as by gender or sex. This is different from the single-sex model, as it does not place any primacy on masculine power. A recent study of burial customs in Norway, for example, has shown that a great many graves do not seem to be overtly gendered at all, and that the identity of the dead can be mediated in many ways. Close study also reveals that assumptions about the connections between gender and activity (problematic in themselves) cannot be applied consistently across Scandinavia; for example, cooking equipment is more common in Norwegian male burials than in female ones. It should also be remembered that the cultures of Viking-Age Scandinavia very definitely recognised degrees of personal freedom, from types of (in)voluntary servitude to full enslavement. These conditions of life were also deeply gendered.

Status can also intersect with gender, raising questions of hierarchy. When other factors are added to the mix, such as relative age and maturity, definitions can become problematic—such as the nature of childhood in the Viking Age and the border to adulthood. What did all this mean in practice for how a person was regarded (even if and when they were a person at all), and what they were permitted or expected to do? There is little evidence that children were automatically regarded as fully social beings from birth in pre-Christian Scandinavia. Children as young as five or so are sometimes found buried with full sets of 'grave-goods', the objects accompanying them in the ground. Mostly they are scaled down for them to have used (tiny jewellery, for example), but sometimes children are interred with adult-sized things. This is especially the case with very young boys and weapons, which implies a confirmation or conferral of status, perhaps linked to the identity of the bereaved family. However, such instances are rare.

Those who survived childhood seem to have gone through a number of rites of passage (such as weaning, naming, and so on) before relatively rapidly joining the workforce in whatever capacity they were able to. At around the age of fourteen or so, any differences between 'children' and 'adults' fade away in the graves, and this seems to have been the threshold of maturity. This would have included marriage and participation in war. It was not a sentimental time.

Bioarchaeological studies of skeletal remains sometimes reveal the signs of childhood malnutrition, and the results are telling. At least in central Sweden, a consistent pattern seems to emerge with up to 7 percent of men having been malnourished as children compared to up to 37 percent of women. Child mortality was high, estimated at between 30–60 percent, which leads to an inescapable conclusion: girls and boys were given different amounts and qualities of food, strongly to the advantage of the boys and to a potentially life-threatening degree for the girls. It is impossible not to read a chilling value system into this discrepancy.

A difficult question concerns the possibility of infanticide, the deliberate killing of unwanted children. This has become a standard trope about the period, but the actual evidence is rare and often equivocal. A man seems to have had the right to reject any child of his wife or concubine, and the inclusion of infanticide in saga narratives suggests it was practised, although to an unknown extent. This is supported by numerous medieval Christian law codes, which include statutes that prescribe punishments for the exposure of children, indicating it persisted well after the conversion.

The recovery of infant remains from middens, cairns, and refuse pits, for example, has been argued to be indicative of the practice. However, even beyond this, nowhere near sufficient numbers of child burials have been found to match the rate of child mortality, which must indicate that not all of them received a conventional grave. Here we also have an external viewpoint from the tenth-century Jewish traveller Ibrāhīm ibn Ya'qūb, who notes that unwanted children at Hedeby, Jylland, were thrown into the sea. Given that the law codes refer to exposure, which would not leave an archaeological trace, we must observe that this agrees with Ya'qūb's account. Selective *female* infanticide is particularly difficult to trace, although there are small suggestions in the archaeology. In the runestone inscriptions of central Sweden, up to six sons might be mentioned from one family, but never more than two daughters. This does not match natural birth rates, although it may be the consequence of prejudice or custom rather than infanticide.

The burial record suggests other parallels for this imbalance among adults too. A study of Scandinavian graves in northern Scotland reveals equal numbers of dead buried with weapons and jewellery, and yet in parts of western Norway the figure is 77 percent and 12 percent respectively. If the gendered assumptions of artefacts hold, this implies radically different treatment of the male and female dead in these two areas, which surely represented a contrast in social attitudes as well.

Notions of gender, and relations between individuals, are also closely bound up with sexuality—not least in terms of orientation and its expression in sexual behaviour, whether socially sanctioned or not.

Heterosexual marriage, sometimes polygynous, was the core manifestation of family values in Viking-Age society, including what was regarded as legitimate sexuality. However, not all liaisons were conducted within the codes of marriage or concubinage, and some were much more informal. Interestingly, while adultery was frowned upon, it was not necessarily grounds for divorce (indeed, intolerance of an open marriage might *lead* to separation). Married women take lovers in several tales, including the *Saga of Grettir*, the *Saga of the People of Eyri*, and the *Saga of Icelanders* (not to be confused with the generic category); in the *Saga of the Ljósvetningas*, a young woman has a whole string of boyfriends.

There were also divine equivalents. In the curious and quite funny Eddic poem *Loki's Quarrel*, the trickster interrupts the gods at a feast in Asgard and proceeds to insult each of them in turn with vivid accusations of a variety of sexual improprieties. It becomes clear that not only is every claim essentially true, but also that nobody much cares. When the goddesses are accused of infidelity, the god Njörd makes an interesting reply: "There's little harm though ladies get themselves a man, a boy on the side, or both". Clearly, although every goddess is married, they have all acted on their desires. Frigg is said to have slept with each of Odin's brothers, and also with a slave in revenge for a slight from her husband; Idun has taken her brother's killer to bed; Gefjon has "laid her thigh over" an unnamed youth (and is therefore on top); Loki has had sex with the wives of Týr, Thor, and indeed Njörd himself; and Freyja has slept with every god in the room, including her brother.

Minus the incest, this may be the practical reflection of concubinage, an accepted licence of female desire though without a comparably formal structure. The legitimacy of women's sexual feelings is mentioned several times in the sources, and the same is true of female supernatural beings, such as the Valkyries, who mourn their dead human lovers. Thus the titular battle-woman in the Eddic *Poem of Gudrún* laments that she misses her man, "in the high-seat and in bed".

Many of the sagas also emphasise mutual attraction as the proper basis for sexual relationships, with a constant element of choice on the part of free (as distinct from enslaved) women. Encounters are initiated by drawing a person close to sit adjacent or on the lap and then proceeding to kisses. This appears in the sagas as consensual behaviour. Sex is described in terms of a passionate embrace, *faðmr* and *faðmlag*, literally encircling a partner with one's arms. Couples "turn towards" each other in bed.

This idea of the sexual freedom of Scandinavian women also surfaces in foreign texts, such as the account of a diplomatic mission from the Muslim emirate in Iberia to the Viking court of what is thought to be southern Denmark, preserved in a thirteenth-century source. In the mid-800s, the ambassador Yaḥyā b. Ḥakam al-Jayyānī, known as al-Ghazāl ('the Gazelle') for his good looks, spent some time with Scandinavian royalty and was a particular favourite of the Viking queen called Nūd in the Arabic, which some scholars have read as the Norse name Aud. According to the text, al-Ghazāl is unnerved by the attention paid to him by such a high-born woman, at which she tells him, "We do not have such things [sexual taboos] in our religion, nor do we have jealousy. Our women are with our men only of their own choice. A woman stays with her husband as long as it pleases her to do so, and leaves him if it no longer pleases her". It is hard to know how much to rely on this—and some scholars have dismissed the entire text as a medieval muddle—but probably at least as much as we can on the sagas. Other Arab sources mention not only what they see as the promiscuity of Scandinavian women but on several occasions how they themselves have the right to initiate divorce; this is quite exact, repeated across several independent texts, and cannot be dismissed as mere prejudice about supposedly loose-living female foreigners. It also correlates well with the Norse sources, including the laws.

The poetic corpus contains several charms to attract the opposite sex, most of them used by gods but clearly a reflection of human concerns. Odin sometimes uses what he calls *mánvelar*, 'love-spells', to seduce groups of women at a time in Eddic poems such as *Harbard's Song*. Similarly, the 'List of Spells' in *Sayings of the High One* includes two of this kind:

I know a sixteenth [spell]:
if I want from a clever girl
to have all her mind and love-pleasure,
I turn the thoughts
of the white-armed woman
and I change her mind entirely.

I know a seventeenth [spell],
so that very late [i.e., never] will
a maiden-young girl reject me.

The sagas also relate several instances of sorceresses being contracted by unhappy lovers to work such magic. There are spells to induce impotence, and its opposite, engorgement to the point of disfunction. Other charms give the recipient the outward appearance of another in order to seduce someone in the guise of his or her preferred partner. A blow from a sorcerer's staff could induce sexual submission or ungovernable desire. A particularly cruel spell allowed a man the favours of all women except those he truly loved, perhaps an insight into Viking-Age social mores. Some of this magic was performed with the aid of runes, three of which had names that meant approximately Lust, Sexual Burning, and Unbearable Need. The sorceresses who possessed such power were themselves held to be sexually predatory and unwise to get to know too well. They were thought to have the ability to shroud a man's mind in a kind of carnal fog.

Of course, sex could also be prosaic, and vulgar. There is another, quite different vocabulary in Old Norse, a coarser world where men boasted to each other of who they'd like to *serða* and *streða*, 'screw' and 'fuck'. They sniggered about "romping on a woman's belly", or "stroking her groin".

The material culture preserves some remarkable archaeological snapshots. There is the rune-inscribed bone from eleventh-century Oslo on which is deeply carved, "Kiss me". One wonders whom it was passed to. Another set of examples comes from a most unlikely place. On the largest island of the Orkneys, off the north coast of Scotland, is the great Neolithic chambered tomb of Maeshowe. Constructed thousands of years before the time of the Vikings, it is one of Europe's finest monuments of the late Stone Age. It also contains the largest collection of runic inscriptions outside Scandinavia, made at the end of the Viking Age and into the early 1100s when Norse settlers broke into the interior, emptied it out, and used its convenient burial niches for quite other purposes than originally intended. Maeshowe was evidently a trysting place—a secluded spot for those seeking privacy out of the wind, with stone alcoves that could quickly be made comfortable with a blanket and a rush light. The inscriptions—often signed—cover a variety of

subjects but include several with crude sexual allusions, one referring to the long, low passage by which one enters the chamber (the
men's names are in italics):

Ingibjörg, the fair widow. Many a woman has gone
stooping in here. A great show-off. [signed] *Erlingr.*

Ingigerd ... sex [?] ... is the most beautiful ... [a fragmentary text next to an engraving of a slavering dog]

Thorný fucked. *Helgi* carved [the runes].

There is otherwise almost nothing in Viking-Age art and iconography with an explicitly erotic theme. Some of the gold foil plaques—
the aristocratic 'business cards' fixed on the posts of halls—have
scenes of chastely embracing and kissing couples. A handful of
male figurines in states of sexual arousal, usually naked except for
a belt clasped in their hands, have been found deposited around
longhouses, but they seem more like emblems of divine (or secular)
virility—sex as power, another dimension of hall culture. The same
may apply to the famous three-dimensional bronze figurine from a
burial mound at Rällinge in Swedish Södermanland that is reproduced in every book on the Vikings and usually labelled as representing the god Freyr. Nude except for a helmet and bracelets, he
is sitting cross-legged, one hand on his knee and the other gripping
his beard, and sporting a prominent erection. Despite the bracing
confidence of the traditional identification, there is simply no way
to know whether he is a god, some other notoriously libidinous
creature such as a dwarf, or a man. The odd posture and specific
clothing details again hint at something beyond a purely sexual
meaning. The context in which it was intended to be used or seen,
or indeed hidden, is similarly unknown—only that it accompanied
someone into the grave.

As far as I am aware, in the whole world of Scandinavian
imagery of the Viking Age, there is only a single depiction of sexual congress. On a runestone from Onslunda in Uppland, Sweden,

11. Sealed with a kiss. Two embracing figures on a gold foil from Sweden, early Viking Age. Such images are the primary evidence for conventions of men's (left) and women's (right) gendered dress. Photo: Gunnel Jansson, Swedish History Museum, Creative Commons.

set up by three brothers in memory of their father, Ófeig, a pair of human figures lie down together, the bearded one on top, their legs improbably entwined. The image appears to be a graffito (although far from casual, as it would have taken effort to carve), added after the stone was raised. It seems unrelated to the primary design scheme and red-painted inscription, although it may have been some kind of comment on the one commemorated.

Finally, there is one puzzling artefact that has undoubted sexual overtones but is of uncertain function. Since before the Viking Age, the southern border of the Jylland Peninsula was protected by a linear fortification, a complex set of ramparts known as the

Danevirke. In one of its ninth-century earthen banks, archaeologists have found a twenty-three-centimetre-long wooden phallus, carved as if erect, and broken at the base. It may have come from an idol of some kind, it may be a sex toy, but like so many such signals from the Viking Age, its real meaning is now obscure.

Not all sexual relations were consensual. The *Grágás* ('Grey Goose', a name of obscure meaning) laws of early Iceland date in manuscript to the 1200s and are almost certainly a compilation from various places and times, but they probably go back at least in part to the tenth century. According to their statutes, a woman can cite as grounds for divorce a wide range of circumstances, including marital violence. This was a major issue that also occurs quite frequently in other law codes, although their medieval date (broadly contemporary with the family sagas) makes it hard to know how closely they reflected Viking-Age realities. They are generally thought to contain remnants of earlier customs, and in some cases, what they proscribe is so defiantly unchristian that it can hardly have been a product of the new faith.

On the assumption that proscription in law is often an accurate guide to what at least some people are actually doing, these texts make for sickening reading. While there is little to indicate that early medieval Scandinavia was exceptional in this regard, the picture is certainly at stark odds with the stereotype of the 'independent Viking woman'. The laws are horribly specific, with penalties spelled out for injuries visible on the face, for limbs so broken as to make movement or work impossible, for the loss of an eye—and so on. A category of 'major wounds' includes those that penetrate the brain, the body cavity, and the marrow. Violence against women is particularly heavily punished when committed in the bedroom, a suggestion that this recognises the concept of marital rape.

The sagas contain a very few instances of practical, negative consequences that domestic violence could have for its perpetrators. In the *Saga of Burnt Njál*, for example, a man named Gunnar

Hámundarson slaps his wife Hallgerd's face during an argument, and she replies that he will one day have cause to regret his action. Years later, when Gunnar is besieged at home by enemies, his bowstring breaks in the middle of the fight, and in desperation he begs his wife to fix him a new one. She refuses, reminding him of the blow he once struck her, and as a result he is overwhelmed and killed.

Sexual assault and rape were legally categorised and prosecuted according to the relative social status of both the abuser and his victim. A high-born rapist was less harshly punished than an enslaved male predator who committed the same crime, but they were both treated with greater leniency if the victim was of low status. By contrast, a wealthy female survivor could demand the ultimate penalty of her attacker, whoever he was.

As in many essentially patriarchal societies, women's honour was a prized possession of their families, to be avenged if lost and to be used as a bargaining chip. According to the *Grágás*, any man who found another in bed with his wife, daughter, mother, sister, foster-daughter, or foster-mother had the right to kill him, regardless of whether a sexual act had taken place. If an unmarried woman became pregnant, it was the father's responsibility to care for the mother and child. If the expectant woman refused to divulge the man's name, her male relatives were legally allowed to employ "force" to compel her answer, as long as they left "no lasting injuries or visible marks" (in the words of the law). That said, it is also clear that there was a very high degree of personal responsibility laid upon men guilty of sex crimes. The rape of a low-born woman was still a more serious offence than consensual adultery committed with a woman of status. Equally, the legal codes do seem to genuinely recognise a woman's claim to the integrity of her body and person—for herself rather than merely as an extension of her kin. There were laws against unwanted touching without violence, with penalties that varied according to the part of the body on which a man laid hands or lips.

The law codes thus both acknowledge female independence and agency, and the individual culpability of perpetrators, but also reinforce the inescapably misogynistic webs of transactional obligation, honour, and social standing in which all were caught.

Broadly speaking, we have little reason to doubt that the majority of people ostensibly conformed to the accepted social norms of behaviour and sexuality—what one Danish scholar has called "the idea of the good". Testaments to such people, in the form of brief but approving biographical summaries, are chiselled onto the runic memorials of the late Viking Age, no doubt with varying degrees of truthfulness. However, Viking lives could be lived in many different ways. There are clear suggestions of queer identities in the Viking Age (with a caveat for the retrospective application of contemporary vocabularies). These can be hard to define, access, and view at a resolution adequate for study, but in some cases it is possible to do so.

Useful data can again be mined from the law codes. Many social norms were manifested in appearance, and clothing was clearly gendered—in cut and style, perhaps in colour, and certainly in decoration and adornment. The correlations of gender and status were also expressed in terms of quality. Although some kinds of jewellery were unisex, most were very much designed for either men or women (which is not to say that such signals could not be subverted). The *Grágás* laws define a clear offence for both men and women wearing clothing or haircuts appropriate to the opposite sex. This not only confirms that there were masculine and feminine norms of personal grooming and appearance, but also that some people evidently contradicted them.

There are hardly any examples of this from the saga literature. One episode, in the *Saga of the People of Laxardal*, set in the ninth and tenth centuries, sees a man divorce his wife on the grounds that she wears trousers "like a masculine woman", having previously complained about all the terrible things that can supposedly happen if "women go about dressed as men". There are also female equivalents, when women end a marriage because of their husbands' supposed effeminacy, as manifested in their wearing shirts cut so low as to expose the chest (it is not irrelevant that—as in this case—married men's clothes were usually made by their wives, which offers intriguing glimpses of agency within a relationship). There are also divine tales of transvestism, in which Thor and other gods end up wearing female attire in scenarios of disguise and deception so convoluted as to be worthy of Shakespeare; here, the effect is usually one of ridicule and mockery. In all these cases, it is clear that such clothing choices are meant to be suggestive of sexual orientation differing from heterodox conventions, and that this was viewed negatively. What any of this means for Viking-Age *practice* is another matter.

There is a possible archaeological image of cross-dressing men on two Gotlandic picture-stones from Lärbro Tängelgårda. These show figures in the flowing dress that typically seems to signal women, some of them holding drinking horns, but a number of them appear to have beards and perhaps helmets. On one of the stones are four of these figures side by side, and the 'beards' are very pronounced, although it is clearly possible this could represent some other convention of local style or artist's preference; gendered signals in this kind of material are so hard to read that they may not be there at all.

Male-bodied individuals buried in conventional women's dress and/or with normatively feminine accessories have conclusively been found at several sites, including Klinta on Öland. There are also such graves from England—for example, at Portway in Andover, southern England, a body identified osteologically as that of a male was buried in a woman's dress, including a full set of jewellery. There are other instances.

There is no doubt that this was a time of extreme homophobia, and we can trace a clear, though chronologically interrupted, path to the Germanic peoples of Tacitus's time. He relates how men found guilty of homosexual acts were pressed into bogs and held down to drown under wicker hurdles. Archaeologists have found many male corpses from the Iron Age in the marshes of Germany and Denmark, often naked, sometimes bound, usually exhibiting various traumatic injuries: slashed throats, blunt-force cranial depressions, garottes around their necks. Some of these victims have been found in pairs and actually covered by wickerwork, just as Tacitus describes.

In the Viking Age, homosexual men were treated with extreme disdain and a complex kind of moral horror, especially those who allowed themselves to be penetrated. Such a man was *ragr*, not only homosexual by inclination and action, but also inhabiting a state of being that extended to ethical and social qualities. This complex of concepts has been extensively studied, and in the words of its leading scholar, "the unmanly man is everything that a man should not be with regard to morals and character. He is effeminate and he is a coward, and consequently devoid of honour".

There are no positive depictions of same-sex relationships in the textual sources, although this is hardly surprising given that they were compiled by medieval Christians. Negative references come mostly in the form of formal insults, what the Norse called *nið* (usually anglicised as *nid*). The legal codes devote a great deal of space to such defamation, indicating the very high price placed on the honour thereby impugned. All such insults and insinuations refer exclusively to men. The saga allusion to 'masculine women' in trousers does not necessarily have to include a sexual dimension, of course, but the implication can arguably be read from it. Female same-sex relations are simply never mentioned at all.

Homophobic insults are employed so numerously in the sagas and poems, and are addressed so frequently in the laws that they must have been relatively common. One archaeological example gives the tedious flavour, a runic inscription scratched on a bone that therein refers to a second inscription, carved into the timber walls of a church. The text takes the form of a dialogue and is written in two different hands (H1 and H2), implying it was passed between two people as they wrote in turn:

H1: What was it that you carved into Cross Church?
H2: Óli has not wiped himself and is fucked in the ass.
H1: That sounded good!

Nid of this kind were classified formally in law. The early medieval Norwegian *Gulathing* laws, for example, describe *tréníð*, 'wood-*nid*', as a carved depiction of two men engaged in a sexual act, or else a runic description of the same (the Cross Church halfwit above would have committed such a crime). There was also verbal *nid*, a slanderous claim of implied homosexual practices. Statements of this kind were *fullrétisorð*—words for which the full penalty must be paid. A further category of 'exaggerated utterance' encompassed accusations of shameful things that could not happen in life but which carried overtones of disgust, such as claiming that a man had given birth. There were more categories of this kind, and all of them carried the penalty of outlawry, the same as for murder and rape. In essence, this punishment was what its name implies: a placement literally outside the law, thus leaving one vulnerable to physical harm without redress.

At the heart of *nid*, and Viking-Age homophobia, was the assumption "that a man who subjects himself to another in sexual affairs will do the same in other respects". The key to such insults was not so much the accusation of perceived sexual perversion as an attack on an opponent's honour. The latter partly defined cultural gender for the Vikings, and also partly depended on it to have meaning. What we would call sexual orientation was, in the Viking Age, completely bound up with much wider and deeper codes of behaviour and dignity, extending way beyond physical and emotional preference. *Nid* linked sexual and ethical concepts, and interlaced them with prevalent notions of the masculine and feminine. None of this implies a contempt for women; to be feminine and effeminated are not the same thing.

Women could, on occasion, take on the social roles of men, in addition to their own specific and important power domains. However, women could not acceptably look like men or try to symbolically be them (as with the trouser-wearer of Laxardal). For men, there was no such blurring of borders, and it was not condoned for a man to take on any aspect of women's lives and duties. Interestingly, it is the man's gender that was limited and intensive, while the gender of women was to a degree unlimited and extensive. At the same time, demonstrative masculinity was a keystone of the sociopolitical foundations. *Nid* challenged this, but also affirmed it because those so accused were required to defend themselves, thereby vigorously upholding the expected norms of gendered power.

Perhaps the greatest potential for the recovery of Viking-Age queerness lies in the analysis of magic and its roles in Viking-Age society. Every level of communication between the community and the other powers was implicated in the practice of sorcery, which only women could acceptably perform. Men could and did practise magic, but at the cost of entering a state of *ergi*—becoming *ragr* and taking upon themselves its full freight of unmanly connotations. There is a broad terminology of male sorcerers, as for their female counterparts, but some of the words are derogatory. There are references to female animals (cows, mares, bitches, and so on) and, again, their capacity to give birth. Whole categories of *nid* were also activated in the context of magic, such as a claim that a man fathered nine wolves on a sorceress.

There seems to have been something in the mechanics and equipment of the rituals that had explicit sexual overtones, gender-appropriate for female performers but which would cast a male sorcerer in an effeminising role. The main tool of the sorcerer was a metal staff that was probably held between the legs and rotated (they apparently served as symbolic distaffs, and were used to 'wind back' the performer's travelling soul, attached to the body by a kind of spiritual thread). Several of the terms for these staffs are synonyms for the male organ; descriptions of the magic-workers speak of them 'riding'; and the body posture is suggestive. Some scholars have also proposed that the staffs were employed in literal sexual penetration, as part of rituals with undoubted carnal object-ives (the sources detail long lists of what is essentially sex magic). Even in medieval woodcuts, there are depictions of naked female witches with distaffs between their legs, very definitely referencing concepts of deviant sexuality.

To ask an obvious question, if the male practice of sorcery brought with it what was effectively a form of social death, and risked actual capital sanction, why would any man choose to openly follow such a path? The answer is that it conferred powers and experiences that could be obtained in no other way; it was imbued with qualities—and perhaps a subversive kind of status—that made it worthwhile even at so steep a price. What is curious is that this sometimes played out in a manner that nonetheless car-ried overtones of social acceptance, going far beyond the conven-ience of 'don't ask, don't tell'. There are several saga examples of kings employing entire teams of male sorcerers for specific magical ends, without any social backlash at all.

The ultimate demonstration of this bargain comes from Asgard itself, the home of the gods. Odin was the master of magic, but in particular he was the lord of precisely this kind of sorcery that made a man *ragr*. To get an idea of how deep the social contradic-tion went, one only has to imagine the god of medieval Christi-anity, with its capital penalties for many kinds of supposed sexual transgression, being clearly described in biblical texts as engaging in same-sex intercourse. Thus we have Odin—lord of the gods, divinity of war and poetry, patron of the royal elites to whom a masculine heterosexual ideal was central—also portrayed as the supreme practitioner of magic that was homophobically shameful for men to perform. A Norwegian scholar got to the heart of the matter some years back in a series of groundbreaking papers on the divine being she referred to as 'Odin the Queer'. The same term surely applies to the men of magic, who were activating social disdain while controlling and weaponising it as power. It may be that *all* the workers of magic and sorcery were differently gendered, at least when seen in the light of their much better documented cousins in the circumpolar cultures of the last three hundred years. In much of Siberia, for example, it has been argued many times that 'shaman' (or its equivalent) constitutes a gender in itself.

Further aspects of sorcery and cult clearly involved sexual performance. There is an extraordinary description of such rituals in the *Story of Völsi*, a prose tale with poetic elements preserved within the fourteenth-century manuscript of *Flateyjarbók* that, on the basis of internal detail, contains authentic information from the Viking Age. It relates a household rite of the early eleventh century, the period when paganism was being suppressed in Norway, and tells how a Christian king and his retinue attend a ceremony in disguise. As part of a communal feast, a long series of rituals are performed in which a preserved horse's penis is passed from hand to hand and spontaneous verses are spoken. The sexual content is explicit, as is the action, for it is made clear that the female servants of the house are expected to employ the object to masturbate:

[*Verse spoken by the eldest son*]
For you, serving-maid,
this phallus will be
lively enough
between the thighs.

[*Reply by an enslaved woman as she takes the object*]
I certainly could not
refrain from
thrusting him inside me
if we were lying alone
in mutual pleasure.

There is more of the same, including the graphic observation that the phallus will "be made wet tonight" by the daughter of the house. Other texts also draw sexual connections between women and horses, and there are a number of misogynistic poems that use the imagery of animals in heat to describe female desire.

These themes and connections can be pursued in the study of graves. Archaeologists determine the sex of the buried dead through analysis of their bones (which is reliable, though not certain) or DNA (which uses a chromosomal definition that is generally uncontroversial, although one should be aware that there are also other ways of making sex based on the genitalia or internal organs). This provides sex determination of male- and female-bodied individuals, but it is not at all the same as gendering them: this is beyond the reach of science.

However, in many cases the deceased were cremated, and the resulting ashes are hard to sex reliably. More often, preservation conditions in the soil are unfavourable to the survival of bone in any state, and there are many graves without human remains at all (although they were evidently originally present). In these cases, for centuries archaeologists have resorted to determining the sex of the dead through association with supposedly gendered objects—thus weapons in a grave are held to suggest a man, jewellery sets denote a woman, and so on. Beyond the obvious problems of conflating sex and gender, and also effectively sexing metal, these readings risk simply piling one set of assumptions on another in what forensic decision-makers call a 'bias snowball' of cumulatively questionable interpretations. Clearly this is unsatisfactory, and at worst can lead to a potentially vast misreading of Viking-Age gender from the literally tens of thousands of burials that have been analysed in this way over the years.

All is not lost; to begin with, it should be acknowledged that while potential caveats should be kept in mind, the majority of these sex/gender/artefact correlations probably do reflect Viking-Age reality. There is no evidence that suggests otherwise. However, not *all* burials conform to such patterns, and an openness to the exceptions—which we know were there—is vital. Without this, one can never hope to do archaeological justice to the gender spectrum discernible in the medieval texts or compare this with Viking-Age empirical reality. More excitingly, the archaeology can turn up evidence for identities and genders that did not make it to the written sources.

The starting point comes in graves with viable bone survival. In such cases, archaeologists occasionally find people buried with objects and clothing that would usually be associated with the opposite sex, following a binary perspective. These include male skeletons wearing what appear to be dresses of the kind more conventionally buried with women, or with the oval brooches that hold the apron together at the breast, and similar combinations. For burials with female bodies, an equivalent is the presence of weapons in numbers sufficient to plausibly suggest a warrior identity for the dead. At Vivallen in Swedish Härjedalen, there was even a male-bodied person buried according to Sámi rituals, in a Sámi settlement, but wearing conventional Sámi man's equipment over a Nordic woman's linen dress, complete with jewellery to match—a crossing of both gender and cultural norms.

The dead proverbially do not bury themselves, and the objects laid in a grave do not necessarily reflect the possessions of the deceased in life. New post-mortem identities can be created through the association of artefacts and the corpse. How can one tell? Is it possible to read an individual's life from the material repertoire of their funeral? Caution is vital; each case should be examined contextually and on equal terms, working towards a balance of probabilities. For a warrior identity, for example, there is the supporting evidence of poems that unequivocally describe real warriors being buried with their arms as a demonstration and affirmation of that role. It is always advisable to revisit the data and question it afresh.

The most prominent example to date usefully combines almost all of Viking gender in a single burial, raising more questions than it answers. In a tenth-century chamber grave designated Bj.581 from an urban cemetery at Birka in Sweden, an expensively dressed corpse was buried seated and surrounded by a full weapon set (which is rare), with two riding horses. This truly spectacular burial was excavated in 1878 and has been held up ever since as a type example of a high-status warrior from the mid-900s, a kind of 'ultimate Viking' of the time. Bj.581 was published as such in generations of standard works. As part of this interpretative package, the deceased was always assumed to have been a man, because warriors were 'obviously' male (conflating sex and gender in the familiar way). In 2011, however, an osteological study suggested the buried person was actually female, and this was confirmed by genomic analysis in 2017—the deceased carried XX chromosomes. The ensuing debate on the apparent 'female warrior' of Birka went viral and now convulses Viking studies, in an at-times vituperative discussion that has little to do with women and war but more concerns underlying fault lines of gendered assumption in the discipline and beyond.

In a sense it does not really matter whether the person in the Birka grave was a female-bodied warrior woman or not (though as one of the lead authors in the research team, I firmly believe she was all those things). This person may equally have been transgender, in our terms, or non-binary, or gender fluid. There are other possibilities, too, but the point is that *they must all be recognised as possible Viking-Age identities* while—crucially—not assuming this must be the case. Not least, in the interpretation of Bj.581, scholars should be careful not to deny the basic agency of women, and their potential to choose one way of life over others; this person does not have to be necessarily different. Furthermore, *all* these intersections of activity and identity were in themselves deeply gendered—from 'warriorhood' to everything else. Importantly, none of this needed to be fixed and permanent. In the later prose texts, difficult sources though they are, one encounters individuals who change names when they embark upon a new path in life—when certain women become warriors, for example. But only sometimes—there are no universals here, and as ever the medieval sources are problematic, late, ambiguous, and uncertain.

Bodies can come in many forms, and there is a major area of Viking life about which relatively little is known: attitudes to (dis) ability. There are literary references to individuals with limited mobility and dexterity, either from natural causes or due to injury. The funerary record also contains several examples of people without limbs or with natural conditions that would have severely constrained their movements; there are also graves containing individuals of restricted growth. What all this clearly implies is that people could survive into adulthood, and be buried like the rest of the population, though they had lived with various forms of physical challenges. From time to time, they must have received care and assistance.

One famous individual, Ívarr hinn beinlausi, Ivar the Boneless, was a ninth-century warrior commander who fought in the British Isles; some saga traditions have him as a son of Ragnar lothbrók. His nickname has been much discussed, and is in any case problematic as it is first attached to him in texts dating to long after his death. A twelfth-century source says, "He was said to lack bones", although the word for 'bones' can also mean 'legs'. *If* the name was real, and *if* it referred (as some believe) to a man who had for some reason lost the use of his legs, then it is intriguing that he was able to rise to such a position of respected command.

Visual impairment, either complete or partial, occurs several times in the mythology—especially in connection with Odin, but also as a motif in the sagas. There are also many metalwork figures, in both two and three dimensions, with eyes that apparently differ from one another; by no means all of these can be readily interpreted as gods. It is hard to unravel the inner meanings of this, but it seems that Viking notions of body normativity were relatively inclusive.

At this point it is also appropriate to remember the distinctly porous border between the nature of humans and the nature of animals, manifested in the potentially shifting qualities of the *hamr*, the 'shape'. Today we recognise and support LGBTQI+ identities, and try to extend that sensitivity to the people of the past, but it is thrilling to consider that the Viking mind went even beyond the boundaries of the human in this respect.

While some of their norms can appear rigid, the Scandinavians somehow applied them in ways that also allowed them to be questioned, undermined, and contradicted. In many ways and for many years, Viking scholars have been naive and simplistic about their acknowledgement and recognition of gender variation in the later Iron Age. Too often our studies have been restricted to admittedly deep explorations of the lives of women, thereby relegating half of humanity to a discrete, ghettoised entity set against a supposed masculine norm assumed by default. In addition to suppressing the obvious presence and agency of women, this also ignores the vast ocean of lives lived on different terms.

Up to a point, one should also resist the urge to categorise: perhaps Viking-Age people chose and renegotiated their identities every day, much as many of us do. Their ideas about gender went far beyond the binaries of biological sex, as scholars are now beginning to understand. Sadly, there has been much less awareness of the privilege required to grant ourselves such innocence for so long.

6

THE PERFORMANCE
OF POWER

THE SLOW EMERGENCE OF NEW Scandinavian institutions from the chaos of the late Migration Period was very much a realignment of power and its intersections with wider society. From the Vendel Period and into the eighth century—the start of the Viking Age—this was the beginning of the long path to unified kingdoms, to a genuine sense of statehood, and ultimately to the Nordic nations that are still recognisable today. But beneath this inevitably irregular process lay something older and more deeply rooted in the Scandinavian cultures—the notion of power as a public entity, something to be seen and debated, spoken and performed. As the political trajectories of the new elites gathered momentum during the eighth to eleventh centuries, their agendas were in constant tension with the remnants of this earlier order. What can in many ways be framed as a social conversation (or perhaps more properly, an argument) about ways to live and rule, forms another of the key motifs in the history of the Viking Age.

The arenas of this conflict—or dialogue, if one prefers a gentler view—were the institutions of popular assembly and the laws that were enacted there, both of which were manifested and embodied in monuments in the landscape. A crucial component of this was communication, principally in oral form. The keeping of records was a matter of memory but also, up to a point, of notation in the form of runic script. Many thousands of runic inscriptions have survived, on wood, bone, and above all on stone, that testify to the importance they held in Viking lives—whether in the everyday round, in politics, or matters of spirituality.

The twin social forces of law and literacy unite in the expression of power, but there was also a third force, one that has in a sense come to stand at the very heart of the popular image of the Vikings: mobility. The peoples of Viking-Age Scandinavia were often on the move, first as individuals and collectives, and ultimately as nations. They travelled over roads and rivers, and on the ice during winter months, but they especially journeyed by sea. The Viking ship, that most clichéd of images, really was one of the primary expressions of their power and the tool of its success.

In exploring these disparate elements in the performance of power, we come closer to the Vikings and their society to understand where they came from, where they were going, and in particular, why and how.

In the aftermath of crisis, and the years of the dust veil with its attendant traumas, the emergence and rapid rise of power structures based on militarised elites has been well established. This included the creation of 'hall culture' built up around rulers and their retinues, and the infrastructure that maintained them. In varying forms, this model of social hierarchy—essentially a pyramid of sorts—would continue into the Viking Age, although the size, shape, and territories of the polities would change.

However, behind these warlords and their petty kingdoms, and the social ladder on which they tried to rise, were the continuities of political life that had been part of Scandinavian culture for centuries. This was the so-called *thing* (Old Norse *þing*), a regular gathering of elected representatives in whom was vested the practical exercise of power at a local level. With roots going back into the prehistoric past at least as early as the Roman Iron Age, the assemblies brought together free men of arms-bearing age to speak on behalf of their communities, resolve issues of mutual concern, and adjudicate in legal disputes. Although varying in precise form by region, the assemblies operated at multiple levels, addressing greater matters of business according to the social and geographical seniority of the *thing*.

In Norway, where the phenomenon has been most closely investigated through archaeological and documentary survey, some thirty or so *thing* sites are known from the first millennium CE. Some are inland, but most cluster along the coast in the areas of densest settlement. Within these, there were apparently three levels of assemblies: the shire (*fylki*), half-shire, and quarter-shire. This tripartite division can also be traced in other parts of Scandinavia, even in quite different contexts; for example, the early third-century 'Norwegian' military force, whose weapons and equipment were sacrificed at Illerup Ådal in Denmark after a defeated invasion, appears to have been clearly divided into three levels of rank—perhaps corresponding with the same social division found in the *thing* sites.

The Norwegian assembly sites resemble courtyards and were once given that name, consisting of a number of longhouse-like structures arranged in an open circle or horseshoe shape around a central space. The buildings were for the temporary housing of delegates, who would travel there for regular meetings held in the enclosed area. In each region, the Iron Age archaeological features correlate remarkably closely to the administrative units of land and populace recorded for the same areas in the law codes and surveys of the early Middle Ages, and even into the early modern period. At the Dysjane site in Tingshaug (literally '*thing*-mound'), Rogaland, for example, the thirty-two structures built around the characteristic courtyard area appear to match the thirty-two ship-districts later recorded for the Ryger region in which the assembly lies. In some cases, even the layout of the building complex actually reproduced the relative geography of the districts each structure apparently represented. The courtyard site thus formed a kind of physical map of the areas from which the delegates had come, so they could walk through the site as if through the administrative landscape that the assembly reflected. Depending on where they were housed (perhaps also combined with distinctive markers in dress or banners), it would have been instantly obvious who each man was and on whose behalf he was present.

Within the bounds of the court, a strictly defined area that was probably guarded, matters were serious, and decisions were made on local disputes all the way to capital crimes. The higher the level of the assembly, the closer to 'affairs of state' and parliamentary functions (in these small worlds) it came. If a matter could not be resolved at one court, it would move up to the next level of assembly, sometimes with a gap of some months.

Delegates would represent their districts, often with spokesmen who were especially gifted at public speaking or legal argument. The speeches were heard by the presiding official—the lawspeaker—who, as his name implies, was obligated with literally memorising and reciting the laws. Drawing on this resource, he was also the judge of the cases presented, although in contentious circumstances it was sometimes necessary to win over the opinion of the assembled delegates themselves. Factionalism was endemic, especially in the later experiments in republicanism as in Iceland, and one of the main duties of the assembly was to place a check on interpersonal or familial feuds before they got out of hand. Such vendettas could be lethal in small communities, and an honour system in which all slights must be either compensated or avenged required very tight controls; many of the Icelandic saga stories revolve around what can happen when feuding grows beyond the law's capacities of restraint.

The *things* were not strictly democratic but were nonetheless focussed on formal ideas of fair representation and an attempt to create neutral spaces where disputes could be heard. It is clear, certainly in Iceland, that the dominant families exercised disproportionate influence over the proceedings (or tried to), and the sagas routinely relate efforts to affect judgements in advance and obtain the most favourable opinion.

Some of the Norwegian assembly sites have slightly different layouts of buildings, while others include enormous linear installations of cooking pits for hosting open-air feasts. In Sweden and Denmark, with milder climates and more hospitable terrain, there seems to have been less need for established sites with semi-permanent standing buildings, and instead there is a focus on open areas where people could conveniently assemble. Many *thing*-mounds (on which the speakers probably stood) still survive in the countryside today, sometimes set aside or as part of cemeteries, and occasionally bounded by water to form a ritual border of the law. A particularly elaborate complex can be found at Anundshög in Swedish Västmanland, where a massive burial mound was surrounded by a smaller cemetery, complex arrangements of stones in the shape of ships, a line of wooden staves, and a runestone. Further up the hierarchy of such sites were those associated with royalty, such as the *thing*-mound on the cemetery ridge at Gamla Uppsala, probably originally a burial but later levelled on top and used for the assembly. Built by the new elites to anchor their rule with the people, such places were established strategically in the midst of their self-affirming monumental landscapes.

Depending on weather conditions, one can imagine small tent cities growing up around the sites, accommodating large numbers of people for short periods. As with any folk gathering, activities were not restricted to the legal and administrative business of the day but would have extended into general socialising at the margins. The assemblies served not only as organs of communal government, but also as an opportunity for the exchange of goods and gossip in an atmosphere reminiscent of a county fair. They also formed an arena for the enactment of public religious rituals.

In Norway, especially (where there is greater resolution of the data), but also in the rest of Scandinavia, the major question is what happened to this system of communal government at its points of contact with the rising power of kings. It is not coincidental that this political friction begins to be felt precisely in the eighth century, at the start of what we call the Viking Age. While their relationship to the lords of the hall and the new monarchies would change over time, the *things* would never entirely disappear. Even today, the Alþingi of Iceland, the *allthing* that was the highest level of assembly for the whole country in the Viking Age, still sits in Reykjavík as the oldest continuous parliament in the world; it shares this honour with the Tynwald of the Isle of Man, also a Norse construction.

One of the key elements in the fabric of power was land ownership, with absentee landholding one of the possible cornerstones of the late Iron Age elites. A major factor in this was inheritance rights, including the transfer of land within families. In the first instance, land always passed through the male line, although women could inherit in the absence of male relatives. If a marriage was childless, property usually reverted to whichever family it had come from. Thus, a childless widower would not inherit his late wife's land even if they had worked it together during their marriage, and it would instead go back to her own kin. A central concept, found in the medieval laws of Norway and Sweden and much disputed as to its possible Viking-Age origins, was the *óðal*, or allodium. If a parcel of land had been owned by members of the same family for a longer period of time (six generations was the convention), their heirs had an inalienable right to it, and sale to others was blocked. One interesting effect of this was to protect the inheritance rights of daughters, who could keep the land over the rights of male relatives outside the immediate family.

One of the primary functions of the later runestones in the eleventh century was to record these rights of inheritance, tracing clear lines of descent and, one imagines, emphasising the legality of claims that had once been (and perhaps were still being) disputed.

185

One stone in particular—from Hillersjö in Uppland—has become justly famous, not only for the unprecedented detail of the familial relationships it describes, but for their outcome:

> Read! Germund got Gerlög, a maiden, as wife. Then they had a son before he [Germund] was drowned and then the son died. Thereafter she got Gudrik as her husband. He [. . .] this [text damaged here, but probably referring to the acquisition of Hillersjö]. Then they had children but only one girl survived, her name was Inga. Ragnfast of Snottsta got her as wife. Thereafter he died and then the son. And the mother [Inga] inherited from her son. Then she had Eirík as her husband. Then she died. Then Gerlög inherited from Inga, her daughter. Thorbjörn the skald carved the runes.

Thus we see Gerlög, twice widowed, who saw all her children and grandchildren die before her, and who in the end reverse inherited the land of three families. What a life, and in microcosm an image of the lives of her Viking-Age contemporaries: child mortality, multiple marriages, early deaths, no certainty, and around it all, the law in its engraved permanence.

Three other examples give the merest sense of the richness to be found in the inscriptions (and there are thousands of them), the intimate bond to the land and the critical nature of ownership, as well as all the human detail in between.

> Östen had this stone raised in memory of Torgärd, his sister, Hallbjörn in memory of his mother.
>
> Bergaholm, Södermanland

> Sibba raised the stone in memory of Rodiaud, his wife, daughter of Rodgair in Anga. She died young, leaving infant children.
>
> Ardre, Gotland

Sibba had this stone made in memory of his and Rodiaud's daughter.

Ardre, Gotland

On the first stone, from Bergaholm, Hallbjörn is underage, which is why his uncle is the main sponsor of the stone; he holds Torgärd's lands in trust and records his inheritance claim should anything happen to the boy. The two 'Sibba stones' from Gotland, raised by the same man to his wife and their daughter, emphasise the rights of infant children to inheritance and also stress that they will inherit from their maternal grandfather: these are the words of a man protecting the future of his line.

The land was not only claimed, but of course also named. Many place-names either refer to obvious topographical features—a stream or spring, a forest, a ford, or a meadow—or join them with someone's personal name. Sometimes whole settlements are associated in this way. Dating names of this (or any) kind is not easy and has occupied an entire field of scholarship for well over a century, but we now have a broad idea of the named landscape of the Iron Age.

Customs varied over time, especially regionally. A certain zoning of function has been discerned, representing not only administrative divisions but also the physical location of the distinctive elements of power. Beyond places connected with royalty, there are -by ('village') names linked to offices and roles, thus situating those people in a network of consolidation, domination, and rapid response across the land. Taking just Swedish examples, we have the villages of the rinkr (a kind of military officer), the karlar (literally 'the men', effectively the retinue itself), even of the smed, the smiths—not an unimportant constituency if you wanted to have ready access to armour and weaponry repair. There are names for administrative power centres and central places themselves, such as tuna and husa and many more.

And then, perhaps above it all or maybe also enmeshed in the same webs of power, were the gods. In what are called theophoric place-names, a divinity is linked to a type of site, most often some kind of cultic place. Examples include -*lund*, a sacred grove, thus Odenslunda, 'the Sacred Grove of Odin'; -*vé*, the name for an enclosed sanctuary, and so Ullevi, 'the Sanctuary of Ull'; -*åker*, some kind of hallowed field, perhaps where offerings took place, and therefore Torsåker, 'Thor's Field'; and so on. Another example is Frösö, 'Freyr's Island', and other kinds of toponym linked to a word for the sacred, thus Helgö, 'Holy Island'. Most of the cultic name types are linked to several of the gods.

The theophoric names vary widely in distribution, with a tendency for specific gods to cluster in particular regions. There are no Ull names in Denmark, but they are thick in eastern central Sweden; Týr names are almost only found in Denmark; Thor places are common in Sweden and Norway; Odin names are rarely found west of the mountains; and so on. Some scholars have argued that this suggests different focal regions for the worship of these divinities, and this may be the case, but differences in customs do not necessarily reflect a shift in the beliefs that underpin them. For example, Jésus is a common man's name in Latin America, whereas one rarely meets a European called Jesus—but this does not mean there are no Catholics in Europe. This may be true of the Norse theophoric names as well.

As we have seen, the main official role at the assemblies was that of the lawspeaker, one of whose tasks it was to recite the laws from memory, thereby acting as guarantor for the legality of the proceedings. The same needs for accurate recall and documentation were answered in the runestone inscriptions. This raises obvious issues of oral record-keeping, and the relationship between the spoken and written word.

The question of literacy is an interesting one in relation to the Vikings. When we use the word today, we most often mean the general ability to read and write, with all that this implies for how we (or others) use these skills in daily life. For the Viking-Age

Scandinavians, however, it had a different sense, much more focussed on specific purposes and circumstances. There were certainly scripts available for use, in the form of runes. These developed much earlier in the Iron Age and are by no means a Viking invention, despite their popular associations. They had prototypes not only in Germanic Europe, but also a clear relationship to Latin.

Runes are deliberately angular signs, designed to be easily cut into hard surfaces, such as stone and especially wood. They were also sometimes painted. There are, broadly speaking, two forms of the Scandinavian runic alphabet, known as the older and younger futhark after the combination of its initial letters. The earlier series had twenty-four signs. The later version, which flourished in the Viking Age, was shorter at sixteen signs, but reused letters from its predecessor:

ᚠ	ᚢ	ᚦ	ᚨ	ᚱ	ᚴ	ᚼ	ᚾ	ᛁ	ᛅ	ᛋ	ᛏ	ᛒ	ᛘ	ᛚ	ᛦ
f	u	þ	ą	r	k	h	n	i	a	s	t	b	m	l	ʀ

Each rune could be used for multiple sounds, as expressed through the filter of different regional dialects. The meaning of the early inscriptions can be especially hard to determine due to changes in the language itself. The sixteen-rune futhark of the Vikings seems to have been a conscious innovation, adapted for the simplification and reduction of the older system—in short, a response to a need. Linguistic fidelity to the phonetic properties of speech was decidedly reduced, but the script was also more accessible, and probably lighter and faster to use. As one of the greatest runologists has emphasised, "It was easy for *the writer* to spell words in this new alphabet but not always easy for a reader to decide what was meant".

There are many local variants, and examples of personal touches (or confusions) brought by individual carvers. Beyond these, however, the younger futhark is found in two forms. The first was an 'ordinary' version of clear, rather formal and decorous characters.

In the Viking Age, these are the signs most often found on monuments such as the runestones, and they are also the ones best known today. The second types were the so-called short-twig runes (there are many alternative names) for rapid use—effectively a kind of runic shorthand—and these were the signs people of the Viking Age used in everyday communications. The runes also had individual names, some of them associated with qualities, although many of the supposed runic 'meanings' popularised today are from relatively modern times or sources of dubious provenance. Runic inscriptions often consist only of a listing of the signs in the futhark itself—either the complete sequence or just the initial letters. Dependent on context, these inscriptions could represent anything from writing practice to an act of ritual significance.

The mythology gives a sacred, mystical origin for the runes, which came to Odin in a trance of ecstatic fervour. After hanging on the World Tree for nine nights, his body pierced with his own holy spear—a literal self-sacrifice ("myself to myself", as he says)—the god has a vision. In the words of the *Sayings of the High One*:

> I took up the runes,
> screaming I took them,
> then I fell back from there.

This association of the runes with magic and religious energies has a long pedigree, and is very prominent in the popular imagination today. Runes were etched on the teeth of Odin's eight-legged horse, Sleipnir, and on the fingernails of the Norns, the spirit-women of fate. It is certain they *could* be used for sorcery and spells when carved into sticks or household items, inscribed on curse poles and the like, or even cut into flesh. They occur several times in this context in the sagas, in scenes of vivid power. One of the Eddic poems, the *Lay of Sigrdrifa*, includes a detailed list of runes for special purposes—for protection in battle, to ease childbirth ("they shall be cut on the palms and clasped on the joints"), to heal, and to travel safely over the sea ("on the prow they must be cut and on the rudder, and burnt into the oar with fire"). There are even 'speech-runes' to give eloquence in legal oratory, and 'mind-runes' for clear thinking. Similarly, they are also found on runic amulets and inscribed slips of metal excavated from graves and in the occupation layers of settlements, serving as prophylactics against harm and ill health, or as active agents of malice against others. Some runestones also preserve magical formulae or cryptic scripts that have to be deciphered before revealing (often rather basic) mythological content, such as the names of gods. However important, in the end they nonetheless represent a peripheral usage of something that at its core was simply script. Obviously, today's Roman letters have also been used for all these purposes and more, but they are not magical in themselves any more than the runes.

In all, many thousands of runic inscriptions have come down to us, mostly in the form of messages carefully engraved onto freestanding rocks—the famous 'runestones' mentioned here many times—in texts set within beautiful borders and other designs of writhing beasts and symbols. Originally painted in bright colours, sometimes the designs and inscriptions were instead cut directly into the smooth surfaces of natural boulders in the landscape. The earliest examples predate the Viking Age and extend as far back as the Migration Period in the fifth century, before increasing in number into the later Iron Age and exploding in popularity during the eleventh century (especially in central Sweden) with the introduction of Christianity. What they almost all have in common is that they are memorials to the dead—occasionally as actual grave markers but more usually set up in prominent places along roads and bridges where they would be most visible. A very few were erected by people in confident acts of self-promotion during their lifetimes. Runes are also found from late Roman times onward, scratched into the surface of metal objects such as bracteate discs, and as ownership marks on weapons and items of jewellery. This practice would continue into the Viking Age.

All this long suggested to scholars that runic literacy was a matter for the elites and a sign of status in itself. Only the relatively well-off could afford to commission a runic memorial to departed family members, and their public display was also a demonstration of social standing. However, this naturally raised the question of who could read them, unless the point was active exclusiveness through an emphasis that some could understand the angular signs whereas most could not. The argument for runes as an elite privilege received a decisive blow in the mid-twentieth century with discoveries in the Norwegian harbour towns of Bergen and Trondheim. Hundreds of small wooden slips, inscribed with runes, were found preserved intact in the waterlogged deposits of the dockside streets. They had served a fascinating variety of functions. Some were merchants' tallies, noting the contents of bags and boxes; there were shopping lists, love notes, name tags denoting ownership, vulgar attempts at humour, and much more. They speak to familiar concerns—"Sigmund owns this sack"; "Ingibjörg had sex with me when I was in Stavanger"; "Gyda tells you to go home" (this one has an attempt at an answer in a different hand, but it is an illegible, drunken scrawl); "Things are bad with me, partner. I did not get the beer or the fish. I want you to know this, and ask you not to press me"—in short, the raw stuff of everyday life, expressed in writing. Not everyone was literate, but a lot of people obviously were, perhaps even children. In more recent decades, similar finds have been made all over the Viking world.

Runestones were produced to order in workshops run by specialists. The actual runic letters were carved by masters, who proudly signed their names. Many inscriptions end with such signatures, and we can trace 'schools' of work across the regions of Scandinavia, even sometimes follow a carver moving around to undertake commissions. For example, Ärnfast and Åsmund were active in Uppland, as was Öpir, who today even has his own scholarly biography; many other carvers' names were recorded. Some of the inscriptions even detail the process, and occasionally we find not only the rune-carver named but also the whole team: one who shaped the stone itself, another who laid out the interlace patterns within which the runes would sit (we know from one such text that they were called something like 'snake-ribbons' or 'snake-eels', although the word is hard to parse), and a third who painted the colours. A beautiful and very elaborate stone from Gotland lists all the workmen in this way, but marvellously also includes some extra, shaky little runes that do not keep to the main design scheme but meander untidily off into what should be a blank space: "and Gairlaiv [did] some as well he can". One wonders if the team was on lunch break and came back to find their hapless assistant enthusiastically bashing away. Never mind—one could always fill it in and paint over, and it is not certain the patron ever knew.

Most of the later inscriptions, almost all Christian in tone, run along similar lines: a list of sponsors and their familial relationships, the name(s) of the one(s) commemorated, perhaps an associated place or profession. Some include short notices of where and/or how a person died—in battle, on an expedition, in the East, with Ingvar in command. In very rare cases, a poem is provided. Often there is a cross and a prayer for the soul. Sometimes the inscriptions mention a commemorative act, like the building of a causeway or the setting up of other monuments such as lines of standing stones or posts. Now and then it is possible to catch glimpses of a locality's history, and through groups of linked stones one can follow the generational fortunes of its leading families. The *Nordic Rune-Name Lexicon* (in Swedish) lists more than fifteen hundred personal names found on the stones—a trove of Viking-Age knowledge that brings us close to the people and their concerns.

The runestones seemed to fit the Vikings' needs for permanent records, while books clearly did not. This is an important point because there is no doubt they understood what these bound stacks of illustrated vellum were, how to make them, and how they worked. Writing Latin with a quill is really not so very far from carving runes with a knife. Nobody knows exactly why the

12. The runestone from Rök. Bearing the longest runic inscription from Scandinavia, this ninth-century stone in Swedish Östergötland preserves cryptic lists of fragmentary stories, bound up with mythological secrets and the commemoration of the dead. Photo: Bengt Olof Åradsson, Creative Commons.

Scandinavians rejected books and the distinctive literary culture that came with them, but it was probably because it gave them nothing they wanted. In the Viking mind, knowledge was a precarious thing. By the same token, the monopoly the Church possessed over both the teaching and employment of writing—holy books, with holy men to interpret them for you—was subtly different, and suffocating, to the Viking sense of what a script was.

The ultimate illustration is the early ninth-century runestone from Rök in Östergötland in Sweden, which carries the longest inscription in all of Scandinavia. A large piece of granite, completely covered in signs on every angle of its surface including the top (which is hard even to see), its long text contains allusions to several stories—deliberately teasing fragments that both presume prior knowledge in some readers and emphasise its exclusivity to others. There are riddles, word games, and references to the deep past of the Migration Period and the mythology of the carver's present. All this in turn relates to the families and concerns of the local area; above all, in its first line, the stone is a memorial set up by a man to his son. Not everyone could read the runes of the Rök stone, and not all those who could might get their deeper meanings, but—like all such memorials and other uses of the runic script—it was deeply socially embedded (and visible) in a way that the book cultures of the Continent never wished to be.

These same features can also be seen among the gods, especially in connection with Odin. It is always clear that his knowledge is bought at great price, and is also contingent: he knows, while others do not; he may pass on what he has learned, but equally may choose to withhold it. Odin teaches the runes (it is no accident that the word also means 'secrets') to the favoured. His spells and charms can be learned by a very few, while his advice is for all. There is an intimidation in this use of wisdom, information, and memory, and their translation into a particularly pure form of power that is nonetheless different from that of the lettered Christian priesthood.

While many people stayed at home, in and around the farm, and never really went anywhere, a fair proportion of the community were at least periodically on the move.

The landscape was crisscrossed by numerous routeways—unpaved dirt tracks and hollow ways, worn clear by constant use and following the terrain as they had done for centuries. People travelled by wagons or wooden carts, with solid wheels locked in place with pins, rolling down the lanes behind a pair of draught animals. Some of the horse gear was extraordinarily fine, with harness bows and distributors to keep the reins from getting tangled, all covered in interlace ornament, animals, and mythical beings; a few were even worked in gold. The wagons were made with detachable cargo bodies that could be loaded up separately and moved around. People rode on horseback (again, with a range of fantastically ornate harness) or simply walked, weaving their way along ridges, around the edges of high ground, or through passes, crossing rivers via fords or bridges where necessary. Some Viking-Age cemeteries still preserve the lines of the paths that traversed them, and similar folkways can still be traced across heaths, circumventing marshes, and through the rural landscape along the routes that have been most obviously sensible and least arduous for millennia prior to modern vehicular transport.

Since the earliest settlement of the region, Scandinavian societies have naturally been characterised by their intimate relationship with water. This connection manifested itself not only in the exploitation of rivers, lakes, and the sea as a means of subsistence and transport, but also in ritual expressions that included the deposition of material wealth, weapons, everyday objects, and even people in peat bogs and other watery contexts.

The importance of water to these communities, however, is most apparent during the Viking Age. A truly maritime culture, the Vikings' reliance on water governed many aspects of everyday life. Changes in sea level, for example, had important consequences throughout the Scandinavian Peninsula, with crucial and continuously evolving implications for communications and settlement. In contrast to the view of many people today, water was not perceived as a barrier to communication and transport but rather as a means of facilitating it. Island and coastal communities would not have been considered remote and inaccessible, but instead as being closely connected to each other through an extensive network of maritime routes.

A key concept is that of time-distance, through which transport is perceived not in terms of the measured physical separation of places but by the time it takes to travel between them. Accustomed as we are to viewing geography through maps (which digitisation has not changed), it can be hard to grasp that England and Norway can be 'closer' in perceptual terms via water than an overland journey of thirty or forty miles. Recent Danish experiments in the *Sea Stallion*, a replica longship based on an eleventh-century example excavated near Roskilde, have demonstrated that with favourable winds it is easily possible to travel from Denmark to the east coast of Britain in just a few days. Weather permitting, a return trip of a fortnight or so is by no means impossible, emphasising just how closely connected the communities of the North Sea were to one another. When these kinds of calculations are applied within Scandinavia, the ubiquity of marine transport becomes clear.

The rivers, fjords, lakes, and coastal channels of the North formed the primary means of movement in Viking-Age Scandinavia, but this travel did not have to be waterborne; a significant amount of journeying was made along the same routes in winter by means of ice transport. Sleds, sledges, and horse-drawn sleighs, including large examples made to accommodate several passengers, have been found in Viking-Age graves. Individuals used ice skates made of cattle bones bound to the shoes with hide thongs; the wearer moved forwards with the aid of a single stout pole much in the manner of a punt on a river. Both humans and animals used iron crampons, folded over and fixed to hooves or footwear. Skis were also used, single or double planks with tapered ends that were often richly carved and, again, propelled with a single pole.

Of all the images associated with the Viking Age, one of the most powerful is that of their ships, especially the great dragon-prowed oceangoing vessels that have been popularised in movies and other media. However, it should be remembered that they represented just one of many kinds of watercraft utilised throughout the period. The most common Viking-Age vessel of all was the humble dugout log boat, a simple craft that could have provided almost anyone access to marine transport and communication routes. Hollowed from a single tree trunk, these could vary in size from a one-person runabout to a larger boat up to ten metres in length and with room for both people and cargo. These vessels are often overlooked in the wider literature on the Viking Age, but their original presence in large numbers testifies to the maritime mobility of the time. Another relatively common vessel was the rowboat or skiff, owned perhaps by prosperous fisherfolk. The important farmers of a district might well have stretched to a sail-powered boat ten metres long or more.

Larger ships would have been commissioned either by major landowners and their families, consortia of merchants, or the nobility. They were long known only from images on coins, wall hangings such as the Bayeux Tapestry, and graffiti. It was not until the late nineteenth century that the post-medieval world got its first glimpse of the real thing. Damaged fragments of an eighteen-metre longship with twelve pairs of oars had been found at Tune in Norwegian Østfold in 1867. These were exciting, but hard to reconstruct; the vessel was later dated to around 910. However, in 1880 at Gokstad in Vestfold, the first of the great intact funeral ships was discovered. Seemingly matching the textual accounts of such burials, it contained an adult male, but most of the accompanying objects had been plundered in antiquity. The ship was twenty-four metres long and five metres amidships, with thirty-two oars. Its regular crew was perhaps forty, but it could carry seventy or so people if necessary. Dendrochronology has dated its construction to c. 890—the reign of Harald Finehair—and it was a true ocean-going warship.

In 1904, a third, even more spectacular ship burial was found at nearby Oseberg, in what is still the richest Viking-Age grave ever excavated. Buried c. 834 when it was a few decades old, the Oseberg ship was twenty-one and a half metres long and five metres across, with fifteen pairs of oars. Slightly smaller and older than Gokstad, it was perhaps an aristocratic barge for offshore use. Oseberg was the grave of two women, one in her eighties and the other some thirty years younger. We do not know which, if either, was the 'primary' burial, but the status of the grave is surely commensurate with royalty. Was this a queen and her maid, and if so, which was which? Or were they social equals? Radiocarbon indicates they died at or about the same time, and isotope studies show they enjoyed similarly rich diets. Recent DNA analyses have suggested the younger woman had quite close family descent from the Middle East, possibly Persia, a testament to the realities of long-distance travel and contact, and an important reminder that—to put it mildly—not everyone in the North was blond-haired and blue-eyed. Both the Gokstad and Oseberg ship funerals were accompanied by lavish animal sacrifices.

Throughout the twentieth century, the corpus of rediscovered Viking ships, mostly preserved only as rivets after the timbers had decayed or burnt, grew exponentially. They include the boat burial fields of Swedish Uppland—initially at Vendel and Valsgärde—but these were joined by comparable graves from Ultuna, Tuna Alsike and Tuna Badelunda, Arboga, and many more, including Gamla Uppsala itself. Boat graves have also been found in the territory of the Götar, in south-western Sweden, showing it was a pan-cultural rite.

In a different context again, in 1962 an innovative coffer-dam excavation revealed five ships that had been deliberately scuttled in the eleventh century to form part of a sunken blockade controlling access to the Roskilde fjord in Denmark. They proved to be of types that had not been seen before in the archaeology, but which expanded the typology of Viking shipping in ways that correlated well with the written sources: a small warship of the *snekkja* type; a bigger, thirty-metre-long war vessel with a draught of only one metre and a crew of up to eighty; and three cargo ships of different sizes, two of them for offshore use and journeys in coastal waters and the third a deep-sea trading vessel of the type known as a *knarr*. The latter was the sort of ship that carried settlers across the North Atlantic—less well-known than the beautiful longships but, in truth, the workhorses of Viking-Age maritime power. Several

13. A Viking workhorse. The remains of the Skuldelev 1 ship, excavated from Roskilde fjord in Denmark but originally made in western Norway c. 1030. A vessel of the *knarr* type, this was the mainstay of Viking-Age shipping, used for open sea voyages and cargo. Photo: Casiopeia, Creative Commons.

other large cargo ships have since been found at Klåstad in Norway, Hedeby in Denmark, and Äskekärr in Sweden.

Work has continued in the same area by the Roskilde Viking Ship Museum that was established to house the five excavated vessels, and has uncovered still more ships, including the largest longship ever found—thirty-two metres long, with a single-watch crew of eighty that could have been doubled for war. Dating to the early eleventh century, it is of the dimensions the sagas give for the highest rank of royal warships.

In Denmark there are also dramatic ship graves from Ladby, Hedeby, and other sites; in Norway numerous examples have been found at Borre, Avaldsnes, and at several locations along the coast. There are now small Viking boat burials from the Orkneys, mainland Scotland, and the Isle of Man, as well as a spectacular example from the Île de Groix, a tiny island off the Breton coast. Most recently, two unprecedented mass graves in boats were found at Salme on the Estonian island of Saaremaa. Dating to c. 750, the larger of the two vessels provides the first conclusive evidence for the use of the sail in Scandinavia; its point of origin seems to have been central Sweden—the same region as the Uppland burials and the heart of the then-emerging Svear kingdom.

The sheer number of remains, together with the organic survival of the Vestfold vessels, provides many clues as to the evolution of Viking ships. The Salme find demonstrates that sailed warships were available to the Scandinavians by at least 750, and that they presumably complemented the rowed vessels found in the Uppland boat graves. Smaller rowing boats like Salme I, perhaps also with the possibility to step a mast, acted as tenders and ancillary vessels. They could certainly accompany the bigger ships into the waters of the Baltic. As one maritime archaeologist has suggested, it is possible that the 'late' introduction of the sail may have actually been just another manifestation of the rising aristocracies in pre-Viking Scandinavia—one more component in their toolkit of dominance. If this was the case, the demonstrable command of sail-driven vessels can be seen as part of the architecture of power no less than the great halls and the monumental grave mounds. Like them, the sail filled a need, and required special technologies that were highly visible both in their application and in the resources needed to create them.

In the late eighth century, it seems that ships became broader and roomier—was this to facilitate oceangoing voyages (especially across the North Sea) rather than the more regional travels of the Baltic that had been the norm until that time? The fluvial waterways of western Europe had not been closed to earlier Scandinavian ships, but the minimal tides of the Baltic would certainly have been more manageable.

Over the course of the ninth and tenth centuries, there was a massive acceleration in the development of shipping technology, in the areas of efficiency, capability, and diversification. Whereas the broader ships of the early Viking Age seem to have been multipurpose, capable of transporting both crews and cargo, from the late 800s, there is evidence of specialised vessels ranging from offshore patrol boats to the equivalent of royal yachts, deep-sea cargo haulers, fishing smacks, and—of course—a range of slim, predatory warships of different sizes. The latter varied from craft suited to defence or pirating along the coasts and fjords, to ocean-going longships designed for major raiding expeditions and real marine warfare. Given these variations in size and function, Viking vessels must have held a crew of anything from a single person to well over a hundred, and in the large warships the complement of crew could be enlarged for short-range combat missions.

Archaeology and visual images provide striking details. Several weather vanes made of gilded copper alloy and designed to be fixed to a ship's prow or mast have been found. Decorated with the 'great beast' typical of the eleventh century, they also have rows of holes from which ribbons would have fluttered in the breeze. One of them even has dents apparently caused by projectiles. An unusual carved bone from Bergen shows the prows of an entire fleet, resting at anchor side by side, and on some of the stems such vanes can be seen. The strakes of ships—the long, horizontal planks of the hull—may have been painted in alternating colours (seen on textiles), and the sails may have been chequered or sewn with the symbols of their captains.

A handful of figureheads have been found dating to the early Iron Age, but none so far is known from the Viking Age itself. However, there are several carved and engraved depictions of such things—dragons' heads and other animals—that extend to a curling tail at the stern. On the Oseberg ship, both stem and stern terminate in the coils of a carved snake, an integral part of the vessel that could not be removed. The Ladby and Groix ships, and perhaps some of the Valsgärde boats, contained a number of iron spirals that match the manes of dragon-figures depicted on metal dress-pins from Birka and other sites; it seems these ships also had dragon prows, which were carved in wood but with metal details picked out.

What resources were needed to sustain this level of maritime power? The obvious need was timber, which would have been grown in managed woodland over many years, with a corresponding requirement of stewardship and forestry skills. Then there was the iron for the rivets and tools, involving a multistage process of resource procurement and manufacture. Among the organic materials, one must remember the rigging and fittings, all the wooden bailers and pins and clamps, the oars and their rowlock covers—in short, the complete equipment of a seagoing vessel. The textile requirements would have included foul-weather clothing for the crew, and something to change into. Above all, of course, the sails. The commitment of time and labour was immense, and was matched by the organisation and investment capacity required to set them in motion. Making a ship and everything it needed was a very serious and expensive undertaking indeed. Building a fleet was an industry.

Ships also had to be maintained once launched. To take just one example, vessels of all kinds needed tar to insulate their hulls and waterproof the woollen sails. The servicing of watercraft would have been a constant feature of dockside activity. Around the jetties at Birka and Hedeby, in particular, archaeologists have found dozens of broken-off brushes with heads of rags and textiles, thickly coated with the tar into which they were presumably dipped just before a careless stroke snapped the shaft and sent it all into the water, where they would be discovered a thousand years later.

Our final image of Viking-Age ships can be a dimmer one, and again, a snapshot of the past that is not usually considered. In the *Saga of Magnús Barelegs*, part of Snorri's *Heimskringla* set in the eleventh century, one can read of the royal ships drawn up in Trondheim fjord:

In spring, near Candlemas, King Magnús set out at dead of night, and stood out with his ships tented and with lights under them [the tents], and sailed to Hefring Head, where they stayed the night, and there made great fires up on the land.

Imagine a Viking fleet riding at anchor for the night, its deck canopies illuminated from within, the water glowing with soft points of light like an Asian river festival.

Let's leave them there in the fjord, and move to different arenas for the performance of power, actually into other worlds—those of the gods and other beings, and their many disturbing points of contact with the realm of the living.

7

MEETING THE OTHERS

THE CONCEPT OF RELIGION, IN the sense that we tend to mean it today, was something that a Viking-Age person might have had difficulty in grasping. This was also one of the tensions between the traditional spiritualities of Scandinavia and the book-based faiths they encountered in the form of Christianity and Islam. The distinction between belief and knowledge is significant for the Vikings' relations with the invisible population with whom they shared their world. However, both these attitudes to the 'other' are also somewhat abstract—they are located in the mind, not in the tangible realm of action and practice.

Put another way, it is one thing to understand how the Vikings thought about their gods and all the other (super)natural beings of the nine worlds that made up the Norse cosmos, but what did they *do* about it? To take examples from some familiar world faiths today, a pious Christian, Muslim, or Jew would be entirely comfortable with the notion of a life structured by religious observance, the enactment of rituals (including prayer), and regular visits to holy buildings, be they churches, mosques, or synagogues. Did the Vikings have an equivalent to this, and if so, what was it?

To navigate this numinous landscape of religious practice is to encounter a world of special places dedicated to communication with the powers. These could be buildings, settings of stone, strange platforms raised on islands in the marshes—or even just groves of trees or fields, their otherness manifested in ways that were not immediately visible. They were sites of sacrifice, of giving up precious objects, or blood, or time, to curry favour with the beings who could bestow it.

These places and rituals could be activated in different ways at various points in the life course, and also by different sorts of intermediaries between everyday folk and the Others. The Vikings had ritual specialists (for want of a better word) who devoted themselves to opening very particular channels of communication—with the gods in general, or one god in particular; with the elves; with the *dísir*; and more. They also had many different kinds of sorcery and magic—and people to practise them—for more personal ends that could be achieved in negotiation with things beyond the human.

For the Vikings, meeting the Others was probably an uncertain or unsettling experience, but it was not an unfamiliar one. In order to understand them, these are encounters we too must entertain.

The closest equivalent to 'religion' found in Old Norse is *forn siðr*, 'the old ways', explicitly contrasting with the new ones brought by the agency of the later Christian kings. However, this is not a formal term for something discrete, but more a way of distinguishing something from its opposite. What did these old ways really entail? Regardless of sectarian differences, many of the world faiths today are at least to some degree religions of the book (in the broadest sense of sacred writings), with orthodoxies and more-or-less rigid rules of behaviour that usually embody concepts of obedience and worship. The latter is important because it also implies unreserved approval of the god(s). The Vikings would have recognised none of this. What we would now isolate as religion was then simply another dimension of daily life, inextricably bound up with every other aspect of existence. This included the gods themselves, who were simply *there* as an unchanging part of the worlds. Granted, one might need to propitiate them to keep on their good side (and on their terms), but you did not have to like them in the process.

A concept that I find perfectly captures the essence of Norse spirituality is that of a 'religiolect'. Just as a dialect encodes a local variant of speech, this term does the same for religion, combining belief and practice in a discrete package that could be activated in particular places or social situations. Specific religiolects might be linked to an ethnic group, the followers of an individual, or a set of contextual circumstances in which specific kinds of spiritual expression were manifested or required. Thus, the main specialist in this field talks of religiolects of the hall, of the farm, of islands, of the coast. One can imagine something similar connected to war, fertility, textile work, or even the linear, time-limited activity-world of long-distance traders. To take a Swedish ethnic example, the Svear and the Götar peoples were probably also different in this respect, and each king's retinue probably had its own codes of ritual behaviour.

A religiolect constitutes difference not only in ritual practices, but also potentially in their underlying ethics and dogma. These variations also cut across other aspects of society, including status or sex, the outdoors or the domestic space, and so on. Religiolects are not necessarily exclusive, but can also be—as the term implies—a means of communication. Perhaps they were in play at the frontiers of belief, for example between the Norse and the Sámi. They capture the core of diversity in the Viking mental landscape.

There is a curious sense in which the very notion of a Norse religion may actually be in part a Christian product. This seems contradictory at first, but has parallels in other cultures where incoming missionaries attempted to supplant traditional beliefs with a regulated church. Something codified, organised, and effectively systemic (everything Norse belief was not) is much easier to oppose, because it is a coherent target and might be suppressed as a single entity. And if this was not already there, then it could be formed in that image. This was the beginning of the process that eventually turned the living, organic story-world of the North into 'the Norse myths'—a kind of pagan scripture that never actually existed. It does not help that the Christians also seem to have misunderstood much of what they encountered and, in turn, incorporated their misconceptions into the retrospective pagan orthodoxy they created.

To truly understand the spiritual universe of the Viking Age, it is necessary to dig beneath those later accretions to reach the original strata of belief and practice.

It can be difficult to approach a spiritual view of things that does not prioritise god(s). Many Christians today still acknowledge saints and their powers of intercession, the very pious might believe in angels as literal truth, and a minority of those especially well versed in the texts might go further to the many other inhabitants of heaven (and the other place) that are in part a product of complicated medieval ecclesiastical hierarchies. However, *none* of these believers would place any other beings more prominently in human affairs than God.

The Vikings did not ignore their gods, by any means, and they certainly had rituals of acknowledgement and need, 'coming to terms' with them. This could be an ad hoc and private process that depended on the individual, like saying a silent prayer. At the level of the body politic, however, there were also 'cultic structures' (the neutral-sounding term archaeologists use to avoid saying 'temple') where such rites were enacted, and ritual specialists to assist. Again, terminology is found wanting because these men and women— especially women—were not 'priests' but instead prominent members of the community whose abilities or connections meant they took on roles as spiritual intermediaries in addition to, or because of, their general social standing.

The 'new elites', whose rise to power in the fifth and sixth centuries in part began the long trajectory of social change that culminated in the Viking Age, had a clearly articulated ideology that served to legitimise their position. One key component of this was their claim of genealogical descent from Odin, Freyr, and the rest. The divine right of kings used to be a literal notion, and it was not confined to Christian monarchs. At the highest level, these sacral kings were themselves agents in the two-way communications with the other worlds, and in some circumstances might personally take on transubstantiated aspects of the gods. In times of dire need and popular unrest—after a succession of failed harvests, for example—the kings might also find themselves being sacrificed by the popular assemblies, given as offerings to their erstwhile patrons in Asgard.

In everyday life, however, people were more concerned with getting along with the invisible population of spirits and nature-beings. All these creatures also required placation, even a form of spiritual bribery. These were transactional, pragmatic relations enacted in a numinous landscape of otherworldly power through which every Viking-Age person had to make their way. The special cultic buildings and constructions for the gods could also serve as portals of access to this teeming world, but there were special festivals dedicated to their service (such as the *álfa-* and *dísablót*), as well as many rituals held in the open air. This, of course, was where these beings lived, and at times it was only polite to come to them.

What did these cult sites look like, and what happened inside them? The written sources preserve the term *hörgr*, which seems to describe small buildings or enclosures where rituals were performed to the gods. Excavations over the years at high-status manorial residences—the great hall complexes—have several times revealed square structures adjacent to the main building and often bounded by a fence. They are clearly not domestic dwellings, and they are often either very clean (and thus obviously kept that way) or else saturated with buried offerings of various kinds. They have been found in Denmark, Norway, and Sweden, and the list of sites is growing all the time. The spatial proximity of these special buildings to the great halls, inside the overall site boundary but also within their own enclosures, almost suggests a function as 'private chapels' of a kind more familiar from the Christian aristocracies. This does not mean the populace had nowhere to commune with the powers, but it would serve to reinforce the militarised hierarchies on which these societies were built, and also to emphasise the rulers' claims of a personal relationship with the gods—the lord needs to talk with All-Father *alone*.

One of these sites is truly extraordinary, not least for its longevity of occupation and degree of preservation. At Uppåkra, in the southern Swedish province of Skåne (which in the Viking Age was part of Denmark), a massive settlement has been excavated that seems to have been a proto-urban power centre and an immediate precursor to what would later become Lund (itself a sacral place-name). Alongside the halls and other structures was a rectangular building that was very cramped inside but also very tall—its roof-bearing interior posts extended for metres into the ground and were essentially tree trunks. The structure almost certainly had either a second floor or perhaps a tower-like projection in the centre, reminiscent of the multiple tiers of the Christian stave churches that still survive in Norway (this may not be coincidental). It had three doors, a functionally unnecessary number that implies they had different purposes or social restrictions; one of them also had a porch-like extension.

The roof-posts and walls of the Uppåkra building were apparently covered in gold foils; more than two hundred of them were found in the postholes and along the wall lines. They would have glittered in the dark, catching the light of the massive central fireplace. It would have been very hot. Inside the main room an iron 'oath-ring' was found, known from written sources as the object on which the most sacred vows were sworn; a second example was recovered outside the building. Buried in the floor was a glass bowl imported from the Black Sea, fragments of several more, and many pieces of gold objects and jewellery, all apparently deposited as offerings during the lifetime of the building. Next to the hearth was a bronze and silver beaker bound in bands of decorated gold—an object of great ritual power. Not only were all these things left there when the structure was finally abandoned, but nobody ever subsequently dared to steal them. The Uppåkra 'temple' (for once the word may be justified) was flanked to the north and south by weapon offerings—mainly broken spears and shields—and other sacrificial deposits that included human remains. Situated at the core of the Uppåkra complex, in a sense functioning also as a reception room like the central chamber of the hall, the cult building had an extraordinary lifespan: its first construction phases date to the third century CE, it went through at least six rebuilds on the same spot, and then continued in use until the Viking Age.

Some ostensibly secular buildings also seem to have had religious purposes, especially the great halls of the leading families. There is now a growing consensus that major landowners and local chieftains may themselves have played a role in cultic ritual, and that the feasting halls of their estates could on occasion host sacrifices and other ceremonies. The Old Norse word for such places was *hof*, a term that in the modern Scandinavian languages has come to mean a royal court. We find it in Viking-Age place-names such as Hofstaðir in Iceland, where evidence was found for animal offerings. This integration of the hall and 'temple' functions seems to have become the norm during the Viking period, as the formerly separated 'private chapels' effectively merged with the residences of the elites.

It may have been something like these buildings, combined with the sheer visual force of Uppåkra, that Adam of Bremen had in mind when he wrote what has become one of the most famous descriptions of the Viking Age. This is the same Adam who wrote of polygyny among the Scandinavians, but his gift to Viking scholars rests largely on another passage in the same work. Adam was a cleric in the service of Archbishop Adalbert of Hamburg; around 1070, while working at the monastery of Bremen in northern Germany, he compiled an official history of the archdiocese, which included its missionary activities in the North. He had many sources, but one of them was the Danish king Svein Ástríðarsson, who passed on first-hand details. It is uncertain to what degree he, or Adam, had a Christian agenda of anti-pagan propaganda. The account includes a lengthy description of the great temple at Uppsala, a huge building hung about with golden chains and containing wooden idols:

> That folk [the Svear] has a very famous temple called Ubsola, situated not far from the city of Sictona. In this temple, entirely decked out in gold, the people worship the statues of three gods in such wise that the mightiest of them, Thor, occupies a throne in the middle of the chamber; Wodan and Fricco have places on either side. The significance of these gods is as follows: Thor, they say, presides over the air, which governs the thunder and lightning, the winds and rains, fair weather and crops. The other, Wodan—that is, the Furious—carries on war and imparts to man strength against his enemies. The third is Fricco, who bestows peace and pleasure on mortals. His likeness, too, they fashion with an immense phallus. But Wodan they chisel armed, as our people are wont to represent Mars. Thor with his sceptre apparently resembles Jove. The people also worship heroes made gods, whom they endow with immortality because of their remarkable exploits, as one reads in the *Vita* of Saint Ansgar they did in the case of King Eric.

He also includes a detail relating to the notion of the halls as temples, in that the Latin word he uses for the room where the rituals took place is *triclinium*, ordinarily the term for the dining chamber of a house—which may have been precisely what he meant.

It is a lengthy treatment in which he also goes on to detail an evergreen tree with great spreading branches, divinatory human sacrifice in a holy well, and a sacred grove. Adam also describes the ritual calendar of Uppsala and a natural 'theatre' surrounded by 'mountains' where the rites were held. The latter may correlate to the plain enclosed by the sweeping curve of the cemetery ridge on which the royal burial mounds were raised—not quite mountains, but nonetheless towering over the surroundings. Adam also mentions that all this was accompanied by festivities so obscene that "it is best to pass over them in silence" (damn).

An entire scholarly industry has tried to parse Adam's text over the years, with varying degrees of credulity and dismissal, but in recent decades the parallels between what he describes and archaeologists' discoveries are growing ever closer. Even the rituals that so worried him seem remarkably like the erotic magic and sexual celebrations that attend gods such as Freyja and Freyr, which would have been enough to send any Christian off to confession. The current feeling is that his account can be trusted in broad terms, although some scholars still strongly disagree. Adam's description also has similarities with Thietmar of Merseburg's account of tenth-century blood sacrifices on an even larger scale at Lejre, the Danish counterpart to Uppsala. These were not isolated phenomena.

In the Old Norse texts, we also find the *vé*, a kind of sanctuary encountered in place-names that appears to have left archaeological traces. At Lilla Ullevi (the 'Little *vé* of Ull') in Swedish Uppland, a rectangular, curbed packing of stones has been found with two linear stone projections that appear to form a kind of forecourt, the whole situated at the edge of a prominent hill. There is evidence for post-built platforms and standing pillars around it, making a further line of enclosure and separation. Around these structures were ritual depositions of buried objects—one assumes gifts to the powers—in the form of weapons, strike-a-lights, and more than sixty amulet rings. These offerings appear to have been made at the very start of the Viking period, with activities on the site stretching back at least a century before that.

A second such Swedish sanctuary has been excavated at Götavi (the 'Gods' *vé*') in Närke, with even more remarkable features.

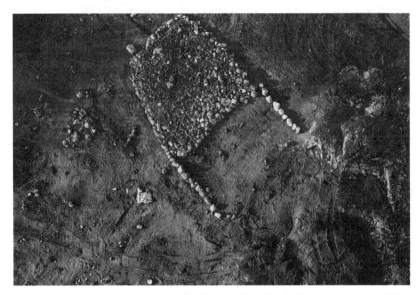

14. Meeting the gods. The open-air ritual site at Lilla Ullevi, Uppland, Sweden. Offerings were dug down into the ground, both in front of the stone platform and around its sides; posts stood beside it. A typically enigmatic 'cult site' from the late Iron Age. Photo by Max Marcus / Hawkeye, used by kind permission.

The name also implies it had a wider spiritual clientele than the sites named after only a single deity—perhaps, like the Pantheon in Rome, a 'temple' of all the Aesir? In the middle of an open and rather marshy plain, nine parallel lines of substantial stone packings had been laid out and then buried beneath a layer of clay. The resulting rectangular construction appears to have had a slightly bowl-shaped depression at the centre and been bounded by a fence. Chemical analyses show that a great deal of blood had been spilled within the enclosure, especially near one end, where great posts had been erected. A connection to animal (and perhaps human) sacrifice seems clear. Around the perimeter of the clay platform, over a long period of time, many fires had been lit. Whatever exactly happened inside the enclosure would have been screened by a wall of smoke, at the same time as the ongoing rituals would have been visible from a considerable distance. This apparent intention to separate the 'initiated' (or whatever one should call them) from a wider group is also reflected in the site's situation, as the clay platform would have essentially formed an island in the boggy ground—not a true swamp, by any means, but nonetheless terrain treacherous enough to make access difficult, a place to carefully watch one's feet.

Unlike Lilla Ullevi, the sanctuary at Götavi is astonishingly late in date, with indications that it was still in use during the eleventh century when, for example, Denmark had already been Christian for more than a century. This would seem to bear out the many literary traditions (and Adam of Bremen) depicting Sweden as resistant to Christian influence for much longer than the rest of Scandinavia.

The nine stone packings at Götavi also raise an important and recurring component of the Viking mind: the sacred number. Nine—and its square root, three—appears numerous times in the mythological tales of the Norse. The sea-deities Aegir and Rán have nine daughters, the spirits of the waves; Heimdall has nine mothers; the giant Baugi has nine thralls; the beautiful Menglod has nine attendants, while her mother, Gróa, protects her with nine charms; Odin has eighteen spells—twice nine; Thrivaldi, another giant who is slain by Thor, has nine heads. Freyr waits for his lover and later wife, Gerthr, for nine nights, the same length of time that Odin hangs on the tree in self-sacrifice, and sweats between the fires in *Grímnir's Sayings*, and makes his long ride to Hel on Sleipnir. In Valhöll, on every ninth night eight rings drop from the great gold ring, Draupnir (thus making nine in all), the source of Odin's wealth. The Muspell princess Laegjárn has a chest that must be closed with nine locks, one by one. The list goes on and on, and is replicated in the human world of Midgard: according to Adam, the great sacrifices at Uppsala last for nine days and are held every nine years, and nine creatures of each kind are killed. (In assessing the veracity of Adam's text, by the way, one might ask how he could have invented just *that* little detail to fit so well with a wider picture he could not have known about.)

And of course, there are nine worlds, and nine layers of Hel, nine leagues under the earth. At the end, at the Ragnarök, the mortally wounded Thor will take nine great paces into death.

Inside all these buildings and enclosures, there must have been a range of ritual activities going on, but central to them all was the *blót*, a term often translated as 'offering' but which meant much more than sacrifice. Closer in nature to a gift, the *blót* was usually an act of killing in which animals (and sometimes humans) were ritually slain and their blood poured into bowls or onto stones. Twigs were dipped in the liquid, and a red spray shaken over onlookers and buildings alike.

The scale of the rites depended on the status of those participating and officiating. At the northern Icelandic temple-hall of Hofstaðir, oxen were decapitated in regular seasonal rituals over many years, and their skulls fixed to the walls of the building—a permanent, visible record of the respectful compact between the dwellers in the hall and the powers around them. Osteological analyses of the bone trauma revealed the animals had been dispatched with sword or axe blows to the neck, striking from the side as the beasts were immobilised by a second person. The method was calculated to produce a great arc of arterial blood—a graphically violent demonstration of commitment, something to be witnessed. The killing of birds, in particular, also seems to have been a common feature of Norse rituals, and there is a suggestion that their deaths functioned as a means of opening a path between the worlds, especially for the dead.

At other sites, deposits of material clearly built up over time, as objects were repeatedly scattered or buried in and around the cultic structures. Examples include not only the weapons and amulet rings mentioned above, but also other objects such as ice crampons (perhaps a prayer for a smooth winter journey), spreads of broken beads, and metalworking slag. It is also clear that food was consumed at these ceremonies—presumably in ritual feasts—and the leftovers sometimes strewn about.

Beyond these cultic buildings and sanctuaries, there is also ample evidence for rituals conducted in the open air and at natural places of sacred significance. Offerings were made in bogs and other watery areas such as marshes and tidal zones. Weapons were deposited in rivers or streams, and often at boundaries—behaviour that has also been observed in the Vikings' overseas colonies. Rings and other costly metalwork were, by contrast, thrown into still water, into lakes and ponds, given to the beings that dwelled under the surface.

In places that were neither land nor water, and thus a kind of liminal space 'betwixt and between', the Vikings built special structures on which to hold their sacrifices. Variants included platforms made of fire-cracked stone or wood, surrounded by the remains of ritual feasts. The animals have been found covered with reeds and rushes, and with bundles of flax. Offerings on the platforms most commonly include cattle, but also pigs, dogs, and especially horses. Most of them were killed with blows to the head, in some cases even with stone axes that date from the Neolithic, made thousands of years before the Vikings. Tools like these were evidently picked up in the fields by Viking-Age people just as they are still found in the countryside today, and there is folklore connecting them with the god Thor. Seeing them as 'thunderbolts', the Vikings may have believed these ancient stone weapons contained special powers, making them an especially charged instrument of sacrifice.

Not all parts of the carcases were used, especially of the horses. In most cases, only the crania and the outer extremities have been found, suggesting these were in fact hides with the head and hooves attached. There are textual descriptions of these grisly artefacts being set up on scaffolds at the edge of sacrificial areas, and it seems that some of the platforms—such as that from Bokaren in Uppland province, Sweden—were ringed by them. On other platforms, ceramic vessels have been found with a hole cut out of the base. Anything poured or placed into these vessels, which stood upright on the inundated timbers, would slowly disappear, melting away as if being consumed by the powers of the water—proof of the offerings' acceptance.

Bog sacrifices had been a constant in Scandinavia from late Bronze Age times onwards, with weapons, items of equipment, precious metalwork, vehicles, and even whole ships deposited in the waters. The people of the Viking Age were thus continuing a long tradition, which significantly had always included the offering of humans. Some people were clearly ritually killed to accompany others in death. However, blood offerings could also be made outside the context of funerals, and it is relatively common to find human remains alongside the bodies of animals that had been given to the gods or other supernatural forces. In Sweden, many of the places where archaeologists have found human sacrifices also reappear in much later folklore and are often associated with a kind of water sprite called the Näcken. This being usually appeared either as a naked man, or sometimes a white horse with unnervingly human eyes, singing or playing a fiddle in a manner that compelled the listener to draw close. Unless appropriate offerings were made, the unlucky visitor would be drawn beneath the water by the Näcken, never to be seen again. Is this a dim memory of those Viking-Age blood rituals, where some of those who came to the place would remain there forever?

Wooden figures of vaguely human form were also set up in the marshes, either as idols or perhaps as proxies for actual people, a kind of permanent sacrifice. These objects have been excavated from the bogs in some numbers and can be very large, taller than humans (perhaps appropriately, if they really are gods). They were often made from trees chosen for some quirk of natural growth in the wood that could be utilised to suggest anatomical detail—such as the male figure on which a jutting branch forms a huge penis. They can even be seen in the poetry. In the *Sayings of the High One*,

Odin is wandering the roads in his outcast persona and makes a curious observation:

> My clothes I gave along the way
> to two wooden men;
> champions they thought themselves
> when they had clothing,
> the naked man is ashamed.

Some of the most dramatic and public sacrificial sites are the sacred groves, the same as appear in the place-names. Adam of Bremen mentions one as part of his account of the Uppsala rituals, a cluster of "divine" trees in which some seventy-two bodies of male animals (nine of each)—including men and large beasts such as stallions—were suspended and left to rot. Similar scenes are depicted on the Gotland picture-stones and on the Viking-Age tapestries from Oseberg. It may not be coincidental that several of Odin's names refer to him as the god of the gallows, and that some of the myths relate how he could wake the hanging dead and interrogate them about the future. Divination played a major part in Viking ritual, and this too may be connected with the sacrificial groves.

The missionaries viewed such displays with particular opprobrium. The Christian cultures of Europe thought it normal to put people to death in a variety of foul and public ways, and yet recoiled in atavistic horror from a tree of hanging animal corpses.

These sites are very hard to trace through archaeology, but something of this kind has remarkably survived at Frösö (the same 'Freyr's Island' we encountered earlier as a place-name) in northern Sweden. When alterations being carried out inside the medieval church required the removal of the floor, directly beneath the altar archaeologists found the well-preserved stump of a birch tree, surrounded by hundreds of bone fragments. Radiocarbon analysis has shown that the tree was cut down in the late eleventh century—in other words, about the time the first wooden church was erected (and close to the date of Adam of Bremen's tale of the Uppsala grove). The bone deposits date from the tenth century, thus dating the activities around the tree firmly to the Viking Age.

The bones represented substantial numbers of animals of several species, and presumably had been offered there over many years—perhaps the bodies were even hung from the branches. In all, the remains of eleven pigs, two cows, and five sheep or goats were found, plus the heads of six elks (the North American moose) and two stags, together with the complete carcasses of five bears. It must have been an extraordinary sight. Body parts from squirrels, reindeer, horses, and dogs also littered the ground. In a disturbing correlation with the texts, the assemblage included human bones— people were among the offerings at Freyr's tree. Recent research on the animal remains from Frösö has shown how the killings were carried out seasonally, especially in the spring, which clearly suggests the rituals there may have been part of a *vårblót*, or spring sacrifice. Some of the pigs (Freyr's sacred animal) were also selected for the unusual length and ferocity of their tusks—once again, the visual spectacle was important.

The tree was certainly meant to be seen, as it was situated at the highest point of the island, with views over the lakes and mountains. The place-name of this spot is also telling: Hov, in other words *hof*, the word for the temple-halls. Similarly, it is no accident that the Christians built their church on this precise site (presumably they had the tree felled, as well), even down to constructing the altar over the stump. Specialists often speak of syncretic religion—the fusion of different traditions or faiths in an easing of transition—but it is rare to find such a thing in the archaeology, although here one might better read the evidence as indicative of violent appropriation. As in other similar situations, it is clear the Christians did not always directly destroy the spiritual customs of the North, but instead tried to convince their adherents that they were a poorly realised precursor of the new faith—that conversion required a movement, an adjustment, not a total rejection of who they were.

The world of sorcery looms large in Viking spirituality, as do the women and *ergi* men who practised it. Their role in Norse life and thought was a crucial one, but it has been much overlooked. More so than those around them, these special women and men were familiar with the sutures of the world. They knew the places where different aspects of reality overlapped, and also the gaps sometimes left between. In their difference from others, these workers of magic seem to have been forced to the edges of society—but it was also there that they found their power. There is a sense in which they straddled the rivers between the realms, leaving footprints on both banks.

It was through the medium of sorcery, not cult, that most of the conversations with the powers were conducted. Much ink has been spilled in vain attempts to classify or define Norse magic, which overlooks the fact that its practitioners probably never really did so, and therefore neither should we. At its simplest, sorcery was a means, or a method, a set of mechanisms by which people tried to influence or compel the Others to do their bidding. In the Viking Age, this was a field of behaviour that lay within the realm of ordinary communities rather than any kind of priestly or royal officialdom.

The evidence for sorcery in the Viking Age is difficult to evaluate, as it comes overwhelmingly from the medieval sagas and poems, but on the other hand these are utterly saturated in magic. To a greater or lesser extent, it appears in almost every story, often in the most vivid terms. Thus, in an episode from the *Saga of the Völsungs* when sorcery was unleashed, we read how "the air and the paths were alive with magic"—it captures the weird power of the Old Norse, the crackling tension of the Other World at its intersection with our own. None of this is direct reportage or anything like it, of course, but it is striking how the literary world of

Scandinavian magic is decidedly *not* a replica of medieval European witchcraft as it was perceived at the time of the saga-writers. In fact, the material culture depicted in the sagas is generally consistent with the Viking-Age world they describe, not the medieval one of their scribal production, arguing strongly for at least a basis in historical circumstances and oral memory.

Another aspect of sorcery that comes through in the sources is its variety. There were different forms of magic—some relatively well defined, others as vague as the terms we use today. These were in turn performed by a huge array of practitioners, some of whom were very specialised indeed.

The highest, most terrible magic—the kind that fell within the skill set of Odin and Freyja (who taught it to him)—was *seithr*. It could be used to see the future, predict fate, improve the harvest, or fill a fjord with fish. *Seithr* could both heal and harm. It could bring good or bad fortune. One could use it to talk with the dead. It could be employed to seduce, charm, or reduce a person to sexual submission. *Seithr* could confuse and distract at a fatal moment, or fog the mind with terror. It could strengthen the limbs or disable them, give someone godlike dexterity, or reduce them to stumbling uselessness. It could make weapons unbreakable or brittle as ice. *Seithr* could injure, it could kill, and with it one could raise the slain. It was the magic of the battlefield, the farm, the field, the body and bedroom, and the mind. There was nothing coincidental about its associations with the divinities of war, sex, and intellect.

There was also *galdr*, a high-pitched singing that, it has been argued, survives to a degree in the cattle-calls that are among the staples of Nordic folk music. Still another magic, *gandr*, was often used by men, and there were many other forms of sorcery, with a reasonably differentiated terminology in Old Norse that we simply cannot translate. All of them could be used singly or in combination, including with *seithr*, to get the job done. Imagine a toolkit full of magical implements selected, in turn, for each stage of a task.

15. Death of a sorceress. Chamber grave Bj. 660 from Birka, Sweden; the burial of a possible worker of spells, identified as such by her iron staff and necklace of amulets. Reconstruction by Þórhallur Þráinsson, used by kind permission.

As the practice of magic was intensely diverse, so too was the range of its practitioners. We have nearly forty different terms for sorcerers from the sagas and poetry. Some have specific roles or connections—they carry staffs; they prophesy; a whole group of them 'ride' in darkness or cold; they use specialised kinds of magic. Other terms have more generalised meanings akin to the modern sense of 'witch' or even 'wizard'. All of this was deeply encoded with sexual overtones.

It is arguably possible to trace these kinds of people in the archaeology, as in the more than fifty graves that contain metal staffs closely resembling the saga descriptions of a sorceress's main attribute, enshrined even in the name of the most common kind of magic-using woman—the *völva*, or 'staff-bearer'. These burials have been gendered as women through the kinds of problematic artefactual associations mentioned earlier, and the bodies certainly wear the 'conventional' female clothing of the Viking Age. However, there was nothing conventional about the sorcerers, and it may be that some of the funerary staff-bearers are cross-dressing men, or trans women, or people who saw themselves in quite different ways. Besides the staffs, these graves include other 'tools of the trade', including hallucinogens, a variety of animal body parts, charms and amulets, and details of dress that are otherwise out of the ordinary. We cannot say for sure that the grave of a *völva*, or any other specific type of magic-worker, has been identified, but the sorcerous practices described in the medieval written sources do seem to have genuine support in the Viking-Age excavated data.

One interpretation of magical practices such as *seithr* has been current for over 150 years, namely the idea that they represent some kind of Norse equivalent to what has elsewhere been called shamanism. The evidence includes the sending out of the soul, Odin's trance, and the sexual rituals of the staff to bring spirits back to the "home of their shapes". These debates continue, but the complex social world of Norse sorcery does seem to find a natural place as an independent cultural tradition within the larger pattern of Northern spirituality.

All these varied practices, and their equally diverse arenas, ultimately concern the living and their attempts to communicate with other types of beings. But the living themselves could also cross one of these boundaries, into the realm of death. In any culture, the treatment of the dead can provide a valuable reflection of attitudes to life—and also of identity, gender, power, status, and much else. The Viking way of death was not only spectacular, but also spectacularly varied. In tracing the outlines of the Viking mind, in exploring the making of Midgard where everyone dwelled, the borders of life itself form the final frontier.

8

DEALING WITH THE DEAD

THE 'VIKING FUNERAL' IS ONE of the most common tropes about these people today: heading into eternity on a burning boat—now *that's* the way to go. Perhaps surprisingly, at least some early medieval Scandinavians really did exactly that. But they also did very much more, and one of the hallmarks of Viking-Age funerary ritual is that almost every grave is unique in its details.

Reviewing the national registers of ancient monuments, some twenty-eight thousand cemeteries are known from the period from 100 to 1000 CE in Sweden and Norway, of which perhaps half date to the Viking Age. To this one must add Denmark, and then Iceland, Greenland, the Faroes, and the colonies in occupied territories across the rest of the diaspora. Together this represents a number of individual burials in the low millions, presenting a 'big data' challenge all its own in terms of analysis and interpretation. This is a task to which archaeology is not yet fully equal.

The research potential of this massive corpus of information—effectively a huge repository of human action, emotion, and belief—is skewed in other ways too. The most dramatic and far-reaching bias in the understanding of Viking-Age death rituals is quite simply the fact that not everyone received a grave of a kind that can be detected archaeologically. Through the tentative correlation of identified settlements, population density on the farms, and the number of recorded burials, some scholars estimate that up to 50 percent of the population are 'missing' from the funerary record in this way.

It is similarly unknown whether these people were of low status, or enslaved, or if there was some other factor that determined their particular manner of disposal in death. Snorri's *Saga of the Ynglingas* makes a rather muddled attempt at explaining the funerary customs of the pagan past, but there he actually says that many of the dead were cremated *and their ashes thrown into water*— perhaps he should simply be taken at his word, as this would certainly explain what is (not) seen in the archaeology. Children's burials are also under-represented.

Most graves contain just a single individual. Occasionally there are two—usually male and female—and sometimes an adult burial might contain the remains of a child (perhaps the result of a difficult childbirth that killed both mother and baby). It is also not unknown for funerary monuments to be revisited, either to deposit a second, or even third, corpse in the same grave as the original occupant, or to make what archaeologists call a secondary burial— for example, by placing the ashes of another body in the side of a mound without accessing the main grave. With the exception of mass graves in connection with battles, executions, or epidemics (none of which are commonly encountered), the rarest of all are those with multiple simultaneous burials. A very few of them are in chambers, but the majority of these multi-person interments are in boats. The Viking way of death never ceases to surprise us.

The Old Norse textual corpus contains very few descriptions of Viking life and belief that are actually written to inform, rather than as narrative from which a scholar can hope to glean something along the way. But there are exceptions, and one such is the first book of Snorri Sturluson's *Heimskringla*, his monumental history of the kings of Norway reckoned from a vague prehistoric past through to the twelfth century. Its introductory saga discusses the dynastic fortunes of the Ynglinga family, the rulers of central Sweden and Norway who were also one of the first of the 'new elites' from the sixth century to leave their mark in literature. Theirs was a Viking-Age success story.

Part of this narrative includes Snorri's attempt to rationalise the pre-Christian gods, especially Odin, casting them as human figures from the remote past who later took on divine aspects in folk belief. It makes for a queasy mix, as Snorri tries to shoehorn pagan belief into Christian sensibilities, but the element of interest here is a list of the so-called Laws of Odin in which he sets out what was supposedly the proper treatment of the dead according to the 'old ways'. It is worth quoting in full:

> Odin established in his land the laws that had previously been observed among the Aesir. He ordained that all dead people must be burned and that their possessions should be laid on a pyre with them. He said that everyone should come to Valhöll with such wealth as he had on his pyre, and that each would also have the benefit of whatever he himself had buried in the earth. But the ashes were to be taken out to sea or buried down in the earth, and mounds were to be built as memorials to great men, and memorial stones were to be raised for all those who were of any account, and this custom lasted for a long time after that.

The Viking-Age truth in this medieval concoction, if any, is very hard to evaluate. However, the Laws actually bear close relation to the funerary world discernible in the archaeology. Among the interesting things to note: *all the things burnt with the dead are their possessions*, which would follow the deceased to the next world; things buried unaccompanied by bodies are also for use after death, and can be selected for that purpose by the living, who make arrangements for their own afterlives; burial mounds are only for special, 'notable' men (it is hard to know how androcentric this statement actually is meant to be); standing stones are for the commemoration of anyone of note; and not all of the dead are treated in the same way.

With this in mind, the whole structure of Viking mortuary rituals can be viewed at three overarching levels, each identified by archaeologists but also corresponding to something that must have been perceptibly real in the past.

The first funerary decision made after a death was the starkest—whether to burn the body, or bury it (or, alternatively, whatever it was they did that left no trace). What people chose to do clearly varied by region, but the reasons for this are unknown. In Sweden, cremation was overwhelmingly the norm everywhere other than in special kinds of places, such as the market centres. In Norway and Denmark, a mixture of cremation and inhumation was practised.

The second key aspect of burial concerned its outer form—what 'type' of grave it was. There was considerable variation here, but within a limited and essentially consistent set of choices that seem to have been made independently of the decision to cremate or inter the deceased. The most common grave form was the earthen mound, which could be constructed in a range of sizes. Stones could also be laid out in patterns—rectangles, circles, ship shapes, and more—and the dead laid to rest within them. Bodies could be interred in underground wooden rooms, or buried inside ships and other vessels. On occasion, these variants can be combined—thus stones in a curb around a mound or set up on top. Archaeologists have a more-or-less precise terminology for this repertoire of funerary choice, writing of 'chamber graves', 'boat burials', and the like. We have little idea what the people of the Viking Age called them, but the grave forms are sufficiently consistent that they must have had a nomenclature that at least approximated ours—or, to put it another way, they would have had a means of saying, "I want one of *those* for my mum", and archaeologists would probably recognise what they were referring to.

The third level of Viking death rituals was the most complex; indeed, it was almost infinite. Inside each individual mound, boat, stone setting, or chamber (and the rest of the dozen or so familiar categories), what was actually done in the course of the rituals was unique in almost every case. The variations were usually very small, although sometimes enormous, but in every case, there is a sense of the individual, of the appropriate way to send a specific person across the border into a different life.

What did that look like? The women buried wearing the skins of lynx, or laid out beneath heavy bear pelts; the swords stuck vertically in a grave; a shield over the face or by the waist; a coin, just one, that was already a century old and worn thin; a line of burials in which every corpse clasps a smooth, white pebble in their hand; a horse led down into a grave, actually standing on the corpse, before being slaughtered; at the foot of the same burial, inside the grave, a standing stone over which the body of a dog has been squashed down, ripping it apart; the man and boy buried crossways to each other in the same oversized grave, their bodies forming a macabre X; the row of spindle whorls carefully arranged along a sword scabbard; a sorceress's staff weighted down under a rock; two horses bisected through the middle, and the halves of their bodies exchanged; a pit full of murdered children, dug down into the side of an army's mass grave; a man in a modest burial on top of which, decades later, a boat full of people would be placed so the keel exactly covered him—a ritual repeated with more men and more boats over the years. One could fill a book with things like this.

This degree of variation applies to both the artefactual assemblages and the rites or ceremonies themselves. The selection, combination, particular type, quality, quantity, and exact positioning of these objects are all factors within Viking-Age mortuary ritual. All across this spectrum of behaviour, details can provide information about the sequence of events, the time they may have taken to perform, and the spatial arena of ritual that in some cases must have extended considerably beyond the grave itself. Some of this might have been spontaneous, some of it planned, still other parts dictated by custom or even law.

In addition to the variation between individual graves, at a larger scale there are also patterns of regional, even local, expression. All this, in turn, must imply at least a degree of variation in the meaning behind these practices, and therefore in the beliefs relating to the treatment of the dead.

Burning the dead was not an easy task, to be attempted ad hoc by grieving relatives. It required specialist assistance, not only in building the pyre of cross-laid logs and kindling in a manner that allowed for the best air circulation and consequent combustion, but also in keeping it going and adjusting the corpse alongside the other things to be cremated. The dead may have been prepared for the pyre, even eviscerated (archaeologists find diagnostic cut marks on some fragments of burnt bone), which would have made for a less gory final process. Once the pyre was constructed, the ready corpse could be laid on top of the wooden construction, sometimes placed inside it, or, most rarely (and inefficiently), burnt directly on the ground.

It was not an ambivalent experience. Poems such as *Beowulf* describe how the fire "consumed the house of bone", how the flesh drew back and skulls cracked open in the flames. Unless held down by the 'funeral managers', a corpse might even sit up in the midst of the pyre. The human bodies were often accompanied by animals, sometimes in very large numbers in the wealthier graves; their corpses also moved, shrivelled, and burst. From the archaeology it is clear that sometimes flint was added to a cremation, and experiments have revealed how this can suddenly explode to produce showers of colourful sparks; this must have been intentional.

Fire and smoke could be seen over long distances, especially if the pyres were on high ground. There are Byzantine eyewitness descriptions of eastern Vikings burning their dead by the light of the full moon—in other words, at night. There are saga accounts of bodies sitting up in illuminated grave chambers, surrounded by 'lights', and the Eddic poem known as *The Waking of Angantyr* mentions 'grave fires' blazing around the barrows. Lamps have also been found in many graves, including several chambers and ship burials—illumination was clearly part of the rites, and the obvious question is why. One answer may be precisely the heightened visual impact of flame and firelight against the backdrop of the dark.

Few people today have seen the immediate aftermath of a cremation, and we tend to be relatively insulated from the corporeal realities of death. The Vikings were intimately acquainted with them. Once a cremation pyre had burnt out, the body was by no means reduced to convenient and tidy ashes. Soft tissue and clothing would have burnt away, but the skeleton itself might have been left substantially intact, though heavily charred and fractured. When excavating the remains of burials, archaeologists can see how the human bones have been retrieved, sorted, cleaned, and sometimes crushed. They are usually kept separate from the remains of the animals laid with them in the flames—also picked out from the debris and treated—but on occasion their ashes are mingled. The remains might be placed in a pottery vessel, or a bag, or a box; piled in a little heap; or simply scattered. This could be done directly on the site of the pyre or dug down into its remains, and a grave constructed over it all in situ. Alternatively, the bones and ash might be moved to a separate site, or several different ones, away from the pyre. There are examples where the same pyre event, for more than one person, resulted in different graves, with the ashes carefully selected and distributed according to a scheme we do not understand.

All this also raises another puzzle. We know that a sizeable proportion of the population did not receive a grave that archaeologists can detect, but added to this, however, is the fact that very few of the cremations we find contain anywhere near enough human remains to equate with an adult body. Only a small, sometimes *very* small, portion of the original burnt corpse was placed in the ground. A modern, professional cremation will reduce an adult male to about seven or eight litres of ashes and bone material, and slightly less for an adult female. The Viking-Age cremations rarely contain more than a litre of remains. Nobody knows what this means. Did the funeral involve a partition of the ashes—some to the family or onlookers and mourners, some for the earth, and so on? Maybe the dead were stored at home, although not in a permanent way that can be traced. Worryingly for the statistics, the remains of a single person might have been buried in multiple monuments, making a sort of distributed grave that has mistakenly been recorded as several individual ones. Perhaps the cremated dead were given to the environment, to Midgard itself—yes, some part of them for the land, but other aspects of their body going to the air and the water. It is hardly likely that all these possibilities will be resolved, but one is left with the nagging feeling that the very definition of what constitutes a Viking-Age 'grave' is open to question.

The dead, both human and animal, were of course not alone on the pyre. The corpses were at the centre of complex arrays of objects, starting with the clothes and personal ornaments worn on the body. At the extremes, these might range from the threadbare shift of the poorest farmhand, a copper brooch and eating knife, to the robes and jewelled regalia of a king. Beyond the body and its coverings, 'grave-goods' at their broadest might encompass almost any aspect of Viking material culture. Some were intact when placed on the pyre, while others—for reasons unknown—were smashed first. All these things found a place (or, by design, did not) in the final grave. Like the human and animal remains, they were picked out from the ashes, cleaned, sometimes broken and twisted in odd ways, and then incorporated into the ongoing rituals of which archaeologists find only the final result. This could also include the deposition of *un*burnt objects along with the pyre debris—yet another stage of the proceedings, and just as opaque to us. A recent study of Swedish graves has shown that birds' eggs were occasionally placed intact into the ashes of cremations, for purposes unknown. At least some were the eggs of ravens, perhaps suggesting a connection with Odin, the god whose mind and thoughts were embodied in these birds.

It is not known why some Viking-Age people chose to bury their dead rather than cremate them. The custom is found to a greater or lesser degree throughout Scandinavia, although with some clustering in time and place. For some, the choice may have been emotional, almost instinctive, while for others it perhaps had clear spiritual overtones. There are saga descriptions of the interred dead 'living' in their graves, including a wonderful episode from the *Saga of Burnt Njál* where men walk past a burial mound at night only to find it somehow open, and inside sits its dead occupant happily singing and looking at the moon.

The Eddic poem mentioned earlier, *The Waking of Angantyr*, relates a daughter's journey to the island of Samsø (equidistant between the Danish regions of Jylland, Sjælland, and Fyn), which is depicted as a strange sort of intermediate place set aside for the dead. Hervör is one of the most well-realised and dramatic shield-maidens in all of Old Norse literature, and she is depicted here seeking her father's grave to retrieve his fatally charmed sword, Tyrfing, intending to use it as an instrument of revenge. The poem is difficult to understand, let alone date; it is not part of the conventional Eddic corpus, although clearly composed in the same style and therefore sometimes collected with the rest. It is notable for its information on attitudes to burial and the nature of life "below the tree roots", as the heroine puts it, and it is worth a moment of our time.

The island appears as an eerie liminal space that is somehow simultaneously part of our world and another; the doors between the two open at night, ringed with flames. Hervör is guided to the grave-fields by a shepherd, who is plainly terrified:

> The herdsman said:
> "Foolish he seems to me, who goes there,
> a man totally alone, through dark night;
> fire is in flight, the mounds lie open,
> earth and bog are burning—let us go quickly!"

> Hervör said:
> "Let us take care not to be frightened by such noise,
> though fires burn throughout the entire island!
> Let's not allow dead warriors
> to quickly frighten us; we shall make conversation."

Determined on her mission of 'conversing' with the deceased, Hervör walks through the mists of flame and smoke, past the corporeal dead standing by their graves, to the mound of her father, who was buried with his bodyguard of berserkers, warriors who fought in an ecstatic frenzy:

> Hervarth, Hjorvarth, Hrani, Angantyr!
> I wake you all below the tree's roots,
> with helmet and mailcoat, with sharp sword,
> with shield and harness, with reddened spear.
> You, sons of Arngrim, violent kin,
> have changed greatly for the heaping up of earth.

The grave's occupants are dismayed. (Dead) Angantyr replies in increasing desperation as he tries to protect his daughter from the consequences of her vengeance: "the door to Hel is open / graves lie open / all the island's surface is seen to be on fire!". Repeatedly the poem talks of the burials 'opening'—the flames everywhere guarding their portals—and twice the grave is described as the threshold of 'the hall(s)'. Nothing works, even when her father warns that the cursed blade will bring the ruin of her house. Hervör stands her ground with a magnificent verse that captures not only the power of Norse poetry but also the concepts of mind (the "*hugr*'s enclosure"). It is worth seeing the original for its intricate wordplay:

Brenni þér eigi bál á nóttum,
svát ek við elda yðra fælumk;
skelfrat meyju muntún hugar,
þótt hon draug séi í durum standa.

You could not light fires in the night,
so that I am frightened by your flames;
the maiden's thought-enclosure does not tremble,
though she sees a ghost stand at the door.

Importantly, Hervör threatens the slain that if she is not given the sword, they will stay fixed in the ground, "dead with the ghosts, rotten in your grave". Clearly, the dead are meant to move on somewhere, at the same time as they also stay put in the burial mound—a contradictory picture that actually makes sense when one looks at the funerary evidence in the archaeology. *The Waking of Angantyr* is a much-neglected source for our understanding of the Vikings' view of death and burial, as well as perhaps one of the best of the Eddic poems. A different translation captures the nature of the place, as Hervör stares unafraid into her doomed future, having already dared what few others have before her:

Now I have walked between the worlds
I have seen the fires circling.

If you stroll through the cemeteries of the Viking Age today, unthreateningly gentle landscapes of grass-covered mounds that can make a nice place for a picnic, you might do well to recall Angantyr's island and its night-time terrors of funeral fire, open graves at the gates of Hel. Hervör did not flinch in crossing this boundary, but on the other hand, her story is not a happy one.

The rituals of inhumation most often involved depositing a body directly into a rectangular grave with or without a coffin or shroud. Different containers could also be used, including the detached cargo bodies of wooden wagons, which seem to have been connected to women of high status. Occasionally there are small piles of human skeletal remains, apparently buried in boxes; these may be the disarticulated remains of people who died while travelling, brought back home to the family. If this is true, it shows an interesting regard for the literal bones, distinct from the body as a whole.

In the majority of cases, the bodies are laid out on their backs, but sometimes they are found on their sides, with legs half drawn up. There is a sense in which the dead are resting or sleeping, reinforced by the finds of 'bedclothes' in the form of pillows under the head, blankets, and coverlets. Sometimes bunches of herbs were buried, perhaps as a mortuary deodorant.

Another feature of the burials is the occasional distortion of the body, with limbs unnaturally twisted or broken, or even missing; a head detached and placed by the torso, an animal jawbone resting on the neck; corpses laid face down in the grave or covered with heavy stones; and many more examples of what archaeologists call 'ritual trauma' in the absence of a better term. These practices used to be considered 'deviant' in the sense of a departure from the norm, but after prolonged study in recent years, they can now be seen as much more common than previously thought; their sheer variety concealed the scale of their collective presence. Whatever such actions meant, they were also a part of the regular irregularity in funerary behaviour.

There were certainly regional preferences, and we see clear indications of a local way of doing things. In parts of Norway and Sweden, the dead were buried in what can hardly be called a coffin—more like an enormous elongated box up to three or four metres long. These were probably built in the grave rather than carried there, but they were nonetheless shallow (like a wooden casket) rather than making a true three-dimensional 'room' as in the chamber graves.

In Iceland, especially in the north of the country, archaeologists have found evidence for wooden posthole structures over the burials—either little buildings or at least arrangements of posts. Were these mortuary houses, residences for the dead, or a place for the living to go and visit them? Beside some excavated Danish graves are postholes sloping inwards towards the burial at a forty-five-degree angle, so the timbers they contained would have jutted out over the resting place of the dead. There is no way to tell what, if anything, was attached to them, and often they have burnt right down to the base of the postholes. Several graves have indications of vertical posts erected over them, more along the lines of a conventional marker. At the close of his account of a burial on the Volga, ibn Faḍlān mentions that a post of birch was set up on top of the grave mound, and 'cut' (rune-carved?) with the name of the dead man and his king.

Inside the inhumations are the same range of funerary gifts (or offerings, or mortuary possessions, or whatever they were) as in the cremations, although for obvious reasons they are better preserved. When one views the remains of the Vikings' funerals in museums today, the contrast between the contorted fragments that had once rested on a pyre and the corroded but relatively intact items from inhumations should not blind us to the fact that the material repertoire of the different burial rites was essentially very similar. There is also what cannot be seen in the cremations, but which one can assume was probably there: the food and drink, the textiles, the furniture, the wooden implements, and containers of all kinds.

The smallest burial mounds were probably never more than just bumps in the ground, less than a metre high. The largest would dwarf modern three-storey houses, roof and all. They sometimes appear singly, but more usually in clusters round a farm or in larger collective cemeteries that served a village or several communities combined. There are regional trends in the scale at which the dead were buried, but even in the biggest grave-fields it can be possible to trace 'family plots' more securely now that DNA can establish such relationships. At the larger market centres, these grave-fields can contain thousands of burials. Such cemeteries should probably be seen less as archaeological site plans and more in terms of land-scapes of experience—places to more easily *feel* the presence of the Others and, perhaps, to communicate with them.

The mounds might be enhanced with stone settings and curbs of various kinds, or rocks set in circles, rectangles, triangles, stars, and other patterns. Others were left either as bare earth that would quickly grass over, or with a thin covering of small stones that gave them the appearance of a cairn. Some of the barrows were sur-mounted by upright stones of all shapes and sizes, united only in their deliberate prominence. They are known as *bautastenar* in the sources. The best example of a cemetery as it originally appeared is found at Lindholm Høje in northern Jylland, where a grave-field was buried by wind-blown sand and has therefore survived intact. Almost every burial is marked by stones, often without apparent pattern but clearly an integral part of the funerary ritual.

Other graves have no mounds over them, just the stone set-tings, following a similar range of patterns to those we have seen. There are also different forms, not least the outline of ships on a scale that can range from a metre or two up to the largest so far found, the 360-metre-long setting at the royal Danish site of Jelling. Sometimes the stones are seemingly randomly chosen, but there are also examples where they have been carefully sorted and arranged in order of size to reproduce the sloping profile of the ship, with the tallest stones at stem and stern. The stone ships occur singly, in pairs, and even in chains of three or four laid out end to end. Inside the ships are one or sometimes several cremations, positioned at varying points around the outline of the 'vessel', and also the remains of fires and feasts. These may not have occurred during the funeral(s), but might point to an ongoing relationship with the burial place.

There are also odd triangular stone shapes with concave sides, known by the Swedish term *treuddar*, 'three-pointers'. They are certainly (usually) graves, but the meaning of the settings is unknown. One archaeologist has speculated that the shape represents the roots of a tree—feasibly the great ash Yggdrasill, and thus a direct link to the mythology and wider ideas of the cosmos.

A unique class of funerary monument, encountered several times already, is made up of the so-called picture-stones. Occurring only on the Baltic island of Gotland and in a handful of places connected with its inhabitants, these are upright slabs of the local limestone, chosen for its ubiquity and also the ease with which it could be detached in flat surfaces eminently suitable for carving. The use of picture-stones on Gotland began early in the Migration Period and extended to the very end of the Viking Age, with a range of forms that changed over time from low rectangular stumps at the beginning of the sequence to massive stelae up to four metres high in the tenth and eleventh centuries. What set them apart from the runestones of the mainland is first their general lack of inscriptions (although these did appear towards the end), but primarily the fact that their surfaces were covered in carved images—hence the name. Outside Gotland, the only other such picture-stones known are one from Uppland, two from Öland, and one from Grobina in Latvia, all thought to commemorate Gotlanders who died there.

The picture-stones were memorials to the dead, and have been found in cemeteries where they seem to have been raised either on or beside burial mounds. Like the conventional runestones, they were also placed along the roads and in other prominent locations where they would be seen. The Gotland stones served much the same purpose as their mainland counterparts, but utilising visual rather than textual media. On the Swedish runestones, the design and colours were enhancements, but the point was conveyed in the inscriptions and their placement (prominent names or words positioned so as to draw the eye, and perhaps picked out in different colours). On the picture-stones, the images told the story.

They are hard to decipher, although many scholars have convincingly traced scenes and episodes from Norse mythology— Odin transforming into an eagle after stealing the mead of poetry; the tale of Völund the smith; Gunnar in the snake pit; and, especially, the epic of Sigurd the dragon-slayer. Not least, the stones thereby provide evidence of the genuine Viking-Age antiquity of the stories that are otherwise only preserved in medieval texts, and they also open up a unique window on the narratives through which the Vikings made sense of their world. The sheer scale of the Gotlandic picture-landscape confirms the importance of the narratives depicted, whether or not we fully understand what each image 'means'. It is vital to acknowledge, however, that all this was bound up with the status of the dead.

Broadly speaking, the picture-stones organise their images in two ways: either jumbled together without a perceptible pattern, or laid out in a stack of horizontal panels rather like a comic strip. These panels can be read sequentially, beginning at the bottom and following the story upwards. Picture-stones were sometimes set up around the borders of a farm, and the upper panel on one stone may be the same as the lower panel on the next in line following their placement around an estate border—in other words, a story 'to be continued'. Because the stones are memorials to the dead, as each generation of monument was added they not only made the clear connection between family and land, but also drew all this together in what was effectively successive pictorial chapters in a dynastic saga. To add a final touch, the stones of this type had a distinctive keyhole-shaped outline that may have represented a door (by comparison with the portals of later, wooden buildings), and thus perhaps an entrance to . . . somewhere else.

Imagine a walk around the land of a wealthy Gotlandic family, marked out by memorials to each generation of owners. That's my father, and there's his father, and the weathered stone by the brook is my great-grandfather. We've always been here, and when my time comes, I know what my story will show. Let's go up to the doors. Shall we look through, and talk to them for a while?

To be clear, not every picture-stone functioned like this, and archaeological understanding is also limited not only by the examples that have survived (only rarely still in their original positions) but also by our limited ability to read the images. They were stories in stone, but they also seem to have had yet another, perhaps simultaneous, purpose that may explain why particular images were chosen, and also the meaning of the apparently haphazard arrangements on some of them. On almost every Viking-Age picture-stone, of either type, the largest single motif is that of a rigged sailing ship, often depicted in careful detail with its crew, its figureheads, and even the design on the sail. On the 'panel-type' stones, the ship covers the lower half of the stone with the story-strips above it. On the deceptively random image stones, it is variously placed but always prominent. In trying to understand the meaning of the ship, it is worth noting that on Gotland—an island, and the literal centre of Baltic trade and its world of maritime contacts— there is not a single boat or ship burial. What if the picture-stones are in a sense *pictorial ship burials*, serving the same ritual functions but spelling out their message in images rather than objects? The mainland boat graves appear to have been only for the highest-status members of the community, which it is reasonable to assume applied to the picture-stones too. Gotland's material culture and customs were different from those of the mainland in almost every other way, so why not in this?

It does not stop here. If the ship-centred picture-stones were symbolic ship burials, some of the smaller grave monuments on the island may have similarly represented wagon burials—another class of funerary rite not found on Gotland. A set of examples comes from the elaborate burial monument of Ailikn, the wife of Liknatr, from Ardre. Four stones form the sides of a container, presumably for her bones or ashes, each stone shaped into a characteristic rectangle with a waving upper edge that is identical to the profile of the wagons depicted on other Gotlandic picture-stones, such as that from Grötlingbo parish. Just as a wagon body was a high-status burial container for women of substance on mainland Scandinavia, so its design equivalent served a similar function on Gotland. The parallel to the pictorial ship burials is exact.

The picture-stones of Gotland probably represent the single widest window onto the thought-world of the actual Viking Age (as distinct from its mediation through medieval texts) that has survived anywhere in the diaspora. Scholars have devoted professional lifetimes to understanding their images, and every year brings new revelations.

Such insular communities have other variations that can illuminate wider traditions. As is perhaps to be expected, the death rituals of Gotland, Öland, Bornholm, and Åland all differ from those of their respective closest mainlands. On Gotland in particular, there was a preference for larger grave-fields that stayed in use for centuries or even millennia, as well as a markedly higher frequency of individual burials with unusual mortuary behaviour that included varieties of ritual trauma. In the Åland islands between Sweden and Finland, the ashes of the dead were accompanied by a unique rite: on top of the ceramic urn containing the human remains, a miniature clay bear or beaver paw was placed. This rite is found only on Åland and in specific clusters of graves on the Volga and Kljaz'ma rivers in Russia—presumably the burials of travelling Ålanders. Thus the Vikings took their varied funerary rituals with them beyond Scandinavia, a diaspora of the dead.

The burials that archaeologists refer to as chamber graves are in reality more like little wooden rooms, constructed underground and usually rectangular in shape. They can be up to four metres long and around two metres wide, and it is not uncommon for them to reach a depth of two metres—just enough for an adult to stand upright. They were roofed with timbered rafters, thereby making a sealed chamber of which the top was most often flush with the original ground surface or slightly lower. In the majority of cases, this was then covered by a mound.

The ritual of chamber burial was known from the centuries before the Viking Age, especially in the Roman Iron Age and the Migration Period, but it reached a zenith in the ninth and especially tenth centuries. By a combination of their size and dignity, the effort required in their construction (especially in the frozen ground of winter), and the quality of the clothing and objects buried with the dead inside, the chamber graves were the resting places of the wealthy or otherwise privileged. Almost always inhumations, they also tend to exhibit a markedly wider frame of cultural contact than most other graves and frequently contain objects and dress accessories imported over long distances. This is usually taken to reflect either the contacts of the deceased (or those doing the burying), or as an indication that this was a travelled individual, or in some cases that the person was actually a foreigner.

They are most common in Sweden, where 111 examples have been found at Birka alone; around 60 are known from Denmark and northern Germany. The latter cluster around Hedeby, and it seems likely the early towns were epicentres for the spread of what became an unusual but interregional burial rite. In Norway the custom was not as widespread, and no such burials have yet been found at Kaupang (the nearest equivalent to Birka and Hedeby). While several examples are known from Vestfold, chamber graves appear for now as a primarily eastern and southern phenomenon.

Inside, the chambers were worlds in miniature. The dead lay in coffins, or on their backs or sides on the chamber floor (which in some cases was a proper deck of timber or at least birch bark matting), sometimes sat in chairs, or were even tucked up in a bed. Around them were often animals, including in some cases one or two horses positioned at the foot of the chamber on a raised platform. Chamber graves are also characterised by the profusion, variety, and quality of objects interred with the dead. Things were piled in the lap of the corpse or placed in their hands; items were propped against the side of the chambers, or rested against a chair; weapons and other pieces were hung from the walls; boxes were full of clothing and bed linen, which could also be piled on the chamber floor; the bodies were fully dressed in rich clothing and jewellery. It is particularly common for objects to have been laid down 'in front' of the dead person, as if for them to see.

Most of the dead interred seated seem to have been female, at least in the chambers; occasionally there were seated men on the decks of buried ships. The seated corpses retained agency. In the burials of this kind at Birka, for example, the dead women were positioned—wherever their grave was located—so that their faces were looking to the settled area, presumably towards their home. The dead man of the *Saga of Burnt Njál* was singing in his chair, and there are other saga episodes where the deceased are sitting down. The *Saga of Grettir*, for example, actually describes the looting of a chamber grave that is a perfect match for the archaeology. When the thief digs down through the mound, he first cuts through the roof timbers and then falls into a foul-smelling space below, landing among horse bones at one end of a chamber. Stumbling forward and groping about in the dark, he feels the back of a chair, and then the shoulder of someone sitting in it—who then *gets up* and . . . Go read the saga.

Some of the chambers are simply baffling. In a pair of examples excavated at Birka, the central chair contains *two* people on top of one another, in each case a woman sitting on a man's lap, held in place by a chain round the bodies. Whatever this meant, like the rest it was not at all random.

Sometimes there are lances thrust vertically down into the chamber floor, or heavily embedded in the horse-platform revetments where they must have been thrown with considerable force. Sometimes lanceheads are stuck into the walls, their shafts now decayed but originally extending into the middle of the chamber to form a kind of meshed lattice over the dead. In one burial, axes had been swung into the chamber sides with such effort that the blades were almost buried in the timber. In one or two Finnish Viking-Age graves, there are coffins nailed shut with spears. These weapon rituals tell their own story, mostly lost, although there are hints in the written sources. For example, there are two references to the act of casting a spear over people as a means of dedicating them to Odin.

At Mammen in Denmark, one of the richest chamber graves of the whole Viking Age was made c. 970 for a man whose clothing has enabled us to reconstruct the dress of society's highest echelons. The chamber itself resembled a hall and even had a pitched roof, all concealed under a great mound. The man was interred with a magnificent axe decorated in a fashion that has given a name to the Mammen style of Viking art. He was laid out in a coffin with a massive candle placed on the top, alight, that continued to burn in the dark until all the oxygen in the closed chamber had gone.

In one of the Hedeby cemeteries, several warrior males were buried in the same chamber, although one of them was separated from the others by a low partition across the floor—one thinks of Angantyr and his berserker companions in the same grave. After all the animals, weapons, and other objects had been placed inside and the chamber sealed, an entire warship was laid across the top before being covered by a mound. Its mast stuck up through the surface, while the bow and stern would have protruded either side of the barrow, like upturned horns.

This chapter began with the stereotypical 'Viking funeral', a grave form that comes up regularly in any discussion of the people and their time. The ship burial was arguably the most spectacular (and revealing) of all the Viking-Age varieties of mortuary behaviour.

That so much is known about ship graves is due partly to the several elaborate examples that have been excavated, but in particular to the most extraordinary written source to have survived from the Viking Age: the mission report of Aḥmad ibn Faḍlān, which we have already seen several times.

In 922, he was sent from Baghdad by the Abbasid caliph on a long and quite hazardous journey to the lands of the Bulghars, whose capital was at the bend of the Volga River. Ibn Faḍlān's account, which exists in several fragmentary second-hand versions and one longer but still incomplete manuscript (none of them are in any sense the 'original'), only covers the outward phase of his trip over hundreds of miles of hostile terrain and multicultural encounters. It also obliquely relates how the dangers of the trek caused so many defections from the diplomatic party that, by stages, ibn Faḍlān seems to have found himself promoted from his original role as essentially an educated bodyguard to become the secretary of the whole mission. He was thereby charged with delivering the caliph's message to the Bulghar ruler, which combined Islamic missionising with a hoped-for trade agreement. The document we have is his report on the outcome, but also perhaps a kind of résumé portfolio for attracting future employment. Ibn Faḍlān was clearly a remarkable person, but unfortunately nothing is known of him beyond this one text—neither his birth nor death, nor even how his great journey ended (clearly he made it home). Although his report contains many passages of almost anthropological interest, and he was both curious and observant, its fame today rests on his descriptions of a people he encountered while at the Bulghar trading post that now lies somewhere near the Russian city of Kazan. He called them *al-Rūsiyyah*, anglicised as Rus', and we know them as the predominantly Scandinavian merchants who plied the Eurasian river trade—in other words, the Vikings in their eastern manifestation.

In addition to general descriptions of the Rus' appearance, clothing, and personal habits, ibn Faḍlān's greatest gift to posterity rests on his detailed observation of the rituals following the death of a Rus' chieftain, culminating in his cremation in a ship. The account was already famous long before the first of the well-preserved Viking ship burials had been excavated. In 1883 ibn Faḍlān's text had even been the inspiration for a dramatic canvas by Polish artist Henryk Siemiradzki that was much admired in the European salons. Combined with the stirring saga stories (then accepted more or less at face value), it was one of the foundations of the romanticising view of the Viking Age that dominated in the late nineteenth and early twentieth centuries. The discovery of the ship graves at Gokstad and especially Oseberg changed all that—it was like seeing the Arabic text come to life: the chamber on deck, the animal sacrifices, even their positions and condition. When a much more complete manuscript of ibn Faḍlān's report was found at Mashhad in Iran in 1923, it fed back into the loop between archaeology and text, supporting both. The parallels continued to appear over decades of new boat burial finds, excavations linking to his report with almost unsettling exactitude—from the expensive dress of the dead to the weapons and other costly possessions laid on board, the animal offerings, and the presence of a human sacrifice—in this case, a young female thrall. The result was that the essentially Scandinavian identity of ibn Faḍlān's Rus' came to be unchallenged, and it remains so today for all but the terminally sceptical.

What the archaeology does *not* record are the events and emotions around the artefacts, but these are at the heart of ibn Faḍlān's writing: the extraordinary unfolding narrative that was enacted in and around the vessel for more than a week prior to its burning, ceremonies of which he left the only eyewitness record. For many reasons his account is, therefore, one of the core texts of the whole Viking Age. The text is very long (thankfully for scholarship) but is well worth exploring in sequence.

When ibn Faḍlān became aware that one of the Rus' leaders had died, he made an effort to attend the funeral because, as he makes clear, he'd heard these things were a sight to see. He was right, although he may have regretted his decision.

The first thing he noticed was that the funeral preparations were so elaborate as to require a full ten days following the man's death. During that time his body was interred in a temporary grave—with temporary grave-goods, including food, drink, and a musical instrument; there is a strong suggestion that all this is intended for his entertainment pending the final funeral, and thus that the dead man is somehow *aware*. The same ten-day period sees continuous festivities in the Rus' camp, involving music, sex, and heavy drinking; almost the entire band is perpetually drunk. Special burial clothes are also made for the dead chieftain, on which no less than a third of his wealth is spent (this has worrying implications for the archaeologist, in that these things are made for the grave). Another third of his wealth goes to the brewing of appropriate quantities of alcohol, while only the remaining third is inherited by his heirs.

All these proceedings are presided over by a middle-aged woman, heavy set and angry, whose title (as ibn Faḍlān understood it through his interpreter) means the 'Angel of Death'. This is interesting in that the term in the text is *Malak al-Mawt*, the Quranic angel whose purpose is to choose the dead and take them to their assigned places—it may not be coincidence that this is very close to what might be said or understood if someone was trying to translate 'Valkyrie' into Arabic. Around the ship, which has been propped up on shore using timbers carved like men, people go back and forth making music and chanting; ibn Faḍlān's interpreter is unfortunately not there that day, so he does not understand what they are saying.

Early on, the dead man's slaves are gathered together and asked which of them will 'volunteer' to be killed; a girl steps forward, and the Arabic implies she is in her mid-teens. This female thrall is thereafter referred to as the dead man's 'bride'; she is dressed in fine clothes and jewellery, and assigned servants of her own (they are the daughters of the 'Angel'). She spends the ten days prior to the burial drinking and feasting, and during this time has sex with many of the men in the camp, particularly the relatives of the deceased.

On the tenth day, the ship is hauled onto the pyre, which is described as a box-like structure of wood (ibn Faḍlān thinks it looks almost like a building, so it must have been substantial). A wooden tent or cabin is set up on the deck, with a bed inside made up with Byzantine gold brocade. The dead man is exhumed—his body has turned black but does not smell—dressed in his mortuary clothes, and brought to the ship, where he is propped up with cushions in a sitting position on the bed. In several successive visits, his possessions (ibn Faḍlān is explicit that this is what they were) are brought on board, and a variety of food, drink, and herbs are laid out around the corpse.

The rituals then intensify. The enslaved girl goes from tent to tent around the ship, having sex with each man, who shouts loudly that he has thereby done what his duty demands of him. A dog is then led to the ship and cut in two, and the halves of its corpse are slung on board. The man's weapons are then placed in the cabin; why are they treated separately from his other possessions? Horses and cattle are then sacrificed—not cleanly slaughtered but instead hacked to pieces with swords. The horses are exercised first, so their bodies glisten with sweat. Some chickens are killed by tearing their heads off; the pieces are first thrown precisely to either side of the ship, and finally onto its deck.

Before entering the ship, the enslaved girl is lifted up by men in order to look over an odd thing—a specially built free-standing door frame that has been set up in the open air. She describes three successive visions of the next world and its inhabitants: a 'Paradise' beautiful and green like a garden, where the girl's dead family is already waiting, and where she sees her dead master calling to her. The daughters of the 'Angel' then remove her jewellery. The enslaved girl then ascends to the deck of the ship by walking on the raised palms of the men with whom she has earlier had sex.

She sings a leave-taking of her fellow thralls, and is made to quickly drink two beakers of strong alcohol. She becomes confused, seems to be trying to lie down, and is reluctant to enter the cabin. When she is forced inside (the 'Angel' grabs her head), the girl begins to scream, but her cries are drowned out by men waiting on the deck, beating staves on shields "which they had brought for that purpose". (These circumstantial details—the girl's drunken distraction, the forethought of the men with their shields and staves—are among the disconcerting features that set ibn Faḍlān's account apart, and why it rings so horribly true.)

The girl is then held down on the bed beside the ten-day-old corpse of the chieftain, and raped by six of the dead man's kinsmen. After this, while four of the men hold her arms and legs, the other two strangle her with a twisted veil. At the same time, the 'Angel of Death' stabs her repeatedly between the ribs "in place after place".

When the living have left the ship, the pyre is then lit by a naked man walking backwards around the vessel; he keeps his face averted and covers his anus with his fingers (all orifices of his body are thus either pointing away from the ship or protected). As the fire consumes the ship and its occupants, fanned by a rising wind, the Rus' talk with approval of how the smoke is being carried high into the sky and that therefore their 'Lord' is pleased. When the ashes cool, a mound is erected over the remains of the pyre and a birch pole set up on top, on which is cut the dead man's name and that of his king. After this, the Rus' leave.

To all this one must add the 'audio-visual effects', to use a callous phrase: the screaming of the animals; their entrails fouling the ship's timbers; the expensive textiles covered in gore; the panic of the girl; the flies in the sticky pools of blood; the mingled scents of recent sex, old death, and violent killing. It is hard to believe anyone could remain entirely calm in the midst of such acts—ibn Faḍlān certainly does not; indeed, he is obliquely threatened by one of the bystanders (who claims that Arabs must be stupid to bury their dead rather than burning them). It must have been nerve-racking for him. As I have earlier stressed, ibn Faḍlān's horrific narrative is an essential corrective for anyone who finds the Vikings admirable.

What does archaeology add to this, or alter?

The rite of boat burial precedes the Viking Age by several centuries and encompasses every type of water craft. People could be interred in little one-person rowboats, in graves cut to look like them, or even just with a plank or two of boat timbers that apparently sufficed to make the same connection with less outlay (it goes without saying that any kind of boat is a very expensive thing to give up to a grave). The great oceangoing ships that have become so famous are the very highest end of the scale, but even they exist in some numbers.

Most of the boats for burial were dragged ashore and laid in shallow trenches, deep enough to keep them stable and upright but leaving substantial parts of the vessel above ground level. The bodies of one or more men and women were placed on board and laid out in various ways—lying amidships or resting in bed, sitting in chairs, or propped up on cushions, sometimes covered by shaggy bearskins. The dead are often deposited in a chamber, usually built amidships (yes, just like ibn Faḍlān says). The ships exhibit the full spectrum of 'grave-goods': weapons, jewellery, tools, household items including looms, agricultural equipment, and a massive range of home furnishings and textiles. Oseberg even had tapestries hanging from the nock of the chamber roof. Boxes, parcels, and bundles of clothing were placed all around. Again at Oseberg, pillows were stacked in a neat pile, a single seed of cannabis placed puzzlingly between each of them. Additional outdoor gear could also be present: tents, sledges, even an entire wagon, and ship's boats for getting to shore. At Oseberg the stepped gangway had been thrown on board. Food and drink were liberally supplied.

The dead were often accompanied by very large numbers of animal sacrifices—up to twenty decapitated horses, for example, were present in the Oseberg grave. Back to ibn Faḍlān: think of the noise and the blood, the ground turning red around the ship. Whole or partial bodies of domesticated livestock such as cattle, sheep, pigs, and goats, have been found. Hunting dogs are often present in the ships; at Kaupang in Norway, there is a boat grave with such a hound that appears to have been carved to pieces with blades, its severed head resting in a bowl on the lap of a seated woman. The blood rituals of the *blót* sacrifice appear to have continued with burials. Birds of prey, absurdly expensive creatures such as falcons and several species of hawk, are also found. Then there are the true exotica: owls, eagles, and cranes, for example. The Gokstad ship burial even contained a peacock.

For ship cremations as opposed to true burials, much of this has to be inferred from sometimes very fragmentary remains. Even in interments, the ships have usually decayed and are visible only as lines of iron rivets that mark where the timbers once lay. Some of the cremations seem to have been the biggest of all: at Myklebost, in Norway, a massive warship was burnt that contained fifty-four shields, their bosses carefully gathered up afterwards from the ashes and deposited in buckets. This was a 'Viking funeral' incarnate.

Beyond the Oseberg, Gokstad, and Tune boat graves, as we have seen, many more are now known in Scandinavia, although the Norwegian finds are by far the best preserved. Overseas, boat burials are found in the British Isles, especially in island communities on the Orkneys, where they are sometimes lined with stones in the prow and stern. On the Scottish mainland, the discovery of a weapon-filled boat grave at Ardnamurchan expands the Viking funerary map. The outlier boat burial on the Île de Groix off the south coast of Brittany was on a quite different scale, encircled by standing stones and with a line of stone uprights that appear to have formed a processional way leading up to it.

The conclusion of the rituals also has something to tell us. Ibn Faḍlān describes a ten-day funeral at the end of which it all seems to hinge on a naked man, who is the only one to approach the pyre, taking precautions as he does so. He seems to expect something to be *active* in there; in protecting all the openings of his body, it seems that he believes it can *move*. The moment he lights the funeral fire, it is apparently safe, and everyone comes forward to add a burning torch to the conflagration.

Oseberg has something reminiscent of this wariness, although the burial is an inhumation rather than a cremation. Most of the objects were deposited with great care and attention, but at the very end most of the larger wooden items—the wagon, sleds, and so on—were literally thrown onto the foredeck, beautiful things just heaved over the side from ground level and being damaged in the process. The accessible end of the burial chamber was then sealed shut by hammering planks across the open gable, but using any old piece of wood that seems to have been at hand. The planks were just laid across at random—anything to fill the opening into the chamber where the dead lay. The nails were hammered in so fast one can see where the workers missed, denting the wood and bending or breaking off the nail heads. Why the need for such haste? Were they afraid, like the kindler of the pyre in ibn Faḍlān?

Some of the other, more behavioural details found in his account may also have matches in the archaeology and in the Old Norse texts. It seems, for example, that the Scandinavians may have had professional mourners, akin to the keening women found in more familiar classical sources. The Eddic poem known as *Guðrúnar-hvöt*, 'Gudrún's Lament', is perhaps a record of such a performance, as the titular character weeps for her murdered daughter, Svanhildr, and encourages her sons to avenge their sister. From the archaeological record, some of the two-dimensional 'female' figurines have mouths stretched in a sort of howling pout, with deep lines etched into the cheeks. It has been suggested that these may be symbols of mourning—the women singing laments and raking their faces bloody. *Beowulf* also mentions women wailing at funerals.

Even the food offerings lead deeper into the rituals. The remarkable range of bread from Birka has been sampled already, but the smallest sort of biscuits almost only come from graves and perhaps were made especially for funerals—bread for the dead. There must have been very specific reasons why it was laid to char on cooling pyres rather than being burnt with the corpses. Even more compelling is the evidence for how the loaves were divided up. Several of them preserve knife cuts in their surfaces, but in most peculiar patterns, marking the bread into many unequal portions in a mixture of radial lines and slices all on the same loaf. Was it measured out according to status, social role, family ties, or something else entirely? Did a ritual specialist apportion the pieces, naming each god or local spirit in turn? We are unlikely ever to know.

The sequential family stories on some of the Gotland picture-stones prompt us to ask what role ancestors may have played in people's lives. Some believe that their worship formed the bedrock of pre-Christian belief in Scandinavia and, therefore, that a relationship with the dead was of the utmost importance to the living. One of the functions of funerary ritual may have been to make a kind of formal introduction of the recently deceased to the collective of the ancestral dead—perhaps in the hope or belief that they could, in turn, aid the living.

Simply being dead did not necessarily make somebody an 'ancestor', which was in some way to be elevated above the norm, effectively to be elected as a role-model for proper behaviour— and not only for the living, but in a curious way perhaps also for the dead. Ancestors were the guardians of tradition, all those 'customs' that the Vikings prized so highly and that were their closest approximation to the concept of religion, and also the arbiters of morality. Crucially, because ancestors were explicitly linked to individuals and families, they resided in the household (or close to it, in their burial mounds). The ancestors thus formed a much more personal avenue of communication between the worlds than 'higher' beings such as the gods and goddesses, and it may therefore be readily understood why it was thought vital to maintain that relationship.

If later folklore can be believed, the family dead were also invited to important festivals among the living—notably the celebration of *jul*, or Yuletide. Elaborate meals would be made for them and set out on the table at night, the scene illuminated by specially made candles. This dinner would be preceded by a *bastu*, a rural wood-fired sauna in a cabin still very common in the Nordic countryside even today, in which the steam-filled room would be prepared and then emptied for the dead to cleanse themselves before eating. As in many other aspects of life in the Viking Age, maintaining good relations with the dead may have been just one more factor of vulnerable living in an unpredictable environment.

How did someone become an ancestor? The answer may lie in the complexity of the funerals themselves. The services afforded to the dead may, in some cases, have embodied the process of fixing the departed in a kind of local ancestral pantheon. Even so, not all ancestors were equal, and social stratification applied to the dead just as to the living. It is significant that so many of the poetic and prose texts tell of human heroes who very much kept their status after death (Adam of Bremen mentions the same thing).

Were graves places to tend and look after, perhaps to pass a few minutes there in contemplation or memory, or were they something else? The evidence tends towards the latter, connected to what the active conduct—the 'service', if you like—of the funerals may have meant in the first place.

It is possible, even likely, that what archaeologists vaguely term 'rituals' were actually the literal performance of stories. The excavated record of burial may in fact document the remains of some kind of graveside drama, publicly conducted with a public message, or several messages, aimed in different ways at different segments of the audience. Think of the stage at the end of a production of *Hamlet*. What does the scene look like when the Dane is dead? It is a Shakespeare tragedy, so there are several bodies, but in material terms these are complemented by their clothes, weapons, and other props, and also the set pieces of the stage itself. This is a complicated environment if one imagines it as an archaeological site, which is the key point. Do the complex tableaux presented in the graves and their contents effectively represent the stage at the end of a play? The dead person(s), the killed animals, all the objects, including even the ships and other vehicles, are perhaps lying where they have ended up after they have played out their roles in the drama of the funeral itself. Returning to *Hamlet*, the scene at the final curtain is complex enough, but leading up to it is the rest of the play. What of all the actors who are *not* present in the final scene but have had major roles in the drama? The same applies to all the different settings, the hours of dialogue, the action, the historical narrative, the deeper themes of the writing, even the humour used to offset the grimmer themes. We may think again of ibn Faḍlān and those ten days of action: what were they really *doing*?

And if each burial was a story, or a play, what of the connections between one funeral and another? This could be what is seen in the apparently dynastic stories of the Gotland picture-stones, and there may have been something similar on mainland Scandinavia though in material rather than visual form. At the cemetery of Gausel in Rogaland, Norway, for example, graves that appear superficially dissimilar (a female coffin burial, a male boat grave, etc.) are actually linked through consistencies between them—in this case, the deposition of a severed horse's head in full bridle, one in each grave. I have referred to this as "funerary motif" while another scholar has called it "mortuary citation", but the effect is the same: the continuation of a set of ideas, repeated between burials separated in time.

Following the idea of materialised narratives embedded in the landscape of burial, it therefore seems these tales may have been connected to discrete social groups, such as families or clans. Individuals at the uppermost strata of society may have had more personalised funerals, the full ship burial, so to speak. Maybe the subject of the story was the telling of their deeds as a means of incorporating the newly dead into a larger, literally ancestral saga.

Such performances could thus relate to the individual, their family and community, broader tales of identity and (spiritual) history, or to the great stories of culture heroes and myths: any or all of these elements combined, altered, and renegotiated into a unique funerary act specific to the deceased—for just *this* woman, *here*, *now*—in turn set within an environment of numinous power.

There are still other layers of meaning that can be found in Viking burials. In some of the boat graves, the relative layout of the objects matches the relative position of different functions in the hall—kitchen equipment at one end, the 'chamber' of the lord in the centre, bedding opposite, and so on. Are the ships also houses or halls of the dead? In this interpretation it is important that the dead stay in the mound, protecting or serving their community with spiritual power—that duality with the opposing idea of death as a journey. There is also no reason why parts of the dead might not travel while other parts stayed; perhaps this is the same notion as lies behind the 'missing' portions of cremated human remains.

All this did not end with the funeral, if one can even be sure when that was really 'over'. Many cultures and religions even today have very long cycles of formal mourning and observance, and it seems the Vikings may have been similar.

The first clue comes with the evident fact that graves were visited and used for a long period after the end of the initial funeral rites. In the great ship burial of Oseberg, it is clear from the excavation records that the burial mound covering it was originally only completed to half its eventual extent, creating a vertical face of earth over the middle of the ship, such as to leave one gable end of the grave chamber open. The environmental remains indicate it stayed this way certainly for weeks and probably months. During this period, the foredeck of the ship was apparently clear. People could access it, move about on it, and even enter the burial chamber to be admitted to the presence of the dead. One can also imagine the decomposition effects of an open grave. This was the situation when the deck was suddenly roughly piled with objects, and the chamber closed in frantic haste.

The same arrangement has been proposed for some of the Valsgärde boat graves, although in their case they may have been housed within a sort of mortuary version of a boat shed, again left open at one end as it emerged from the cemetery hill.

More humble graves were also opened on occasion and objects either moved around or taken. It is clear this could happen very soon after the funeral, because the corpses were still articulated and had not yet decayed. Equally, it is hard to imagine such 'grave robbing' (as it used to be termed) being a secret activity. How could one dig through metres of soil, dismantle stone constructions, and even cut through wooden components in silence, only a few metres from dwellings? Not least, in small communities such as these, it would have been impossible to walk about with somebody's grandfather's sword and expect no one to notice. There may be several explanations, of which one is a sort of sanctioned plundering, whereby things too valuable to really give to the ground would be deposited for form's sake during a funeral but then discreetly retrieved afterwards, while the community agreed to look the other way. Another possibility is that these were aggressive acts committed as desecrating ploys in the context of feuds, or at a higher scale as part of dynastic warfare. The Norwegian boat graves were opened in this way, and recent dating of the spades used to dig the access holes indicates it took place during the reign of Harald Bluetooth, a predatory Danish king with his eye on Norway. Perhaps he was taking out rivals among his opponents' ancestors, and thereby also weakening their grip on land and power through an attack on their family honour.

One obvious factor in understanding Viking burials is the question of where the individual dead were thought to go. Despite the stereotypes of Valhalla/Valhöll, actually relatively little is known of specific afterlife beliefs, and what there is contains many contradictions. The graves provide small clues, although they are hard to interpret. For example, the buried dead, and even the accompanying horses, sometimes wore crampons on their feet—does this imply the funeral took place in winter, or are the dead travelling to somewhere cold? The written sources mention special 'Hel-shoes' to speed the dead on their way—is this something similar? One of the bodies in the boat burial from Scar on Sanday, Orkney, was that of a man whose feet had both been broken and twisted round to face backwards; was this to prevent him from following the others on their way, or to stop him coming back to haunt the living?

The textual sources are very clear on beliefs concerning the restless dead—*draugar* in Old Norse. They were conceived in deeply tangible terms as reanimated corpses coming back to a kind of life. In the tales there is little rationale behind who returns in this way and who does not, although most often in life they were troublemakers, witches, and generally bad sorts. Some *draugar* grow in size, beyond the human, and gain strength and power from their undead state; in the sagas, they are often pitted against heroes, who rid a district of their haunting. A minority of these revenants are actually helpful—for example, dead women who return to cook and clean in a farmstead, usually to the horror of its living residents. It is usually ambiguous *how* the dead come back. They do not often seem to physically claw their way out of the grave, but more frequently just appear like ghosts, despite their corporeal state. On occasion they escape from living pursuers by sinking into the ground. Burials are sometimes discovered in which the corpse has been pinned down under rocks or mutilated, and archaeologists have speculated this may have been a means of ensuring they stayed put. The written sources also mention legal proceedings that could be used to formally forbid the door to *draugar*, summoning them individually to hear judgement and be returned to death.

When vehicles, especially ships, are involved in burials, it is often assumed that death was therefore a journey, and that the deceased would travel by boat, wagon, or sled into the next world. This may be true, but these might just represent exceptionally expensive possessions of the dead (or their living relatives) alongside all the other artefacts. In the greatest ship burial of all, Oseberg, the vessel was actually moored in the grave by a hawser tied to a massive boulder; apparently the intention was that it should not 'travel' anywhere at all.

There is no reason to expect consistency, because the Vikings themselves certainly did not. To take just one, by now familiar, example, a Rus' bystander at the ship funeral witnessed by ibn Faḍlān says clearly to him that the dead are burnt (rather than buried) so as to enter 'Paradise' immediately, and that the 'Lord' of the deceased played a role in sending a strong wind to ensure this happened. There is no reason why we should not take this seriously; it would provide an entirely sensible rationale for the cremation rite.

Funeral rituals probably included at least some kind of intentional preparations for the world to come, perhaps even arranged in such a way as to make one posthumous future more likely than others. This did not even have to involve a burial at all, or at least not of a body. One example of this is the phenomenon of hoard deposition, the concealment of wealth (usually silver) in the ground. Generations of numismatists have viewed these hoards essentially in economic terms—a very basic form of financial protection in the absence of banking, the earthen equivalent of stuffing your money under the mattress. To some extent this is probably true, and the cliché of 'buried treasure' is sometimes a reality. But in places like Gotland, where at least one silver hoard has been found on almost every farm, this cannot be the only explanation: it is simply not credible that virtually all homeowners concealed their family cash in the backyard and then died before telling anyone about it. There were probably many concurrent explanations for hoarding behaviour, but it may relate to mortuary ritual either in the absence of a corpse or in addition to one disposed of elsewhere. There is also an alternative, concerning the actions of a person in advance of her or his own death. Some ambitious individuals were capable of erecting runic memorials to themselves in their own life-times, which recalls Snorri's suggestion that hoarded wealth could be buried by the person who had accumulated it in order to enjoy it themselves in the afterlife. Scholars have often been too ready to dismiss details of the *Ynglingasaga* account, and yet this is the kind of telling observation that is at least as likely to reflect Viking-Age reality as it is Snorri's imagination.

The divine realm of Asgard held two primary destinations for the dead: Valhöll and Sessrúmnir, the latter being Freyja's hall in her fields of Fólkvangr. The poetry and later texts are clear that both of these were reserved for the warrior dead—half to Odin and half to Freyja.

Sessrúmnir, 'Seat-Room', was "large and beautiful", according to Snorri, and it does seem that this was truly a parallel Valhöll. In the *Prose Edda* he even calls the goddess herself Valfreyja, 'Freyja of the Slain', a similar formulation to that of the Valkyries themselves. This tallies with a passage in the Eddic poem *Grímnir's Sayings* where Odin clearly states that each day Freyja *chooses* half of the slain, and that she does so first, while he 'has' the other half. Fólkvangr means 'field of the host', a kind of supernatural parade ground, where the poems claim the goddess decides who shall sit on the benches of her hall. Freyja's role as a deity of war is often overlooked.

Valhöll appears in the sources as a remarkable place, rising on a plain and shining from a distance. Its rafters are the shafts of spears, "and golden shields covered its roof like shingles", in Snor-ri's words. Instead of blankets or rushes, its benches are covered in chainmail (quite uncomfortable, one would think). A wolf, the beast of battle, hangs over its threshold while an eagle circles above. There is a hint in the Eddic poems that Valhöll contains other halls within it, but this is unclear.

Inside, there are animals. The goat, Heidrún, can be milked for mead of divine quality, producing it by the vatful. From the antlers of a stag, Eikthyrnir, drips dew that is the purest water in the worlds. It is clear that in Valhöll are all the trappings of hall life in Midgard, but writ large. Servants gather kindling for the fires; there are pigs to be fed; horses graze outside; and hunting dogs are at the ready. The *einherjar*—the immortal warrior dead—drink, play board games, and fight. If they are killed, they rise again each evening in time for supper: choice cuts of pork from the boar, Saehrímnir, roasted every day and whole again the next.

Valhöll has 540 doors (the same as Thor's hall), from each of which some eight hundred *einherjar* will pour forth to fight the Ragnarök. It has been speculated that this image may have been influenced by a dim folk memory of seeing the Colosseum in Rome—an imposing structure of staggering size, covered by arched openings, within which warriors fought in an endless show. The notion has gone out of scholarly favour now, but there might be something to it; Roman templates were nothing new in the North.

Odin's hall, and Freyja's, hold "all men who have fallen in battle since the beginning", but they will be too few "when the wolf comes", as Fenrir inevitably will at the Ragnarök. Kings and their retinues are therefore especially welcome, with the Valkyries serving wine for such a royal entrance. One poem—among the earliest sources for the hall of the slain—sums it up. This is the *Eiríksmál*, 'Words for Eirík', composed on the orders of Queen Gunnhild, sorceress widow of King Eirík Bloodaxe of York. Killed in an ambush at "a certain lonely place" in 954, Eirík was one of the ultimate Vikings, in the best and worst senses, and his fame has not faded from the tenth century through today. In the poem, Odin and his servants hear a mighty host approaching Valhöll, a lord with kings in his train, the greatest of guests who has earned his place:

Heill nú, vel skalt hér kominn ok gakk í höll
Hail to you, be welcome here and come into the hall!

The other main realm of the dead was Hel (pronounced approximately like the English word 'heal'), with a problematic etymology that may or may not relate to its Christian near-namesake. Located in the north, it was ruled by a being of the same name—a woman whose body is half that of a beautiful goddess and half blue and dark, the colour of a corpse. She is Loki's daughter by one of his complicated liaisons, and is said to be gloomy and downcast. Her halls are 'high', very large, and very many (which implies the need for space and a growing population). The most detailed descriptions come from Snorri and other late texts, but both the place and its host are also mentioned in Eddic and skaldic poetry.

The long and difficult road to Hel appears as a specific motif several times in the poems. This is the path taken by Odin on Sleipnir, desperate to find an explanation for the troubling nightmares that have disturbed his son Baldr. He wakes the dead sorceress by the eastern doors of Hel's hall to ask about Baldr's dreams (which have their own poem of that name), only to be horrified as he sees the benches inside being cleared for the boy's reception. There is even an Eddic poem called *Brynhild's Hel-ride*—the tale of a dead, lovelorn Valkyrie who travels there in the wagon in which she was burnt on her pyre.

Whether Hel really was a 'bad' place has long been a central question in the untangling of the Norse afterlife. There are many negatives—its ruler's appearance and demeanour, the connotations that the north held in the Viking mind, and the long road 'down' to it, nine levels deep into the dark and mist. It doesn't *sound* nice. But on the other hand, these may be Christian interpolations of the later texts, especially given the similarities of the name. It might have been hard for the medieval authors to make it anything other than the opposite of Valhöll, a concept they understood. This is emphasised by the rhetorical flourishes Snorri can't help but add: Hel's knife is called Famine, her bowl is Hunger, she sleeps in Sick-Bed, the portal of her hall is Stumbling-Block, her servants are Lazy-Walkers, and so on. No other aspect of the Norse afterlife, or any divine abode, is described using this kind of blunt-instrument vocabulary.

In fact there is no early indication that Hel was an unpleasant place; indeed, there is very little to indicate one's deeds in life affected where one went after death (other than battlefield heroics). Not least, Baldr, the brightest god, goes to Hel after he is slain by his brother Höd, and even Egil Skalla-Grímsson—saga hero, quintessential Viking, warrior-poet, and Odin worshipper par excellence—says himself that Hel is waiting for him "on the headland of his old age". In the earlier poetry, dying men are said to be entering "Hel's embrace". There is every suggestion that a lot of people went there, that they expected to do so, and that they were in no way depressed by the thought. We should be wary of equating 'Valhalla' with some kind of Christian heaven, or Hel with its dark twin.

One unsettling fact that emphasises just how little is known of Norse 'religion' is that we have little idea where women went after death. Presumably most journeyed to Hel, just like the majority of men, but does this explain the many high-status female burials that are in every way the equal of the male equivalents? Perhaps the female counterparts to the *einherjar* were also welcomed by Freyja, travelling to her halls in the wagons that are found in their graves. A single female character in the *Saga of Egil Skalla-Grímsson* says as much, but this is the only instance. Alternatively, this may be the proof that Hel (the place) was not negative or dark, simply a different destination that welcomed allcomers.

As if to further emphasise the gaps in our knowledge, a single line in the Eddic poem *Harbard's Song* suggests a whole world, with attitudes and assumptions behind it of which nothing is known. As the poem says (with my italics):

Odin has the noblemen who fall in battle
and *Thor has the race of thralls.*

So, there was an eternity for the enslaved, too, apparently in the care of the storm god.

There was also an afterlife of the sea, set apart for those who died there. The drowned—all of them—were caught in a net by Rán, the sea goddess married to Aegir, lord of the ocean. Their unnamed underwater hall may have been in some senses a marine equivalent of Valhöll or Hel, although it is not known if a terrestrial death was actually a requirement to go to those places (what of a great warrior who died in a sea battle, for example?). The water deities were old, as they are mentioned in both Eddic and skaldic poetry. Rán had nine daughters, the embodiment of the waves, who sometimes carry a suggestion of the slight erotic charge that attaches to the Valkyries. In the texts, their father, Aegir, seems friendly enough, hospitable and generous, whereas his wife personified the treacherous, unpredictable nature of the sea.

Just as the *einherjar* would fight for the gods at the Ragnarök, the drowned also had their station, although a terrible one that they do not seem to have earned. As all the powers gather at the end, something will stir on the ocean floor, the greatest Viking ship ever made. Its name is Naglfar, 'Nail-Ship', so called because it is built from the fingernails of everyone who has ever died; the vessel thereby naturally grows larger by increments over the millennia until by the time of the Ragnarök it will be vast beyond imagining. As the roosters begin to crow, announcing the coming battle, Naglfar breaks loose from the sea bed and rises to the surface, its waterlogged timbers green and rotten. Its cargo will be all the dead of Hel; its captain is the giant Hrym; Loki stands at the helm. The drowned are its crew.

Finally, there are also episodes in the Icelandic sagas that present more terrestrial afterlives—physical places in Midgard where some of the dead reside (beyond the localised sense of them 'living' in their graves). These are almost always mountains or strangely shaped hills, outcrops that rise suddenly from flat plains and the like. Their names are usually some variant of Helgafell, 'Holy Mountain', and there are several such places in the Icelandic landscape that you can still visit today. Each is clearly linked to

16. Holy Mountain. The site of Helgafell on the Snæfellsnes peninsula in Iceland is one of several such sacred outcrops, that in the Viking Age were believed to function as abodes of the dead. The heroine of the *Saga of the People of Laxardal*, Gudrún Ósvifrs-dóttir, is supposedly buried below the rock. Photo: Creative Commons.

a particular district, and often to its leading clans. In essence, the holy mountains function as a sort of family vault combining the familiar connections with the land and an actual afterlife destination. This may be the kind of place that lay on the other side of the 'doors' opened by the Gotland picture-stones. One wonders if this is a relic of an older, more personal set of beliefs, and susceptible to a greater degree of local control than the more abstract afterlives of Asgard, Hel, and the halls of Rán. In any event, the world inside the holy rock seems pleasant and is depicted as a feast of warmth, food, and drink—a scene of literal life after death.

Attractive though some of these places sound, there was nothing 'deserving' about most of the Norse afterlife. It is hard to find a moral scheme in the Viking mind or in the actions of their gods. Anybody can drown, and not everyone is a battlefield hero—and yet the inhabitants of both Hel's and Aegir's halls end up fighting for evil at the doom of all things. For the living, it must have been strange to imagine where a family member lost at sea really was, and what would happen to her or him in time.

The Vikings' knowledge concerning the ultimate destination of their souls (for want of a better term), of the fate of every person— their *doom*, in the proper sense of the word—and the coming war of the Ragnarök gave them a very different outlook from anyone alive today.

This difference was one of spiritual beliefs and death rituals, of worldview and how reality itself was perceived; it extended further still, across the social strata and inside every individual. But what happened when that difference met the outside world of their own time?

Of course, the Scandinavians had connections with the surrounding regions going back far into the Iron Age and still deeper into remote prehistory. They were no strangers to foreign parts, and to an extent they were familiar figures immediately beyond the diffuse borders of the North. But in the middle decades of the eighth century, a number of factors came together to both propel and draw the Vikings overseas in new ways, and in ever greater numbers.

They would appear in the annals first as raiders and pirates, a threat that eventually escalated to the scale of fleets and armies. As traders they moved farther than ever, ultimately into the depths of the Eurasian steppe. As colonists they established themselves across western and eastern Europe, while as voyagers they settled new lands in the North Atlantic all the way to the shores of the Americas.

To get inside this 'Viking phenomenon'—to understand how it began and then slowly rolled across the northern world—requires nuanced thinking. There is no point in seeking illusory 'triggers' and 'smoking guns' where they did not exist. Instead, we should explore the rationale for the raids; the nature of the market forces that drove them; and the political economics of warrior culture that underpinned it all.

In short, it is time to put the 'Viking' in the Viking Age.

THE VIKING
PHENOMENON

9

INROADS

THE START OF THE VIKING Age is often visualised by means of a map, not least in books such as this one. It will use arrows to show the routes, dates, and targets of the 'first raids', usually broken down into discrete chunks of time—a half century, say—and thereby also tracing the progression of the maritime attacks that for so many define these three centuries. The movements of 'Vikings' are most frequently shown in a rather abstract sense, perhaps indicating a point of origin, and thus also successive 'waves' of assault.

Many of these maps have as their starting point the raid on the insular monastery of Lindisfarne off the coast of Northumbria in northern England, which was attacked in June 793—the first securely recorded example. Thereafter, on further maps, follows an escalating series of attacks on other monastic houses, vulnerable settlements, and eventually whole regions accessible from the coasts and rivers of the British Isles and the north-western European Continent. Many scholars have tried to divide the Viking Age into phases, usually determined by changes in the patterns of maritime violence. The conventional view sees an initial period of sporadic raiding from c. 789 to 805, and then a focussed shift to targets in Ireland and Scotland until 834, before the rise of true Viking armies with overwintering campaigns after that date.

This is a pattern I tend to follow, although I am constantly aware that it is an imposition of hindsight, not reflective of life as lived. And of course, we know that there was much more to the Viking Age than this, not least in the centuries that lay behind its ostensible beginnings. These were people with their own richly textured cultural world, the inheritors of sophisticated Scandinavian traditions, practices, and worldviews built up over millennia. Vikings had their own motivations and rationales for what they did. Not least, their actions overseas fitted with political trends and ideologies that were entirely embedded in the societies at home in Scandinavia.

In human history it is occasionally possible to discern what systems theorists call singularities—relatively small social changes in themselves but with long-term and large-scale impacts. They can be hard to get a grip on, often the result of many separate elements suddenly coming together in what may be a more-or-less random manner. Once set in motion, however, they can be difficult or even impossible to reverse—the proverbial tipping point. Archaeology deals with material culture, literally with things that have survived from the past into the present, and as such the buried record rarely preserves singularities directly. With effort and care, though, they can be discerned in the patterns that form around them, and this is possible for the beginnings of the Viking Age.

Before venturing there, however, there is something else, almost a moral imperative. The 'cartographic' Viking Age, the raids-as-mapped, is a useful but comfortably distant way to approach these events. A violent reality check is needed—a corrective and necessary acknowledgement of what that maze of dates and place-names and labelled arrows really meant.

At their most immediate, on the spot, on the day, for many the raids were the most bitter of endings. Behind every notation on our maps lay an urgent present of panic and terror, of slashing blades and sharp points, of sudden pain and open wounds; of bodies by the wayside, and orphaned children; of women raped and all manner of people enslaved; of entire family lines ending in blood; of screams and then silence where there should be lively noise; of burning buildings and ruin; of economic loss; of religious convictions overturned in a moment and replaced with humiliation and rage; of roads choked with refugees as columns of smoke rose behind them. Of utter, ruthless brutality, expressed in all its forms.

In explaining their overseas attacks, it should never be forgotten who and what Vikings—*actual* Vikings—really were, beyond the compelling intricacies of their worldview and the wonderful fact that they each carried within them the personification of luck and a female spirit-guide. In poetry, the English called them *wælwulfas*, 'slaughter-wolves', and with good reason—but the Vikings even said it themselves. Here is the great tenth-century Icelandic warrior-poet Egil Skalla-Grímsson, describing his raiding experiences (in an effort to impress a woman at a feast, which also tells you something about him):

Farit hefi ek blóðgum brandi
svá at mér benþiðurr fylgði,
ok gjallanda geiri;
gangr var harðr af víkingum.
Gjǫrðum reiðir róstu,
rann eldr of sjǫt manna,
ek lét blóðga búka
í borghliðum sœfask.

I have gone with bloody blade
where the wound-partridges [ravens] followed,
and with screaming spear;
Vikings fought fiercely.
Raging we gave battle,
fire ran through men's houses,

I let bloody bodies
sleep in town gateways.

In the latter decades of the eighth century, a singularity composed of intricate, intersecting streams in Scandinavian society—and its interaction with the wider world—began to emerge. There was no convenient single event or factor that set 'the Viking Age' in motion; instead there were many of them in combination. In seeking to understand what all these components were, and how they came together with such large-scale and violent drama, the emphasis must always be on multicausality and complexity.

Crucially, at the core of it all was an export of the trends and behaviours that had already been happening *inside* Scandinavia for centuries—the long trajectory from the end of the Migration Period to the eve of the Viking Age. This cultural package had long included international contacts and interactions. In practice, the Viking raiders were never a bolt from the blue, unknown barbarian sails on a North Sea horizon. Their victims had encountered Scandinavians many times before, but as traders rather than agents of chaos; the surprise was in the violence, not the contact.

By the eighth century, the conflict that had been endemic among the petty kingdoms of Scandinavia for most of the late Iron Age had become unsustainable, especially along the Norwegian coasts. Tensions escalated to the point of requiring a larger arena for their resolution. It is not hard to see the expediency in seeking material wealth overseas to the west, using such ventures to expand the military forces available, and sustaining them through the promise of reward. There were also economic stimuli in the mercantile ambitions of the Norwegian sea-kings and also their counterparts in Denmark and Baltic Sweden. Looking both west and east, they saw opportunity in proactive overseas trade. Coupled with this were social pressures—the effects of polygyny creating an underclass of young men disenfranchised by the laws of inheritance and with minimal marriage prospects. A summer or two of maritime violence offered the potential for life-altering change in many directions. Lastly, there was the traditional Scandinavian worldview itself, and its weaponised expression in an assault on the Christian cultures that really were bent on its destruction.

But before exploring these underlying causes over the following chapters, it is first necessary to understand their effects.

In approaching the individual events of the early Viking Age, rather than at the level of longer-term processes, it is easy to slip into a kind of tyranny of written sources. More-or-less contemporary texts such as the *Anglo-Saxon Chronicle* preserve handy lists of annals, stating clearly what apparently occurred and when (such as the Lindisfarne raid in 793). For all the scholarly critique there has been of detail, it is unsurprising that the picture they contain has become the focus of attention.

However, the earliest actual evidence for a Viking raid is not textual at all, but archaeological. Crucially, considering that it predates the Lindisfarne attack by more than forty years, it does not come from the West and the British Isles, but from the East, and the Baltic.

Around the middle of the eighth century, c. 750, a Swedish maritime expedition came to violent grief on or near the island of Saaremaa off the coast of Estonia. We know this because of the chance discoveries from 2008 to 2012 of two boats full of dead warriors, buried by the seashore in what is now the village of Salme. They had been set up parallel to the water some forty metres apart on an isthmus, at a strategic point where ships would pass. The graves would have been a visible landmark—they were intended to be seen, and remembered. Before the excavation of the Salme find, the largest number of bodies previously known from a Viking boat burial was four, arguably five. The first of the Salme vessels, the smaller of the two, contained the corpses of seven men; astonishingly, the second Salme ship contained no fewer than thirty-four bodies. Taken together, the Salme boat graves are unique, not least for the insights they provide into the earliest raids, and are therefore worth taking time to explore.

The smaller of the two vessels was a rowing craft approximately eleven and a half metres long and two metres wide, perhaps a sort of ship's boat. Its mortuary crew had been placed sitting up on the benches: six of them in three pairs at the oars, and the seventh, and oldest, at one end—probably the steersman in the stern. The men were buried with a variety of tools and utensils, a few weapons (although not enough for each of them), large quantities of meat, and the headless bodies of two hawks.

The second vessel was much larger: a true oceangoing ship seventeen metres long and three metres across the beam. At one end of the boat, probably the prow, thirty-four men were buried in four layers, laid side by side down in the hull. On and around them were at least forty-two swords, many of high-quality workmanship with jewelled hilts and gold decoration. One of them even had a blade inlaid with designs in gold, something entirely unknown before the Salme find. The men wore jewellery of simple cloak pins, implying practical, hard-wearing gear for use at sea—nothing fancy. The exceptions were a few wearing beads and two with necklaces of bear's teeth; they would have looked striking. The bodies were strewn with gaming pieces. Some had fish carefully placed over them; others held sea birds in their arms. Some of the men had chops of veal, mutton, and pork stacked on their breast. The deck was heaped with cuts of beef and pork.

The whole pile of bodies was covered by a wooden 'burial mound' made from shields, placed with overlapping boards to form a timber dome over the dead. Each shield boss had been hammered flat, the boards were slashed, and many of the weapons were deliberately bent. The mound had been covered by a single piece of coarse textile, and the only such item large enough presumably would have been a sail. It had been weighted down with a curb of stones. Three birds of prey had been laid over the 'shield mound'. Six dogs, cut to pieces, had been draped over the shields around the perimeter. Two swords were stuck vertically in the top of the mound.

The Salme burials had clearly been preceded by fighting of some kind. Many of the bodies, especially in the upper layers of the 'shield mound' and in the smaller boat, exhibited either blade, penetration, and/or blunt-force trauma, with slashes to the face and arms, arrow wounds to the hips, and more. In the centre of the mound lay a man with some of the worst injuries and also the finest weapons, including a ring-hilt sword—the mark of a *very* high-status leader. Unlike the other bodies, his had not been covered with gaming pieces; instead, he had only one, the king, and it had been placed in his mouth.

The dead ranged in age from late adolescence to maturity, with the majority in their thirties—they were men in their prime. They were also unusually tall. Isotope studies of the teeth suggested that (with only a handful of exceptions) their place of origin was somewhere in the Mälar Valley of central Sweden, a conclusion supported by the parallels between the Salme weapons and equipment and those of the Uppland boat graves.

The clear suggestion, reinforced by massive wounds on many of the bodies, is that the Salme burials resulted from a Svear maritime expedition that ended in violence—in other words, a raid. It has also been argued that this was a diplomatic mission; hawks were commonly used as prestige gifts and were extraordinarily difficult to keep alive in transport. If this was the case, the diplomacy must have failed, to put it mildly.

The care taken with the dead, the time and effort, and the resemblance to the ship rituals of the Swedish mainland all suggest that the dead were buried by their friends, and thus that whatever had occurred, the Swedes ultimately prevailed. DNA studies also show a broad pattern of relationships implying that most of them came from the same, albeit very extended, local and familial background. Four were actually brothers, buried together in a group. Taken together, this looks very much like part of one of the family dynasties that formed the main power blocks in the eighth century.

That the Austmarr—the 'Eastern Sea', as it was called in Old Norse—was a key arena of Scandinavian maritime power play, including raiding, should not surprise us in the least. Snorri's semi-mythical history of the Ynglinga dynasty clearly describes the central Swedish kingdom's operations there. The Danes had probably been doing something similar along the southern Baltic coast. The conclusion needs to be stated again: Viking raids, in the literal and exact sense of the term, were initially a phenomenon not of the West, but of the East. They were also, to a great extent, a 'domestic' activity that occurred in Scandinavian 'territorial waters', to use a modern anachronism that nonetheless fits. This is why, even later in the period, there are runestones that speak of guarding *against* Vikings: they were equal opportunity predators.

One of the Ynglinga kings, Yngvar, even died on such an expedition, as Snorri says:

> King Yngvar made peace with the Danes, and then began to raid around the Baltic [Austrvegr]. One summer he took out an army and went to Eistland [Estonia] and raided during the summer, at the place called Steinn. Then Eistr [Estonians] came down with a large army, and they had a battle. The native army was so numerous that the Svíar could put up no resistance. Then King Yngvar died and his army fled. He is buried in a mound, close by the sea. This was in Adalsýsla district. The Svíar went home after this defeat. So says Thjódólf [the poet of the 'List of the Ynglingas']:

> It was said
> that Yngvar was
> by Sýsla people
> put to death,
> and off 'Sea's Heart' [sea's heart: rock: Steinn]

the host of Eistr
slew the leader,
the light-hued one,
and the eastern sea
sings the lay
of Gymir to cheer   [Gymir: personification of the sea]
the fallen king.

The Adalsýsla district is the mainland directly opposite Saaremaa, but the location of Steinn, the rock in the heart of the sea, is uncertain. It may be that the answer can be found in the *Historia Norvegiae*, a Latin history of Norway older than Snorri's *Heimskringla*, and which explicitly says Yngvar "was killed by the inhabitants while campaigning on an island in the Baltic called Eysysla". The place-name is the origin of the modern Ösel, the Swedish name for Saaremaa—in other words, when these sources are combined, Yngvar seems to have died and been buried *in a mound by the sea on that island*. Yngvar's reign is usually dated to the early seventh century, a hundred years before the Salme burials, but one wonders nonetheless, not least in view of the man with the gaming king-piece in his mouth.

If this initial eastern, rather than western, focus is understandable, it is equally clear that the idea of launching serious long-distance expeditions over the open sea and thus beyond the Vikings' immediate cultural comfort zone (as it were) was directed westwards to the British Isles and almost simultaneously south-west to Frankia, what is today France and the Low Countries.

The Vikings ominously enter the written record in the pages of the *Anglo-Saxon Chronicle*, the court record of the Wessex kingdom, for the year 789:

Here Beorhtric took King Offa's daughter Eadburh. And in his days came first three ships of Northmen from

Hordaland: and then the reeve rode there and wanted to compel them to go to the king's town because he did not know what they were; and then they killed him. These were the first ships of the Danish men which sought out the land of the English race.

The *Annals of St. Neots* specify the location as "the island which is called Portland", which lies just off the Dorset coast near Weymouth. It must be said that the date is not secure, in that this only locates the event in the period of the Wessex king's reign, 786–802; the encounter was therefore not necessarily in the year of the annal, which was compiled retrospectively. It is also not entirely clear whether Portland was a raid at all, rather than some kind of customs-control misunderstanding, or why shiploads of Scandinavians would have come so far south without previously making landfall. The confusion is increased by the identification of their origin as Hordaland in western Norway, but at the same time, the scribe says they were "Danish". The catch-all of *Dani* (and *pagani*, 'pagans') for Scandinavians would repeat throughout the English sources on the period. Finally, the entry contains a blatant error, perhaps a deliberate untruth: we know Scandinavians had already been in contact with the English for at least a century and probably much longer. The possible reasons for the *Chronicle's* discretion here will become apparent.

The *Chronicle's* version of the earliest raids needs to be supplemented by the evidence from contemporary letters and charters, which suggest Portland might not even be the first of them. In 792 a charter of King Offa of Mercia refers to Kent, and the need for military service against "seaborne pagans" (who can only be Scandinavians) in migratory fleets that had presumably been active for some time.

The first securely recorded western raid came in the following year, and is of course the famous assault on Lindisfarne, the Northumbrian monastery dedicated to Saint Cuthbert and located on Holy Island, which was connected to the mainland by a tidal causeway. As the *Anglo-Saxon Chronicle* puts it:

> In this year fierce, foreboding omens came over the land of the Northumbrians, and the wretched people shook; there were excessive whirlwinds, lightning, and fiery dragons were seen flying in the sky. These signs were followed by great famine, and a little after those, that same year on 6th ides of January, the ravaging of wretched heathen men destroyed God's church at Lindisfarne.

The *Annals of Lindisfarne* amend the date to June 8, which makes more sense in terms of weather. This second description of the attack, more a reaction, is also among the most-quoted passages of the whole period. In a letter written to the king of Northumbria by the English cleric Alcuin, then in temporary residence at the Frankish court, one can read:

> Never before has such terror appeared in Britain as we have now suffered from a pagan race, nor was it thought that such an inroad from the sea could be made. Behold, the church of St. Cuthbert spattered with the blood of the priests of God, despoiled of all its ornaments; a place more venerable than all in Britain is given as prey to pagan peoples.

Later accounts describe how the monks were killed outright, thrown into the sea to drown, or enslaved, and the church plate was carried off.

Alcuin returned to the Lindisfarne raid several times in his letters and notes, but one theme emerges consistently—the idea of surprise, the sense that this had never happened before. Scholars used to press regularly on this point, but it began to be challenged already in the 1980s, when the first real archaeological evidence was found of pre-Viking North Sea trade, implying close links between the peoples that predated the raids. Attention turned to another passage in Alcuin's *same letter* to Aethelred of Northumbria:

> Consider the dress, the hairstyle, and the luxurious habits of the princes and people. Look at the hairstyle, how you have wished to imitate the pagans in their beards and hair. Does not the terror threaten of those whose hairstyle you wished to have?

In other words, the Lindisfarne raiders came from a people already familiar enough to their victims that they had once been seen as fashionable role-models—which, of course, requires close observation. Scholars have long argued over the word *navigium*, conventionally translated 'inroad from the sea', as above, as evidence of an unprecedented act. Another hand in the manuscript has amended it to *naufragium*, a 'disaster', and while this is probably a later addition, the sense may be the same: Alcuin meant an *aggressive* marine incursion, not just maritime contact of any kind. What astonished Alcuin and his contemporaries was that their Scandinavian friends brought swords, not goods to trade, and it is this that marks the real behavioural turning point of the Viking phenomenon—at least in its overtly violent aspects, as outsiders saw them. When Alcuin offered to negotiate the return of the hostages taken at Lindisfarne, in his letter to its bishop, Higbald, it is evident he somehow had a line of communication to their captors, which again suggests he knew them.

The Vikings were back the following year, and they knew what they liked: isolated, undefended, but very rich monastic houses. They were probably well familiar with them from trading ventures, as markets were sometimes held near such institutions. Any Scandinavian entering a church of this kind—rather drab on the outside and served by ineffectual-looking men with silly haircuts—must have been astounded at the gold and silverwork within. Motivation is not an issue here. Another monastery was hit, the twin Northumbrian houses of Monkwearmouth-Jarrow. During the raid, one of the Viking commanders was killed, and some of the ships were "broken up" by bad weather that drowned a few of those aboard; when the surviving crews staggered ashore, they were massacred by the locals. Even at this early date, these were not entirely one-sided affairs.

In 794 the *Annals of Ulster* record massive raids in Britain, although in general terms. After the Monkwearmouth setback, conventional wisdom has it that the Vikings' attention turned to Scotland, and in 795 the island abbey of Iona was sacked with many casualties among the monks (struck again in 802 and 806, it was eventually abandoned). However, by 797 Alcuin was writing to the citizens of Canterbury to lament how he saw "a pagan people becoming accustomed to laying waste our shores with piratical robbery", which does not sound like the reflection of only a handful of raids in distant Scotland and across the Irish Sea. He records fighting with maritime aggressors in Frankia in 799, and only a few years later, there is a mention of an astonishing two hundred ships attacking Frisia (today's Netherlands).

Ireland was first assaulted in 795, the same year as Iona, at a similar site on the Isle of Rathlin. The raids continued on the *west* coast, also at more insular monasteries—Inishmurray and Inishbofin. Holmpatrick on the east coast was assaulted in 798. By the early 800s, Ireland was being raided almost continually, when again and again coastal monasteries were targeted as easy prey. In 808 the *Royal Frankish Annals* note how pirates captured a papal envoy for ransom; as the aftermath of Lindisfarne makes clear, there was some form of diplomatic relations with the Vikings. The same Frankish sources also mention particularly intensive attacks in Ireland between 811 and 813.

At the same time in southern England, the picture becomes clearer still, when Kentish charters covering the period from 811 to 822 on several occasions mention defences against the Vikings, who seem to be moving west along the coast. There is a suggestion of fortifications and possibly shipborne deterrents. One charter of 811 even refers to the *destruction* of camps, implying the Vikings had actually set up some kind of landward bases; other charters make it clear that there were fortifications against the pagans and others that were made by them. In 814 the charters make similar references to anti-pagan defences, suggesting repeated incursions presumably each summer. The raids were beginning to accelerate in frequency. In 822, attacks are mentioned at Milton, which is fifteen kilometres inland. This same charter refers to "pagan enemies", which raises the question as to whether there might also have been pagan 'friends'. All the charters refer to the construction of bridges, which might have served as river blockades (a tactic used with success fifty years later in Frankia).

Interestingly, none of this appears in the *Anglo-Saxon Chronicle*, which first mentions escalating Viking attacks from the mid-830s onwards. However, the *Chronicle* was the court propaganda arm of the Wessex dynasty. It seems that certain kinds of news were unwelcome, or perhaps the aim was to skate over the ineffective defences of the early ninth century in favour of Wessex's 'heroic' efforts against the Danes decades later. Despite this, in the charter evidence the same pattern repeats in Mercia in the English Midlands. The suggestion of negotiations with the Vikings, and the odd silences of the *Chronicle*, have even led one historian to suggest that Ecgberht of Wessex's takeover of Mercia in 824 might have been achieved with Scandinavian military assistance.

An obvious question concerns where the Scandinavians were coming from, and how. The first raiders were primarily from the west coast of Norway, but it has always been assumed their route to Britain was directly south to the Northern Isles of Shetland and Orkney. From there, it was thought the raiders sailed either to the east down the English coast to the Northumbrian monasteries, or to the west and into the Irish Sea, in either case turning back afterwards for home. In view of the new interpretations of the Kent coast charters, utterly missing from the *Chronicle* and thus distorting our perceptions of events, it has plausibly been suggested that the Norwegian raids instead hugged the European coast past the shores of Denmark and the Low Countries, before heading across to the British Isles by the shortest route. From there they cruised northwards back to Norway, either directly along the English east coast and past Northumbria, or into the Irish Sea from the south (occasionally even passing to the west of Ireland), thereby looting their way home.

An isolated attack on the mouth of the Loire in 819 sounds very much like a side effort on one of these westward voyages around the south-west of Britain before it headed up into the Irish Sea. Dorestad, the great Frisian trading centre, reached its zenith in the 830s, and for that reason was also thereafter the site of frequent Viking attacks, which makes sense if the raiding fleets were travelling this southern route.

The combination of the Salme boat graves and new work from Britain represents a radical revision of how the early Viking impact unfolded. From the Baltic to the North Sea, this in turn was inevitably linked to where those raiders came from and why—all of which was intimately bound up with the political economy back in Scandinavia. In addition, market forces, demographics, and ideology all played a role, and it is in this constellation of contributory factors that the real origins of the Viking Age can be found.

10

MARITORIA

THE VIKING RAIDS WERE VIOLENT, brutal, and tragic. They were also very profitable indeed, albeit with inherent risks. As such, the raids were deeply political and also represented the manifestation of economic policy—often in ways that many of their participants (as distinct from their commanders) might not have recognised at the time.

The centuries prior to the start of the Viking Age saw the rise of what might best be called *maritoria*, a form of power that combined the aspirations of petty kings with the control of territory, closely connected to a new form of market, and all linked by a relationship with the sea. The reasons for the raids can be found in these special polities and their underpinnings.

As with so much of the early history of the North, these developments had their roots in the gradual decline of the Western Roman Empire, and in the changes that rolled over Scandinavian societies as the imperial institutions to the south contracted or failed. The rising aristocracies—those 'new elites' with their hall culture, skaldic self-honour, and monumental burial mounds—were only part of the picture. Set alongside them, but intimately meshed with their ambitions, was the revival and reorientation of the post-Roman economy. It was the revolution in these market

286

forces, as much as the rise of the warlords, that laid the foundations for the Viking Age.

By the sixth and seventh centuries, at the latest, the Scandinavian elites were already expanding beyond localised economies and subsistence strategies to embrace more organised, long-distance activities. Thus a North Atlantic right whale caught off the Norwegian coast supplied a local market with oil, blubber, and meat, while its hide and especially its eminently carveable bones were exported to the rest of Scandinavia. These connections extended still further, both to the nascent European empires that remade themselves along pseudo-Roman models, and also to the east with the trade routes of the maritime Silk Roads through the Persian Gulf to the Indian Ocean and ultimately even to distant China. The key to all this was control of the system, which was exercised through the establishment of specialised market centres, founded as deliberate strategies of economic power with an eye to both domestic and foreign trade.

This reorientation, from networks of redistribution and gift exchange to more disembedded trade, was not an isolated development. The new mercantile horizons of Scandinavia were a reflection of a general north-west European phenomenon: the resurgence of the post-Roman economy with an international platform. In England and Frankia, new 'emporia' of this kind were known as *wics*, a component preserved today in east-coast town names such as Ipswich (Gipeswic) and Norwich (Norvic). They included Hamwic (today's Southampton) and Lundenwic (London, centred south-west of the Roman city), and also extended into other, more northern kingdoms such as Northumbria, with sites like Eoforwic (York).

In a form of settlement known as 'ladder development', several of these places initially took the form of two streets running parallel with the shore, one above the other, with cross streets (the 'rungs' of the ladder) connecting them at intervals. The waterside thoroughfare linked directly with the incoming marine traffic, which was either drawn up on the sand itself or, later, served by docks and jetties. It is no accident that the main street of Lundenwic was *strond* (now cocooned within the city of Westminster as the Strand)—literally 'the beach', as the name implies. On the street behind stood the residences, workshops, and commercial heart of the settlements. The 'ladders' soon expanded by adding more streets both away from the water and along its frontage.

Within the Frankish Empire, there was a similar market centre at Quentovic, a now-lost settlement on the Canche River near Étaples in the Pas-de-Calais, its trading activities primarily directed across the Channel to Kent. In addition to Quentovic, Frisia— roughly the modern Netherlands—emerged as a particular fulcrum of the north-west European trade. Frisia was central precisely because it was also liminal, bordering the territories of the Franks, Saxons, and Danes, and thus critical to them all—especially as a conduit of trade. It had maritime connections west and south, north-east to the base of Jylland, and also to the lands of the Germans. The key site here was Dorestad, located in the Utrecht region near a crucial fork of the Rhine that afforded excellent communications. From the seventh century onwards, it grew rapidly into the primary northern market and port of the Frankish Empire. By far the largest entrepot of its kind, Dorestad developed into an extraordinary linear development running for several kilometres along the river. Its broad timber jetties stretched far out into the stream and were so tightly packed as to essentially form a wooden, overwater extension of the market itself.

By the early 700s the same phenomenon was appearing in Scandinavia.

In Denmark, the earliest Scandinavian region to consolidate higher political authority, this development centred on Ribe in south-west Jylland, close to the border of the kingdom. Probably the first of the expanding Scandinavian emporia, it seems to have been founded early in the eighth century, stimulated by proximity

17. The first market. A reconstruction of early Ribe, as it looked in the late eighth century—small plots, divided by low fences with simple workshops and craft activity. This place would grow into one of Scandinavia's first towns. Image by and © Flemming Bau.

to the English and Frankish *wics*, and the Frisian trade in particular. Within a few years, a series of long, regular plots were laid out along a basic street system, bounded by low fence lines and containing workshop areas for the production of beads, metalwork, and other crafts. It was probably not much to look at initially, and perhaps was only seasonally occupied, but Ribe was the beginning of an economic and political experiment that was to have far-reaching consequences.

By around 770 or so, a second major Danish market had been founded on the opposite coast of Jylland at Hedeby (now Haithabu in northern Germany, but at the time firmly in Viking-Age Denmark). Situated on the Schlei River, Hedeby lay farther south than Ribe and was integrated into the Danevirke defensive rampart that guarded the border. A note in the *Royal Frankish Annals*, one of the official court histories of Charlemagne's empire, relates how in 808 the Danish king, Godfred, had been raiding in the Slavic territories to the east, where he destroyed the trading settlement of Rerik (modern Groß Strömkendorf in northern Germany). Allied at the time with the Franks and serving as a sort of free port, Rerik was essentially a kind of West Slavic Ribe, and it is clear Godfred appreciated its potential. Rather than occupying a site far from his home base, the *Annals* record how Godfred simply 'transferred' its merchants wholesale to Hedeby, installing them there under his patronage.

The same process was playing out elsewhere in the North. In Sweden, something similar was set up on an island in Lake Mälaren, which was some distance from the sea but provided a sheltered, deep-water harbour and ready access both to the Baltic and to the river routes inland. In this settlement of Birka, the earliest occupation layers date to around 750—somewhere between the foundation of Ribe and Hedeby. What may perhaps have been a local market site was quickly made permanent with houses, workshops, and streets arrayed in a crescent with its open edge against the water, the lanes running down to stone-founded wooden jetties that extended into the lake. The first Christian mission to Sweden reached Birka in 829 under the leadership of a senior priest (and later archbishop) named Anskar, and the records of his largely unsuccessful efforts also contain details of the market. It was apparently under royal stewardship, run by an agent while the local king had one of his hall complexes across the water on a neighbouring island. Archaeology tells us that the interior of the settlement was cramped, full of small structures, and probably unsanitary. At Birka's northern periphery, a number of large longhouses stood apart, each on its own artificial terrace elevating it above the lake—perhaps the 'villa' community of wealthier inhabitants who did not want to mix with the dirt and squalor of the main settlement. A defended hillfort was established at one end of the settled area, and soon the entire market centre would be enclosed by a wall that also divided it from the growing numbers of cemeteries outside.

These beach emporia and markets—sites such as Hedeby and Birka—were manifestations of the changing economic history of post-Roman Europe, as it was rewritten by upwardly mobile societies. In the new academic vocabulary, they are seen as 'nodal points' in international networks, connecting different petty kingdoms and allowing them to trade as peers. In the course of the Viking Age, some of them would grow into true urban centres.

There was a clear hierarchy of markets, at its lower end the everyday transactions made amongst the rural population, either between themselves or through itinerant peddlers. Right from the beginning of the later Iron Age, at least, there were interconnected webs of smaller trading places—anything from a single jetty with sales made directly over the side of a boat, to local fairs and markets. An in-depth study of Gotland, for example, has shown that the entire coastline of viable landing places was covered by tiny harbours—some fifty sites in all—most of them just a stone-set slipway, an area with a cleared path to the sand, and little more, but sufficient for local needs.

As regional trading places, they could also act as intermediaries for the wider distribution of goods from the bigger markets. In the same way, all the major coastal and riverine installations not only served the primary maritime trade, but also acted as connectors—gateways, as economic historians term them—into the overland mercantile routes of the interior. These in turn fed into the pre-existing networks of local exchange that had probably been there for millennia, thus ensuring that the long-distance commodities that arrived in, say, Ribe, could make their way to rural communities and farms.

One function that the larger markets such as Birka and Ribe clearly served was as ports of trade for the importation of goods from overseas. However, numerous layers of exchange operated through early Viking-Age societies. An emphasis on the controlled import of foreign goods both exotic and mundane can tend to over-shadow the value of domestic production, which of course can also be managed and appropriated. There also seems to have been a concept of 'commodity money', whereby produce and raw materials of various kinds—whether textiles, combs, or even foodstuffs—were exchanged at agreed-upon rates literally as money, not as barter. In the eighth century, with the rise of the emporia, these things were produced in the countryside and moved into the markets; later in the Viking Age proper, the market towns themselves would take over this production.

The archaeology of the major markets brings out one of their qualities above others—namely that they were carefully planned in regular plots, often laid out on a basic street grid, with fences demarking clear zones of property and control. In short, these places were organised, although whether by a central authority or through collective, communal endeavour is another matter. It is not hard to see how this zoning could also take on other dimensions, in the form of exclusive rights of trade or even a form of protectionism.

Given this level of organisation, a perennial question in Viking studies has concerned the roles played by elites in the establishment of these early market centres. While economic impetus was provided by patrons among the petty kings and other regional rulers, places like Ribe were also driven by larger patterns of trade. The introduction of the sail into Scandinavian shipping technology seems to coincide with the rise of these mercantile centres, and was thus another possible component of these economic developments.

Many market centres also doubled as assembly sites, and the dual function brought people together in ever-greater numbers; Birka was a major one, for example. It is hard to be sure, but some of the names of the regular regional markets also hint at cultic overtones, such as the Disting, 'the *Dísir* assembly', held in Uppsala. Perhaps the beings connected with such occasions also functioned as something akin to a patron saint of commerce.

Through association with the assemblies, this 'democratic' baseline is important. It seems clear that the paramount force for regional and international trade was not the will of the political elites, but the agency of merchants and craftworkers. This was linked, in turn, to a clear perception of supply in response to demand, intertwined with the variables of taste and fashion. In this respect the kings were more like entrepreneurs, investing in a likely venture, and perhaps in a better position than others to seize an opportunity. In the power structures of the Scandinavian polities at the eve of the Viking Age, there was a web of relationships governing the production, distribution, and consumption of goods, not only by and for the elites but extending to all levels of society.

Another related question concerns who actually lived in Ribe, Birka, and the rest. Local exchange was a very different matter to large-scale international trade conducted with a foreign ship, and each form of transaction required a different infrastructure. This was reflected in the settlements that grew up around these sites as they developed, with populations that, broadly speaking, were more closely integrated into the mercantile activity that came to dominate all other aspects of the place. These emporia also saw the creation of what would effectively become a genuine professional class—artisans specialising in craft manufacture, and shopkeepers dedicated to its sale.

These fledgling towns were not only aspirational centres of early trickle-down economies. All such places have their darker sides—their diversions, subversions, and illegalities. Drinking was a sufficiently popular activity to require dedicated taverns, even if they are hard to detect in the archaeology; the same probably applied to sex work. It is also likely that criminal activities took new and different forms in the markets. No doubt raiders home from the sea could find other sources of income in the bustling streets ("nice workshop you got here, be a shame if something happened to it"). Any surge in trade involving physical valuables also requires security, bodyguards, insurance of a sort—a different kind of townies. The Viking Age definitely had its underworlds, and its shadows.

These new roles, prompted by the new markets, sometimes took very parochial forms. On Gotland, for example, jewellers expressed their local allegiances with distinctive kinds of dress accessories found only on the island, but incorporating designs and symbols from other traditions and cultures. The result was an insular identity, signalled on the person, but acknowledging the wider context in which the islanders happily operated. The same can be said of Ribe, Hedeby, Birka, and other such sites. At the same time, in all these market centres, it is clear that the population had regular and early access to non-local products, with implications for their contacts to a wider hinterland connecting the rural and 'urban' populations. Meat and produce were brought in from the country. Fish could be caught locally, but at some sites, such as Birka, there was also an extensive exploitation of bird resources such as eider—hunting them in the spring out into the archipelago of islands.

There is also a marked mobility in these people, and isotopic studies of the early Birka burial grounds have shown a particular trend for individuals to move around the age of thirteen or fourteen—perhaps the threshold of adulthood. The geographic range seems to span up to one hundred kilometres in any direction.

The early markets acted, then, as conduits for commerce and gateways for foreign contacts. In the seventh century and the first decades of the eighth, these contacts were almost entirely coming *to* Scandinavia; trade did not take the form of Northern merchants venturing outwards. This changed in the mid-eighth century, and the people of the North started to move *towards* the trade and to exercise direct control over it. This was one of the key contributing factors to the singularity of the Viking Age—the economic motor running beside and behind the force of the raids.

Remembering the first evidence of such activity, the Salme ships and the violent end of the men within them, we will explore this mercantile world first in the east, through the Baltic. After this, we can follow the chronology of the raids—Portland, Lindisfarne, and the rest—and turn to the west.

The Baltic, the 'Eastern Sea' for the Norse (and still the Swedish name for it, Östersjön), had been a trading ground throughout prehistory, with goods flowing into and out of the North since at least the Bronze Age. The islands of its western rim—Gotland, Öland, and Bornholm—were culturally Scandinavian, albeit with their local quirks and expressions of identity as in every other region.

The economic revolution of the West, seen in the establishment of organised emporia, also had its eastern counterpart; the same trends appeared in the Baltic at precisely the same time. These Vikings of the West and East were all the same people, acting in much the same way across the range of their travels and contacts, though with behaviour that naturally varied according to local conditions and contingencies.

There was clearly an active trade with what is now Finland, probably via the Åland archipelago that in the Viking Age was virtually a Scandinavian cultural outpost, albeit a little more distanced than Gotland. Copper alloy was a major import, used for the distinctive bronze ornaments in female jewellery. Finnish circular brooches turn up on Gotland, at Birka, and elsewhere in the Mälar Valley, while Scandinavian oval brooches are found in the Finnish interior.

On the southern Baltic shore, a Slavic resurgence can be detected between the Oder and Vistula Rivers, beginning around 650 and manifested in the establishment of something resembling the emporia of the North Sea. Larger markets were coming into being—such as Rerik, which played a role in the foundation of Hedeby—but there were also many smaller ones. Archaeologists have found some fifteen trading sites along the North German and

Polish coastline—all of which had a Scandinavian presence by the eighth century. These West Slavic sites were characterised by partly subterranean pit-houses, organised along similar lines to the Scandinavian emporia though with a local touch.

There seems to have been almost a Scandinavian colony at Grobina in modern Latvia, and it is at this time, the mid-eighth century, that the major trade routes took perceptible form. There was an 'amber way' for the mercantile flow of this prized commodity, running along the Visla River via Truso (in modern Poland) and Grobina, that connected to Scandinavia through Gotland. This was paralleled by an eastern route from the Mälar Valley, perhaps via Åland, to the Estonian shore. The whole coast of today's Baltic states was important in this context because it provided access to the eastern European interior via a series of rivers—the Nemunas, the Venta, the Daugava, and others. They were often guarded with hillforts along their length and thus required complex negotiations (and tributes or taxes) to pass, in successive stages as the waterways cut through the territories of different tribes.

In the eighth-century Baltic, the key mercantile venture for the Scandinavians was the decision to move east—all the way east—through the Gulf of Finland and into what today is the territory of the Russian Federation. There is no doubt that this represented a development of existing cultural and commercial contacts; it was in no way terra incognita for the Scandinavians. Individuals from at least mainland Sweden and Gotland had journeyed there many times, but there is no evidence for large-scale travel in any organised sense, and certainly not of settlement. This is what would change around 750, simultaneous with the same development in north-western Europe.

The focus of this eastward move was at a place now known as Staraja (Old) Ladoga, located at the mouth of the Volkhov River where it discharges into Lake Ladoga, Europe's largest body of freshwater. Access from the Baltic and the Gulf of Finland was direct, along the Neva River on which St. Petersburg would be founded a millennium later, thence along the shore of Ladoga and upriver a few kilometres to the settlement. The Volkhov was the prime means of access to the river systems farther south that led to and from the Russian interior, but also ultimately into the Dniepr system, which could be followed all the way through what is now Ukraine to the Black Sea, and to the richest market of them all: Byzantium.

The first traces of occupation at Ladoga date to 753, a precision achieved with tree-ring chronologies of the first timber structures preserved in the waterlogged soil. Thus, we see the same founding date as the other emporia of this kind, this same shift in the balance of society, trade, and power. By the end of the century, the camp was thriving.

Laid out along the Volkhov at the confluence of a smaller tributary, Ladoga was a strongly linear development that followed both banks. The core area was where the waters met, with a mixture of square timber structures typical of the Slavic peoples, and rectangular longhouses of Norse type. This ethnic mix was there right from the start, with Slavs, Scandinavians, Finns, Balts, even Sámi, and others all jostling in the market as it steadily expanded. The settled area was ringed with basic defences, and some kind of fortress seems to have been constructed early on atop the promontory overlooking the confluence.

The riverbanks outside the core area, and the fields behind the settlement, were covered in cemeteries, apparently ethnically zoned and with grave types typical of the different traditions among Ladoga's citizenry. Over time, these signals began to merge and blend, no doubt like the lives of the people who made them, but it was the Scandinavians who seem to have founded the market and dominated it from the start.

We might picture places like Ladoga as similar to the frontier settlements of the American West, growing rapidly from a few tents with ships' supplies and basic necessities to the rudiments of small towns. They were probably rough, potentially violent, and also exciting, if that was to your taste: somewhere to make your fortune and then either stay or move on, provided you survived the risks. Think of a muddy, riverine Deadwood with greater ethnic variety, plus swords and a multitude of gods, and it's probably not so far from the truth. The East was somewhere to make a new start, to shape a different life, and perhaps to forget a previous one. These endeavours should not be seen solely in terms of success. Imagine all the hopeful Scandinavian rubes eager to build a future on the eastern rivers, welcomed with open arms by the sharp-faced hustlers of Ladoga. Need supplies? Step over here. Thirsty? Of course, shipmate. No funds? Well, luck is always capricious, but fortunately we have credit, and on *such* good terms. The Ladogans are your new-found friends, a slap on the back and a horn of ale—and suddenly three more on the table, so generous!—but their eyes never smile. You shake on the deal, and then that big Slav moves to block the doorway. There was probably nowhere easier for someone to disappear, willingly or not, and there would have been a lot of unmarked graves.

These fantasies are fun to entertain, but this really was a world of genuine opportunity. The markets and bazaars were ethnic melting pots, filled with a babble of languages that was probably smoothed out in the lingua franca of trade. Interactions operated at two levels of institution. In formal terms, mercantile exchange must have been bounded by jurisdictions, regulations, codes of conduct, and laws. Informally, these were shot through with the expectations of equally local traditions, cultural norms, ritual observations, and so on. Perhaps the most fundamental of all was the provision of a secure environment where all this could take place—a market wholly without guards would not last long. The currencies of these exchanges were furs, silver, and slaves—a trinity that would repeat for centuries.

In the 700s, the eastern river trade was not yet fully controlled by Scandinavians—their influence would expand in the ninth century before reaching its zenith in the tenth. Ladoga was the start—the foot in the door—but for at least the latter half of the eighth century and perhaps well into the ninth, these water routes were probably something of a challenge.

Raiding and commerce were two components, almost two varying expressions, of the same phenomenon: the pursuit and consolidation of power, expressed through the acquisition and redistribution of portable wealth. The expansionist ambitions of the Svear kings of Sweden produced places like Ladoga—but also events like those behind the Salme boat graves and the violent end of that arguably royal maritime expedition.

In the West at the same time, specifically on the coast of Norway, the realities of power were very personal indeed, and it is here that politics merged fully with economics to produce something sudden and violent: the raids. This is the same pattern as that seen dimly in the East, but coming into much sharper focus.

By the mid-eighth century, perhaps some fifteen small 'kingdoms' had coalesced along the Norwegian shorelines—through competition (violent or otherwise), absorption, expansion and alliance—some of them stretching inland along the fjords to the small areas of fertile farmlands. Within these structures, however, a more specialised sociopolitical pattern emerged, related to the region's unique topography and economic potential, and differing in significant ways from the comparable groupings in the rest of Scandinavia.

The region that Snorri Sturluson referred to as the Midlands, stretching from Rogaland in the south to Nordmøre in the north, has produced particularly good data. In the agricultural heartlands of Jæren is the key site of Avaldsnes, which together with the adjacent land along the Karmsund Strait makes a useful lens through which to shine light on this critical time and place. There is evidence of an intriguing two-tier political system. In the inland regions on fertile soils, there were over thirty manors and large estates—magnate farms, essentially—with agrarian subsistence economies that took advantage of the available resources. This is more or less the same settlement pattern and political structure as in the rest of Scandinavia. However, there was *also* an outer coastal elite, with ten or so manors based on islands and offshore locations—apparently with an eye to the maritime traffic along the shore. The latter seem to be something new in late Iron Age Scandinavia.

One major piece of corroborating evidence for this differentiated power structure comes in the form of the 'courtyard' assembly sites that formed the basic level of governance. A new dating project has shown that most of the assembly places in Rogaland (the area around Avaldsnes) declined and were abandoned in the eighth century. In other areas, such as Hålogaland farther north, the *things* continued in use until the Viking Age.

In practical terms, this means that the central-southern part of the west coast—the shore facing Britain—underwent a dramatic change in power relations in the course of the 700s. This is, of course, the same period as the establishment of the market centres farther south and east, in Denmark and Sweden, and when the Russian rivers were opening up.

It seems likely that the early Iron Age assemblies played a role in electing leaders, perhaps even the first of the kings, a function that naturally came into question when the new elites of the post-Roman period began to shape their own futures. However, as royal power grew to overtake the governmental role of the *things*, the assemblies began to confine their business to legal proceedings. In Rogaland, this seems to have gone even further, with the kings taking on this jurisdiction as well—a clear centralisation of power in the hands of the elites.

Clearly, the nature of government was shifting along the Norwegian coast, but in a different way, and perhaps more rapidly, than in the rest of Scandinavia. Here, the eighth century saw the rise of another new kind of ruler, and the Old Norse sources have even preserved a name for him (they were all men): the *sækonungr*, the sea-king. They are mostly mentioned in the legendary sagas, in the metaphoric imagery of skaldic poems, and occasionally in the lists of poetic synonyms, as well as in Snorri's *Saga of the Ynglingas*, where there is this interesting definition: "At that time [. . .] there were many sea-kings who commanded large troops and had no lands". It is clear that their 'kingship' depended not on lineage—which had become entrenched by the eighth century—but on maritime military power in its own right.

In the 1930s a list was compiled of all the sea-king personal names from the written sources, sorting out those with origins in the ninth century or earlier. This work is of immense importance in understanding who these men were. As their compiler states, the names are "miniature historical pictures", hardly fit for the kings of the later sagas but eminently suitable as real-world descriptors of violent war leaders. They almost stride from the page: Áti, 'Messmate'; Beiti, 'the Cruiser'; Ekkill, 'He Who Sails Alone'; Geitir, 'the Goat'; Gestill, 'the Little Guest'; Jalkr, 'Screamer'; Mysingr, 'the Mouse'; Maevill, 'the Seagull'; Rökkvi, 'He Who Sails at Dusk'—and some seventeen more. These are pirate names. One thinks of Blackbeard, Calico Jack, and the rest, analogies that are actually quite viable. The key point is that these are Viking names in the proper sense of the word, the real thing.

Each of the sea-kings' territories was a genuine maritorium, encompassing an entire community culturally oriented towards the ocean. Crucially, they were not based upon the control of land, beyond what was needed to supply the core manors with their needs. Places like Avaldsnes were thus *warrior* manors—bases for the warlords of the sea, with hinterlands that kept them in food and drink, as well as the raw materials to equip and maintain the ships. The farms of the surrounding districts could provide men for emergency defence and a ready supply of crews for the ships themselves.

The greatest of the sea-kings was Harald Finehair, the man who would attempt to unify Norway in the ninth century and begin the process of state formation that would reach completion two hundred years later; Avaldsnes was one of his manors. Significantly, earlier in his career as a sea-king, Harald went by a different name: Lúfa, 'Mophead', another of the piratical, gang-leader epithets, later tidied up to form his royal nickname. Harald was notorious for his many wives and concubines, and one scholar has even suggested that these relationships were a means of linking the different regions of his hinterland in the web of alliances necessary to support his seaborne power. It is a compelling picture.

Unlike their southern neighbours, the growing polities along the Norwegian North Sea coast lacked direct access to the Frisian markets and had no Ribe-type trading sites of their own. The sea-kings of the Norwegian Midlands seem to have compensated for this with an investment in the long-distance trade in Arctic raw materials and products—including furs, down, walrus ivory, and especially whetstones, positioning themselves as key brokers in this lucrative commodity. The trade seems to have taken off around the 720s, with peak production in the last decade of the eighth century—which coincides with the first serious raids on western Europe.

The consolidation of the sea-kings' power involved securing the marine passageways along the Norwegian coast, which protected shipping and ensured the continuance (and control) of trade. Their influence may have gone deeper still. In Rogaland, the courtyard *thing* sites seem to disappear at exactly the time when the sea-kings were entrenching their rule. If the rights of the popular assemblies were transferred to the person of the king, this was a dramatic appropriation of authority, expressed in terms that would have been felt among the populace and manifested in the abandoned gathering places that had served their communities for generations. The Icelandic family sagas speak vividly of the disaffection among many of the Norwegians, who were unhappy with the new royal order that drew more and more power to itself—at the expense of the agricultural class. In the retrospective (and surely biased)

The Viking image. A digitally reconstructed warship of the late Viking Age, based on excavated examples, embodying the stereotype but reflecting reality. Reconstruction by and © Arkikon.

Dressed to impress. A modern reconstruction of armour and regalia from boat graves at Valsgärde and Vendel, Uppland, Sweden, showing the appearance of the new warlords who rose to power after the Migration Period crisis. Photo: Lindsey Kerr, Wulfheodenas Living History group, used by kind permission.

The place of power. A drone photo of the Vendel and Viking-Age royal power centre at Gamla Uppsala in Sweden, seat of the Ynglinga dynasty. The monumental burial mounds can be clearly seen along the ridge, while the great halls were on terraces where the medieval church is now located. Photo: Daniel Löwenborg, used by kind permission.

House and home. A Viking-Age farm of middling status in a rainy autumn, based on excavated examples. Image by and © Arkikon.

A lady of means. The reconstructed dress of a wealthy Viking-Age woman buried in a boat at Gamla Uppsala, Sweden. Reconstruction by Þórhallur Þráinsson, used by kind permission of Gamla Uppsala Museum.

A set of jewellery of the kind sometimes found in women's burials; two oval brooches with a necklace between, and two other clothing-fasteners. Photo: Lennart Larsen, © National Museum of Denmark, used by kind permission.

Silver armrings, neckrings, and brooches, from various Viking-Age hoards on Gotland. Photo: Katarina Nimmervoll, Swedish History Museum, Creative Commons.

Stories in stone. A Viking-Age picture-stone from Lärbro on Gotland, with images organised in sequential strips; are these scenes from mythology, heroic tales, or tributes to the dead? Photo: Neil Price.

Funerary theatre. The Oseberg ship burial, c. 834, as it may have looked during the rituals, the vessel only half-buried to leave an open arena for interaction with the dead. Reconstruction by and © Anders Kvåle Rue, used by kind permission.

Deadwood on the Volkhov. An aerial view of Staraja Ladoga, the gateway to the Russian rivers. The Viking-Age settlement was based at the confluence of the main channel and a smaller tributary, now spanned by the medieval fortress and the modern village. Photo Lev Karavanov, Creative Commons.

Mikligard. The city of Constantinople, capital of the Byzantine Empire and the greatest metropolis in the world, seen here as it might have looked at the very end of the Viking Age. The 'Great Place' was the primary goal of the Scandinavian travellers in the east. Image: © Byzantium 1200 Project and Tayfun Odner, used by kind permission.

An Iberian adventure. The interior of the Mezquita, the Great Mosque of Córdoba in Spain, and one of the best-preserved Viking-Age buildings in the world; this was the power centre attacked by örn and his raiders in the 50s. Photo: Ronny Siegel, Creative Commons.

The town on the heath. Hedeby, Jylland, from the air. The great arc of its rampart can still be seen overgrown with trees, enclosing the urban settlement; cattle and buildings provide scale. Now open fields, in the tenth century this was the main market centre of the North, with mercantile links across Europe and beyond.

Photo: © State Archaeological Department, Schleswig-Holstein, used by kind permission.

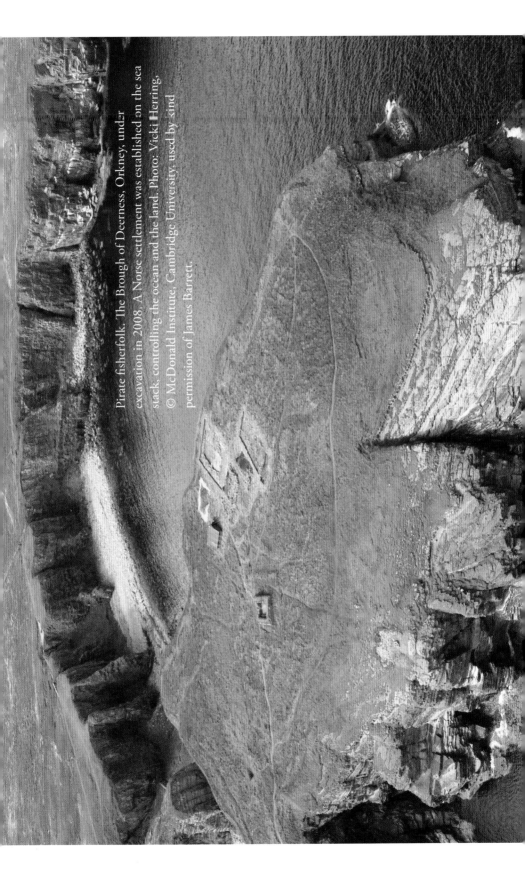

Pirate fisherfolk. The Brough of Deerness, Orkney, under excavation in 2008. A Norse settlement was established on the sea stack, controlling the ocean and the land. Photo: Vicki Herring, © McDonald Institute, Cambridge University, used by kind permission of James Barrett.

Rise of the Rus'. The Golden Gate in Kiev, a Soviet reconstruction in situ of the eleventh-century fortified gateway, preserving a cross-section through the city wall, now with timber features to restore its original appearance. Photo: George Chernilevsky, Creative Commons.

A military monarch. The ring-fortress at Trelleborg in Denmark, one of at least five such installations built by King Harald Bluetooth in the late tenth century. Photo: Thue C. Leibrandt, Creative Commons.

A king's capital. Reconstruction of the royal centre at Jelling in Jylland, with the great mounds built by King Harald and the complex of

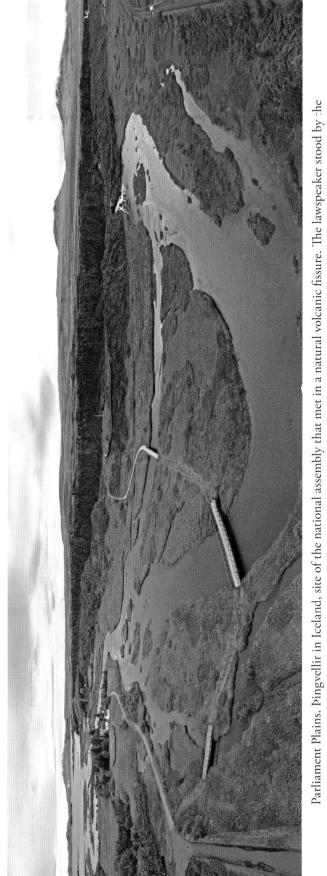

Parliament Plains. Þingvellir in Iceland, site of the national assembly that met in a natural volcanic fissure. The lawspeaker stood by the white flagpole, his voice echoing off the great lava wall, while delegates were housed in booths along the flatlands by the river. Photo: Bob T, Creative Commons.

Christ comes to Greenland. The chapel built for Thjodhild, wife of Eirík the Red, at their home at Brattahlid. This replica stands next to the original, on the site of the farm with Eiriksfjord (now called Tunulliarfik) behind. Photo by Claire Rowland, Creative Commons.

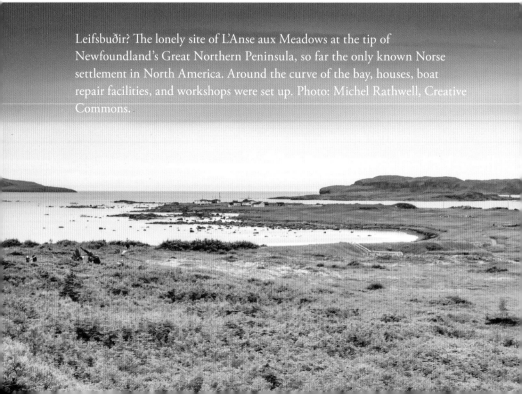

Leifsbuðir? The lonely site of L'Anse aux Meadows at the tip of Newfoundland's Great Northern Peninsula, so far the only known Norse settlement in North America. Around the curve of the bay, houses, boat repair facilities, and workshops were set up. Photo: Michel Rathwell, Creative Commons.

history of the medieval saga-writers, these independent-minded landowners were some of the key movers behind the decision to settle a new colony in the North Atlantic, and establish the republic of free farmers that would become Iceland.

The sea-kings were critical to the beginnings of the Viking Age in the West, and their attempts to expand their power along the whole coastal ribbon form the political backdrop to the raids. The Lindisfarne raiders came from this area. This was the social environment that created and motivated them. It was also the home to which they returned with ships full of loot—enormous sums of portable wealth that in turn sustained the world of the sea-kings.

At this point we should briefly consider some of the other theories that have been put forward as explanations for the raids, and therefore as catalysts for the Viking Age itself. Each of these 'triggers' either has inherent problems or else is an insufficient explanation in isolation.

One of the most persistent relates to technology, specifically Scandinavian shipping design. The argument is that innovations in watercraft—the introduction of the sail and the creation of shallow-draught vessels constructed of overlapping clinker-built planks for speed and manoeuvrability—made it practically possible for the Vikings to sail abroad in this way; they would perhaps have launched the raids earlier, but did not have the ability to do so. Following this line of thinking, advances in boatbuilding provided a 'push factor' that drove the Scandinavians out into the world: they had the ships, so they were going to use them. There are several problems with this. First, maritime warfare was nothing new in the late eighth century, or even the 750s. The bog sacrifices of Denmark indicate serious levels of naval engagement even in the early Iron Age, and it is no great step from the Danish shore to the rest of the European coast. Similarly, the Oseberg-style boats of the early

Viking Age were certainly marvellous craft, but the truly lethal warships were a development of the later ninth and tenth centuries. There is no doubt at all that the Scandinavians were master mariners, and their ships were indeed markedly better than those of the surrounding cultures of north-west Europe, but sea travel had been a commonplace for centuries, and piracy and maritime military ventures were hardly Viking inventions. Ships and sea power were at the core of what real Vikings *did*, but they do not alone explain the *why* and *when*.

Then there is an environmental argument that sees a warming of the climate making new ventures into previously inhospitable environments like the North Atlantic suddenly more viable and attractive. As part of the effect, it is claimed, the outgoing Scandinavians engaged in raiding and settlement elsewhere on their travels. However, the much-debated Medieval Warm Period did not begin to manifest until over a century *after* the raids began—perhaps even longer. Iceland and Greenland were already settled by the time the temperature began to rise. The climatic influence of the sixth-century 'dust veil' is clear, and we have explored its contributions to the society that would eventually generate the Viking phenomenon, but by the mid-eighth century it was buried deep in the mix.

Some scholars see the European emporia not as part of a larger economic realignment, but as a 'pull factor' corresponding to the supposed 'push' of the ships. The argument is simple: the Vikings started raiding because there was a rapid expansion in places worth plundering—what today's militaries call a target-rich environment. However, this does not fully align with the chronology. It is clear that the emporia *were* repeatedly raided (Dorestad was especially unfortunate) and that as conduits for the manufacturing wealth of the import-export trade they made for both tempting and profitable objectives. But it would be wrong to see these kinds of long-distance commercial networks as solely a development of the eighth century when the raids really began, and one should not forget that the Scandinavians also themselves traded in such places as well as burning them down.

It is when the role of the emporia is combined with the politics of Scandinavia itself that the situation in the mid-eighth century begins to come into focus.

The internecine and aggressive nature of power in Scandinavia's hall cultures has already been established. Some see the rise of the sea-kings along the Norwegian coast as the crystallisation of that society's predatory aspects. As their grip on the region was consolidated, the sea-kings may have stood as guarantors of general security and thus gradually curtailed the opportunities for 'domestic' raiding within Norway. The idea is that the raiders' reduced prospects at home pushed them abroad instead, and thus initiated the classic attacks on the British Isles.

There is no doubt that the raiders who hit the shores of England in the late 700s, and shortly thereafter those of Scotland and Ireland, came from this region of Norway—finds of insular loot and monastic treasure, often broken and repurposed, are abundant in the contemporary burials there. However, this does not address who these 'Vikings' actually were and why they were not integrated into the societies these new sea-kings were building—after all, one person's pirates can easily become someone else's navy. By contrast, I believe we can see the sea-kings as the actual *originators* of the western raids, and that the 'Vikings' were a fully integrated part of their power-base; there was little daylight between them. In any case, whether as catalysts for Viking aggression or as active participants in the raids, the effects of the sea-kings' ambitions were much the same.

Something similar can be seen in the Svear drive east and south across the Baltic. The economic stimuli included the role of the eastern river routes as sources of potentially enormous wealth, revealed in the course of the early eighth century through a growing number of expeditions into this region and interactions with the people there. From the 750s onwards, the petty-kingdoms of Scandinavia were ready and able to act on this information.

At the same time as these 'kings and Vikings' were actively looking for opportunity beyond Scandinavia's borders, the people they were looking *at* were experiencing a time of unprecedented vulnerability. At the level of relatively small-scale communities in England and Frankia, civil defence was disorganised and wholly unprepared against fast-paced attack. At a state level, both the Empire and the English kingdoms were either at the point of civil war or simply not able to react rapidly enough. However, it also went the other way. Notwithstanding the traditional focus on Viking aggression, for much of the period, the peoples of southern Scandinavia were under near-constant threat from the belligerence of their Christian neighbours. The Frankish Empire was being carved out at the point of a sword by Charlemagne's expansionist wars in the late eighth century, and the North would have been feeling these social pressures at the time of the first raids (the 'great man' died in 814, decades after the seaborne attacks had begun). The ninth-century division of the Empire following years of civil war did nothing to alleviate the tensions along the Danish frontier, and there is little to suggest the slowly expanding Viking polities ever felt entirely safe from southern assault even into the new millennium. Scandinavian military endeavours almost always included an element of proactive defence alongside their more immediately mercenary ambitions.

Taken together, this presents us with a total worldview of encultured violence and expansive competition that stretched from the Danish heartlands along the respective coasts of Norway and Sweden. But with Salme and Ladoga as symbols of something larger, we begin to see an underestimated component of the Viking phenomenon, namely that by the mid-eighth century this had already begun to be projected outwards, not to the west but to the east, in what were essentially home waters. The raiding, trading, and land-taking that would become familiar features of the Scandinavians' western adventures were already established patterns of behaviour in the Baltic, the 'Eastern Sea' of the Norse world.

The intersection of all these socio-economic factors, converging from the mid-700s until the end of the century, explains what was happening. Against the background of long-term trends towards political consolidation both within Scandinavia and among its neighbours, the competitive kingdoms of the North needed sources of revenue and portable wealth to fuel their expansive ambitions at home. The surrounding cultures were politically fragmented even within their larger state structures, and largely unable to mount coordinated defences against rapid hit-and-run attacks. The result was a perfect storm of opportunity and desire, supply and demand.

The same date range—the years around the middle of the eighth century, 750 or so—recurs again and again in all these discussions, forty years *before* the Lindisfarne raid. This is when Birka was founded in Sweden, following Ribe's example in Denmark. This is when Ladoga was established as a gateway to the eastern rivers. This is also when the Norwegian sea-kings were making fast their hold on the coast and gradually starting to extend their range overseas to the west. And this is the date of the Salme expedition. Economics, politics, and their 'extension by other means', maritime violence: it was a powerful combination.

The final component of the Viking raids is in many ways the most obvious: the raiders themselves. At a time when the notion of the individual was socially elevated and acknowledged—in poetry, ritual advice, moral codes, and runic epitaphs—personal agency was also critical. It is to them we now turn.

11

WARRIORHOODS

A SINGLE PROFITABLE RAIDING EXPEDITION—ONE need not necessarily be away from home for more than three weeks—might change a life (and end many others, of course). Its beneficiaries spanned a range of social classes, and what they got out of it, their priorities, differed accordingly. But there was much more to this than opportunism, and individual greed was activated within the bigger schemes of others. The enterprise was directed, to a greater or lesser degree.

This is important because we must dispense with the notion of spontaneity, of an element in the Viking 'character' that sent them out raiding. Any such action requires considerable planning in terms of resources, logistics, and personnel. It also presupposes the possibility to spare the ships' crews from activities at home and the willingness of others who could take up their responsibilities while they were away. There were also considerable technological necessities and constraints—and all this when any violent encounter was still on the distant horizon.

The Viking raids were not only about material reward, a matter of loot and plunder. In a culture that privileged fame, prowess, and demonstrable achievement, they also offered opportunities for gaining all these things. As one scholar puts it, "The act of acquiring silver was as important as the silver itself". A mentality geared for war, and the deeply ingrained militarism that accompanied the rise of the new elites, combined with clear notions of preordained fatalism to produce a frame of mind that drove the Viking attacks with militant fervour—almost a form of holy war.

This may have been almost literally the case, in the context of countering expansive Christian missionary ambitions in the late eighth century, generating a need to appropriate and weaponise the traditional beliefs of the North in the service of the elites. As individuals bought in to this ethos, they became an effective medium of its aggressive expression.

There was also a personal level to these processes. Take the raids on targets such as Lindisfarne, places where Scandinavians had been trading and thus had seen with their own eyes not only the wealth of the monasteries but also how unprotected they were. It is not hard to imagine some young merchant—or perhaps that merchant's bodyguard—thinking hard about his situation in life, how it could be improved, and then tentatively suggesting to his friends, "Why don't we just *take* it?" Why not, indeed? After a winter of brooding on the idea, it must have become more tempting by the day. Perhaps they even believed they had thought of it themselves, as the local sea-kings discreetly kept the notion alive in their minds.

Being a warrior in the Viking Age was a matter of status as well as action. Deeds were done with a view to their immortalization and a concern for the afterlife of reputation. Warriorhood could be symbolic as well as practical, conferred through identification with its attributes—especially weapons. Burials containing large amounts of armaments may be the graves of actual warriors, or of those who bore the trappings without 'living the life', or even of people for some reason given this identity solely in death.

All this can be seen in runic inscriptions, which provide a glimpse of the martial ideal in the form of memorial texts for the dead. A selection can give the flavour of this warrior ideology, and reveal much of how it was expressed and reinforced through such very visual monuments. Again and again one sees runestones erected by survivors in memory of fallen comrades, honouring the dead and at the same time themselves through association; often those commissioning the stone are mentioned more prominently in the inscription than the one commemorated.

The Battle of Fýrisvellir, fought near Uppsala in the 980s between the Swedish king Eirík and his nephew Stýrbjörn, seems to have left a particular mark on the consciousness of the time, even though its historical truth shades into legend. Here is one of three stones from Hällestad in Skåne, now part of Sweden but then in Viking-Age Denmark:

> Áskell placed this stone in memory of Tóki Gormr's son,
> to him a faithful lord.
> He did not flee at Uppsala.
> Valiant men placed in memory of their brother
> the stone on the hill, steadied by runes.
> They went closest to Gormr's Tóki.

Two other stones at the same site also mention retainers of the same Tóki. Fýrisvellir is referred to again on one of the three Högby runestones from Östergötland, although this time it is probably a man on Eirík's side who is commemorated. The stone is also notable in that it records the violent fates of an entire family:

> The good man Gulli got five sons.
> The brave valiant man Ásmundr fell at Fœri [Fýris];
> Assurr met his end in the east in Greece;
> Halfdan was killed at Holmr [Bornholm?];

Kári was [killed] at Oddr [probably north-west Sjælland];
also dead [is] Búi.

Another runic allusion to Fýrisvellir is one of the most well-known
stones of all and comes from Karlevi on Öland. Combining prose
with the oldest recorded example of a skaldic verse in the metre fit
for princes, it seems from the dating to have been raised (perhaps
on their way home) by the retinue of a Danish lord who had died
in the battle. The Karlevi stone also includes among its wonderful
kennings the name of a Valkyrie. It is one of the most spectacular
'war memorials' of the Viking Age:

This stone is placed in memory of Sibbi the good, Fuldarr's
son, and his retinue placed on [. . .]
    He lies concealed,
    he who was followed
    by the greatest deeds
    (most men knew that),
    a battle-tree of Þrúðr[1]
    in this mound;
    Never again shall such a battle-hardened
    Viðurr-of-the-Carriage of Endill's[2] mighty dominion,
    rule unsurpassed over land in Denmark.

In addition to basic comradeship, and the ambiguous meaning of
'brother', inscriptions of this kind often take care to place the living in social relationship to their lord. This applied whether he was
alive (demonstrating loyalty) or dead (honouring his achievements

---

[1] Þrúðr: a Valkyrie; her battle-tree: *chieftain*
[2] Viðurr: Odin name, 'killer' or 'warrior'; Endill: sea-god; his carriage: ship;
ship-warrior of the sea

and thereby keeping their oaths). Something similar is recorded on another famous Skåne runestone from Sjörup:

> Saxi placed this stone in memory of Ásbjörn Tófi's son, his partner. He did not flee at Uppsala, but carried on killing as long as he could hold a weapon.

'Partner' here carries the sense of shipmate, resonant of a phrase on the stone from Aarhus in Denmark that was probably raised to a man who died at the Battle of Svöldr in 999. In the crucial context given in its closing words, it is among the most concise of properly Viking memorials:

> Gunúlfr and Øgotr and Aslakr and Hrólfr set up this stone in memory of Fulr, their comrade-in-arms. He found death [. . .] when kings were fighting.

The notion of military fraternities—brotherhoods of warriors—has been around a long time in Viking studies. There are slight indications of such things in the sagas, with all the usual caveats, including a somewhat lurid tale of an entire tenth-century community of them supposedly based at Jómsborg, near Wolin in what is now Poland. As we have seen, several runestones mention the notion of comradeship, of brothers-in-arms, but it is hard to pin this down any closer, compelling though they are. On the other hand, clear archaeological evidence exists for a symbolism of masculine skill in battle: a culture, almost a cult, of decorated weapons and war-gear, with connections to the poetry of violence and divine inspiration for its underpinnings.

Deeper exploration of the topic has long been hindered by the enthusiasm for such military 'secret societies' exhibited by the Nazis (and their modern successors) as part of their general infatuation with the Vikings. These attitudes are politically compromised in the worst ways, bracingly free of factual connection with the past, and they can be dangerous—but they should also not be allowed to distract from what actually occurred around the business of war in the Viking Age.

The central concept in the organisation of Viking warrior groups—as one scholar calls them, 'bands of brothers'—seems to have been the *lið*, a term that cannot be precisely defined but is usually taken to refer to a shipborne host or team of warriors sworn to a leader whose responsibility it was to feed, equip, and reward them for their service. The size and nature of *lið* appear to have ranged from a couple of ships' crews up to forces numbering one to two hundred individuals. These groups likely formed the core of the early raiding parties and, later, the smallest components of the large Viking 'armies', which were coalitions of *lið* rather than united groups under the command of a single leader. The *lið*'s discrete and autonomous nature is emphasised in the *Annals of St. Bertin*, which in 861 describe Vikings in a fleet made up of *sodalitates*, 'brotherhoods', that dispersed from the main force to overwinter in various ports along the river Seine. A *lið* can thus be considered an armed fighting group, loyal to a single autonomous leader, that operated on a seasonal or permanent basis.

The formation of a *lið*, and its effective activities, could have only taken place with significant levels of cooperation, manifested in various ways including through material culture. Although the *lið* represents one of the most basic forms of armed collective—a warband in its literal sense—it cannot be said with any certainty whether its formation was based on familial or other social relationships (remember the four brothers in the Salme ship grave), or whether it comprised individuals who shared no pre-existing social or political ties at all. Recruitment into these groups transcended not only kinship but also ethnicity; a *lið* might have incorporated individuals from multiple locations within Scandinavia itself and beyond.

There is a sense in which raiding was a way to relieve domestic social tensions that might otherwise get out of hand. This could even be the case within and between the *lið*, caused by the delicate networks of 'friendship' and kinship. These carried with them such complex webs of mutual obligation, extending across the borders of political rivalries, as to hamper the expansionist policies of the elites when they competed with each other 'at home'. However, warriors who did not have to worry about fighting their 'friends' could be harnessed as a unified force for the outward projection of power. This could also snowball, creating turbulence in the political balance in Scandinavia. If one kingdom started to do this, the others may have wished, or needed, to follow suit.

The leading specialist in the rigid codes of Viking friendship has speculated that one additional rationale for the raids was precisely because the likely targets excluded those who might fall within the protective frameworks of the Scandinavian social compact. By extension, plunder abroad could be used to further cement such relationships at home and even to extend one's circle of 'friends' in this specific sense. Linked to this is the disturbing conclusion that the primary export of Viking-Age Scandinavia was not commerce, but violence—a sort of capitalism of aggression. From the Vikings' own perspective, seen from within their embedded mind-set of a militarised society, theirs was the 'best' sort of violence, the preferred choice of destruction. This must have been a major incentive for the elites, a social safety valve that could be harnessed to their benefit.

The violence associated with the raids could take other, even uglier forms, for reasons that were rooted in social custom and connected to the warrior life.

A very early idea about the reasons for the raids focussed on a supposed rapid rise in population across Scandinavia, beyond what the land could sustain, especially in the marginal agricultural regions of Norway. This also shaded uncomfortably into the notion of a 'wave of advance', whereby the Germanic peoples somehow irresistibly expanded and conquered, and even that it was somehow 'in their nature' to do so. There is an uneasy feeling here of inherent colonialism that is, to put it mildly, best avoided in connection with the Vikings, whose culture has already been so politically abused. Demographics is perhaps the least convincing of the explanations put forward for the raids, not least in that there is no real evidence of population pressure at all. If anything, the region was still recovering from the massive decline of the Migration Period, and the population would also grow much greater *after* the Viking Age with no truly dramatic shifts in agricultural production. An abstract notion of 'land pressure' and legal arguments around inheritance patterns do not explain the raids either. There was a transition to absentee landholding, up to a point, but there was no sudden tipping point of disinherited youth.

However, there *was* an important connection between landholding and wealth, which were intertwined with honour, status, and the essence of self-respect. All this was, in turn, connected to the family and the things that held it together, especially marriage. One aspect of this was relevant to the raids above all others.

As we have seen, Viking-Age societies practised polygyny, whereby men could each legitimately marry more than one woman, but women could only have one male partner. If we assume an equal number of men and women (the ratio should be approximately 1:1 given normal birth rates), then polygyny will leave a significant proportion of the male population without socially sanctioned possibilities to form partnerships with the opposite sex. In terms of social practicality rather than physical possibility, this results in an imbalance in the relative numbers of sexually active men and women who are able to form liaisons. As Viking-Age culture also included the institution of concubinage, on a similarly male-dominant basis and *in addition* to the possibility of having multiple wives, this biased the ratios still further. Even when accounting for sexual orientation and preference, and the fact that illicit relationships could occur, the conclusion is still inescapable: potentially *very* large numbers of Viking-Age men could not hope to marry or find partners at home.

As we have seen, there is at least some evidence that Viking-Age communities also practised infanticide. If it was biased towards male children, this introduces the possibility that the balance of the sexes was uneven to begin with, resulting in a population with more men than women in absolute terms. The evidence for selective female infanticide is shaky, but there are certainly signs of the differential treatment of children in terms of nutrition. If all this was combined, the situation might have become truly serious.

This could have manifested in two ways, of which the first would be a search for portable wealth to use as bride-price, and thus to 'move up' in the hierarchies of marriageable men; if there was an inflation of bride-wealth at this time, it would only have exacerbated these conditions. And if the currency of bride-price changed, perhaps as a result of the new forms of portable wealth entering the Scandinavian system from abroad following the raids, this too could have led to massive inflation. If young men provided their own means of payment in this system—for example, through plunder—this would have led to greater independence from their families, but also effectively disenfranchised their offspring. The circular feedback of this process is obvious, with equally clear implications as one of several factors behind an escalation of the raids.

The second possible result of sexual imbalance is among the nastiest aspects of the Viking Age, and we have encountered it before. If a man could not find a woman willing to marry or cohabit with him, or if he could not meet the agreed economic expectations of such an arrangement, the raids offered opportunities to take women by force in sexual slavery. There is abundant evidence that many men chose to do exactly that.

If the 'socio-sexual economy' *was* becoming unbalanced, then by the 750s it could have caused real social stress. It would have affected the cohesion of the family, and the sustainability of political structures that were in any case largely maintained only by armed force. This is not to suggest that male attempts to improve their marriage prospects were a primary trigger for the raids, but neither can they be ignored. Not least, this was occurring in soci eties driven by an ideological predisposition towards (and with a long pedigree of) maritime predation.

Slaving, including for the purposes of sexual trafficking, was one of the worst practical aspects of the raids—the most brutal of profit motives combined with misogynistic gratification. But the expeditions had other tangible elements, too, not the least of which was the actual process of maritime fighting, supported by a material culture of weapons and armour.

We need to know what a raid *looked like*.

A key component in the Viking image is also embodied in the reality of the raiders: the bearing of arms. As in so many other aspects of Viking life, their weapons too have been subject to stereotype.

The effective use of Viking weaponry relied on very much more than brute force, the opposite of the crude barbarian cliché still propagated so widely. Men would train from a young age, spending years constantly honing their abilities with a variety of weapons, each of which required different skills. To use them in combination was a kind of lethal dance, a choreographed interplay of movement, balance, dexterity, and strength—all while wielding deadly tools to cut or pierce.

In addition to personal knives, which were ubiquitous but used only as a last resort, the most basic weapon, available more or less to all, was the common axe. It is important to distinguish between tools made for farmyard use and actual weapons—they were not interchangeable. The typology of axes is quite broad, but in general they developed into specialised weapons of war as the shafts got longer (eventually requiring a double-handed grip) and the axe-head grew heavier with a progressively longer and more vicious cutting edge. At the extreme, the great war axe of the Danes could bring down a horse and rider with a single blow. They were neither difficult to forge nor especially expensive, and thus relatively widely

18. A silver pendant figure from Klahammar, Sweden, a unique depiction of a warrior armed with axe and sword. Photo: Max Jahrehorn, Oxider AB, used by kind permission.

used. In the sagas, axes are sometimes given the names of trolls—suitably blunt for a brutal but effective killing machine.

Spears were also comparatively cheap weapons—although not necessarily of low status—and while their heads were sometimes richly decorated with inlaid silver or even with intricately welded blades, the basic kind was not much more than a flattened or pointed piece of metal with sharp edges and a riveted socket. They came in different lengths with varying widths of spearhead, adapted for throwing or, more commonly, for use with both hands as a weapon of close combat. The slimmest lances had lean, pointed profiles and ash shafts of up to two metres, suited for a clean cast or a mounted charge. The heavier varieties had thicker heads and wider blades, sufficient to cause deep, broad, penetrating wounds. The largest added a crossbar behind the blade, giving weight to the thrust and also making it easier to pull out after a strike. To judge from depictions on metalwork, this kind could also be used on horseback, pinned between a rider's leg and the horse's flank, and presumably used in shock combat.

Viking swords required time and skill to manufacture. A very basic example would not necessarily have cost the earth, but at the extremes of investment, they were the ultimate badges of military prowess and prestige. Swords were slashing weapons, designed to cut rather than stab. In the early Viking Age, it was slightly more common to use single-edged types, whereas double-edged blades became the norm later on. Most sword hilts ended in a heavy pommel, the best of them made to exactly counterbalance the weight of the blade. A variety of forging techniques could be used, of which the finest was pattern-welding, where separate bars of iron were repeatedly heated and folded together before being hammered flat. The result was a flexible, lethal blade with high tensile strength, but also an extraordinarily beautiful object, as the coils and layers in the metal were visible as fine lines. The effect is mentioned in poetry, as 'snakes' writhing in the iron. The edges were hardened, sharpened steel. Every part of the hilt might also be decorated— the guard, the pommel, even sometimes the grip itself if it was made from tightly bound wire or plates of metal rather than the more common leather or horn.

Scabbards were made of wood panels bound or glued together, often lined with greased wool containing lanolin that would naturally oil the blade inside. The sheaths were sometimes covered in leather, tooled with intricate designs that might also be painted on the wood. A metal chape protected the pointed end of the scabbard, while the mouth and other sections of the sheath could be reinforced with bronze mounts. The scabbard was either suspended from a belt or worn on a baldric that crossed the body diagonally over one shoulder. Any or all of the ensemble could be decorated, and the highest end of the scale was a twisting mass of figures comparable to the prestige weapons of the Migration and Vendel Periods.

These high-status objects were the kind of swords that might acquire names, about which tales were told—weapons with life histories, even a kind of material biography. Egil Skalla-Grímsson had Dragvandil, a name that probably refers to a blade so long it dragged on the ground. The eleventh-century Norwegian king Magnús Óláfsson Barefoot had a sword with the prosaic name of Legbiter. The sagas and poems are full of magical blades: Angrvadall, 'Stream of Anguish', that glowed brightly in war but shone with a pale light in peacetime, its blade inscribed with runes; there is Gramr, 'Wrath', the sword of Sigurd the dragon-killer; Hrunting, the supposedly invincible sword that failed Beowulf in his fight with Grendel's mother; Skofnung, the unnaturally sharp sword of Hrólf kraki, in which were bound the souls of twelve berserkers; Tyrfing, the weapon that Hervör wrested from her dead father Angantyr, a sword forged by dwarves, with a blade that shone like flames. There are many more, sometimes with a supernatural edge guaranteed to kill a man each time they were drawn, but often with fatal consequences for the wielder. In the mythological world, Heimdall's sword is called Man-Head; *The Lay of Svipdagr* mentions a blade called Damage-Twig, and so on.

A feature of the Salme boat burials raises several questions about bladed weapons: the surprising fact that there are more swords than men. It is possible they are there as symbols, gifts of honour to the dead, stand-ins for individuals whose bodies are missing, or any other explanation that does not directly link them as the possessions of the men in the boats. On the other hand, these may be the weapons they owned in life, following them into death; some of them were placed in the dead men's hands. Swords are usually reckoned as elite armaments reserved for the wealthy, due to their sheer expense—the 'average' Viking warrior wielded lowlier weapons, such as spears and axes. But what if this is wrong, as one reading of Salme would suggest? Another possibility is that our perception of swords as costly items is correct, and that the Salme expedition was therefore a *very* high-ranking, even royal, affair.

The most coveted swords were products of Frankish smiths, imported to the North as blades and fitted with hilts there. One particularly famous Rhineland workshop that began operations in the ninth century can be recognised by the name *Ulfberht* inlaid into its blades. Originally (one presumes) the signature of its master smith, it became an early logo in an almost modern sense, and swords bearing it continued to be produced for another two hundred years. There were also many fake versions of lower quality and sometimes even with the name misspelled—the market-stall rip-offs of the Viking Age. More than one hundred genuine Ulfberht swords have been found, the majority in Scandinavian graves but also extending out into the diaspora as far as the Volga.

The Viking preference for Frankish blades is easy to understand. Renowned for their workmanship, and particularly their flexible toughness, this was war-gear to which one literally entrusted life and limb. In Notker the Stammerer's biography of Charlemagne, there is an episode in which some domestically produced Scandi-navian swords are offered to the emperor as tribute and are then tested for quality. Charlemagne tries to bend a blade so that its point touches the hilt, but it snaps and he rejects it in disgust. Unsheathing his own sword, he performs the task with ease "and then let it gradually straighten itself again". These were the Frank-ish swords that ibn Faḍlān witnessed among the Rus', the best that could be obtained.

A second blade weapon became increasingly common in the later Viking Age. It does not have a formal name, being often referred to as a fighting-knife or battle-knife, and it was essentially a development of the one-handed, long *seax* knife of the Migra-tion Period. A single-edged blade with a thick back that added weight to a short, stabbing blow, it seems to have been intended as a back-up weapon. By the tenth century, battle-knives had elaborate scabbards that were worn horizontally along the belt, allowing them to be drawn across the body from behind a shield if the sword was gone; a variant hung down at an angle from an elaborate harness. It seems they may also have been worn on the back—again for a swift, over-the-shoulder draw.

The bow was the final component of the full, 'conventional' set of offensive weapons. The common form in Scandinavia was a shorter variant of what would become the medieval longbow: a straight piece of ash wood bent to be strung and capable of firing an arrow over long distances with great penetrating power. In the tenth century, following the rise of Rus' culture and eastern influences, we also see the importation of specialist shorter bows of recurved type, combined with wide-angle quivers of the kind used by the steppe nomads. Made to be rapidly fired from a horse, these were deadly weapons that required considerable training to use effectively.

Arrows came in many shapes and forms—from broad cutting heads designed to cause copious bleeding in unprotected flesh, to narrow, pointed bodkin-like types for piercing between the links of chainmail. The most common multipurpose form had a leaf-shaped head; archaeologists occasionally find very specialised types, such as a pronged 'trident' used for carrying burning cloth into the sails and rigging of ships (there was one in the Salme burials). There were many more forms adapted for hunting, with types specific to individual animals.

For defence, the basic shield was a circular wooden affair made of thin planks bonded together, usually covered with leather, and with a rim holding it all in place. Inserted into a central hole was a round boss of iron, riveted onto the board and with a crossbar wooden handle inside that extended across the reverse; this was the grip and a protector for the hand. Some shields were closely matched to their owners, bespoke items fitted to the individual. From both archaeology and literature, it is clear that the boards were painted either a single colour (black, yellow, red, and white are recorded) or with patterns—a swirl of curved lines radiating from the boss seems especially common. In some graves of mounted warriors, there are two shields, and in metalwork images of riders, there are depictions of a second shield slung along the horse's flank.

Shields were offensive as well as defensive weapons, used to disarm opponents or push aside their weapons, often in combination with swords or axes. If the edge was struck with force into an enemy's neck, a shield could kill. There are also descriptions of later, more desperate stages of fighting after the wooden boards of a shield had been hacked away, leaving only the boss enclosing its owner's fist—still deadly in a close-combat iron punch.

Armour was mostly organic, made of padded leather or in the form of quilted jackets that provided a modicum of protection, especially from blunt-force blows or glancing cuts. Chainmail was certainly known, and would have been worn over textiles by those who could afford it. Made of thousands of interlocking rings, each of which had to be made separately and then joined, a full shirt of mail was a very expensive thing. It could be waist-length, or in the later Viking Age worn almost down to the ankles. Within the Baltic region, especially at Birka, there is evidence for the use of lamellar armour, formed of rectangular plates of iron sewn onto fabric to form a flexible, articulated defence. Worn as extended shirts, and also as protectors for the extremities, this was an Eastern tradition that probably entered Scandinavia along the river routes.

Relatively little is known of Viking-Age helmets. Only one approximately complete example has ever been found, at Gjermundbu in Norway. This is a rounded skull cap of iron with a face protector that covered the nose, surmounted by a spectacle-shaped eye guard. The neck and probably also the lower face were covered by a curtain of mail. Helmets of this kind are shown on picture-stones, although it is possible they were of hardened leather. A few other helmet fragments have been found on settlement sites or in burials, and are shown in a wide range of images, including three-dimensional carvings. From this, two things are clear. First, helmets (of all kinds, including the cheapest) were relatively common, which is not surprising given the obvious need to protect the head in combat. Second, at least the metal varieties were considered so valuable that they almost never accompanied their owners into the grave. Needless to say, *none* of them had horns.

One of the most enduring components of the Viking myth can be found in the berserkers—the frenzied warriors who fought naked, consumed with uncontrollable fury while out of their minds on mushrooms. This is, as they say, a truth with modification.

There is no doubt that the *berserkir* were a Viking-Age reality, but almost every other aspect of their nature is open to interpretation. The word itself refers to a shirt (*serk*) with either a *bear-* or *bare-* prefix, thus giving an image either of an ursine warrior or a man shirtless in the sense of being unarmoured or even naked. That the bear connection may be the more relevant of the two is reinforced by a lupine counterpart to the berserkers in the form of the *ulfheðnar*, meaning 'wolfskins'.

In the archaeology there are the famous 'weapon dancer' images, men either naked or clad in wolf pelts and wielding swords and spears. These occur particularly on Migration and Vendel Period war gear, but also extend to Viking-Age objects, tapestries, coins, and a picture-stone. There are comparable images of armed figures with heads like boars or bears on metalwork such as pendants, on textiles, and even on a runestone depicting an animal-warrior, complete with floppy ears. At Hedeby, two rather unsettling animal masks made of felt were found rolled up and used as caulking in a sunken ship, and may also have been part of a berserker's equipment; they most closely resemble dogs or bulls.

Something related may lie behind the inscription on a runestone from Istaby in Blekinge, Sweden, which lists three generations of men in the same family, all of whom have names combining battle terms with a wolf element. Perhaps this implies some form of totemic animal running down the generations:

Hathuwulfr [Battle-Wolf],
son of Heruwulfr [Sword Wolf],
cut these runes in memory of Haeriulfr [War-Host-Wolf].

There are also contemporary written accounts from outside Scandinavia that describe Vikings in combat, including some suggestive details. A Byzantine chronicle of wars against the Rus' includes descriptions of warriors howling like animals, and a commander fighting with a frenzied abandon so extreme as to resemble literal insanity; the imperial veterans had never seen anything like it. Similarly, wolf imagery is sometimes employed when discussing Scandinavian forces in the field. This may be poetic convention or, perhaps, something more.

The earliest Norse literary reference to such warriors is in the skaldic praise poem *Haraldskvæði* by Thórbjörn hornklofi. It in part describes the Battle of Hafrsfjörðr that took place c. 872; the poem was probably composed around 900. The details are graphic beyond the normal conventions of skaldic verse— the warriors are described as drinking blood, for example—and they were clearly seen as something separate from other types of combatant:

They [the ships of Harald's fleet] were loaded with farmer-chiefs and broad shields, with Vestland spears and Frankish swords; *berserkir* screamed, the battle was on, *ulfheðnar* howled and shook their spears.

Of the *berserkr*-fury I would ask, about the drinkers of the corpse-sea [blood]: what are they like, these men who go happy into battle?

Ulfheðnar they are called, who bear bloody shields in the slaughter; they redden spears when they join the fighting; there they are arranged for their task; there I know that the honourable prince places his trust only in brave men, who hack at shields.

The most often-cited description is much later, and comes from Snorri's *Saga of the Ynglingas*:

> His [Odin's] men went [into battle] without mail-coats and were as wild as dogs or wolves, they bit their shields, were as strong as bears or bulls; they killed people, but they themselves were hurt by neither fire nor iron; this is called going berserk.

There is no evidence whatsoever, in archaeology or text, for the berserkers' use of hallucinogens, entheogens, or any other form of mind-altering drug or chemical, including the consumption of fly agaric (despite the fact that Wikipedia's entry for berserkers recommends the reader also look up 'Dutch Courage' and, indeed, 'Going Postal').

The term *berserksgangr* (generally translated as 'going berserk', as above) literally describes a way of moving, 'berserk-walking', and not a fighting rage at all—something that might fit well with the strangely formal postures of the 'weapon dancers' and the pelt-wearing warriors on the metalwork. This could be a ritual, a sort of militarised performance, and one scholar has suggested that these theatrics were the real root of berserker-hood—effectively a symbolic preparation for war rather than reflecting any actual behaviour on the battlefield. The one need not rule out the other, especially given the generally dramatic nature of other Viking rituals perceptible in the archaeology. We must remember Þórbjörn's poem and the non-Scandinavian descriptions of actions that truly sound like fighting rage.

In the sagas, berserkers appear mostly as stock villains—useful antagonists for the heroes to kill—although in the kings' sagas they are sometimes present as regular parts of a royal retinue, a sort of Viking special forces. Interestingly, the motif of biting the shield, usually dismissed as a literary fantasy, is actually encountered *earlier* than most of the Icelandic texts in the form of the 'warders' in the Lewis gaming sets, ivory sculptures that probably date to the twelfth century. Difficult though they are to approach (something probably true at the time, too), for all the problems of interpretation, these unusual men must nonetheless be given their place as part of the Viking war machine.

Alongside the berserkers, another persistent symbol of Viking-Age warfare is the shield-maiden. They appear conflated with Valkyries and other female warriors several times in the heroic poems of the Eddic tradition, in skaldic poems, and with some frequency in the poetic citations of Snorri's *Edda*. In the sagas of Icelanders, by contrast, armed women are not encountered at all other than in isolated contexts of self-defence, momentary rage, or planned revenge. However, shield-maidens do appear frequently in the legendary sagas: in the figure of Hervör retrieving her father Angantyr's sword, and also in the *Saga of Ragnar lothbrók*, the *Saga of Hrólf Gautreksson*, and several others. Early parts of Saxo's *History of the Danes*, begun in the late twelfth century, also includes many dramatic descriptions of shield-maidens. In several of these sources, the action is set not just in the Viking Age, but also in the centuries preceding it as far back as the Migration Period.

In the sources, such women may appear singly or in small bands—the latter sometimes specifically composed of female warriors—or more integrated into general fighting forces. In individual cases, they can assume positions of command by leading armies and directing campaigns. Occasionally these women are described as having different and sometimes transgressive attributes of appearance (wearing male clothing, for example). They fight both with and without armour. For some of these women, taking on this identity involves a change of name, and even of grammatical gender in that masculine forms of words are used. The tales adopt a variety of moral and social viewpoints, sometimes framing the women as rare exceptions to their sex, and in other instances giving little sign that they were regarded as out of the ordinary.

19. Warrior woman? A reconstruction of the person buried in Birka chamber grave Bj.581, based on the excavated data and with clothing details extrapolated from other Birka burials and contemporary graves in the Caucasus. Image: Tancredi Valeri, used by kind permission.

For all their literary qualities, however, it is clear that none of these sources represent anything close to a faithful historical record. The legendary sagas are particularly problematic, and textual specialists have almost universally interpreted the figure of the shield-maiden as a later literary product, developed within narratives that reflect the social preoccupations of the time. The existence of *actual* warrior women in the Viking Age, as opposed to a simulacrum of them sprung from a kind of medieval fiction, has been much debated.

This changed in 2017 when DNA analyses were conducted on the seated body from a Birka chamber grave discussed in chapter

5, confirming that this 'warrior' was female. The controversies that ensued from this claim, and their implications for the gendered study of the Vikings, have been reviewed earlier. In terms of further archaeological comparisons, among burials with a female sex determination on osteological grounds alone, there are some fifteen or so with single axes and a handful more with a spear or a knife, perhaps a few arrows, and occasionally a shield. In the conventional interpretations applied to male graves, not many of these would be considered 'warrior' burials. There are only a very few with full weapon sets like the Birka grave.

The exceptional nature of the Old Norse stories does not prove they were based on real-life individuals, at however great a remove, not least since such figures only appear in certain genres of saga-writing and not others. However, they certainly do not refute the existence of real female warriors. In truth, the medieval texts are interesting, but strictly speaking unnecessary, for the interpretation of the excavated data. These burials are decidedly *not* medieval saga, legend, or poetic licence but empirically observable Viking-Age reality.

Weapons in themselves do not necessarily determine or define a warrior, and neither does gender; there are always alternative possibilities. Some scholars attempt to draw fine distinctions between types of combatant that are often skewed in odd ways as they intersect with identity. After a certain point, these debates become absurd in the context of Viking-Age reality (one pictures a couple of monks peering over the monastery wall at an advancing troupe—"What do you think, *are* they warriors, or more like *militia*?"—as the chapel goes up in flames). But we must ensure that the same standards of data, evidence, and logic should apply regardless of sex, with our minds resolutely open to complexity. If scholars are prepared to claim that even a single male-bodied individual buried with numerous weapons can be gendered as a man and interpreted as a warrior (and there are hundreds of such examples across the Viking diaspora that are accepted with little controversy), then they must be prepared to come to the same conclusion if the sex determination is different.

Taking a clear-eyed look at the archaeological data, it seems that there really were female warriors in the Viking Age, including at least one of command rank. They were never numerous, and few have been even tentatively identified, though this may change as we re-examine our sources and our consciences. They were rare exceptions—unusual people, to be sure—but they were there.

It is hard to know what a Viking-Age raid, or battle, was actually like. Several books have been written claiming to give detailed treatments of tactics, battlefield formations, and the like, but these are almost entirely drawn from later practice applied retrospectively, and often from literal readings of textual sources with debatable reliability. In reality, we know comparatively little other than the impressions of noise, chaos, and violence that are conveyed so vividly in poetry and in the names of the Valkyries.

A basic division seems to have been between collective engagement and single combat; the former won battles while the latter enhanced prestige.

The primary battlefield strategy involved the shield-wall, in which a force formed up in a line several men deep with overlapping shields. As a cohesive unit, it could be used to advance and push opponents back by sheer impetus, while spears and knives could be employed to stab forward between the ranks. Swords and axes could also come into play, and the legs of anyone facing a shield-wall were especially vulnerable from underhand thrusts. The formation's strength lay in unity as a collective and the greater degree of protection afforded from frontal attack. Shields could also be raised to deflect incoming arrows.

The flying wedge formation, known in Old Norse as *svínfylking* (the 'boar's snout'), also seems to be of ancient origin. Although it is described mainly retrospectively in medieval texts, according to the first-century Roman author Tacitus it was also employed by the Germanic tribes of his time. The confluence of such independent sources a millennium apart suggests the Vikings practised this tactic, just as the sagas say. The 'boar' would see armoured warriors forming up in a triangular array, with the point towards the enemy, moving forward at speed and using momentum and weight to punch through the opposing ranks.

In combat at sea, the strategy was much the same as on land, and sometimes a line of ships was even roped together to form a mobile, floating platform so as to make a maritime fight as much like a terrestrial one as possible. Such ship platforms could then be rowed against each other, the jagged lines formed by the prows clashing and interlocking, creating an even larger wooden field of combat. The fighting proceeded from ship to ship, and the sagas reveal how each vessel would be 'cleared' in turn. Casualties were left where they fell or thrown into the sea. All such battles were accompanied by showers of arrows and other projectiles.

Individual duels are recorded not only on the battlefield, but also as a means of formally resolving insults, as in many cultures. In such cases, combatants used whatever weapons they preferred. Single combat in war was especially praiseworthy, appearing in poetry and sagas—such as the lone Norwegian who allegedly held the English army at, and literally on, Stamford Bridge in 1066. Fighting with an axe, he supposedly kept the river crossing until he was stabbed from the water below with a spear.

Ultimately, any experience of war was personal. In the late eighth century, an expedition such as Lindisfarne might well have been a young Viking's first taste of such things. If he survived, it was a memory that would never leave him, and this too we should remember. None of this was without context or rationale.

We're on the west coast of Norway. The second or third son of the farm, not much hope of a landed inheritance but just about content with his lot. He's been walking out with Sigrid from up the valley—they've kept each other company since they were children, and 'everyone knows' they'll get married. But now she's suddenly wearing a new brooch with that curling ornament they have over the sea, and she's spending time with the boy from the big house, the stocky one who borrowed his father's sword and sailed off with the lads last summer.

Faced suddenly with a whole different future, it's not hard to see how our man starts to adjust his plans for the following season and begins to make enquiries among the ship owners. The same situation can be viewed from other perspectives, including that of the family at home.

You heard about the Christ-house that the Vikings burnt, the river of gold that flowed back with them—well, it was our *boy* who killed the boss man there, *the one with that funny stick. Good to see our youngest getting his act together,* making *something of himself, you know? He doesn't realise, but of course it was me who set it up, got him a place on board; the lord's always listened more to me than to my husband.*

Or the women who feel their prospects shifting—their choices expanding—with each boat that returns, with every present and proposal. Some of it is just baubles and glitter, offered by the usual idiots who can't grasp that they're out of their league with someone much brighter than they are. But there are also openings, windows onto what could be a different life, in a bigger house, on better land, with a world of possibilities.

And there's that tall one again, good-looking despite the scar, with the gold-hilted blade (which he didn't have last year). This is the third ship he's sailed with, and he's got another stripe on his teeth. Ignore that frightened girl he brought home with him—that's just to be expected,

and anyway she can't even speak the language; and he does keep look-
ing at you. But you'll be the judge of where that might lead.

And then there are the ship-lords, the planners—with the helmets
and the rings and the brightly coloured cloaks—who take the biggest cut but also the financial risk (Ólaf lost a whole crew last season). They enjoy the plunder but see it as a means to an end, as the
fuel for their fame, as power.

You've told your boat-builder to start laying down a new keel—or why
not two?—and you've put the word out that a poet could find a wel-
come in your hall. Last year, that sea-king from Jæren walked straight
past you at the assembly, but next time he'll look you in the eye.

These are speculations, of course, but they are not unreasonable.
Though some of this may be unpalatable to us, there is nothing
overtly mercenary or mechanistic here, just people living their lives
and hoping to improve them. Their norms were not necessarily
ours, at all, and none of this should be applied uniformly across
society—why would anyone imagine that?

The 'Viking Age' was never a process, something with a firm
direction. This was not a Blitzkrieg or, yet, an assault on the West
(or East). Instead, these were initially isolated events occurring over
a matter of days once or twice a year, across vast spans of territory.
It might take weeks or months to hear the news that they had happened at all. Over thirty years, this would not dominate anyone's
everyday concerns.

But this was only the start, the very first raids. Within a decade
or so, the nature of these expeditions would change. For some of
the Scandinavians, it would be a ride they were glad to share, a
flow they slipped into for the profit and, yes, the adventure. Initially, it took some people away from home, and brought them
back altered; it also changed the lives of those who stayed behind.

Before too long, the definition of 'home' would be fluid, mobile, before coalescing again around quite different places across the sea. For others in the North—just a handful, at first, but in growing numbers—all this was a path they dreamt of, pursued, and shaped. Perceptible to us but probably only to a very few of them, it was the beginning of something new.

12

HYDRARCHY

T HE RAIDS ON THE NORTHUMBRIAN monasteries seem to have
been isolated events along the northern coasts (though who
knows what the compilers of the *Anglo-Saxon Chronicle* chose to
discreetly omit). For southern England, they were a prelude to
Viking assaults clearly severe enough to require the construction of
defences against them.

In Ireland, the raids definitely got worse, beginning with
attacks on Inishmurray and Roscam in 807. There are references
to military successes against the Vikings in 811 and 812, in Ulster
and Munster, but also of Irish defeats at Connaught in the latter
year. Howth, in the north of Dublin Bay, and Wexford Harbour
were both attacked in 821. There are general references to widespread raiding.

It is hard to know how much, if any, of this affected Frankia.
The English cleric Alcuin, chronicler of the Lindisfarne raid, mentions attacks in Aquitaine (south-west France) in 799, which may
have been what prompted Charlemagne to strengthen the security
of the coast the following year. The exception is that allusion in the
Royal Frankish Annals to a fleet of two hundred Danish ships raiding Frisia in 810. The figure is such an enormous escalation of the
smaller forces implied in all other raiding accounts of this period

that it is difficult to interpret, and can reasonably be regarded as suspicious. Ten years later there was another burst of activity in Frankia, with attacks in Flanders, Aquitaine again, and the Seine estuary.

The raids during the first three decades of the ninth century seem individually to have been of similar character and size, and presumably were driven by similar kinds of initial motors as their predecessors. A successful formula was repeated—with even greater profit but for essentially the same combination of individual motives and the sociopolitical aims of local elites—but still within relatively modest parameters. A clear escalation *can* be seen in the Irish and Frankish raids, collectively involving dozens of ships, at least, and perhaps more. This is certainly implied by the attack on Frisia, an imperial buffer zone and already an area of border tensions between the Franks and Danes. Whether or not the Viking fleet that ravaged the region in 810 really numbered two hundred vessels, it was big enough to demand payment of one hundred pounds of silver after defeating the Frisians three times in open battle. By the time the Franks could respond by sending troops, the Danes had already left (to add to the disappointment, the emperor's pet elephant suddenly died at the same time—one of those useless bits of historical information that tell us the past was real).

The organisation of these ventures—and the fact that at least in Ireland the raiders are described as coming in 'flotillas', with caveats for what that might mean in reality—also indicates that the scale of the Viking attacks was increasing into the 820s. At the same time, we should remember that this was thirty years after the first recorded western raids, and seventy years after Salme. In context, this is actually a generation or two, which gives the lie to any sense of 'waves' of attacks overwhelming western Europe. Nonetheless, the Vikings were developing a system of sorts, and it clearly worked in relation to their objectives. They excelled at hit-and-run tactics and ambushes, and had proved themselves unexpectedly capable of assaulting fortified targets. They followed very different rules from their victims.

The notion that, before the raids, the Scandinavians were ignorant of what lay 'west over the sea' is nonsense. They probably had a good idea of life at least along the east coast, in particular around the markets and monasteries—but this is not the same as complete familiarity with England, its people and landscapes, its politics and culture. It may be that much of this early period was essentially one of tentative exploration, mapping out vulnerabilities while ensuring relatively safe lines of supply and retreat.

However, in Scandinavia the early raids were having an effect. A growing number of men may have improved their social standing, personal wealth, longer-term economic outlook, and perhaps their marriage prospects. These men were not isolated from their communities at home, but of course fully integrated within them. The raids very much played across borders of gender. Every woman with whom the raiders were connected, in any way, thus played a part in the changes set in motion by the flow of foreign loot. Other people also arrived in Scandinavia—the newly enslaved—whose lives were changed forever, the women's most (and worst) of all.

The results and proceeds of the raids were not limited to the raiders themselves. The elites who financed the expeditions made other kinds of gains: their coffers filled, perhaps augmented still further by demanding a cut of the general take (although 'their fair share' sounds nicer, doesn't it?). They could activate these economic rewards to entrench and expand their positions, including through the funding of more raids that would drive the cycle forward. Their retinues grew, along with their strength and status. This might not have been solely positive, for with affluence comes rivalry and jealousy, and with increasing power comes envy on the part of those who would like to usurp it. The internecine politics of Scandinavia and its petty-kingdoms were probably enflamed rather than soothed by the North Sea adventure.

And of course, some of the raiders never came back at all—perhaps even quite large numbers of them on unlucky occasions, such as the Monkwearmouth fiasco when most of the ships foundered and their crews were massacred. The Viking life was a risky one, even for a fortnight. This too had its consequences, but given the militarised ideologies and honour systems of the North, it is likely that such hazards were not a primary concern, and certainly not much of a deterrent.

The raiding of the early ninth century was intense but sporadic; this situation changed in 834. There is no evidence that the events of that year, as recorded in the *Anglo-Saxon Chronicle*, were the result of a coordinated and deliberate shift in strategy. It is only in retrospect that they appear as a watershed, a divider between what came before—a few boatloads at a time, just a *lið* or two of warrior brothers—and what would follow.

After 834, the Scandinavians regularly came in fleets numbering hundreds of ships, carrying thousands of men. Their depredations would bring the major western European powers to the very brink of destruction, and they would also acquire names in the chronicles and annals of those regions: the Great Heathen Army or the Great Raiding Army; the Armies of the Seine, the Somme, and the Loire; the Great Summer Army; and more. Their stories were complex ones, but they are key to understanding the following two centuries of Viking activities across Eurasia.

Just as with the coastal attacks that began decades earlier, the nature and motivations of these new ventures were intimately connected with the political economies of Scandinavia. But this time there was a key difference, something that set the fleets and armies apart from the first raids: *in the early ninth century, there was no single polity, kingdom, or other social entity in Scandinavia sufficiently large to launch maritime ventures of this kind.* In other words, none of these forces can be understood in simple ethnic or political terms. They were not 'the Danes', 'the Norwegians', or even 'the sea-kings'; in fact, they were not 'the anybodies'. They were something else, and the challenge is to find out what that was.

Getting inside these escalating Viking groups is now a possibility, through archaeological excavations in the remains of their camps, their burials, the detritus of their daily lives—much of it with startling implications. Aside from confirming that they really did number in the thousands, it seems these 'armies' also included women and children—families—and that they had entire economies of manufacturing and exchange. They were by no means just fighting forces, although raiding was always at the heart of their operations. Going deeper, inside their heads, one finds new vistas of bold social experiments, political resistance, and attempts to create a different kind of life.

All this suggests that the large-scale, mobile Viking conglomerates of the ninth century were neither 'armies' nor 'warbands', but continuously evolving migratory communities. They were not on their way to anywhere, but were an end in themselves, justified through action. In essence, *these forces were polities in their own right*.

As the fleets grew bigger, as the forces swelled in size and became more diverse, as they hit tougher targets, and above all as they began to stay away from Scandinavia for ever-longer periods, something significant occurred. Where raiding had once been an activity, something for a few weeks or a summer, it now effectively became, at least for some, a lifestyle. To be a Viking in this context was a frame of mind; a belief system; a career strategy; a ritual act; of course a livelihood, if a violent and risky one; but most of all, a choice.

It's not that the profits to be made in the West were unknown before, it's just that now something has moved and come together in their minds—not collectively and simultaneously, of course, but meshing gradually through grapevine communications, the talk in the ports, and not least, the persuasive qualities of visible success. In time, a short *time, the practical understanding of just how rich a potential lies beyond the marine horizons, in almost every direction, will transform their world.*

One must begin with *what* happened, and only then can the *why* and *how* become apparent.

In the year 834, Dorestad, the wealthy emporium at the fork of the Rhine about one hundred kilometres from the Dutch coast, was attacked and burnt, apparently by a force from Denmark. It was an astonishing move—this was no monastery or isolated community, but one of the most important places in the trading networks of northern Europe. This would be like physically assaulting one of today's great financial hubs. The Vikings slaughtered at will and took shiploads of slaves. The surrounding region was devastated. The same was to happen every single summer for the next four years, in the face of ineffectual Frankish responses that included failed peace negotiations. The Vikings seem to have played a careful hand, combining feigned diplomacy supported by the raiding they never had any intention of renouncing.

By 837, the *Annals of St-Bertin* were resignedly describing the "usual surprise attack" on Frisia. Utrecht and Antwerp were hit repeatedly, and the same Viking fleets crossed the Channel to raid the Isle of Sheppey in the Thames estuary. There is a suggestion that the Scandinavians followed a similar south-coast route as in previous decades and headed into the Irish Sea from the south. As before, while en route they also tried their luck in Frankia with a probing attack on the Loire in 835 in which the monastery on the island of Noirmoutier was overrun. This would be a harbinger of much worse to come.

Ireland was heavily and constantly attacked from the mid-830s onwards for the next fifteen years. Raiding along the coasts and also inland along the rivers, the Vikings hit more than fifty named targets (many several times), and there are records of more regional impacts. Monasteries were again focal points of the raids, but markets and settlements had now become targets too. The fleets established temporary bases on the rivers, defences for their ships, and camp sites from which they raided at will in the countryside.

England seems to have been left in relative peace in the 830s, although this is possibly a distortion resulting from deliberate omissions in the *Chronicle*. In 839, for example, there is a strange ecclesiastical record of dreams that troubled the sleep of the king of Wessex, images of pagans devastating his land. This nocturnal vision was so disturbing that he pledged to make a pilgrimage to Rome to ask for divine intercession. Viking raids evidently weighed so heavily on the mind of southern England's most powerful monarch that he thought his kingdom hung in the balance. This is not only suggestive of considerable Viking activity in England at this time, it is also a very long way from the burning of a church on Lindisfarne.

In any case, this would change decisively in 840 and 841, when another shift can be detected. The Irish west coast was raided repeatedly, and expeditions were made to the interior. Camps were founded at Dublin (probably in the Kilmainham area), Annagassan, and other sites, and a seasonal Viking presence became entrenched in these areas. The eastern and southern coasts of England also came under attack, with at least a dozen raids in two years, each of which probably ranged widely. The Vikings were now a fixture of the English experience, and the financial impact of their activities had real political weight. The human toll, in lives lost both literally and to enslavement, was growing.

The real catalyst for the surge in Viking activity was civil war in Frankia—the Carolingian Empire named after its founder, Charlemagne. In 840, his successor, the emperor Louis the Pious, died. The turbulent relations between Louis's three surviving sons, barely kept in check during the emperor's declining years, boiled over on his death. Charles the Bald, Lothar, and Louis the German began to fight it out for control of the Empire, in a conflict that spilled over into every sector of the realm, from the Iberian border to the Alps, all the way to southern Denmark and the Rhine. The state apparatus was riven with disunity and factionalism, as minor nobility, city governors, local magnates, and even bishops formed their own militias and took sides (often simply their own).

The Vikings poured into the gap left by the distraction and destabilisation of the Empire, and would not leave for twenty years. The great rivers of Frankia—the Seine, the Somme, and the Loire—acted as watery motorways into the heart of the Empire. This was no longer a matter of coastal attacks and peripheral economic damage: the Vikings brought war to the Franks, striking hundreds of kilometres inland up the rivers. It is evident that there were many different groups, each with their own commanders and agendas, sometimes combining in larger constellations. What they had in common was the ability to insert themselves deftly into the political chaos.

Mobile Viking bands fought the forces of the three imperial claimants, singly or sometimes in alliance. They also raided local municipalities and took on the militias, or just whatever ragtag defence the peasantry could muster in the face of indifferent central leadership. Vikings were also hired as mercenaries by any and all of these factions, to fight their civil enemies or even other Vikings; in many cases, the Scandinavians then pooled their forces to turn on their erstwhile employers. None of this took place in a vacuum of knowledge, nor was it a matter of haphazard reaction: the Vikings knew exactly what they were doing, where they were doing it, and who they might be likely to encounter in the process. This mastery of reconnaissance in depth—an awareness of the value to be placed on prior knowledge—showed throughout their campaigns in Frankia and later in England. The Viking commanders were active political agents, stirring the civil war to effect maximum destabilisation, which in turn fed the Scandinavians' own twin objectives of moveable wealth in the form of plunder, and mobile labour through the taking of captives.

Even God was enlisted in the struggle, as seen in an antiphonal (a piece of music for a church service) made for use in the imperial chapel of Charles the Bald, which records a prayer sung for protection against the raids: *de gente fera Normannica nos libera, quae nostra vastat, Deus, regna*: "Grant us freedom, Lord, from the wild Northern people who lay waste our realms".

The graves of western Norway and Denmark from this time are full of Frankish metalwork and coinage—the fruits of the raids. It is possible to discern a hierarchy of insular objects in the burials, activated in new Scandinavian contexts. One can almost perceive the relative status of different participants in the raids, manifested in the materials and quality of the looted items. Jewellery seems to have been particularly popular and was preserved either intact or else reused as pendants and the like. Carolingian disc brooches are common finds, whereas silver was mostly melted down and recast into objects more to Norse tastes.

In 843, the three main Carolingian factions agreed on peace and a tripartite division of the Empire—Charles ruled Francia Occidentalis, from the Pyrenees to the Pas-de-Calais; Lothar governed Francia Media, a north-south strip of territory that included most of the Low Countries, Burgundy, and Provence with an extension into northern Italy; Louis got the east, Francia Orientalis, with lands in what is now western Germany; the small 'Celtic' province of Brittany remained fiercely independent.

The Viking response to the treaty was considered, and worrying. In that same year, a fleet overwintered in Frankia for the first time, setting up a base (on Noirmoutier, again) at the mouth of the Loire with good access to the open sea. This set the pattern for decades to come and was repeated in England from 851 onwards. Usually located on estuarine islands or other easily defended marine sites, these camps would sometimes serve for a year or two before being abandoned, but over time some of them developed into more-or-less permanent bases. Three major and distinctive groups of Vikings would congregate at such enclaves on the Loire, Seine, and Somme, and were thereafter referred to as the 'armies' of those regions. By the 850s, the points of entry to all three major water routes into Frankia were essentially under Viking control.

The 'raids', which had long since become seasonal campaigns, now evolved into a continual Viking presence. The armies were still uniquely mobile, never far from their ships, and their operations in the field year on year are unparalleled for this period. Ever since the 830s, the fleets had also been increasing in size. Sixty-seven vessels—an unusually exact number—are mentioned at Nantes in 843. Two years later, Paris itself was attacked by a fleet of 120 ships that had fought its way up the Seine; this was the raid led by one of the most famous Vikings of all, Ragnar lothbrók. He was an effective if vicious commander, and his followers were given a staggering seven thousand pounds of silver and gold bullion in order to finally leave the city in peace. It would be the first of many such payments.

After Paris, the size of the raiding fleets only increased still further, no doubt prompted by the demonstrable profits such ventures could produce. Into the 850s, there are records of a 252-ship raid in Frisia; 105 ships at the Île de Bièce and 103 in the Vilaine, both in Brittany.

On Lothar's death in 855, the Empire again experienced periods of unrest, with Louis making a move on his brother Charles through an invasion of the west. Although Charles survived and, in time, would come to rule as sole emperor, the weakness of the imperial defences was again an open invitation to the Vikings. They were not slow to exploit it. In 860, the situation was vividly described by Ermentarius of Noirmoutier, a monk who had been driven from his monastery when the Vikings took it over as their base on the Loire:

> The number of ships grows: the endless stream of Vikings
> never ceases to increase. Everywhere the Christians are the
> victims of massacres, burnings, plunderings: the Vikings

conquer all in their path and nothing resists them: they seize Bordeaux, Périgeux, Limoges, Angoulême and Toulouse. Angers, Tours and Orléans are annihilated and an innumerable fleet sails up the Seine and the evil grows in the whole region. Rouen is laid waste, plundered and burned: Paris, Beauvais and Meaux taken, Melun's strong fortress levelled to the ground, Chartres occupied, Evreux and Bayeux plundered, and every town besieged.

On the Seine in 861, the *Annals of St-Bertin* lost count of a Viking fleet at 260 ships. There was no such thing as a 'standard' longship, so it is impossible to know how many people each one held, but on average, scholars usually find thirty or so to be a reasonable number. This was now a matter of *thousands* of Vikings in the field, moving across multiple regions in different groups.

Even when local defences managed to block the raiders' advances, they simply moved somewhere else. It was not until 862 that Charles the Bald, having achieved a modicum of stability in his kingdom, was able to organise sustained resistance in the form of an innovation that had instant and practical effect. He ordered the construction of fortified bridges across the main arterial rivers, controlling access along their passage by leaving only small openings blocked by moveable barriers and chains. The remains of one of them have been excavated at Pont de l'Arche on the Seine near Pîtres, revealing a complex structure with a fortress on each bank of the river, spanned by a massive defended bridge that also blocked a tributary. The outlay must have been enormous, and it is clear why administrative calm was a necessary prerequisite for such a project.

The impact of the bridges was rapid. The fleet sizes quoted by the annals rapidly fall. On the Loire and the Seine, there were only forty and fifty ships by 865, rather than the hundreds of a few years earlier. The success of the imperial strategy was not appreciated in England. In that year, the Viking fleets collectively withdrew from

Frankia and crossed the Channel in a massive invasion. In the process, and over the following decades, the English records provide us with our highest-resolution images, from anywhere in the world, of the Vikings at war.

When a large fleet landed at Thanet in 865 and quickly moved to East Anglia, the Vikings encountered a very different political scene than they were used to in Frankia. Although the Empire had been divided, it was at least nominally a functioning imperial bureaucracy. England, by contrast, was made up of several separate kingdoms, some more powerful than others; the largest were Mercia in the Midlands, Northumbria in the north of the country, East Anglia on the east coast, and Wessex to the south. They were often in uneasy alliance, but sometimes in openly expansionist competition. England had been converted to Christianity a couple of centuries earlier, and thus its sociopolitical structures were radically different from those of Scandinavia, but there were nonetheless similarities in the network of interlinked, rival kingdoms. The Vikings seized on this to their immediate advantage.

For the next fifteen years, what the *Anglo-Saxon Chronicle* calls either the 'Great Heathen Army' or sometimes the 'Great Raiding Army' fought its way across the English kingdoms. From the beginning in East Anglia, one can observe aspects of the Vikings' interactions in supposedly hostile territory that throw new light on the nature of their campaigns. The *Chronicle* records without comment that "there the army was provided with horses". In other entries over the years, the raiders were given supplies of various kinds, including food, and allowed safe havens where their families (explicitly mentioned, which has interesting implications) could remain protected. Even in the period of the earlier, intermittent raids, there had been signs of something similar—in 838, for example, the Vikings had made an alliance with the people of Cornwall. There are other signals of such relations. A splendid gospel book, the *Codex Aureus*, was donated to Christ Church

Canterbury with an inscription adding that it had been ransomed from a Viking army by a pious English couple—something surely impossible without relatively sophisticated lines of communication and at least some degree of trust.

It is very clear that—albeit perhaps as the least of several evils—by no means all the English were necessarily opposed to the Vikings. The expansionist ambitions of Wessex were no secret, and in some regions the Scandinavians might have been seen as a bulwark against the aggression of the southern kingdom. In any case, their presence was inescapable. Only a few years later, an ecclesiastical grant of food rents, allocating the produce of tax levied in kind, makes provision for dislocation in supply on account of heathen attacks—in other words, the Vikings had already become encoded into legal documents as possible disruptors, along the same lines as 'acts of God' in today's insurance policies.

The army had multiple commanders—among them men who were possibly the sons of Ragnar lothbrók, including Ivar the Boneless, Halfdan, and Ubbe—and it was, like the fleets in Frankia, a conglomerate of smaller units. These were the same *lið* of the early raids, but multiplied. We should envision a hierarchy of Viking groups—some loyal to a single ship's captain, others forming a small flotilla or two of loose affiliation, or loyal to even larger units, all placed within networks of allegiance and agreed support under the nominal command of one or more 'jarls' (as they are called in the English sources). There was no 'king of the Vikings', no single person with whom the English could negotiate. Even in Frankia, when emissaries sought the leader of a Viking army, the response came that they had none, but made their decisions collectively.

Having wintered in East Anglia, the army headed north and in 866 took the emporium of Eoforwic—York—after fighting all along the Roman walls of the city. For almost a century afterwards, Jorvík, as it became known, would be *the* main Viking stronghold of the north, ruled first by puppet kings and then directly by Scandinavians.

Thanks to the *Anglo-Saxon Chronicle*, the path of the Vikings can be followed with great precision, at times month by month. In 867 they made an attempt on Mercia, wintering in Nottingham, but were bought off after Wessex came to the Mercians' aid, and the army returned to York for another winter. In late 869 the Vikings were back in East Anglia, where they stayed for a year. Its king, Edmund, resisted and was captured and killed—becoming England's first official martyr at Scandinavian hands. Thereafter, East Anglia, like Northumbria, passed into effective Viking control.

The Vikings were masters of what one scholar has aptly called "longboat diplomacy". In the course of years spent in the field, the Vikings had shown themselves to be completely in tune with the English systems of defence. They knew all about the networks of strategic communications in the form of *herepaths*, or 'army-roads', and used them to their advantage. They understood the signal beacons on high ground, which they sometimes lit themselves to confuse the local militias.

With renewed strength, in 871 the Vikings invaded Wessex itself, where they were reinforced by a second Viking fleet—the 'Great Summer Army', as the *Chronicle* calls it. King Aethelred of Wessex, and his young brother, Alfred, led the English levies in eight or nine battles with the Vikings over the following months, with neither side gaining the upper hand through a succession of defeats and victories. Three months after a Wessex triumph at Ashdown, Aethelred died, and Alfred was crowned. He paid off the Vikings in some desperation, and they wintered in London, before spending the next three years pacifying Northumbria, overrunning the small kingdom of Lindsey (in present-day Lincolnshire), and finally taking Mercia.

It should be stated clearly: in just nine years, an invading Scandinavian force had effectively destroyed all but one of the English kingdoms. By 874, only Wessex remained as an independent realm. And again, the Great Army was in no sense a national entity, or a politically directed military strategy.

At this point the Viking host divided. Some headed north with Halfdan, who took them raiding even into southern Scotland. Returning to York in 876 they did something new: in a startling single line that echoes through the rest of English history, the *Chronicle* says that "they divided up the land of Northumbria, and they were ploughing and providing for themselves". The meaning is clear: *the Vikings had begun to settle down*, and the nature of their contact with the British Isles thereby changed forever.

The southern branch of the army, under Guthrum and two other commanders, went back to war. The kingdom of Wessex's desperate four-year fight against the Vikings is a cornerstone of English history, spawning as much myth and legend as fact, but the events are nonetheless solidly underpinned by the *Chronicle*. The Vikings crisscrossed southern England with forays north to Mercia, and penetrating as far east as Cornwall. Alfred's Wessex forces fought or ran, and even attempted to confront the Scandinavians at sea (with little success), until by 878 they had been pushed to the brink. In a final effort, Alfred rallied what was left of his troops and led them to an unexpected victory at Edington. Both sides had fought each other to a standstill, and agreed on a peace treaty dividing England in a manner that left Wessex in control of the south and west, while the east and north of the country was formally ceded to the Vikings in a recognition of de facto political realities. Although it would not acquire the name until slightly later, this region became known as the Danelaw—literally the land under the legal code of the Danes. The Viking armies dispersed throughout this area and into Mercia, and again began to settle.

In the year of the Treaty of Wedmore that created the Danelaw, in Frankia there was a strange repeat of what had happened in 865. The Carolingian emperor, Charles the Bald, had died in 877, followed soon after by his son, plunging the Empire back into yet another conflict over the succession. As they had done decades before, the Vikings turned their eyes to Frankia. While most of the Great Army stayed in England, some chose to cross the Channel for the chance of renewed plunder; they were aided by a third Viking force that had recently arrived at Fulham in London, which rapidly turned around for the Continent. This does not need to have been a stark choice, as there is every likelihood individuals moved back and forth between the Frankish raids and a Danelaw home. The armies were distinctly fluid entities.

Over the next six years, a second Viking assault washed over the Empire, with fleets ranging far up the Rhine and even taking the Frankish capital at Aachen. The imperial palace was occupied and its chapel humiliatingly used as a stable for the Vikings' horses.

Paris was besieged for a year from 885 to 886—an event illuminated for us by the eyewitness account of Abbo, a monk who watched the fighting on the walls from the nearby monastery of St-Germain-des-Prés. He relates how the Seine around the Île de la Cité—where Notre-Dame stands today—was choked with so many Viking ships that you could cross the water on the wooden river of their decks. The fleet was backed up downstream for kilometres. Abbo vividly describes the fight for the bridges, duels of archery around the towers, and the Vikings' use of siege engines (perhaps even mounted on their ships). As the city walls were set ablaze, he says, the night sky above "turned the colour of copper". Ultimately, the siege was lifted by the arrival of an imperial army, but the Vikings were so feared that even the emperor did not engage them, instead paying them to go away (much to the disgust of the Parisians who had held out for so long).

Again, it is worth pausing to reflect on this. Less than a century earlier, perhaps a few dozen men ran up a beach to burn the monastery at Lindisfarne in an attack that was probably over in less than a day. At Paris, a fleet of thousands of Vikings, in hundreds of ships, besieged one of the greatest cities of Europe for a year, and fought pitched battles with the best soldiers the Empire could field. The speed and scale of the escalation is breathtaking.

In the following years, the Frankish Empire again began to stabilise, with the same effect of dramatically and quickly improving defensive measures against the Vikings. By 890, the fleets had dispersed as quickly as they had coalesced, either heading back to Scandinavia or returning to the Danelaw.

This Frankish coda to the century of the great raids also provides a moment to review their real cost, and to try to understand their true scale from a different perspective. The damage to the imperial economy was without parallel. If the data from the Continental written sources is combined, the protection money paid to the Vikings during the ninth century totalled about thirty thousand pounds' weight of silver, most of it in cash: a sum equivalent to seven million silver pennies over a period when the estimated total output of the Frankish mints was in the region of fifty million coins. This equates to approximately 14 percent of the entire monetary output of the Frankish Empire—*for a century*—evaporated in the payment of extortion demands that produced no tangible positive gain and, in many cases, failed to appease the Vikings anyway. In addition even to that, the Scandinavians were given grain, livestock, produce, wine, cider, horses, and other commodities as part of their terms for not attacking— literally for not doing anything—and, of course, the same things were often lost when they did. Between 830 and 890 in Frankia, some 120 named settlements were sacked and destroyed, besides the unspecified accounts of regional devastation. And of course, the human cost was incalculable. Ermentarius of Noirmoutier did not exaggerate in choosing imagery reminiscent of a Viking apocalypse.

For many years, the Scandinavian depredations of the 830s through the 880s tended to be studied from discrete geographical or political perspectives—the Vikings in England, in Ireland, in Frankia, and so on. But the key point is that these were in large part the same forces moving, dividing, and reforming. If one area managed to organise sufficient resistance to impede the Vikings' progress, they simply shifted somewhere else. Even Alfred of Wessex, in most cases, did not actually defeat them—they just moved on, and may well have done so anyway.

In a cautionary tale for all archaeologists, in the absence of written sources we would never dare to postulate the scale of the Viking invasions of England and Frankia from their material remains alone—with one exception. The inner workings of the armies have already been glimpsed: their constituent parts of 'brotherhoods', their complex command structures, communal decision-making, and propensity to division. However, in the last three or four decades, archaeology has begun to reveal previously unsuspected aspects of these armies in the remains of their camps.

These establishments seem to have appeared first in Ireland in the late 830s, and then in Frankia a few years later. In the Irish sources (via Latin), they are termed *longphuirt* (sing. *longphort*), meaning roughly 'ship-landing', and also *dúnad* and *dún*, both of which have connotations of fortification. Vikings are also mentioned as coming from specific places, as if they were some kind of semi-permanent bases. Focussing on the east coast, 'camps' of this kind are found at Lough Neath, Strangford Lough, Carlingford Lough, Dublin, Waterford, Wexford, and Cork, amongst other locations; in all, some twenty such sites are named. Most are in locations with good water access, and it has been suggested that each was within a day's sail of its nearest neighbour. Parts of one such camp have been excavated at Woodstown near Waterford, and a second surveyed at Annagassan. In Frankia, with the exception of a fortification at the Camp de Péran in Brittany, all are known mostly from the written record—the Île de Bièce in the Loire, Oissel in the Seine, Neuss on the Rhine, and others, including monastic houses taken over as strongpoints.

The most productive archaeological examples have been explored in England, of which the first was excavated at Repton in Derbyshire. Recorded in the *Anglo-Saxon Chronicle* as the location of an overwintering of the Great Army from 873 to 874, Repton was also the site of a Mercian royal mausoleum, located next to an impressive church. In the 1970s and 1980s, excavations around this building unexpectedly located three key elements of the winter camp: a D-shaped enclosure with its straight side against the bank of the river Trent, incorporating the church itself as a fortified gateway; a series of clearly pagan Viking burials around the church; and a massive charnel deposit of disarticulated human bones that had been built into the looted mausoleum.

The charnel represents at least 264 individuals, including nearly 20 percent women. Many exhibited weapon trauma. It is a single deposit, although it is harder to tell if the bones had been assembled over a year or two, perhaps by gathering the dead from fields of battle to be finally interred at a main camp. However, it can definitely be associated with the presence of the army through radiocarbon dating, finds of coins dating to 872 and 873, and weapons of Viking type. In the Repton discovery, archaeologists had a chance to explore the actual members of a Viking force for the first time. Work is still ongoing, but the isotopic data reveals that the majority of individuals came from all over Scandinavia, with some also from the British Isles and the Continent, perhaps even as far south as the Mediterranean. The burials clustered around the church all have Scandinavian isotopic signatures. The same data reveals significant changes of diet over time, which suggests these people moved around a great deal. The men fall within an age range of about eighteen to forty-five.

The whole charnel deposit was covered by an earthen mound, with a double curb made of deliberately smashed-up English sculpture and querns from the monastery. There seems little doubt that this was a defiantly non-Christian Viking occupation. A number of postholes and pits filled with offerings suggest elaborate rituals, and several children were buried by the approaches to the mound in what appear to be sacrificial acts.

A few kilometres away at Heath Wood, lies one of the only later mound cemeteries from England; excavations have revealed it to be a Scandinavian cremation grave-field, so far unique in Britain. The remains were relatively meagre and hard to interpret, but included at least one woman who seems to have been buried with weapons. The excavators speculated that the site may have had a relationship to the Repton army—perhaps an offshoot or faction of the Viking force burying their dead in a different way.

From 2011 to 2015, a second major Viking camp was excavated at Torksey in Lincolnshire, the location of the army's overwintering in the year before it arrived at Repton. The project revealed a totally different picture to the relatively small enclosure at Repton that had hitherto been the model for what a camp was thought to look like. Torksey does not appear to have had formal defences; instead, it was located on a marshy island that provided natural protection. The Vikings clearly adapted to circumstance. Most important, it was vast—some fifty-five hectares, with space for thousands of people; at last the implications of the written sources were matched by the archaeology. Inside the camp was a revelation: evidence of craftwork and manufacturing, trade with the local environs, fishing, and clear proof of the presence of women. Numerous coins, weapons, and other artefacts securely dated the site, and suggested the army had spent up to six months there. In short, Torksey revealed not just an army, but an entire mobile community with a degree of self-sufficiency and its own economy.

A third army camp at "a riverine site near York" (abbreviated ARSNY, the location kept confidential at the landowner's request) was also investigated at about the same time. The material signals there mirror the finds from Torksey with the same emphasis on physical scale (this time thirty-three hectares), manufacturing and trade, local exchange networks, and the presence of women. The 'winter' camps were also entirely serviceable, and often occupied, in the spring, summer, and autumn. At both ARSNY and Torksey, something not far from a small town arose, with all this implies for the nature of the population that built it.

The apparent discrepancy in scale between these sites and Repton may have a relatively simple explanation. It has been suggested that the sites of Repton and Heath Wood may be part of the same entity, but widely dispersed in the landscape. In this model, the Repton enclosure might have formed a sort of defended citadel or ship-shelter within a larger camp. And if Torksey and ARSNY have given us the sites and activities, Repton has shown us the inhabitants themselves.

Both Repton and Torksey saw continued activity even after the army had departed, suggesting the legacy of their presence resonated for many years in a conflicted landscape. At Repton this took the form of further burials in and around the great charnel mound, a clearly Christian cemetery where isotopes show that at least half of those interred were local people. At Torksey, the site developed into a town renowned for its pottery industries.

The Irish *longphuirt* were not quite the same as the English winter camps, but they can still be usefully studied together. Not least, Woodstown also showed indications of a similar internal economy to Torksey, with a pattern of silver hoards that reflect a close relationship with the Irish kingdom of Osraige in which it was situated.

From decades of excavations at the winter camps, an entirely new picture of the Viking 'armies' has begun to emerge. The key data comes from the isotopic signatures suggesting where the buried dead originally came from, the gendered artefacts, the sheer scale of the sites, and the material indicating the different kinds of activities that went on there.

First, the Viking forces were clearly multi-ethnic, not just 'Scandinavian', a picture that fits with their conglomerate and organic nature. Even the 'Scandinavians' in the armies—the majority of their members—were from all over the region and had no focal point of origin. Women were part of these communities, and the armies really were as massive as the written sources imply—several thousand individuals at a minimum. Clearly, they did not restrict themselves to military activities but also pursued craftwork, manufacturing, and trade. There can be no doubt that these entities and their activities go far beyond anything that could merely be called 'raiding': the Vikings' mobile forces had long since become something else.

The presence of women is particularly telling, and here there is also supporting evidence from beyond the camps. A comprehensive analysis of female jewellery of Scandinavian design, recovered with metal detectors throughout eastern England, suggests there were very large numbers of women wearing foreign fashions in the Danelaw. It does not seem that the brooches and other items were all imported, but rather were made to Scandinavian taste using partly local materials. Of course, the iconography of jewellery is not the same as ethnicity, and anyone can wear a brooch—is this indicative of 'Danish fashion' becoming popular (or even advisable) in an area under Scandinavian control? This was tested through a DNA survey, and a strong Scandinavian signature was found—in other words, there really *were* numerous foreign women in these areas. The numbers of individuals involved are startling in themselves: at a conservative guess up to thirty to fifty thousand Scandinavian immigrants of both sexes may have arrived over the three decades following the establishment of the Danelaw. This is a revolutionary conclusion.

It seems likely that the women mostly settled in secondary immigrations after the wars with Wessex had died down, but the Repton charnel and the other camps confirm there were also (perhaps different) women actually moving as part of the armies. Even in battle, the Viking forces may have been more mixed affairs than previously thought. There is, of course, the tentative evidence for female warriors, but at the siege of Paris in the 880s, Abbo specifically mentions that Danish women were present on the field—not fighting as such, but close enough to physically push their men back into the fray if they showed signs of hesitation.

The conclusion is still a little unfocussed but nonetheless clear in outline: after the initial impetus of the attacks in the 830s and

840s, once a kind of beachhead had been established across the east and south of England, there were significant numbers of Scandinavian women (and presumably children) in the armies. They did not 'accompany' the men and were not 'camp followers' of male Vikings. Instead, their presence was integral to what these forces really seem to have been: not raiders writ large with their wives and girlfriends in tow, but in effect armed family migrations. This movement of people would also rapidly grow in scale.

There is no avoiding the fact that fighting was absolutely central to this endeavour, including the maintenance of Scandinavian control once the Danelaw had been won. These groups were violent and dangerous, and it seems everyone within them was accepting of that—but war and plunder were not their only objectives. The longships were not still carrying the same kinds of 'raiders' as forty years before. These Vikings of the ninth century were different: men and women who shattered the political structures of western Europe, but who did not represent any of the individual Scandinavian polities or power blocs.

It seems necessary to find a new vocabulary, a different terminology, to describe these forces—ironically, it may be useful to return to one of the oldest clichés about them: the idea of the Viking as pirate.

This notion is not only inherent in the most common understanding of the word itself, *víkingr*, but has also been one of the key components of their image since at least the early seventeenth century. Here is the great British historian Camden, in his monumental work *Britannia* from 1610:

[The Danes] were by the writers that penned in Latine the histories of England named *Wiccingi* for that they practised Piracie: for *wiccinga* in the Saxon tongue, as Alfricus witnesseth, doeth signifie a Pirat that runneth from creeke to creeke.

357

But pirates, like Vikings, have also been subject to misleading stereotype. They were not 'loveable rogues' in the mould of Long John Silver or Jack Sparrow, created by the popular writers and filmmakers of later times, but actually something much more interesting and sophisticated—as Camden himself probably knew. The famous pirate fleets of the Atlantic and the Caribbean (and their counterparts in the China Seas, for example), which have been extensively researched, can be understood as one of the best comparative paradigms for studying the peripatetic, large-scale Viking forces we see in the ninth-century West.

What emerges most of all is the sense of piracy as inhabiting, and shaping, its own constructed social world. It provided a consciously alternative lifestyle, with an improvised but nonetheless pronounced egalitarian spirit that was profoundly at odds with the state-sanctioned norms of the pirates' respective homelands. There was a levelling of hierarchy, in that authority ultimately rested with the crew. Captains were elected, and plunder divided according to skill or duty. And all this was active and conscious, a deliberate reorganisation of maritime social relations to create a 'masterless' existence. The pirates even had a name for it: "the new government of the ship".

Piracy brought with it chronic instability, though also a sense of continuity from crew to crew. It was not a system that could sustain prolonged or severe internal conflict. On occasion, the activities of the so-called Golden Age pirates (broadly speaking in the period from the 1650s to the 1720s) could be sponsored by state actors, often to achieve objectives with which the state could not be associated—but they never operated at a national level. Despite being obviously of the maritime world, pirates could and did intervene in affairs on land.

The pirate life was sustained by tales and rumours of its own success. Pirates affirmed their special identities through the use of visual media such as the famous flags; one leading scholar has even described the images on them—crossed bones, dripping blood, hourglasses, and the like—as forming "a triad of interlocking symbols: death, violence, limited time". They also employed specific combinations of material culture, and its expression in their own dances, shanties, magic, and ritual. Loyalty was above all to the community itself—the flexible life of choice that it offered, fuelled by the social insights provided by travel and encounter. Pirates also tended to have a different view of the marginalised, and of minorities, than the states from which they had come.

Those who fought the pirates also had opinions about all this, of course. For our purposes, the most important is encapsulated in a term that was coined to describe the difficulties of engaging with and neutralising a pirate threat. It seems to have first been used in 1631 by Richard Braithwaite, who described the typical mariner in the convoluted language of his time:

> They will have it valiantly when they are ranked together, and relate their adventures with wonderful terror. Necessary instruments are they, and agents of main importance in that Hydrarchy wherein they live; for the walls of the State could not subsist without them; but least useful are they to themselves, and most needful for others supportance.

The key word here is 'hydrarchy', which was expanded in the eighteenth century to become a general label for the revolutionary fulcrum of dangerously radical social ideas represented by the Atlantic maritime community. The situation the term tries to capture is one in which there are no overall leaders with whom to negotiate (there was never a pirate monarch, which was part of the point), no state structures to oppose, and indeed no formal organisation to fight. The mythical hydra, the multiheaded beast of Greek legend, was a challenge to defeat because every time one of its heads was severed, two more grew to take its place. Likewise, sinking individual pirate ships or killing notorious captains did little to dent the nature of the enemy—and yet, through it all, 'the pirates' as a collective source of grave political peril remained entirely valid and operative, just like the supposedly unkillable hydra.

In my opinion, the application of this concept to the Viking Age represents a real breakthrough in understanding what was going on with the ninth-century 'armies'. Using the terminology of hydrarchy to describe these forces soon reveals that the points of comparison are compelling. There are textual references to named Viking leaders, but no kings or real nobility; indeed, there are explicit descriptions of collective decision-making. The 'armies' were confederacies of *lið*, as in the 'brotherhoods' of the *Annals of St-Bertin*. In a later entry for 861, the same source describes how in the spring, "the Danes made for the open sea, and split up into several flotillas which sailed off in different directions according to their various choices". They were also made up of networks of oath-driven relationships, and short-term contractual bonds for mutual benefit. Just like the pirates, the Viking armies had limited internal cohesion and could exhibit rapid fluctuations in size. This is reflected in the nature of their camps—transitional and expedient spaces, perfect for the working out of new identities and different ways of life.

In search of settlement opportunities with plunder, the Viking forces were never coherent wholes and, equally, did not represent a coordinated move outward from Scandinavia. There was never any single motivation behind this phenomenon. Some scholars believe the key factor was a dramatic expansion of Baltic trade, spreading around the coasts of Europe. Bigger targets for raids presented themselves at the same time that the profitability of attacking isolated sites such as monasteries probably declined. It is not hard to see that the evolution of larger Viking groups—true fleets and real armies—would make sense in response to these trends. This is easy to suggest but harder to map out in practice, although it would have provided both motivation and direction for a movement that would soon coalesce around mobile forces on a massive scale. On the other hand, the internal politics of the North provided ample reasons for people to want to leave—whether as a result of backing the wrong party in a domestic conflict, or simply to seek an alternative, many might choose to join one of these new social experiments. There is every indication that this was a fluid decision, not necessarily a permanent one.

This was what the Vikings of the West had become. Operating beyond the borders not only of Scandinavia but also of its political structures, for much of the ninth century a Viking hydrarchy extended across the British Isles and the Frankish Empire.

A hundred years away from Lindisfarne, and now well into the Viking Age, the Scandinavian mark on the political map of Europe was already indelible. In essence, the rise of the great armies in Frankia and England marked the emergence of Vikings—real Vikings—as an independent force for the first time. Just as with the false dichotomy of 'western' and 'eastern' Viking Ages, so the same pattern is repeated here: while the expansion towards the British Isles and the Continent was unfolding, other (and sometimes the same) Scandinavians were also moving in all directions.

This gradual and unplanned expansion across the Eurasian world was never a one-way process (or really a process at all), but more a matter of mutual feedback. People came home and journeyed away again, often many times; other peoples came *to* the North, sometimes in greater numbers than those leaving it. All these travellers carried with them, and left behind, a great many things: not only objects—the 'material culture' beloved of archaeologists—but also ideas, attitudes, and information. At the most intimate levels of interaction, they also left their genes, and their families acquired new ones.

This was the beginning of the Viking diaspora, and it is now time to follow them there.

13

DIASPORA

THE TWIN POLES OF THE Viking experience, as traditionally perceived, were raiding and trading. Both embody the act of movement, of expansion, of the drive into the world beyond Scandinavia that has always been a hallmark of the Viking Age. What is often overlooked is that they were also complementary.

The raids on the West initially boosted the personal economies, and prospects, of individuals. At the same time, they fuelled the ambitions of elites and provided them with the material currency with which to keep and increase their hold on power. Ultimately, the raids amplified trends and behaviours that had long been developing inside Scandinavia, and projected them outwards and overseas. The feedback that then kicked in was the flow of looted objects—quite literally portable wealth—that was converted into status as well as comfort. In time, that influx of the new also included ideas, some of which (like Christianity) would prove to be unsettling for the established norms of the North.

The raiding became something else—and mutated into the hydrarchies of the ninth century—in part because the political situation in Scandinavia had been changed by the raids themselves. There were winners and losers in these power games, for example among the sea-kings, just as there had been in the centuries prior to the Viking Age. The great raiding armies and fleets provided a lucrative and, perhaps, somewhat nostalgic alternative to this changed reality that in a short time offered something more permanent: not just profitable adventures but settlement and a new life. Both the consolidation of the expanding kingdoms in Scandinavia, and the opportunities offered by campaigning overseas gradually reshaped the North. The Vikings changed the places through which they moved, often violently, but they were themselves transformed in the process.

But the West was not the only focus of Viking activity—the East, too, and in time the South, would draw the Scandinavians. In the course of the ninth century, at the same time as the fleets cruised the waterways of western Europe, the river routes from the Baltic shore were beginning to be opened up. Places like Ladoga, our riverine Deadwood, would expand and soon become only the first link in a chain that stretched thousands of kilometres eastwards—not only to Byzantium, but as far as the Eurasian steppe and even connecting with the Silk Roads of land and sea. In the south, the Viking forces in Frankia would gather at the base on the Loire in a move to strike Iberia, and also to sail into the Mediterranean.

Like the European operations, the roads to the East would eventually also lead to settlement opportunities, indeed to the establishment of colonies even bigger and longer-lasting than those of the West. We do not know whether all this was an objective or an unexpected dividend. What is clear is that by the mid- to late 800s, the Scandinavians had begun to look at the surrounding world in a different way. This was an unfolding series of events, one thing evolving from what had come before. A Viking diaspora had begun to take shape.

Until the twenty-first century, scholars had always talked of an 'expansion', almost in an imperial spirit of Scandinavians spreading across a 'Viking world'. Starting a decade or so ago as individual studies and coordinated projects, this perception shifted into something more diffuse but also realistic. The concept of the diaspora has now taken root in Viking studies and is today recognised as a much more useful way of looking at the geopolitical spread of Scandinavian settlers, raiders, traders, and influence.

As it was first introduced to Viking research, the notion of a diaspora was very much built on the social sciences and heavily mediated through textual source material. Many of the concepts derive from recent history—linked to themes of migration and transnationalism—but they can usefully be applied to the Viking-Age past. In the process, the diaspora also opens up new ways of understanding the period. It is actually quite a specific term, and relates as much to the arguable concept of a Viking 'homeland' as to where (and how, and why) the Scandinavians travelled.

A diaspora, including that of the Vikings, can involve several features, most obviously dispersal from an original starting point. This can be traumatic, but can also involve a search for better prospects of various kinds, or the furtherance of colonial ambitions. Over time, the diaspora can foster a collective memory, even myth-making, about the notion of 'home', which can also become idealised. This does not mean that movement in a diaspora was only in one direction—there may be constant contact, reverse migration, or at least "a continuing conversation". There may be a strong ethnic group consciousness, sustained over long periods of time and extending across the diaspora beyond its constituent regions. This may lead to tensions with the original inhabitants of the diasporic settlement areas, but, equally, it can manifest in the positive evolution of new, creative interactions.

To a greater or lesser degree, all these features can be found in the Viking diaspora. From the ninth century onwards, this flow of people, things, and ideas certainly involved violence—a great deal of it, in fact, especially in the West. But underneath these currents of raiding aggression ran the constant undertow of trade and more peaceable interaction. At one level this was catered for by the networks of emporia, nodes in the still broader webs of markets and commercial sites that operated at so many levels. This, too, extended into the East with the river trade.

The routes into the eastern European interior developed early in the Viking Age, if not before, either through the Gulf of Riga or particularly the Gulf of Finland. This was driven, in part, by an internal expansion within Finland from the coasts to the interior, and in general it is clear that Finnish-speaking peoples played a major role in the opening up of the rivers. They acted as Baltic brokers for the Volga route down to the Caspian, and exerted great influence over the northern hunting grounds that partially drove the riverine traffic. One of the leading experts in Viking-Age Finnish interactions likens the eastern Baltic to the Hudson Bay area—both were water worlds with the fur trade at their core.

For the first half of the ninth century, furs seem to have been the mainstay of the eastern merchants. In the North, not least in Finland and among the Sámi, control of hunting was critical, including the management of potential resource depletion. Raw materials and products typical of central Sweden have been found far up the Finnish river valleys, providing clues as to the points of long-distance connections between actors in the trade.

The largest concentration of early Viking-Age finds in the Eurasian interior comes from Staraja Ladoga, the frontier-style settlement on the Volkhov River, where Finns were clearly influential. As perhaps the principal gateway between Scandinavia and the eastern world, it is not surprising that the Ladoga emporium expanded during the early ninth century and continued to do so into the tenth, likely reflecting the growth of increasingly intensive mercantile connections with the lands to the south. Evidence of metalworking, craft activities in antler and bone, and glass making, as well as finds of silver dirhams, attest to the function of the settlement as a major port of exchange. Sites such as Staraja Ladoga remained important throughout the Viking Age, and would soon also become jumping-off points for journeys to the south. While many of the groups operating in the East would have traded along the Volkhov, Dniepr, and Volga rivers, or with the tribes living in the regions either side of these major arteries, for many the ultimate goal was to reach the Black Sea and so travel onwards to Constantinople—the heart of the Byzantine world.

There were many ways to reach it, but perhaps the most well-travelled route went up the Volkhov past Staraja Ladoga, across Lake Ilmen into the Lovat River. Once the limits of its navigable passage were reached, an overland portage to the Dniepr was necessary. From here, the great waterway flowed south to the Black Sea. Perhaps the most crucial and dangerous part of the journey came relatively near its end, in the middle reaches of the Dniepr. Before it was dammed by the Soviet Union in the 1930s, there existed a system of rapids, extending seventy kilometres south from the area of Dnipropetrovsk. Varying from seven to twelve in number depending on the time of year in which they were encountered, they prevented shipping from moving along the river. During the Viking Age, this necessitated portaging the ships around each individual rapid, which provided the nomadic Pechenegs with ample opportunities to attack and plunder merchant travellers.

A remarkable tenth-century Byzantine document testifies to the Scandinavians who made the trip. *De Administrando Imperio*, 'On the Administration of the Empire', was a secret manual of governance written by the Emperor Constantine Porphyrogenitus as a guide for his son and successor. Combining confidential tips on foreign policy with a wealth of information about trading partners, it also contains reports of the strange Northerners who came to Constantinople. Their path took them through the Dniepr rapids, and at some point they must have described them to the court scribes because the names of each patch of churning water are rendered in what is clearly Old Norse embedded in the Latin text. Wonderfully illustrative of the dangers that lay in wait for any crew that for some reason did not disembark upstream of the falls, they include Essupi (*supa*, 'The Drinker'), Gellandri (*gjallandi*, 'The Yeller'), and Aifor (from *eifors*, meaning 'Ever Fierce'). The latter is also named on a Gotland runestone that commemorates a man named Ravn who had previously travelled in the East.

Such were the hazards associated with this part of the river that at least some Northern voyagers felt driven to offer sacrifices to the gods on St. Gregory's Island, which lay just to the south of the rapids, as a token of gratitude for their safe passage through. Excavations in the northern part of the island suggest a settlement may have existed here during the ninth and tenth centuries, possibly as a waystation for groups beginning or ending their passage along the portage route. Having passed through the lower stretches of the Dniepr and into the Black Sea, ships could traverse the western shore, towards Constantinople.

The city had been established as the capital of the Eastern Empire in the late fourth century by Emperor Constantine (which is why it bears his name), and had functioned as the imperial seat for over five hundred years. It had been expanded, refortified, and otherwise augmented numerous times as a result of public work schemes introduced by emperors who were eager to leave a permanent legacy of their rule. By the eighth century, it had grown into one of the largest metropolises in the world, with a population in excess of half a million—probably more than in all of Scandinavia at the time.

The city jutted out into the Bosporus between the Sea of Marmara and the Golden Horn at the gateway to Asia. Both its landward and seaward sides were protected by an immense system of fortifications. Upon entering through one of its monumental gates, any Scandinavian visiting for the first time would have been confronted with vast public forums and markets, towering churches and governmental buildings, and public structures such as racetracks, all of which were built from stone. Many had been in use since the time of the Romans, and a Northerner visiting Constantinople must have wandered the streets in awe.

In time, a new kind of society would develop along the riverine routes to the south, an ethnic conglomerate that evolved as a manifestation of the trading life. Known as the Rus', these were the people from whose name the modern 'Russia' derives. Their real rise came in the tenth century, but it is clear that even in the first half of the ninth, a sufficiently distinctive identity was emerging that a label was required to describe it.

The earliest record of the name is from the *Annals of St-Bertin* in 839, when a Byzantine delegation to the Frankish emperor included among its members a group of people called *Rhos* in the Latin text, although the word appears to be Greek (presumably it was what the envoys called them). According to the Byzantines, these men had experienced such difficulties with hostile tribes on their journey to Constantinople that it was safer for them to travel home via western Europe instead, and the Eastern emperor appealed on their behalf for Frankish assistance. According to the annals, the Franks made enquiries and finally determined that the men were Swedes (and accordingly detained them as spies); the text even records that their king was called Hákon. It is perhaps telling that this first mention of Rus' not only implies that they were sufficiently frequent visitors to Constantinople for the Byzantines to find a term for them, but also that they were not yet powerful enough to be able to guarantee their own security.

The Rus' are also mentioned in the *Homilies of Photios* written in 860 by the Byzantine patriarch of that name, but the main historical source for their ninth-century activities is the so-called *Russian Primary Chronicle*, which was probably compiled in Kiev in the early twelfth century. It describes the Rus' as arriving on the shores of the eastern Baltic around the 860s and quickly imposing a tribute system on the indigenous Slavs. They were driven off, but—so the story goes—after a period of infighting, the Slavic tribes allegedly sent emissaries to the Rus' asking them to bring order to their land. Three brothers—Rurik, Truvor, and Sineus—are said to have been chosen to rule. Rurik occupied an island north of what would later become Novgorod (*Holmgarðr* in Old Norse) and would take control of his brothers' territories upon their deaths. There is clearly a fair degree of retrospective legitimising in the *Primary Chronicle*, but that there was some kind of organised Scandinavian move into the Volkhov system in the ninth century is more than supported by the archaeology.

In the Arabic narratives, the Rus' appear as *al-Rūsiyyah*, but it is obvious that a single original term must have been behind all these labels that are consistent across cultures. It was presumably self-applied, and there has been much discussion of what it was. Attention has focussed on Roslagen, a district on the eastern coast of central Sweden whose name means approximately 'the rowing country'. While few believe the Rus' actually came specifically and only from that region, it is plausible in that it implies an explicit connection with Sweden (as in the *Annals of St-Bertin*) and with travel by oared boat. The same word is ultimately at the root of the modern Finnish name for Sweden itself, Ruotsi. Perhaps the Norse term for the travellers on the eastern rivers originally meant something like 'the rowers', an interestingly small-scale collective noun for expeditions of a few individuals reliant on each other while voyaging largely alone and unprotected into a great vastness. The meaning would have been clear to those they met, and it is easy to see how the name might stick.

Who are you? We're from the boat, we're the crew, me and the lads. Maybe the Rowers will come again next year, with more of those wonderful things to sell? Let's hope so.

Over time, the sense of the word clearly changed, from what was originally perhaps a workaday description to an all-embracing ethnonym for the river traders—and, crucially, for the men who backed their ventures with armed muscle. What is fascinating is how the idea of the Rus' became associated with a specific identity of mercantile water travel in the East. One should be cautious about ahistorical comparisons, but there is a startlingly close parallel with the Métis of Canada and parts of the northern United States, an identity that combined people of varied origin unified by a way of life—in this instance, the fur trade of the great interior—and changing over time. Beyond their emotional bonds, marriages and other unions with local people provided incoming trappers with protection, privileged knowledge, and access to kinship networks with their associated benefits. This is exactly what we see with the Rus' in much the same context, and the fusion of cultures on the rivers. They, too, were *voyageurs*.

The Rus' were not purely of Scandinavian origin, clearly, but they were always an obvious and dominant presence (probably mainly from Sweden), including in command positions. Two Arab sources explicitly equate the Rus' with the Scandinavians, making it very clear they regarded the two peoples as interchangeable. However, use of the Rus' term could also be applied more vaguely, meaning something like 'northern foreigners'.

In the ninth century, the river trade had both individual and collective aspects. As the Viking phenomenon gathered pace, and the market emporia formed static points on the trading networks, so ships and riverine traffic became mobile connectors—a form of 'high-speed rail' between Scandinavia and Europe. However, there is another dimension, too. One obvious consequence of Viking activities was the massive influx of portable wealth to Scandinavia, but this was not the same as having *usable* wealth. You can make an expensive gift of looted jewellery and the like a few times, but you cannot easily go shopping with the equivalent of a thousand hundred-dollar bills. The economic context for all this, in the background but overshadowing the trade, was the financing of Scandinavian political competition, and this is borne out both by the written sources and the patterns revealed in the archaeology.

The logistics of this system were complex. As the fur trade declined after about 860 or so (it may not be coincidence that this is when Rurik was supposed to have assumed control at Ladoga), there emerged on the eastern rivers what economic historians call 'high-power money'. This is a currency (that does not have to be literally coinage) with a value that is universally regarded to be more stable than the alternatives. In today's world, the US dollar widely holds such a position, but for the Viking-Age river trade, it was silver. For most of the ninth century, the source of silver was the mines and mints of the Abbasid Caliphate in today's Middle East. Importantly, so long as the standard was agreed upon, silver did not even have to be universally available, although there hardly seems to have been a shortage of dirham coins for much of the period.

They are found mostly in the form of buried silver hoards, usually kept in the form of coins but sometimes also melted down and recast. More than a million dirhams have been recovered from Scandinavia and the Baltic, especially on the island of Gotland. It is extraordinary to think that the vast majority of all the dirhams that survive anywhere, some 81 percent, come from Europe; only 9 percent of them are from their points of origin in the Caliphate. An entire industry of coinage is preserved in the legacies of Viking trade. Many of the Gotland hoards contain silver arm-rings— sometimes dozens of them—both decorated as jewellery and completely plain. Much work has been done on the economics of such 'ring money', a portable form of payment you could both wear and spend.

Around this river traffic one can infer an infrastructure of commerce without which the trade would have been very hard to maintain. Alien though they may seem to our Viking stereotypes, these traders must have had concepts of time-limited exchange in the more seasonal markets, coupled with the problems of liquidity. Perhaps they used some kind of bills of exchange, drawn on important markets and protected by the potential for expulsion with consequent exclusion from the trade. Just as a gentleman of the British Raj could issue a note in Delhi to be drawn on his bank in London, perhaps there was a Rus' equivalent for Birka or Bulghar, the settlement at the Volga bend. At the centre of all this is the notion of credit, which may even have governed the majority of transactions. Nor should we forget the carriage of samples, goods to try out before placing larger orders.

The trade was made by individual agents, but probably with collective responsibility for their actions in foreign markets. Mechanisms like this would have kept the peace in the edgy confrontations and negotiations along the rivers, perhaps policed by a form of local security. It is even possible this was originally the service, or one of them, that the Rus' provided.

All the trade networks, whether to the East or elsewhere, incorporated processes of feedback. What was selling well on the river last year had an effect on the domestic markets back in Scandinavia. The fluctuations of supply and demand are eternal constants, for the Vikings as for anyone else. In a deeply modern sense, even people who never left their farms in Uppland were both aware of, and implicated in, the events and economic trends of a wider world. Nor would this have been something abstract; everyone would have seen things brought back from the river journeys or other trips into Europe and the West. Even the thralls were within earshot of travellers' tales told round the fire.

Stories were told of other regions too, not only the riches to be had on the eastern rivers, but also of the fabulous wealth of the Muslim world. While the majority of Viking activity on the European continent was confined to modern-day France and the Low Countries, some Viking fleets were drawn farther south by the prospect of plunder, bringing them into contact and conflict with the people of the Iberian Peninsula.

During the Viking Age, the modern-day countries of Spain and Portugal were divided into several discrete polities. In the north, lying along the coast of the Bay of Biscay and abutting the Pyrenees, lay a handful of Christian states, of which the largest was the Kingdom of Galicia and the Asturias. Most of Iberia, however, had been under Muslim control since the late 700s after an invasion from North Africa. Following a coup that brought a new dynasty, the Abbasids, to power in the recently founded city of Baghdad, a breakaway emirate formed in southern Spain, al-Andalus, with its capital at Córdoba. An uneasy peace persisted between the Christian and Islamic kingdoms, broken by small-scale skirmishing and occasional outright warfare.

The first Viking attacks on Spain are recorded as taking place during the mid-ninth century. Having sailed south in 844 from their base at Noirmoutier at the mouth of the Loire, a large Viking fleet conducted raids along the northern Iberian coast before heading south into Muslim territory. The Scandinavians sacked targets in what is now Portugal and southern Spain, including Lisbon, Cadiz, and Algeciras, before turning to enter the Guadalquivir River. Their eventual target may have been Córdoba itself, but in their path first lay the city of Seville. The subsequent assault is documented by Aḥmad ibn Muḥammad al-Rāzī, who tells us of the seven days that raiders spent sacking the city, killing the men, and enslaving the women and children. As word spread into the surrounding countryside, the emir, 'Abd a-Raḥmān, mustered a large army and marched to meet the Viking force, which was now ensconced on the Isla Menor. The Vikings were drawn out of their camp and the city by decoy troops who led them to Tablada, some two miles south of Seville, where they were ambushed and slaughtered by the bulk of the Muslim army. The surviving members of the Viking force fled to their ships and departed, leaving thirty vessels behind, while the dead were hung from the palm trees of Seville.

No other major raiding expeditions were made until 859, when a second force set out from the Loire—a fleet that later sources place under the command of Hástein and one of the most famous

Vikings of them all, Björn Ironside. He was almost certainly a real person, although layers of associations grew up around his memory as his reputation morphed into the stuff of legend and saga. Possibly one of the many alleged sons of Ragnar lothbrók, he acquired his nickname (again, in a very late source) because he emerged remarkably unscathed from combat.

His great southern raid left so many echoes in later written sources that it is now difficult to disentangle myth from reality. The fleet is supposed to have numbered sixty-two ships, although one source has a nice round hundred. Like the force that preceded it in 844, the fleet seems to have first raided the northern Iberian coast, attempting and failing to take the town of Santiago de Compostela in Galicia. The raiders continued to southern Spain, again attacking Seville, Cadiz, and Algeciras, in turn. In the autumn of 859, the fleet then passed unopposed through the Straits of Gibraltar; as far as is known, they were the first Scandinavians ever to do so.

According to twelfth-century sources, the Norse word for the Mediterranean was Miðjarðarhaf, the 'Midgard Sea', and even the gateway into it had mythological overtones. The Gibraltar passage was called Nörvasund, which some scholars translate as the 'Straits of Odin', in his persona as Nörr, the brother of Night. That the Vikings chose names of this kind may mean that they regarded the region as unknown territory, as they headed 'off the map' and into an almost legendary realm.

Once through the straits, the fleet made for the North African coast and its first real success. Mazimma, in the small Moroccan state of Nekor, was sacked and occupied for eight days. Two of the royal women—we even know their names, Ama al-Raḥmān and Khanūla—were captured, and a large ransom was paid by the emir of Córdoba for their return. The Vikings then crossed back to Spain and ravaged Andalucía and Murcia before harrying northwards along the Mediterranean coast. There are hints in the sources that they divided into smaller flotillas to do so, reminiscent of the 'brotherhoods' that fought in Frankia.

The Balearic Islands of Formentera, Ibiza, Majorca, and Minorca were all raided. The fleet then continued into southern Frankish territory, assaulting monasteries and towns before wintering in the marshy Camargue region in what is now Provence. In the spring of 860, the Vikings raided along the Rhône but were forced back to the sea, at which point they sailed for Italy. We have fairly credible sources for an attack on Pisa, but it is at this point that the legend takes over. Later texts, originating in eleventh-century Normandy, conjure a stirring tale in which the Vikings launched a successful assault on what they believed to be Rome itself, only to discover it was in fact the small Tuscan settlement of Luni. Apart from the sheer unlikeliness that men who had seen Byzantium would mistake a village for the former imperial capital, the tale also includes elements repeated in other, similarly fabulous stories; sadly, it is almost certainly fiction. However, this does not mean that Luni, and also Fiesole (mentioned in another source), were not plundered in reality. Moreover, after their north Italian raids the entire fleet disappears from the record for nearly a year, and from the sources we have, it is clear they were headed into the eastern Mediterranean. Tenth- and eleventh-century chronicles have them in Constantinople and Greece, while one Arab source even puts them credibly in Alexandria, raising the extraordinary possibility that the Vikings reached Egypt.

They are recorded as attempting to return to the Atlantic via the Straits of Gibraltar in 861. On this occasion, however, they were intercepted by a large Muslim fleet. Two thirds of the Viking ships were destroyed, but the remainder—supposedly under Björn's command—ran the blockade and fought their way through to the open sea. They finally returned to the Loire in 862 after a further episode of raiding in northern Iberia, their ships so laden with booty and slaves that, according to yet another later text, their gunwales were almost underwater. At least some of the survivors must have managed to retain their captives from the early raids in North Africa, as the Irish chronicler Duald Mac-Fuirbis records that "after that the Norsemen brought a great host of Moors in captivity with them to Ireland . . . long were these dark people in Ireland".

Following Hástein and Björn's raid, Viking activity in Iberia remained minimal until the mid-tenth century. At this time, new attacks targeted the Christian kingdoms in northern Spain, with Galicia bearing the brunt of the raiders' aggression during three major assaults in 951, 965, and 966. Although it is clear that the Vikings were not universally successful in their endeavours, in 968 a raiding fleet established a base on the Ulla River, near Santiago de Compostela, and spent the next three years plundering the Galician countryside. Whether the ultimate motive was to establish a permanent settlement is unknown, but the modus operandi of the Viking force is immediately recognisable as that which had long been used, with great success, on the Loire, Seine, and Somme rivers. Further raids were conducted in the early 970s, following which there was a hiatus in attacks until the eleventh century.

Very little evidence of Viking contact with the peoples of the Iberian Peninsula—either peaceful or violent—remains today. Encounters between Scandinavian seafarers and both Christian and Islamic populations were almost certainly more frequent than contemporaneous sources would have us believe, yet the only evidence for diplomatic contact is limited to a purported Umayyad embassy to the court of an unnamed Scandinavian king. There is also a single deer-antler box dating from the late tenth century, now in the Museo de la Real Colegiata de San Isidoro in León, which may well have been a Scandinavian royal gift. No evidence for the plunder gathered in Iberia by Hástein and Björn, or by any other raiding fleets, has been found in Scandinavia or the overseas colonies. It is possible that the mixed fortunes of those raiding groups that did venture south discouraged attempts to establish more permanent bases that would draw Iberia into the long-distance networks of trade and redistribution that the Vikings operated elsewhere. It is possible, however, that the Viking presence simply has not yet been identified in the archaeological record. Even if the raids did not take place on the same scale as in France, it is difficult to believe that there is no evidence to be found. Further research is clearly necessary if we are to better understand this peripheral but nonetheless important corner of the Viking world.

There is a beautiful coda to these southerly ventures, an example of something so strange as to be scarcely credible, but also a demonstration of what archaeology and science can really achieve together. One of the things biologists study in connection with human migrations is the movement of animal proxies. In other words, even if people prove elusive to locate, it may be possible to track the presence of the domesticated species and parasites that moved with them. In some cases, traces of them at a certain place and time are suggestive of a larger event. One such study has mapped the presence of the common house mouse, especially those with a particular genetic signature associated with Denmark, in different areas of Europe. Tenth- or eleventh-century mouse bones of this species—which at that date are *only* found in places where Vikings had travelled—have now been confirmed from Madeira. There is no written record of a Viking presence there, but the brief landing of a Danish ship is the only explanation that fits, and it would not be geographically surprising. For a culture so fixated on memory, on the legacy of achievement, how ironic it is that the only trace of 'Viking Madeira' should be a mouse.

The Atlantic was also the stage for another significant feature of the early diaspora: the Scandinavian discovery and settlement of first the Faroe Islands and then Iceland. Over the following centuries, the North Atlantic would prove to be one of the central zones of Norse activity, not only for the establishment of the long-lasting Icelandic commonwealth, but also for the settlement of Greenland and the first European landfall in North America. In short, while Viking raids in the British Isles and Continental Europe would continue, the northern reaches of the Atlantic Ocean would experience a different kind of Viking Age.

According to the written sources, the Norse settlement of Iceland—the so-called *landnám*, or land-taking—occurred somewhere around 870. The first to stay were supposedly exiles who refused to live under the rule of the Norwegian king Harald Finehair, the most successful of the west-coast sea-kings. Until recently, this was largely supported by a form of scientific analysis that in the Viking world is unique to Iceland, in that the horizontal deposits of volcanic tephra resulting from the island's frequent eruptions can be closely dated, very usefully if they happen to seal archaeological remains. For a long time, all known evidence for the settlement of the country post-dated a layer of tephra that fell in 871, plus or minus two years.

There has been a long-standing debate, however, as to whether Iceland had been home to isolated communities of Irish hermits prior to the arrival of the Norse settlers. This suggestion has been based on the writings of an early ninth-century cleric named Dicuil, who wrote in his *Liber de Mensura Orbis Terrae* that the North Atlantic islands had been inhabited for over one hundred years by monks—the *papar*, or 'fathers'—who had travelled north to seek solitude. The twelfth-century *Íslendingabók*, the 'Book of Icelanders', tells a similar story, although it is possible there is an element of Christian revisionism as the land thus appears consecrated by the former presence of the monks. Iceland could have been seen by the medieval writers as having been 'originally' Christian, with the new faith as something latent and waiting for the settlers to later rediscover. This version ignores possible conflicts between the monks and the pagan ancestors of the later Christian Norse, and in emphasising that the *papar* depart prior to the settlers' arrival, it gives them a conveniently clean slate on which to begin their own journey towards God.

While the claims of both Dicuil and *Íslendingabók* have yet to find confirmed support from the archaeological record, after many years of controversy, there is now clear and accepted evidence of pre-Viking cereal cultivation on the Faroes, with the discovery of charred grains of barley preserved in burnt peat under windblown deposits at a site on the island of Sandoy. Dating to the fourth through sixth centuries, these cereals seem likely to represent the basic subsistence practices of a small community, and this would certainly fit with the presence of presumably Irish monks. There is now also some evidence to suggest an earlier Norse presence on Iceland. Recent excavations at Stöðvarfjörður, on the eastern coast of the island closest to the British Isles and Scandinavia, have yielded exciting evidence for what appears to be a Scandinavian longhouse dated by radiocarbon to around 800. However, it is uncertain whether the structure was inhabited permanently, and it could have been occupied seasonally by groups participating in fishing or whaling expeditions.

The Norse colonists who settled in the North Atlantic islands first established their farms on the coast. The Faroes had the potential for great productivity at the time of the initial colonisation, and animals were able to winter outside. Indeed, the first settlers found the islands to be inhabited by large numbers of sheep, which might conceivably have been brought there by the monks. Early farms have been excavated at sites such as Niðri á Toft near Kvívík, and Á Toftanesi in the village of Leirvík, all with a distinctly Scandinavian layout. Following the initial period of *landnám*, the settlement pattern seems to have remained relatively static. Although little is known about the Faroes compared to other North Atlantic colonies such as Iceland, their position on the main sailing route from Scandinavia and the British Isles meant that they would have been frequently visited. There is clear excavated evidence for a variety of long-distance trading contacts. In the maritime world of the Vikings, the Faroes were anything but remote.

In Iceland, the main area of initial settlement was on the west coast. It has recently been argued that colonists were drawn to this part of the island by large colonies of walrus, whose ivory was a valuable trading commodity. The initial *landnám* period is regarded as lasting until 930, when the first general assembly was established. During this time the settlement pattern was quite dynamic. Detailed studies of regions such as Mývatnsveit in the north of the country reveal a steady process of farm abandonment over time. The initial settlements of the ninth and tenth centuries seem to have been almost experimental, as the colonists sought the best way to adapt to their new environment. Around 20 percent of the early farms were soon abandoned, and another 30 percent disappeared over the following hundred years or so. However, this picture can be deceptive, as the pattern seems to reflect a process by which population distribution became more concentrated over time. The organisation of the landscape was also adjusted in response to environmental factors and to maximise the economic sustainability of agriculture and pasture, combined with subtle shifts in the nature of chiefly authority and its relationship to the land. In other areas of the country, such as Skagafjörður, almost no abandonment is seen in the archaeological and landholding records, and the settlers there seem to have achieved an effective balance almost immediately after the *landnám*.

When the evidence from texts, genetic studies, and personal names is combined, it becomes clear that people travelled to Iceland from all regions of Scandinavia, including Gotland. There were Sámi colonists in considerable numbers—perhaps to be expected in a Norwegian context—which reinforces the suggestion that communities there were much more integrated than has traditionally been understood. Small numbers of Franks and Saxons also seem to have gone to Iceland, but this is not surprising: the Viking world was a cosmopolitan place, and people travelled for much the same reasons of economy, opportunity, and affection as they do today.

Such freedom of choice may not have applied to all the settlers. Unlike Viking-occupied England, which seems to have included Scandinavians of both sexes, in the more marginal environments of the North Atlantic colonies a very different picture emerges. Genetic research reveals that a very large proportion—even the majority—of female settlers in Iceland were of Scottish or Irish heritage, with a particular focus on Orkney and the Hebrides. While a good many multicultural relationships can be expected, it is nonetheless striking that the first colonists seem to have been comprised very much of 'Scandinavian' men (mainly Norwegians) and 'Celtic' women. The rosy view of this would see hundreds or even thousands of Irish Sea women suddenly finding Norse boyfriends with whom to start afresh in the North Atlantic. However, there is a surely more likely, and frighteningly coercive, explanation in light of the already noted imbalance that may have developed in the Scandinavian sex ratios. There was certainly at least some element of slave-taking during the raiding and Norse overlordship in these areas of Britain, and it might also be that Viking chieftains in the Hiberno-Scottish region freed local captives in order to build up a mobile following.

Within decades of its settlement, Iceland would grow into another social experiment, a republic of farmer chiefs. This was only the first of several 'new worlds' that the Scandinavians would establish across their diaspora from east to west and that would unfold within radically changing structures of society and political life. The new religion, Christianity, was beginning to have real impact in the North from the mid-ninth century onwards, and in time would fuse with the rising power of kings to create the distinctively Scandinavian nations that still exist today.

NEW WORLDS,
NEW NATIONS

14

THE GOLDEN AGE OF THE SHEEP FARMER

NEW WORLDS ARE MADE THROUGH ambition and effort, with a measure of risk, sometimes with violence, and often by accident. They can be shaped by the many or by the few (often at the expense of the rest). Above all, they are created and maintained through economics. This was especially true for the later Viking Age, as the diaspora gathered momentum in the course of the tenth century. That expansion brought with it deeper changes in Scandinavian society, which were manifested at the most basic level of the community, in the organisation and management of the land itself, and in the ways people lived upon it.

As the Scandinavians travelled ever farther afield, their trading networks grew, providing sustaining fuel for the Viking-Age economy; the hierarchical nature of the market centres and emporia became more pronounced. By the late 800s, the largest of them had developed into something that can reasonably be called towns—the first in the North, and the beginnings of the long urban trajectory of the Middle Ages.

When one looks closer, the real power, and the means of producing it, can take unexpected forms. Some years ago, a prominent historian despaired of the constant focus on the Vikings as maritime warriors, and instead stressed the fact that most of the Scandinavian population stayed home on the land and never did any harm to anyone. The time of the Vikings, he claimed, was really "the Golden Age of the pig farmer". He had a point, though he got the animal wrong: the Scandinavian landscape of the late Viking period was a world of sheep.

Clearly, one of the primary components of the Viking phenomenon was the ship. The rapid developments in the technologies of water power were by no means a sole 'trigger', but the Scandinavian ventures into the wider world could not have happened without them. This was not just a matter of improved design, of faster ships with shallower draughts and better handling—these things brought with them a demand for raw materials and resources. Chief amongst these factors, because by its very nature it was critical to the success of Viking shipping, was the introduction of the sail.

Although obviously common in the classical cultures of the Mediterranean, sails seem to have first appeared in the North during the eighth century, as seen in the Salme find. A great deal went into their manufacture, especially in their absolute need for wool and fibres such as hemp or flax. Viking ships seem to have carried square sails woven in woollen twill, sewn together from several strips of cloth either in parallel lines or on a diagonal. To make them less permeable to air flow, the sails would be greased with tallow, fish oil, or other substances, especially tar. For small craft, a cloth weight of 0.3–0.75 kilograms per square metre is needed, while larger vessels needed heavier sails of 0.95–1.05 kilograms per square metre. Double-coated Norse sheep of the kind common in the Viking Age produce 1–2.5 kilograms of wool per year.

Textile archaeologists have calculated the amount of cloth that would have been required to equip the Ladby ship, a good example of a medium-sized warship found in a burial mound on the island of Fyn in Denmark. Based on a sail size of eighty square metres (probably a conservative estimate), it would have taken two person-years of ten-hour days to make just one mainsail weighing about fifty kilos, and nobody would put to sea without reserve sail-cloth that might save their lives. This workload is also something of an ideal figure, so the reality would have been closer to three or even four person-years *for one sail*. This was not solo work, of course, but the permutations of time for increasingly large teams of textile workers are easy to calculate.

Then there were the sea-clothes. As far as we can tell, these were multi-layered assemblies of coarse, thickly lined, insulated fabric able to withstand the weather of the open ocean. The Ladby ship had a crew of thirty-two, judging by the oar positions. Using the same ten-hour-day production pace as for the sails, it would have taken perhaps twenty-four person-years to fit out the crew. And added even to this are rugs, tents, a variety of other clothing (including a change of clothes for wet conditions), plus ropes, cord-age, and the like.

The numbers start to blur at this point, but we might realis-tically speak of a year's constant work for about thirty people to fully equip a ship and crew. By the tenth century, fleet sizes of two hundred vessels or even more were not uncommon in the Euro-pean riverine campaigns. In this light, the ability to marshal and harvest the necessary resources became a statement of power in its own right. It required nothing less than a reorganisation of the landed economy.

Archaeologists have calculated that by the early eleventh cen-tury, the total sailcloth requirements of the warships, cargo vessels, and fishing boats of Norway and Denmark would have amounted to around one million square metres—in other words, the annual production of some two million sheep. Added to this is the wool required for all that warm, water-repellent clothing and bedding, the yield of three sheep being required to make the shifts of cloth-ing needed by one person for a fishing season. A thick, heavy rug might take the annual yield of seven to fifteen animals. This

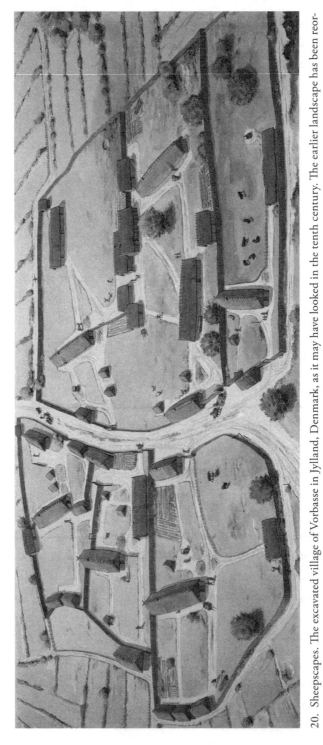

20. Sheepscapes. The excavated village of Vorbasse in Jylland, Denmark, as it may have looked in the tenth century. The earlier landscape has been reorganised into larger estates, cleared for sheep farming. Image by and © Flemming Bau.

extraordinarily high demand for wool makes clear that a substantial portion of the land in Viking-Age Scandinavia must have been given over to sheep farming. This is confirmed in the archaeological record, which shows massive programmes of farm consolidation at this time, with fewer but larger units of settlement.

What appears in the later Viking Age as farm 'abandonment', long interpreted as some kind of population contraction (perhaps due to migration overseas), is now understood as simply a reorganisation of the landscape, presumably with larger family groups occupying the farms. To serve the wool needs of the community, especially for sailcloth, it is clear that the products of many estates must have been combined and that there was a social system for doing this—with somebody in charge. These colossal numbers of sheep would have been primarily confined to grazing land at the margins, especially heathland, which expanded dramatically in the Viking Age; approximately one hectare of heathland would provide fodder for about one to two kilograms of wool yield per year. Alongside wool production, good arable land was given over to the cultivation of fibre plants, such as hemp and flax—again with a primary use in sails, rope and rigging.

Sails capture the wind, providing a vessel with speed and manoeuvrability, but of course they are secondary to the most obvious and fundamental element of all: the ship itself. This introduces another key resource demand, the need for timber. The later Viking Age of Scandinavia was in many ways a sheepscape (to coin a term), but it was also a wooden world.

The construction not only of ships, but also of buildings, aspects of infrastructure, and defensive works, required time, expertise, and immense amounts of timber from carefully managed woodlands. Subsistence farmers and professional artisans alike would have depended on regular and reliable access to raw materials, and would have devoted serious effort to their acquisition, working, and use.

To illustrate the sheer scale of the materials needed, there is the example of the Skuldelev 2 warship, built near Dublin or Waterford but scuttled outside Roskilde in Denmark in the eleventh century. This ship was painstakingly reconstructed, using traditional techniques, by the shipwrights at Roskilde, from which it was deduced that the ship would have taken 2,650 person-days to build and an extra 13,500 hours of work on the iron for rivets and other fittings. The entire process would have also used more than two kilometres of ropes and 120 square metres of sail, in addition to other necessary components.

We should not imagine Viking-Age people simply strolling out to limitless forests to cut down a few trees. Different species were selected and maintained for their strength, flexibility, endurance, and form in relation to their intended use. Ash and lime were used for bows, shield boards, and the shafts of weapons, while hazel from regularly pollarded trees was cut for wattle-work wall panels and fencing. Oak, elm, birch, and pine were employed for buildings and ships, either as full logs or in planks radially split from the trunk. Interior details and roofing shingles were also made from wood. Wagons, sledges, dugout boats, and other vehicles further consumed vital woodland resources. Timber was also needed for everyday household vessels such as bowls and cups as well as furniture, including beds, looms, and benches, or in wealthier households, the throne-like *kubbstolar* chairs made from hollowed-out stumps. In short, the need for timber saturated Viking society at every level—from its greatest hall buildings and longships to lean-to shelters and brushwood for a simple fire.

Access to forested land and the right to exploit it were therefore major factors in the economy and were handed down through the generations. The management of complex woodland environments required long-term planning and investment, as a full-grown oak tree felled for a ship might have been planted sixty years earlier or more with just such an end use in mind. The possession of such resources formed a crucial component of family estates, and sometimes gave rise to conflicts over inheritance. The control of timber and woodland labour was thus linked to status and social standing, with a potential influence on power relationships in the community. This can be seen particularly clearly in the later North Atlantic colonies, where the rapid clearance of timber in Iceland had a major impact on the settlers' lives, making them dependent on imports of wood from Scandinavia and increasing the importance of driftwood rights. Some of the 'Vinland voyages' to North America were probably undertaken to exploit the rich woodlands of the eastern seaboard.

When the pastoral economy of millions of sheep is combined with the enormous demands of managed woodland, with the aim of turning these raw materials into finished products, one further resource inevitably springs to mind: the need for labour on a truly massive scale. This included the people who tended the animals, took care of the pastureland, and kept up the droveways; the people who sheared the sheep, gathered the wool, and prepared it for working; the people who carded and spun the wool, and turned it into cloth; the people who managed the woodlands, felled the trees, and did the heavy work of trimming, sawing, and splitting before the master boatwrights or carpenters got to work; and the same for all the related industries—obtaining the bog iron, smelting the ore, making the nails and rivets and tools. And on and on. All these workers, in turn, had their own needs of housing and sustenance.

Textile work provides just one vivid example of the scale of labour required. We have already seen the calculations for the production of a sail, suggesting years of spinning and weaving time for one person. Obviously, these would be group activities, but even so, the work involved is staggering when considered over the entire scale of maritime and household requirements. It is almost impossible to overstate the importance of textile production to the Viking economy, permeating every aspect of life. Although some products, such as sails, lasted for many years, a very large proportion of the Viking-Age population must have spent their time in textile manufacture.

In the written sources, it is abundantly clear that this work was primarily within the social sphere of women—but which women? The free female population did not suddenly expand exponentially in the course of the Viking Age. This suggests that many of these textile workers would very likely have been enslaved.

This may go some way towards explaining the numerous sunken-floored weaving huts found clustered around the halls or at settlement boundaries on sites throughout Scandinavia—buildings that proliferate just when the landed estates are expanding in size. The conditions inside the sheds would have been horrendous. In excavations of these structures, archaeologists find lines of circular weights by the doors, where they had fallen from the looms left in place when the buildings were abandoned. The close, repetitive work was done in what light could be had, a narrow shaft of illumination surrounded by near darkness. Years spent in such dimness, trying to pick out the threads and different vegetable dyes, would have ruined the women's eyesight. All day, tiny floating particles of wool would gradually accumulate around the work, drawn into the lungs with every breath. By evening, the air inside the huts was probably opaque and filled with the sound of coughing. In the winter darkness, it would all have been even worse, working by rushlight alone. The work was vital, the experience appalling.

The source of this unfree labour, and not just for textile work, was intimately connected with the Viking phenomenon itself and was a crucial element in the creation of the diaspora. If raiding and trading were two components of the same whole, they came together in the institution of slavery. In many cases, the Vikings' maritime piracy produced one commodity above others: human beings, captured and enslaved.

This is not hard to understand. The raiding was in part *for* slaves, who were then sold on into the existing trade networks (for which they also provided a sustaining rationale) both within Scandinavia and beyond. The labour of the enslaved in turn enabled the *escalation* of these same activities, because it was the unfree who made it all possible. Behind the Viking fleets and crews, apparently appearing so spontaneously in the annals, lay this elaborate and cyclical system that created more of the same.

As one historian has put it, slaving was at the very core of Viking-ness. The raids were an economy in their own right.

That same economy had other outlets and conduits. One of the key social and economic transformations often said to define the Viking Age is the slow development of urbanism in Scandinavia, which paralleled similar institutional change around the shores of the Baltic and the North Sea. While there clearly was a move into towns on the Continent and in England, this was largely a legacy of the Roman urban centres that in many cases were literally still standing, waiting to be taken up again. The European cultures also retained at least some measure of active relationship to former imperial sites—whether spatial, social, or psychological. Scandinavia, by contrast, lay beyond the frontiers of the Empire and thus lacked the pre-existing (albeit decaying) urban models of Roman Europe.

It is surely significant that while the Viking-Age Scandinavians had terms for 'market' and 'trading place', they did not have a word for what we would call towns. This applies not only to such places in their homelands, where the need for an urban definition is in any case arguable, but even to the massive centres the Vikings encountered on their travels. Instead, the term *garðr*—usually applied to the basic unit of settlement, the individual farmstead—was employed in conjunction with qualifying words that can seem to us remarkably modest. The most extreme example is one we have already encountered: Constantinople, modern Istanbul, the capital of the Byzantine Empire and during the Viking Age the greatest metropolis in the world. It was certainly the largest settlement any

Viking would ever have seen, but they called it simply Miklagarðr, the 'big garðr' or perhaps the 'Great Place', surely one of history's more spectacular understatements and an epithet deeply sugges-tive of the Viking attitude to human habitations and their relative scale. Other examples include Novgorod, called Holmgarðr, or the 'Settlement on the Island', and so on. In most instances there is nonetheless a sense of boundedness and enclosure not found in places given other kinds of names.

The societies of England and Carolingian Frankia, with which the Scandinavians had intensive contacts, were firmly urban, as were the Arab Caliphates in the Middle East and Iberia. Techno-logically and socially, the Viking-Age Scandinavians could easily have developed towns like these, but for some reason chose not to do so. They travelled to cities such as Constantinople and yet in their homelands made do with single-street beach markets for centuries. The Scandinavians' urban needs were adaptive to cir-cumstance, and what they saw and eagerly engaged with overseas may simply not have been of much use to them at home.

This raises interesting questions as to how Viking-Age Scandi-navians thought about these places, and how (or if) they saw the difference between 'town' and 'country'. What did they tell each other about their experiences of urban life? What did those who had never seen a 'town' think such a thing looked like? Did living there confer reputation, and if so, to whom and in what way? Just as disadvantaged individuals today may dream of escaping rural poverty for life in the 'big city'—a place that exists as much, if not more, in the mind as in reality—perhaps some Viking-Age people had similarly bruised aspirations.

Some of the Scandinavian centres occupied a middle ground between the beach emporia and the larger sites that would last into the eleventh century. In Vestfold, Norway, at the beginning of the ninth century, a settlement was founded at Kaupang. The inhabited area, spread along the shore of a protected bay a few kilo-metres from the mouth of the river Lågan, was divided into plots in the years around 800. Excavations have revealed few waterlogged deposits, with the exception of some latrines and wells with preserved wood, but these were enough to produce dendrochronological dates ranging from 808 to 863, a solidly ninth-century lifespan for the settlement. It covered at least five to six hectares and was set out in regular plots divided by trenches, with small structures within. The manufacturing capacities of the site can be seen in the evidence recovered from workshops, where the remains of production in bronze, silver, lead, and gold are preserved, as well as exceptional finds of moulds and crucible fragments. Lead weights were clearly a growth industry at Kaupang—several hundred have been found—and were used in everyday transactions, implying the very widespread use of bullion as a means of payment. Kilos of raw lead, used to make the original models from which clay moulds were produced, have also been recovered. One such lead piece reveals some sharp (but familiar) business practices in that it was fashioned into a form of brooch usually encountered as a high-end import to Scandinavia—in other words, the locals were making and selling their own 'imported' jewellery, something akin to suspiciously cheap Rolexes. Amber was also extensively worked on-site, and many objects in this material have come up in the excavations. Imports to the site included glass, carnelian beads, jet bracelets, and pottery from the Rhineland—the latter perhaps containing luxuries such as wine or oil.

But no more than that. This is what sets the tenth-century heyday of the great proto-urban centres of Scandinavia apart from the smaller markets of the 800s. The very earliest Scandinavian emporium, at Ribe, continued to expand into the ninth century, with increasing numbers of buildings and eventually a defensive ditch around the settlement. Places like Birka and Hedeby spread in every direction. (Beyond the faintly ludicrous checklists of 'urban characteristics' once beloved of archaeologists trying to define towns, my own criterion is very simple: lacking even the most basic sense of direction, I just ask myself if a Viking-Age settlement was so large and complex a place that I could get lost in it—if the answer is yes, it's probably a town.)

In all these places, whole blocks of housing and workshops were springing up, and new wooden streets were being laid down. It is clear there were frequent changes to the settlements' layout and form. Buildings tended to be short-lived, being torn down and rebuilt on the same plots. Fire was also a constant hazard, leading to a fair degree of unintended urban renewal. By the tenth century, the general pattern seems to have been for workshops to front the streets, with dwellings in the yards behind—a design repeated in Viking market centres both at home (as at Sigtuna) and abroad (as in York).

At Hedeby and Birka, the defences were strengthened and extended into the water as barrages to control access. The settlement areas themselves slowly rose too, as the ground simply built up with the combined waste and detritus of urban life. When a house was pulled down, a new one was built on the flattened remains of the old, all trodden down into the mud together with the food waste, faeces, and general rubbish of the place. Sanitary it was not—you could probably smell these places a kilometre off.

Slaving was certainly present at these sites—though this does not mean they were 'slave fortresses' of the kind familiar from the West African coast in the early modern period. If the slave trades of later periods are any guide, no dedicated slave markets were necessary as transactions could take place almost anywhere in a settlement—on the stoops of private houses, even on street corners. Such small-scale trade, when conducted regularly, could dispose of hundreds of captives every year.

At Hedeby, for example, most of the finds of shackles and chains have come from the harbour area, presumably dropped when the enslaved were transferred onto the quays. One of the site's investigators is convinced that most of the trading actually took place on the wharves themselves—in Hedeby's case, those broad wooden platforms extending into the water so close together as to effectively make a floating marketplace. Some of these sales were probably seasonal—after the summer raids and before the harvest—although the trade probably continued at some level all year round.

By the tenth century, the larger seagoing boats had to moor end-on at the very limit of the platforms. Remarkable archaeological survivals enable us to see life in Hedeby harbour in close detail—from the swords that seem to have been thrown into the water as each new jetty was dedicated, to a snapshot of the market under attack. Around the year 990, a major warship burnt right in front of the jetties, perhaps in battle, so close that the fire spread to the timber platforms. Because the ship was blocking the harbour access, half of it was broken up, probably using poles pounded down into the wreck from smaller boats, and the pieces floated away to clear the path for shipping. The harbours would have required repair each spring to mend the damage of the previous winter's ice.

And then there is the population itself, in death as in life. To continue with the Danish example, some 1,350 burials are known from Hedeby, distributed across seven cemeteries. The majority are situated outside the wall to the south and contain a mix of cremations and inhumations, the latter sometimes located between mounds. Dating from the late ninth and tenth centuries, these burials clearly include some Christian graves. Most do not include any grave-goods, although the area also holds spectacularly pagan monuments. A core group of 350 burials—including high-status chamber graves—extended from the harbour area into the settlement. The hillfort is associated with about sixty cremations under mounds, while a northern cemetery holds inhumations dating from the mid-ninth to the mid-tenth centuries.

The towns of Scandinavia were home to true urban professionals—housebuilders, carpenters, thatchers; ditch diggers and manual labourers; night-soil folk, who emptied the latrines; and of course, the whole range of craftworkers, metalsmiths, jewellers, wood-turners, potters, and the like.

There is compelling evidence that the larger market centres also had major implications for the lives of women. In Norwegian rural cemeteries, for example, female graves make up about 20 percent of the total where sex determinations can be made, but in Birka town the proportion is up to 60 percent across its several grave-fields. In other markets such as Hedeby, the figure is lower, at 38 percent, but still significantly higher than in the countryside. What does this 'urban' visibility of women mean? It has been suggested that it might depend on textile production and the shift of very special-ised, high-end spinning to the new urban centres—perhaps that this was in fact one of the main rationales for their creation.

These fledgling towns were not only places for the produc-tion and sale of goods, but also meeting places for the exchange of information and knowledge. Much of it would be familiar even to us. A stroll along Birka's streets would have taken you through the scents of different dinners, perhaps with a variety of spices and fla-vours representing international cuisine. *Feel like a Frisian meal this evening? Try Radbod's tavern by the docks—those Saxon merchants we met last month in Hedeby said it was amazing. And you should taste Ulf's beer next door, he uses heather!*

The same is true of language; your walk would also have brought you past the polyglot conversations of others—merchants from the empires of the Franks and Germans, from the eastern waterways, from Rus', and from the Caliphate of the Arabs. Adam of Bremen mentions Norwegians, Slavs, Prussians, and others in Birka. In the Hedeby excavations, weapons were found from the Volga-Bulghar area and of Magyar origin. There must have been a lingua franca, even forms of creole, and probably everybody knew many words for *silver, furs,* and *slaves.* Here and there in the streets, you might even meet a few far-travelled *blámenn,* 'blue people', whom we would know as people of colour. There is little evidence of racism in Viking society and, as far as I am aware, not a single example of a denigrating epithet or attitude on the basis of skin colour. It sounds idealistic in the twenty-first century, but for the

Vikings, who you proved yourself to be, rather than your outward shell, really does seem to have counted for something. We all have a *hamr*, a shape, but it is the *hugr*, the mind or soul, that counts more.

The urban mind in Scandinavia was another product of the Viking Age, a changed perspective on lifestyle and economy that would continue for centuries as another gift to the North. But what of the wider world with which this all connected? How did this change and develop in the tenth century and into the later Viking Age?

15

SILVER, SLAVES, AND SILK

IT IS NO EXAGGERATION TO say that the last thirty years of academic study have enlarged the Viking world dramatically, as the artificial barriers of the post-war years slowly faded. Two aspects of this are paramount. In the East, a new understanding of the organic creation of social and political identities along the rivers, expressed in the developing ethnicity of the Rus', has led to an acknowledgement that their range extended beyond Byzantium and even the Arab world, onto the Asian steppe itself to connect with the fabled Silk Roads. In the West, Viking contacts with the British Isles have been illuminated by archaeological finds that have changed how their activities there are perceived, with implications for all western Europe.

Crucially, in order to make sense of the diaspora as it expanded during the late ninth and tenth centuries, this geographical dichotomy must be erased and the 'Viking world' restored to a unified whole—the way it was actually experienced by those who lived in it. In practical terms, we need to recapture a time when silk purchased by an intrepid Scandinavian in the markets of Persia could end up being made into a bonnet for a woman living in the towns of the Danelaw—and moreover, that while this might have been thought luxurious or expensive, nobody would have been surprised.

This globalised Viking Age also connects with the development of new economies in Scandinavia, as we have seen—shipbuilding on an unprecedented scale, underpinned by urban transformation, all connected with a growing slave state. This, too, was part of the diaspora. Scandinavian territorial ambitions fuelled the mercantile networks and a near industrial acceleration of naval power, but the one also enabled the other.

In the West, three areas above all show the lasting effects of Scandinavian migrations and political contact, ranging from among the earliest of their overseas ventures to the latest: the maritime worlds of Scotland and the Northern Isles of Orkney and Shetland, the Irish Sea, and the Channel coasts of Frankia. The Viking diaspora, by definition, involved a conscious maintenance of links back to Scandinavia and an active notion of original belonging. The process by which these ties were expressed, supported, and eventually let go is one that charts the overall trajectory of the Viking Age itself.

The west coast of Scotland is one of only two truly sheltered coastlines in western Europe, and in terms of cultural connections, it is significant that the other is the west coast of Norway. It is hardly surprising that these maritime environments were in contact.

Due to their proximity to the Norwegian coast, the 'Northern Isles' of Shetland and Orkney have often been assumed to be among the first territories to feel the impact of Viking raiding and seaborne expansion. Their geographical relationship is best appreciated by turning a map of the North Sea upside down, to view the natural sailing route of shortest open-water distances from the 'North Way' across to the Isles, then to the coast of the Scottish mainland, and thence south and west past the Hebrides (the 'Western Isles') and into the Irish Sea.

The nature of this region's interaction with Scandinavia is still unclear, especially concerning relations between the incoming

Norse and the indigenous Picts, descendants of the Iron Age tribes of Scotland mentioned by Roman authors. Interpretations range from relatively peaceable exchange through to enslavement and subjection, all the way to outright genocide. There was raiding at vulnerable, insular Hebridean monasteries early in the ninth century, so the Vikings were definitely there, but there is a real shortage of clear sources for what happened in the Isles. Perhaps the very silence of the record is eloquent. The larger picture, however, is of a steady trickle (occasionally a stream) of Scandinavian immigration to Scotland, and especially the Isles, developing over time into a distinctive regional culture of the Viking diaspora.

In the Orkneys and Shetland, the earliest secure evidence for Norse settlement is from the mid-800s, but there may have been earlier contact. The surviving textual sources for the Isles are all medieval, and indeed the main ones are explicitly framed as legitimating hindsight histories of the Orkney earls. The most comprehensive of them, *Orkneyinga saga*, is a wonderful read, but its veracity is problematic. It is not even certain if there really *was* an Orkney earldom until the Middle Ages, when a retrospective sheen may have been applied to what were essentially raiding enclaves. Over the longer term, it is clear that the Norse established themselves throughout the Isles, often building sizeable farms of the familiar type with longhouses of turf and stone along with ancillary buildings.

The Viking presence in mainland and eastern Scotland is less well represented. Interestingly, the folklore traditions of the east coast preserve many tales about Vikings, mostly concerning raids and battles, with other stories of 'Danish' camps and burials. While this region was not subject to the serious Scandinavian settlement that we find elsewhere, contacts were nonetheless frequent, and it is obvious the Norse brought their institutions with them. At Dingwall on the Scottish mainland, recent investigations have identified a potential *thing* site—an assembly place—comprising a mound and surrounding ring ditch. A number of other potential *thing* sites have been identified across Scotland, not only on the mainland but also in the Northern and Western Isles.

Unlike the Scandinavian settlements in England and Ireland, no urban centres were founded here. Instead, there are traces of beach markets—relatively simple affairs of basic, temporary structures along the strand at reliable harbours and waterways. Probably dating back to Norse contacts with Scotland in the pre-Viking period, these deceptively rudimentary sites were conduits for trade and exchange, not least in timber, which seems to have been a major commodity. As in the Western Isles, the Scandinavian settlers seem to have intentionally situated their new homes in close proximity to pre-existing Pictish settlements, as at Old Scatness and Jarlshof in the Shetlands, and at Buckquoy and Pool in the Orkneys. In the extensive cemetery at Westness on the island of Rousay, the men buried with Norse objects are significantly taller than the average males in unequivocally Pictish burials elsewhere, so the populations can be clearly distinguished.

The nature of the interactions between Norse and local peoples has left faint traces in the archaeology, especially that of Orkney. The Scandinavian settlement at Buckquoy has produced objects decorated with Pictish art styles, suggesting that, in at least some cases, the Vikings settled among the indigenous population rather than displacing or removing them. At Quoygrew, on Westray, it seems the indigenous inhabitants quickly adapted to imported goods such as soapstone vessels and Norse-style combs. Traditional pastoral and agricultural practices also survived, implying quite close interaction between new arrivals and the existing population. This argues against the notion of a 'Pictish genocide', at least for Orkney.

Elsewhere, the picture was more violent, as seen at the Brough of Deerness, a spectacular sea stack (a near-offshore pillar of natural rock, produced by the erosion of sea and wind) towering above the water on Orkney's mainland and joined to the cliffs by a narrow path. Once thought to have been a monastic settlement, excavations have shown it to have been a residence of a Norse chieftain, with longhouses and what appears to have been a private chapel. From the tenth century onwards, Deerness clearly had an armed garrison and perhaps functioned as part of a chain of off-shore watch stations. The group based there may have had other tasks, including actively monitoring or patrolling shipping lanes. According to the medieval *Sverre's saga*, Earl Harald actually cites piracy as one of the key sources of revenue needed to maintain his power in Orkney. Coupled with this is an explicit recognition that he cannot afford to exercise too much direct control on the raiders for fear they will turn against him—an uneasy alliance of 'pirate fishermen'. Deerness may have been the kind of base from which these seaborne predators operated, under variable degrees of higher sanction. *Orkneyinga saga* has some fascinating descriptions of *várvíking* and *haustvíking*—literally 'spring-viking' and 'autumn-viking'—showing the seasonal cycle of raiding that operated in places like this.

In the Hebrides, despite more than a millennium of earlier Celtic occupation, there are no non-Norse place-names at all. This suggests a total break without any continuity of habitation, and provides disturbing support for the theory of total population removal or replacement. In the Scottish islands as a whole, there is a high proportion of female genetic lineages shared with Norway, implying that Scandinavian women eventually settled in large numbers.

Over time, the settlements in the Northern Isles took on a distinctly Norse character. On the Bay of Skaill in Orkney, for example, near the famous Neolithic village of Skara Brae, a substantial farm has been excavated with evidence for far-flung contacts with regions as distant as Normandy. Some of the buildings contained runic inscriptions and tally marks scratched into the stonework, as have been found at other Orcadian sites. It was a site of some status, and it is clear that Skaill's inhabitants expressed their social standing through impressive architecture and landscape engineering.

Great artificial mounds were made with rubbish, consolidated with earth and stone. These strange creations were a distinctly colonial endeavour, and mounds like them have been identified in a number of other North Atlantic colonies, including the Faroes. Just as Scandinavian rulers demonstrated their status through the building of royal halls and monumental burial mounds, so these Orkney magnates did likewise on a smaller scale, creating cenotaph-like copies to project their ambition. It was a distinctly Norse visual language of power.

The establishment of Scandinavian colonists in the Scottish Isles also transformed the economies of the region. Flax production increased, as did dairying (although not in the Hebrides) and agricultural investment in general. Fishing also intensified and extended into new areas of the ocean, and there was an increase in the intake of fish protein all across society, showing how the resources of the sea were utilised more than ever as a central part of the everyday diet. This overwhelmingly marine economy was probably an introduction from Norway during the ninth century, the period of the first major Norse migration to the Northern Isles.

The close links that communities shared with the sea are reflected in the relatively high number of boat burials that have been identified in Scotland. While these are almost unknown elsewhere in the British Isles, six boat graves are known from the Hebrides, three from the Northern Isles, and one from the mainland. Rather than true ship burials, the Scottish boat graves contain small, coastal craft up to five metres long of the type known as a *færing*. Powered by oars and a small sail, such vessels were the main means of transport around the offshore waters of the Isles, and were a natural symbol of status for those accorded such a boat as their last resting place.

In 2011 the first Viking boat burial from the Scottish mainland was found at Ardnamurchan, near the westernmost point of island Britain. Sometime in the tenth century, an individual had been interred in a five-metre-long boat, with a bent sword and spear by his or her side. Other finds included a drinking horn, a shield, and tools associated with agriculture and smithying—an assemblage that would not be out of place in graves on the Norwegian coast. Like other Scottish boat burials, the *færing* at Ardnamurchan seems to have been carefully filled with stones as part of the funerary rituals. Isotopic analysis of the person's teeth suggests the buried individual originated from Scandinavia, although north-eastern Scotland or eastern Ireland are also possibilities.

The central belt of mainland Scotland, stretching roughly across the country from modern Glasgow to Edinburgh, was also an arena of Norse operations, though the evidence has mostly survived as burials and remnants of plunder. Here are the north-ernmost finds of a special kind of stone grave marker known as hogbacks, a uniquely colonial monument that seems to have been commissioned by the Norse elites. There is also a group of elaborate Viking-Age burials at Loch Lomond, near Dumbarton, and a spec-tacular tenth-century hoard of silver, gold, and jewellery in Gal-loway. The ecclesiastical nature of a number of the hoarded items indicates they may well have been plundered from a monastery.

The west coast of Scotland was part of a much wider arena of Norse activities, facing as it did onto the Irish Sea. This body of rough but shallow water drew several kingdoms and small states into its orbit. To the west was Ireland, fragmented into warring clans; to the north, Scotland and the Western Isles of the Hebrides; to the east, Wales and the whole coast of England; in the centre, occu-pying a key strategic position, was the Isle of Man. To a greater or lesser degree, all these regions came under Scandinavian influence in the course of the Viking Age: the Irish Sea was the most impor-tant axis of Norse activity in the West.

Its north-eastern shoreline was a gateway to one of the endur-ing Viking power blocs of the ninth and tenth centuries—the com-bined strength of the Kingdom of York and the Danelaw. These were the polities carved out by the hydrarchy, the 'Great Army', and the other Viking forces that had fought the English to stalemate, and then proceeded to settle the lands they had won.

In practice, by the late 800s, the eastern half of England, and most of the north, was under Scandinavian control. The Danelaw boundary with Wessex and the lands of the southern English is well known from the treaty agreed between King Alfred and the Viking leader Guthrum at some point between 878 and the latter's death in 890. This famously records the border between Wessex and Scandinavian-held East Anglia as travelling "up the Thames, and then up the Lea, and along the Lea to its source, then in a straight line to Bedford, then up the Ouse to Watling Street", although one imagines that the reality was a messier, shifting zone of cross-border conflict.

Inside the Danelaw, power seems to have been divided between numerous autonomous political factions whose bases were distributed among the regional settlements. In the Midlands, a group of townships known as the Five Boroughs began to flourish as market centres: Derby, Nottingham, Lincoln, Stamford, and Leicester were tightly connected with the surrounding countryside in webs of settlements dominated by Scandinavians. Even today, some of their road names end in -gate, still the modern Scandinavian word for street (gata or gade).

The Danelaw seems to have had its own economy, which was necessary for maintaining its independence from the English kingdoms across its borders. Silver bullion seems to have been in general circulation, and hoards suggest the Danelaw must have had a general weight standard, although individuals would have personalised their own weights. There is also evidence of attempts to introduce coinage that mimicked the currency of English Mercia and Wessex. The York coinage made explicit use of Viking symbolism, with issues showing the raven banner, sometimes alongside a Christian cross. However, this new silver money does not seem to have found widespread use outside the urban hinterlands, perhaps indicating the realistic limits of Viking power.

There is also good evidence for the manipulation of cultural identity through the creation and use of new material styles. People wore mass-produced dress accessories with a mix of Scandinavian, English, and European influences, speaking to the formation of cosmopolitan identities. There are even brooches made with component parts manufactured in both England and Scandinavia. The same hogback tombstones found in Scotland are present in northern England in much larger numbers, and here too they seem to have been a way for an Anglo-Scandinavian aristocracy to express their multicultural affiliations. This was the diaspora in practice— fitting in to a new home, but never forgetting the old.

It is certain that many Scandinavian settlers came to some accommodation with the Church, still a dominant force and deeply embedded in English social structures which the Vikings could not (and perhaps did not wish to) fully replace. They may have quickly adopted Christianity alongside or in preference to their existing beliefs. To take but one example, a free-standing stone cross in the churchyard at Gosforth in Cumbria incorporates images of the Ragnarök into its depiction of what is presumably the Day of Judgement—Odin, Fenrir, and others are clearly visible. Many Thor's hammer pendants have been found in England, mostly from women's graves, so the old gods were clearly kept alive by at least some of the Danelaw Vikings. Cultic place-names, such as Toreswe (originally *Torsvé*) in north Lincolnshire, show that the Norse deities were not only known but actively worshipped in Viking-Age England. Weapons and other metalwork were offered in rivers, streams, and bogs in a way that connects to the Scandinavian ritual concern with wetlands that went back centuries. The symbol of Thor's hammer also appears on more than thirty examples of coinage minted in the Viking Kingdom of York. On the later issues, it is shown alongside a sword that may represent the weapon of St. Peter, thus combining images of divine protection to cover everyone's bets.

Despite the widespread settlement of Scandinavians, they were under constant pressure from the English kingdoms, who had never forgotten what had been lost in the wars of the ninth century. Gradually, the control the Vikings exercised over eastern and northern England began to fray, especially at the edges of the Danelaw. The Vikings had tried to build border fortifications, mirroring the Saxon *burhs*—defended townships—that Alfred had earlier constructed on the frontier, but in the late ninth and tenth centuries the English began to push back.

As the Wessex armies chipped away territory, they consolidated their gains by building more *burhs*. In a reversal of the situation they had once taken advantage of in Frankia, the Vikings' division and lack of political cohesion meant they could not mount a concerted, organised resistance. Alfred's early efforts to annex the southern portions of the Scandinavian territories were continued by his children, Edward the Elder and Aethelflaed, following his death in 899. Year by year, decade by decade, the Danelaw was retaken, and by the late 900s it had ceased to exist in practical terms.

A hundred years after the establishment of the Danelaw, the polity itself was gone, but its demographic impact would be permanent. The Scandinavian settlers mostly remained, assimilated into the wider population. There are also linguistic signals of continuity, such as the poorly understood 'Danish tongue' that appears in contemporary documents to denote what was obviously a lingua franca in England among people of Scandinavian descent.

Importantly, what resulted from the reconquest was not a reconstitution of the former English kingdoms the Vikings had destroyed—instead, the liberated Danelaw was in effect transformed into greater Wessex. Edward the Elder would come to inherit the throne of Mercia on the death of his sister, Aethelflaed, in 918, and further territorial gains by his successor, Aethelstan, would see all of England come under the rule of Wessex in 927. In a curious sense, then, the Vikings were responsible for the creation of England itself, perhaps the element of their legacy that in later centuries would prove to have the greatest consequences for the world.

The boundaries of the so-called Kingdom of York in Northumbria were never fully defined, including a somewhat blurred border with the Danelaw, but it was all part of a contiguous region of Viking dominance. At the heart of the York kingdom lay the fortified mercantile centre of Jorvík itself, its Scandinavian name an adaptation of its earlier English one, Eoforwic. From the mid-ninth to mid-tenth centuries, the Viking rulers of York governed an area that stretched south to the Humber River and north to the Yorkshire Wolds—essentially spanning the north of England from coast to coast. Areas of north-western England, including the modern-day counties of Lancashire and Cumbria, have yielded evidence for Scandinavian settlement, and the Wirral Peninsula seems to have acted as a major entry point to the Danelaw from the Irish Sea.

Archaeologically, the city of York is one of the best known in the entire Viking world. Excavations at Coppergate (the 'street of the cup-makers') in the 1970s, and later at many more sites in the city, have revealed a densely packed, truly urban centre of timber buildings, many with cellars, organised into zones of manufacturing and craftwork. With a river frontage on the Ouse, and utilising the layout of the ruined Roman town, Jorvík was a major capital of the North and maintained trading connections in all directions. One of the glories of its archaeology is that many of the cultural deposits are waterlogged, preserving organic materials such as textiles and wood almost unchanged. Buried metres below the modern streets, whole cellars had survived nearly to waist height; the excavators could walk in through the doors. Clothing, musical instruments, furniture, and all kinds of household items and foreign exotica—even Chinese silks—have made Jorvík a baseline for our understanding of Viking urbanism.

Its most famous ruler was Eirík Haraldsson, more usually known by his nickname—Eirík Bloodaxe. One of Harald Fine-hair's many sons, he inherited the sea-king's life and seems to have ruled parts of Norway for a brief time, but was later driven into exile for the murder of several of his family members (hence the name). He then carved out a fortune for himself in a career of violence that took him from western Norway to his own kingdom in York. His consort, Queen Gunnhild, was almost as notorious, rumoured to be a sorceress and shape-changer of exceptional viciousness. Eirík's court kept the Viking-Age gossipmongers busy for a decade, and his life could fill a biography of his own. Although he resisted the English move northwards, Eirík was eventually killed at Stainmore in 954, and the Kingdom of York died with him.

The York kings ruled in a state of constant tension with their counterparts in Dublin, across the Irish Sea. Sometimes allies, occasionally enemies and rivals, these twin factions steered the fortunes of the whole region for more than a century.

Unlike England, Ireland did not witness a large-scale influx of colonists. However, there were clearly fleets based in the Irish Sea from the early ninth century that perhaps also operated from bases in mainland Britain, such as the Bristol Channel or the Somerset region. The *Anglo-Saxon Chronicle* for 835, for example, records a *micel sciphere*—a 'great ship-army'—in Cornwall, and it does not seem likely that this kind of raiding was launched from the North Sea.

From the 840s, the Viking presence in Ireland becomes more concrete. At this time historical sources begin to document the establishment of the so-called *longphuirt* in coastal and riverine areas. Though subtly different from the winter camps of England, they fulfilled many of the same functions. Some, such as those established at Dublin, Cork, Wexford, Waterford, and Limerick, would evolve to become Ireland's principal cities.

According to the *Annals of Ulster*, the *longphort* at Dublin was set up in 841. The area had previously been the focus of native Irish settlement, so although the Vikings did not actually found the city, the Scandinavian presence certainly marked a new phase in its development. In the ninth century, the Viking settlement took the form of a defended enclave around the 'black pool' that gives Dublin its name, with a possible harbour or jetties. In the tenth century, settlement continued there but was concentrated around the Wood Quay district, another defended site with water on three sides.

At the time of the *longphort*'s founding, burials from the area suggest that the groups operating there included not only Scandinavians but also individuals from the British Isles, implying some of the Vikings' early victims may have thrown their lot in with the raiders. The largest cemetery, however, can be linked directly to the *longphort*: most of the graves at this site, Kilmainham, are those of men, often accompanied by full sets of weapons including large numbers of single-edged swords. These burials are very clearly those of fighting forces, equipped for serious military operations. In line with this, there is a remarkable element of trauma evident in the Dublin skeletons, with more than a third of the adult males exhibiting signs of injury from blade weapons and blunt force. In the tenth- and eleventh-century deposits at Fishamble Street, some seventeen skulls were found scattered across the site in pits and latrines. Several of these crania were clearly the result of decapitations, and some bear the marks of stakes or poles—it seems the riverbanks were lined with heads. Such trophy displays were long a part of Irish war customs, and it may be that these practices were adopted by the Dublin Norse. For the first century of its existence, at least, Dublin was clearly a hard town, an appropriate base for a piratical fleet.

This ties in with the bigger picture. Of the nearly four hundred burials with Scandinavian material culture in Britain and Ireland, fully *half* contain weapons. Another indication that trade may not have been at the heart of the Viking urban experience in Ireland is the simple fact of the Norse confinement to the coasts. This may not have been their wish, but expansion inland could have been limited militarily by the Irish clans.

During its early years, Dublin seems to have had a pronounced rural economy, albeit with an organised street plan along the banks of the River Liffey and extending up the slopes behind. Later, the settlement was divided into neighbourhoods with clearly differing qualities of housing—a familiar picture from modern towns. At its Viking-Age height, Dublin was probably home to a population numbering in the low thousands. Excavations have revealed a range of domestic structures, ranging from small houses with benches and central hearths, to buildings that probably functioned as store-rooms. Finds from their interiors have provided detailed insights into daily life in the Viking-Age town. These include gaming pieces and improvised boards; children's toys, such as miniature wooden ships and swords; and detritus from craft activities that attests to the settlement's long-distance trading connections.

Pig pens have also been found in Dublin, along with animal bones that indicate the settlement was being supplied with beef from outside its walls—a similar pattern to the food economy of the Scandinavian market centres at home. Dublin enjoyed a good relationship with the surrounding farms for the first years of its existence, with the choicest cuts of meat being brought in (though this may also reflect some degree of coercion towards their produc-ers). By the early tenth century, however, possibly because of the increasingly tense relationship between the Dublin Vikings and the indigenous population, things had clearly deteriorated, and only inferior-quality meat was being sold in the town.

It is hard to say how many Vikings were operating in Ireland, though the numbers of *longphuirt* suggest a number perhaps in the low thousands. Fleets are listed that range in size from a few tens of vessels to a maximum of three hundred, escalating into the tenth century, when conflicts with the Irish were at their zenith. By the early eleventh century, the full-force fleet of the Dublin Norse is reckoned to have numbered around two hundred ships, and the city was able to field an army of six to ten thousand men. The same period saw frequent fighting, not only with the Irish but also with other Vikings, in addition to raids across the sea to England. In order to maintain numbers, a steady flow of new recruits would have been needed.

This level of violence, which was clearly a prevalent feature of life in Viking-Age Ireland, raises serious questions about the Scandinavian presence. Not all the *longphuirt* developed into towns, but it is possible they were much more than military enclaves. Some may have been multifunctional trading centres intended to facilitate the movement of goods. It is useful to remember that those Vikings who engaged in maritime piracy and warfare would likely have been the same individuals who appeared at market sites and emporia to sell or trade what they had obtained through force only a short time previously. Perhaps the *longphuirt* represent the centralised redistribution of wealth, no matter its origin or the legality of its acquisition. If so, this may go some way to explaining the settlement pattern of Viking forces in Ireland, which seem to have been largely confined to the immediate hinterlands of the *longphuirt*.

While it is possible that Scandinavians did settle at least to some degree in the wider landscape, adopting local housing styles and material culture in a way that would make them archaeologically 'invisible', Vikings may have found it more beneficial to harness Ireland's economic potential without seeking any form of direct rule. Irish social power had never been based on control of land—other than certain symbolic sites of prehistoric fame—but rather on the overlordship of people. This meant that the Vikings might adopt a different approach to that employed in other regions, by creating gateways through which trade and wealth could flow into and out of the Irish interior. The Scandinavian elites based in these coastal settlements could then make a profit from the redistribution of imports (including captives), which in turn allowed them to dominate maritime trading routes.

The instabilities of Ireland's politics continued into the tenth century, with increasing conflict between ostensibly 'Irish' and 'Scandinavian' communities whose ethnicity was becoming blurred. However, one should be wary of convenient terms for hybrid identities such as the 'Hiberno-Norse' (or the 'Anglo-Scandinavians', for that matter), not least because they somehow assume there were previously 'pure' ethnicities that later blended. This ignores the universal nuances of personhood, allegiance, background, and all the other components of identity. We should rather see these polities, effectively little 'city states', as building single communities from multiple identities.

For the Dublin 'Vikings', the balance of power was finally tipped in 980 by their failed invasion of Meath in the eastern midlands, which ultimately led to a concerted Irish effort to curtail their strength. In 1002 something very unusual occurred; the Irish were united under a High King, Brian Bóruma, who over the next decade built up a massive coalition against Dublin. In practice, Scandinavians were present in both camps, as were people from all over the Irish Sea world and beyond. In 1014, the Dublin forces were decisively defeated at the Battle of Clontarf outside the city, although Brian was killed. In practice, the Scandinavians retained control of the town itself, but thereafter the real power lay with the Irish.

Situated between York and Dublin in the middle of the Irish Sea, the Isle of Man was also heavily impacted by the Vikings, who first settled there during the mid-ninth century. One scholar has suggested that Man was in effect a pirate kingdom, which its central location would certainly make feasible.

Little is known of the settlement process itself, but early graves imply at least a measure of threat and aggression on the part of the first Norse colonists. One of the more notable burials is that from

Balladoole, where an early tenth-century boat grave seems to have been deliberately built over and through a number of pre-existing Christian graves. Whether this reflects an act of deliberate desecration or a more general attempt to place burials within a ritually powerful location is hard to tell, but in either case the Balladoole burial physically established the presence of the settlers in a symbolic statement of land-taking.

Traces remain of the familiar Scandinavian legal systems and structures of assembly, including the unique Tynwald *thing*-mound on which the Manx legislature still meets on formal occasions. As in Ireland, there is little evidence for the Scandinavian-style longhouses that are so commonly found in the North Atlantic colonies. There are only a few structures that are distinctly recognisable as 'Norse', of which perhaps the best preserved is a bow-sided longhouse discovered at a site called the Braaid. Hillforts and defended promontories suggest a not entirely peaceful existence. Unfortunately, much of the basic settlement pattern of Norse Man is an archaeological blank, but the island is relatively small, and it can be assumed the incoming Scandinavians took over the agricultural landscape of the indigenous Manx.

One of the most fascinating aspects of the Viking settlement on Man is the clear evidence for a fusion of traditional spiritual ideas and Christianity. The early Viking burials there have a particularly 'pagan' flavour. In addition to that at Balladoole, notable graves include the one at Ballateare where a woman had been sacrificed, and a female burial at Peel Castle on St. Patrick's Isle. The woman at Peel is notable for the large number of grave-goods accompanying her, including two knives (one with a handle decorated in silver wire), a comb, a goose wing, an ammonite fossil, a necklace of jet and amber beads, and an object that has been interpreted variously as a cooking spit or perhaps a magic staff of the type used by a *völva* sorceress. The manner in which all these people were buried conforms to the wider pattern of pre-Christian funerary rite observed in Scandinavia. Later in the tenth century, however, religious identities seem to have started taking new shapes. As in England at places like Gosforth, a number of Manx carved stones portray Christian iconography alongside images that seem to derive from Old Norse cosmology. Perhaps the best example of this is Thorwald's Cross, from Kirk Andreas, which appears to depict Odin being devoured by the wolf Fenrir at Ragnarök. On the other side of the cross is an image of a figure (perhaps Christ?) trampling a serpent. This implies that, within a few generations, the settlers had begun to adapt to new belief systems and cultural traditions, though perhaps while maintaining aspects of their own traditional worldviews.

The last few decades have also seen increasing efforts to understand the Viking presence in Wales. There is still much to learn about this enigmatic part of the Viking world, and for the most part the evidence does not extend beyond possible Scandinavian influences in place-names and some specific references to attacks in historical and literary sources. Until recently there was little archaeological evidence for the Viking presence, with the exception of a small number of hoards and some tentatively identified pagan burials situated near the coastline.

However, it is now known that Scandinavians settled on the island of Anglesey off the north-west coast (the name of which is Onguls-ey, or 'Ongul's Island', in Old Norse) early in the Viking Age, and by the late ninth century a Hiberno-Norse elite were based at Penmon in the east of the island. On current evidence, the native population of Anglesey does not seem to have been removed or killed by the Vikings. Excavations at Llanbedrgoch have revealed enigmatic traces of Norse activities that hint at the nature of their contacts with the locals. Perhaps a one-time royal centre, it seems to have been a multicultural (though defended) place where Scandinavians mixed not only with the Welsh but with others coming from all over the British Isles. There are a number of tenth-century burials, and stable isotope analysis on their teeth reveals they spent their childhood years in places as far apart as western Norway,

Brittany, and Herefordshire. Other sites, such as Red Wharf Bay on the north-east coast of Anglesey, appear to have been way stations and refitting bases for Scandinavian seafarers—an essential resource in the stormy waters of the region.

In western Europe, the Irish Sea was only one of several water-worlds the Scandinavians made their own. The North Sea and, closer to home, the Baltic are other obvious examples, but they were not alone. In the diaspora that developed out of the time of the hydrarchs, there was a fourth such maritime environment where, almost ironically, the Viking presence would leave the most lasting imprint of all: the Channel coast of what is now France.

The Frankish Empire had suffered two prolonged periods of Viking assaults during the ninth century, the second coming in the 880s with a concerted campaign that left its mark from Paris to the upper reaches of the Rhine. The respite after the raiders had, at last, been expelled from the rivers was not a long-lasting one, though the political context of what would follow was distinctly different.

The Viking fleets began to return in the early years of the tenth century, bigger and now also driven by what seems to have been a lack of targets in the rest of Europe—there was not much mileage in Scandinavians attacking England, Ireland, or the Scottish isles unless it was in direct alliance with their countryfolk who were already there. In Frankia, the new raids were much more focussed than before and hit the estuary of the Seine repeatedly. The situation grew so quickly unstable that, following a battle at Chartres in 911, the Frankish king, Charles the Simple, was forced to negotiate with the Vikings, and in the process made a fatal mistake that was to shape his nation even down to our own times. In some desperation, and with considerable lack of foresight, Charles granted the Scandinavians a swathe of territory in what was then called Neustria, along the northern coast of the kingdom facing England. Because of its new overlords, it would soon gain a new name, one that it has kept to the present day: *Nordmannia*, 'the land of the Northmen', the province we call Normandy.

A charter from 918 records that the Scandinavian settlers there were under the command of a leader called Hrólfr (to the Franks he was Rollo, the name by which he is more commonly known today), who seems to have combined diplomacy with the constructive use (or threat) of violence to such a degree that in 924 his lands were augmented with additional territories. In return for these concessions, Rollo and his descendants were charged with preventing further attacks into the Frankish interior along the Seine—the idea being essentially to turn poachers into gamekeepers. It worked to a limited degree, at first, but soon had the opposite effect, with the Seine Vikings simply welcoming their Scandinavian comrades from overseas and allowing them to settle in ever increasing numbers, thereby further entrenching their grip on the region. The Seine was also the highway to Paris, riverine access to which had thus been actively granted to the Vikings.

It seems the colonists integrated fairly rapidly with the indigenous population, and as a result the material evidence for the early occupation of Normandy is sparse. Weapons have been dredged from the major rivers of the province, which, as in England, suggests these rituals of watery offerings arrived with the Scandinavians. A single burial containing an individual thought to be a Scandinavian woman has been identified at Pîtres, not far from the site of Charles the Bald's bridge across the Seine at Pont de l'Arche.

As in several areas of the British Isles, the greatest evidence for the Scandinavian presence comes in the form of their placenames, which cluster in Normandy. There are also Norse elements preserved in aspects of Norman law, and the legislature was clearly firmly in Viking hands—as one would expect. Excavations in the major centre of Rouen, however, have shed light for the first time on the development of the city, revealing that the tenth-century housing plots were divided into long, thin tenements similar to those identified in Viking-Age contexts in the British Isles. Evidence for destruction at the cathedral there, as well as at the monastery at Jumièges, some twenty kilometres to the west, may also be attributed to a more aggressive Viking presence.

Rollo died around 930, but the colony lived on under the rule of his son, William Longsword, who had succeeded his father before his death. William would be granted additional lands by the Franks in 933, extending Normandy's territories to the Cotentin Peninsula and making it a dukedom. Its borders are still those of Normandie today (in the French spelling), a permanent reminder of Viking heritage; the region even has a long-cross flag reminiscent of the modern Nordic national colours.

Within a few generations, the direct Scandinavian influence in Normandy began to fade as first, second, and subsequent generations of immigrants continued to integrate into Frankish society. William was murdered in 942, but he was succeeded a few years later by his son following a short period of conflict with the Franks. The duchy continued to grow in power, and in 1066 a dispute over the English throne led Rollo's descendant, William the Bastard (better known to history as 'the Conqueror' and William I of England), to launch a successful invasion across the Channel; in doing so, he shaped the course of history in the British Isles. This remarkable achievement ensured not only that Normandy was the only Viking colony in western Europe to survive the Viking Age itself, but also that it would thrive, expanding its influence into southern Europe and the Mediterranean during the eleventh and twelfth centuries.

The Viking Age was also a formative period for Brittany. Situated to the west of Normandy, at the north-western edge of modern-day France, the region had always asserted an independent and complex identity. Its population spoke a Celtic language and had close affinities to the indigenous Britons of Cornwall and Devon just across the water.

The Bretons had maintained somewhat frosty relations with the Franks since long before the first Viking raids. Brittany as a united territory, recognised by the Empire, seems to have emerged when it was made a Carolingian duchy in the 830s, but this was very dependent on personal connections between the Breton leaders and the crown. When Emperor Louis the Pious died in 840—a catalyst for the civil war the Vikings would exploit so effectively—the Bretons also seized the moment and sought to reassert their autonomy. This led them to manage a complex network of diplomatic allegiances with both Carolingian and Viking leaders; the latter became a powerful and growing influence in regional politics during the second half of the ninth century. This would not only result in Breton and Viking forces combining to launch assaults on the Carolingians, but would also break out as conflict between the Bretons and the Vikings themselves—most often the Scandinavian 'army' that established itself at the mouth of the Loire.

Further turmoil in the region was fuelled by internal rivalries among the Breton elite that culminated in a civil war in 874. In the late 880s, Brittany came under intensive attack, and dissention among the Bretons allowed the Loire Vikings temporarily to occupy western Brittany. They were pushed out by Alain of Vannes in the 890s, leading to a period of relative calm until his death in 907. Viking attacks then again intensified and were further driven by the ceding of Normandy to Rollo around 911, which pushed non-aligned Scandinavians operating on the Seine—more of those brotherhoods, the *lið*—to make for the Loire. From 914 Brittany experienced four years of intensive attacks, followed by the arrival of another large Viking fleet that came ashore at Nantes in 919. The combined Viking forces were overwhelming, and in 920 the province was entirely overrun. The following year, Robert I ceded the capital city of Nantes to the Viking leader, Røgnvaldr.

The Scandinavian colony in Brittany survived for about twenty years. While this is a short time by comparison with the Danelaw, the Irish towns, or Normandy, two decades was still a long time as lived experience. Røgnvaldr apparently spent much of his rule fighting, and he seems to have died shortly after 925. Conflict erupted again in 927 and 930, and in 931 the Vikings in Brittany assembled a large army with the intention of attacking east into Frankia, but a (failed) Breton revolt curtailed these plans. Another rebellion, this time led by Alain Barbetorte, occurred in 936. Alain had grown up as a Breton noble in exile at the English court, having fled there when Brittany fell. He returned at the behest of other Breton leaders-in-waiting, tasked with driving the Vikings out of the region. Nantes was recaptured, but Scandinavian resistance sputtered on until 939, when a large Viking force was defeated in battle at Trans. Viking activity in Brittany would continue into the 940s and beyond, but the Scandinavians had lost the province forever.

Given Brittany's uniquely short but violent life as a Viking colony, it is not surprising that much of the surviving archaeological evidence is of a militaristic nature. Possible evidence for Viking raiding has been identified in destruction layers at the abbey of Landévannec, and there are spectacular traces of combat at the Camp de Péran fortress in the north of the province. Excavations of the circular enclosure there found that the fortification had been either occupied or attacked by a Viking force. Numerous weapons were found under the burnt remains of the collapsed rampart, along with a coin of St. Peter that was minted in York c. 905–925. Structures were also found inside the fortification, perhaps allowing some insights into the nature of accommodation constructed by Viking armies while on campaign. The date of the coin fits well with the results of radiocarbon dates obtained from the wall surrounding the site (915 plus or minus twenty years), which suggests the encampment may have been attacked during the Breton reconquests of the 930s.

Several Viking burials are also known from the region, the most dramatic being one on the Île de Groix, a rocky island off the southern Breton coast. Here, two males—an older individual and a young adult—were cremated in a ship along with dogs and birds. Burnt with them were swords, an axe, archery equipment, and spears, as well as some two dozen shields and other items; the warlike tone is obvious. The shield bosses are particularly interesting in that they are of a type so far unknown outside Brittany, having been discovered only here and in more recently excavated Viking graves at the island monastery of l'Île Lavret. Perhaps this was equipment manufactured 'in house' by Vikings operating on the Loire during the early tenth century—in other words, similar to the activities seen in the winter camps of the Great Army in England. The range of other equipment within the grave, however, implies the dead men possessed a wide network of connections that stretched as far as England, northern Germany, and central Sweden.

While the Viking occupation of Brittany was short-lived, the developments taking place in this small territory were to have significant impacts on the longer-term trajectory of the Viking Age. The frequent rebellions of the Bretons and the wars they fought against their Frankish neighbours served, again and again, to draw much-needed resources away from other areas of the Empire, which contributed to the weakening of the great kingdom Charlemagne had secured only a few generations before. Many of the Viking groups that were operating across northern Europe would have cut their teeth in the frequent battles against the Bretons and the Franks, and the region also served as a springboard for further raids south. It was the place where some of the most prolific leaders of the Viking Age, such as Hástein, earned their reputations. Brittany played a formative role as a catalyst of conflict and change.

The Île de Groix ship burial is a good place to observe the realities of the Viking world, seen as an arena of fluidly mobile activity rather than as artificially separated western and eastern theatres of operations. In this case, a single object from the grave can illustrate the globalising connections that joined the component regions of the diaspora, and in the process lead us back into the East to examine developments that were proceeding there in parallel with the opening of the Danelaw, the Irish Sea kingdoms, and places such as Normandy. One of the Groix sword scabbards had a decorated chape (the metal protector over the point of the blade) depicting a diving falcon. This symbol was known across the Viking world as the sign of the Rus'. It is found in greatest numbers among the equipment of the warriors who garrisoned Birka, the market centre in Sweden, and some of the chapes appear to have been manufactured there. The falcon sigil is seen in graves all over Scandinavia, and above all it appears along the arterial river systems of Russia, Ukraine, and Eurasia. Somebody in the Groix burial had eastern connections, and in that he would not have been in the least unusual.

The Rus' appear in many written sources, as we have seen—in Frankish annals, Greek homilies, and imperial Byzantine bureaucracy; in the *Russian Primary Chronicle* of the eleventh century; and even in the works of the Icelandic historian Snorri Sturluson. The richest, most detailed descriptions of their activities are found in Arab texts, many of which are eyewitness accounts. It is also important to understand that the texts generally refer to two fundamentally different spheres of Rus' activity—the Arab descriptions connect them to the Volga and the Don, while the Byzantine and European sources relate to their travels along the Dniepr system.

The historical narrative for their origins as presented by the *Primary Chronicle*—the arrival of Rurik and his brothers in Ladoga—has been hotly debated, especially regarding their ethnicity. For many decades, opinions were largely divided between a so-called Normanist camp that advocated a strictly Scandinavian ancestry, and others that argued for a more Slavic background. The argument was complicated by an intense politicisation of these issues in the former Soviet Union, where an authentically 'Russian' historical identity was anything but an academic question.

This politicisation, which has thankfully now largely subsided, also affected perceptions of the people the Rus' encountered in the lower reaches of the Volga, the Dniepr, and other routes into the Black and Caspian Seas. On the steppe, the most important confederacy of peoples was that of the Khazars, who had migrated into the lower Volga region during the seventh century. Their presence had stopped Islamic northward expansion for three hundred years; they had even made incursions into the Caliphate on occasion. Other key players were the Volga Bulgars, who were initially one of the primary trading contacts for Scandinavian merchants. To the south and west, around the shores of the Black Sea, lay the lands of the Pechenegs and the Magyars. It has only been since the downfall of the USSR that these semi-nomadic steppe tribes have been widely recognised as a significant political and cultural factor in the Viking Age.

The mobile Scandinavians; the settled Byzantines, Slavs, and Bulghars; the nomadic Khazars, Pechenegs, and Magyars: all these peoples were moving parts in the vast machine of eastern trade, diplomacy, and the frequent warfare that erupted.

After the establishment of Ladoga, one of the next settlements to grow up on the rivers was Gorodishche, an island around 175 kilometres south of Staraja Ladoga on the Volkhov River, just to the north of Lake Ilmen. This was probably the early Rus' trading post recorded as *Holmgarðr*. The modern name means 'little fort', and the site was protected by a fortification of logs laid in ditches. Its emergence may indicate a logistical shift southward on the part of the Rus' themselves, in order to accommodate the rapid growth of their influence.

Evidence for the role of Scandinavian merchants in moving goods along the Volkhov can be seen in the form of a complete walrus tusk uncovered during the excavations. It probably came from the Arctic waters north of Russia, and may even have been obtained from the Sámi. The tusk could have been intended for the European trade and was perhaps to be a prestige gift. All of the more than thirty cultic objects found at the site are of Norse origin. There is now general agreement that the Scandinavian element at Gorodishche was both very large and unusually socially diverse. Judging by the material culture, they appear to have primarily come from central Sweden and the Mälar Valley—the heart of Viking-Age Svealand. Despite their significant numbers, these Scandinavian immigrants seem to have merged rapidly with the Slavic population. This transition in material expressions of identity may represent the formation of a class-based community, in which expressions of ethnicity were not prioritised as a means of identifying between different groups.

Some nine hundred kilometres to the south of Staraja Ladoga in modern Ukraine, another major node on the river trade grew up on the Dniepr, at what is now Kiev. According to the *Primary Chronicle*, it was founded by one Oleg (Helgi), a Scandinavian relative of Rurik, who expanded the Rus' territories along the river and needed a more southerly base. This was to have long-lasting effects; as the fledgling state continued to grow, it would come into increasing contact and conflict with the steppe nomads inhabiting the area to the south along the Volga River. These peoples, as well as others on the lower reaches of the Dniepr and Dniestr Rivers, were themselves vying for power while attempting to maintain an amicable relationship with the Byzantine Empire, which was also concerned with strategically expanding its territories in the Black Sea region. By the late tenth century, Kievan Rus' was a power to be reckoned with.

Kiev seems to have developed as a fortified centre at some point during the late ninth century, and expanded rapidly thereafter. The settlement began as a series of small villages that slowly grew and eventually converged. A fortified centre was established on Starokievskaja hill, and on the banks of the Dniepr lay the waterfront community in what is now the Podil neighbourhood. While there seems to have been a minority Scandinavian elite presence in the city, here again there also seems to have been a relatively rapid assimilation of local culture.

Around the year 900, the hillfort at Staraja Ladoga was destroyed and replaced by a wall that enclosed the whole settlement. The 'Deadwood' of the East had become almost respectable—a consolidated, fortified strongpoint at the entrance to the Volkhov. Around the same time, another river route opened up along the Daugava through what is now Latvia, guarded by systems of hillforts.

In the fifty years from around 875 to 925, western European merchants gradually stopped coming to places like Birka and the Mälar Valley, and new contacts emerged almost wholly oriented towards the east. In Denmark, however, the trade remained focussed west and south. These shifts are reflected in many proxies, such as the fashion for Frankish clothes in the ninth century, overtaken by baggy pantaloons of eastern cut in the 900s.

In the early to mid-tenth century, the settlement at Gorodishche expanded to the nearby site of modern Novgorod, literally the 'new fortress', though to the Vikings it was still Holmgarðr. The settlement that lies on the two southernmost hills there, one on each bank of the Volkhov, has been dated to the 950s, with the earliest phases of occupation on the kremlin hill some twenty years later. Excavations since the time of Stalin have uncovered deeply stratified, waterlogged deposits that have preserved minute details of life in the city during the Viking Age and the medieval period. These included superimposed layers of wooden planked streets, laid down on top of each other as the ground rose within the settlement due to the accumulation of waste and everyday detritus. Structures within fenced enclosures were preserved to such a degree that it is possible to identify porches, yards, and even evidence for different architectural techniques. These included various types of timber joins, as well as several different models of wooden guttering that were installed by the citizens of Novgorod on the roofs of their houses. Also preserved are more personal items—including musical instruments, masks, toy weapons, and dolls—allowing daily life within the settlement to be reconstructed with vivid clarity.

The tenth century also saw the rise of another major Rus' settlement, at Gnezdovo, near modern Smolensk at the confluence of the Dniepr and Svinets rivers. This was the point at which boats were portaged from the Volkhov and Lovat system a short distance south to enter the main Dniepr flow, allowing them to travel all the way to the Black Sea. Gnezdovo supported the familiar multi-ethnic population, with Scandinavians predominating, and grew eventually almost to the size of urban Hedeby in Denmark. It had several focal centres surrounded by cemeteries of different character, and the feel of the place would have been familiar to travellers from the North. Gnezdovo was somewhere to resupply, refit, and rest before continuing the journey north or south, but it was also a destination in its own right—a trading site where one could make a living. Like early Ladoga, it was probably pretty rough.

From the mid-tenth century onwards, many of the Scandinavians who made the journey south arrived in Constantinople seeking employment in the armies of the Byzantine Empire. In time, the emperors' personal bodyguard would come to consist almost entirely of Scandinavian warriors. This so-called Varangian Guard was named after the Old Norse word for an oath, *vár* (as in the English 'vow'). Identifiable by their characteristic battle-axes (and famed for their drinking), the guard was constituted in the late tenth century and remained dominated by Scandinavians for a hundred years, until increasing numbers of English exiles began to join in the wake of the Norman conquest.

Numerous sagas record individuals travelling to Constantinople to join the guard, and a number of runestones from Sweden also name individuals dying abroad in 'Greece', most probably in the service of the Empire. One of these, from Kyrkstigen in Uppland, is dedicated to a man named Ragnvaldr, who was apparently a commander of a troop within the guard itself. Of all the Scandinavians who ventured south to fight for the emperor, the most famous was Harald Sigurdsson, later King Harald 'Hard-Ruler' of Norway. Having earlier found employment in the armies of Kiev, he served as a captain in the Varangian Guard for several years during the 1030s and 1040s (and was even rumoured to have had an affair with the empress) before returning to Norway to make his bid for power.

While little physical evidence for the Scandinavian presence in Constantinople is evident today, some striking examples have survived in the Ayasofya, or Hagia Sophia, cathedral. Originally built as an Orthodox basilica in the sixth century, Hagia Sophia was converted into a mosque following the Ottoman conquest of the city in 1453; today it serves as a museum. In the Viking Age, it was the main place of worship for the imperial family. Several runic inscriptions have been found there, scratched into column bases and the like, including many etched into the balustrades of the upper gallery. This is where the imperial family were seated when attending public ceremonies, and they would have been accompanied by the Varangians. One imagines guard members standing on watch—bored by yet another interminable service in a language they didn't understand—using a palmed blade to surreptitiously carve their names for posterity.

The Rus' saw military service not only in Byzantium but also in Kiev, where they furthered the expansionist policies of the local dynasties and quickly settled. Their military structures are still poorly understood. In Khazaria, the realm of the steppe nomads by the Caspian Sea, Rus' had been captured in battle and then incorporated into the Khazar armies as something not far from slave-soldiers, as seen in the *Russian Primary Chronicle* and the important account of al-Mas'ūdī. There seems to have been a 'Varangian Guard' there too, perhaps even earlier than its counterpart in Byzantium. Rus' mercenaries also served in Georgia, among the Volga Bulghars, even in Poland and Hungary. Many Viking weapons have been recovered from the Danube, and two swords have been found during excavations in the far south of Turkey along the eastern Mediterranean coast—one at Patara, the ancient capital of the Lycia region, and a second at Yumuktepe in Muğla. These are sparse traces, to be sure, but they are nonetheless material evidence of Rus' activity along and beyond the imperial frontiers.

From the early 900s onwards, there were also a number of large-scale raids in the Caspian Sea region. Al-Mas'ūdī, writing in his *Meadows of Gold and Mines of Jewels*, notes that around 912 the Rus' came from the Sea of Azov, where they had a base, and devastated the lands around the Caspian. His account includes many interesting details. We learn that the Rus' were made up of several different groups, that they lived in the lands of the Khazars and around the Caspian littoral, that they had many merchants but no king, and that they burnt their dead on enormous pyres. Crucially, al-Mas'ūdī seems to have heard of the great raids on Iberia launched from the Loire bases, and he is one of the writers who explicitly says that these people—that is, Scandinavian Vikings—were the same as the Rus'.

Another Rus' eastern raid, in 943, seems to have been conducted with the intention of establishing hegemony over the Caspian. During this raid the Rus' captured the city of Bardha'a, in modern-day Azerbaijan, where they spent several months plundering the city and the surrounding countryside. It was only due to an outbreak of dysentery among the fleet that Islamic forces were able to drive the Rus' out of the region. A leading scholar of Viking warfare has perceptively suggested that there is actually little difference between these large, mobile military expeditions of the Rus' and the pirate polities of the West, such as the Great Army. Researchers have become accustomed to using different terminologies to describe them, but in reality they may well have been very similar. Just as the Rus' evolved politically, there may have been many variants of the form that their power took, and perhaps there were hydrarchies in the East as well.

These raids almost certainly contributed to tensions between the Rus' and the Khazars, through whose lands the Rus' had to pass in order to access the Caspian. In the 960s, Sviatoslav of Kiev—a man of clear Scandinavian descent—went to war against the Khazars and destroyed their capital at Atil, paving the way for Rus' dominance over the entire length of the Volga. Raiding expeditions into the lands that lay between the Black Sea and the Caspian Sea would continue into the eleventh century, at which time, during the reign of Jaroslav I, Kiev was enclosed within a massive circuit of earthen defences. Its walls were pierced by elaborate and monumental fortified gateways, one of which, the Golden Gate, still survives in heavily reconstructed form, topped by an Orthodox church.

As the power of the Rus' grew, the influence of the eastern routes to the Khazars diminished, and the north-south riverine trade was reorganised and streamlined as a mercantile venture with Kiev as one of its major focal points (the other one being Novgorod). It is at around this time that a true state-based Rus' identity seems to have emerged. The late tenth century would see the Rus' polity become a leading actor in an increasingly complex and fluid political arena of diplomatic negotiation, betrayal, and warfare. Crucially, it was deeply integrated with Europe, and from the tenth century onwards the rulers of eastern Scandinavia were sending their daughters to new husbands among the princes of Novgorod and Kiev. The river route even had a specific name in Scandinavia, Garðariki, 'land of the settlements'.

The political machinations of this period have left other monuments, too, such as the unique group of more than thirty runestones in central Sweden that record men who died "in the east with Ingvar". A commander of that name is the subject of a particularly fanciful legendary saga, where he is given the nickname 'the Far-Travelled', but there are other sources that enable a fragmentary picture to be pieced together. Ingvar seems to have been a young leader from central Sweden who in 1036 led an unusually large fleet into the East. The stones clearly commemorate a real expedition; it was obviously something out of the ordinary, different from the regular Rus' journeys to the Black Sea. Ingvar seems to have headed to the Caspian and then somehow gone beyond the borders of the known Rus' world and thus, in the Viking mind, into a sort of semi-mythical place. This may explain the drama of his saga, the impact that it had back home (as we can see from the runestones), and also, not least, the fact that in 1041 Ingvar died out there with most of his men. More prosaically, his expedition has been interpreted as a concerted political act, conducted with an aim of expanding the Rus' sphere of influence into the area of modern-day Georgia.

Ingvar's expedition clearly lived a very long time in the memory of the North, and rumours of it must have spread far and wide (even Adam of Bremen mentions it, thirty years after Ingvar's death). There is no runestone to Ingvar himself, but one to his brother Harald survives at Gripsholm on the southern shore of Lake Mälaren in central Sweden. It is a rare example of a runic inscription with a verse of poetry, and in its laconic elegance is one of the finest epitaphs of the Viking Age:

Tóla had this stone raised in memory of her son Harald,
Ingvar's brother.
They travelled like men far for gold,
and in the east gave [food] to the eagle.
[They] died in the south, in Serkland.

Over time the Rus' grew more belligerent and aggressive in asserting their rights to the river trade. Although they depended on the markets of the Byzantine Empire for their continued survival, disputes between the Rus' and the imperial forces led to frequent conflicts, and Byzantine sources record them as conducting several major attacks on Constantinople itself. After one such assault, having been unable to breach the massive walls of the city, the Rus' leader is said to have nailed his shield to the gates in contempt.

A magnificent though rather inadvertent monument to the Rus' survives in the form of the monumental Piraeus Lion, a massive marble statue of the fourth century BCE that is now outside the Arsenal in Venice (plundered in an early modern war) but which once stood on the dockside at the harbour of Athens. Its shoulders and sides are covered with several very elaborate runic inscriptions that must have taken time, effort, and skill to carve. In a new interpretation, they read:

> They cut [the runes], the men of the host [. . .] but in this harbour those men cut runes after Haursi, the farmer [. . .] Svear men applied this on the lion. He fell before he could receive payment.
>
> Young warriors cut the runes.
>
> Åsmund carved these runes, they, Eskil [?], Thorlev and [. . .]

One can almost see it—the Aegean sun on the water, the great lion on the quayside, and perhaps the locals looking on nervously as a group of young Varangians climbed all over it, chiselling away in honour of their dead friend. This was a memorial that nobody who came to the port of Athens could miss. This is relevant because the Piraeus inscriptions testify to other qualities and priorities too. The fact that a man was honoured appropriately—noting that he had fulfilled his oaths and would have been paid, had he not been killed—was important, as was the fact that his memorial was made on so prominent a landmark (the port was even known as the 'harbour of the lion') that it could have been visited in the future. The group of Varangians also clearly included a poet, again pointing to the weight placed upon a proper record. Scandinavians who served abroad did so in the knowledge that, if they never came back, someone would still remember them.

At least in the early tenth century, it is possible that some of the Rus' were essentially river police, the guards who guaranteed the trade. Recalling the people in the Birka chamber burials—the mounted archers with their recurved bows and special thumb rings—the Rus' appear as military elites who have adopted the best equipment and tactics of those they might have to fight. Ornate silks and kaftans have been found in graves across Scandinavia, and depictions on Gotlandic picture-stones of warriors wearing the wide, baggy trousers that characterised Persian and Arab fashion similarly imply that Viking dress codes were infused with an element of foreign flair. The same individuals also had armour of Byzantine type, as well as the lamellar that was particular to the mounted steppe nomads of Eurasia—all while the isotopes and genomic analyses indicate they themselves were of Scandinavian origin. In a way, this almost appears to be a uniform—not in the sense of identical clothes but in a recognised repertoire of symbolism and style, what one scholar has called a "Turkic military outfit". As before, one image stands out: the chapes of their sword scabbards marked with a falcon swooping to attack, the badge of the Rus'.

Numerous runestones, such as this one from Turinge in Swedish Södermanland, evocatively record men who died in the East:

> Ketil and Björn, they raised this stone in memory of Thorstein, their father; Ônund in memory of his brother and the huskarls [i.e., the retinue] in memory of the [. . . and] Ketiley in memory of her husbandman.
>
> These brothers were
> the best of men
> in the land
> and abroad in the *lið*,
> held their huskarls well.

21. The sign of the Rus'. A bronze scabbard chape found in the urban area at Birka, Sweden. Its design combines the diving falcon motif characteristic of the Rus', with a human figure transforming into the bird—perhaps the god Odin stealing the mead of poetry. Photo: Gabriel Hildebrand, Swedish History Museum, Creative Commons.

> He fell in battle
> in the east in Garðar [Russia],
> commander of the *lið*,
> the best of landholders.

Here is another, also from Södermanland:

> Styrlaug and Holm raised the stones next to the path in memory of their brothers. They met their end on the eastern route, Thorkell and Strybjörn, good retainers.

Other runestones give us glimpses of a dangerous life in the river towns, as in the monument raised to one Sigvíth, who "fell in Holmgarðr [Novgorod], the ship's leader with the seamen".

Even those who came home were altered by what they had seen and done in the 'land of settlements'. Although they are a late source, several sagas describe the difficulties experienced by men who returned to Iceland from lengthy periods spent out East on Varangian service. They seem to have acquired qualities abroad that set them apart from their former neighbours, a different moral compass perhaps, even a legacy of battlefield trauma that we might call PTSD. These eastern veterans had problems fitting in, finding themselves changed men in an unchanged land.

In the East itself, burials throughout the river systems also show the presence of the Rus'. Excavations at settlements and cemeteries, including Staraja Ladoga and Gnezdovo, have identified Scandinavian-style finds. At least twenty-four sites on the upper Volga contain Scandinavian material, often in great quantity, including weapons, jewellery, and amulets relating to Norse beliefs. Graves there exhibit burial rites familiar from the Viking homelands. New archaeological work has shown that the distribution extended well beyond the proto-urban centres, indicating how the Rus' expanded their control over the river basins. On the waterways themselves, small fortifications probably acted as customs points.

Several tenth-century graves with clear Scandinavian material components contain double interments of a man and woman together. Their body positions are hard to interpret but suggest an intimate relationship between the people in life, and moreover one that was deliberately signalled. In the Shestovytsya grave-field near Chernihiv, in Ukraine, for example, a chamber grave contains a man with his left arm around the shoulders of a woman laid out beside him, both dressed in eastern fashion. At Podgortsy, near L'viv, a man with Scandinavian weaponry was buried linking arms with a woman; in another grave from the same cemetery, a couple hold hands. In several cases the women are substantially smaller than the men—perhaps teenage girls. Are these gestures of affection, of possessive control or literal ownership, of intimacy or coercion, or of still other relationships?

For the Scandinavians operating in Kievan Rus', life in the East, as in the other Viking colonies, introduced new challenges and possibilities. Cultural traits and social customs can develop their own unique trajectory when part of a frontier lifestyle, and it has been suggested that women might have adopted new roles among the mercantile groups of the East. They are mentioned several times in ibn Faḍlān's description of the Rus', with his first-hand observations of their fashions and jewellery. This implies that parties of Scandinavian merchants travelling south to the Byzantine Empire, like those who lived among the large raiding fleets of ninth-century Europe, included families—an interesting observation that has not received the attention it deserves. Interactions went both ways, of course. A famous Viking of the late ninth century, a man called Geirmund Hjørson, was the son of a Norwegian trader and a Samoyed woman from northern Siberia. He was so dark and unusual in his looks that he earned the nickname *heljar-skinn*, 'black-skin'. Not only did he suffer no notable social detriment, he became one of the leading men of Iceland.

Over time, the river world of the Rus' changed dramatically—from its origins as the arena of Viking *voyageurs* to a mighty state that would ultimately play a part in the evolution of Russia itself. The decisive shift came in the late tenth century, when the Rus' *archon* (war leader) Vladimir married into the Byzantine royal family, accepted baptism, and adopted Christianity as the religion of the state. The Rus' would be further drawn into the Byzantine world. The emergence of the word 'Varangian', used by them to denote new arrivals from Scandinavia, suggests that by then they wanted to explicitly distance themselves from their Baltic roots: the Kiev state was shaping its own future, and in the process perhaps judiciously rewriting its past. By the end of the Viking Age, the lands of Kievan Rus' extended from the Black Sea to Lake Ladoga.

Having reached the Byzantine Empire and the south-eastern shores of the Caspian Sea, the Scandinavians found themselves on the very doorstep of the great Abbasid Caliphate. At the height of its power in the ninth century, a great swathe of territory from modern-day Tunisia to Uzbekistan was ruled from Baghdad.

There is no knowing how many Scandinavians made the journey into the interior of the Caliphate, but some certainly did so. Several runic inscriptions commemorate individuals who travelled to Serkland—'Saracen Land'—the same place named on the Ingvar stones. This was a vague term for what was probably a rather vague region, at least as seen from a Swedish farm. Just as with the ambiguities of the Rus' label, Serkland seems to have referred to somewhere 'way out east', although with general connotations of Arabia.

As early as the 840s, in his *Book of Itineraries and Kingdoms*, the Arab geographer ibn Khurradādhbih noted that Rus' merchants would bring their goods overland to Baghdad by camel from the Caspian Sea shore. They had Slavs with them who served as interpreters when they wanted to speak to Arabs, but there are also signs that some Scandinavians also spoke Arabic. The script became part of their visual culture, when it was written (usually incorrectly) on merchants' weights—an indication of how 'proper' balances 'ought' to look. In Baghdad, ibn Khurradādhbih goes on, the Rus' pretended to be Christians so as to pay lower taxes as monotheists—even in the heart of the Middle East, they had useful local knowledge that enabled them to game the system. The implication is that by the early ninth century, the Rus' were already quite well known around the Caspian and the region north of the Caucasus.

Just as with the Scandinavian encounter with Byzantium, the sheer impact of a place like Baghdad must have been enormous. It had been established by the Abbasids in the early 760s and was thus a relatively young settlement. Visitors would first pass through extensive suburbs, irrigated via canals that drew precious water from the Tigris. The city itself was entered by four monumental gates that pierced a double wall of defences. Inside, the main commercial and residential areas of the city formed two concentric rings within the fortifications. In their centre—surrounded by extraordinary gardens—lay the caliphal palace, the administrative buildings, and the main mosque. At its zenith during the ninth century, Baghdad and its hinterland supported a population of up to nine hundred thousand people, making it one of the largest cities in the world at the time and even bigger than Constantinople.

Scandinavian contacts with the Caliphate have left few material traces, but those that remain can be dramatic in their implications. The inscription on a rather nondescript runestone from Stora Rytterne in Swedish Västmanland records a most unusual place-name:

> Gudleif placed the staff and these stones
> in memory of Slagvi,
> his son, who met his end in the east, in Karusm.

The last word has been read as an Old Norse approximation of Khwārazm, an oasis area south of the Aral Sea in what is now Uzbekistan—a long way to go for a young man from a Mälar farm. The very modesty of the stone is telling in that this was not a record of an extraordinary journey; it was something normal. Moreover, the very fact of its existence not only testifies to a youthful adventure with a tragic end; it also shows that somebody else made it back to tell the family. Like many such memorials, the stone was set up in the absence of a body; the story came home to Sweden when the man did not.

Some scholars have seen evidence for a failed Islamic mission to Scandinavia in the large numbers of imported Arab objects found there, often inscribed with religious messages. These include a censer and a number of bronze flasks excavated in Sweden and the Åland islands, all bearing Islamic religious inscriptions. It is possible that these were originally made for some liturgical function—perhaps to purify the water used in washing before prayer. Not least, every single Arab coin carried an exhortation to God.

22. Journey to the Aral Sea. Eleventh-century runestone Vs 1 from Stora Rytterne in Västmanland, Sweden, set up by a father to commemorate his son Slagvi, who died at the Khwārazm oasis in what is now Uzbekistan. Photo: Berig, Creative Commons.

Although hard to prove, such an endeavour would be in keeping with similar efforts to convert the steppe peoples to Islam.

Some travellers from the Middle East clearly did visit Scandinavia. There is the woman apparently of Persian origin in the Oseberg ship burial, who it should be remembered was jointly afforded the most extravagant funeral ever documented in Scandinavia. Other Arab visitors also met a favourable reception, as seen in the affections lavished in Denmark on the handsome Andalusian diplomat al-Ghazāl, 'the Gazelle'. There must have been exceptions, of course, but tolerance seems to have been a Viking virtue.

The core of the trade with the Caliphate was in silver. It has been estimated that up to 125 million dirhams, representing approximately 340 tons of metal, moved into northern and eastern Europe in the tenth century. It is unsurprising that many other middlemen between Arabia and the Baltic wanted a cut of the trade. The Rus' exchanged with them all, at markets where merchants of all lands gathered to buy and sell. It was at one such place, in 922, that ibn Faḍlān recorded the pragmatic prayer of one of these Rus' travellers, who was making offerings to wooden pillars at the Bulghar market by the Volga shore:

> I want you to bless me with a rich merchant with many dinars and dirhams, who will buy from me whatever I wish and not haggle over any price I set.

The dirhams were brought to Scandinavia in packages direct from the mints, without being separated, as can be seen from the die-linked sequences of coins. The island of Gotland was the primary Baltic node in the routes to the east. During the tenth century in southern Denmark, Hedeby formed another of the vital European conduits for the dirham trade. As well as providing tax and border tolls, the town connected Scandinavia, the Continent, and the Baltic, all areas into which the eastern silver was redistributed. Arab silver has even been found in the ingots of the Danelaw, perhaps brought over as bullion by southern Scandinavian immigrants to England. There was a hiatus in the flow of silver for the last thirty or forty years of the ninth century, before it resumed in the form of Sāmānid dirhams. From around 890 to 930, the silver stream to Scandinavia was continuous, and massive. Most of the examples from Gotland and Estonia are whole coins, while they get progressively more fragmented as one moves, in turn, through mainland Sweden to Denmark, Poland, and what is now the Czech Republic. The trade route moved anticlockwise around the Baltic, with Sweden (and probably Birka) as the key point of entry after the transit through Gotland.

These locations may also mark the intermediaries of the slave trade, for which the flow of silver provides a detectible proxy. It left other signs, too, for example the massive programme of hillfort construction in the Polish Pyast state, which links to the influx of the first dirhams there in 940. It seems the Poles were building defences against the predatory slave-raiding of the Rus' that is mentioned in the Arab sources.

The sale of captives could bring a variety of goods in return, especially on the eastern routes—including livestock, textiles and clothing, even salt and spices. However, slaves were always a risky commodity, prone to ill health and potentially dying en route. For this reason, slaving was most often a component in a more diversified trade. This aspect of the Viking economy, and the mind-set behind it, can be traced throughout their diaspora, but nowhere more so than in the East.

There were, of course, other wares, especially silk. It has even been suggested that the word 'Serkland' itself may have referred to the fabric, as denoting the place where (silk) shirts, *serkr*, came from. Some twenty-three sites with excavated silk are known from Scandinavia, all from the ninth and tenth centuries. The number of individual finds is staggering, impressive in themselves, but all the more so because of what they imply about how much was originally there. At Birka alone, there are sixty-one graves containing silk, mostly from the Near East and Byzantium, with some that had travelled all the way from Tang Dynasty China; silk is present in about 30 percent of all Birka burials in which textiles survive. In the magnificent Oseberg ship burial, there are more than one hundred silk fragments, from up to fifteen different fabrics of varying quality. Some of the pieces had been reused, showing the high value placed on even tiny scraps. Even the burial chamber on the deck was lined with silk. At Valsgärde in Swedish Uppland, most of the Viking-Age boat graves contain silk clothing details used to trim cuffs and collars, or to provide facings on jackets. The mixture of styles suggests that the meaning of the motifs had not been transferred along with the fabric.

The Tang silks may have come to the North via the Persian Gulf. As ever, the evidence is very sparse, but it has been suggested that the best explanation of rock carvings found overlooking the waters at Jabal Jusasiyah in northern Qatar is that they depict Viking oared ships. There is no certainty here, but they would not be out of place given what we know of the Rus' connections to trade routes extending farther east to the Indian Ocean and beyond.

Two twinned objects illustrate the breadth of the diaspora, linking East and West in the most human of ways.

In the Viking-Age colonies in England, some decades ago archaeologists excavating well-preserved, waterlogged deposits made two remarkable finds. In the urban centre of York, and also in Lincoln (one of the Danelaw's Five Boroughs), tenth-century occupation layers produced fragments of silk that originally were part of delicate caps worn by women over their hair. Repeatedly repaired and well cared for, they must have been precious things indeed. The cloth seems to have originated in Persia or, just possibly, China. Almost incredibly, analysis of an unusual fault in the weave has shown that *the pieces come from the same bale of silk*. The sheer improbability of making two independent discoveries that connect in this way is one thing, but it also suggests that the trade may in fact have been relatively small. A single enterprising merchant, with luck and judgement, could have brought back a bolt of cloth big enough to go a very long way when sold in modest lengths.

Goods journeying from the Silk Roads to northern England: it would be hard to find a better image of the Scandinavian achievement over just two centuries, and of individuals' places within it. The final acts of the era, however, focussed inwards. A new faith and new models of rulership would combine to permanently transform the North itself, and, in the process, bring an end to the age of the Vikings.

16

THE EXPERIMENTS OF MONARCHY

THE TWIN POWERS OF CHURCH and state, and the degree of separation advisable between them, have been two of the basic building blocks of western European nationhood for at least fifteen hundred years. They were no less fundamental in the rise of the Nordic nations and in the consolidation of their rulers as monarchs at the head of unified kingdoms. As ever, behind these forces of social and political change were other drivers rooted more crudely in the economics of profit, and the power to use it. The cycle of raiding, slaving, and trading fed the diaspora and was in part responsible for it—but it also enabled transformation back in Scandinavia itself. The later Viking Age saw a far greater *direction* of cause and effect than in the ninth and early tenth centuries—a deeper understanding of the governmental demands that new forms of overseas ventures could supply. This political awakening harnessed and activated the new economic potential of the North, and set Scandinavia on the path to Nordic monarchies in the arena of literate, Christian Europe.

There was no linear process of mission and conversion in the transition to a new faith, nor can we necessarily speak of the replacement of one religion by another, even in the late Viking Age. That some people believed in a single God, his ever-living son, the Holy Spirit, and the community of saints was known to Scandinavians from at least the seventh century and probably much earlier. They would have encountered the Christian pious abroad in their travels as merchants, and would have seen priests in the settlements they visited. Christians occasionally appeared at home, too—foreigners were nothing new in late Iron Age Scandinavia, and the beliefs of such visitors encompassed a whole spectrum of different gods, including the one they called the White Christ. In fact, this conversation had been going on in Europe at least since the days of the later Roman Empire, when Christianity, Judaism, and an array of alternatives had been offering their own competing propositions on the Other World(s) to a populace that in practice usually preferred to pick and mix.

Even in the first raids, the monasteries were chosen as targets precisely because the Vikings knew what they were, or at least had a good idea what they contained. It must have been clear that the cloisters and chapels had to do with religion and the worship of a deity, and the notion of ritual buildings where one entered the presence of the divine was entirely intelligible.

There seems to have been a modest attempt to bring Christianity to Scandinavia even before the raids, in the early eighth century. The Danes' proximity to the faithful of the European Continent ensured they were the first recipients of the Word. Alcuin, the same English cleric who wrote with such outrage about the attack on Lindisfarne in 793, also compiled biographical notes on past evangelicals, including Willibrord of Northumbria, who crossed the Danish border in about 710. Willibrord does not seem to have convinced many, but he was nonetheless allowed to leave with some thirty youths who presumably were to be trained in the gospel. For a century after Willibrord, there are no records of missionary activity in the North, and by then the raids had not only begun, but had started to escalate.

This is important because it is clear that monks and lay brothers were among the captives taken on the Vikings' plundering expeditions. We do not know what happened to these people, but it is conceivable—even likely—that for some in Scandinavia, the nervously expressed ideas of their new thralls were a first contact with the Christian faith. In the 820s, Archbishop Ebbo of Reims was sent into Denmark at the behest of not only the Frankish emperor but also the pope himself. During his year there, he managed to baptise a few converts; a modest beginning, it is true, but this was more than any of his known predecessors had been able to do.

The Christian message could also be communicated through objects, either actively or by chance. A high-status settlement on the island of Helgö, in Lake Mälaren, Sweden, was occupied into the early Viking Age, and finds from the excavations there include a Coptic scoop and an Irish crozier head. The latter is especially striking as it must have been the personal property of a bishop, and hardly an item to be willingly given or traded. How these items arrived at Helgö is unknown, but it is possible they came as loot with raiders returning from the west. Equally, it could be that the sacral nature of these objects was known to the Scandinavians, and this is why they were taken. Helgö actually means 'Holy Island', and other ritual artefacts from different faiths had also found their way there. The most spectacular was a sixth-century bronze statue of the Buddha, made in the Swat Valley on the Afghan border and presumably brought to Scandinavia along the early versions of the eastern trade routes. The Buddha had been adapted to Northern religious taste, being provided with leather rings around its arm and neck, just like the contemporary wooden figures found in Danish bogs, presumed to represent deities.

The Christian powers of Continental Europe used any method available to effect conversions. Three years after Ebbo of Reims came back from Denmark, a political exile named Harald Klak turned up at the Frankish court. He claimed to have been forced from power following a civil conflict in Denmark and requested assistance from the emperor. The imperial response was apparently to make practical aid contingent on baptism, and Harald and his followers were duly welcomed into the faith. Heading back to Denmark, his party was accompanied by the missionary Anskar, who founded some kind of monastery in the region north of the Elbe River. This man was to play an important role in the conversion story.

The main source for Anskar's mission is a biography by his contemporary, Rimbert. It relates how, in 829, Anskar was invited to visit Birka as a guest of King Björn, who seems to have been in charge there. He spent eighteen months in and around the trading centre and baptised many people, including the royal agent. He returned to the Frankish Empire in 831 and was appointed archbishop of Hamburg, which was amalgamated with the see of Bremen following a Viking attack on the city in 845. Anskar maintained an interest in evangelising the North and returned to Sweden twice before his death in 865. Further missions to the region were conducted by his later successor, Gautbert.

At Uppåkra in southern Sweden, the long-lived cult house went out of use in the early ninth century, perhaps the result of a targeted Christian mission. Among the finds on the site were several objects with Christian symbolic themes, and this could be evidence of an attempt to actively influence the religious thought of the local people.

It was probably no accident that all the initial missions seem to have been pitched through Scandinavian rulers. Viking-Age elites held both secular and ritual power, and were thus potentially able to influence their people's view of such things. The Church was careful to work first on them, attempting to accelerate the conversion of the North by working from the top down (as had happened in the Roman Empire itself in the fourth century). The patronage of a baptised Scandinavian king would lead to thousands of ordinary converts, as the missionaries were quick to realise.

Anskar's successes at Birka may have left a trace in a number of graves near the hillfort that have been argued to reflect Christian practice. The burials include both adults and children, also unusual for the site. Cross pendants have been found in some graves, along with a type of cross-decorated jug from the Rhineland that some scholars see as a liturgical vessel. But these were modest achievements, and it is clear that for all Anskar's efforts, Birka never became a Christian settlement but remained firm in its adherence to the old beliefs.

Fascinating insights into the nature and reality of the early missions can be had from sources such as Widukind's *History of the Saxons*, written around 968, which describes the conversion of a later Danish king. From the ambiguous way in which he charts the context of the royal baptism, it is clear that while the Danes are in many senses Christians, they also happily retain many of their earlier beliefs. The task of the missions was not conversion, as such, but the practical demonstration of Christ's power through action.

There is a remarkable glimpse of how this worked in practice through a document known as *Heliand*, 'The Saviour'. Written in Old Saxon during the first half of the ninth century, it is a paraphrase of the gospel for a Germanic audience, tweaked for their sensibilities and pitched almost as a Norse saga though with biblical heroes. Thus we read of Jesus's birth in Galileeland, his later travels to Jerusalemburg, and how the Lord lives in a great hall in the sky (clearly Valhöll). The Lord's Prayer is in 'secret runes', Peter is given command over the gates of Hel (with one L), and so on. Satan's temptation of Christ takes place in a northern wilderness filled with vague forces, 'powerful beings' that seem to live among the trees, and one wonders what this implies of the traditional Northern beliefs that were known to the Christian clerics. By the same token, Jesus's disciples are 'warrior-companions', framed in the language of a warlord's retinue, and the Last Supper is the 'final mead-hall feast'. Even God is called by Odinnic epithets such as 'Victory-Chieftain' and 'All-Ruler'. This is the kind of message that was taken into Scandinavia by the first missionaries—a doctrine meshed with the ancestral stories of the North and following a model found in many other conversion histories.

It has sometimes been suggested that the Scandinavians' adoption of Christianity was mostly a veneer—lip service to the outward trappings of belief combined with regular church attendance, but in reality merely a thin covering over the old ways that persisted beneath. In all the debate concerning afterlives and the varying destinations offered by the traditional customs and the new religion, one wonders whether Viking-Age people might actually have *decided* where they wished to go after death. If so, what did they make of a faith in which the fate of a person's immortal soul was dependent on living a certain kind of life? It is hard to overstate how alien this concept may have seemed, although a cornerstone of many world faiths today.

The religious context of the sources is crucial here and affects the material culture as well. Much of what is known about the pre-Christian thought-world of the Vikings comes to us through the writings of, precisely, Christians. Even the framing story of this book—the creation of Ash and Elm—is relevant to this retrospective filter: how much of a coincidence is it that the 'first couple' in Norse cosmology have names beginning with A and E? Although the meaning of Askr/Ash is unequivocal, Embla is less certain. 'Elm' is the most commonly accepted translation, but the actual noun for an elm tree (*almr*) is masculine, and the etymology is convoluted. 'Vine' is another possibility, though this requires an ultimate derivation from Greek, and from there the scholarly debate starts to meander into the thickets of postulated Indo-European linguistic heritage. This kind of unresolved confusion—the ambiguities, contradictions, and possibilities—are all typical of the Viking-Age spiritual palimpsest, as we see it dimly in the rear-view from more than a millennium in its future.

The influence exercised by Christianity in the North was closely related to regional politics. Throughout the Viking Age, the number of small polities across Scandinavia was steadily decreasing, as the leading players in the region's power games absorbed the territories of their neighbours and rivals. Seen from the other end of that equation, other statelets found themselves coming under the rule of these rising kings. As part of the same process, the relative size of the Viking-Age polities increased. While the overall trajectory towards an eventual unification of the Nordic kingdoms seems relatively clear, what happened along the way was anything but linear and straightforward, and its progress is not easy to track. To take but one example, King Harald Finehair supposedly brought Norway under his control in the 870s, but it is obvious that practical power was retained at a local level until well into the tenth century.

Ascribing a date to the political unification of Denmark and Sweden is more difficult. In Denmark, centralised rule seems to have been achieved by the mid-tenth century, although by whom is uncertain. Danish kings such as Godfred were evidently able to initiate large-scale public works by the early 800s, and the consolidation of the kingdom at this time cannot be ruled out. However, the extensive political upheaval and civil war that is recorded as taking place in Denmark during the mid-ninth century implies there was still much to fight for in terms of power and territory. Sweden would remain fragmented well into the Middle Ages, despite the efforts of successive kings to assert their power over strongly independent regional elites. This situation is probably reflected in the fact that real progress in Christian conversion does not seem to have been made until the tenth century—in most regions, the catalyst for the spread of the new religion was the baptism of the kings themselves.

Christianity was attractive to Scandinavian rulers, although not necessarily to those they ruled, for several reasons. One was the more efficient collection of tax, made possible by the ordered division of territory that followed the establishment of parishes and dioceses. Stewardship of these entities lay in the royal gift, and provided another layer of incentive with which to motivate the retinues that ultimately buttressed a monarch's power. The impact on the populace was more profound, as the Church would come to restructure their lives, beginning with the rhythm of the day itself. A ringing bell was an aural imposition that could not be ignored, and was clearly resented (at Hedeby, a bell has been found in the harbour, where it must have been thrown; such an expensive object would otherwise have been recovered). The Christian ritual calendar was tightly regulated, governing what people could eat and how they worked and behaved; even the intimacies of their lives came under ecclesiastical scrutiny. This was a potent tool of power, as the kings were quick to recognise. At the highest level, the position and rights of the king were also given divine sanction, in a subtly different way than the descent they had earlier claimed from Odin and the other Norse gods.

The Church gained political influence through advising the crown, and in time became indispensable to the administration of the kingdom. Churches and monasteries ensured that the presence of Christian power was widely distributed, and these institutions were sometimes populated by men who in practice were secular elites and their kin.

Although this relationship between a would-be incoming Church and a burgeoning state might seem secure, the reality was more vulnerable—not least because of pushback from a rural populace that might have quite different ideas about the nature of power, where it came from, and how it should be wielded and distributed. Changes in the balance of regional forces, civil war, and political assassinations all had the potential to disrupt or even halt the spread of Christianity until rulers more congenial to the Church's objectives rose (or were assisted) to power.

The consolidation of the Danish kingdom in the tenth century shows how this worked in practice. Geographical location ensured that Denmark would see the first sustained efforts within Scandinavia for organised religious missions, with proximity to the German bishoprics providing easy access across the border. However, these seem to have met with relatively little success for the whole of the ninth century (Anskar's establishment of a church at Hedeby in 850 apparently did not last—remember that bell). The key change seems to have occurred a century later, with the accession of a new king who had very clear ideas of where he wanted Denmark to go. Around 960, Harald Bluetooth inherited power from his long-lived father, Gorm the Old, and appears to have been baptised only five years later. Harald's reign was characterised by the spread of Christianity across his kingdom, as well as by a marked cementation of royal authority expressed through an extraordinary programme of monumental engineering.

The core of Harald's power lay at Jelling, in the middle of the Jylland Peninsula. Effectively a capital, it was founded on land that was already well-settled, and there had been villages throughout the Jelling valley from pre-Viking times. Major excavations there have revolutionised our understanding of what Harald did at this site. Today, the most visible monuments at Jelling are two massive mounds—the construction of the northern barrow is dendrochronologically dated to 958–959 and its southern counterpart to the 970s. The northern mound, itself built over an existing Bronze Age funerary monument, may have been the original grave for Harald's father, but archaeological investigations revealed the burial to have been emptied in the Viking Age—possibly in order to extract Gorm's remains and place them inside the church that Harald later built between the mounds. The south barrow never contained a burial, which has been the cause of much speculation. Was it originally constructed in advance for Harald himself, but abandoned as a pagan monument after the king converted? Or was it simply part of the site's ritual symmetry?

Jelling was the site of the national assembly of the Danes, and lay no more than four days' travel from anywhere in the kingdom. Harald's first great project was an administrative centre rather than a royal residence, signalling acceptance of Christianity but on local terms. Its monumentality also evinced a rather nervous relationship with the imperial powers of Europe, modelled after their trappings of power but with a clear eye to 'authentically Danish' traditions. A link to the past was provided by a runestone set up by the late king:

King Gorm made this monument in memory of
Thyre, his wife, Denmark's adornment

Harald chose to build upon this in a similar medium, with what has become the ultimate symbol of the site: the famous Jelling runestone. Raised between the two mounds, in honour of his parents (and himself), the inscription reads:

King Harald ordered this monument made in memory of Gorm, his father, and in memory of Thyre, his mother; that Harald who won for himself all of Denmark and Norway and made the Danes Christian.

Most telling of all is the stone's unique design: the runes are laid out in horizontal lines, unlike every other regular stone, but exactly like a Latin text. The interlace motifs even act like the illuminated initials found in manuscripts. Harald was not only proclaiming his sovereignty and conversion of the country, he was doing it on a stone book.

Whether Harald truly 'won' all of Denmark, instead of expanding or merely inheriting his lands upon his father's death, is open to debate, and in this the Jelling stone should probably be seen as a piece of political propaganda rather than a realistic record of his own achievements. Harald was an expert at self-promotion.

The king's new model power centre enclosed the mounds within a massive palisaded enclosure, around twelve and a half hectares in size. Wood remains dated using the preserved tree rings give a range of 958–985 for the enclosure; the later dates probably indicate timbers used for repairs. Over a thousand trees, each at least a century old (and thus the product of careful management), were felled to make the palisade. Harald clearly commanded immense resources.

Around the inside of the enclosure walls, and aligned parallel to them, were longhouses of a new type that began to be built all over Denmark at this time. It seems that the royal taste was influential—either through emulation and fashion, or by command. Excavations have shown that the two mounds were built over the longest stone ship setting ever recorded in Scandinavia, some 360 metres in length and about 70 metres 'amidships'. Perhaps this was the 'monument' to Gorm's wife, mentioned on the stone he commissioned as her memorial. The north mound was sited exactly where the 'mast' of the stone ship would have been, and at the precise centre of the palisaded enclosure.

Administration aside, it is not entirely clear what the Jelling complex was actually for. Its date coincides with the refortification of the Danevirke, the defended earth and timber rampart along Denmark's southern border. It was at this time that its line was linked up with the walls of Hedeby, thus integrating the market centre into a coordinated frontier installation. At least in its earliest incarnations, Hedeby seems to have formed a kind of discrete cultural island south of the Danevirke, and may even have been a politically neutral free trade zone. It later became a key element in the defensive system of which the Danevirke was a part. The land route it controlled at the base of the Jylland Peninsula was critical due to the extreme natural hazards of the shipping passage through the Skagerrak into the Baltic. The Danish kingdom faced increasing threats from the Ottonian Empire to the south, and the construction of the enclosure at Jelling can in part be seen as a show of force for the benefit of this German audience.

Given Harald's ambitions and the attention he evidently paid to the trappings of power elsewhere in Scandinavia, the empty south mound at Jelling was possibly the start of an attempt to shape his own royal capital along the 'proper' model of much earlier foundations such as Gamla Uppsala and Lejre. Some twenty-two hectares of turf were dug up to construct the south mound at Jelling, representing the deliberate destruction of arable land—a significant demonstration and commitment. Even the location of a ship setting adjacent to a mound can be paralleled at places such as Anundshög in Swedish Västmanland, another site within the traditional territory of the Ynglinga dynasty. If the combination of hall buildings and ancestral barrows was the going fashion, Harald may have decided to join the kingly club on a monumental scale unrivalled in Scandinavia—a pattern of dictatorial architectural egotism familiar from more recent times.

King Harald's energetic commissions did not stop with Jelling. Towards the end of his reign, he expanded his programme of monumental constructions with an extravagance that indirectly led to the rebellion that eventually toppled him. While building work was still ongoing at Jelling, he also ordered a huge bridge to be set up some ten kilometres to the south-west at Ravning Enge. Like the stone ship, it is the largest of its kind ever found in Scandinavia: 760 metres long and 5 metres wide, broad enough for two carts to pass each other. Made of a timber walkway elevated on piles sunk into marshy ground, the posts were so large as to essentially be shaped tree trunks. The strangest thing about the bridge is that it takes an unnecessarily long route across the marshy valley. Could it have been a deliberate folly, or purely a statement of power?

The most spectacular remnants of Harald's reign (or megalomania) are the famous Trelleborg-type fortresses, of which five are known so far. These include Trelleborg itself and Borgring on Sjælland, Nonnebakken on Fyn, and Aggersborg and Fyrkat in northern Jylland. A sixth fortification of uncertain relationship to the others has left traces at Borgeby in Skåne, southern Sweden, which was then part of Denmark. All of them were exactly circular with massive ramparts, faced on both sides with vertical logs and topped by palisaded walkways. Inside, each had a cruciform plan made of intersecting streets leading to gates at the points of the compass. Exactly surveyed courtyards were laid out in the four quadrants of the interior, filled with high-end longhouses of the same type as at Jelling. Most of the fortress ramparts still stand and are of near identical dimensions, about 120 metres in diameter, the exception being Aggersborg, which is much larger at 240 metres. All of them are prominent in the landscape and served as highly visible symbols of power.

They all seem to have been constructed at the same time, in the early 980s. The political situation in Denmark deteriorated towards the end of Harald's reign, with tensions on the German border and civil unrest. The fortresses may have been staging points for a planned invasion of Schleswig, or defensive sites designed to protect Harald's territory from external threats. They might even have been intended to suppress the Danish population itself, which would explain why all the known fortresses were situated in relatively densely populated areas, with good access to land routes and waterways.

Exactly who was housed in the fortresses is also unclear—they were administrative as well as military centres, and their population certainly included women (one of them, at Fyrkat, was buried with all the trappings of a pagan sorceress, which sheds light on the realities of Harald's claim to have converted the Danes). An isotope study of eleven individuals from a mass grave within the cemetery at Trelleborg has revealed that a number of the dead were not locals, but came from the Slavonic and north German coast, and perhaps even from southern Norway—all areas under Danish control during Harald's reign. It may be that, as in medieval armies, King Harald relied on mercenaries to support his rule.

He also seems to have targeted his rivals, and perhaps dissenting citizenry, through their means of ritual expression and identity. As we have seen, the opening and plundering of the presumably royal ship burials of Vestfold in Norway has been dated precisely to his reign, so it seems as if Harald was neutralising the ancestors of the people he tried to bring under his sway—a confirmation of the role these monumental graves played in the psychological landscape.

Late in his reign, Harald was aided in his ambitions by a decisive change in the regional balance. In 983 the focus of Ottonian imperial attention shifted emphatically to the south, and thus removed what had for centuries been a critical factor in the limitation of Danish royal power. The imperial German court was a model as well as an enemy. This perhaps explains some of the developments at Jelling, which has the air of an 'imperial' monument to God and to Harald himself, constructed in emulation of the European—specifically German—pattern of Christian kingship.

In the two decades of Harald's rule, the Danish kingdom was transformed into a centralised, nominally Christian state—but not without opposition and backlash. Perhaps as a result of the extensive and sweeping changes Harald introduced, and because of the horrendous labour costs they must have required, the 980s saw increasing political turmoil in Denmark. Harald's own son, Svein Forkbeard, led an open rebellion around 987. At some point during the resulting civil war, Harald was killed, and many of his monuments were attacked and demolished. The Trelleborg fortresses and the Jelling palisade were burnt. The locus of power in Denmark then moved eastwards from Jelling to Sjælland, which saw a pagan revival in the late tenth century in opposition to the advance of Christianity (the Odin cult seems to have particularly prospered at this time, which also indicates that it never really went away).

The Christianisation process elsewhere in Scandinavia is harder to piece together. According to the later sources for Norway, especially the kings' sagas, the first ruler actively to attempt to spread Christianity there was Hákon the Good, who reigned during the 940s and 950s, but the new religion does not seem to have become deeply entrenched until the 990s and the advent of kings who were not afraid to use force to effect conversions of the aristocracy.

There is a late tenth- or early eleventh-century runestone from Kuli near Trondheim that combines a conventional memorial text with the evocative statement that "for twelve winters had Christianity been in Norway". There is otherwise little archaeological evidence with which to augment the literary narrative of the conversion process.

In some especially independent-minded parts of the Viking world, such as Gotland, the faith took centuries to find a foothold. On this Baltic island, many of the dead were still being buried with full pagan ritual into the end of the twelfth century, while Christians on neighbouring farms used their own rites. Even the opening sentence of the *Guta Laws*, dated c. 1220, states as the first legal stipulation "that we shall refuse heathendom and accept Christianity", implying this was far from the norm even then. At times both religions are represented on the same funerary monuments, either hedging the bets of the deceased or perhaps attesting to a genuine fusion of beliefs.

Similar patterns can be observed in the Scandinavian colonies of the diaspora. Ottonian missionaries were sent to Rus' in 946 at the request of Olga (Helga) of Kiev, who was ruling as regent following the death of her husband, although Olga's baptism at the Byzantine royal court at some point in the 940s or 950s implies links both with the Catholic and Eastern Orthodox churches. Her grandson Vladimir (Valdemar) consolidated the rule of Kiev, and in the process explored the potential benefits of a number of different faiths, but he was finally baptised a Christian as part of his marriage to a Byzantine princess around 988. In the 990s he ordered the construction of a massive church and palace in Kiev, and imported Byzantine builders and craftsmen for the job. In so doing, he created a new focal point of Christian royal power from which to command. By the twelfth century, the influence of Christianity had spread outwards from the main riverine arteries of the Rus' kingdom and into the countryside. Soon, however, new power centres began to emerge. In addition to expressing their political autonomy, some settlements began to assert their own religious independence. In Novgorod, for example, the power of the diocese and the archbishops that controlled it grew dramatically throughout the twelfth and early thirteenth centuries, contributing to the eventual fragmentation of the Kievan Rus' polity.

In Sweden, where the consolidation of the country would not take place until much later, there seem to have been some attempts by regional kings to introduce Christian models of kingship. Despite the intermittent success of early missionaries in preaching at a local level, however, the evidence for continued sacrificial rites at Götavi (and not least, Adam of Bremen's lively description of the rituals at Uppsala) demonstrate that pre-Christian beliefs remained popular as late as the eleventh century.

This is not hard to understand. The basic instrument of conversion was the rite of baptism, administered by churchmen as a means to nominally bring an individual or group into the Christian fold. However, a genuine change of faith on the part of the baptised was not compulsory. Even forced baptisms, such as those commanded by tenth-century kings in Norway, were considered valid by the Church. As such, while baptism was evidently an important rite, it cannot be taken as an indication of religious conversion in the sense that we understand it today. Priests seem to have been more concerned with harvesting souls than effecting long-term change on individuals.

It was not until the eleventh century that Christianity really began to transform daily life in Scandinavia. People seemed to have followed both the old and new ways in the same communities for many decades, apparently without major tensions. The first churches, simple one-room affairs made of timber, were very small and suitable only for the elite families who commissioned them. Formal worship in a consecrated building was for the rich, and it is clear that this attitude was at least initially shared by both Church and state.

23. House of a new god. A stave church reconstructed at Moesgård Museum, Denmark, and based on an excavated eleventh-century example from Randers. Photo: Sten Porse, Creative Commons.

The manifestations of all this in everyday experience have left some remarkable traces. In the late tenth century at Trendgården on Jylland, some enterprising smith was catering to his or her customers by casting Christian crosses and Thor's hammers in the same soapstone mould. That it could simultaneously produce two crosses but only one hammer provides an insight into patterns of supply and demand, and also illuminates the open duality of religious practices in the years when Christianity began to make itself felt in Danish society. Also of interest are a number of so-called Thor's hammer crosses—rather ambiguous objects that seem to have been intentionally made to be taken either way. Such items could have been worn to signal adherence to multiple belief systems, which might have been advantageous according to context.

While unfurnished inhumations are not necessarily indicative of Christian burial rites (those prescriptions would come centuries later), towards the end of the Viking Age they clearly began to replace cremations and furnished inhumations, albeit with an extended period of transitional burial practices. A striking insight into ideological negotiation and transition can be seen at Birka in an elaborate chamber burial dating from the mid-tenth century. It contained a woman accompanied by a number of objects (including an iron staff) that marked her out as a possible sorceress. Around her neck, however, was a silver pendant crucifix that seems to have been strung on a necklace of beads together with decidedly non-Christian amulets. The presence of the crucifix is not incompatible with the interpretation that the woman was a practitioner of *seithr* magic. Given that Christianity would have likely been regarded as exotic at that time in Sweden, maybe the inclusion of the cross in the woman's ensemble was intended to harness the arcane powers of the new religion, enhancing her ability to practise her magical art.

In other cases, freshly converted Christians may have buried their parents with appropriate rites of the new faith but also included elements of the old religion that they knew their loved ones might really have preferred. In a society that does not seem particularly prejudiced against innovative spiritual ideas, many combinations are possible, and there is no reason why all members of a family needed to share the same beliefs (indeed, there are many saga accounts of multifaith households). Adding to this are some regional trends that are hard to interpret. For example, in the Swedish Götaland provinces it seems that Christian burial appears in the mid-tenth century—much earlier than elsewhere. Perhaps an unknown mission was active there.

In the eleventh century, there was a surge in the erection of runestones, the majority bearing Christian inscriptions. In total, around 3,500 runic inscriptions are known from Scandinavia, of which some 2,400 are from Sweden, 450 from Denmark, and about 140 from Norway. The practice seems to have been particularly intensive in central Sweden; thirteen hundred stones were raised in Uppland alone. This geographical focus on one of the areas that converted *latest* may either be explained as reflecting a successful drive of missionary enthusiasm, or perhaps the opposite in that there were so many pagans the Christians felt obliged to proclaim their faith as visibly as possible.

One feature of the stones' distribution and content provides a clue. A consistent 2 to 3 percent of the stones have non-lexical inscriptions—either using proper runes that do not make intelligible words, or else made up of angular signs that resemble runes but are not the real thing, as if someone was trying hard to imitate the visual impact of a script they did not actually understand. Interestingly, these illegible stones are definitely *not* poor-quality affairs; their decoration and design are just as elaborate as that of the 'regular' runestones. Significantly, these strange non-lexical inscriptions are found at the outer periphery of areas where 'regular' runestones are most common. The implication is Christians were gathering together in communities apparently with some wealth and influence, at least sufficient to make those around them want to imitate their signals. At the very least, it shows that runestones had a visual function in their own right, partly independent from the content of their inscriptions.

Now grey and weathered, the runestones were originally brightly coloured—their lines picked out in black (derived largely from soot) and with panels in red and white based on lead oxide. Most take the form of upright stones that were raised in a specific place, but in some cases inscriptions were carved into the faces of boulders. They commonly feature designs of crosses and prayers for the preservation of the dead person's soul.

Some of the stones may represent attempts to consecrate ground before it was possible to build a church. Maybe the presence of a runestone in itself signalled a form of Christian burial in cemeteries in which old-style traditional funerals were still taking place. It is not uncommon to find runestones reused in the fabric of the first medieval churches. There is no doubt that people knew what these memorials were, and it is as if the ancestors were being brought into the fold of an established Christian community that could, at last, afford a place of worship and a real churchyard.

Some runestone images suggest a real depth of knowledge of biblical stories, such as depictions of Calvary on the Timmele stone in Västergötland, and the four animals from Daniel 7:3–7 and Revelations shown on the Måsta stone from Uppland. Such motifs are not superficial or casual. There are also runestones that confirm Scandinavians were making pilgrimages to Jerusalem in the eleventh century, which is also recorded in the Icelandic sagas. This would have been a truly enormous undertaking, and hardly represents the actions of people with only a limited understanding of their faith. A remarkable stone from Stäket in Swedish Uppland, now lost, provides context:

> Ingirún, Hard's daughter, had these runes carved for
> herself. She wants to travel east and abroad to Jerusalem.
> Fót carved the runes.

Not only is this woman making a clear declaration of her intentions ('want' is synonymous with 'will' in these inscriptions), but her decision to erect a runestone before heading out was also a kind of testament to the hazards of the journey: she might not come back, and may not have intended to. It seems likely that Ingirún had connections on the eastern route, people who might have been able to smooth her passage. Let's hope she got there safely.

There are also indications that not everyone was happy with the spread of the new faith. Several runestone texts incorporate invocations to Thor, and there is even an example where the usual central motif of the cross has been replaced with a large hammer— no doubt a deliberate response to Christian custom.

The social position of women also altered with the conversion. Several scholars have argued that Christianity brought a focus on the individual in contrast to the patriarchal norms of traditional Viking-Age society. It is interesting that all the cross pendants known from Birka were found in women's graves. Christian perspectives on the afterlife, which offered hope of a happy and permanent existence in heaven and the ability to influence one's destiny through actions undertaken in life, may have also appealed to women, given that the conditions for entering Valhöll and Sessrúmnir seem to have favoured men. Evidence for increased gender equality as a result of a shift in religious belief might explain the number of runestones erected by women, or recording their sponsorship of bridges as a symbol of the soul's journey to God.

On the other hand, the Church was hardly egalitarian, and curbed women's agency in many ways. The traditional spirituality of the North gave women considerable power and control of access to the other worlds, all of which was removed by Christianity. Their status within the household was also demoted. At its core, this was part of the Church's strategy of gaining access to the family unit—by usurping female dominance in that sphere—and thus to the kinship networks that were central to the real exercise of power in Scandinavian life. In this way, the new faith was able to create a space for itself between the general populace and the elites, thereby making the Church the only gateway to the divine.

The impact of the conversion process, however, went even further than a reformation of political and social relationships. In some regions, even economies of subsistence were being reshaped by the demands that the Church placed on communities. The introduction of a stringent religious calendar—with a large number of holy days and periods of abstinence from certain foods, for example—had a significant impact on fishing practices. There is clear fishbone evidence for riverine fishing of freshwater species all the way through the Viking Age, as well as exploitation of the marine 'outlands', but it is not until the eleventh century that real quantities of saltwater fish begin to appear everywhere in the archaeological record. Especially in the North Sea, there is a new emphasis on deep-water fishing coincident not only with Christian demand but also linked to urban expansion and perhaps the potential for trade. The same process created a new market for the international exchange of dried fish products.

The growth of unified kingdoms, the influence of the Church, and the economic motors that bound them together also provided impetus for another development of the late Viking Age: the establishment of true urban centres. They were distinctively different from the 'proto-urban' markets such as Hedeby and Birka that had expanded beyond their original limits to become crucial nodes of trade. Instead, these new towns were deliberate foundations made to express the Christian power of kings, in useful service to both God and mammon.

Several of them involved a spatial shift within a small region, the new foundation gradually assuming the functions of an older market that was slowly abandoned. Around the turn of the eleventh century, for example, Roskilde was established in Denmark as a successor to nearby Lejre. The same thing happened in central Sweden in the 980s, when Birka was eclipsed by Sigtuna. In both cases, churches were built soon after the founding of the new centres, sometimes followed closely by a mint. Sigtuna, for example, was producing coins for its founder, King Olof Skötkonung (his nickname rather bluntly means 'tax king'), from around 995. In Norway, new royal towns were founded at what would become Oslo, and most prominently at Nidaros (modern Trondheim) on the west coast.

Trade does not seem to have played a major role during the early years of Sigtuna or Roskilde: they and other towns were established primarily as royal administrative centres rather than marketplaces. The shift from Birka to Sigtuna was not a direct transfer of people and function but a discontinuous process— because this new town was not an emporium but the symbolic focus of a new kind of power. It is no coincidence that the founding of Sigtuna was almost exactly contemporaneous with Harald

Bluetooth's grandiose projects in Denmark, and in different ways both undertakings reflect the ambitions of young Christian rulers who subscribed to new models of kingship.

The process of state formation may have been a collaborative undertaking shared between monarchs, loyal nobility, the Church, and the new urban centres. Towns were focal points for Christian burials and services, and the prime locations for churches, shrines, and sites of pilgrimage. The association of urban centres with the cult of saints was encouraged by the Church, and the early royal heroes of the conversion were rapidly canonised in order to serve as national figures and rallying points for religious unification. These late towns can be seen as 'ports of faith': secure entry-points for Christian ideas and practices under royal patronage and protection, supported by an authority that emphasised the official line in belief.

The new towns had eclectic populations. The people of Sigtuna contrast sharply with those of rural communities, in that they came from a wide geographic area from northern, central, and eastern Europe, and the British Isles. Crucially, this is a product of mobility—people moving around in their daily lives—not a matter of permanent migration. Roughly half of the Sigtuna citizens were non-local, with a tendency for women to travel more than men. Runestones in the town mention what appear to be guilds from Frisia (the modern Low Countries), joining the Baltic and Finnish diaspora that had been expanding in southern Scandinavia for centuries.

This new urbanism did not mean that all power had been wrested from the countryside and secured in the hands of the king and Church. Local chieftains retained the loyalty of their communities, and tensions between these different levels of society are evident long into the Middle Ages.

Perhaps because of their old links to the rural population, the earlier market centres such as Birka and Hedeby had long half-lives. At least some kind of activity continued there after their primary mercantile functions had moved on. The last coin was minted in Hedeby in 1086, and the town's products continued to turn up along the familiar trade routes. The hierarchy of markets was still alive, with the difference that these once-grand emporia had been overtaken by the royal towns.

As Scandinavian society changed under all these external influences, the new rulers were presented with both opportunities and challenges. In the late tenth and early eleventh centuries, at least within their North Sea world, it is no exaggeration to say that the new Viking kings began to entertain imperial ambitions.

Harald Bluetooth was among the first of them, consolidating his hold not only on modern-day Denmark but also over parts of southern Sweden and Norway. But as we have seen, the heavy-handed exercise of authority that must have accompanied his enormous construction projects, and perhaps his muscular view of conversion, ended in his deposition and death. However, things would go better for the man who brought him down—his son Svein Forkbeard.

Late tenth-century Scandinavia was riven by a new series of civil conflicts, a seemingly unchanging situation in the North. In a sense these were large-scale versions of the inter-kingdom rivalries that had always been a part of the late Iron Age political scene, but this time played out as wars between what were fast becoming nation states. Denmark's crown holdings in Norway, the manifestation of Harald Bluetooth's claims, had been held in trust by the Lade jarls—the rulers of a semi-independent territory of that name in the north of the country. However, around 975 their leader, Hákon Sigurdsson, cut ties with Denmark and for that reason did not come to Harald Bluetooth's aid during the rebellion.

While Svein Forkbeard was consolidating his reign in Denmark, from the 980s onwards, Viking attacks on England began again. Unlike those of the late eighth and ninth centuries, however, the assaults that took place during this period were perpetrated by large, well-organised fleets under the command of Scandinavian royals, new and powerful players in the North Sea region.

In 991, the *Anglo-Saxon Chronicle* records the arrival of a Viking leader named Óláf Tryggvason. A descendent of Harald Finehair who had spent his youth in exile in Kievan Rus', he commanded a fleet of ninety-three ships in a series of raids against southern and eastern England. Óláf's campaign culminated in a battle at Maldon in Essex, immortalised in an Old English poem, where he destroyed a large army of local militias and was subsequently paid ten thousand pounds to leave. This was the first of many bribes—termed *danegeld*, 'Dane-payment', in the sources—that were made to Viking groups over the following years. The scale of the extortion would increase rapidly over time, as attested by the large number of hoards of eleventh-century English coinage found in Scandinavia.

These raids have left violent evidence in the archaeology. At Weymouth and Oxford, both in the south of England, two mass graves of execution victims seem to represent reprisals against Scandinavians. In the Weymouth burial, the decapitated bodies of fifty men had been thrown in an old quarry pit. The grave has been dated to 970–1025, with isotopic analysis indicating that the majority of the men came from regions as varied as Arctic, subarctic, and southern Scandinavia; northern Iceland; Russia; and the Baltic coasts. This is a very similar geographical spread to some of the large armies from the days of the hydrarchy, a century earlier. At another site in the grounds of what is now St. John's College, Oxford, thirty-seven men had been brutally slain and then dumped in a ditch. Radiocarbon dates indicate that they were murdered at some point around the year 1000, and given their broad 'Viking diasporic' origins, it seems likely that they were raiders whose *hamingjur* luck spirits had abandoned them.

For ambitious and successful warlords without a crown, men like Óláf Tryggvason, the large payments made by the beleaguered English could provide the means for an attempt on a Scandinavian throne. In 995 Ólaf did just that, returning to Norway and establishing himself as king following the death of the Lade jarl Hákon Sigurdsson. During Ólaf's rule, the first coins were minted in Norway. Based heavily on contemporaneous English issues (familiar to the Vikings for all the wrong reasons, because they had been bribed with so many of them), Ólaf's coins featured Christian iconography and an inscription proclaiming him to be king of the Norwegians.

Ólaf's reign proved to be short, and he was consumed by the same internecine politics that had brought him to power. Sources like the *Anglo-Saxon Chronicle* make it possible to follow Viking movements of the ninth century fairly well over a period of months, with a level of resolution that provides a basic orientation in the forces and commanders involved. A hundred years later, it is a measure of change that events now emerge as recognisable 'history', albeit largely of the drier kings-and-battles variety; the medieval saga material also fills in the detail, with varying reliability.

The war that brought Ólaf down was complex and vicious, but a close look at its intricacies reveals the inner workings of these late Viking-Age kingdoms.

Ólaf had made many enemies. In taking the Norwegian crown when Jarl Hákon died, Ólaf had alienated the natural successor, Hákon's son Eirík. Fleeing to Sweden ahead of Ólaf's assassins, Eirík took shelter with Ólof the Tax-King in Sigtuna. At the same time, Svein Forkbeard had not forgotten the territories in Norway that had once belonged to *his* father, Harald Bluetooth. These three men—a displaced Norwegian heir, an ambitious Swede hungry for land, and a Dane nursing a grudge—formed an alliance against King Ólaf of Norway.

The crunch came in the late summer of 999, or perhaps the following year (the sources are unclear). At Svöldr in the southern Baltic, Ólaf was ambushed at sea by a combined fleet of Danes, Norwegian exiles, and their Swedish allies. It was commanded by Eirík in his flagship, the *Iron Ram*. The resulting sea battle was one of the largest of the Viking Age and lived long in saga memory. Faced with overwhelming odds, all but eleven of Ólaf's seventy ships fled, leaving him outnumbered more than ten to one by the opposing fleet. King Ólaf Tryggvason made a final stand on the deck of his flagship, the *Long Serpent*, but seeing the battle was lost, he leapt into the sea in full armour. With Ólaf's death, Norway was divided between Svein Forkbeard and the Swedish king, Olof, but much of it was held in fief by Eirík Hákonsson and his brother (confusingly also called Svein).

Svein Forkbeard then turned his attentions to England, where he conducted a number of large raids that escalated from 1004. Other Vikings, such as the famous warrior Thorkell the Tall, led their own attacks from 1009 to 1012. Some scholars regard this period as effectively a second Viking Age: a new period of catastrophic raiding but unfolding in a totally different political context to the assaults of a century earlier. The attacks grew steadily worse; in 1013, Svein Forkbeard launched a full invasion of England.

It was a feature of the first large-scale raids, in the ninth century, that the political targets were either empires riven with civil war and therefore divided into factions (like Frankia), or regions containing many small kingdoms (like England). In either case, the effect was the same—advantage to the Vikings but also a strange form of protection in that if one polity, province, or river valley fell to the Scandinavians, it was a regional rather than national loss. Svein's invasion of a united England was itself partly a long-term result of earlier Viking attacks, but it also meant that success in war would have dramatic consequences.

The Danish forces advanced rapidly, seizing strategic targets and generally spreading chaos in a country already weakened by years of massive attacks. East Anglia, where they landed, went down quickly, followed by Northumbria and Lindsey in the north. The old Danelaw territories, full of people of Scandinavian descent, pledged allegiance to Svein. The Viking army divided into two divisions—led by Svein and his son Knút—for a two-pronged assault on the south. Winchester fell, but the Londoners resisted; in an ironic throwback to the confusion of the old Frankish campaigns, they were assisted by Thorkell the Tall, whose Vikings had signed on with the English as mercenaries. It was not enough. Svein threw his whole army against London (the famous nursery rhyme, 'London Bridge is falling down', is supposedly a memory of the Viking attack on the strategic link across the Thames). The city surrendered. One consequence, after years of raids, was that the people had lost confidence in their leaders, especially the king, Aethelred, and as a result the English monarchy collapsed. The royal family escaped abroad.

Having won Denmark by force in fatal rebellion against his father in the late 980s, and regained his lost Norwegian inheritance at Svöldr in 999, Svein became the first Viking king of England fourteen years later.

The bizarre coda is that he died, apparently of natural causes, just five weeks afterwards in February 1014. The result, predictably, was decades of dynastic fighting that would engulf the thrones of England, Denmark, Norway, and Sweden.

At first, the English rallied and Aethelred returned, driving Svein's son Knút back to Denmark, which was under the temporary rule of Knút's brother Harald. By 1015 the family were ready to go west again, and together they led another invasion of England with the whole Danish fleet. Aethelred died at this time and was succeeded by his son, Edmund Ironside, who led months of fierce resistance to the Vikings. In October 1016, however, Knút won a decisive battle, and Edmund Ironside himself died soon afterwards, possibly of wounds sustained in combat. With Knút on the throne, England was once again in Danish hands.

In 1018 or 1019, Harald died back in Denmark, and in order to secure the kingdom, Knút travelled home that year. To pay for the costs of his fleet, he levied a massive tribute from the English that even left its mark on Swedish runestones. On a memorial from

Orkesta in Uppland, one can read of a man named Ulf who "took *geld* in England" from three leaders—Tosti, Thorketil, and finally Knút himself.

Upon accepting the Danish crown, Knút gained control of what was, in reality, a North Sea empire, which he ruled as a true Christian monarch in the European style. Norway was reabsorbed into the Danish holdings in 1029. Knút's ambitions, his projections, are commemorated in one of the most extraordinary images of the Viking Age: a confraternity book donated by the king and his wife to Winchester New Minster (effectively the national cathedral) in 1031 as a demonstration of lay support for the Church. On the dedication page of the *Liber Vitae* is the first from-life portrait we have of a Viking king. Knút is shown standing by the minster altar, a crown being placed on his head by an angel pointing upwards to God in heaven; the king rules with direct blessing of the divine. Knút's right hand grasps a huge altar cross that he has given to the monks; the gold leaf still shines today. His royal generosity is evident, a model patron of the Church and the arts. But his other hand firmly grips the hilt of his sheathed sword: he goes armed in the minster—the realpolitik that backs up his claim. To add still further to the scene, on the other side of the altar stands Knút's wife, Emma, the widow of King Aethelred, against whom he first fought for the kingdom; in marrying his late enemy's wife, the Viking legitimates his 'Englishness'.

Knút remained on the English throne until his death in 1035, but his empire had already begun to loosen in his lifetime and did not survive him. The largest territory ever controlled, up to that time, by a single Scandinavian ruler was once again divided. Norway and Denmark had been given by Knút to two of his sons during his lifetime, but they either died or were deposed within a few years of his death. A third son, Hardaknút, inherited England and made an uneasy treaty with the new king of Norway, Magnús Ólafsson, stating that their combined territories would be ceded to whichever of them lived longest (hardly a recipe for peace).

In 1042, Hardaknút died of a stroke while drinking, and Magnús accordingly laid claim to Denmark. The English nobility seized the opportunity and took back their throne, installing Edward the Confessor, Queen Emma's son by her first marriage to King Aethelred. Edward reigned for more than twenty years, but after his death in 1066, the resulting claims on the English throne—from Norway, via the descendants of Magnús; from Normandy, via a somewhat tortuous connection with English royalty; and from the Saxon nobles themselves—would set the stage for the twin invasions of Harald Hard-Ruler and William the Conqueror. Two hundred and seventy years from Lindisfarne, more than three hundred from Salme, western European history would swing on a pendulum between a Norwegian former commander of the Varangian Guard and a fifth-generation Viking descended from Rollo's army of the Seine.

The Viking Age, even in its artificial sense of a historical construct, was never a straight narrative sequence.

In the arena of Scandinavian politics, its end really began with Svein's death and was completed with the passing of his son, Knút. Even these men were quite familiar—if not quite yet as equals—to the European royalty of the Continent. The same can be said of Scandinavia itself. At one level it was transformed beyond recognition from the mass of tiny polities that had clawed their way up and out from the crisis years of the sixth century. By the mid-eleventh century, Norway, Sweden, and Denmark were political realities, with only parts of Svealand and its centre at Uppsala holding out against at least a formal adoption of Christianity.

But, at another, deeper level, the North still ran in the old ways of thinking, and of being. The descendants of the diaspora still prospered in other lands, and not all of them were under the sway of the Scandinavian kings—a different, older Viking Age was still alive. Some people had not yet forgotten their *fylgjur*, the spirit-women inside every person, and the final chapter of the Viking saga concerns a place where they still reside today.

17

LANDS OF FIRE AND VINES

WHILE NEW NATIONS WERE BEING constructed in Scandinavia, combining the idea of a single kingdom with power that ultimately derived from the Christian God, entirely new worlds were being opened up in the North Atlantic.

From its settlement in the ninth century, Iceland grew and grew, offering a chance for a bold social experiment that was in many ways the direct opposite of what was happening in the Vikings' homelands. Like the militant hydrarchies before them, the Icelanders too were shaping a social order of their own, something different and new. The wild and fiery landscape of the island, dotted with volcanoes, great plains of black lava, and glaciers, suited the culture that would emerge there.

Iceland was also a staging ground for exploration and colonisation even farther west over the ocean. The Norse travelled for familiar reasons, in search of land, resources, and wealth, but also for the winning of a reputation worthy of praise and remembrance. Voyaging over rough seas, uncharted coasts of ice-bound rock and fresh grass were found first in Greenland. When its valleys and fjords were thickly settled with farms, some went west again— sailing past a shore of broken stone and miraculous kilometres of white beaches, to finally arrive in a place they called Vinland, the 'land of vines'. Although they never knew it, the Norse had reached the continent of North America.

As with most undiscovered territories, the North Atlantic was an arena where people could remake themselves, or at least try to do so. Here, the Vikings experienced tensions with the lives they had left behind them, with who others wanted them to be. They also encountered the unexpected, in meeting the inhabitants of places they soon realised had not been empty after all.

Of all the territories of the diaspora, Iceland, in particular, cut across the social and political currents that were swirling around Scandinavia. It was never an easy combination—an island of pioneer settlers, established without rulers in an age of monarchs, a republic of independent-minded farmers in a time of burgeoning nation states. These tensions were already apparent when it was first colonised in the late ninth century, against the background of the sea-kings' growing power. Iceland's founding population was a complex mixture, as we have seen—men from Norway and from the settlements in the Scottish Isles, some Scandinavian women but many more from the Irish Sea region. Within a century of the *landnám*, the land-taking, more and more settlers had homesteaded along the rivers and fjords.

These districts became worlds in miniature, their families rising and falling in prominence and leaving their mark in the sagas. The tidal pool and inlet around which Reykjavík would later develop was inhabited early on, and the remains of several longhouses have been found by the water, but soon the whole of the west coast was covered in settlements. The Snæfellsnes Peninsula, slightly to the north, is especially rich in history, folklore, and legend; Laxárdalr, in nearby Breiðafjörður, was home to some of the most prominent families; and so on round the country, every valley claimed and worked.

Iceland's increasing prosperity in the tenth century attracted not only the envy of the Norwegian kings, but increasingly too the attention of the Church. When the marginal agricultural economy and climate were added to the mix, it is clear that the Icelanders faced a number of challenges.

Resources were always an issue in the North Atlantic. Investigation of the post-*landnám* flora shows the opening of the land and tree felling on a massive scale. It is important to understand that the dramatic and barren landscape that attracts tourists today was not at all what the Vikings found: it was what they created. When the Norse arrived, Iceland was heavily forested, but the trees were quickly cut for building materials—an entire society needing to construct places to live and work—while the scrub cover was exhausted for use as fuel. Within a generation of the first landfall, the nature of the place had changed irrevocably. In addition to causing accelerating soil erosion, this also led to a constant demand for timber that increased sharply from the tenth century onwards. With the trees gone, driftwood became a vital resource, and the rights to gather it were strictly partitioned and controlled. Driftwood is useful for many household purposes but very difficult to work, being both hard and also impregnated with too much sand and soil.

The earliest structures on the island were built of local timber, but thereafter it had to be imported. Some of the wealthiest settlers even brought their homes with them, as portable 'kit' structures: they could be disassembled into their component parts in only two or three days by a team of workers. In prefabricated form, they were transported to Iceland from Norway, and later also onwards to Greenland. This partly explains why the basic size of the structures is broadly constant across the North Atlantic colonies.

A combination of necessity and the practicalities of insulation and waterproofing meant that turf became the main material used in the construction of dwellings and other structures. In a typical North Atlantic longhouse, the basic housing unit of the region under Norse settlement, between 1,000 and 1,500 square metres of cut turf were required to construct its walls. Even today, especially in Greenland, large expanses of turf cuttings can still be seen in the vicinity of Viking Age farms; it is clear that the management and extraction of turf resources were carefully supervised activities. A farm might consist of a main building and several outhouses— workshops and byres, maybe a smithy, perhaps quarters for the thralls. In the later Viking Age, and more so on into the Middle Ages, these ancillary spaces were incorporated into the main farmhouse for increased warmth, resulting in complex modular structures of conjoined buildings.

Throughout the North Atlantic, peat was also an important resource, commonly used as household fuel, in metalworking, and as a building material. As with turf, large-scale peat cuttings are identifiable even today around the Viking-Age settlements, and it seems that special areas in the landscape were set aside for the purpose.

Iceland never adapted to a monetary economy in the Viking Age, and there are very few silver hoards. Other commodities played a leading role in its systems of exchange, foremost of which was probably *vaðmál*—the rather coarse and heavy wool twill cloth, also known as tabby, that was employed universally in the Viking world as the basic textile for household use. It was therefore not only a viable and easily traded product for the domestic market, but also a valuable item for onwards exchange. The island was never isolated, and conducted a lively trade to the other North Atlantic colonies and back to Scandinavia. The sagas are full of passages to Norway in particular, despite political tensions with the royal powers there, and contact was always maintained.

Thinking of the diaspora as a mental condition as much as a physical one, it is interesting that *Landnámabók*, the 'Book of Settlements', lists the Scandinavian origins of only about 10 percent of the first homesteaders in Iceland. As in many frontier narratives, the forward-looking new lives that people made for themselves were often deemed more important than what was left behind in the 'old country'.

The settlement of the North Atlantic colonies also precipitated the institution of a new type of legal system. This drew on the traditional use of *thing* sites that had long been a feature of life in mainland Scandinavia. In contrast to the situation in Norway, where kings were asserting their authority over the assemblies, governance in Iceland was placed almost entirely in the hands of parliaments, where legislation was created and renewed, and legal cases were heard. One of the first was on Þingnes, a windswept peninsula near Reykjavík, and there were regional assemblies around the country. Around 930, a national parliament, the Alþingi, was established at the location now known as Þingvellir—a spectacular rift valley formed by the divergent movements of the Eurasian and North American Continental plates. The law of the Alþingi was upheld by thirty-six *goðar*, or chieftains, who became the major players in Icelandic politics. In 960, the system was redeveloped when the island was divided into four quarters, each of which was made up of three regional assemblies, which in turn were led by three *goðar*.

Despite the aspirations of the Icelanders to devise a new system of government, their brave new world was far from a peaceful utopia. The core narratives of many saga accounts describe the long and bloody feuds that developed between competing families and political factions along the valleys, neighbourly quarrels that escalated to theft and killings. As the power of the *goðar* grew into the medieval period, so did the stakes in these disputes, propelling the feuds forward. The resulting civil conflicts would ultimately prove to be the end of the Icelandic republic, as the continuing spiral of violence was finally terminated when direct control was asserted from Norway in the thirteenth century.

Another serious threat to social stability was posed by outlaws, especially due to their stock raiding. A number of their hideouts are known, and some have attracted a rich accretion of folklore. Such tales are, of course, a fundamental part of the Icelandic narrative—literally so in the form of the famous sagas encountered throughout this book. The individuals who populate the stories are true Viking-Age characters, albeit filtered through the medieval prose of the saga-writers, with the variable reliability of an assumed oral history on which the whole edifice rests. For a modern Icelander, reading the Old Norse of the sagas has about the same level of difficulty as Shakespearean prose for an English speaker. Many Icelanders today trace their descent from saga protagonists and the early settlers, and the corpus of stories is, in every sense, a national treasure.

There is Aud the Deep-Minded, stranded as a widow in Caithness on the north Scottish shore, who commissioned her own ship and captained it first to Orkney and then to the Faroes and Iceland; she became one of the country's great landholders, and one of its first Christians. And Flosi Thordarson, who burnt his enemies in their hall after a reluctant campaign of revenge, only to hear someone chanting poetry down among the flames. "Was Skarphedin alive or dead when he spoke that verse?" asks one of his men, and Flosi's reply, "I shall not make any guesses about that." There is Gudrún Ósvífrsdóttir, widowed four times after a tangled cycle of love, vengeance, and feud—at the end of a long life, she looks back on her late husbands with the most famous line in the sagas, "I was worst to the one I loved the most"; people still debate who she meant. Or Thorodd the Tribute-Trader, who drowned with his men on a fishing expedition, their bodies never found; every night of the funeral feast, he and his companions walked in to sit by the hearth, water streaming from their clothes, "until the fire began to burn very low, then they went away". And Gunnhild, sorceress-queen of Jorvík, who once perched in a window in the shape of a bird, twittering all night trying to break a poet's concentration. Then there's the outlaw anti-hero Grettir Ásmundarson, who fought the terrible revenant Glam, and always said the only thing that ever frightened him was the sight of the undead man looking up to stare at the moon.

Some of these people were definitely real, others perhaps not. Few of them can have done *precisely* the things ascribed to them in the texts—but in a sense, it does not really matter. Please, read the sagas.

The Viking-Age experience behind the literary lives of the medieval texts can be vividly revealed by archaeology. The site of Hofstaðir in northern Iceland can serve as a useful window onto the colony. An unusual and extraordinary place with strong ritual overtones, excavations there revealed a remarkable level of preservation: in the floor deposits, for example, it is possible to see the imprints of furniture and household effects, and even the curving scrape made every time a badly fitting door was opened. Hofstaðir was settled soon after 940 with the construction of a hall, a smithy, and a sunken-floored building. Between the 980s and the 1030s, the hall was greatly expanded. The main building was lengthened, a smaller one was constructed nearby, a larger smithy was built, and a new latrine was dug.

From this second phase onwards, there are indications of a much bigger population for the complex, but also a suggestion that this was something seasonal, and that the hall was purpose-built for large gatherings of people on specific occasions. This is supported by the size of the hearth, which was not sufficient to heat the structure, and also by specialised butchery patterns in the animal bones that imply the meat was brought to the site already processed for feasting. Environmental studies on the animal bones reveal the pigs kept on-site were being fed on trout, a diet that produces exceptionally fatty pork. This is an uncommon practice, with no other regional parallels, and indicates that the pigs were being purposely reared for their meat to be used in high-status feasting. Hofstaðir is also the only site to preserve evidence for the consumption of suckling pig, another delicacy.

This was the place where bulls were sacrificed, two-person teams killing them in great spectacles of blood, as we saw earlier. The skulls of the cattle seem to have been afterwards fixed around the walls of the hall. Up to thirty-five crania were recovered from the excavation, bearing witness to many years of such rites—radiocarbon dating suggests the sacrifices may have been spread out over as much as a century. It also appears this was done in the second half of June; these were summer rituals during the period of permanent sunlight. Most of the sacrificial bulls did not come from the Mývatn area, but were brought to Hofstaðir from outside the district—another expensive practice. The killing of cattle seems to have come to an end at the same time as the adoption of Christianity, suggesting an obvious link between the introduction of the new faith and the decline of such public pagan events (even if non-Christian rites continued behind closed doors for a time).

Many other finds testify to Hofstaðir's unique status, although some are hard to interpret; for example, the site has large concentrations of cat bones, which are found nowhere else. The settlement was dismantled and abandoned in the 1070s, when the buildings were taken apart and each structure was ritually closed with burials of animal skulls.

Iceland officially converted to Christianity around the year 1000, although there is a complex story behind it. The new faith had been infiltrating the island for decades, arriving actively or passively with every new ship, as rumour or conviction. The progress of conversion in Scandinavia, not least in Norway, made itself felt in Iceland too. The settlers looked to the future and debated their options accordingly. The *Book of Icelanders* records that the decision to accept the Christian religion was made by the lawspeaker of the Alþingi, in response to increasing unrest resulting from friction between adherents of the new beliefs and stubborn traditionalists. Having meditated under a cloak in something resembling a shamanic trance, the speaker came down on the side of conversion but with some interesting provisos: Icelanders would thenceforth call themselves Christians, but could still practise the old rituals in private, eat horseflesh, and expose unwanted children if they wished (which, not least, implies they were really doing these things). As in mainland Scandinavia, early Christianity seems to have been a relatively private affair, with many farmsteads possessing their own churches—a situation that would continue into the Middle Ages.

The latter half of the tenth century saw Icelanders venturing even farther west, leading to the colonisation of Greenland in the 980s. The reasons for this remain a matter of debate, but it is possible that the areas in Iceland available for settlement were being steadily locked in by established chieftains. The story of the Norse presence in Greenland, and later the New World, is preserved in two Icelandic tales—the *Saga of Eirík the Red* and the *Saga of the Greenlanders*. They differ substantially in the details, but convey a broadly similar big picture of the westward expansion.

Greenland was discovered accidentally by travellers blown off course in a storm. On their return to Iceland, they told others of what they'd seen, and the news of a great land to the west began to circulate. This coincided with a local drama in the west of the country, when a sentence of outlawry—exile literally beyond the law—was pronounced on a man called Eirík the Red, as a result of a series of killings in a neighbourly feud. A difficult, violent, but intrepid man, with limited options, Eirík decided to try his luck in these new lands and sailed there with a small group of followers. A year later he was back in Iceland, full of tales of the wonderful place he had decided to call Greenland—chosen, according to the saga, because people would want to go there if it had a nice name.

Eirík's persuasions found a ready audience. It must have been tempting to head out there to an unsettled country (as Iceland had been only a century earlier) in search of new lands for colonisation. In addition to pasture, the availability of game, including reindeer, seal, and walrus, also acted as a draw for new settlers. This first Norse presence, which would become the so-called Eastern Settlement (Eystribygð), was established around the southern tip of Greenland. Archaeologists have recorded some five hundred farms there, spreading northwards along the coast and extending to a smaller community sometimes known as the Middle Settlement.

Its social and political centre was at Brattahlíð, the site of Eirík's farmstead complex on what he characteristically had named the Eiríksfjord (today the place is known by its Inuit name, Qassiarsuk, and the fjord is Tunulliarfik). Remains of Eirík's house have been found; it was an imposing structure with a flagstone floor, surrounded by ancillary buildings, including byres for animals. Nearby stood a tiny turf church, made (according to the sagas) for his wife, Thjodhild. Eirík never shared her faith and remained faithful to the old traditions until his death, and their spiritual differences caused tensions between them. At an unknown location near Brattahlíð was the site of the first *thing* assembly in Greenland. This district would continue in prominence for centuries, with a later Christian focus around the bishopric at Garðar, founded in the twelfth century on the next fjord to Brattahlíð.

Another major site in the Eastern Settlement was at Herjolfsnes; it was located away from the main centre but cleverly placed to form the natural first landfall of ships arriving from Iceland. Founded by Herjólf Bárdarson, who came over in the first ships with Eirík, Herjolfsnes thrived effectively as a port of transit—receiving the first news from the east and doing a brisk trade in outfitting travellers with the things they didn't know they needed.

Farther north, up the coast, a second Norse colony was soon founded and became known as the Western Settlement (Vestribygð). Around one hundred farms have been identified here. In both settlements, the Norse sited their settlements in the more temperate areas along the coast, where the fjords and valleys allowed a pastoral agricultural system. As elsewhere in the North Atlantic, they adhered to their cultural roots when constructing and managing their homes. The turf and stone farmhouses still visible as ruins there today were, in many respects, similar to those found in Iceland and the Faroes, as was the continued use of the infield/outfield farming methods whereby the areas closest to the dwellings were cultivated while the land farther away was used for pastured grazing. An important part of the economy was the annual walrus hunt, conducted far to the north in the waters of what is now Disko Bay. This hazardous trip to the northern hunting grounds (Norðrsetur) took many weeks, but provided the raw materials for the colonists' own use and to keep trade going with Iceland and Scandinavia.

In other ways, too, the harsh environment demanded that the colonists adapt their way of life in order to survive, and there is some evidence they tried to do so. In the Western Settlement, around eighty kilometres from the modern-day Greenlandic capital of Nuuk, excavations by Danish archaeologists at a site they named *Gården Under Sandet* (Farm Beneath the Sand), or GUS, found eight phases of superimposed occupation, revealing compound structures combining dwellings, animal stabling, and outhouses in conglomerate buildings that maximised heat retention and warmth. At GUS there is a constant sensitivity to the environment, as buildings of different kinds changed usage to fit the season and the climate. Both in Iceland and Greenland, the ability to feed livestock over the winter was of fundamental importance. Fodder plants unsurprisingly predominate in the environmental record, and in the faunal record there is a high proportion of goats, useful as hardy animals that could be fed on woody fibres such as twigs. Preserving food was an equally important part of the annual cycle, especially for the winter months, and the settlers applied their ingenuity to this as to all other challenges of their new home. There is good evidence, for example, for the use of seaweed ash as a source of salt, which was vital to the preservation process.

It is now possible to use increasingly sophisticated scientific analyses to examine the environmental impact of the Norse settlers in the North Atlantic colonies. In Greenland, the colonists left their own 'footprint' on the landscape, and it is visible in the archaeological record. It has been estimated that up to 5 percent of the

Greenland flora is of Norse origin, imported with the settlers and distributed across the pasturelands surrounding the settlements.

The Greenland Norse certainly signalled a Scandinavian identity, but as in the Faroes and Iceland, there are some undeniably local adaptations to the immediate environment. Literacy seems interestingly high, for example, as runic inscriptions are comparatively more common there than elsewhere in the Viking world and are moreover applied to a much greater range of objects than is usually the case. A number of items bear ownership marks, including a spade from Vatnahverfi inscribed with "Gunnar owns" and a spindle whorl from the same area featuring the words "Sigrid made". While fairly mundane in themselves, these inscriptions demonstrate a high level of everyday runic fluency; clearly, fast and accurate communication was in wide demand. The inscriptions from late Norse Greenland also reveal the existence of a developed cult of the Virgin Mary, whose name can be found inscribed on everyday things such as spindle whorls—perhaps evidence for the kind of frontier religion that can take root with great conviction.

In contrast to the many runic inscriptions preserved in the medieval levels of Norwegian towns such as Bergen and Stavanger, in Greenland there are almost none directly relating to trade. However, a profusion of tally sticks seems to indicate that the Greenlanders spent a lot of time counting things, presumably commodities of various kinds. It is hard not to sense an obsessive need here, repeatedly making sure they had enough to get by.

Life in Greenland, as in the other Norse Atlantic colonies, was harsh and sometimes short. The margins of subsistence were clearly, at times, very small; for example, at the GUS site, the land around became progressively denuded as the environs of the farm were overexploited. A particularly traumatic record of the realities of farmstead life survives in the thin layers of accumulating soils inside the buildings there, and in the environmental evidence they contain. Careful analysis has revealed that the GUS inhabitants almost certainly starved to death in the houses. The record shows a brief but very significant rise in the presence of carrion flies—an outdoor species that for a short period came inside. No bodies were found at GUS, so it appears someone removed them at a later date. As the environmental analyst of the site observes, three successive bad years in Greenland would have been enough to take out even the most well-prepared farm.

The sheer toughness of life on the margins of the North Atlantic—the risk and vulnerability—goes much further towards explaining the extraordinary oceanic voyages of discovery than any supposedly innate sense of Norse adventure. The Faroes, Iceland, and Greenland were all found by accident when ships were driven off course in bad weather; nobody just set out for a far horizon. It is also important to remember that many of these Viking voyagers were simply never seen again. No sagas were written for them, and they just vanish from history into the waters of the Atlantic. That this was seen as a natural hazard of maritime life can be understood from the shockingly laconic (to a modern mind) notations of such ship losses that we find in the sagas. From the *Saga of the Greenlanders*:

> In the summer in which Eirík the Red set off to colonize Greenland, twenty-five ships sailed from Breidafjord and Borgarfjord [in Iceland], but only fourteen reached there.

Curiosity, but also a degree of necessity, played a role in probably the most famous incident in the creation of the Viking diaspora: the first European encounter with North America. Our textual sources for this are meagre indeed—only the two sagas already mentioned, which contain a wealth of detail but also many contradictions. While both tell a similar story, they differ in a number of respects. For example, while the *Saga of the Greenlanders* credits Bjarni Herjólfsson (son of the local magnate at Herjolfsnes) as first sighting North America in 986, when his ship was storm driven while attempting to reach Greenland, the *Saga of Eirík the Red* (perhaps unsurprisingly, given his family) credits Leif Eiríksson as discovering it when coming back from Norway. According to both sagas, the initial sightings induced later attempts to explore the newly discovered lands.

In a sense, the Vinland voyages were marginal events involving only a few ships and a couple of hundred individuals, and there is no particular indication that they were important to the Norse as anything more than an epic story (that the tale *was* famous is shown not only by the sagas, but also by the fact that the voyages were clearly remembered for centuries). However, they also marked something else: the unique moment in human history when the populations that had begun expanding out of Africa hundreds of thousands of years earlier finally linked up from east and west, completing the full circle of settlement and encounter around the globe. It is a story worth examining in some detail.

In the sagas, the North American region settled by the Norse is referred to as Vinland, 'vine-land', due to the settlers' discovery of wild grapes. The way to reach it is charted in the texts: one initially sailed north up the west coast of Greenland, way beyond the Western Settlement, before turning west to head across open water for two days. According to the sagas, on reaching the far coast, Norse explorers turned south, first passing a land of flat stones (referred to as Helluland, likely Baffin Island) and one of dense forest (Markland, probably Labrador). There is a description of endless beaches with dazzlingly bright sand that also fits this course. Vinland, the focus of Norse activity in the sagas, is encountered south of Helluland and Markland, but exactly where it was is unclear. It is here the two texts diverge most dramatically, both in the nature of the voyages and where they went.

In the popular imagination today, the Vinland voyages are primarily associated with Leif Eiríksson—Leif 'the Lucky'—but in both sagas it is clear that the main Norse explorers were the married couple Thorfinn karlsefni and Gudríd Thorbjarnardóttir.

In the *Saga of Eirík the Red*, Leif discovers Vinland but does not land there. Only one settlement voyage is made, led by Thorfinn with three ships and 140 (or 160) men made up of various relatives and retainers of Eirík the Red, including Leif's brother and sister. Two separate settlements are founded in Vinland—one at 'Straumfjörðr', where the group overwinters, and a second at 'Hop', which seems to have lasted longer. Here they encounter indigenous peoples whom the texts refer to as *skraelingar*—a derogatory term meaning something like 'savages'. After a cautious first meeting, the locals return in large numbers and begin to trade, although they are afraid of the Norse bull, an animal they have never seen. This seems to sour relations, and after a period of absence the indigenous people return and attack the Norse camp. The explorers are saved by Leif's sister, Freydís, who seizes the sword of a fallen man and bares her breast, which according to the saga so startles the attackers that they retreat. A complicated series of episodes follows, involving more murders of indigenous people and the death of Leif's brother at their hands, squabbles among the Norse, and a rather drawn-out voyage back to Greenland. The dream of Vinland is abandoned. The region is ambiguously described in Eirík's saga, and its geography does not make internal sense. Its northern limit is a headland the saga calls Kjarlarnes, but the same text also mentions that some of the Norse wish to *look for* Vinland to the west of that point.

The *Saga of the Greenlanders*, by contrast, is more detailed in many ways and describes several separate journeys to the New World. Its events seem to have been rather awkwardly compressed into the single voyage of the other saga. The chronology is also shifted slightly later, in that Bjarni waits several years before reporting his sighting of a new land, and it is not until c. 1000 that Leif Eiríksson hears of it and sets out to go there. In this text, he is the one who first lands. Adding to the difficulties of interpretation, only *one* settlement is mentioned in the *Saga of the Greenlanders*. This place is built by Leif and is named, accordingly, Leifsbuðir

('Leif's Houses'); he lends the site to the voyagers that follow him, although he personally does not return to Vinland.

When Leif gets home to Greenland, a new expedition is launched by his brother Thorvald. They, too, reach Leifsbuðir, and in fact stay there over three winters while they spend the summers exploring the coast. According to this version, it is clear that the Norse gained considerable knowledge of the region and also that they ranged far from their base—which has implications for the archaeological data, as we shall see. This mission ends in disaster when the Norse unexpectedly encounter (as Leif never did) people whom this saga also calls *skraelingar*; unlike the Eirík's saga account, the contact is violent from the start. Thorvald and his men kill several of them, before being attacked in numbers and making a fighting retreat to the ships. In the process, Thorvald is killed by an arrow, as he is in the 'combination voyage' of Eirík's saga.

The ships eventually make it back to Greenland, and their exploit is followed by the voyage that is the focus of the *Saga of the Greenlanders*—when Thorfinn karlsefni and Gudríd travel to Vinland accompanied by sixty men and five women. They bring with them trade goods and livestock, intending to stay, and initially their encounters with the indigenous people are peaceable. They barter for milk and cloth (the colour red seems especially popular), but soon there is a misunderstanding when one of the locals tries to grab a Norse weapon and is killed. Here the account seems to converge with that of the *Saga of Eirík the Red*, as the Norse are attacked in force but manage to fight their way out and return to Greenland. The saga includes a final coda, with an additional voyage (making four in all) jointly led by Leif's sister, Freydís. This has clear links to the Eirík's saga narrative, but here ends in murderous discord between the settlers (several of whom Freydís personally kills with an axe—she is clearly her father's daughter).

In both sagas, Leif's other brother, Thorstein, leads an abortive voyage to find Vinland, spending months lost at sea before being driven back to Greenland and dying of illness. He is married to

Gudríd Thorbjarnardóttir at the time, and it is in her widowhood that she meets her future husband, Thorfinn.

In both sagas, the indigenous people are described in some detail: moving in small flotillas of skin boats, whirling some kind of noise-makers, wielding bows and arrows, sleeping in skin 'bags'. The tragic details of colonial first encounter are familiar from later times, and convincing for that reason: initial trade, with very different value systems (the Norse can't believe the locals are willing to trade beautiful furs for nothing more than milk), but soon turning violent and deadly, often in relation to supposed 'thefts' of weapons. There is even the kidnapping of people to be taken home and taught the ways of 'civilisation'—change the names and these could be episodes from Cook's journals. Given the saga geography and the archaeological data, the scholarly consensus today is that the First Nations people encountered by the Norse were probably the ancestors of the Beothuk, recorded in early modern times as living throughout Newfoundland. Their later history was one of colonial damage and loss; the Beothuk were declared extinct in 1829, although some individuals may have survived longer into the nineteenth century.

Over the centuries, the memory of the Norse expeditions to Vinland dimmed and then faded altogether. It was not until the 1960s, following years of searching, that excavations identified a Norse site at l'Anse aux Meadows, at Épaves Bay on the northern tip of Newfoundland. The remains of eight buildings were found, grouped into three complexes. These included both dwellings and workshops, one of which was a smithy where bog iron had been processed. There was also evidence for wood-working activity and ship repair, in something resembling a boat shed. The architecture of the settlement is classic Norse in the North Atlantic style, familiar from the Faroes to Greenland.

The finds are fairly meagre but include a ringed pin cloak fastener of a kind that is diagnostically Norse. There was also a spindle whorl and a fragmentary bone needle—evidence for (perhaps female?) textile working—as well as a glass bead. Pieces of wood were excavated that had clearly been shaped by iron tools, that the indigenous people did not possess.

The buildings at L'Anse aux Meadows were burnt, either by First Nations people after the departure of the Norse or perhaps by the latter as an act of ritual closure. The site is generally dated to around 1000, but some of the material found appears to be earlier, implying the settlement may have been established prior to the Norse explorations recorded in the sagas (although the chronology is admittedly vague).

The site at l'Anse aux Meadows could have potentially housed around one hundred people, but does not seem to have been occupied on a permanent basis. Rather than seeking to establish a colony, the wish to secure valuable timber supplies may have been the main motivation for the foundation of the settlement. Contrary to the story in the sagas, no evidence has yet been found for cattle, barns, or byres, which were essential to the long-term survival of any new colony. No graves have been discovered, either, which also indicates a relatively short-lived settlement. That said, new environmental work at the site suggests the Norse occupation, whether intermittent or not, may have lasted for up to a century.

Several scholars believe l'Anse aux Meadows was, instead, essentially a way station used for resupply and boat repair between longer expeditions into the interior. The clear references to wild grapes—and indeed the name itself—imply that Vinland was not located in Newfoundland, as the northernmost latitude at which wild grapes grow is much farther south, around New Brunswick. The identification of butternuts and butternut wood at l'Anse aux Meadows, which also have their northern growth limits in the New Brunswick region, supports this suggestion. If the Norse *did* voyage farther south, then they potentially could have penetrated relatively deep into the St. Lawrence River in what is now Quebec Province, or headed south along the coast of Maine. Given the distance from their homes in Greenland and Iceland, and the vagueness of their geographical knowledge, perhaps Vinland was a name given by the Norse to the whole region.

L'Anse aux Meadows today is an extraordinary place, precisely because its remains are so modest—the outlines of turf buildings as bumps in the grass around the bay, a reconstructed longhouse, an excellent museum—at the same time, the mind reels at what it represents. And all unknown to the people concerned. The Norse did not know where they were, and the First Nations people they met had no idea whom they'd encountered or where they had come from. The first time I ever saw the Northern Lights was in the skies above St. Anthony, the nearest modern settlement, and the whole site lives long in any visitor's memory.

Brief hopes of finding another site were raised when a satellite-based survey seemed to locate some kind of Norse outpost at Point Rosee, situated at the opposite, western end of Newfoundland. Some months later, however, follow-up excavations confirmed that the 'cultural remains' were all entirely natural in origin. The researchers had, quite properly, tested their initial hypotheses, found them to be erroneous and said so, and this is the way science sometimes goes. For now, the potential extent of any exploratory voyages into the south must remain a matter of speculation.

It is clear that the Norse went back to Vinland repeatedly, and also that they had further contacts with the local people while there. Excavation of a grave in the Western Settlement of Greenland has revealed a man who died as a result of an arrow wound; the tip was still embedded in his body and was of First Nations manufacture. He had presumably been shot over there but made it home before succumbing to his injury. In another Greenland grave, traces have been found of a robe made from the hide of a North American buffalo—a species native to the plains. This can only have reached the east coast via internal trade, before finally going home with a Norse Greenlander, who may have liked it enough to be buried in it.

Turning north from l'Anse aux Meadows, however, the situation is very different. In recent years, evidence has been growing for Norse contact with the peoples of Arctic Canada and the far north-western reaches of Greenland—the Dorset Palaeo-Eskimos and, later, the Thule Inuit. Trading contacts are suggested by a number of finds identified at sites associated with aboriginal peoples. These include whetstones and soapstone artefacts from Baffin Island and northern Labrador, as well as small pieces of metalwork that have been found on the coast of Hudson Bay and the Hudson Strait. It seems that at least one Norse ship wrecked in the high Arctic on the Canadian shore, as scavenged materials including iron tools and the characteristic clench-nails used to hold the planks of the hull together have been found on Inuit sites. Some of these nails tell a tragic story, as they bear signs of heating— presumably the crew's desperate repair attempts that failed as they could not make a fire hot enough to do the job.

Possible indications of a fleeting Norse presence have also been identified at Nanook on Baffin Island. Here, excavations of a structure that has no clear parallels in indigenous or Norse architecture yielded a small crucible used for smelting copper, as well as cordage and whetstones used for sharpening metal implements. Could this represent the second known Norse occupation site in North America? If so, then it is conceivable that the Greenland colonists may have expanded the Norse sphere of influence even further than had previously been believed, making North America the last truly unexplored archaeological frontier of the Viking world. In a specialist's bookcase, nearly a metre of shelf is taken up with 'Viking America' despite the fact that, as yet, there is still only L'Anse aux Meadows and a handful of signals from farther north along the Canadian seaboard. Beyond this, there is really nothing more, and the Vinland voyages slowly fade out here.

If the American seaboard was a Viking terminus of sorts, it was nonetheless an extremity of a regional endeavour in the North Atlantic that, in some ways, lasted longer than Norse colonies elsewhere. We have followed the Vikings from their distant origins in the turmoil of the sixth century, through their political consolidation in the eighth and ninth centuries, to their diaspora of raiding and trading across Eurasia and the western sea. How did their world end?

18

THE MANY ENDS OF THE VIKING AGE

S OME WOULD HAVE THE VIKING Age beginning on June 8, 793, with the attack on Lindisfarne; others would have it draw to a close with the Battle of Stamford Bridge in Yorkshire on September 25, 1066, when King Harald Hard-Ruler of Norway died leading the charge against the English line, an arrow in his throat.

As ever, it was not nearly so simple.

Even in the unified nation states of the old homelands, with their divinely sanctioned Christian kings, the path ahead was not smooth. Norway and Denmark remained relatively stable as political entities, but far into the Middle Ages they were riven by civil wars that were really not so altered from those of the Viking Age. The main difference was the factional fighting for single countries and their crowns, rather than dynastic conflicts for swathes of land and little states. Overseas raiding continued, but as international politics rather than piratical ambition; in a sense this latter died with Svein Forkbeard, who so briefly enjoyed his successful conquest of England in 1014. That said, it probably felt little different on the receiving end.

In a curious way, the medieval Scandinavian kings also continued the Viking raids in a new context—that of the Crusades. These sacred wars of the later eleventh century onwards were prosecuted close to home, among the Baltic tribes who still resisted Christianity, and of course away in the Holy Land itself. Only a generation after Stamford Bridge, the Norwegian king Sigurd led his fleet along the coast of Frankia and into the Mediterranean, plundering as he went, just like his Viking forebears. Arriving eventually in Palestine, he was instrumental in helping the king of Jerusalem capture the city of Sidon. Sigurd then turned for home, stopping at Constantinople where he was welcomed by Emperor Alexios, to whom he gave his ships. He was provided with overland transport back to Scandinavia, but in true Varangian tradition many of his men decided to stay on as mercenaries of the Byzantine Empire.

In its overseas territories, the Norwegian crown maintained tentative control of the Hebrides until the 1260s, but assumed de facto government of Iceland at the same time, ending its centuries of commonwealth. Orkney and Shetland remained firmly Scandinavian—islands of proudly self-sufficient pirate fisherfolk—until their annexation by Scotland in the fifteenth century.

Unlike Norway and Denmark, the Swedes would take centuries to finally come together, either as a country or (up to a point) as Christians. Olof the Tax-King had his little power base in Sigtuna, but that was far from the whole realm. The tribal enmities of the Svear and Götar peoples ran deep, and still divided the country from the central plains to the lake lands. The power of the Church gripped the south, which would remain under the rule of the Danish throne until the seventeenth century. In the Mälar Valley, however, it was another matter—the old beliefs lived on alongside the new until the 1100s, and probably, behind closed doors, for much longer than that. Adam of Bremen wrote his alarmingly graphic description of the Uppsala temple, and its pagan festivities so obscene that he could not bring himself to relate them,

only twenty-nine years before the fall of Jerusalem in the First
Crusade.

The fate—in a very Norse sense—of the Viking diaspora was different again. As might be expected, the social, political, economic,
and ideological motors that drove the Scandinavian transformation of the eighth to eleventh centuries wound down in different
ways, at different times and paces, in different regions. There are
several ways of accessing this.

One is through the 'archaeological' view of Viking-ness, the
difficult connections between social change and material culture.
The fallacy of making a simple equation of this kind—identifying
a 'Viking' necklace, say—was exposed long ago when types of
beads that had always been firmly associated with Viking-Age settlements began to turn up on Danish excavations dated fifty years
before the traditional 'start' of the period; did the Viking Age begin
earlier than we thought? This is what prompted the scholarly debate
on the Migration Period crisis and its long-term consequences, the
fundamental changes of the mid-eighth century, and a more subtle
understanding of history than one that rested on the burning of a
monastery at Lindisfarne.

The same is true for the trajectories of material culture in the
late Viking Age and after, with everything that this implies. In central Sweden, for example, runestones of classic late Viking-Age type
continued long into the 1100s. On Gotland, jewellery of exactly
the same kind as Viking-Age people wore was clearly still fashionable in the 1200s. In Scotland and the Isles, the transition to
a medieval economy should really be placed in the late thirteenth
century, mainly on the grounds of changes in the fishing industry
and a serious shift to a deep-water catch. In Dublin and the other
Irish 'city states', decorative patterns common in the eleventh century, especially the twisting beasts and interlace of the so-called
Ringerike and Urnes art styles, were actively being used a hundred years later. Then there are all the 'hybrid' identities. When did

the Vikings on the Seine start to become 'Normans', for example? Judging by how they signalled their identity, this happened within about a decade of Rollo's first land grant in 911. In the territories of Kievan Rus', on the other hand, there is a material continuity of recognisably Scandinavian elements at least into the 1200s.

The key is the illusory conflation of identity and things. Yes, of course, objects can be used to signal status, affiliation, preference, and more, but they can also be ambiguous, ironic, even used to mock what they ostensibly affirm. There is only limited sense in talking of a 'Viking' sword and a 'medieval' one, and we must turn to larger social processes.

Alone among the former Viking colonies, Normandy's boundaries have remained intact, and there is, even now, a strong sense of contrast to the rest of France—an identification with the Scandinavian origins of the province that can at times become politically charged. The dukedom continued into the medieval period proper, naturally aided by the fact that its ruler also occupied the throne of England. In the British Isles, Yorkshire and the north would retain an underlying Scandinavian character for centuries, a fierce independence that was a legacy from the time when Eirík Blood-axe held out against the southern English; it was no accident that the north largely joined Harald Hard-Ruler's invasion in 1066. In a more diluted form, the same was true of the former Danelaw territories. The cultural and linguistic heritage of the Great Army settlers never entirely disappeared, but instead fused with the rising notion of England (a concept in part forged in resistance to the Vikings) to shape new settlements, new trading connections, and new lives. In Ireland, the Norse coastal enclaves became the primary urban foundations of the Middle Ages, as the economy and politics of the country gradually integrated. However, the town-and-country dichotomy would persist into modern times.

In all these areas, the Vikings live on today primarily as tourist magnets, as the draw of heritage trails and 'experiences'. The

Scandinavians of the Viking Age were acutely concerned with memory; they might have been happy at this.

The world of the Rus' followed a different route, separate from Scandinavia but nonetheless fully integrated into European politics. The East was never separated. The continuing rise of Kiev made its princes into powers to be reckoned with. Their northern counterpart, and occasional rival, was in time even ennobled with its own aristocratic title bestowed on the city itself: Lord Novgorod the Great. Its furs kept English monarchs warm into Tudor and Elizabethan times. The Viking roots of the riverine *voyageurs* who had founded the trade were never fully lost, and that link was occasionally activated in alliances and the like. It was difficult family history: even as late as the Soviet 1950s, the Communist Party felt it necessary to deny that the origins of Russia lay with Scandinavian ambition, rather than Slavic enterprise.

It is in the North Atlantic that 'Norse culture' continued longest, to the extent that for many years books on the Vikings continued to reference Icelandic settlements and material culture that were solidly medieval in date. (I have done so here, a little, in the Norse contacts with the high Canadian Arctic.)

These were not static societies. The social codes came increasingly under the mantle of the Church, although they were necessarily adapted to the unique sensibilities of the region. Iceland's politics became ever more tightly bound with those of Norway. The age of the saga-writers—Snorri Sturluson not least among them—was also a time of intense manoeuvring for power among the country's leading families. Archaeologists can tell how rural architecture and life on the land changed with new social conditions in Iceland and the needs of a colder climate, but at the same time there were real continuities with the Viking Age. It is no accident that the medieval saga-world and the ancestral Viking past can feel so similar on the page. Still today, Iceland is probably the region of the diaspora that most consciously and approvingly preserves its connection to the past.

In Greenland, the Norse occupation did not last, but the end was drawn out and is still an enigmatic puzzle to researchers. A reorientation of the ivory trade to India and Africa in the thirteenth century affected the demand for walrus tusks—the colony's prestige export item—and, in general, European merchants chose to do business with more accessible places closer to home. This was a major economic blow, in a place where life was never far from marginal at the best of times. The ships from Iceland and Norway grew fewer by the year. Nonetheless, the settlers clung to their farms into the 1300s, their numbers dwindling slowly. For much of that time, they still kept up with European fashion and political trends; the annual trading vessels were a rich source of information and gossip. Greenland was remote, but not a complete backwater even so. Several runic inscriptions record voyages of hunting and exploration far into the frozen north of the country and across into Arctic Canada, all the way up to Ellesmere Island. Into the Middle Ages, however, a steady deterioration in the climate meant that viable agricultural subsistence became unreliable at precisely the time when the Norse needed to depend on it more than ever. There are also unproven suggestions of conflict with Thule groups moving into Greenland from the north. Over time, people moved away, or died, and the farms just ran down.

The destiny of Norse Vinland was linked to that of its explorers' homelands, but there is a brief coda. In 1121, a bishop in Greenland "left to seek Vinland" and thereby disappeared from history. In 1347, a storm-tossed ship arrived in Iceland, blown off course while on its way home to Greenland—its crew had been collecting timber along the Labrador coast, the 'Markland' of the Norse. The memory of the far West was evidently kept alive in the North Atlantic if, by the fourteenth century, it could be noted without much interest that people were felling trees there. But after that

24. The very end. On the banks of the fjord at Hvalsey near modern Qaqortoq in south Greenland lies the now-ruined church where Sigrid Björnsdóttir married Thorstein Ólafsson on September 16, 1408. A report of their wedding is the last reference we have to the Norse occupation of Greenland that began in the Viking Age. Photo: Neil Price, taken on the 600th anniversary of the marriage.

the record is silent, until Norwegian researchers found L'Anse aux Meadows more than half a millennium later.

The last message from the Greenland colony is a strange one. At Hvalsey church, near modern Qaqortoq, on September 16, 1408, Sigrid Björnsdóttir married Thorstein Ólafsson, the captain of a ship that had arrived from Iceland. We know of this because the legitimacy of their marriage was questioned when the couple sailed back to Thorstein's home. It is clear that nobody in Iceland seems to have thought there was still a functioning clergy in Greenland. This sceptical note is the very last reference to the Norse occupation that began in the Viking Age, and it also includes other details brought back by that last ship—a lethal witch trial, complicated with sexual jealousy and the vicious micropolitics of a small community where enmities can get out of control. The outpost to the west was in terminal decline, and its ultimate abandonment cannot have been far off.

Hvalsey church is surprisingly well-preserved today, surrounded by the tumbled stones of the settlers' farms with the water stretching away in front. Exactly six hundred years to the day after the wedding, in September 2008, I was with a group of Viking scholars visiting the spot to mark this distant anniversary. In a curious and moving echo, we were accompanied by a descendant of the original couple. The clouds were low and grey, icebergs dotted the fjord, and on the way in a whale had surfaced close to the boat. It was a forbidding and lonely place, the ruined church roofless and open to a dark sky.

Through the second and third sections of this book, from the Viking phenomenon to new lands and nations, the early medieval Scandinavians have emerged more as they are conventionally perceived: as travellers in pursuit of profit, loot, fame, or a new home. Their world was vast.

A person born in Swedish Uppland could have walked the streets of Baghdad's round city, the centre of the Islamic world. More importantly, they could then have gone home and told everyone about it, and shown them the wonderfully smooth, flowing cloth of shining colours they'd bought. More striking still is the fact that their family and friends might have compared that silk unfavourably with the nicer stuff that Cousin Eirík had traded from the gulf of the southern sea the year before, after it had made a long journey through many hands from somewhere improbably farther east where (so they say) people had differently shaped eyes.

A person born in Denmark could have cruised with Vikings through the waters of Frankia and fought on the Seine beneath the burning walls of Paris, before heading out for the Midgard Sea from a base on the Loire. They could have passed the great rock at its entrance and plundered all the way to—just possibly—Alexandria, and back. Think of the tales, the stories told in the taverns of Europe, of the dazzling mosque of Córdoba and of the stone gods with animal heads in the delta of the Nile.

One individual from the later Viking Age can stand for them all, here at the end, someone we have already met. Shortly after the year 1000, Gudríd Thorbjarnardóttir coasted the shores of Helluland and Markland before landing in Vinland with her husband, Thorfinn karlsefni, and their crew. They were probably not the first Norse visitors and likely followed the path taken by others before them. Gudríd was pregnant, and while in Vinland, she gave birth to the first European child born in North America (and how appropriate to future history that he should be called Snorri). She had already come a long way, of Norwegian family from Iceland via Greenland, and from one set of beliefs to the new faith. She met First Nations people, and later—making a pilgrimage to Rome—she would almost certainly meet the pope; she had eaten wild grapes in Vinland, and she would taste Mediterranean wines under the Italian sun. By the time she reached old age as a Christian nun in Iceland, Gudríd was probably the most travelled woman on the planet.

These are all familiar figures of the 'Viking world', or more properly of the diaspora, updated in the archaeological details but nonetheless the people we know. But we should not forget the first section of the book, when we saw who they really were. That traveller in Baghdad was grateful that their *hamingja* was so powerful, that their luck-spirit got them home safe. The raider in Andalucía made blood offerings to the gods of lightning and war, and trusted that the *valkyrjur* would always be there, watching and waiting. Even Gudríd knew the right songs to summon otherworldly beings at the call of a *völva* sorceress, before turning away from them to a vision of the White Christ. Her descendants would be bishops. Perhaps even she was content that her *hugr* had, in the end, truly found its home.

503

The Viking mind is far away from us today, but occasionally just about tangible. When we walk through a forest at night, or watch the moon rise over a black field of *hraun* lava, or greet the spring in the unnervingly still waters of a lake, we can touch its workings for a moment or two.

Beyond the stereotypes, the Viking Age (and not just in Scandinavia) was a time of horrifying violence and equally awful structures of institutionalised, patriarchal oppression. Men and women, along with people who adopted a remarkably broad spectrum of different gendered identities, lived within and through these networks—building, perpetuating, and supporting them, but also tearing them down, resisting and subverting, creating anew.

The same Viking Age was also a period of social innovation, a vivid and multi-cultural time, with considerable tolerance of radical ideas and foreign faiths. It was a period of flourishing arts, with an explicit acceptance that travel and cultural encounter broadened one's outlook. If people today bring anything away from a meeting with the Viking Age, it should be this. We should never ignore or suppress the brutal realities behind the clichés—the carnage of the raids, the slaving, the misogyny—but there was much, much more to the Vikings. They changed their world, but they also allowed themselves to be altered, in turn; indeed, they embraced those connections with other peoples, places, and cultures.

Their most respected values were not only those forged in war but also—stated outright in poetry—a depth of wisdom, generosity, and reflection. Above all, a subtlety, a certain play of mind, combined with a resilient refusal to give up.

There are worse ways to be remembered.

EPILOGUE: GAMES

THIS IS A VISION OF the future, because the Ragnarök is still to come.

First the heavenly bodies will go dark. Sól, the shining sun-woman, is swallowed whole, the lamp of the day extinguished forever. The moon is caught at last by the howling wolf Mánagarm, 'Moon-Dog', that has been on its trail for aeons. Máni is chewed up, his dying light spattering the world like blood as it dims to black. Cold grips Midgard; frost chills the ground in a winter that does not end. The mountains tremble, the dwarves moaning and keening in their halls. Trees shake loose from the earth, and Yggdrasill itself shudders and groans.

The roosters begin to crow—in Asgard, in Hel, in the distant forest at the edge of things. Heimdall's horn is heard across the worlds, warning of the coming horror.

Every bond, every fetter, every chain, loosens and breaks. All the forces of the dark begin to stir, and move into the gloom towards Asgard and the final battle.

On the sea floor, the Nail-Ship slips free and rises to the surface in a choking wreath of weed and decay, water streaming from the deck. The drowned sit at its oars, the ranks of the dead stand packed in its hull, and Loki is at the helm.

Bifröst, the rainbow bridge that has stood since the creation, will fail at last as it breaks beneath the sons of Muspell when they ride to the Ragnarök. Shards of colour fall and fade behind them, while the frost giants ford the mighty rivers of the other world to reach the plain of combat. The fire giants' battle array is very bright, and it stretches for a hundred leagues in every direction.

Odin rides to meet them from the doors of Valhöll, his helmet made of gold, his spear levelled for the charge. Sleipnir's eight legs eat up the distance, the ground speeding beneath him. Behind the lord of the gods, the einherjar pour from every gate, their long-awaited war come at last.

The plain darkens with the countless millions of beings fighting across it—gods, giants, monsters, spirits of all kinds, and humans both living and dead. The rising noise, a vast scream echoing through the worlds, drowns all sound.

The ocean boils and churns as the Midgard Serpent twists itself onto the land. Its venom sprays over Thor even as he kills it, his hammer falling as he takes nine great paces into Hel. Loki and Heimdall—the trickster and the guardian of the bridge—each slay the other. Týr fights the hellhound, Garm, and they are both torn to pieces. Freyr is forced to battle without his sword and is killed by Surt, whose own blade shines brighter than the sun. The jaws of the great wolf, Fenrir, open wide to scrape the earth and sky, and Odin is eaten alive. But the beast does not live long, its head ripped apart by All-Father's son. The worlds are awash with blood, but all has happened as it should—as it was foretold.

When the Ragnarök is done, everything is dead. The gods and their foes lie paired, slain together in mutual fury. Around the plains of Vígríthr, the field is strewn to the horizon with all the bodies of the human race and the invisible population with whom they shared their world. There is no light because the sky is black and empty, the celestial bodies dissolved. A cold, dark fog covers the worlds, and the very fabric of creation is streaming away into the void. The end of all things, death after the afterlife, an eternal absence.

But it is not, in fact, the End.

A new earth, verdant and green with flowing waterfalls, rises from the ocean. A new sun, daughter of the old, brings light to the heavens. Somehow, the sons of Odin and the sons of Thor have survived, the latter inheriting his hammer. Baldr returns from Hel, as does Höd, the brother who slew him by mistake. They gather in the ruins of what was Asgard, on the field of Ithavölr. The first thing they see? A set of golden chess pieces "that in the old days they had owned", shining in the meadow. A wonderful new hall appears on a hill, with fields of self-sown corn springing up below it, for "the worthy warrior bands" who will live there (in the words of the Seeress's Prophecy*). It seems that humans will populate this place again.*

And now we see them: a man and a woman who have hidden from the Ragnarök in the depths of the forests. The woman is Lif, 'Life'; the man is Lifthrasir, 'Lover of Life'. They emerge from the trees, into the sunlight.

It is all ready to start over, with a new first couple; they are the parents of new people—new children—to come.

It would be hard to conceive of a greater cataclysm—apocalypse with a capital *A*—which is probably why the story of the Ragnarök continues to resonate in the popular imagination today. This is a Viking funeral for the entire cosmos.

The rebirth of the world after the final battle may possibly be a Christian addition, a vision of 'Viking heaven' on a biblical model to replace the multiple realms of death in the traditional beliefs, the one coming after the other just as the new faith supplanted what went before. A later source's ambiguous reference to the arrival of a "Powerful One" may refer to the risen Christ, adding to the sense of a (somewhat clumsy) medieval reworking of the original story. On the other hand, as we have seen, if the Fimbulwinter really was a memory of the sixth-century dust veil, then this too eventually passed and life began again.

An alternative interpretation sees the Ragnarök as reflective of Icelandic concerns with the ever-present harshness of their environment. In this ecocritical view, the whole of Norse mythology—most of which comes to us through Icelandic texts—is not unreasonably seen to exhibit "an intense preoccupation with the idea of an onrushing and unstoppable apocalypse", embodying the anxieties of a life that, at times, was close to the margins of viable subsistence.

Ultimately, the exact nature of the Ragnarök is one more of the ambiguities that surround the thought-world of the Norse. Whether or not the Scandinavians of the Viking Age originally believed that Ragnarök really was the end of all things, by the Middle Ages, when the stories were frozen into the form that has reached us, there is no doubt of their continuation in the medieval mind. And so the worlds will begin again, with a game of chess in the grass.

This book began with a metaphor, an attempt at a new reading of the Vikings on their own terms, trying to see them as they saw themselves—hence my choice of title. Here at the end, which also concerns the final chapter of that cosmology, we can take the same phrase but apply a more literal meaning. We should not forget that all the Children of Ash and Elm were also, once, simply children: ten generations of small people who grew up in what we call the Viking Age—another shift of perspective away from the wild marauders of stereotype. They are gone, of course, but we can still just about make them out in the things they used; in their

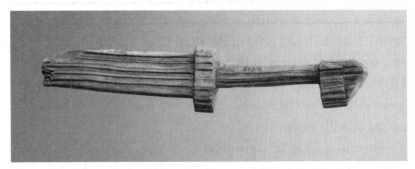

25. Playing Viking. A wooden toy sword from ninth-century levels at Staraja Ladoga, Russia. Photo: Vladimir Terebenin, © State Hermitage Museum, St. Petersburg.

graves, buried too soon with their little treasures; in the places they lived; and in the later texts, the poems and sagas.

We can see them at their games, playing. Galloping a wooden horse on an earthen floor in Dublin. Bouncing a ball made of rags along Novgorod's timber streets. Watching over a smaller sibling, wriggling about in a barred chair like the one from Lund. Battling with carefully crafted miniature wooden swords, made to match the bigger versions with the blades they weren't supposed to touch. We can see them in the rain and mist of the Faroes, sailing their toy boats on the spring melt and waiting for the tide.

26. A child of Ash and Elm. A facial reconstruction by Oscar Nilsson, based on the excavated skeletal remains of a six-year-old girl, buried at Birka, Sweden. Photo: Swedish History Museum, Creative Commons.

REFERENCES

T HE ACADEMIC AND POPULAR LITERATURE on the Vikings is truly vast, and
inevitably only a small selection can be given here. The relevant specific
sources are cited individually by chapter in the following, but the reader may
also be interested in general works, any of which can serve as inroads to wider
study.

1. GENERAL BACKGROUND

Perhaps the best one-volume academic treatment of the period ever written is
now a half century old and inevitably outdated in some ways, but still rewards
a close reading. *The Viking Achievement* by Peter Foote and David M. Wilson
(Sidgwick & Jackson, London, 1970) will probably never be surpassed in this
respect.

The standard academic source book is currently still *The Viking World*
(Routledge, London & New York, 2008), edited by Stefan Brink and myself,
containing nearly fifty chapters by the leading specialists in the field and covering most aspects of the period. For the latest authoritative syntheses of the
Viking Age, see Else Roesdahl, *The Vikings* (3rd edn., Penguin, London, 2016);
Jörn Staecker and Matthias Toplak (eds.), *Die Wikinger* (Propyläen, Berlin,
2019); and Jeanette Varberg, *Viking* (Gyldendal, Copenhagen, 2019). For an
excellent survey of the Vikings' material world, see Steve Ashby and Alison
Leonard, *Pocket Museum: Vikings* (Thames & Hudson, London & New York,
2018).

In addition, any of the following (including some older classics) will provide useful overviews up to their publication dates:

Gunnar Andersson (ed.), *We Call Them Vikings* (Swedish History Museum, Stockholm, 2016).

James Graham-Campbell, *The Viking World* (2nd edn., Francis Lincoln, London, 1989).

James Graham-Campbell, Colleen Batey, Helen Clarke, R. I. Page, and Neil Price, *Cultural Atlas of the Viking World* (Andromeda, Oxford, 1994).

Richard Hall, *The World of the Vikings* (Thames & Hudson, London & New York, 2007).

Dick Harrison and Kristina Svensson, *Vikingaliv* (Natur & Kultur, Stockholm, 2007).

Lotte Hedeager, *Iron Age Myth and Materiality: An Archaeology of Scandinavia AD 400–1000* (Routledge, London & New York, 2011).

Judith Jesch, *The Viking Diaspora* (Routledge, London & New York, 2015).

Gwyn Jones, *A History of the Vikings* (Oxford University Press, Oxford, 1984).

Alexander Koch (ed.), *Die Wikinger* (Minerva, Munich, 2008).

Anna Lihammer, *Vikingatidens härskare* (Historiska Media, Lund, 2012).

F. Donald Logan, *The Vikings in History* (3rd edn., Routledge, London & New York, 2005).

Julian D. Richards, *The Vikings: A Very Short Introduction* (Oxford University Press, Oxford, 2005).

Else Roesdahl and David M. Wilson (eds.), *From Viking to Crusader: Scandinavia and Europe 800–1200* (Nordic Council, Copenhagen, 1992).

Birgit Sawyer and Peter Sawyer, *Die Welt der Wikinger* (Siedler, Berlin, 2002).

Peter Sawyer, *The Age of the Vikings* (2nd edn., Arnold, London, 1971).

Peter Sawyer, *Kings and Vikings* (Methuen, London & New York, 1982).

Peter Sawyer (ed.), *The Oxford Illustrated History of the Vikings* (Oxford University Press, Oxford, 1997).

Gareth Williams, Peter Pentz, and Matthias Wemhoff (eds.), *Viking: Life and Legend* (British Museum, London, 2014).

Anders Winroth, *The Age of the Vikings* (Princeton University Press, Princeton, 2014).

Although it has been superseded by subsequent work, honourable mention should also be made of David M. Wilson's *The Vikings and Their Origins*

(Thames & Hudson, London & New York, 1970), as it is the only English-language work prior to this one which truly tries to set the Vikings in their longer-term context.

For readers interested in following avenues of enquiry with specialist help, two monumental encyclopaedic works are essential. The first is the *Kulturhistoriskt lexikon för nordisk medeltid* ('Cultural Historical Lexicon of the Nordic Middle Ages'), a trilingual work in the Scandinavian languages that appeared in twenty-two volumes between 1956 and 1978, consisting of thousands of short entries by leading scholars. German speakers may consult a similar work, the *Reallexikon der Germanischen Altertumskunde*, of which several editions exist: the initial four volumes from 1911 to 1919; the massive new series from 1968 to 2008, with more than one hundred supplementary specialist volumes that are still appearing as this book goes to press and which together comprise more than fifty thousand pages of text; and its internet successor, *Germanische Altertumskunde Online*, available by subscription from De Gruyter, which includes everything previously published together with continual updates.

PRIMARY SOURCES

Reference is given here to accurate translations in English, wherein the interested reader will find a full guide to the critical editions of the original works.

There are a number of good translations of the *Poetic Edda*, but my personal favourite is by Carolyne Larrington (Oxford University Press, Oxford, 1996). See also *The Elder Edda: A Book of Viking Lore* by Andy Orchard (Penguin, London, 2011). An excellent scholarly edition with the Old Norse text and parallel English translation is by the late Ursula Dronke, *The Poetic Edda* (3 vols., Oxford University Press, Oxford, 1969–2011). If this book prompts no other response in you than this, read the *Poetic Edda*! Unless otherwise noted, translations of Eddic poems in this book are from Larrington's edition.

Snorri Sturluson's works are of central importance. The best English translations of his *Prose Edda* are by Anthony Faulkes (Everyman, London, 1984) and Jesse Byock (Penguin, London, 2005). The *Heimskringla*, Snorri's collected histories of the kings of Norway, is translated by Alison Finlay and Anthony Faulkes (3 vols., Viking Society for Northern Research, London, 2011–2015).

The Complete Sagas of Icelanders (Including 49 Tales) have been translated in five volumes under the editorship of Viðar Hreinsson for Leifur Eiríksson Publishing (Reykjavík, 1997). Selections from this set, as a slightly smaller collection and as individual sagas, have been published separately since then by

Penguin, London. Translations of individual legendary sagas are referenced by chapter in the following.

The corpus of skaldic poetry is being steadily published in definitive new editions, including translations, edited by Margaret Clunies Ross, *Skaldic Poetry of the Scandinavian Middle Ages* (8 vols., Brepols, Leiden, 2008–).

A different kind of early medieval work, *The History of the Danes* by Saxo Grammaticus, has been translated by Hilda Ellis Davidson and Peter Fisher (2nd edn., Brewer, Cambridge, 1996).

The Book of Settlements, Landnámabók, is translated by Hermann Pálsson and Paul Edwards (University of Manitoba Press, Winnipeg, 2006); *Íslendingabók*, the Book of the Icelanders, is translated by Siân Grønlie (Viking Society for Northern Research, London, 2006).

A small number of books provide a general taster of the Old Norse written sources. *Chronicles of the Vikings: Records, Memorials and Myths* (British Museum Press, London, 1995), by the late Ray Page, is a marvellously eclectic collection. Page was one of the best prose stylists that Viking studies has ever produced, and his commentary on the difficult interpretation of written sources combines both insight and wit. Textual primary sources of all kinds are usefully collated by Angus A. Somerville and R. Andrew McDonald (eds.), *The Viking Age: A Reader* (3rd edn., University of Toronto Press, Toronto, 2020). A wider net is cast by the *Longman Anthology of Old English, Old Icelandic and Anglo-Norman Literatures,* which also sets the Norse material in its cultural context (eds. Richard North, Joe Allard, and Patricia Gilles, Longman, Harlow, 2011). For elegant samples of the verse, see R. G. Poole, *Viking Poems on War and Peace* (University of Toronto Press, Toronto, 1991) and Judith Jesch, *Viking Poetry of Love and War* (British Museum Press, London, 2013).

Runic inscriptions are designated in this book according to Scandinavian convention. In Sweden, each inscription is lettered by the province where it occurs (the most common being U, for Uppland) followed by a sequential number as each text was recorded in turn; Danish and Norwegian inscription numbers are prefixed by DR and NIyR respectively. The Swedish runic texts, which form the majority by far, are mostly covered by *Sveriges Runinskrifter*, published in fifteen volumes (some with several parts) from 1900 to 1981; updates on new finds can be found online from the Swedish National Heritage Board's 'runverket'. The easiest point of access to the entire corpus is through the online Scandinavian Rune-Text Database from Uppsala University. When runic inscriptions are mentioned in this book, references are given below to their identifying numbers, which can then be consulted in the aforementioned works.

A general introduction can be found in Martin Findell, *Runes* (British Museum Press, London, 2014). For overviews of the Scandinavian inscriptions, see Sven B. F. Jansson, *Runes in Sweden* (Gidlunds, Stockholm, 1987); Terje Spurkland, *Norwegian Runes and Runic Inscriptions* (Boydell, Woodbridge, 2005); and Lisbeth M. Imer, *Danmarks Runesten* (National Museum of Denmark, Copenhagen, 2016). These works contain hundreds of translated inscriptions, and I recommend browsing any of them to get the raw flavour of life in the Viking Age.

Most of the primary English and Continental sources on the Vikings have been translated, and all quotes from these texts come from the following editions:

The Anglo-Saxon Chronicle, ed. and trans. Michael Swanton (2nd edn., Phoenix, London, 2000).

Carolingian Chronicles [Royal Frankish Annals & Nithard's Histories], trans. Bernard Walter Scholtz (University of Michigan Press, Ann Arbor, 1972).

The Annals of St-Bertin, trans. Janet L. Nelson (Manchester University Press, Manchester, 1991).

The Annals of Fulda, trans. Timothy Reuter (Manchester University Press, Manchester, 1992).

Ottonian Germany: The Chronicon of Thietmar of Merseburg, trans. David A. Warner (Manchester University Press, Manchester, 2001).

Adam of Bremen, *History of the Archbishops of Hamburg-Bremen*, trans. Francis J. Tschan (Columbia University Press, New York, 1959).

The Annals of Ulster (to AD. 1131), eds. S. Mac Airt and G. Mac Niocaill (Dublin Institute for Advanced Studies, Dublin, 1983).

The War of the Gaedhil with the Gaill or The Invasions of Ireland by the Danes and Other Norsemen, trans. J. H. Todd (Longmans, Green, Reader, and Dyer, London, 1867).

The main Arab, Byzantine, and Russian sources are also available in excellent editions:

Aḥmad ibn Faḍlān, *Mission to the Volga*, ed. and trans. James E. Montgomery, in Tim Mackintosh-Smith and James E. Montgomery (eds.), *Two Arabic Travel Books* (NYU Press, New York, 2015), 165–298.

Ibn Fadlān and the Land of Darkness: Arab Travellers in the Far North, trans. Paul Lunde and Caroline Stone (Penguin, London, 2012); also includes ibn Hayyān, Ibrāhīm ibn Yaʻqūb, Miskawayh, and others.

Þórir Hraundal, *The Rus in Arabic Sources: Cultural Contacts and Identity* (University of Oslo, Oslo, 2013).

Constantine VII Porphyrogenitus, *De administrando imperio*, eds. and trans. Gyula Moravcsik and Romily Jenkins (Dumbarton Oaks, Washington, DC, 1967).

John Skylitzes, *A Synopsis of Byzantine History 811–1057*, trans. John Wortley (Cambridge University Press, Cambridge, 2010).

The Russian Primary Chronicle, trans. and ed. Samuel Hazzard Cross and Olgerd P. Sherbowitz-Wetzor (Medieval Academy of America, Cambridge, MA, 1953).

A much earlier, Roman text is mentioned several times in these pages as a vital source for the European heritage of the North. Cornelius Tacitus's study of *Germania* is often published together with his book on Britain, the *Agricola*:

Tacitus, *Agricola, Germany*, trans. A. R. Birley (Oxford University Press, Oxford, 1999).

2. CHAPTER NOTES

Needless to say, like any academic my knowledge is to a very substantial degree reliant on the work of others. The names of individual scholars have been omitted from the main text to improve flow, but it is important that the ideas discussed here are correctly attributed if they do not originate with me. The following notes credit these fellow Viking specialists and provide references to these secondary sources and points of entry for readers wishing to travel deeper into the Viking world.

PROLOGUE: DRIFTWOOD

I have chosen to begin this book with a brief retelling of the Norse creation story, but others have done so before me, and undoubtedly better. References to academic works on this theme can be found under chapter 1, following, but these same tales have also been recast in more literary form, to be enjoyed as such rather than as scholarly treatments. The best examples can be found in Kevin Crossley-Holland's *The Norse Myths: Gods of the Vikings* (Deutsch, London, 1980) and *Norse Myths: Tales of Odin, Thor and Loki* (Walker Books, London, 2017); A. S. Byatt's *Ragnarok: The End of the Gods* (Canongate, Edinburgh, 2011); and Neil Gaiman's *Norse Mythology* (Bloomsbury, London, 2017). My description of the gods on the beach is faithful to the Old Norse texts but has conscious echoes of the Haida origin myth in the lovely version by Bill Reid and Robert Bringhurst, *The Raven Steals the Light* (Douglas & McIntyre, Vancouver, 1988), when Raven finds the First Men wriggling in a clam shell on the sands of Rose Spit and frees them to play in his "wonderful, shiny new world".

There is an extensive literature on the Vikings' long, difficult historiography of appropriation and distortion. See Else Roesdahl and Preben Meulengracht Sørensen (eds.), *The Waking of Angantyr: The Scandinavian Past in European Culture* (Aarhus University Press, Aarhus, 1996); Andrew Wawn, *The Vikings and the Victorians: Inventing the Old North in Nineteenth-Century Britain* (Brewer, Cambridge, 2000); Catharina Raudvere, Anders Andrén, and Kristina Jennbert (eds.), *Myter om det nordiska—mellan romantik och politik* (Nordic Academic Press, Lund, 2001); Stefan Arvidsson, *Draksjukan: mytiska fantasier hos Tolkien, Wagner och de Vries* (Nordic Academic Press, Lund, 2007); Heather O'Donoghue, *From Asgard to Valhalla: The Remarkable History of the Norse Myths* (I. B. Tauris, London, 2010); and Jón Karl Helgason, *Echoes of Valhalla: The Afterlife of the Eddas and Sagas* (Reaktion, London, 2017), all with references for further reading. It is important to note—not least for professional students of the past—that in this the Vikings are far from alone. To take but one example, readings of the antique world have also been drawn into the same depressing narratives of prejudice and hate; see Mary Beard, *Women and Power: A Manifesto* (Profile, London, 2017) and Donna Zuckerberg, *Not All Dead White Men: Classics and Misogyny in the Digital Age* (Harvard University Press, Cambridge, MA, 2018). For a recent overview of where we are, see Sarah Croix's excellent essay, 'The Vikings, victims of their own success? A selective view on Viking research and its dissemination', *Danish Journal of Archaeology* 4:1 (2015): 82–96.

The Norwegian visitor to King Alfred's court was named Ohthere (probably Óttar in his own tongue); a full text and discussion of his account can be found in Janet Bately and Anton Englert (eds.), *Ohthere's Voyages* (Viking Ship Museum, Roskilde, 2007).

INTRODUCTION: ANCESTORS AND INHERITORS

The runestone mentioning the 'Viking watch' is U 617 from Bro in Uppland. For a summary of alternative readings of *víkingr*, see Frands Herschend, 'Wikinger', *Reallexikon der Germanischen Altertumskunde* 34 (2006): 55–59.

The exasperated Cambridge scholar who despaired of loose Viking terminology was Ray Page, his comment coming from an even more exasperated review in *Saga-Book of the Viking Society for Northern Research* 21 (1985): 308–311. The historian who unfortunately settled on 'Norsemen' was the late Eric Christiansen in his interesting but eccentric book *The Norsemen in the Viking Age* (Blackwell, Oxford, 2002: 1–9). Scepticism as to the impact of the Vikings, and even their existence outside the saga imagination, came to the fore in Fredrik Svanberg's *Decolonising the Vikings* (University of Lund, Lund, 2003) and in Richard Hodges's provocative 2004 essay, 'Goodbye to the Vikings?' *History Today* 54:9. A couple of my comments here echo my article, 'My Vikings and *Real Vikings*: Drama, documentary and historical consultancy', in Tom Birkett and Roderick Dale (eds.), *The Vikings Reimagined: Reception, Recovery, Engagement* (De Gruyter, Berlin, 2020: 28–43).

Turning to methods and sources, the thinking on time periods as vantage points resonates with Tom McCarthy's *Satin Island* (Knopf, London, 2015), an unnerving meditation on the impossibility of writing history. Readers interested in an overview of archaeological approaches can turn to Martin Carver, *Archaeological Investigation* (Routledge, London & New York, 2009). For the written sources, the main English and Continental texts are listed above; others are cited as necessary by chapter. There are several outstanding guides to the world of Old Norse sagas and poetry that include extensive discussion of genre, critical issues, and interpretation. I recommend Jónas Kristjánsson, *Eddas and Sagas: Iceland's Medieval Literature* (Hið íslenzka bókmenntafélag, Reykjavík, 1988); Heather O'Donoghue, *Old Norse-Icelandic Literature: A Short Introduction* (Blackwell, Oxford, 2004); Rory McTurk (ed.), *A Companion to Old Norse-Icelandic Literature and Culture* (Blackwell, Oxford, 2007); Margaret Clunies Ross, *The Cambridge Introduction to the Old Norse-Icelandic Saga* (Cambridge University Press, Cambridge, 2010); and Carolyne Larrington, Judy Quinn, and Brittany Schorn (eds.), *A Handbook to Eddic Poetry: Myths and Legends of Early Scandinavia* (Cambridge University Press, Cambridge, 2016).

The idea that the Codex Regius may have been the work of an amateur collector comes from conversation with Terry Gunnell. J. R. R. Tolkien's pithy comments about early medieval texts can be found in *The Monsters and the*

Critics, and Other Essays (Allen & Unwin, London, 1983). For a few words on the social context of the sagas, I have drawn on the translator Ben Waggoner's perceptive remarks in his introduction to *The Sagas of Ragnar Lodbrok* (Troth, New Haven, 2009). Useful meditations on the interactive experience of reading the Old Norse texts include M. I. Steblin-Kamenskij, *The Saga Mind* (Odense University Press, Odense, 1973) and Vésteinn Ólason, *Dialogues with the Viking Age* (Heimskringla, Reykjavík, 1998). The reading of Egil Skalla-Grímsson through a Christian lens is by Torfi Tulinius, *The Enigma of Egill* (Cornell University Press, Ithaca, 2015).

CHAPTER 1: THE HOME OF THEIR SHAPES

Beyond the *Poetic Edda*, anyone wanting to approach the world of Norse mythology, that reservoir of the Viking mind, should first turn to three fundamental source books that may be consulted for detail: Rudolf Simek, *Dictionary of Northern Mythology* (Brewer, Cambridge, 1993); Andy Orchard, *Dictionary of Norse Myth and Legend* (Cassell, London, 1997); and John Lindow, *Norse Mythology: A Guide to the Gods, Heroes, Rituals, and Beliefs* (Oxford University Press, Oxford, 2001).

Detailed studies of the Norse conception of the worlds have been published by Anders Andrén, *Tracing Old Norse Cosmology* (Nordic Academic Press, Lund, 2014) and Christopher Abram, *Evergreen Ash: Ecology and Catastrophe in Old Norse Myth and Literature* (University of Virginia Press, Charlottesville, 2019). Excellent works in Scandinavian languages include Henning Kure's *I begyndelsen var skriget: vikingetidens myter om skabelsen* (Gyldendal, Copenhagen, 2010) and the collection by Anders Andrén et al. (eds.), *Ordning mot kaos—studier av nordisk förkristen kosmologi* (Nordic Academic Press, Lund, 2004). The speculations on Snorri's motivations in recording pre-Christian lore and the idea of Yggdrasill as the Milky Way come from the work of Gísli Sigurðsson, research professor at the Árni Magnússon Institute for Icelandic Studies in Reykjavík; this book is the better in many ways for countless conversations with Gísli over the years. The quotation on the celestial bodies in the *Seeress's Prophecy* is from Jesse Byock's translation of the *Poetic Edda* referenced above.

A well-referenced overview of Norse mythology and cosmology can be found in Carolyne Larrington's *The Norse Myths* (Thames & Hudson, London, 2017). This is one of the most intensively studied aspects of Viking culture, and the literature here is vast. Among the still-relevant highlights are two timeless classics published the same year: H. R. Ellis Davidson, *Gods and Myths of*

Northern Europe (Penguin, London, 1964) and E. O. G. Turville-Petre, *Myth and Religion of the North* (Weidenfeld & Nicolson, London, 1964). Good collections of the latest thinking can be found in Margaret Clunies Ross, *Prolonged Echoes: Old Norse Myths in Medieval Northern Society* (2 vols., Odense University Press, Odense, 1994 & 1998); Merrill Kaplan and Timothy R. Tangherlini (eds.), *News from Other Worlds* (North Pinehurst Press, Berkeley, 2012); Timothy R. Tangherlini (ed.), *Nordic Mythologies: Interpretations, Intersections, and Institutions* (North Pinehurst Press, Berkeley, 2014); and Pernille Hermann, Stephen A. Mitchell, Jens Peter Schjødt, and Amber Rose (eds.), *Old Norse Mythology: Comparative Perspectives* (Harvard University Press, Cambridge, MA, 2017).

The gods are treated collectively in several of the above works, but see also Jean Renaud, *Les dieux des Vikings* (Ouest-France, Rennes, 1996). On Odin, see H. R. Ellis Davidson, *The Battle God of the Vikings* (University of York, York, 1972); Kris Kershaw, *The One-Eyed God* (Institute for the Study of Man, Washington, DC, 2000); and Annette Lassen, *Odin på kristent pergament* (Museum Tusculanum, Copenhagen, 2011). On Thor, see Richard Perkins, *Thor the Wind-Raiser and the Eyrarland Image* (Viking Society for Northern Research, London, 2001); Maths Bertell, *Tor och den nordiska åskan* (Stockholm University, Stockholm, 2003); Lasse Christian Arboe Sonne, *Thor-kult i vikingetiden* (Museum Tusculanum, Copenhagen, 2013); and Declan Taggart, *How Thor Lost His Thunder: The Changing Faces of an Old Norse God* (Routledge, London, 2018). On Baldr, see John Lindow, *Murder and Vengeance Among the Gods: Baldr in Scandinavian Mythology* (Academia Scientarum Fennica, Helsinki, 1997). On Loki, see Folke Ström, *Loki, ein mythologisches Problem* (Gothenburg University, Gothenburg, 1956); Georges Dumézil, *Loki* (Wissenschaftliche Buchgesellschaft, Darmstadt, 1959); Anna Birgitta Rooth, *Loki in Scandinavian Mythology* (Gleerup, Lund, 1961); and Yvonne S. Bonnetain, *Der nordgermanische Gott Loki aus literaturwissenschaftlicher Perspektive* (Kümmerle, Göppingen, 2006). On Freyja and the goddesses, see Britt-Mari Näsström, *Freyja—The Great Goddess of the North* (University of Lund, Lund, 1995) and *Nordiska gudinnor: nytolkningar av den förkristna mytologin* (Bonnier, Stockholm, 2009) and Ingunn Ásdísardóttir, *Frigg og Freyja: Kvenleg goðmögn í heiðnum sið* (Hið íslenska bókmenntafélag, Reykjavík, 2007).

The possible precursors of Norse religion in other traditions have been extensively discussed. The Indo-European hypothesis was first developed extensively by Georges Dumézil, *Mythes et dieux des Germains* (Leroux, Paris, 1939) and most recently has been explored by Anders Kaliff in several important works, including *Fire, Water, Heaven and Earth: Ritual Practice and Cosmology in Ancient Scandinavia: an Indo-European Perspective* (Riksantikvarieämbetet, Stockholm, 2007) and *Källan på botten av tidens brunn. Indoeuropeiska rötter till fornnordisk religion* (Carlssons, Stockholm, 2018). Anders Hultgård has investigated possible Vedic parallels in a large number of publications, all referenced in his magisterial book *Midgård brinner: Ragnarök i religionshistorisk belysning* (Royal Gustav Adolf Academy, Uppsala, 2017). For more general observations on comparative religion, including these traditions, see Neil MacGregor, *Living with the Gods: On Beliefs and Peoples* (Penguin, London, 2018).

The observation that the Norse 'pantheon' is something of an illusion comes from Terry Gunnell, 'Pantheon? What pantheon? Concepts of a family of gods in pre-Christian Scandinavian religions', *Scripta Islandica* 66 (2015): 55–76. The rituals practised by the gods themselves are discussed by Kimberley C. Patton, *Religion of the Gods: Ritual, Paradox, and Reflexivity* (Oxford University Press, Oxford, 2009: ch. 7). For the relationship of gods and giants, see two works by Gro Steinsland, 'Giants as recipients of cult in the Viking Age?', in Gro Steinsland (ed.), *Words and Objects: Towards a Dialogue Between Archaeology and History of Religion* (Instituttet for sammenlignende kulturforskning, Oslo, 1986: 212–222) and *Det hellige bryllup og norrøn kongeideologi* (Solum Forlag, Oslo, 1991); also Tommy Kuusela, *'Hallen var lyst i helig frid'. Krig och fred mellan gudar och jättar i en fornnordisk hallmiljö* (Stockholm University, Stockholm, 2017).

The meditations on fate closely follow the work of Karen Bek-Pedersen, the leading specialist in this field. References can be found in her book, *The Norns in Old Norse Mythology* (Dunedin, Edinburgh, 2011), which is also the best treatment of these beings.

The Valkyries are uniquely fascinating and have accordingly attracted an extensive literature. I have discussed them in my book *The Viking Way: Magic and Mind in Late Iron Age Scandinavia* (Oxbow, Oxford, 2019: 274–288), where readers can also find an annotated list of their names. For further reading in depth, see Folke Ström, *Diser, nornor, valkyrjor* (Royal Academy of Letters, Stockholm, 1954); Judy Quinn, '"Hildr prepares a bed for most Helmet-Damagers": Snorri's treatment of a traditional poetic motif in his *Edda*', in Pernille Hermann, Jens Peter Schjødt, and Rasmus Tranum Kristensen (eds.), *Reflections on Old Norse Myths* (Brepols, Turnhout, 2007: 95–118); Luke John Murphy, *Herjans dísir: valkyrjur, Supernatural Femininities, and Elite Warrior Culture in the Late Pre-Christian Iron Age* (unpublished MA thesis in Old Norse religion, University of Iceland, Reykjavík, 2013); Régis Boyer, *Les Valkyries* (Les Belles Lettres, Paris, 2014); and Karen M. Self, 'The Valkyrie's gender: Old

Norse shield maidens and Valkyries as a third gender', *Feminist Formations* 26:1 (2014): 143–172. The line about their lethally mesmerising appearance is from Jesse Byock's translation of *The Saga of the Völsungs* (University of California Press, Berkeley, 1990). The 'Web of Spears' poem is preserved in the *Saga of Burnt Njál* and discussed at length by Russell Poole, *Viking Poems on War and Peace* (University of Toronto Press, Toronto, 1991).

For all the 'invisible population'—spirits, *dísir*, and others—and Viking soul beliefs, see the individual entries in the three mythological dictionaries referenced above.

On the elves and dwarves, in particular, see two papers by Terry Gunnell, '*Hof*, halls, *goðar* and dwarves: An examination of the ritual space in the pagan Icelandic hall', *Cosmos* 17 (2001): 3–36 and 'How elvish were the álfar?', in John McKinnell, David Ashurts, and Donata Kick (eds.), *The Fantastic in Old Norse/Icelandic Literature* (International Saga Conference, Durham and York, 2006: 321–328); also Rudolf Simek, 'On elves', in Stefan Brink and Lisa Collinson (eds.), *Theorizing Old Norse Myth* (Brepols, Turnhout, 2017: 195–223). Rudy has also written on the *dísir*: 'Goddesses, mothers, dísir: Iconography and interpretation of the female deity in Scandinavia in the first millennium', in Rudolf Simek and Wilhelm Heizmann (eds.), *Mythological Women* (Fassbaender, Vienna, 2002: 93–123). Anyone interested in trolls has two excellent books to choose from: John Lindow's *Trolls: An Unnatural History* (Reaktion, London, 2014) and Rudolf Simek's *Trolle: Ihre Geschichte von der nordischen Mythologie bis zum Internet* (Böhlau, Cologne, 2018). The Bornholm 'trolls' are reported in Danish by René Laursen and Margrethe Watt, 'Guldhullet', *Skalk* 2011/4: 3–9 and Flemming Kaul, 'Folkminderne og arkæologien 2', *Skalk* 2018/5: 20–27.

The 'List of Spells' is incorporated into the 'Sayings of the High One' in the *Poetic Edda* and can be found in the aforementioned editions.

CHAPTER 2: AGE OF WINDS, AGE OF WOLVES

The political problems of the Western Empire's decline and the migrations have been explored from fundamentally different viewpoints by Guy Halsall in his *Barbarian Migrations and the Roman West, 376–568* (Cambridge University Press, Cambridge, 2007) and Peter Heather's *The Fall of the Roman Empire* (Oxford University Press, Oxford, 2007) and *Empires and Barbarians: Migration, Development and the Birth of Europe* (Pan Macmillan, London, 2009). See also Julia Smith, *Europe After Rome: A New Cultural History 500–1000* (Oxford University Press, Oxford, 2005) and Chris Wickham, *The Inheritance* of Rome: A History of Europe from 400 to 1000 (Allen Lane, London, 2009). For an excellent comparative exercise, see Giusto Traina, 428 AD: An Ordinary Year at the End of the Roman Empire (Princeton University Press, Princeton, 2009). For Roman relations with Scandinavia, see Kent Andersson, I skuggan av Rom: romersk kulturpåverken i Norden (Atlantis, Stockholm, 2013) and Sergio Gonzalez Sanchez and Alexandra Guglielmi (eds.), Romans and Barbarians Beyond the Frontiers: Archaeology, Ideology and Identities in the North (Oxbow, Oxford, 2017).

There are a number of good general overviews of Scandinavian later prehistory, including landscape perspectives. For Denmark, see Jørgen Jensen, Danmarks Oldtid (4 vols., Gyldendal, Copenhagen, 2006); for Norway, see Bergljot Solberg, Jernalderen i Norge (Cappelen, Oslo, 2000); for Sweden, see Stig Welinder, Sveriges Historia 13000 fKr–600 eKr (Norstedts, Stockholm, 2009). For agrarian (pre)history, see Janken Myrdal and Mats Morell (eds.), The Agrarian History of Sweden: 4000 BC to AD 2000 (Nordic Academic Press, Lund, 2011); Per Ethelberg et al., Det sønderjyske landbrugs historie: jernalder, vikingetid og middelalder (2nd edn., Museum Sønderjylland, Haderslev, 2012); and Frode Iversen and Håkan Petersson (eds.), The Agrarian Life of the North 2000BC–AD1000 (Portal, Oslo, 2017). All this is usefully placed in the biggest of big pictures by Barry Cunliffe, Europe Between the Oceans, 9000 BC–AD 1000 (Yale University Press, New Haven, 2008).

The Danish bog sacrifices are summarised in Jørgen Ilkjær, Illerup Ådal—et arkæologisk tryllespejl (Jysk Arkæologisk Selskab, Moesgård, 2000) and Lars Jørgensen, Birger Storgaard, and Lone Gebauer Thomsen (eds.), The Spoils of Victory: The North in the Shadow of the Roman Empire (National Museum of Denmark, Copenhagen, 2003). The Hellvi mask is published by Neil Price and Per Widerström, 'Bronsmasken från Hellvi', in Paul Wallin and Helene Martinsson-Wallin (eds.), Arkeologi på Gotland 2 (Uppsala University, Uppsala, 2017: 199–208).

For social structures and rural settlement of the Roman Iron Age and Migration Period, see Peder Mortensen and Birgit Rasmussen (eds.), Fra stamme til stat i Danmark (2 vols., Jysk Arkæologisk Selskab, Moesgård, 1988 & 1991); Charlotte Fabech and Jytte Ringtved (eds.), Samfundsorganisation og regional variation: Norden i romersk jernalder og folkevandringstid (Jysk Arkæologisk Selskab, Moesgård, 1991); Lotte Hedeager, Iron Age Societies (Blackwell, Oxford, 1992); Ulf Näsman, 'Från Attila till Karl den store: Skandinavien i Europa', in Michael Olausson (ed.), Hem till Jarlabanke: jord, makt och evigt liv i östra Mälardalen under järnålder och medletid (Historiska Media, Lund, 2008: 19–47); and Frands Herschend, The Early Iron Age in

South Scandinavia (Uppsala University, Uppsala, 2009). For the European context, see Hubert Fehr and Philipp von Rummel, *Die Völkerwanderung* (Theiss, Stuttgart, 2011). An excellent overview of Migration Period material culture can be found in Wolfgang Pülhorn (ed.), *Germanen, Hunnen und Awaren: Schätzte der Völkerwanderungszeit* (Germanisches Nationalmuseum, Nuremberg, 1987).

The massacre at Sandby borg is reported by Clara Alfsdotter, Ludvig Papmehl-Dufay, and Helena Victor, 'A moment frozen in time: Evidence of a late fifth-century massacre at Sandby borg', *Antiquity* 92 (2018): 421–436. The possible, and controversial, influence of the Huns has been considered by Lotte Hedeager, 'Scandinavia and the Huns: An interdisciplinary approach to the Migration Period', *Norwegian Archaeological Review* 40:1 (2007): 42–58 and in her book, *Iron Age Myth and Materiality: An Archaeology of Scandinavia AD 400–1000* (Routledge, London & New York, 2011).

The dismissive comment on "the latest Great Disaster theory" was by historian Chris Wickham in his book *Framing the Early Middle Ages* (Oxford University Press, Oxford, 2005: 549), although in fairness he wrote this before the full range of environmental proxies truly became clear. Many scholars are currently working on the sixth-century crisis and in particular the 'dust veil'; I thank, in particular, Ulf Büntgen, Matthew Collins, Svante Fischer, Ingar Gundersen, Hans Göthberg, Frode Iversen, Arild Klokkervoll, Fredrik Charpentier Ljungqvist, Daniel Löwenborg, Ester Oras, Felix Riede, Dagfinn Skre, Sara Westling, Mats Widgren, and Torun Zachrisson. Particularly important early works include Joel D. Gunn (ed.), *The Years Without Summer: Tracing AD 536 and Its Aftermath* (BAR, Oxford, 2000) and Antti Arjava, 'The mystery cloud of AD 536 in the Mediterranean sources', *Dumbarton Oaks Papers* 59 (2005): 73–96. An overview of scholarship up to 2015 can be found in Neil Price and Bo Gräslund, 'Excavating the Fimbulwinter? Archaeology, geomythology and the climate event(s) of AD 536', in Felix Riede (ed.), *Past Vulnerability: Volcanic Eruptions and Human Vulnerability in Traditional Societies Past and Present* (Aarhus University Press, Aarhus, 2015: 109–132). See also Arne Anderson Stamnes, 'Effect of temperature change on Iron Age cereal production and settlement patterns in mid-Norway' and Frode Iversen, 'Estate division: Social cohesion in the aftermath of AD 536–7', both in Frode Iversen and Håkan Petersson (eds.), *The Agrarian Life of the North, 2000 BC–AD 1000* (Portal, Oslo, 2017: 27–76). Scientific analyses of the dust veil's cause appear at such a steady rate that comprehensive citation here would soon be outdated, but see M. Sigl et al., 'Timing and climate forcing of volcanic eruptions for the past 2,500 years', *Nature* 523 (2015): 543–549; Ulf Büntgen et al., 'Cooling and societal change during the Late Antique Little Ice Age from 536 to 660 AD', *Nature Geoscience* 9 (2016): 231–236; Matthew Toohey et al., 'Climatic and societal impacts of a volcanic double event at the dawn of the Middle Ages', *Climatic Change* 136 (2016): 401–412; and Robert A. Dull et al., 'Radiocarbon and geologic evidence reveal Ilopango volcano as source of the colossal 'mystery' eruption of 539/40 CE', *Quaternary Science Reviews* 222 (2019). The Justinian plague is treated by Lester K. Little (ed.), *Plague and the End of Antiquity: The Pandemic of 541–570* (Cambridge University Press, Cambridge, 2007).

The "ruin of the moon" comes from Jesse Byock's translation of the *Seeress's Prophecy* as contained in Snorri's *Edda* (ch. 12). The translations from the *Kalevala* are by J. M. Bosley (Oxford University Press, Oxford, 1989) while the verses from the earlier version are by Francis Peabody Magoun, *The Old Kalevala and Certain Antecedents* (Harvard University Press, Cambridge, MA, 1969).

The Sámi have attracted an extensive literature. For a general history, see Lars Ivar Hansen and Bjørnar Olsen, *Samernes historie fram til 1750* (Cappelen, Oslo, 2004); for its wider dimensions, see Carl-Gösta Ojala, *Sámi Prehistories: The Politics of Archaeology and Identity in Northernmost Europe* (University of Uppsala, Uppsala, 2009). For a crucial work on Sámi identity and ritual, see Birgitta Fossum, *Förfädernas land: en arkeologisk studie av rituella lämningar i Sápmi, 300 fKr–1600 eKr* (Umeå University, Umeå, 2006). The classic work on Sámi-Norse interaction is by Inger Zachrisson (ed.), *Möten i gränsland: samer och germaner i Mellanskandinavien* (Statens Historiska Museum, Stockholm, 1997); see also Neil Price, 'Drum-Time and Viking Age: Sámi-Norse identities in early medieval Scandinavia', in Martin Appelt, Joel Berglund, and Hans Christian Gulløv (eds.), *Identities and Cultural Contacts in the Arctic* (National Museum of Denmark, Copenhagen, 2000: 12–27). Their religion is also treated at length, in the comparative context of the Norse beliefs, by Thomas A. DuBois, *Nordic Religions in the Viking Age* (University of Pennsylvania Press, Philadelphia, 1999) and my own *The Viking Way: Magic and Mind in Late Iron Age Scandinavia* (2nd edn., Oxbow, Oxford, 2019: ch. 4). All these works contain extensive references.

One of the first to chart the rise of the 'new North' after the fifth- and sixth-century crisis was Peter Bratt, *Makt uttryckt i jord och sten: Stora högar och maktstrukturer i Mälaradalen under järnåldern* (Stockholm University, Stockholm, 2008), and the figures for monumental mounds in the Mälar Valley can be found in this work. A similar picture for western Sweden is presented by

Annelie Nitenberg, *Härskare i liv och död: social exklusivitet och maktstrategi i Vänerbygd under yngre järnålder* (Göteborg University, Göteborg, 2019). For wider studies, see Svante Norr, *To Rede and to Rown: Expressions of Early Scandinavian Kingship in Written Sources* (University of Uppsala, Uppsala, 1998) and John Ljungkvist, *En hiar atti rikR: om elit, struktur och ekonomi kring Uppsala och Mälaren under yngre järnålder* (Uppsala University, Uppsala, 2006). The historian who described the new elites as "violent chancers" was Guy Halsall, quoting one of his students, in his book *Warfare and Society in the Barbarian West, 450–900* (Routledge, London, 2003: xiii); this work is also an excellent source for the history and ideology of these warlords. An English and European context for this process is provided by Nicholas Howe, *Migration and Mythmaking in Anglo-Saxon England* (Yale University Press, New Haven, 1989); Martin Carver (ed.), *The Age of Sutton Hoo* (Boydell, Woodbridge, 1992); and Martin Carver, *Formative Britain: An Archaeology of Britain, Fifth to Eleventh Century AD* (Routledge, London, 2019).

For primary sources on the new elites, one must inevitably begin with *Beowulf;* a good English translation is by Michael Alexander (rev. edn., Penguin, London, 2003); a flowing, poetic reading has been made by Seamus Heaney, *Beowulf: A New Translation* (Faber & Faber, London, 1999). The latest scholarship on the poem, especially relating to its historicity as a source for the late Migration Period, can be found in Bo Gräslund, *Beowulfkvädet: den nordiska bakgrunden* (Uppsala University, Uppsala, 2018). Other texts on the royal families of the North are treated in the works above and referenced for chapter 10, following, but a key source is the *Saga of the Ynglingas*, the first book of Snorri's *Heimskringla*.

On the martial image, see Paul Trehearne, 'The warrior's beauty: The masculine body and self-identity in Bronze-Age Europe', *European Journal of Archaeology* 3:1 (1995): 105–144. The Valsgärde site and its publications are summarised in Svante Norr (ed.), *Valsgärde Studies: The Place and Its People, Past and Present* (Uppsala University, Uppsala, 2008) and Kent Andersson, *Krigarna från Valsgärde* (Atlantis, Stockholm, 2017). The Vendel Period is otherwise poorly served with syntheses for Scandinavia, and nothing has yet superseded two publications that appeared some time back: Ann Sandwall (ed.), *Vendeltid* (Statens Historiska Museum, Stockholm, 1980) and Jan Peder Lamm and Hans-Åke Nordström (eds.), *Vendel Period* (Statens Historiska Museum, Stockholm, 1983). A brief, popular overview can be found in Charlotte Hedenstierna-Jonson, John Ljungkvist, and Neil Price, *The Vikings Begin* (Uppsala University, Uppsala, 2018). The birch-bark shrouds on some of the

References

Valsgärde boat graves, of probable Sámi origin, are discussed by Karolina Pallin in her undergraduate thesis in art history, *Vendeltida båtkapell: textilt näverhantverk i Valsgärdes båtgravar* (Uppsala University, Uppsala, 2016).

Hall culture and architecture are discussed by Frands Herschend, *Livet i hallen* (Uppsala University, Uppsala, 1997) and Johan Callmer and Erik Rosengren (eds.), *". . . gick Grendel att söka det höga huset . . ." Arkeologiska källor till aristokratiska miljöer i Skandinavien under yngre järnålder* (Hallands County Museum, Halmstad, 1997). A useful study of the hall's less tangible qualities can be found in A. C. Antoniades, *Epic Space: Towards the Roots of Western Architecture* (Wiley, London, 1992). For the militant ideologies of the hall, see Michael J. Enright, *Lady with a Mead Cup: Ritual, Prophecy and Lordship in the European Warband from La Tène to the Viking Age* (Four Courts, Dublin, 1996) and Stephen S. Evans, *Lords of Battle* (Boydell, Woodbridge, 1997).

The royal centres that underpinned these fledgling polities have been published by Tom Christensen, *Lejre bag myten* (Jysk Arkæologisk Selskab, Moesgård, 2015); Bjørn Myhre, *Før Viken ble Norge* (Vestfold Fylkeskommune, Tønsberg, 2015); Olof Sundqvist and Per Vikstrand (eds.), *Gamla Uppsala i ny belysning* (Gävle College, Gävle, 2013); and Kristina Ekero Eriksson, *Gamla Uppsala: människor och makter i högarnas skugga* (Norstedts, Stockholm, 2018). For the Götar equivalent, see Martin Rundkvist, *Mead-Halls of the Eastern Geats: Elite Settlements and Political Geography AD 375–1000 in Östergötland, Sweden* (Royal Academy of Letters, Stockholm, 2011), and for the south, see Fredrik Svanberg, *Vikingatiden i Skåne* (Historiska Media, Lund, 2000). For the massive hall at Borg, see Gerd Stamsø Munch, Olav Sverre Johansen, and Else Roesdahl (eds.), *Borg in Lofoten: A Chieftain's Farm in North Norway* (Tapir, Trondheim, 2003). The 'Shining Hall' of Kaupang is discussed by Dagfinn Skre in volume 1 of the *Kaupang Excavation Project* (4 vols., Oslo University / Aarhus University Press, Norske Oldfunn 22–25, 2007–2016) while the latest on Tissø is published as Sandie Holst, Lars Jørgensen, and Egon Wamers, *Odin, Thor und Freyja: Skandinavische Kultplätze des 1. Jahrtausends n. Chr. und das Frankenreich* (Schnell & Steiner, Regensburg, 2017).

The quotation from *Beowulf* comprises lines 2633–2642, given here in Seamus Heaney's poetic translation.

The ocular effects of helmets in firelight are discussed by Neil Price and Paul Mortimer, 'An eye for Odin? Divine role-playing in the age of Sutton Hoo', *European Journal of Archaeology* 17:3 (2014): 517–538. The gold-foil figures, so-called *guldgubber*, are best encountered through the many publications of Margrethe Watt; by way of introduction in English, they are addressed in the context of their greatest find spot on Bornholm: Christian Adamsen et al. (eds.), *Sorte Muld: Wealth, Power and Religion at an Iron Age Central Settlement on Bornholm* (Bornholms Museum, Rønne, 2009). A major new study appeared as this volume went to press, Alexandra Pesch and Michaela Helmbrecht (eds.), *Gold Foil Figures in Focus* (Centre for Baltic and Scandinavian Archaeology, Schleswig, 2019). Their clothes have been discussed by Ulla Mannering, *Iconic Costumes: Scandinavian Late Iron Age Costume Iconography* (Oxbow, Oxford, 2017), a book that also reproduces hundreds of the foils.

International trade, and Baltic interaction, is referenced under chapters 10 and 14, following, but see also Søren Sindbæk and Athena Trakadas (eds.), *The World in the Viking Age* (Viking Ship Museum, Roskilde, 2014). For the new understanding of the 'outlands' and their importance for trade, see Steve Ashby, Ashley Coutu, and Søren Sindbæk, 'Urban networks and Arctic outlands: Craft specialists and reindeer antler in Viking towns', *European Journal of Archaeology* 18 (2015): 679–704. In particular, several major works on this have been published by Andreas Hennius, 'Viking Age tar production and outland exploitation', *Antiquity* 92 (2018): 1349–1361; Andreas Hennius et al., 'Whalebone gaming pieces: Aspects of marine mammal exploitation in Vendel and Viking Age Scandinavia', *European Journal of Archaeology*, 21(2018): 612–631; and Andreas Hennius, 'Towards a refined chronology of prehistoric pitfall hunting in Sweden', *European Journal of Archaeology* (2020, in press); his forthcoming doctoral thesis is set to fundamentally rewrite our view of these economies. For this section, I have also benefitted from John Moreland's timeless essay 'Concepts of the early medieval economy', originally from 2000 but collected in his *Archaeology, Theory and the Middle Ages* (Duckworth, London, 2010: 75–115).

CHAPTER 3: THE SOCIAL NETWORK

Scandinavian social structure is explored by Jón Viðar Sigurðsson, *Det norrøne samfunnet* (Pax, Oslo, 2008); for family life, in particular, see Birgit Sawyer, *Kvinnor och familj i det forn- och medeltida Skandinavien* (Viktoria, Skara, 1992) and Liv Helga Dommasnes, 'Women, kinship, and the basis of power in the Norwegian Viking Age', in Ross Samson (ed.), *Social Approaches to Viking Studies* (Cruithne Press, Glasgow, 1991: 65–73). Further insight into kin relations can be found in Tara Carter, *Iceland's Networked Society* (Brill, Leiden, 2015). The comment about the property owning the owners is from Eric Christiansen, *The Norsemen in the Viking Age* (Blackwell, Oxford, 2002).

On marriage, polygyny, and concubinage, see Auður G. Magnúsdóttir, *Frillor och fruar: politik och samlevnad på Island 1120–1400* (Gothenburg University, Gothenburg, 2001) and 'Women and Sexual Politics', in Stefan Brink and Neil Price (eds.), *The Viking World* (Routledge, London, 2008: 40–48). See also Ben Raffield, Neil Price, and Mark Collard, 'Polygyny, concubinage and the social lives of women in Viking-Age Scandinavia', *Viking and Medieval Scandinavia* 13 (2018): 165–209. The Arab writers who describe polygyny are discussed by Þórir Hraundal, *The Rus in Arabic Sources: Cultural Contacts and Identity* (University of Oslo, Oslo, 2013). Adam of Bremen's account is referenced above; the relevant section on the Danish king's vices is in book 4, chapter 21, and book 3, chapter 11. The saga and poetic texts mentioned here are reviewed in more detail in the paper by Raffield et al., referenced above. I am grateful to Steinunn Kristjánsdóttir for her discussions on polygyny from an Icelandic perspective. The runestones mentioning multiple wives are Sö 297 from Uppinge in Södermanland and U 1039 from Bräcksta in Uppland.

The complex mechanics of *vinátta*—friendship—are explored by Jón Viðar Sigurðsson, *Viking Friendship: The Social Bond in Iceland and Norway, c.900–1300* (Cornell University Press, Ithaca, 2017).

The quote from the *Sayings of the High One* recommending leaving your dog for a neighbour to feed comes from strophe 83. A superb illustrated survey of the Viking-Age household and most other aspects of daily life can be found in Kurt Schietzel, *Spurensuche Haithabu* (4th edn., Wachholtz, Neumünster, 2018). For a representative sample of rural settlement studies, see Sten Tesch, *Houses, Farmsteads, and Long-Term Change* (Uppsala University, Uppsala, 1993); Hans Göthberg, Ola Kyhlberg, and Ann Vinberg (eds.), *Hus och gård i det förurbana samhället* (2 vols., Riksantikvarieämbetet, Stockholm, 1995); and Karin Rosberg, *Vikingatidens byggande i Mälardalen* (Uppsala University, Uppsala, 2009).

Viking food culture is discussed by Sven Isaksson, *Food and Rank in Early Medieval Time* (Stockholm University, Stockholm, 2000); Per Widerström, 'Järnålderns mat—en annan smakpalett', *Gotländsk Arkiv* 91 (2019): 106–113; for the late Viking Age in the West, see also Ditlev Mahler (ed.), *Gruel, Bread, Ale and Fish: Changes in the Material Culture Related to Food Production in the North Atlantic 800–1300 AD* (National Museum of Denmark, Copenhagen, 2018). The thesis on Viking bread is by Liselotte Bergström, *Gräddat: brödkultur under järnåldern i östra Mälardalen* (Stockholm University, Stockholm, 2007). Another thesis has been written just on meat spits and skewers: Susanne Bøgh-Andersen, *Vendel- och vikingatida stekspett* (Lund University, Lund,

1999). Viking-Age drinking glasses are discussed by Kent Anderson, *Glas från romare till vikingar* (Balderson, Uppsala, 2010).

For Viking entertainment, see Mark Hall, 'Board games in boat burials: Play in the performance of Migration and Viking Age mortuary practice', *European Journal of Archaeology* 19 (2016): 439–455; John Birdsagel, 'Music and musical instruments', in Phillip Pulsiano (ed.), *Medieval Scandinavia: An Encyclopedia* (Garland, New York, 1993: 420–423); and Leszek Gardeła, 'What the Vikings did for fun? Sports and pastimes in medieval northern Europe', *World Archaeology* 44 (2012): 234–247. The child's chair from Lund is published in Else Roesdahl and David M. Wilson (eds.), *From Viking to Crusader: Scandinavia and Europe 800–1200* (Nordic Council, Copenhagen, 1992: 376). The cosy neck support from the Mammen grave is described by Charlotte Rimstad, 'En komfortabel, evig søvn', *Skalk* 2019/5: 12–15.

Combs are discussed by Steven P. Ashby, *A Viking Way of Life* (Amberley, Stroud, 2014). The complaint about well-groomed Scandinavians is from John of Wallingford; see Richard Vaughan, 'The chronicle attributed to John of Wallingford', *Camden Miscellany* 21 (1958): 1–74.

A reconstruction of the stylish Scandinavian officer in Byzantium—actually Svjatoslav of Kiev—can be found in Ian Heath, *The Vikings* (Osprey, Oxford, 1985: plate G) after the description by Leo the Deacon. Aḥmad ibn Faḍlān's account is referenced in the general section above.

The main work on Viking-Age dental modification is by Caroline Ahlström Arcini, the osteologist who first identified the practice. Her ideas are collected and referenced in her book, *The Viking Age: A Time of Many Faces* (Oxbow, Oxford, 2018). Ibrāhīm ibn Ya'qūb's writings are also referenced above in the general section.

Most of the general works and exhibition catalogues listed above are picture driven, often in colour, aiming to illustrate the Viking Age in a way this book is not. Two works, in particular, are designed to do precisely that and they do it well: *Viking Artefacts* by James Graham-Campbell (British Museum Press, London, 1980) and *Pocket Museum: Vikings* by Steve Ashby and Alison Leonard (Thames & Hudson, London, 2018). The latter includes many images of three-dimensional figures with various hairstyles, including those mentioned in the text.

The Hårby and Revninge figures have only been preliminarily published as Mogens Bo Henriksen and Peter Vang Petersen, 'Valkyriefund', *Skalk* 2013/2: 3–10 and Claus Feveile, 'Revninge-figurens gåder', *Skalk* 2015/1: 3–8. For Viking-Age clothing, see Inga Hägg, *Kvinnodräkten i Birka* (Uppsala University, Uppsala, 1974) and *Textilien und Tracht in Haithabu und Schleswig* (Wachholtz,

Kiel, 2015); good colour images can be found as noted above in Kurt Schietzel, *Spurensuche Haithabu* (4th edn., Wachholtz, Neumünster, 2018). I am indebted to costume designer Linda Muir for observations on the potential sensual qualities of Viking clothing, the fruit of several enjoyable discussions.

The literature on jewellery and craftwork (including in metals) is enormous, and only a selection can be given here. The standard work on oval brooches is Ingmar Jansson, *Ovala spännbucklor* (University of Uppsala, Uppsala, 1985) while its equivalent for beads is Johan Callmer, *Trade Beads and Bead Trade in Scandinavia ca. 800–1000 AD* (Lund University, Lund, 1977). Major studies of metalworking, with their respective regional focus but wider referencing, can be found in the work of Gustaf Trotzig, *Craftsmanship and Function* (Statens Historiska Museum, Stockholm, 1991) and Unn Pedersen, *I smeltedigeln: finsmedene i vikingtidsbyen Kaupang* (University of Oslo, Oslo, 2010). Pendant figurines are discussed by Michaela Helmbrecht, *Wirkmächtige Kommunikationsmedien: Menschenbilder der Vendel- und Wikingerzeit und ihre Kontexte* (Lund University, Lund, 2011). The unique material culture of the Gotlanders is collected by Lena Thunmark-Nylén, *Die Wikingerzeit Gotlands* (4 vols., Royal Academy of Letters, Stockholm, 1995–2006), with reference to her own work on jewellery and that of Anders Carlsson.

Sources for agrarian practices and history have been noted above. The complete equipment of a smith has been published by Greta Arwidsson and Gösta Berg, *The Mästermyr Find: A Viking Age Tool Chest from Gotland* (Royal Academy of Letters, Stockholm, 1983). Textile work has been referenced above, but see also Marianne Vedeler, *Silk for the Vikings* (Oxbow, Oxford, 2014). The notion of pictorial textile weaving as a domain of female power is explored by Lena Norrman in her book *Viking Women: The Narrative Voice in Woven Tapestries* (Cambria Press, Amherst, 2008).

For artistic traditions, the latest synthesis, excellent and well-illustrated, is James Graham-Campbell's *Viking Art* (Thames & Hudson, London & New York, 2013). As one of the world's leading art-historical archaeologists of the Viking Age, James has also addressed aesthetics, and their economics, in many other general works (listed in the introduction to this section) and specialist regional studies, especially of Scotland; these are noted in the appropriate sections that follow. See also David M. Wilson, *Vikingatidens konst* (Signum, Lund, 1995).

CHAPTER 4: THE PURSUIT OF LIBERTY

Possible Bronze Age Scandinavian precedents on slaving are treated by Johan Ling, *Elevated Rock Art: Towards a Maritime Understanding of Bronze Age Rock*

Art in Northern Bohuslän, Sweden (University of Gothenberg, Gothenberg, 2008).

Foote and Wilson's *The Viking Achievement* (1970), noted above, was the first major work of synthesis to discuss slavery in early Scandinavia; it is still sound, and I have drawn on it in several places here (they are also the authors of the line about the enslaved owning and leaving nothing). More recently, slavery in the Viking Age has been discussed by Ruth Karras, *Slavery and Society in Medieval Scandinavia* (Yale University Press, New Haven, 1988); in the Swedish-language collection edited by Thomas Lindkvist and Janken Myrdal, *Trälar: ofria i agrarsamhället från vikingatid till medeltid* (Nordic Museum, Stockholm, 2003); and in Stefan Brink's *Vikingarnas slavar: den nordiska träldomen under yngre järnålder och äldsta medeltid* (Atlantis, Stockholm, 2012). The wider context to the west is provided by David Wyatt, *Slaves and Warriors in Medieval Britain and Ireland, 800–1200* (Brill, Leiden, 2009). A new field of research on Viking-Age slavery is being opened up by Ben Raffield, 'The slave markets of the Viking world: Comparative perspectives on an "invisible archaeology"', *Slavery and Abolition* 40 (2019): 682–705.

For the names of the enslaved from the *List of Ríg*, I have used translations of the *Poetic Edda* by Carolyne Larrington (1996) and Ursula Dronke (1997), with some minor amendments of my own. The runestones preserving the voices of the enslaved are U 11 from Hovgården in Swedish Uppland and DR 58 from Hørning in Denmark. Viking shackles have been studied by Ny Björn Gustafsson, 'För folk och fä: Vikingatida fjättrar och deras användning', *Fornvännen* 104 (2009): 89–96. The Weston stone is illustrated in Else Roesdahl et al. (eds.), *The Vikings in England* (Anglo-Danish Viking Project, London, 1981: 61). The burnt 'tomb of the thralls' at Tranders is published by Lise Harvig, J. Kveinborg, and Niels Lynnerup, 'Death in flames: Human remains from a domestic house fire from Early Iron Age, Denmark', *International Journal of Osteoarchaeology* 25 (2015): 701–710.

The Ballateare burial is published by Gerhard Bersu and David M. Wilson, *Three Viking Graves on the Isle of Man* (Society for Medieval Archaeology, King's Lynn, 1966: 35–62). The research on the diet of the enslaved is by Elise Naumann, Maja Krzewińska, Anders Götherström, and Gunilla Eriksson, 'Slaves as burial gifts in Viking Age Norway? Evidence from stable isotope and Ancient DNA analyses', *Journal of Archaeological Science* 41 (2013): 533–540. The study relating slavery to dental modification is by Anna Kjellström, 'Spatial and temporal trends in new cases of men with modified teeth from Sweden (AD 750–1100)', *European Journal of Archaeology* 17:1 (2014): 45–59.

References

CHAPTER 5: BORDER CROSSINGS

Studies of gender in the Viking Age have only recently begun to seriously branch out beyond binary discussions, most of which have emphasised studies of women. Major works include Judith Jesch, *Women in the Viking Age* (Boydell, Woodbridge, 1991); Jenny Jochens, *Women in Old Norse Society* (Cornell University Press, Ithaca, 1995); Eva-Marie Göransson, *Bilder av kvinnor och kvinnlighet: Genus och kroppspråk under övergången till kristendomen* (Stockholm University, Stockholm, 1999); Nancy Coleman and Nanna Løkka (eds.), *Kvinner i vikingtid* (Scandinavian Academic Press, Oslo, 2014); and Jóhanna Katrín Friðriksdóttir, *Valkyrie: the Women of the Viking World* (Bloomsbury, London, 2020). Works mainly focussing on Old Norse literature include Jenny Jochens, *Old Norse Images of Women* (University of Pennsylvania Press, Philadelphia, 1996); Rudolf Simek and Wilhelm Helzmann (eds.), *Mythological Women* (Fassbaender, Vienna, 2002); Sarah Anderson and Karen Swenson (eds.), *Cold Counsel: Women in Old Norse Literature and Mythology* (Routledge, London & New York, 2002); and Jóhanna Katrín Friðriksdóttir, *Women in Old Norse Literature: Bodies, Words and Power* (Palgrave Macmillan, New York, 2013). Most of these works also take up the more specific themes that follow.

More general studies include Tove Hjørungdal, *Det skjulte kjønn: patrialkal tradisjon og feministisk visjon i arkeologien belyst med fokus på en jernalderskontekst* (University of Lund, Lund, 1991); Elisabeth Arwill-Nordbladh, *Genuskonstruktioner i nordisk vikingatid* (Gothenburg University, Gothenburg, 1998); and Henric Bagerius, 'I genusstrukturens spänningsfält: Om kön, genus och sexualitet i saga och samhälle', *Arkiv för Nordisk Filologi* 2001: 21–63; see also Katherine Hauptmann, 'Slaget om vikingatiden—en ojämn kamp mot forna stereotyper', in Katherine Hauptmann and Kerstin Näversköld (eds.), *Genusförbart: inspiration, erfarenheter och metoder för mångfald i museiarbete* (Nordic Academic Press, Lund, 2014: 61–71).

The runestone from Fläckebo in Västmanland is Vs 24. The 'single-sex' model is from Carol Clover's influential paper, 'Regardless of sex: Men, women, and power in early Northern Europe' *Speculum* 68:2 (1993): 1–28. The best work on shared traits, with the burial study mentioned in the text, has been undertaken by Marianne Moen, *Challenging Gender: A Reconsideration of Gender in the Viking Age Using the Mortuary Landscape* (University of Oslo, Oslo, 2019), building on her earlier book *The Gendered Landscape: A Discussion on Gender, Status and Power in the Norwegian Viking Age Landscape* (BAR, Oxford, 2011) and also explored in her paper 'Gender and archaeology: Where are we now?', *Archaeologies* 15/2 (2019): 206–226. Excellent wider studies that adopt a fruitful, integrated approach to gender include Michèle Hayeur Smith, *Draupnir's Sweat and Mardöll's Tears: An Archaeology of Jewellery, Gender and Identity in Viking Age Iceland* (BAR, Oxford, 2004) and Marianne Hem Eriksen, *Architecture, Society, and Ritual in Viking Age Scandinavia* (Cambridge University Press, Cambridge, 2019).

For childhood in the Viking Age, see Else Mundal, 'Forholdet mellom børn og foreldre i det norrøne kjeldmaterialet', *Collegium Medievale* 1 (1988): 9–26; M. Lindqvist, 'Barn på vikingatiden', *Gotländsk Arkiv* 76 (2004): 74–77; Chris Callow, 'First steps towards an archaeology of children in Iceland', *Archaeologia Islandica* 5 (2006): 55–96; Lotte Mejsholm, *Gränsland: konstruktion av tidig barndom och begravningsritual vid tiden för kristnandet i Skandinavien* (Uppsala University, Uppsala, 2009); Marianne Hem Eriksen, 'Don't all mothers love their children? Deposited infants as animate objects in the Scandinavian Iron Age', *World Archaeology* 49:3 (2017): 338–356; Dawn M. Hadley, 'Children and migration', in Sally Crawford, Dawn M. Hadley, and Gillian Shepherd (eds.), *The Oxford Handbook of the Archaeology of Childhood* (Oxford University Press, Oxford, 2018: 404–428); and Ben Raffield, 'Playing Vikings: Militarism, hegemonic masculinities and childhood enculturation in Viking-Age Scandinavia', *Current Anthropology* 60 (2019): 813–835.

Differential malnutrition in childhood is analysed by Anna Kjellström, 'People in transition: Life in the Mälaren Valley from an osteological perspective', in Val Turner, Olwyn Owen, and Doreen Waugh (eds.), *Shetland and the Viking World* (Shetland Heritage Publications, Lerwick, 2016: 197–202); there are other possible interpretations of the *cribra orbitalia* data—for example, that the condition was caused by high infection pressure—but this should exhibit an even distribution in the population rather than one skewed by sex; I am grateful to the author and to Marianne Hem Eriksen for discussion here. On infanticide, see the above and also papers by Nancy Wicker, 'Selective female infanticide as partial explanation for the dearth of women in Viking Age Scandinavia', in Guy Halsall (ed.), *Violence and Society in the Early Medieval West* (Boydell, Woodbridge, 1998: 205–221) and 'Christianization, female infanticide, and the abundance of female burials at Viking Age Birka in Sweden', *Journal of the History of Sexuality* 21 (2012): 245–262.

The study comparing male and female burials in Scotland and Norway is by Frida Espolin Norstein, *Migration and the Creation of Identity in the Viking Diaspora: A Comparative Study of Viking Age Funerary Rites from Northern Scotland and Møre og Romsdal* (unpublished MA thesis in archaeology, University of Oslo, Oslo, 2014).

On Viking-Age sexuality, see Jenny Jochens, 'The illicit love visit: An archaeology of Old Norse sexuality', *Journal of the History of Sexuality* 1 (1991): 357–392; Neil Price, 'Anstößige Körper? Sexualität in der Eisenzeit Nordeuropas', in Villem van Vilsteren and Rainer-Maria Weiss (eds.), *100.000 jahre sex: über Liebe, Wollust und Fruchtbarkeit* (Helms Museum, Hamburg, 2004: 54–63) and 'Sexualität', *Reallexikon der Germanischen Altertumskunde* 28 (2004): 244–257. The lines from *Loki's Quarrel* and *Sayings of the High One* are from Ursula Dronke's translation.

The much-discussed caliphal mission to the Vikings is treated by Sara Pons-Sanz, 'Whom did al-Ghazāl meet? An exchange of embassies between the Arabs from al-Andalus and the Vikings', *Saga-Book of the Viking Society for Northern Research* 28 (2012): 5–28, with extensive references. Sexual magic, the Rällinge figure, the Danevirke phallus, and burials of male-bodied individuals with normatively feminine accessories are all discussed by Neil Price, *The Viking Way: Magic and Mind in Late Iron Age Scandinavia* (Oxbow, Oxford, 2019: 172–183). The Maeshowe runes are discussed and translated by Michael Barnes, *The Runic Inscriptions of Maeshowe, Orkney* (Uppsala University, Uppsala, 1994); the quoted inscriptions are numbered as Farrer VIII, XXIII, and IX respectively. The Onslunda runestone is U 1043.

Sexual crime and legal strictures are discussed by Ben Raffield, Neil Price, and Mark Collard, 'Polygyny, concubinage and the social lives of women in Viking-Age Scandinavia', *Viking and Medieval Scandinavia* 13 (2018): 165–209; see also Fredrik Charpentier Ljungqvist, 'Rape in the Icelandic sagas: An insight in the perceptions about sexual assaults on women in the Old Norse world', *Journal of Family History* 40 (2015): 431–447. The Grágás codes are translated in two volumes as *Laws of Early Iceland* by Andrew Dennis, Peter Foote, and Richard Perkins (University of Manitoba Press, Winnipeg, 1980 & 2000).

The Danish scholar with *The Idea of the Good in Late Iron Age Society* is Frands Herschend (Uppsala University, Uppsala, 1998). The cross-dressing woman comes from chapter 35 of the *Saga of the People of Laxardal*, and the images on the picture-stones (numbers I and IV from Lärbro Tängelgårda) are discussed by Eva-Marie Göransson, prior.

Homophobia and the *nid* complex are discussed by Preben Meulengracht Sørensen, *The Unmanly Man: Concepts of Sexual Defamation in Early Northern Society* (Odense University Press, Odense, 1983), still the primary work on this, from which I quote here. For Norse insults, see Bo Almquist, *Norrön niddikt-ning* (2 vols., Almqvist & Wiksell, Stockholm, 1965 & 1974). The homophobic runic inscription mentioning the Cross Church carving is translated by James

Knirk (with a small amendment), reproduced in 'Nið and the sacred' by Preben Meulengracht Sørensen in *Artikler*, the Norrønt Forum edited collection in his honour (Norrønt Forum, Aarhus, 2000: 78–88).

Analyses of magic making interesting use of queer theory include work by the Norwegian scholar mentioned in the text, Brit Solli: 'Odin—the *queer*? Om det skeive i norrøn mytologi', in Ingrid Fuglestvedt, Terje Gansum, and Arnfrid Opedal (eds.), *Et hus med mange rom: vennebok til Bjørn Myhre på 60-årsdagen* (Stavanger Archaeological Museum, Stavanger, 1999: 393–427) and *Seid: Myter, Sjamanisme og Kjønn i Vikingenes Tid* (Pax, Oslo, 2002); see also Neil Price, *The Viking Way*, as above, which includes a study of the *Story of Völsi*. A major, if controversial, work envisioning a queered Iron Age is Ing-Marie Back Danielsson, *Masking Moments: The Transitions of Bodies and Beings in Late Iron Age Scandinavia* (Stockholm University, Stockholm, 2007).

The Vivallen grave is discussed in my book *The Viking Way*, p. 222ff. References to the debate on female Viking warriors and the so-called shield-maidens can be found in the following for chapter 11; see also the 2019 paper 'Gender and archaeology' by Marianne Moen, noted prior. All these works include extensive references on the complex gendering of graves.

On Viking-Age (dis)ability, see Lois Bragg, 'From the mute god to the lesser god: Disability in medieval Celtic and Old Norse literature', *Disability and Society* 12 (1997): 165–177 and *Oedipus Borealis: The Aberrant Body in Old Icelandic Myth and Saga* (Fairleigh Dickenson University Press, Madison, 2008); Annette Lassen, *Øjet og blindheden i norrøn mytologi og litter*atur (Museum Tusculanum, Copenhagen, 2003); Elisabeth Arwill-Nordbladh, 'Ability and disability: On bodily variations and bodily possibilities in Viking Age myth and image', in Ing-Marie Back Danielsson and Susanne Thedéen (eds.), *To Tender Gender: The Pasts and Futures of Gender Research in Archaeology* (Stockholm University, Stockholm, 2012: 33–60); and Christopher Crocker, 'Disability and dreams in the medieval Icelandic sagas', *Saga-Book of the Viking Society for Northern Research* XLIII (2019): 37–58. (Dis)ability studies are a relatively new feature of Viking research, and I would like to acknowledge the pioneering and important work done here for the contemporary English and Germanic cultures by Christina Lee and her colleagues.

CHAPTER 6: THE PERFORMANCE OF POWER

For extensive discussions of assemblies, law, and justice, see Olwyn Owen (ed.), *Things in the Viking World* (Shetland Amenity Trust, Lerwick, 2012) and especially Alexandra Sanmark, *Viking Law and Order: Places and Rituals of Assembly in the Medieval North* (Edinburgh University Press, Edinburgh, 2017). Two important papers by Marie Ødegaard are 'Thing sites, cult, churches, games and markets in Viking and medieval south-east Norway, AD c.800– 1600', *World Archaeology* 50 (2018): 150–164 and 'Tinginstitusjonens alder i Skandinavia belyst ved arkeologi og stedsnavnsgransking—samsvar eller ikke?', *Viking* 2018: 89–116. Frode Iversen discusses the Norwegian courtyard sites in 'Emerging kingship in the 8th century? New datings of three courtyard sites in Rogaland', in Dagfinn Skre (ed.), *Avaldsnes—A Sea-Kings' Manor in First-Millennium Western Scandinavia* (De Gruyter, Berlin, 2018: 721–746). Literature on feuding can be found in the following in connection with chapter 17 and the sociopolitics of Iceland.

Inheritance rights are discussed in many of the general works listed above, but a number of specialist studies address the relationships between land and family and the ways in which this was manifested in the landscape—for example, through ritual depositions and other activities along boundaries. Torun Zachrisson's *Gård, gräns, gravfält* (Stockholm University, Stockholm, 1998) is excellent, and later developments and challenges to the allodium system are addressed by Johan Runer, *Från hav till land, eller Kristus och odalen* (Stockholm University, Stockholm, 2006). The inheritance dimensions of runic inscriptions are discussed in detail by the late Birgit Sawyer, *The Viking-Age Rune-Stones: Custom and Commemoration in Early Medieval Scandinavia* (Oxford University Press, Oxford, 2000: chs. 3–4), where the Hillersjö text from U 29 and its complex family tree are discussed on pp. 49–50; the inscription is given here in Sawyer's elegant translation. The three other quoted inheritance inscriptions are respectively from runestones Sö 302, Bergaholm, Södermanland; G 111, Ardre, Gotland; and G 112, Ardre, Gotland.

A classic work on place-names and landscapes of power is Stefan Brink, 'Political and social structures in early Scandinavia: Aspects of space and territoriality—the settlement district', *Tor* 29 (1997): 389–438. A recent and important study of *huse* names is by Lisbeth Eilersgaard Christensen, Thorsten Lemm, and Anne Pedersen (eds.), *Husebyer—Status Quo, Open Questions and Perspectives* (National Museum of Denmark, Copenhagen, 2016). Theophoric names are addressed by Per Vikstrand, *Gudarnas platser: förkristna sakrala ortnamn i Mälarlandskapen* (Royal Gustav Adolf Academy, Uppsala, 2001) and in the edited volume by Sæbjørg Nordeide and Stefan Brink, *Sacred Sites and Holy Spaces: Exploring the Sacralization of Landscape Through Time* (Brepols, Turnhout, 2013), the latter containing references to Brink's many papers on this topic.

Major works on runes and runic literacy are listed in the general section above, to which may be added Birgit Sawyer's volume already cited. The great runologist whose pithy observations are quoted in the main text was Sven B. F. Jansson, whose work revolutionised their study. For the runic lore in the *Lay of Sigrdrifa*, I have quoted Carolyne Larrington's translation. For the magic use of runes, see John McKinnell and Rudolf Simek, *Runes, Magic and Religion: A Sourcebook* (Fassbaender, Vienna, 2004) and Mindy MacLeod and Bernard Mees, *Runic Amulets and Magic Objects* (Boydell, Woodbridge, 2006). Sofia Pereswetoff-Morath's book *Viking-Age Runic Plates* (Royal Gustav Adolf Academy, Uppsala, 2019) is the standard work on these objects. The runesmith with his own biography is Öpir: Marit Åhlén, *Runristaren Öpir, en monografi* (Uppsala University, Uppsala, 1997). The Gotlandic runestone mentioning the "snake-eels" is G 203 from Hogrän. The personal names on the runestones are collected by Lena Peterson, *Nordiskt runnamnslexikon* (Institute for Language and Folklore, Uppsala, 2007). The stone from Rök in Östergötland is designated Ög 136.

Viking-Age horse-holding is discussed by Anneli Sundkvist, *Hästarnas land* (University of Uppsala, Uppsala, 2001). The concept of time distance is elaborated for the late Iron Age by Martin Carver, 'Pre-Viking traffic in the North Sea', in Seán McGrail (ed.), *Maritime Celts, Frisians and Saxons* (Council for British Archaeology, York, 1990: 117–125). The trials of the *Sea Stallion* are published as Anne-Christine Larsen et al. (eds.), *The Sea Stallion from Glendalough* (Viking Ship Museum, Roskilde, 2008). A variety of Viking-Age transport methods are reviewed in Kurt Schietzel, *Spurensuche Haithabu* (Wachholz, Neumünster, 2018: 534–537). A useful overview of sea craft is provided by Ole Crumlin-Pedersen, *Archaeology and the Sea in Scandinavia and Britain* (Viking Ship Museum, Roskilde, 2010) and Gareth Williams, *The Viking Ship* (British Museum Press, London, 2014); these works also contain details of weather vanes, figureheads, and ship depictions in other media. A range of ship types are reviewed by Ole Crumlin-Pedersen and Olaf Olsen (eds.), *The Skuldelev Ships I* (Viking Ship Museum, Roskilde, 2002); Ole Crumlin-Pedersen, *Viking-Age Ships and Shipbuilding in Hedeby/Haithabu and Schleswig* (Viking Ship Museum, Roskilde, 1996); and Ole Crumlin-Pedersen and Hanus Jensen, *Udspændte både fra vikingetid og jernalder* (Viking Ship Museum, Roskilde, 2018).

For the funerary ships from Oseberg, Gokstad, Ladby, and Hedeby and the later graves at Valsgärde, see Nicolay Nicolaysen, *Langskibet fra Gokstad ved Sandefjord* (Hammermeyer, Kristiania, 1882); A. W. Brøgger, Hjalmar

Falk, and Haakon Shetelig (eds.), *Osebergfundet* (4 vols., Universitetets Old-saksamling, Oslo, 1917–1928); Arne Emil Christensen, Anne Stine Ingstad, and Bjørn Myhre, *Osebergdronningens grav* (Schibsted, Oslo, 1992); Michael Müller-Wille, *Das Bootkammergrab von Haithabu* (Wachholtz, Neumünster, 1976); Anne C. Sørensen, *Ladby: A Danish Ship-Grave from the Viking Age* (Viking Ship Museum, Roskilde, 2001); and Svante Norr (ed.), *Valsgärde Studies: The Place and Its People, Past and Present* (Uppsala University, Uppsala, 2008). The intangible aspects of ships are discussed by Ole Crumlin-Pedersen and Birgitte Munch Tyhe (eds.), *The Ship as Symbol in Prehistoric and Medieval Scandinavia* (National Museum of Denmark, Copenhagen, 1995). The comment on the introduction of the sail as a tool of power is by Ole Kastholm of Roskilde Museum.

CHAPTER 7: MEETING THE OTHERS

The practice of Norse 'religion' has attracted an extensive literature. In addition to the works cited above under chapter 1, a good inroad is Thomas A. Dubois, *Nordic Religions in the Viking Age* (University of Pennsylvania Press, Philadelphia, 1999) and, for readers of Norwegian, Gro Steinsland's *Norrøn religion: myter, riter, samfunn* (Pax, Oslo, 2005). Two major multi-volume works are also of relevance here: Anders Andrén, Catharina Ruadvere, and Kristina Jennbert (eds.), *Vägar till Midgård* (16 vols., Nordic Academic Press, Lund, 2001–2014) and John McKinnell, Margaret Clunies Ross, and John Lindow (eds.), *The Pre-Christian Religions of the North* (7 vols., Brepols, Turnhout, 2018–).

The leading specialist in religiolects is Maths Bertell, who introduced the term into Viking-Age discourse; see his forthcoming paper, 'Into a hall, out to an island: The Iron Age hall culture religiolect as a case study of religious change and diversity'. I thank him for permission to discuss the concept here. The primary work on religious ideologies of power is by Olof Sundqvist, *Freyr's Offspring: Rulers and Religion in Ancient Svear Society* (Uppsala University Press, Uppsala, 2002). On cultic sites and structures, the classic work, outdated but still essential, is Olaf Olsen, *Hørg, hov og kirke* (Gad, Copenhagen, 1966). For more recent publications, also embracing the ritual specialists themselves, see Olof Sundqvist, *Kultledare i fornskandinavisk religion* (University of Uppsala, Uppsala, 2007); Gunnar Andersson and Eva Skyllberg (eds.), *Gestalter och gestaltningar—om tid, rum och händelser på Lunda* (Riksantikvarieämbetet, Stockholm, 2008); Olof Sundqvist, *An Arena for Higher Powers: Ceremonial Buildings and Religious Strategies for Rulership in Late Iron Age Scandinavia*

(Brill, Leiden, 2016); Anders Kaliff and Julia Mattes, *Tempel och kulthus i det forna Skandinavien* (Carlssons, Stockholm, 2017); and Sandie Holst, Lars Jørgensen, and Egon Wamers, *Odin, Thor und Freyja: Skandinavische Kultplätze des 1. Jahrtausends n. Chr. und das Frankenreich* (Schnell & Steiner, Regensburg, 2017). The Uppåkra 'temple' is reported by Lars Larsson, *Continuity for Centuries: A Ceremonial Building and Its Context at Uppåkra, Southern Sweden* (Lund University, Lund, 2004). The translation from Adam of Bremen, on the Uppsala temple, is from the edition by Francis Tschan, modified by Olof Sundqvist.

The sites at Lilla Ullevi and Götavi are discussed by Neil Price, 'Belief and ritual', in Gareth Williams, Peter Pentz, and Matthias Wemhoff (eds.), *Vikings: Life and Legend* (British Museum, London, 2014: 162–195). *Blót* sacrifices are reviewed by Britt-Mari Näsström, *Blot: tro och offer i det förkristna Norden* (Norstedts, Stockholm, 2002). For the Hofstaðir rituals, see Gavin Lucas and Tom McGovern, 'Bloody slaughter: Ritual decapitation and display at the Viking settlement of Hofstaðir, Iceland', *European Journal of Archaeology* 10:1 (2007): 7–30. On the wider practice of ritual, see Torsten Capelle and Christian Fischer (eds.), *Ragnarok—Odins verden* (Silkeborg Museum, Silkeborg, 2005) and Anders Andrén and Peter Carelli (eds.), *Odens öga—mellan människor och makter i det förkristna Norden* (Fälth & Hässler, Värnemo, 2006).

At a personal level, the use of figurines and amulets is discussed by Bo Jensen, *Viking Age Amulets in Scandinavia and Western Europe* (BAR, Oxford, 2010); Michaela Helmbrecht, *Wirkmächtige Kommunikationsmedien. Menschenbilder der Vendel- und Wikingerzeit und ihre Kontexte* (Lund University, Lund, 2011); and Leszek Gardeła, *Scandinavian Amulets in Viking Age Poland* (University of Rzeszów Institute of Archaeology, Rzeszów, 2014).

For water offerings, see Julie Lund, *Åsted og vadested: deponeringer, genstandsbiografier og rumlig strukturering som kilde til vikingetidens kognitive landskaber* (University of Oslo, Oslo, 2009); Anne Monikander, *Våld och vatten: våtmarkskult vid Skedemosse under järnåldern* (Stockholm University, Stockholm, 2010); Ben Raffield, '"A river of knives and swords": Ritually deposited weapons in English watercourses and wetlands during the Viking Age', *European Journal of Archaeology* 17:4 (2014): 634–655; and Torun Zachrisson, 'Händelser vid vatten: om näcken vid Lutbron och de förkristna dödsoffren i sjön Bokaren, Uppland', *Saga och Sed* 2014: 69–91. For the Frösö tree, see Ola Magnell and Elisabeth Iregren, 'Veitstu hvé blóta skal? The Old Norse blót in the light of osteological remains from Frösö church, Jämtland, Sweden', *Current Swedish Archaeology* 18 (2010): 223–250.

With mild embarrassment, I have to say that the standard work on Viking-Age sorcery is still my own *The Viking Way: Magic and Mind in Late Iron Age Scandinavia* (2nd edn., Oxbow, Oxford, 2019). It contains all the spells, saga references, and archaeological correlates with reconstructions of the possible sorcerer graves and, in general, provides a four-hundred-page overview of the place of magic in the Norse mental universe. The book also provides extensive references for further reading. Essential works include Lotte Hedeager, *Skygger af en anden virkelighed* (Samleren, Copenhagen, 1997); Dag Strömbäck, *Sejd* (2nd edn., Royal Gustav Adolf Academy, Uppsala, 2000); Catharina Raudvere, *Kunskap och insikt i norrön tradition—mytologi, ritualer och trolldomsanklagelser* (Nordic Academic Press, Lund, 2003); François-Xavier Dillmann, *Les magiciens dans l'Islande ancienne* (Royal Gustav Adolf Academy, Uppsala, 2006); Eldar Heide, *Gand, seid og åndevind* (University of Bergen, Bergen, 2006); Clive Tolley, *Shamanism in Norse Myth and Magic* (2 vols., Academia Scientarum Fennica, Helsinki, 2009); Stephen A. Mitchell, *Witchcraft and Magic in the Nordic Middle Ages* (University of Pennsylvania Press, Philadelphia, 2011); and Leszek Gardeła, *(Magic) Staffs in the Viking Age* (Fassbaender, Vienna, 2016).

The social world of everyday magic, not least at a time of its waning in the face of new ideas and technologies, is compellingly captured by Hannah Kent in her novel of rural Irish folk belief, *The Good People* (Picador, London, 2017); I draw on some of her resonant phrases here in speaking of the power that could come of being forced to the margins. The translation from the *Saga of the Völsungs* about the crackling tensions of magic is by Jesse Byock.

CHAPTER 8: DEALING WITH THE DEAD

The first serious study of Viking-Age death rituals is still one of the best, although it is oddly neglected today; going far beyond the literary framework of its title, see Hilda Ellis, *The Road to Hel: A Study of the Conception of the Dead in Old Norse Literature* (Cambridge University Press, Cambridge, 1943).

The translation from chapter 8 of Snorri Sturluson's *Ynglingasaga* is from Alison Finlay and Anthony Faulkes's edition of *Heimskringla* (Viking Society for Northern Research, London, 2011).

The burial customs of the Viking Age form one of my own primary research fields, and, unsurprisingly, this section draws heavily on my own work as well as that of others. Besides others listed later in this section, my publications here include 'Dying and the dead: Viking Age mortuary behaviour', in Stefan Brink and Neil Price (eds.), *The Viking World* (Routledge, London & New York,

2008: 257–273); 'Nine paces from Hel: Time and motion in Old Norse ritual performance', *World Archaeology* 46:2 (2014): 178–191; and 'Death ritual and mortuary behaviour', in Anders Andrén, Jens-Peter Schjødt, and John Lindow (eds.), *Pre-Christian Religions of the North: Histories and Structures* (Brepols, Turnhout, 2020). These works include references to the major cemetery excavations at Birka and Kaupang, on Öland and Gotland, and more.

The intricate properties of the cremation pyre are explored by Mogens B. Henriksen, *Bålets betydning. Ligbrænding i Danmarks oldtid belyst ved arkæologiske fund og ligbrændingsexperimenter* (2 vols., Copenhagen University, Copenhagen, 2016). For the Byzantine text describing nocturnal funerals, see Alice-Mary Talbot and Denis F. Sullivan (trans.), *The History of Leo the Deacon: Byzantine Military Expansion in the Tenth Century* (Dumbarton Oaks, Washington, DC, 2005); Leo discusses the Rus' in books eight and nine of his *History*. The study of birds' eggs in Viking-Age graves is by Anna Jelicic, *En hårdkokt historia: en studie av äggskalfynd från vikingatida gravkontext med särskilt focus på Uppland och Gotland* (MA thesis in archaeology, Uppsala University, Uppsala, 2017).

Funerary archaeology is admirably synthesised by Sarah Tarlow and Liv Nilsson Stutz (eds.), *The Oxford Handbook of the Archaeology of Death and Burial* (Oxford University Press, Oxford, 2013). The intriguing ambiguities of early medieval burials have been explored by many scholars, but see, in particular, the authors of the theme issue of *Current Swedish Archaeology* 24 (2016), with special reference to the works of Alison Klevnäs, and also the collection by Duncan Sayer and Howard Williams (eds.), *Mortuary Practices and Social Identities in the Middle Ages* (University of Exeter Press, Exeter, 2009); for useful English comparisons, see Howard Williams, *Death and Memory in Early Medieval Britain* (Cambridge University Press, Cambridge, 2006).

The long quotations from *The Waking of Angantyr*, which is preserved in the *Saga of Hervör and Heidrek*, are given here in the translation of Todd Krause and Jonathan Slocum, with my minor amendments. The excerpt about the circling fires is from Patricia Terry's translation.

Burials in wagon bodies are discussed by Inga Hägg, 'Om vikingatidens vagnskorgsgravar', *Saga och Sed* 2009: 91–99. 'Deviant' burials are discussed extensively in the many papers of Leszek Gardeła, summarised in, 'The dangerous dead? Rethinking Viking-Age deviant burials', in Leszek Słupecki and Rudolf Simek (eds.), *Conversions: Looking for Ideological Change in the Early Middle Ages* (Fassbaender, Vienna, 2013: 96–136); see also Andrew Reynolds, *Anglo-Saxon Deviant Burial Customs* (Oxford University Press, Oxford, 2009). For aspects of Icelandic burials, see Þóra Pétursdóttir, 'Icelandic Viking Age graves: Lack in material—lack of interpretation?', *Archaeologia Islandica* 7 (2009): 22–40 and references to chapter 17 following. The Lindholm cemetery is published by Thorkild Ramskou, *Lindholm Høje gravpladsen* (Lynge, Copenhagen, 1976). An excellent survey of regional customs is by Fredrik Svanberg, *Death Rituals in South-East Scandinavia AD 800–1000* (University of Lund, Lund, 2003).

The main catalogue of the Gotland picture-stones is by Sune Lindqvist, *Gotlands Bildsteine* (2 vols., Wahlström & Widstrand, Stockholm, 1941–1942); the latest synthesis is Maria Herlin Karnell (ed.), *Gotlands bildstenar* (Gotland Museum, Visby, 2012). For the story stones, the idea of pictorial ship burials, and door symbolism, see also Anders Andrén, 'Doors to other worlds: Scandinavian death rituals in Gotlandic perspective', *Journal of European Archaeology* 1 (1993): 33–56; the wagon stones are discussed by Þórgunnur Snædal, 'Ailikn's wagon and Óðinn's warriors: The pictures on the Gotlandic Ardre monuments', in John Sheehan and Donnchadh Ó Corráin (eds.), *The Viking Age: Ireland and the West* (Four Courts, Dublin, 2010: 441–449).

The chamber grave ritual has been discussed extensively; see Silke Eisenschmidt, *Kammergräber der Wikingerzeit in Altdänemark* (University of Kiel, Kiel, 1994); Nils Ringstedt, *The Birka Chamber-Graves* (Stockholm University, Stockholm, 1997); Frans-Arne Stylegar, 'Kammergraver fra vikingtiden i Vestfold', *Fornvännen* 100 (2005): 161–177; and Neil Price, 'Wooden worlds: Individual and collective in the chamber graves of Birka', in Charlotte Hedenstierna-Jonson (ed.), *Birka nu* (Riksantikvarieämbetet, Stockholm, 2012: 81–94). For the use of chairs, see Heather Robbins, *Seated Burials at Birka: A Select Study* (MA thesis in archaeology, University of Uppsala, Uppsala, 2004).

The Finnish graves nailed down with spears are discussed, along with other funerary rituals from the region, by Anna Wessman, *Death, Destruction and Commemoration: Tracing Ritual Activities in Finnish Late Iron Age Cemeteries (AD 550–1150)* (Finnish Antiquarian Society, Helsinki, 2010). The Mammen burial is published by Mette Iversen, *Mammen: grav, kunst og samfund I vikingetid* (Jysk Arkæologisk Selskab, Aarhus, 1991). For the Hedeby graves, see Ute Arents and Silke Eisenschmidt, *Die Gräber von Haithabu* (2 vols., Wachholtz, Neumünster, 2010); the boat grave is published by Michael Müller-Wille, *Das Bootkammergrab von Haithabu* (Wachholtz, Neumünster, 1976).

References to the crucial account by Aḥmad ibn Faḍlān are given in the introductory section above. His description of the Rus' ship burial has been discussed by archaeologists and others on numerous occasions, including in my own papers listed at the start of the section for this chapter. For a guide to the archaeological literature on this subject, see Neil Price, 'Vikings on the Volga? Ibn Fadlan and the rituals of the Rūssiyah', in Jonathan Shepard and Luke Treadwell (eds.), *Muslims on the Volga in the Viking Age: Diplomacy and Islam in the World of Ibn Fadlan* (I. B. Tauris, London, 2020). I am grateful to James Montgomery for many discussions over the years about this central source. The concept of the hostile dead in the mound, perhaps referencing the cautious kindler of the pyre, is treated by Jan Bill, 'Protecting against the dead? On the possible use of apotropaic magic in the Oseberg burial', *Cambridge Archaeological Journal* 26 (2016): 141–155.

References for the major Scandinavian ship burials are given above for chapter 6. For a sample of Scottish boat graves, see Olwyn Owen and Magnar Dalland, *Scar: A Viking Boat Burial on Sanday, Orkney* (Historic Scotland, Edinburgh, 1999) and Oliver Harris et al., 'Assembling places and persons: A tenth-century Viking boat burial from Swordle Bay on the Ardnamurchan Peninsula, western Scotland', *Antiquity* 91 (2017): 191–206. The Groix burial is published as part of Michael Müller-Wille's 1976 paper on the Hedeby boat, referenced above, and also in my book, *The Vikings in Brittany* (Viking Society for Northern Research, London, 1989).

The interpretation of certain 'female' figurines as mourners has been put forward by Frog and Eila Stepanova. For Viking-Age concepts of the ancestors, see Andreas Nordberg, *Fornnordisk religionsforksning mellan teori och empiri: kulten av anfäder, solen och vegetationsandar i idéhistorisk belysning* (Kungl. Gustav Adolfs Akademien, Uppsala, 2013) and Triin Laidoner, *Ancestors, Their Worship and the Elite in the Viking Age and Early Medieval Scandinavia* (PhD thesis in Scandinavian studies, University of Aberdeen, Aberdeen, 2015).

For ritual drama, see the fundamental work by Terry Gunnell, *The Origins of Drama in Scandinavia* (Brewer, Woodbridge, 1995). For the performance of funerary stories, see my papers 'Bodylore and the archaeology of embedded religion: Dramatic licence in the funerals of the Vikings', in David Whitley and Kelley Hays-Gilpin (eds.), *Belief in the Past: Theoretical Approaches to the Archaeology of Religion* (Left Coast Press, Walnut Creek, 2008: 143–165); 'Passing into poetry: Viking-Age mortuary drama and the origins of Norse mythology', *Medieval Archaeology* 54 (2010): 123–156; and 'Mythic acts: Material narratives of the dead in Viking Age Scandinavia', in Catharina Raudvere and Jens Peder Schjødt (eds.), *More than Mythology: Narratives, Ritual Practices and Regional Distribution in Pre-Christian Scandinavian Religions* (Nordic Academic Press, Lund, 2012: 13–46). For the concept of mortuary citation, a term coined by Howard Williams, see 'Mortuary Citations: Death and Memory in the Viking World', a theme issue of *European Journal of Archaeology* 19:3 (2016).

The funeral ship as a metaphor for the hall is discussed by Frands Herschend, *Livet i hallen* (Uppsala University, Uppsala, 1997). The 'unfinished' burial mound at Oseberg was discovered in the archives by Terje Gansum and published in his book *Hauger som konstruksjoner—arkeologiske forventninger gjennom 200 år* (University of Gothenburg, 2004). On 'grave robbing', see Jan Bill and Aoife Daly, 'The plundering of the ship graves from Oseberg and Gokstad: An example of power politics?', *Antiquity* 86 (2012): 808–824 and Alison Klevnäs, 'Abandon ship! Digging out the dead from Vendel boat-graves', *Norwegian Archaeological Review* 48 (2015): 1–20 and her paper in the 'Mortuary Citations' volume listed above. An active relationship to the past in a funerary context is explored by Eva Thäte, *Monuments and Minds: Monument Re-use in Scandinavia in the Second Half of the First Millennium AD* (University of Lund, Lund, 2007) and Ann-Mari Hållans Stenholm, *Fornminnen: det förflutnas roll i det förkristna och kristna Mälardalen* (Nordic Academic Press, Lund, 2012).

Rituals against the returning dead are discussed in the works on deviant burial above. For notable literary episodes, see especially the *Saga of the People of Eyri* (which includes the door court, forbidding access to the dead) and *Grettir's Saga*.

For a discussion of silver hoards as a form of banking for the afterlife, see Jacek Gruszczyński, *Viking Silver, Hoards and Containers* (Routledge, London & New York, 2019). The *einherjar* in Valhöll are discussed by Andreas Nordberg, *Krigarna i Odins sal: dödsföreställningar och krigarkult i fornnordisk religion* (Stockholm University, Stockholm, 2003). For afterlife beliefs in general, see Hilda Ellis, *The Road to Hel*, referenced at the start of this section. The line about the afterlife of slaves is from strophe 24 of *Harbard's Song*.

CHAPTER 9: INROADS

The reference to *wælwulfas* comes from the Old English poem known as *The Battle of Maldon*, ed. and trans. Bill Griffiths (Anglo-Saxon Books, Pinner, 1991). Egil's own battle poem comes from chapter 48 in his eponymous saga. The Old Norse text is quoted here after Bjarni Einarsson's edition (Viking Society for Northern Research, London, 2003); the translation is by Christine Fell (Dent, London, 1975), with my minor amendments.

The Salme boat graves are not yet fully published, but an overview can be found in Jüri Peets, 'Salme ship burials', *Current World Archaeology* 58 (2013): 18–24; the latest technical reports are Jüri Peets et al., 'Research results of the Salme ship burials in 2011–2012', *Archaeological Fieldwork in Estonia* 2012

(2013): 1–18 and Marge Konsa, 'Two Vendel era ship burials at Salme on the island of Saaremaa', *Estonian Cultural Heritage. Preservation and Conservation* 1 (2013): 152–154. The isotopic studies suggesting that the buried men came from central Sweden are published by T. Douglas Price et al., 'Isotopic provenancing of the Salme ship burials in Pre-Viking Age Estonia', *Antiquity* 90 (2016): 1022–1037. The DNA studies of the Salme men, with their kinship relations, can be found in Ashot Margoyan et al., 'Population genomics of the Viking world', *Nature* 2020, in review.

There is also a slightly different reading of the Salme ships given by Marika Mägi in her book, *In Austrvegr: The Role of the Eastern Baltic in Viking Age Communication Across the Baltic Sea* (Brill, Leiden, 2018: 232–241). She sees the collective rituals of the first boat, in particular, as reminiscent of similar communal burials found elsewhere on the island and argues this might suggest the Salme graves were made by local people rather than Scandinavians. I disagree, as not only the ship burial rite itself, but also details of the rituals (such as shooting arrows into the boat), are precisely paralleled at Ultuna in Sweden, the same site that has exact parallels to the Salme sword harness; this is, therefore, not necessarily a Saaremaa rite at all but fits perfectly with the Salme men's home ground. The quoted prose and verse about Yngvar's death are from *Ynglingasaga*, chapter 32, the first part of Snorri's *Heimskringla*.

Basic narrative histories of the early raids in the British Isles and Frankia can be found in any of the general works listed in the first section above, which also lists translations of the regional primary records written by their victims. For the Lindisfarne attack, Alcuin's key texts can be found in Colin Chase (ed.), *Two Alcuin Letter-Books* (Centre for Medieval Studies, Toronto, 1975). The important implications of his fixation with Viking haircuts were first raised by John Hines in 1984 in his thesis on earlier contacts across the North Sea, *The Scandinavian Character of Anglian England in the Pre-Viking Period* (BAR, Oxford). Recent work on Scandinavian familiarity before Lindisfarne can be found in Aina Margrethe Heen-Pettersen, 'The earliest wave of Viking activity? The Norwegian evidence revisited', *European Journal of Archaeology* 22 (2019): 523–541.

The historical research going beyond the well-thumbed pages of the *Chronicle*, in the process revolutionising our understanding of the first raids, derives primarily from the groundbreaking studies of Clare Downham, on which I rely here. Her major work of revisionism has been published as 'The earliest Viking activity in England', *English Historical Review* 132 (2017): 1–12. She is also the historian who suggests that the Wessex takeover of Mercia may have had Viking assistance. The equally important idea of the 'southern route' for the first raiders into the Irish Sea was put forward by David Griffiths, 'Rethinking the early Viking Age in the West', *Antiquity* 93 (2019): 468–477.

CHAPTER 10: MARITORIA

The hunting of the North Atlantic right whale has been discussed by Andreas Hennius et al., 'Whalebone gaming pieces: Aspects of marine mammal exploitation in Vendel and Viking Age Scandinavia', *European Journal of Archaeology*, 21 (2018): 612–631.

The revolution in understanding the trading emporia of the north-west European coasts largely began in 1982 with Richard Hodges's *Dark Age Economics: The Origins of Towns and Trade AD 600–1000* (Duckworth, London; updated in 2012 and subtitled *A New Audit*); the same author collaborated with David Whitehouse, in 1983, on *Mohammed, Charlemagne and the Origins of Europe* (Duckworth, London), with inspiration for both books derived from the works of Henri Pirenne. For later overviews, with references to excavations in the English and Frankish emporia, see Michael McCormick, *Origins of the European Economy: Communications and Commerce AD 300–900* (Cambridge University Press, Cambridge, 2001); Tim Pestell and Katharina Ulmschneider (eds.), *Markets in Early Medieval Europe: Trading and 'Productive' Sites, 650–850* (Windgather Press, Oxford, 2003); and Chris Wickham, *Framing the Early Middle Ages: Europe and the Mediterranean, 400–800* (Cambridge University Press, Cambridge, 2005). For discussion on the nature of early Viking-Age markets and proto-urbanism, I am grateful to the URBS research cluster at Uppsala University, especially Anton Bonnier, Joakim Kjellberg, and Filmo Verhagen.

The Dutch archaeologist working on Frisia is Nelleke IJssennagger, with her book, *Central Because Liminal: Frisia in a Viking Age North Sea World* (Groningen University, Groningen, 2017); this also includes references to the extensive excavations at Dorestad.

The Ribe emporium is summarised by Claus Feveile, *Viking Ribe: Trade, Power and Faith* (Sydvestjyske Museer, Ribe, 2013); for Hedeby, see Kurt Schietzel, *Spurensuche Haithabu* (Wachholz, Neumünster, 2018); an overview of Birka can be found in Bente Magnus and Ingrid Gustin, *Birka och Hovgården* (Riksantikvarieämbetet, Stockholm, 2009) and in Jim Hanson et al., *Birkas skepp: vikingatid på östersjön* (Medströms, Stockholm, 2018).

Søren Sindbæk is the primary specialist in nodes and trading networks, with several important publications. These include *Ruter og rutinisering: Vikingetidens fjernhandel i Nordeuropa* (Multivers, Copenhagen, 2005); 'The small world of the Vikings: Networks in early medieval communication and exchange', *Norwegian Archaeological Review* 40 (2007): 59–74; 'Close ties and long-range relations: The emporia network in early Viking-Age exchange', in John Sheehan and Donnchadh Ó Corráin (eds.), *The Viking Age: Ireland and the West* (Four Courts, Dublin, 2010: 430–440); 'Silver economies and social ties: Long-term interaction, long-term investments—and why the Viking Age happened', in James Graham-Campbell and Søren Sindbæk (eds.), *Silver Economies, Monetisation and Society in Scandinavia, AD 800–1100* (Aarhus University Press, Aarhus, 2011: 41–66); 'Northern emporia and maritime networks: Modelling past communication using archaeological network analysis', in J. Preiser-Kapeller and F. Daim (eds.), *Harbours and Maritime Networks as Complex Adaptive Systems* (Römisch-Germanischen Zentralmuseum, Mainz, 2015: 105–118); and 'Crafting networks in Viking towns', *Medieval and Modern Matters* 4 (2016): 119–132. For a specifically western perspective, see Zanette T. Glørstad and Kjetil Loftsgarden (eds.), *Viking-Age Transformations: Trade, Craft and Resources in Western Scandinavia* (Routledge, London & New York, 2017).

The Gotland harbours have been researched by Dan Carlsson, *Vikingahamnar: ett hotat kulturarv* (Arkeodok, Visby, 1998). Gotland's special culture in the Viking Age is summarised in Gun Westholm (ed.), *Gotland Vikingaön* (Gotland Museum, Visby, 2004); see also Ny Björn Gustavsson, *Casting Identities in Central Seclusion: Aspects of Non-Ferrous Metalworking and Society on Gotland in the Early Medieval Period* (University of Stockholm, Stockholm, 2013).

For observations on the Birka bird hunting, I thank Per Ericsson of the Natural History Museum in Stockholm. Studies of mobility among the Birka population can be found in Charlotte Hedenstierna-Jonson, 'Foreigner and local: Identities and cultural expression among the urban people of Birka', in Val Turner, Olwyn Owen, and Doreen Waugh (eds.), *Shetland and the Viking World* (Shetland Heritage Publications, Lerwick, 2016: 189–196) and T. Douglas et al., 'Isotopes and human burials at Viking Age Birka and the Mälaren region, east central Sweden', *Journal of Anthropological Archaeology* 49 (2018): 19–38.

Useful collections on Viking-Age Baltic interactions include Birgitta Hårdh and Bozena Werbart (eds.), *Contacts Across the Baltic Sea During the*

Late Iron Age (University of Lund, Lund, 1992); Ingmar Jansson (ed.), *Archaeology East and West of the Baltic* (Stockholm University, Stockholm, 1995); and Johan Callmer, Ingrid Gustin, and Mats Roslund (eds.), *Identity Formation and Diversity in the Early Medieval Baltic and Beyond* (Brill, Leiden, 2017); see also two books by Marika Mägi, *In Austrvegr: The Role of the Eastern Baltic in Viking Age Communication Across the Baltic Sea* (Brill, Leiden, 2018) and *The Viking Eastern Baltic* (Arc Humanities Press, Amsterdam, 2019). Two important collections also summarise the eastern littoral: Joonas Ahola and Frog with Clive Tolley (eds.), *Fibula, Fabula, Fact: The Viking Age in Finland* (Finnish Literature Society, Helsinki, 2014) and Joonas Ahola, Frog, and Jenni Lucenius (eds.), *The Viking Age in Åland* (Finnish Academy of Science and Letters, Helsinki, 2014).

Ladoga has been extensively published in Russian, but useful summaries can be found in Simon Franklin and Jonathan Shepard, *The Emergence of Rus 750–1200* (Longman, London, 1996: 3–49); Wladyslaw Duczko, *Viking Rus* (Brill, Leiden, 2004: 60–95); and Fedir Androshchuk, *Vikings in the East* (Uppsala University, Uppsala, 2013: 16–20). The meditations on the economic structures of settlements like this are based on the work of Anders Ögren, which is set to revolutionise the field of Viking economics; I thank him for permission to discuss his ideas here, and for many enjoyable years of conversations.

Two key early texts, marking a real paradigm shift in the archaeology of Viking-Age Norway (and, like all such, massively controversial at the time), are by the late Bjørn Myhre: 'The beginning of the Viking Age—some current archaeological problems', in Anthony Faulkes and Richard Perkins (eds.), *Viking Revaluations* (Viking Society, London, 1993: 182–204) and 'The archaeology of the early Viking Age in Norway', in Howard Clarke et al. (eds.), *Ireland and Scandinavia in the Early Viking Age* (Four Courts, Dublin, 1998: 3–36). I attended both the conferences from which these books derive, and am so glad that Bjørn lived to see the vindication of his ideas two decades later.

The work on Snorri's Midlands, and especially at Avaldsnes, has proceeded for many years under the direction of Dagfinn Skre; I have drawn heavily on his work for this chapter, with thanks and acknowledgements for many years of discussions. His detailed meditations on the power of the sea-kings have emerged through numerous publications culminating in his two monumental edited volumes, *Avaldsnes—A Sea-Kings' Manor in First-Millennium Western Scandinavia* and *Rulership in 1st to 14th Century Scandinavia* (De Gruyter, Berlin, 2018 and 2020), which contains extensive references to his previous work; it also includes Frode Iversen's important work on the assembly sites. Alongside the essays by Dagfinn and others in that collection, for specific reference to the whetstone trade see also Irene Baug, Dagfinn Skre, Tom Heldal, and Øystein Jansen, 'The beginning of the Viking Age in the West', *Journal of Maritime Archaeology* 14 (2018): 43–80. The crucial collection of sea-king names can be found in Björn Sigfússon, 'Names of sea-kings (*heiti sækonunga*)', *Modern Philology* 32:2 (1934): 125–142.

Previous attempts at untangling the menu of determinism often put forward to explain the raids include two important papers by James Barrett: 'What caused the Viking Age?', *Antiquity* 82 (2008): 671–685 and 'Rounding up the usual suspects: Causation and the Viking Age diaspora', in Atholl Anderson et al. (eds.), *The Global Origins and Development of Seafaring* (McDonald Institute, Cambridge, 2010, 289–302).

CHAPTER 11: WARRIORHOODS

The comment on the ideological benefits of raiding is by Steve Ashby in 'What really caused the Viking Age? The social content of raiding and exploration', *Archaeological Dialogues* 22:1 (2015): 89–106.

Military ideologies and their material manifestations are discussed by Mattias Jakobsson, *Krigarideologi och vikingatida svärdstypologi* (Stockholm University, Stockholm, 1992); Anne Nørgård Jørgensen, *Waffen und Gräber. Typologische und chronologische Studien zu skandinavischen Waffengräbern 520/30 bis 900 n.Chr.* (Royal Society of Northern Antiquaries, Copenhagen, 1999); Charlotte Hedenstierna-Jonson, *The Birka Warrior: The Material Culture of a Martial Society* (Stockholm University, Stockholm, 2006); Lena Holmquist Olausson and Michael Olausson (eds.), *The Martial Society: Aspects of Warriors, Fortifications and Social Change in Scandinavia* (Stockholm University, Stockholm, 2009); and Anne Pedersen, *Dead Warriors in Living Memory: A Study of Weapon and Equestrian Burials in Viking-Age Denmark, AD 800–1000* (National Museum of Denmark, Copenhagen, 2014).

The three runestones from Hällestad in Skåne are DR 295–297. The Högby runestone is Ög 81, and the Karlevi stone is Öl 1. The Sjörup runestone is DR 279, and the Aarhus stone is DR 66. Judith Jesch's *Ships and Men in the Late Viking Age: The Vocabulary of Runic Inscriptions and Skaldic Verse* (Boydell & Brewer, Woodbridge, 2001) also contains much of interest in this context.

On the *lið* and the social organisation of Viking raiders, see Ben Raffield, Claire Greenlow, Neil Price, and Mark Collard, 'Ingroup identification, identity fusion and the formation of Viking warbands', *World Archaeology* 48:1 (2015): 35–50 and Ben Raffield's important paper, 'Bands of brothers: A re-appraisal of the Viking Great Army and its implications for the Scandinavian colonization of England', *Early Medieval Europe* 24 (2016): 308–337. Jón Viðar Sigurðsson's observations on Viking 'friendship' have been referenced for chapter 3, above, as has the background data on the practice of polygyny. For the social impact the practice may have had in the context of maritime violence, see Ben Raffield, Neil Price, and Mark Collard, 'Male-biased operational sex ratios and the Viking phenomenon: An evolutionary anthropological perspective on late Iron Age Scandinavian raiding', *Evolution and Human Behavior* 38:3 (2017): 315–324.

The best overview of military material culture is by Gareth Williams, *Weapons of the Viking Warrior* (Osprey, Oxford, 2019). Notker's description of the Frankish emperor bending swords comes from book 2, chapter 18, in David Ganz's translation, *Einhard and Notker the Stammerer: Two Lives of Charlemagne* (Penguin, London, 2008).

The many sources on the berserkers are summarised in Neil Price, 'The Lewis "berserkers": Identification and analogy in the shield-biting warriors', in David Caldwell and Mark Hall (eds.), *The Lewis Chessmen: New Perspectives* (National Museums Scotland, Edinburgh, 2014: 29–44). See also Roderick Dale's comprehensive treatment, *Berserkir: A Re-examination of the Phenomenon in Literature and Life* (unpublished PhD thesis, University of Nottingham, Nottingham, 2014), which contains his observations on what he rather wonderfully calls the "berserker strut". The runestone with the floppy-eared 'berserker' is Vg 56 from Källby in Västergötland, Sweden. The Istaby runestone is DR 359. The Byzantine account is from John Skylitzes, referenced in the general section above.

Birka chamber grave Bj.581 is discussed by Charlotte Hedenstierna-Jonson et al., 'The first female Viking warrior confirmed by genomics', *American Journal of Physical Anthropology* 164:4 (2017): 853–860 and by Neil Price et al., 'Viking warrior women? Reassessing Birka chamber grave Bj.581', *Antiquity* 93 (2019): 181–198—both articles with online supplementary materials. The second paper debates the controversies, and they both include extensive references. To this should be added Agneta Ney, *Drottningar och sköldmör. Gränsöverskridande kvinnor i medeltida myt och verklighet ca 400–1400* (Gidlunds, Södertälje, 2004); Lydia Klos, 'Wanderer zwischen den Welten: Die Kriegerinnen der Eisenzeit', in Edith Marold and Ulrich Müller (eds.), *Beretning fra femogtyvende tværfaglige vikingesymposium* (Aarhus University, Aarhus, 2006: 25–43); Leszek Gardeła, 'Warrior-women in Viking-Age Scandinavia: A preliminary archaeological study', *Analecta Archaeologica Ressoviensia* 8 (2013): 273–340; and Luke

John Murphy, *Herjans dísir: valkyrjur, Supernatural Femininities, and Elite Warrior Culture in the Late Pre-Christian Iron Age* (unpublished MA thesis in Old Norse religion, University of Iceland, Reykjavík, 2013).

The most comprehensive synthesis of warfare at this time is by Kim Hjardar and Vegard Vike, *Vikings at War* (Oxbow, Oxford, 2016), and Gareth Williams's book mentioned above is also an excellent guide. For weaponry, see also Fedir Androshchuk, *Viking Swords* (Swedish History Museum, Stockholm, 2014).

CHAPTER 12: HYDRARCHY

The early phase of western raiding is described by Clare Downham, *The Viking Kings of Britain and Ireland: The Dynasty of Ívarr to A.D. 1014* (Dunedin, Edinburgh, 2007) and David Griffiths, *Vikings of the Irish Sea* (History Press, Stroud, 2010). These also deal with the period after 834, but, for the Continent in the ninth century, see also Jean Renaud, *Les Vikings en France* (Ouest-France, Rennes, 2000); Élisabeth Ridel (ed.), *Les Vikings en France: une synthèse inédite* (Dossiers d'Archaeologies, Dijon, 2002); Anne-Marie Flambard Héricher (ed.), *La progression des Vikings, des raids à la colonisation* (University of Rouen, Rouen, 2003); Pierre Bauduin, *Le monde franc et les Vikings* (Albin Michel, Paris, 2009); and Élisabeth Ridel (ed.), *Les Vikings dans l'Empire franc* (Orep, Bayeux, 2014). The siege of Paris is discussed by Nirmal Dass (ed. & trans.), *Viking Attacks on Paris: The Bella parisiacae urbis of Abbo of Saint-Germain-des-Prés* (Peeters, Paris, 2007). For the life of Ragnar lothbrók, see Elizabeth Ashman Rowe, *Vikings in the West: The Legend of Ragnarr Loðbrók and His Sons* (Fassbaender, Vienna, 2012).

The Frankish loot turning up in Scandinavian graves has been studied by Maria Panum Baastrup, *Kommunikation, kulturmøde og kulturel identitet: tingenes reise i Skandinaviens vikingtid* (Copenhagen University, Copenhagen, 2012) and Hanne Lovise Aannestad, *Transformasjoner: Omformning og bruk av importerte gjenstander i vikingtid* (Oslo University, Oslo, 2015).

The Viking activities in Britain are probably the most intensely studied aspect of the entire diaspora. In addition to the prior works by Downham and Griffiths, for overviews see Alfred P. Smyth, *Scandinavian Kings in the British Isles 850–880* (Oxford University Press, Oxford, 1977); Henry Loyn, *The Vikings in Britain* (Batsford, London, 1977); Else Roesdahl et al. (eds.), *The Vikings in England* (Anglo-Danish Viking Project, London, 1981); Dawn Hadley, *The Vikings in England: Settlement, Society and Culture* (Manchester

University Press, Manchester, 2006); Julian D. Richards, *Viking Age England* (2nd edn., History Press, Stroud, 2007); and Thomas Williams, *Viking Britain* (Collins, London, 2017). A number of important papers can also be found in John Hines, Alan Lane, and Mark Redknap (eds.), *Land, Sea and Home* (Maney, Leeds, 2004). Regional studies include Sue Margeson, *The Vikings in Norfolk* (Norfolk Museums, Norwich, 1997); B. J. N. Edwards, *Vikings in North West England* (University of Lancaster, Lancaster, 1998); Paul Cavill, Stephen E. Harding, and Judith Jesch, *Wirral and Its Viking Heritage* (English Place-Name Society, Nottingham, 2000); Heather O'Donoghue and Pragya Vohra (eds.), *The Vikings in Cleveland* (University of Nottingham, Nottingham, 2014); Derek Gore, *The Vikings in the West Country* (Mint Press, Exeter, 2015); Stephen E. Harding, David Griffiths, and Elisabeth Royles (eds.), *In Search of Vikings: Interdisciplinary Approaches to the Scandinavian Heritage of North-West England* (CRC Press, Boca Raton, 2015); Ryan Lavell and Simon Roffey (eds.), *Danes in Wessex: The Scandinavian Impact on Southern England, c.800–c.1100* (Oxbow, Oxford, 2016); and Rebecca Gregory, *Viking Nottinghamshire* (Five Leaves, Nottingham, 2017). Reading on York and the Danelaw can be found in the following under chapter 15.

The notion of 'longboat diplomacy' was coined by Gareth Williams. The Viking manipulation of English defensive systems is discussed by John Baker and Stuart Brookes, *Beyond the Burghal Hidage: Anglo-Saxon Civil Defence in the Viking Age* (Brill, Leiden, 2013).

For the late ninth-century Viking assault on the Low Countries and the Rhine, see Rudolf Simek and Ulrike Engel (eds.), *Vikings on the Rhine* (Fassbaender, Vienna, 2004) and Annemarieke Willemsen, *Wikinger am Rhein 800–1000* (Theiss, Stuttgart, 2004).

The Woodstown camp in Ireland is published by Ian Russell and Maurice F. Hurley (eds.), *Woodstown: A Viking-Age Settlement in Co. Waterford* (Four Courts, Dublin, 2014). The Camp de Péran in Brittany is described by Jean-Pierre Nicolardot, 'Le Camp de Péran et les Vikings en Bretagne', in Ridel's 2002 synthesis referenced above, pp. 60–69. The Repton camp has been published by Martin Biddle and Birthe Kjølbye-Biddle, 'Repton and the Vikings', *Antiquity* 66 (1992): 36–51 and 'Repton and the "great heathen army", 873–4', in James Graham-Campbell et al. (eds.), *Vikings and the Danelaw* (Oxbow, Oxford, 2001: 45–96) and by Catrine L. Jarman et al., 'The Viking Great Army in England: New dates from the Repton charnel', *Antiquity* 92 (2018): 183–199. The Heath Wood burials are published by Julian Richards et al., 'Excavations at the Viking barrow cemetery at Heath Wood, Ingleby', *Antiquaries*

Journal 84 (2004): 23–116. For the Torksey camp, see Dawn Hadley and Julian Richards, 'The winter camp of the Viking Great Army, AD 872–3, Torksey, Lincolnshire', *Antiquaries Journal* 96 (2016): 23–67 and 'In search of the Viking Great Army: Beyond the winter camps', *Medieval Settlement Research* 33 (2018): 1–17, where they have speculated on the relationships between the different camps. The ARSNY site is published by Gareth Williams (ed.), *A Riverine Site Near York: A Possible Viking Camp?* (British Museum Press, London, 2020).

The groundbreaking analysis of female jewellery in the Danelaw is by Jane Kershaw and can be found in her book, *Viking Identities: Scandinavian Jewellery in England* (Oxford University Press, Oxford, 2013) while its genetic counterpart is published as Jane Kershaw and Ellen Røyrvik, 'The "People of the British Isles" project and Viking settlement in England', *Antiquity* 90 (2016): 1670–1680. The initial Viking presence, including that of women, is also treated extensively by Shane McLeod, *The Beginning of Scandinavian Settlement in England: The Viking 'Great Army' and Early Settlers, c.865–900* (Brepols, Turnhout, 2014).

I have explored the notion of the Viking as pirate in two works: Neil Price, 'Ship-men and slaughter-wolves: Pirate polities in the Viking Age', in Leos Müller and Stefan Amirell (eds.), *Persistent Piracy: Historical Perspectives on Maritime Violence and State Formation* (Palgrave Macmillan, Basingstoke, 2014: 51–68) and 'Pirates of the North Sea? The Viking ship as political space', in Lene Melheim, Håkan Glørstad, and Zanette Tsigaridas Glørstad (eds.), *Comparative Perspectives on Past Colonization, Maritime Interaction and Cultural Integration* (Equinox, Sheffield, 2016: 149–176); these papers introduced the notion of hydrarchy to Viking studies and, incidentally, also include the references to Camden. Other scholars looking at Norse piracy are Benjamin Hudson, *Viking Pirates and Christian Princes: Dynasty, Religion, and Empire in the North Atlantic* (Oxford University, Oxford, 2005) and Christian Cooijmans, *Of Monarchs and Hydrarchs: A Conceptual Development Model for Viking Activity Across the Frankish Realm (c. 750–940 CE)* (unpublished PhD thesis, University of Edinburgh, Edinburgh, 2018).

The leading scholar of pirate communities is Marcus Rediker, whose work I draw on substantially here (he also made the remark about the triad of symbols). His publications are referenced in my own papers above, but the following are of particular relevance: *Between the Devil and the Deep Blue Sea: Merchant Seamen, Pirates and the Anglo-American Maritime World, 1700–1750* (Cambridge University Press, Cambridge, 1987) and *Outlaws of the Atlantic: Sailors, Pirates, and Motley Crews in the Age of Sail* (Beacon Press, Boston, 2014). See also Peter

Linebaugh and Marcus Rediker, *The Many-Headed Hydra: The Hidden History of the Revolutionary Atlantic* (Verso, London, 2000), the primary work on pirate hydrarchies, which includes the quote attributed to Braithwaite. I thank Marcus for his correspondence with me on these issues.

CHAPTER 13: DIASPORA

The idea of a Viking diaspora—as opposed to the traditional 'expansion'—has many roots but, above all, is found in the work of two scholars. The primary publications are by Lesley Abrams, 'Diaspora and identity in the Viking Age', *Early Medieval Europe* 20 (2012): 17–38 and three by Judith Jesch: *The Viking Diaspora* (Routledge, London & New York, 2015); 'The concept of "homeland" in the Viking diaspora', in Val Turner, Olwyn Owen, and Doreen Waugh (eds.), *Shetland and the Viking World* (Shetland Heritage Publications, Lerwick, 2016: 141–146); and 'Diaspora', in Jörg Glauser, Pernille Hermann, and Stephen A. Mitchell (eds.), *Handbook of Pre-Modern Nordic Memory Studies* (De Gruyter, Berlin, 2018: 583–593). Jesch is carefully specific in her use of the term, more so than many who have subsequently taken it up and employed it more loosely. In her research projects on this theme, based at the University of Nottingham, she has focussed on the definitions drawn from social science—for example, the work of Robin Cohen, *Global Diasporas: An Introduction* (2nd edn., Routledge, London & New York, 2008). The latter is the source of the observation about a continuing conversation, and the list of diasporic characteristics in my text is drawn from both Cohen and Jesch. For a recent overview of the Viking diaspora in a global context, see David Abulafia, *The Boundless Sea: A Human History of the Oceans* (Allen Lane, London, 2019: chs. 18–21).

The latest overview of eastern Baltic trade has been referenced above but is relevant here, too: Johan Callmer, Ingrid Gustin, and Mats Roslund (eds.), *Identity Formation and Diversity in the Early Medieval Baltic and Beyond* (Brill, Leiden, 2017); two key papers therein reference the fur trade with the Finns (Mats Roslund, who also made the Hudson Bay analogy) and Ladoga's role in the silver stream (Søren Sindbæk). Further Baltic interactions are discussed in Mats Roslund's book, *Guests in the House: Cultural Transmission Between Slavs and Scandinavians 900–1300* (Brill, Leiden, 2007). The link to the eastern rivers is taken up by Line Bjerg, John Lind, and Søren Sindbæk (eds.), *From Goths to Varangians: Communication and Cultural Exchange Between the Baltic and the Black Sea* (Aarhus University Press, Aarhus, 2013).

For the connections with Constantinople, see Fedir Androshchuk, Jonathan Shepard, and Monica White (eds.), *Byzantium and the Viking World*

555

(Uppsala University, Uppsala, 2016). An old work that still repays attention is H. R. Ellis Davidson, *The Viking Road to Byzantium* (Allen and Unwin, London, 1976). The Rus' are also discussed in chapter 15, but for general sources, see Simon Franklin and Jonathan Shepard, *The Emergence of Rus 750–1200* (Longman, London, 1996: 3–49); Wladyslaw Duczko, *Viking Rus* (Brill, Leiden, 2004); and Fedir Androshchuk, *The Vikings in the East* (Uppsala University, Uppsala, 2013). The delegation to the Frankish court and the reading of Hákon are discussed by Ildar Garipzanov, 'The Annals of St. Bertin (839) and *Chacanus* of the *Rhos*', *Ruthenica* 5 (2006): 7–11. The Métis analogies for the Rus' have been extensively discussed by Charlotta Hillerdal, *People in Between: Ethnicity and Material Identity—A New Approach to Deconstructed Concepts* (Uppsala University, Uppsala, 2009).

The Gotland hoards are discussed by Jacek Gruszczyński, *Viking Silver, Hoards and Containers* (Routledge, London & New York, 2019). For the river trade, see papers in James Graham-Campbell and Gareth Williams (eds.), *Silver Economy in the Viking Age* (Left Coast Press, Walnut Creek, 2007) and James Graham-Campbell, Søren Sindbæk, and Gareth Williams (eds.), *Silver Economies, Monetisation and Society in Scandinavia, AD 800–1100* (Aarhus University Press, Aarhus, 2011). Market forces are explored by Ingrid Gustin, *Mellan gåva och marknad* (University of Lund, Lund, 2004), and I have again benefitted greatly from discussions with Anders Ögren.

For the Vikings in Iberia, see Eduardo Morales Romero, *Historia de los Vikingos en España* (Miraguano Ediciones, Madrid, 2004); Christopher Bo Bramsen (ed.), *Vikingerne på den Iberiske Halvø* (Embassy of Denmark, Madrid, 2004); Neil Price, 'The Vikings in Spain, North Africa and the Mediterranean', in Stefan Brink and Neil Price (eds.), *The Viking World* (Routledge, London & New York, 2008: 462–469); and especially Ann Christys, *Vikings in the South: Voyages to Iberia and the Mediterranean* (Bloomsbury, London, 2015). The translations of the Norse names for Mediterranean localities are by Elena Melnikova. The work on Madeiran mice is by Jeremy Searle et al., 'Of mice and (Viking?) men: Phylogeography of British and Irish house mice', *Philosophical Transactions of the Royal Society B* 276 (2009): 201–207.

Excerpts from the main sources for the settlement of the North Atlantic were collected by Gwyn Jones, *The Norse Atlantic Saga* (2nd edn., Oxford University Press, Oxford, 1986). For archaeological surveys, including the sites mentioned in the text, see William Fitzhugh and Elizabeth Ward (eds.), *Vikings: The North Atlantic Saga* (Smithsonian, Washington, DC, 2000); James Barrett (ed.), *Contact, Continuity, and Collapse: The Norse Colonization of the North*

Atlantic (Brepols, Leiden, 2003); and Andras Mortensen and Símun V. Arge (eds.), *Viking and Norse in the North Atlantic* (Faroese Academy of Sciences, Tórshavn, 2005). The excavations at Stöðvarfjörður by Bjarni Einarsson are still ongoing and as yet unpublished, although they have been widely reported in the media. For other perspectives on the first settlement, see Margrét Hermanns-Auðardóttir, *Islands tidiga bosättning* (Umeå University, Umeå, 1989) and Bjarni F. Einarsson, *The Settlement of Iceland: A Critical Approach* (Hið íslenska bókmenntafélag, Reykjavík, 1995). The controversial origins of Iceland's founding population have generated a vast literature continually growing as more genetic studies are undertaken; the debate largely began with J. T. Williams, 'Origin and population structure of the Icelanders', *Human Biology* 65 (1993): 167–191 and continued with the extensive work of Agnar Helgason and his team over many publications; this is all fully referenced in the latest study: Maja Krzewińska et al., 'Mitochondrial DNA variation in the Viking Age population of Norway', *Philosophical Transactions of the Royal Society B* 370 (2015): 20130384.

CHAPTER 14: THE GOLDEN AGE OF THE SHEEP FARMER

The historian who remarked about the pig farmers was Eric Christiansen, *The Norsemen in the Viking Age* (Blackwell, Oxford, 2002: 6).

For the resource implications of the sail, see Lise Bender Jørgensen, 'The introduction of sails to Scandinavia: Raw materials, labour, and land', in Ragnhild Berge et al. (eds.), *N-TAG Ten: Proceedings of the 10th Nordic TAG Conference* (BAR, Oxford, 2012: 173–181). For work since then, see Morten Ravn et al. (eds.), *Vikingetidens sejl* (Saxo Institute, Copenhagen University, Copenhagen, 2016) and Morten Ravn, *Viking-Age War Fleets* (Viking Ship Museum, Roskilde, 2017); the figures for sailcloth and wool cited here are from Eva Andersson Strand, and I also thank Frans-Arne Stylegar for sharing his ideas on this. The Ladby vessel used in these examples is published by Anne C. Sørensen, *Ladby: A Danish Ship-Grave from the Viking Age* (Viking Ship Museum, Roskilde, 2001).

The expansion of the landed estates can be seen throughout Scandinavia but perhaps most clearly in Denmark at settlements such as Vorbasse and Trabjerg; see Steen Hvass, 'Vorbasse: The Viking-Age settlement at Vorbasse, central Jutland', *Acta Archaeologica* 50 (1980): 137–172 and Lise Bender Jørgensen and Palle Eriksen, *Trabjerg: en vestjysk landsby fra vikingetiden* (Jysk Arkæologisk Selskab, Aarhus, 1995). Useful regional studies that place this in a wider context can be found in Steffen Stummann Hansen and Klavs Randsborg (eds.), *Vikings in the West* (Munksgaard, Copenhagen, 2000) and Palle Eriksen et al., *Vikinger i vest: vikingetiden i Vestjylland* (Jysk Arkæologisk Selskab, Aarhus, 2011).

The Skuldelev 2 ship is published in Ole Crumlin-Pedersen and Olaf Olsen (eds.), *The Skuldelev Ships I* (Viking Ship Museum, Roskilde, 2002: 141–194). The description of life in the weaving sheds owes a debt to Pat Barker's feminist reimagining of the *Iliad* story, *The Silence of the Girls* (Hamish Hamilton, London, 2018). References for the raiding-slaving-trading trinity can be found above for chapter 4 and in relation to the impacts of polygyny in chapter 11. A clear example of a settlement with a 'Big House' and many small sheds that may be the quarters of the enslaved is Sanda in Uppland, Sweden; see Torun Zachrisson, 'De osynliggjorda: om trälar i arkeologisk forskning', in Thomas Lindkvist and Janken Myrdal (eds.), *Trälar: ofria i agrarsamhället från vikingatid till medeltid* (Nordic Museum, Stockholm, 2003: 88–102). The historian who sees slavery at the core of Viking-ness is Peter Heather, as expressed in a rather profound remark during conference discussion.

References for Hedeby and Birka can be found under chapter 10, above. An overview of Kaupang can be found in Dagfinn Skre and Frans-Arne Stylegar, *Kaupang vikingebyen* (Oslo University, Oslo, 2004) while the new excavations there have been published as Dagfinn Skre (ed.), *Kaupang Excavation Project* (4 vols., Oslo University/Aarhus University Press, Norske Oldfunn 22–25, 2007–2016). The last general survey of Viking urbanism was by Helen Clarke and Björn Ambrosiani, *Towns in the Viking Age* (2nd edn., Leicester University Press, Leicester, 1995), but references to current debates can be found in Lena Holmquist, Sven Kalmring, and Charlotte Hedenstierna-Jonson (eds.), *New Aspects on Viking-Age Urbanism c. AD 750–1100* (Stockholm University, Stockholm, 2016). The work mentioned at Hedeby is by Sven Kalmring, 'The harbour of Hedeby', in Svavar Sigmundsson (ed.), *Viking Settlements and Viking Society* (University of Iceland, Reykjavík, 2011: 245–260). The suggestion about the importance of high-grade textile work as a female function of urban life is by Ingvild Øye, whose many publications in this field provide an outstanding overview of a gendered profession in the Viking Age.

CHAPTER 15: SILVER, SLAVES, AND SILK

Two recent works treat the notion of a post–Cold War, globalised Viking Age. See Søren Sindbæk and Athena Trakadas (eds.), *The World in the Viking Age*

(Viking Ship Museum, Roskilde, 2014) and Neil Price, 'Distant Vikings: A manifesto', *Acta Archaeologica* 89 (2018): 113–132.

The observation about the sheltered coastlines of Scotland and western Norway is by Arne Kruse. The literature on the Picts is vast, but, for an overview, see Martin Carver, *Surviving in Symbols: A Visit to the Pictish Nation* (Historic Scotland, Edinburgh, 1999) and Gordon Noble and Nicholas Evans, *The King in the North: The Pictish Realms of Fortriu and Ce* (Birlinn, Edinburgh, 2019).

Orkneyinga Saga is translated by Hermann Pálsson and Paul Edwards (Penguin, London, 1978). For general works on the Vikings in Scotland and the Isles, see Barbara E. Crawford, *Scandinavian Scotland* (Leicester University Press, Leicester, 1987); Anna Ritchie, *Viking Scotland* (Batsford, London, 1993); James Graham-Campbell and Colleeen E. Batey, *Vikings in Scotland: An Archaeological Survey* (Edinburgh University Press, Edinburgh, 1998); and Olwyn Owen, *The Sea Road: A Viking Voyage Through Scotland* (Canongate, Edinburgh, 1999).

For the Orkneys, in particular, see Barbara E. Crawford, *The Northern Earldoms: Orkney and Caithness from AD 870 to 1470* (John Donald, Edinburgh, 2013); for excavations, see Christopher D. Morris, *The Birsay Bay Project* (2 vols., University of Durham, Durham, 1989 & 1996); James Barrett (ed.), *Being an Islander: Production and Identity at Quoygrew, Orkney, AD 900–1600* (Oxbow, Oxford, 2012); and David Griffiths, Jane Harrison, and Michael Athanson, *Beside the Ocean: The Bay of Skaill, Marwick, and Birsay Bay, Orkney* (Oxbow, Oxford, 2018). The excavations at Deerness, by James Barrett, are now being prepared for publication, as is the work by Jane Harrison on the artificial mounds of Skaill. For Shetland, see Val Turner, Olwyn Owen, and Doreen Waugh (eds.), *Shetland and the Viking World* (Shetland Heritage Publications, Lerwick, 2016) and individual sites in J. R. C. Hamilton, *Excavations at Jarlshof, Shetland* (HMSO, Edinburgh, 1956); Barbara E. Crawford and Beverley Ballin Smith, *The Biggings, Papa Stour, Shetland: The History and Archaeology of a Royal Norwegian Farm* (Society of Antiquaries of Scotland, Edinburgh, 1999); and Stephen Dockrill et al., *Excavations at Old Scatness, Shetland I: The Pictish Village and Viking Settlement* (Shetland Amenity Trust, Lerwick, 2010). For the Hebrides, see Niall Sharples, *A Norse Farmstead in the Outer Hebrides* (Oxbow, Oxford, 2005) and Alan Macniven, *The Vikings in Islay* (John Donald, Edinburgh, 2015). Caithness is covered in several general works, but see Colleen E. Batey, Judith Jesch, and Christopher D. Morris (eds.), *The Viking Age in Caithness, Orkney and the North Atlantic* (Edinburgh University Press, Edinburgh,

1993) and Christopher D. Morris, Colleen E. Batey, and James Rackham, *Freswick Links, Caithness: Excavation and Survey of a Norse Settlement* (Historic Scotland, Edinburgh, 1995).

Scottish boat burials have been referenced above for chapter 8. A rare example of a child's burial is reported by Colleen Batey and Caroline Paterson, 'A Viking burial at Balnakeil, Sutherland', in Andrew Reynolds and Leslie Webster (eds.), *Early Medieval Art and Archaeology in the Northern World* (Brill, Leiden, 2013: 631–659). The metal economy is presented by James Graham-Campbell, *The Viking-Age Gold and Silver of Scotland* (National Museums of Scotland, Edinburgh, 1995).

The politics of the Scottish mainland in the Viking Age are discussed by Alex Woolf, *From Pictland to Alba, 789–1070* (Edinburgh University Press, Edinburgh, 2007). For excavations at a major east-coast monastic site attacked by Vikings, see Martin Carver, Justin Garner-Lahire, and Cecily Spall, *Portmahomack on Tarbat Ness: Changing Ideologies in North-East Scotland, Sixth to Sixteenth Century AD* (Society of Antiquaries of Scotland, Edinburgh, 2016).

The Irish Sea cultural sphere has been referenced above, but see, in particular, Alfred P. Smyth, *Scandinavian York and Dublin* (Irish Academic Press, Dublin, 1987); Clare Downham, *The Viking Kings of Britain and Ireland: The Dynasty of Ívarr to A.D. 1014* (Dunedin, Edinburgh, 2007); and David Griffiths, *Vikings of the Irish Sea* (History Press, Stroud, 2010).

All the above contain extensive references to individual towns and polities. Beyond this, for York and the Danelaw, see Richard Hall, *Viking Age York* (Batsford, London, 1994); Dawn Hadley, *The Northern Danelaw: Its Social Structure, c.800–1100* (Leicester University Press, Leicester, 2000); James Graham-Campbell et al. (eds.), *Vikings and the Danelaw* (Oxbow, Oxford, 2001); Dawn Hadley and Letty Ten Harkel (eds.), *Everyday Life in Viking-Age Towns: Social Approaches to Towns in England and Ireland, c.800–1100* (Oxbow, Oxford, 2013); and Matthew Townend, *Viking Age Yorkshire* (Blackthorn, Pickering, 2014). The final publication of the major Viking excavations in York, including references to the long series of reports, is Richard Hall, *Anglo-Scandinavian Occupation at 16-22 Coppergate: Defining a Townscape* (Council for British Archaeology, York, 2014).

For the economy of Scandinavian England, see James Graham-Campbell, *The Cuerdale Hoard* (British Museum Press, London, 2011); Mark Blackburn, *Viking Coinage and Currency in the British Isles* (Spink, London, 2011); and Jane Kershaw and Gareth Williams (eds.), *Silver, Butter, Cloth: Monetary and Social Economies in the Viking Age* (Oxford University Press, Oxford, 2019). Social expression in the Danelaw has been referenced above, but see Jane Kershaw,

Viking Identities: Scandinavian Jewellery in England (Oxford University Press, Oxford, 2013) and Steven P. Ashby, *A Viking Way of Life* (Amberley, Stroud, 2014). Hogback grave covers have been catalogued by James Lang, 'The hogback: A Viking colonial monument', *Anglo-Saxon Studies in Archaeology and History* 3 (1984): 83–176; see also Richard N. Bailey, *Viking Age Sculpture* (Collins, London, 1980) and the ongoing publications of the *Corpus of Anglo-Saxon Stone Sculpture* from the British Academy in London.

The latest work on the Viking Age in Ireland can be found in several collections: Howard B. Clarke, Máire Ní Mhaonaigh, and Raghnall Ó Floinn (eds.), *Ireland and Scandinavia in the Early Viking Age* (Four Courts, Dublin, 1998); Anne-Christine Larsen, *The Vikings in Ireland* (Viking Ship Museum, Roskilde, 2001); John Sheehan and Donnchadh Ó Corráin (eds.), *The Viking Age: Ireland and the West* (Four Courts, Dublin, 2010); Emer Purcell et al. (eds.), *Clerics, Kings and Vikings* (Four Courts, Dublin, 2015); and Howard B. Clarke and Ruth Johnson (eds.), *The Vikings in Ireland and Beyond* (Four Courts, Dublin, 2015).

For the Irish city states and Dublin in particular, see Ruth Johnson, *Viking Age Dublin* (Town House, Dublin, 2004); Patrick F. Wallace, *Viking Dublin: The Wood Quay Excavations* (Irish Academic Press, Dublin, 2016); Howard B. Clarke, Sheila Doohey, and Ruth Johnson, *Dublin and the Viking World* (O'Brien Press, Dublin, 2018); and the ongoing series of *Medieval Dublin Excavations* published by the Royal Irish Academy in Dublin (which includes a major collection on the funerary evidence for the Viking presence by Stephen Harrison and Raghnall Ó Floinn). Clare Downham has written thoughtfully on '"Hiberno-Norwegians" and "Anglo-Danes": Anachronistic ethnicities and Viking-Age England', *Medieval Scandinavia* 19 (2009): 139–169. Exciting work on the military forces of Viking-Age Ireland is underway by Tenaya Jorgensen and her colleagues at Trinity College Dublin, and is set to significantly increase our knowledge here.

For Manx material, see Christine Fell et al. (eds.), *The Viking Age in the Isle of Man* (Viking Society for Northern Research, London, 1983) and David M. Wilson, *The Vikings in the Isle of Man* (Aarhus University Press, Aarhus, 2008). For ritual life on the island, see Gerhard Bersu and David M. Wilson, *Three Viking Graves on the Isle of Man* (Society for Medieval Archaeology, King's Lynn, 1966) and Leszek Gardeła and Carolyne Larrington (eds.), *Viking Myths and Rituals on the Isle of Man* (University of Nottingham, Nottingham, 2014). The archaeologist who sees Man as a 'pirate kingdom' is James Barrett, and I agree.

For the Celtic West, see Henry Loyn, *The Vikings in Wales* (Viking Society for Northern Research, London, 1976) and Mark Redknap, *Vikings in Wales* (National Museums and Galleries of Wales, Cardiff, 2000).

For Normandy, see David Bates, *Normandy Before 1066* (Longman, London, 1982); Jean Renaud, *Les Vikings et la Normandie* (Ouest-France, Rennes, 1989); Lucien Musset, *Nordica et Normannica* (Société des études nordiques, Paris, 1997); and Katherine Cross, *Heirs of the Vikings: History and Identity in Normandy and England, c.950–c.1015* (York Medieval Press, York, 2018). Other recent studies can be found in the synthetic works referenced above for chapter 12. An important paper in this context is Simon Coupland, 'From poachers to gamekeepers: Scandinavian warlords and Carolingian kings', *Early Medieval Europe* 7 (1998): 85–114.

The main sources for Brittany in English are my own publications: Neil Price, *The Vikings in Brittany* (Viking Society for Northern Research, London, 1989); 'The Viking conquest of Brittany', in Stefan Brink and Neil Price (eds.), *The Viking World* (Routledge, London & New York, 2008: 458–461); and 'Viking Brittany: Revisiting the colony that failed', in Andrew Reynolds and Leslie Webster (eds.), *Early Medieval Art and Archaeology in the Northern World* (Brill, Leiden, 2013: 731–742). See also Jean-Christophe Cassard, *Le siècle des Vikings en Bretagne* (Gisserot, Quintin, 1996).

The Rus' symbol of the diving falcon has its own book by Björn Ambrosiani (ed.), *Birka Studies 5. Eastern Connections: The Falcon Motif* (Riksantikvarieämbetet, Stockholm, 2001). Appropriately, in stylised form it continues to serve as Ukraine's coat of arms.

Unsurprisingly, the majority of work on the Vikings in the East is published in Russian or Ukrainian. References to this literature—which is truly enormous—may be found in the works cited here, but, for ease of access, these notes are restricted to material in English. For overviews, see Simon Franklin and Jonathan Shepard, *The Emergence of Rus 750–1200* (Longman, London, 1996: 3–49); Pär Hanson (ed.), *The Rural Viking in Russia and Sweden* (Örebro bildningsförvaltning, Örebro, 1997); Wladyslaw Duczko, *Viking Rus* (Brill, Leiden, 2004); Ulf Fransson et al. (eds.), *Cultural Interaction Between East and West* (University of Stockholm, Stockholm, 2007); Fedir Androshchuk, *The Vikings in the East* (Uppsala University, Uppsala, 2013); and Pierre Bauduin and Alexander E. Musin (eds.), *Vers l'Orient et vers l'Occident: regards croisés sur les dynamiques et les transferts culturels des Vikings à la Rous ancienne* (University of Caen, Caen, 2014). For contacts with eastern peoples, see Jakub Morawiec, *Vikings Among the Slavs* (Fassbaender, Vienna, 2009); Tsvetelin Stepanov, *The Bulghars and the Steppe Empire in the Early Middle Ages* (Brill, Leiden, 2010); and Boris Zhivkov, *Khazaria in the Ninth and Tenth Centuries* (Brill, Leiden, 2015). For Novgorod, see Mark Brisbane (ed.), *The Archaeology of Novgorod, Russia* (Society for Medieval Archaeology, Lincoln, 1992) and his edited series *The Archaeology of Medieval Novgorod* (4 vols., Oxbow, Oxford, 2006–2019).

For Byzantium and the Varangian Guard, see H. R. Ellis Davidson, *The Viking Road to Byzantium* (Allen and Unwin, London, 1976); Sigfús Blöndal, *The Varangians of Byzantium* (Cambridge University Press, Cambridge, 1978); Raffaele D'Amato, *The Varangian Guard 988–1453* (Osprey, Oxford, 2010); and Fedir Androshchuk, Jonathan Shepard, and Monica White (eds.), *Byzantium and the Viking World* (Uppsala University, Uppsala, 2016); the latter work contains a great many papers of interest. The runestone mentioning a guardsman is U 112 from Kyrkstigen in Uppland, Sweden.

In his MA thesis in medieval studies, Csete Katona has made a major study of the Rus' activities as mercenaries, which has been most useful here: *Co-operation Between the Viking Rus' and the Turkic Nomads of the Steppe in the Ninth–Eleventh Centuries* (Central European University, Budapest, 2018). The two Viking swords from southern Turkey are recent finds and have not yet been fully published. The comments on al-Mas'ūdī are by Þórir Hraundal, *The Rus in Arabic Sources: Cultural Contacts and Identity* (University of Oslo, Oslo, 2013). The scholar who sees the Rus' in similar terms to the armies of the west is Gareth Williams.

The latest work on Kiev is summarised in two books by Christian Raffensperger: *Reimagining Europe: Kievan Rus' in the Medieval World* (Harvard University Press, Cambridge, MA, 2012) and *The Kingdom of Rus'* (University of Amsterdam Press, Amsterdam, 2017). For Ingvar's expedition, see two books by Mats G. Larsson, *Runstenar och utlandsfärder* (Lund University, Lund, 1990) and *Ett ödesdigert vikingatåg: Ingvar den vittfarnes resa 1036–1041* (Atlantic, Stockholm, 1990). His saga is translated in *Vikings in Russia* by Hermann Pálsson and Paul Edwards (Edinburgh University Press, Edinburgh, 1989). The runestone commemorating Ingvar's brother is Sö 179. The new interpretation of the Piraeus inscription, by Thorgunn Snædal, is in Fedir Androshchuk, Jonathan Shepard, and Monica White (eds.), *Byzantium and the Viking World* (Uppsala University, Uppsala, 2016).

On the Rus' as military elites, see Charlotte Hedenstierna-Jonson, *The Birka Warrior: The Material Culture of a Martial Society* (Stockholm University, Stockholm, 2006). Their material culture is also reviewed by David Nicolle, *Armies of Medieval Russia 750–1250* (Osprey, Oxford, 1999). The scholar referring to the "Turkic military outfit" is Þórir Hraundal. The runestones mentioning Rus' are Sö 338, Sö 34, and Sö 171, all from Södermanland in Sweden. The meditations on Varangian PTSD come from the as-yet unpublished work of Rue Taylor, whom I thank for permission to discuss them here.

For Scandinavian burials in the East, see Kirill Mikhajlov, 'Chamber-graves as interregional phenomenon of the Viking Age: From Denmark to Rus'', in Mariana Rębkowskiego (ed.), *Ekskluzywne Życie-Dostojny Pochówek w Kręgu Kultury Elitarnej Wieków Średnich* (Wolin, 2011: 205–223) and especially Fedir Androshchuk and Vladimir Zotsenko, *Скандинавские древности Южной Руси—Scandinavian Antiquities of Southern Rus'* (Collège de France, Paris, 2012, with English summaries). The work on Rus' women as traders is by Anne Stalsberg, 'Women as actors in North European Viking Age trade', in Ross Samson (ed.), *Social Approaches to Viking Studies* (Cruithne Press, Glasgow, 1991: 75–88) and 'Visible women made invisible: Interpreting Varangian women in Old Russia', in Bettina Arnold and Nancy L. Wicker (eds.), *Gender and the Archaeology of Death* (Alta Mira, Walnut Creek, 2001: 65–80). The story of Geirmund Hjørson is told by his (literal) modern descendant, Bergsveinn Birgisson, in *Den svarte vikingen* (Spartacus, Oslo, 2014).

For the Vikings in Arabia and the Caliphate, most of the discussion has been confined to the texts. The best modern survey has been mentioned several times here: Þórir Hraundal's *The Rus in Arabic Sources: Cultural Contacts and Identity* (University of Oslo, Oslo, 2013); many of the observations in my book draw on his inspirational work. An earlier set of translations into Norwegian also contains much of interest, Harris Birkeland, *Nordens historie i middelalderen etter arabiske kilder* (Dybwad, Oslo, 1954), as does Stig Wikander, *Araber, Vikingar, Väringar* (Svenska humanistiska förbundet, Lund, 1978). See also several papers in Søren Sindbæk and Athena Trakadas (eds.), *The World in the Viking Age* (Viking Ship Museum, Roskilde, 2014). The runestone with the Khwārazm inscription is Vs 1. The notion of an Islamic mission to Scandinavia has been put forward by Egil Mikkelsen, 'The Vikings and Islam', in Stefan Brink and Neil Price (eds.), *The Viking World* (Routledge, London & New York, 2008: 543–549).

The merchant's prayer from ibn Faḍlān is given here in James Montgomery's translation. The silver trade generates an ever-growing literature of papers, especially relating to the Gotland hoards. Major works, with references, have been noted above, but for the East, in particular, see also Thomas S. Noonan, *The Islamic World, Russia and the Vikings, 750–900: The Numismatic Evidence* (Routledge, London & New York, 1998); the papers by Christoph Kilger in the second volume of the Kaupang excavation reports, Dagfinn Skre (ed.), *Means of Exchange* (Aarhus University Press, Aarhus, 2007); and Fedir Androshchuk, *Images of Power: Byzantium and Nordic Coinage c.995–1035* (Laurus, Kiev, 2016). The many papers of Gert Rispling are also central to our understanding of the dirham trade.

The link between silver and slaves is being explored by the Dirhams for Slaves project at Oxford University with the work of Jacek Gruszczyński, Marek Jankowiak, Jonathan Shepard, and Luke Treadwell. I would also like to acknowledge the important contributions being made by Viacheslav Kuleshov.

Charlotte Hedenstierna-Jonson is one of very few to have explored the Vikings' travels even farther east; see her important paper, 'With Asia as neighbour: Archaeological evidence of contacts between Scandinavia and Central Asia in the Viking Age and the Tang Dynasty', *Bulletin of the Museum of Far Eastern Antiquities* 81 (in press). The silk trade is discussed by Marianne Vedeler, *Silk for the Vikings* (Oxbow, Oxford, 2014). The possible Viking boats on Qatari rock carvings are discussed by Guy Isitt, 'Vikings in the Persian Gulf', *Journal of the Royal Asiatic Society* 17:4 (2007): 389–406. This should be set against the larger picture of East–West trade and cultural exchange, on which the best recent and well-referenced work is Peter Frankopan, *The Silk Roads: A New History of the World* (Bloomsbury, London, 2015); and Susan Whitfield (ed.), *Silk Roads: Peoples, Cultures, Landscapes* (Thames and Hudson, London and New York, 2019).

The linked silk fragments from 5-7 Coppergate in York and Saltergate in Lincoln are discussed by Richard Hall, *The Viking Dig* (Bodley Head, London, 1984: 88).

CHAPTER 16: THE EXPERIMENTS OF MONARCHY

For overviews of the conversion of Scandinavia, see Bertil Nilsson (ed.), *Kontinuitet i kult och tro från vikingatid till medeltid* (Lunne, Uppsala, 1992); Anne-Sofie Gräslund, *Ideologi och mentalitet: Om religionsskiftet i Skandinavien från en arkeologisk horisont* (Uppsala University, Uppsala, 2001); Martin Carver (ed.), *The Cross Goes North: Processes of Conversion in Northern Europe, AD 300–1300* (Boydell, Woodbridge, 2003); Alexandra Sanmark, *Power and Conversion: A Comparative Study of Christianization in Scandinavia* (Uppsala University, Uppsala, 2004); Jón Viðar Sigurðsson, *Kristninga i Norden 750–1200* (3rd edn., Det norske samlaget, Oslo, 2012); Anders Winroth, *The Conversion of Scandinavia* (Yale University Press, New Haven, 2012); and Sten Tesch (ed.), *Skiftet: vikingatida sed och kristen tro* (Artos, Skellefteå, 2017). For the 'pick and mix' approach to European religion, see Keith Hopkins, *A World Full of Gods: Pagans, Jews and Christians in the Roman Empire* (Weidenfeld & Nicolson, London, 1999).

The sources for the missions include Rimbert's *Vita* of Anskar, which has not been translated into English for many years; see Charles H. Robinson, *Anskar: The Apostle of the North 801–865* (Society for Propagation of the Gospel in Foreign Parts, London, 1921). For other key works, see also Widukind of

Corvey, *Deeds of the Saxons*, trans. Bernard S. Bachrach and David S. Bachrach (Catholic University of America Press, Washington, DC, 2014) and *The Heliand: The Saxon Gospel*, trans. G. Ronald Murphy (Oxford University Press, Oxford, 1992). For an overview of the debate on the names of Askr and Embla, see Lennart Elmevik, 'Embla: Ett bidrag till diskussionen om den nordiska urmoderns namn' (*Saga och Sed* 2012: 47–54).

The political history of Denmark is covered in two general works, now quite old but still sound, each taking a slightly different approach: Klavs Randsborg, *The Viking Age in Denmark* (Duckworth, London, 1980) and Else Roesdahl, *Viking Age Denmark* (British Museum Press, London, 1982). More recent surveys can be found in volume 4 of Jørgen Jensen, *Danmarks Oldtid* (Gyldendal, Copenhagen, 2006) and in the relevant sections of the general works on the Viking Age referenced above.

The 'stone book' at Jelling is discussed by Else Roesdahl, 'Jellingstenen— en bog af sten', in Ole Høiris et al. (eds.), *Menneskelivets mangfoldighed* (Aarhus University Press, Aarhus, 1999: 235–244). Harald's great circular fortresses are published as Poul Nørlund, *Trelleborg* (Nordiske Fortidsminder, Copenhagen, 1948); Olaf Olsen, Holger Schmidt, and Else Roesdahl, *Fyrkat, en jysk vikingeborg* (2 vols., Lynge, Copenhagen, 1977); Andres Dobat, *Kongens borge* (Jysk Arkæologisk Selskab, Moesgård, 2013); Else Roesdahl et al. (eds.), *Aggersborg: the Viking-Age Settlement and Fortress* (National Museum of Denmark, Copenhagen, 2014); and Helen Goodchild, Nanna Holm, and Søren Sindbæk, 'Borgring: The discovery of a Viking Age ring fortress', *Antiquity* 91 (2017): 1027–1042. The distinctive longhouses are discussed by Holger Schmidt, *Building Customs in Viking Age Denmark* (Kristensen, Copenhagen, 1994).

The analysis that revealed Harald's mercenaries is by T. Douglas Price et al., 'Who was in Harald Bluetooth's army? Strontium isotope investigation of the cemetery at the Viking Age fortress at Trelleborg, Denmark', *Antiquity* 85 (2011): 476–489. The Danevirke and its environs are most recently surveyed by Matthias Maluck and Christian Weltecke (eds.), *The Archaeological Border Landscape of Hedeby and the Danevirke* (State Archaeological Department of Schleswig-Holstein, Schleswig, 2016). The bell in Hedeby harbour is discussed by Björn Magnusson-Staaf, 'For whom the bell tolls', *Current Swedish Archaeology* 4 (1996): 141–155. Harald's presumed robbing of Norwegian royal burials is reviewed by Jan Bill and Aiofe Daly, 'The plundering of the ship graves from Oseberg and Gokstad: An example of power politics?', *Antiquity* 86 (2012): 808–824. The later histories of Gotland and Kievan Rus' are all referenced above.

The Trendgården mould, early crucifixes, and cross-hammer pendants can all be found in *Pocket Museum: Vikings* by Steve Ashby and Alison Leonard (Thames & Hudson, London, 2018). Birka grave Bj.660 is discussed in Neil Price, *The Viking Way: Magic and Mind in Late Iron Age Scandinavia* (Oxbow, Oxford, 2019: 85–88). Christian burial practices, including the early evidence from Götaland, are discussed by Jhonny Thérus, *Den yngre järnålderns gravskick i Uppland* (Uppsala University, Uppsala, 2019); see also Gunnar Andersson, *Gravspråk som religiös strategi* (Riksantikvarieämbetet, Stockholm, 2005).

Runestones have been referenced for chapter 3, above, but in the context of conversion and gender, see also Anne-Sofie Gräslund, *Runstensstudier* (Uppsala University, Uppsala, 1994); Lars Wilson, *Runstenar och kyrkor* (Uppsala University, Uppsala, 1994); Linn Lager, *Den synliga tron: runstenskors som en spegling av kristnandet i Sverige* (Uppsala University, Uppsala, 2002); and Cecilia Ljung, *Under runristad hall: tidigkristna gravmonument i 1000-talets Sverige* (Stockholm University, Stockholm, 2016). The non-lexical runestones and their implications are discussed by Marco Bianchi, *Runor som resurs: vikingatida skriftkultur i Uppland och Södermanland* (University of Uppsala, Uppsala, 2010). The Christian knowledge revealed by runestones comes from the work of Henrik Williams. The Timmele stone is Vg 186; the Måsta stone is U 860; Ingirún's Jerusalem declaration is on U 605; and the stone with the large Thor's hammer is Sö 111 from Stenkvista in Södermanland.

The impact of the Christian ritual calendar is discussed by Alexandra Sanmark in her book referenced above. For changes in the fishing industry, see James Barrett and David Orton (eds.), *Cod and Herring: The Archaeology and History of Medieval Sea Fishing* (Oxbow, Oxford, 2016).

The new urbanism of the late Viking Age has generated a significant literature. As above, a general overview to the mid-1990s can be found in Helen Clarke and Björn Ambrosiani, *Towns in the Viking Age* (2nd edn., Leicester University Press, Leicester, 1995), updated with the papers in Lena Holmquist, Sven Kalmring, and Charlotte Hedenstierna-Jonson (eds.), *New Aspects on Viking-Age Urbanism c. AD 750–1100* (Stockholm University, Stockholm, 2016). The latter volume includes the latest work on Sigtuna by Sten Tesch, who led excavations there for many years. Ongoing work in the town is presented in the *Situne Dei* series from Sigtuna Museum, which has also published reports from the many excavations in the settlement. See also Jonas Ros, *Sigtuna: staden, kyrkorna och den kyrkliga organisationen* (Uppsala University, Uppsala, 2001) and *Stad och gård: Sigtuna under sen vikingatid och tidig medeltid*

(Uppsala University, Uppsala, 2009). In Denmark, Aros (Viking-Age Aarhus) is discussed in Annette Damm (ed.), *Viking Aros* (Moesgård Museum, Aarhus, 2005) and Hans Skov and Jeanette Varberg (eds.), *Aros and the World of the Vikings* (Moesgård Musuem, Aarhus, 2011). The many excavations in the towns of Trondheim, Bergen, and Oslo can be explored through the reports published by the Norsk Institutt for Kulturminneforskning (NIKU). The idea of the towns as 'ports of faith' is from the work of Sæbjørg Walaker Nordeide. The demographics of Sigtuna are discussed by Maja Krzewińska et al., 'Genomic and strontium isotope variation reveal immigration patterns in a Viking Age town', *Current Biology* 28:17 (2018): 2730–2738.

For later Viking-Age political history, see Niels Lund, *Fra vikingeriger til stater: træk af Skandinaviens politiske udvikling 700–1200* (Museum Tusculanum, Copenhagen, 1993); Andres Dobat, 'The state and the strangers: The role of external forces in a process of state formation in Viking-Age South Scandinavia (c.900–1050)', *Viking and Medieval Scandinavia* 5 (2009): 65–104; Sverre Bagge, *From Viking Stronghold to Christian Kingdom: State Formation in Norway c.900–1350* (Museum Tusculanum, Copenhagen, 2010); and Jón Viðar Sigurðsson and Anne Irene Riisøy, *Norsk historie 800–1536* (Det norske samlaget, Oslo, 2011). An excellent corrective to the kings-and-battles perspective can be found in Anna Lihammer's study, *Bortom riksbildningen: människor, landskap och makt i sydöstra Skandinavien* (Lund University, Lund, 2007). Svein Forkbeard has his own biography by Poul Skaaning, *Sven Tveskæg* (Hovedland, Copenhagen, 2008); and Knút has several, of which the best is Timothy Bolton, *Cnut the Great* (Yale University Press, New Haven, 2017). The social impact of the later raids is discussed with insight and eloquence by Thomas Williams, *Viking London* (Collins, London, 2019). A somewhat controversial overview is also provided by Angelo Forte, Richard Oram, and Frederik Pedersen, *Viking Empires* (Cambridge University Press, Cambridge, 2005). The Orkesta runestone is U 344. The last of the dynasty is discussed by Ian Howard, *Harthacnut: King of England* (History Press, Stroud, 2008).

CHAPTER 17: LANDS OF FIRE AND VINES

For Iceland, in addition to the general works on the North Atlantic referenced for chapter 13, above, a good starting point is Jesse Byock's book *Viking Age Iceland* (Penguin, London, 2001), linking with the same author's *Medieval Iceland: Society, Sagas, and Power* (University of California Press, Berkeley, 1988). The early settlements (and the diaspora in general) are discussed by Orri Vésteinsson, Helgi Þorláksson, and Árni Einarsson, *Reykjavík 871±2* (Reykjavík City Museum, Reykjavík, 2006) while the classic archaeological survey of Icelandic farms is by Mårten Stenberger et al., *Forntida gårdar i Island* (Munkgaard, Copenhagen, 1943). Among recent work is Davide Zori and Jesse Byock (eds.), *Viking Archaeology in Iceland* (Brepols, Turnhout, 2014), along with regular archaeological reports published by the Institute of Archaeology in Reykjavík and in the journals *Archaeologica Islandica* and *Árbók Hins Íslenzka Fornleifafélag*.

A massive programme of work has been undertaken on human-environmental interaction in early Iceland, much of it within the orbit of the North Atlantic Biocultural Organisation (NABO; www.nabohome.org) and in their online *Journal of the North Atlantic*. On Icelandic legal structures and the nature of feud, see Jesse Byock, *Feud in the Icelandic Saga* (University of California Press, Berkeley, 1982) and William Ian Miller, *Bloodtaking and Peacemaking: Feud, Law, and Society in Saga Iceland* (University of Chicago Press, Chicago, 1990). Icelandic burials are surveyed by Kristján Eldjárn, *Kuml og haugfé úr heiðnum sið á Íslandi* (3rd edn., National Museum of Iceland, Reykjavík, 2016), augmented by the work of Adolf Friðriksson.

Aud Ketilsdóttir, known as the Deep-Minded, appears in many sources, including the *Book of Settlements*, the *Saga of Burnt Njál*, the *Saga of the People of Laxardal*, and others. Flosi is the leader of the Burners in the *Saga of Burnt Njál;* the man who spoke the verses, alive or dead, was Njál's son Skarphédinn. Gudrún Ósvífrsdóttir is the complicated heroine of the *Saga of the People of Laxardal*. Thorodd appears in the *Saga of the People of Eyri*, a tale rich in hauntings of every kind. Freydís Eiríksdóttir features in the two Vinland sagas. Grettir has his own saga of that name. Gunnhild Gormsdóttir, also known as the Mother of Kings, features strongly in the *Saga of Egil Skalla-Grímsson* (the poet she tried to distract) and other sagas.

Hofstaðir is published as a book of that name, edited by Gavin Lucas (Institute of Archaeology, Reykjavík, 2009). For the conversion of Iceland, see Jón Hnefill Aðalsteinsson, *Under the Cloak* (Uppsala University, Uppsala, 1978) and Steinunn Kristjánsdóttir, *The Awakening of Christianity in Iceland* (University of Gothenburg, Gothenburg, 2004).

There are many papers on Greenland in the North Atlantic volumes referenced above. For syntheses, see Kirsten A. Seaver, *The Frozen Echo: Greenland and the Exploration of North America ca. AD 1000–1500* (Stanford University Press, Stanford, 1996) and *The Last Vikings* (I. B. Tauris, London, 2010); see also Jette Arneborg, Georg Nyegaard, and Orri Vésteinsson (eds.), *Norse Greenland*

(Eagle Hill, Steuben, 2012). The Danish series *Meddelelser om Grønland*, published 1879–1979 by the Commission for Scientific Studies on Greenland, contains most of the early archaeology—work continued since by the scholars at the National Museum of Denmark and their SILA unit. See especially Jette Arneborg and H. C. Gulløv (eds.), *Man, Culture and Environment in Ancient Greenland* (National Museum of Denmark, Copenhagen, 1998).

The environmental work at the GUS site has generated many papers, but for an overview, see Paul C. Buckland and Eva Panagiotakopulu, 'Archaeology and the palaeoecology of the Norse Atlantic islands: A review', in Andras Mortensen and Símun V. Arge (eds.), *Viking and Norse in the North Atlantic* (Faroese Academy of Sciences, Tórshavn, 2005: 167–181). For general ecology, see Kevin J. Edwards, Egill Erlendsson, and J. Edward Schofield, 'Is there a Norse "footprint" in North Atlantic pollen records?', in Svavar Sigmundsson (ed.), *Viking Settlements and Viking Society* (University of Iceland, Reykjavík, 2011: 65–82), which contains extensive references to the same team's important work in Greenland and elsewhere in the region. For runes, see Lisbeth M. Imer, *Peasants and Prayers: The Inscriptions of Norse Greenland* (National Museum of Denmark, Copenhagen, 2017).

The *Saga of the Greenlanders* and the *Saga of Erik the Red* are translated together as *The Vinland Sagas: The Norse Discovery of America*, by Magnús Magnússon and Hermann Pálsson (Penguin, London, 1965). The early excavations at L'Anse aux Meadows are published by Anne Stine and Helge Ingstad, *The Norse Discovery of America* (2 vols., Norwegian University Press, Oslo, 1985) while the later seasons are summarised, with a very comprehensive bibliography, by Birgitta Linderoth Wallace, *Westward Vikings: The Saga of L'Anse aux Meadows* (Parks Canada, St. John's, 2006). The new environmental work at the site is by Paul M. Ledger, Linus Girdland-Flink, and Véronique Forbes, 'New horizons at L'Anse aux Meadows', *Proceedings of the National Academy of Sciences* 116 (2019): 15341–15343. The follow-up report on the search for Norse occupation at Point Rosee is unpublished, but was lodged with the provincial government of Newfoundland and Labrador by Sarah Parcak and Gregory Mumford on November 8, 2017.

For general overviews, see Erik Wahlgren, *The Vikings and America* (Thames & Hudson, London & New York, 1986); Birthe Clausen (ed.), *Viking Voyages to North America* (Viking Ship Museum, Roskilde, 1993); and Shannon Lewis-Simpson (ed.), *Vinland Revisited: The Norse World at the Turn of the First Millennium* (Historic Sites Association of Newfoundland and Labrador, St. John's, 2003). A work that explicitly takes up Norse interactions with First

Nations peoples is Kevin E. McAleese, *Full Circle, First Contact: Vikings and Skraelings in Newfoundland and Labrador* (Newfoundland Museum, St. John's, 2000); see also Ingebjorg Marshall, *A History and Ethnography of the Beothuk* (McGill-Queen's University Press, Montreal, 1998). Several papers on Norse activities in the high Arctic can be found in William Fitzhugh and Elizabeth Ward (eds.), *Vikings: The North Atlantic Saga* (Smithsonian, Washington, DC, 2000).

CHAPTER 18: THE MANY ENDS OF THE VIKING AGE

The later political history of Scandinavia is referenced for chapter 16, above, and the longer-term regional trajectories of the Viking diaspora (not least the North Atlantic colonies) can be found in the studies of those areas in the respective sections of the book.

Readers interested in the dramatic life of Gudríd Thorbjarnardóttir can turn to her lively biography by Nancy Marie Brown, *The Far Traveler: Voyages of a Viking Woman* (Harcourt, Orlando, 2007).

EPILOGUE: GAMES

The story of Ragnarök and its aftermath is related in several of the Eddic poems, especially the *Seeress's Prophecy* and *Vafthrudnir's Sayings*, as well as in Snorri's *Prose Edda;* references to all these can be found above. The two best modern works are Terry Gunnell and Annette Lassen, *The Nordic Apocalypse: Approaches to* Vǫluspá *and the Nordic Days of Judgement* (Brepols, Turnhout, 2013) and Anders Hultgård, *Midgård brinner: Ragnarök i religionshistorisk belysning* (Royal Gustav Adolf Academy, Uppsala, 2017). The problems of the pastoral sequel to the Ragnarök, and its ecocritical dimensions, are imaginatively explored by Christopher Abram in his *Evergreen Ash* (see references to chapter 1, above).

ACKNOWLEDGEMENTS

Tᴴɪꜱ ʙᴏᴏᴋ ᴡᴀꜱ ᴘʀᴇᴘᴀʀᴇᴅ ᴡɪᴛʜɪɴ my research project *The Viking Phenomenon*, running from 2016 to 2025 at Uppsala University. My grateful thanks to the Swedish Research Council for their generous funding, and to my colleagues on the core team: Charlotte Hedenstierna-Jonson, John Ljungkvist, and Ben Raffield. I would also like to particularly thank Ben for his assistance with background research on the closing chapters when deadlines loomed. From the broader project group, I would like to acknowledge Andreas Hennius, Karin Ojala, Sofia Prata, Gareth Williams, and Anders Ögren.

I've had the title of this volume in mind for many years, partly as an antidote to the endless stream of books called *The Vikings* or something similar (some of them written by me, so nobody should take this personally) and partly stimulated by another work. *The Children of Aataentsic*, written by Bruce Trigger in 1976, is still the seminal history of the Huron people of the Eastern Woodlands, and I've always been impressed not only by its ambition and scope but also by its wonderfully reader-hostile title that is so committed to an emic view of its subjects.

The Children of Ash and Elm is very much my own synthesis of the Viking Age, but it is also the product of more than three decades of interaction with the wider world of Viking scholarship. By editorial policy, the main text is free of direct references, but I hope the bibliographic notes reflect the enormous debt I owe to the work of others and give appropriate credit to its appearance here in summarised form. For decades of inspiration, information, conversation, and company I would like to express my thanks to the wide community of Viking research: the delegates of the Viking Congress; the Viking Worlds initiative; the members of the Centre for Viking-Age Studies (ViS) at Oslo, a place that feels like a second home; the extended archaeological and folklore communities of Iceland (the other place that feels like a second home); the national museums, or their equivalents, of the Nordic countries; and all the nodes of Viking scholarly excellence across the universities of the world. I would also like to acknowledge the Kyngervi group focussing on the 'others' of the Viking Age, and the Norse Queer and Gender Studies Network from which it emerged. Special honour should be paid to all the postgraduate scholars and *doktorands* with whom the future of Viking studies rests; may they find the jobs and careers they richly deserve, and may we all help them to do so.

To my teachers, colleagues, and students, past and present, at the universities of UCL, York, Wits, Oslo, Stockholm, Aberdeen, and Uppsala—nothing in my career would have been the same without you. Thanks for all of it.

Some acknowledgements, however, must be made by name. In various ways large and small, over many years, the following individuals have made an especially positive difference in my professional life: Hanne Lovise Aanestad, Lesley Abrams, Adolf Friðriksson, Aiden Allen, Magnus Alkarp, Anders Andrén, Fedir Androshchuk, Martin Appelt, Jette Arneborg, Steve Ashby, Graeme Barker, James Barrett, Colleen Batey, Anna Bergman, Maths Bertell, Jan Bill, Geoff Blundell, Stefan Brink, Jesse and Gayle Byock, Sophie Bønding, Claus von Carnap-Bornheim, Martin Carver, Tom Christensen, Mark Collard, Kevin Crossley-Holland, Keith Dobney, Clare Downham, Kevin Edwards, Gunnel Ekroth, Phil Emery, Ericka Engelstad†, Marianne Hem Eriksen, Charlotte Fabech, Bill Fitzhugh, Peter Foote†, Terje Gansum, Leszek

Gardeła, Helen Geake, Gísli Sigurðsson, James Graham-Campbell, David Griffiths, Jacek Gruszczyński, Anne-Sofie and Bo Gräslund, Terry Gunnell, Guðmundur Ólafsson, Guðrún Sveinbjarnardóttir, Dawn Hadley, Richard Hall†, Helena Hamerow, Joe Harris, Stephen Harrison, Michèle Hayeur-Smith, Lotte Hedeager, Heimir Páulsson, Knut Helskog, Pernille Hermann, Frands Herschend, Hildur Gestsdóttir, John Hines, Tom Horne, Anders Hultgård, Eva Hyenstrand, Lisbeth Imer, Ingunn Ásdísardóttir, Frode Iversen, Marek Jankowiak, Cat Jarman, Jenny Jochens, Jóhanna Katrín Friðriksdóttir, Wayne Johnson, Jón Viðar Sigurðsson, Lars Jørgensen†, Anders Kaliff, Hirofumi Kato, Jane Kershaw, Simon Keynes, Anna Kjellström, Alison Klevnäs, Rick Knecht, Rune Knude, Kristian Kristiansen, Anna Westman Kuhmunen, Magnus Källström, Carolyne Larrington, Shannon Lewis-Simpson, David Lewis-Williams, John Lindow, Irene García Losquiño, Julie Lund, Niels Lynnerup, John McKinnell, Lene Melheim, Karen Milek, Steve Mitchell, Mjöll Snæsdóttir, Marianne Moen, James Montgomery, Paul Mortimer (and all at Wulfheodenas), Leos Müller, Michael Müller-Wille, Agneta Ney, Gordon Noble, Svante Norr, Evgeny Nosov†, Michel Notelid, Ulf Näsman, Heather O'Donoghue, Adrian Olivier, Bjørnar Olsen, Orri Vésteinsson, Maria Panum Baastrup, Anne Pedersen, Unn Pedersen, Peter Pentz, Aleks Pluskowski, Russell Poole, Catharina Raudvere, Andrew Reynolds, Julian Richards, Mike Richards, Howell Roberts, Else Roesdahl, Steve Roskams, Håkan Rydving, Alexandra Sanmark, Birgit and Peter Sawyer††, Duncan Sayer, Jens Peter Schjødt, Sarah Semple, John Sheehan, Jonathan Shepard, Rudy Simek, Paul Sinclair, Søren Sindbæk, Dagfinn Skre, Ben Smith, Kevin Smith, Brit Solli, Matthew Spriggs, Gro Steinsland, Steinunn Kristjánsdóttir, Frans-Arne Stylegar, Olof Sundqvist, Pat Sutherland, Žarko Tancosić, Þóra Pétursdóttir, Þórir Jónsson Hraundal, Kalle Thorsberg, Iain Torrance, Luke Treadwell, Torfi Tulinius, Helle Vandkilde, Andrew Wawn, Pat Wallace, Jenny Wallensten, Anna Wessman, Susan Whitfield, Dave Whitley, Nancy Wicker, Per Widerström,

Jonas Wikborg, Willem Willems†, Henrik Williams, Michael Wood, Inger Zachrisson, and Torun Zachrisson. My heartfelt thanks to you all and apologies to anyone who should have been on this list but is not (thirty years is a long time!).

Needless to say, any and all errors that remain in this book are my own.

The Vikings are a perennially popular media topic, and I have been more fortunate than most in my collaborators and employers in that field; their conversations, ideas, and insights have very much fed into this book. In addition to some of the academics who appear above, my thanks to Ágúst Guðmundsson, Mark Caswell, Mike Fillipov, Peter Findlay, Sam Hanson, Michael Hirst and the cast of *Vikings*, Bettany Hughes, Lars Knudsen, Craig Lathrop, Linda Muir, Heather Pringle, Dan Snow, Rebecca Snow, Kenton Vaughan, and Michael Wood. Special thanks to Robert Eggers.

Most of the maps were produced by Ben Raffield and Daniel Löwenborg—my thanks to them both. Map 2 was made by Ingvild T. Bøckman and Frode Iversen, Museum of Cultural History, University of Oslo; it was originally published in Frode Iversen's chapter 'Between Tribe and Kingdom—People, Land, and Law in Scandza AD 500–1350' in Dagfinn Skre (ed.), *Rulership in 1st to 14th century Scandinavia* (Ergänzungsbände zum Reallexikon der Germanischen Altertumskunde, vol. 114. De Gruyter, Berlin, 2019: 245–304), and I am very grateful for their kind permission to reproduce it here.

I am grateful to all the copyright holders who generously gave permission to reproduce images, and who assisted in sourcing them. Special thanks to Caroline Ahlström Arcini, James Barrett, Tom Christensen, Julie Lind, Lindsay Kerr, Ole Kastholm, Viacheslav Kuleshov, Chris Lowe, Max Marcus, Peter Pentz, Anneli Sundkvist, and Per Widerström. Those who know me or my work will be aware of my long-standing affection for reconstructions, and I would like to thank here Ragnar Børsheim and the team at Arkikon; Flemming Bau; Anders Kvåle Rue; Franziska Lorenz and Jochen Stuhrman; Tancredi Valeri; and especially Þórhallur Þráinsson, my artistic collaborator of many years.

My head of department at Uppsala University, Susanne Carlsson, has been fantastic in allowing me to rearrange my regular work schedule, and my colleagues have been very kind. I would especially like to thank Anneli Ekblom, who, unasked, saved me a whole week of time on an urgent report at a critical moment; that's a *lot*.

Beyond my office and home (they are not quite the same thing, yet), this book has been written and revised in a variety of places. My grateful thanks to the American Swedish Institute, Minneapolis; the Nordic Museum, Seattle; the University of Iceland, Reykjavík; the many facilities of UCLA; Birka Museum, Björkö; and a succession of American, Canadian, Hawaiian, Japanese, Nordic, and Spanish hotels. On far too many occasions, my desk has been a seat table on a Scandinavian Airlines long-haul flight, and I would like to extend my warm appreciation to the onboard staff who have never been less than patiently accommodating to a stressed archaeologist.

These acknowledgements would not be complete without my nightmare fuel, the fiction reading I did in small bursts—usually at about 1:00 a.m.—to decompress before bed while nonetheless maintaining the edge of stressed paranoia that I somehow seem to require in order to write. In that context it will surprise no one that I'm a longtime fan of James Ellroy. His *L.A. Quartet* did the job back in the early 2000s when I was writing up my doctorate; for the final month of work on the first draft this time, I started with a reread of *Perfidia* and got to the finish line with *This Storm*, hot off the press. *Dear God, such glee.*

I have been fortunate in working with two outstanding editors. At Basic in New York, this book's first home, Lara Heimert has improved the text immensely and also provided a firm hand on the tiller when necessary (and it was sadly necessary). Her team—Jessica Breen, Allison Finkel, Kait Howard, Amber Hoover, Roger

Labrie, Katie Lambright, Olivia Loperfido, Abigail Mohr, Melissa Raymond, Megan Schindele, and Michelle Welsh-Horst—also have my grateful thanks. At Penguin in London, Stuart Proffitt made a close reading of the final manuscript, valuable indeed, ably assisted by Alice Skinner; my thanks also to Isabel Blake, Ania Gordon, and Julie Woon. Patrick Walsh, my unflappable agent, has believed in the Children and smoothed their path since our first serendipitous meeting. As ever, I owe a great debt to Tom Holland for that introduction.

For familial and moral support, my thanks to Ingrid and Jörgen Qviström, Louise and Richard Dennerståhl, and Nathalie and Anders Le Bouteillec-Ögren—and of course to my late parents, Jean and Geoffrey Price. Whether late at night at the kitchen table in Uppsala or on our Gotland veranda looking out at the sea, or for what felt like every single weekend, there were too many times when my laptop seemed always open. For several months I neglected my family for this book, and whatever its merits (or otherwise), there is really no excuse for that. Linda, Lucy, and Miranda not only have all my love but are also quite simply the most thoroughly decent human beings I know.

Neil Price
Uppsala, December 15, 2019

INDEX

Page number in bold indicate image of that page of the colour insert. Page numbers followed by *fig* indicate an illustration on that page.